SAVING TRUTH

Saving Truth from Paradox

HARTRY FIELD

UNIVERSITY PRESS

OXFORD
UNIVERSITY PRESS

Great Clarendon Street, Oxford OX2 6DP
Oxford University Press is a department of the University of Oxford.
It furthers the University's objective of excellence in research, scholarship,
and education by publishing worldwide in
Oxford New York
Auckland Cape Town Dar es Salaam Hong Kong Karachi
Kuala Lumpur Madrid Melbourne Mexico City Nairobi
New Delhi Shanghai Taipei Toronto
With offices in
Argentina Austria Brazil Chile Czech Republic France Greece
Guatemala Hungary Italy Japan South Korea Poland Portugal
Singapore Switzerland Thailand Turkey Ukraine Vietnam

Oxford is a registered trade mark of Oxford University Press
in the UK and in certain other countries

Published in the United States
by Oxford University Press Inc., New York

© Hartry Field 2008

The moral rights of the author have been asserted

Database right Oxford University Press (maker)

Reprinted 2011

All rights reserved. No part of this publication may be reproduced,
stored in a retrieval system, or transmitted, in any form or by any means,
without the prior permission in writing of Oxford University Press,
or as expressly permitted by law, or under terms agreed with the appropriate
reprographics rights organization. Enquiries concerning reproduction
outside the scope of the above should be sent to the Rights Department,
Oxford University Press, at the address above

You must not circulate this book in any other binding or cover
And you must impose this same condition on any acquirer

ISBN 978-0-19-923074-7

Printed in the United Kingdom by
Lightning Source UK Ltd., Milton Keynes

For Julia Wrigley and Elizabeth Wrigley-Field

Either the sentence on this page isn't true, or this book will be made into a major motion picture, coming soon to a theater near you.

Preface

This book is an opinionated survey of philosophical work on paradoxes of truth and of related notions such as property-instantiation; with occasional forays into related topics such as vagueness, the nature of validity, and the Gödel incompleteness theorems. A *highly* opinionated survey: there is a particular approach that I make no secret of advocating. Still, I recognize that my favored approach has its own costs, and that the alternative views have considerable attractions and are worth exploring in their own right (not just as foils for my favored approach). I don't know of any book that adequately surveys the options and compares their virtues on a range of issues, and this book is an attempt to fill that gap.

Philosophical work on the paradoxes tends to be highly technical, and there is good reason for that: to ensure that one has evaded paradox one needs a consistency proof. (Or at least a non-triviality proof: this weaker formulation is needed to encompass "paraconsistent dialetheism", which embraces "controlled inconsistency.") Nonetheless, I have tried to keep this book fairly non-technical. (The technical underpinnings of my own work are presented elsewhere; in the book I try to convey the general flavor of them without going into all the messy details.) This isn't to say that the book is light reading, and in places I assume some knowledge of various topics in mathematical logic which may be unfamiliar to some of my intended audience; but I hope that readers will be able to skim over parts they find difficult and pick up the general thread of discussion at later points. I would have liked to have been able to write a book with all the technically easier parts first, but didn't see how to do it: especially since the main focus isn't on technical issues, but on philosophical ones, and neither the order of philosophical familiarity nor the order of philosophical simplicity are at all the same as the order of technical simplicity. I suspect many readers will find, for instance, that Chapter 1 is harder going than many of the chapters that follow it.

Although this book is on a topic on which I have published quite a bit in the last few years, I have written it mostly from scratch, partly in order to force myself to rethink some issues and partly to ensure that it was written at a less technical level. I have however cribbed a bit from two of my papers: from "This Magic Moment: Horwich on the Boundaries of Vague Terms" in Chapter 5, and from "Variations on a Theme by Yablo" in Chapter 16.

Also, I should note that while the title is similar to that of my article "Saving the Truth Schema From Paradox," the theory advocated has only a slight resemblance to the one advocated there. My later papers on the paradoxes introduced a major shift, and it is the position advocated in them that is developed in this book.

Over the last twenty years or so, there has been a huge amount of important technical work on a topic I shall *not* discuss: the proof-theoretic strength of various arithmetic theories to which a truth predicate has been added. I take considerations of proof-theoretic strength to be quite relevant to the choice of one particular truth theory of a given type over others *of that type*: for instance, one classical gap theory over another classical gap theory, or one weakly classical theory over another weakly classical theory. (These terms are explained in the body of the book.) But these considerations are far less relevant to the choice of one *type* of truth theory over another, and it is that question that is the focus of this book. Indeed, I'll be arguing for a type of truth theory quite different from those whose proof-theoretic strength has mostly been investigated; for this reason, few of the papers in this important literature will be mentioned. It isn't that I think that these issues are philosophically uninteresting: indeed, I'd be glad if the type of theories I advocate were eventually subjected to the kind of detailed proof-theoretic investigation that classical theories have been subjected to. But that is work for the future—and for people other than me, since it exceeds my competence. My putting these issues aside has an advantage for the non-technical reader: it means that much less attention to the formal details of particular theories will be required.

Three apologies in advance. First, there are some points that I make more than once—in some cases, more than twice. One reason for this is that I myself rarely want to read a book through in order, but prefer to skip around a bit. I suspect that many of my readers will be like me in this regard, and so it seems worth repeating some things in places where they are relevant again. Another reason is that the points I repeat are mostly those whose lessons have been vastly underappreciated in the literature on the paradoxes, and which are absolutely essential to a proper understanding of the issues.

Second, while I have tried to provide many citations to other literature (and I thank a referee for Oxford University Press for a great deal of help with this), the literature is far too vast for me to have done so very comprehensively. Many claims that appear without citation have been made by others as well, and citations I do provide may not always be to the first published instance. By and large my policy has been to cite things that I believe may be useful to the reader, rather than to try to document priorities (something that in any case I would be ill-equipped to do).

My final apology is to sticklers about use and mention. I identify with the author—I can't remember who it was—who quipped "In matters of use and mention I follow the conventions of *Principia Mathematica*." My sloppiness on this score is not purely due to laziness: following strict policies on use and mention requires really ugly formulations that I hate to read, and I'm sure I'm not alone. Of course I try to be careful where confusion might otherwise result, which can be a genuine danger in this subject (as for instance in matters of ordinal numbers *versus* ordinal notations; though even here my initial formulations are careless, and full rigor is imposed only when it really matters, which is in Chapter 22).

A book like this is obviously much influenced by prior work in the field, and the way I work is too unsystematic for me to know everything that has influenced me. But aside from the really obvious influences (Tarski and Kripke), I'd say that what really got me started seriously thinking about this subject was the seminal paper of Friedman and Sheard. Perhaps it is most famous for its contribution to the issues of proof-theoretic strength mentioned above, but what interested me was their beautiful cataloging of the possibilities for those classical solutions of the paradoxes that meet some very natural conditions (such as declaring that all tautologies are true and that modus ponens preserves truth). This had a profound impact on my research, both during the 1990s when I was trying to work with classical solutions, and later in effecting my conversion to non-classical theories. I should also mention Graham Priest's work, not so much for its specific details but for helping create an environment where it was easier to challenge classical orthodoxy—though my own departure from classical logic is in a rather different direction from his.

In addition, I've talked to a lot of people about issues related to the paradoxes over the past few years, and quite a few have made comments or observations that have influenced my presentation in this book or in some of the papers that led up to it. I don't know if I can remember them all, but they include Robert Black, Eliza Block, John Burgess, Kit Fine, Michael Glanzberg, Joel Hamkins, Thomas Hofweber, Paul Horwich, Matt Kotzen, Hannes Leitgeb, Tim Maudlin, Vann McGee, Agustin Rayo, Greg Restall, Stephen Schiffer, Lionel Shapiro, Stewart Shapiro, Scott Sturgeon, Alan Weir, Philip Welch, Crispin Wright, Steve Yablo, Elia Zardini, and two anonymous referees for Oxford University Press. Four others deserve special mention. I have discussed a number of issues in the book with JC Beall, and he has been a valuable sounding board and has offered much encouragement. Kevin Scharp pressed me very hard on worries about lack of a unified defectiveness predicate in my favored theory, and thinking about his criticisms led me to realize that my original version of the hierarchy of defectiveness predicates (in Field 2003a) was modeled too closely on the Church–Kleene theory of ordinal notations and could be substantially extended and improved (as it was in Field 2007, which I follow here). Josh Schechter has offered extremely detailed criticisms at several stages along the way; in addition, it was he who called Restall's argument (Section 21.4) to my attention, and pushed me to improve upon my initial attempts to reply to it. And again, Graham Priest, whose persistent criticisms on a variety of issues have sharpened my appreciation of hurdles to overcome, and with whom I have had many discussions that have probably influenced me in ways I don't fully realize.

In addition, I thank Peter Momtchiloff for his support of the project—indeed for his support of an impressive amount of good philosophy in his years with Oxford University Press.

And apologies to Chris Peacocke: I've taken what was a very amusing story of his and mangled it to make it relevant to paradox.

Contents

Introduction   1
   1 Grelling's paradox   1
   2 Russell's paradox for properties   1
   3 ... *v*. Russell's paradox for sets   2
   4 Solution routes to Russell's paradox for properties   4
   5 Grelling again   11
   6 Change of logic and change of meaning   14
   7 Some connections to other issues   18

PART I. A SELECTIVE BACKGROUND

1 Self-Reference and Tarski's Theorem   23
   1.1 Self-reference and Gödel–Tarski diagonalization   24
   1.2 Tarski's "Undefinability Theorem"   27
   1.3 Tarski's "Undefinability Theorem" states more than undefinability   30
   1.4 Another form of Tarski's theorem   32
   1.5 Can set-theoretic truth be defined?   33
   1.6 Inductive characterizations and restricted truth definitions   36
   1.7 Further remarks on explicit definition   39

2 Validity and the Unprovability of Soundness   42
   2.1 Validity and the necessary preservation of truth   42
   2.2 Truth in a model   43
   2.3 The Kreisel squeezing argument   46
   2.4 The unprovability of soundness   48

3 Kripke's Theory of Truth (Strong Kleene Version)   56
   3.1 The Kripke construction for restricted languages   58
   3.2 The Kripke construction for unrestricted languages   62
   3.3 Conservativeness   65
   3.4 Does truth coincide with semantic value 1 even for restricted languages? (KFS *v*. FM)   68
   3.5 Gaps and gluts   70

3.6 The weaknesses of Kripke's construction	72
3.7 Acceptance and rejection in KFS	73
3.8 Defectiveness again	76
Appendix: Kleene logic and other deMorgan logics	79

4 Adding a Conditional? Curry and Lukasiewicz — 83

4.1 The Curry paradox	83
4.2 Continuum-valued semantics	86
4.3 What do the semantic values mean?	88
4.4 Determinate truth in continuum-valued semantics	89
4.5 Ultimate failure: quantifiers	92
4.6 Indeterminacy and rejection	94
Appendix: The Conservativeness Theorem	97

5 Interlude on Vagueness, and the Paradoxes of König and Berry — 100

5.1 Must vague predicates have sharp boundaries?	100
5.2 Penumbral connections and higher order vagueness	102
5.3 Must higher order vagueness collapse?	104
5.4 Linear order?	105
5.5 The König and Berry paradoxes	106
5.6 The role of a classical meta-theory for a non-classical language	108

PART II. BROADLY CLASSICAL APPROACHES

6 Introduction to the Broadly Classical Options — 117

7 Truth-Value Gaps in Classical Theories — 121

7.1 Gaps and (T-OUT)	121
7.2 Kleene-style gaps versus supervaluation-style gaps	124
7.3 Declaring one's axioms untrue	130
7.4 Propositions to the rescue?	132
7.5 Truth-of, heterologicality, and properties	134
7.6 Restricted (T-OUT)	135
7.7 Does declaring one's axioms untrue destroy the purpose of truth?	138

8 Truth-Value Gluts in Classical Theories — 142

8.1 Gluts and (T-IN)	142
8.2 (T-IN) theories	143
8.3 What do glut theories say about themselves?	146
8.4 Evaluation of gluts *v.* gaps	147

Contents

9 A Second Interlude on Vagueness … 150
   9.1 Indeterminacy in classical theories … 150
   9.2 Supervaluationism … 153

10 Introduction to Supervaluational Approaches to Paradox … 156
   10.1 The simplest supervaluational fixed points … 156
   10.2 Indeterminacy, weak validity, and reasoning by cases … 160
   10.3 The status of the truth rules … 162
   10.4 Indeterminacy again … 164
   10.5 Boolean-valued semantics … 166
   10.6 Strong validity, and weak validity revisited … 169
   10.7 Yogi Berra's advice and ignorance interpretations … 172

11 A Survey of Supervaluational and Revision-Rule Theories … 176
   11.1 Simple supervaluationism is very weak … 176
   11.2 General supervaluational fixed point theories … 177
   11.3 Avoiding the problems of simple supervaluationism … 181
   11.4 Rule-of-revision theories … 186
   11.5 Soundness proofs revisited … 190

12 Are Supervaluational and Revision Theories Self-Undermining? … 192
   12.1 What do strong supervaluational and strong revision theories say about themselves? … 192
   12.2 What do medium supervaluational and medium revision theories say about themselves? … 196
   12.3 Are even the strong theories really "self-undermining"? … 199
   12.4 Gödel's Second Incompleteness Theorem … 200
   12.5 Conclusion … 204

13 Intersubstitutivity and the Purpose of Truth … 205
   13.1 Harmless gaps … 206
   13.2 Acceptance and rejection in weakly classical theories … 208
   13.3 The rest of the iceberg … 209

14 Stratified and Contextual Theories … 211
   14.1 Contextual theories and "Strengthened Liar reasoning" … 211
   14.2 Stratified gap and glut theories … 214
   14.3 "The ghost of the Tarski hierarchy": stratified internal fixed point theories … 222
   14.4 Stratified determinacy predicates for weakly classical theories … 225

PART III. PARACOMPLETENESS

15 What Is To Be Done? — 231
- 15.1 A framework for generalizing continuum-valued semantics — 231
- 15.2 Determinateness and the Liar hierarchy — 235
- 15.3 More on the never-collapsing hierarchy of determinately operators — 239

16 Fixed Points and Revision Rules for Conditionals — 242
- 16.1 Yablo fixed points — 244
- 16.2 Revisionism — 249
- 16.3 The transfinite Liar hierarchy and other examples — 253
- Appendix: The Fundamental Theorem — 257

17 More on Revision-Theoretic Conditionals — 259
- 17.1 Algebraic semantics — 259
- 17.2 Conservativeness and schemas — 262
- 17.3 Modal semantics — 264
- 17.4 Laws and non-laws — 266
- 17.5 Variations — 271

18 What Has Been Done — 275

PART IV. MORE ON PARACOMPLETE SOLUTIONS

19 Validity, Truth-Preservation, and the Second Incompleteness Theorem — 281
- 19.1 Another form of Curry's paradox — 281
- 19.2 The validity argument — 284
- 19.3 The Second Incompleteness Theorem — 286

20 Other Paradoxes — 291
- 20.1 Paradoxes of denotation — 291
- 20.2 The naive theory of properties, relations, and propositions — 294
- 20.3 Set theory — 296
- 20.4 Paradoxes of truth and validity — 298
- 20.5 "Non-bivalent" validity? — 303

21 Do Paracomplete Solutions Depend on Expressive Limitations? — 309
- 21.1 Boolean negation and "exclusion negation" — 309
- 21.2 Intuitionist negation and the intuitionist conditional — 312
- 21.3 Wright's argument — 314
- 21.4 Restall's argument — 316

22 Determinateness, Hyper-Determinateness, and Super-Determinateness — 325

22.1 Transfinite iteration made rigorous — 326
22.2 Hyper-determinateness: the problem — 331
22.3 Hyper-determinateness: the solution — 333
22.4 Expanding the language? — 338
22.5 Higher-order resources — 340
22.6 Super-determinateness — 343

23 Determinateness, Stratification, and Revenge — 347

23.1 Stratified truth *v.* iterated determinacy — 347
23.2 Genuine costs — 350
23.3 Trying to get revenge — 353

PART V. PARACONSISTENT DIALETHEISM

24 An Introduction to Paraconsistent Dialetheism — 361

24.1 Dialetheism, the truth schema, and intersubstitutivity — 361
24.2 Acceptance, rejection, and degree of belief — 363
24.3 Gluts, gaps, and intersubstitutivity again — 364

25 Some Dialetheic Theories — 368

25.1 Priest's LP — 368
25.2 Dualizing paracomplete theories — 369
25.3 Priest's conditionals — 371

26 Paraconsistent Dialetheism and Soundness — 376

26.1 The first incompleteness theorem, Curry's paradox, and truth-preservation — 376
26.2 Can we get even restricted truth-preservation? — 380

27 Hyper-Determinacy and Revenge — 384

27.1 Model theory, designated values and truth — 384
27.2 Sole truth and sole falsehood — 386
27.3 Extended paradox? — 390

References — 393
Index — 399

Introduction

1. GRELLING'S PARADOX

The predicate 'red' is true of all and only the red things; and the predicate 'has mass greater than 10 kilograms' is true of all and only things that have mass greater than 10 kilograms. More generally, for any (simple or complex) predicate of our language that one substitutes for the letter '*F*', the following holds:

(TO)   '*F*' is true of all and only the things that are *F*.

Or so it seems. But consider the predicate 'is not true of itself'. (TO) yields

'Is not true of itself' is true of all and only those things that are not true of themselves.

But this is inconsistent according to standard (i.e. classical) logic. For it yields

'Is not true of itself' is true of 'is not true of itself' if and only if 'is not true of itself' is not true of itself;

which is to say,

'Is not true of itself' is true of itself if and only if it is not true of itself.

This has the form

B if and only if not-*B*,

which is contradictory according to standard logic.

This is often called Grelling's paradox, or the heterologicality paradox. (Its inventor Grelling used the term 'heterological' as an abbreviation of 'is not true of itself'.)

2. RUSSELL'S PARADOX FOR PROPERTIES

Grelling's paradox concerns linguistic expressions, but it is arguable that underlying it is a more basic paradox concerning properties, one that is in essence due to Russell. The property of being red is instantiated by all and only the red things; the property of having mass greater than 10 kilograms is instantiated by all and only things that have mass greater than 10 kilograms. More generally, for any (simple or complex) intelligible predicate of our language that one substitutes for the letter '*F*', the following would seem to hold:

(INST) The property of being *F* is instantiated by all and only the things that are *F*.

But again, there's a problem: consider the "Russell property", the property of not instantiating itself. (INST) yields

The Russell property is instantiated by all and only those things that don't instantiate themselves.

In particular,

The Russell property instantiates itself if and only if it doesn't instantiate itself.

Again this has the classically contradictory form

B if and only if not-*B*.

3. ...*v*. RUSSELL'S PARADOX FOR SETS

When writers today speak of Russell's paradox they usually mean not quite the paradox above, but a paradox involving the mathematical notion of set. The paradox is analogous, with 'is a member of' instead of 'instantiates': it seems that there is a set whose members are precisely those things that are not members of themselves; but then in anology with the above we argue that this set is a member of itself if and only if it isn't, which is classically contradictory.

Russell's paradox for sets has a standard solution: there simply is no such set. This is not an *ad hoc* solution, for there is a natural picture of sets according to which it is inevitable. On this picture, the sets form a hierarchy, the rank hierarchy. Putting aside the empty set for simplicity, we have at the bottom layer the "rank 1" sets, whose members aren't sets (but things like apples, people, and particles). At the next layer we have "rank 2" sets, all of whose members are either non-sets or sets of rank 1, with at least one of the latter. (The last condition is to ensure that no rank 2 set is also rank 1.) In general, the sets of each layer have members only of preceding layers (and for each preceding layer, they have a member of that layer or higher). This ensures (i) that no set can be a member of itself. That in turn ensures (ii) that there can be no universal set, i.e. no set of which everything is a member; for then it would have to be a member of itself, which we've just seen is ruled out. Finally, (iii) there can be no Russell set, i.e. no set of all things that are not members of themselves; for by (i) it would have to be a universal set, but by (ii) there is no universal set.

This solution to the Russell paradox is motivated by the hierarchical picture of sets. And that picture is not only natural, it is mathematically fruitful: it provides the framework for virtually all of contemporary mathematics. Indeed, there is reason to think that this was the picture underlying set theory from the beginning (in Cantor's work), even prior to the discovery of Russell's paradox.[1] The notion of set is primarily a mathematical notion, so it would be hard to criticize this solution to the paradox.

Kurt Gödel is reported to have remarked "There never were any set-theoretic paradoxes, but the *property-theoretic* paradoxes are still unresolved."[2] The idea behind the first part of his remark is presumably that the notion of set was hierarchical from the start, so that it should have been obvious all along that there was no Russell set (in the mathematical sense of 'set'). The idea behind the second part is that this obvious resolution of Russell's "paradox" for sets simply doesn't carry over to the paradox for properties.

And this seems correct, at least for the notion of property that Gödel had in mind. I make that qualification because the term 'property' is used in more than one way. One use of the term is for *natural properties*. On this use, what properties there are is something discovered in part by science: e.g. science tells us that there is no such property as being de-phlogisticated, but that there are properties like spin and charm. But Gödel presumably had in mind a quite different use of the term 'property'. Properties in this second sense are sometimes called *concepts*, but that term too is ambiguous: it is often used for mental entities, whereas what is intended here is an objective correlate of mental entities. I'll instead use the term *conceptual property*. The whole point of the notion of conceptual property is that there is a conceptual property corresponding to every intelligible predicate. 'Identical' is intelligible, so there is a 2-place conceptual property of *being identical to*. (That is, a conceptual *relation*: relations are multi-place properties.) From this we can form a one-place conceptual property of *being identical to itself*; this is a universal property, so the hierarchical picture simply can't apply to conceptual properties. Similarly, 'instantiates' is intelligible, so there is a conceptual relation of instantiation, and a conceptual property of instantiating itself. And there is another conceptual property of *not* instantiating itself, which is the Russell property. If this is right, then the standard solution to Russell's paradox for sets simply doesn't carry over to the paradox for conceptual properties.[3]

(By the standard solution to Russell's paradox for sets I mean the solution embodied in set theories such as Zermelo-Fraenkel. Russell himself offered a slightly different solution, the theory of types, in which there is no single membership predicate, but a whole hierarchy of different ones. Similarly, one might offer a resolution to the property-theoretic analog according to which there is no single instantiation predicate, but a whole hierarchy of different ones.

---

[1] See Lavine 1994, pp. 76 ff.   [2] See the opening sentence of Myhill 1984.
[3] The paradox Russell himself had in mind was probably closer to the property paradox than to the paradox for mathematical sets. Russell originally raised the paradox in connection with Frege's theory of extensions. Extensions were supposed to be like mathematical sets in obeying an axiom of extensionality: no two extensions were instantiated by exactly the same things. But they were to be like conceptual properties in that every predicate had one, and that they didn't fall into a hierarchy of ranks.

I will consider theories like this in due course,[4] but for now I merely say that they have been almost universally abandoned for sets, and are unattractive for properties for the same reasons and more.)

One possible reaction to this is that we should, with Quine (1960, sec. 43), simply declare there to be no such things as conceptual properties. That's certainly a possible view (for which there may be some motivation independent of the paradoxes), but it is not ultimately of much help in the present context since the apparently analogous heterologicality paradox, which involves only linguistic expressions, would still remain. Another possible reaction is that our common-sense conception of conceptual properties should be replaced with a hierarchical conception; though that would be a very radical alteration of the common-sense conception. Fortunately there are other possibilities.

4. SOLUTION ROUTES TO RUSSELL'S PARADOX FOR PROPERTIES

We've seen that one possible reaction to Russell's paradox for (conceptual) properties is

Non-existence Solution: There is no such thing as "the Russell property", i.e. "the (conceptual) property of not instantiating itself". (Put loosely: There is no (conceptual) property corresponding to the predicate 'doesn't instantiate itself'. I take this as just an informal way of putting what's in the first sentence. Note that talk of "correspondence" doesn't appear in the official formulation.)

The idea is to decompose the schema (INST) into two components: a correct component

(INST$_w$) *If* there is a property of being F, *then* it is instantiated by all and only the things that are F;

and a component that needs restriction

(COMP)   There is a property of being F.

According to the Non-existence Solution, (INST$_w$) holds for all intelligible predicates F, but (COMP) fails for some of them, e.g. 'doesn't instantiate itself'. There will need to be many other failures of (COMP) too, if other paradoxes like Russell's are to be handled along similar lines. A serious theory that incorporates the Non-Existence Solution will have to tell us for which F's (COMP) holds and for which ones it fails.

I've suggested, following Gödel, that the Non-Existence solution isn't very attractive (for anyone who doesn't just reject conceptual properties out of hand).

---

[4] At least, I will consider analogous theories of truth-of, and will suggest a general method for getting from any theory of truth-of to a corresponding theory of properties.

Conceptual properties aren't like sets, and it would violate their *raison d'etre* to suppose that for an intelligible predicate like 'doesn't instantiate itself', there is no corresponding property of *not instantiating itself.*

This is doubtless too quick, for one possibility would be to grant that every *intelligible* predicate has a corresponding property, but to deny that 'doesn't instantiate itself' is intelligible. On the most obvious version of this, we maintain the original (INST) (and hence (COMP)), for any intelligible predicate F. But there's something very odd about holding that 'doesn't instantiate itself' isn't intelligible. It can be brought out by asking "What part of 'doesn't instantiate itself' don't you understand?" It seems that if you accept (INST) (restricted to intelligible predicates), then you must regard the predicate 'instantiates' as intelligible, since it is used in the formulation of (INST)! Presumably 'not' and 'itself' are intelligible too, so how can 'doesn't instantiate itself' fail to be intelligible? 'Intelligible' would have to be given a very special reading for this to make any sense. Of course we can always give it the special reading 'expresses a property', but (COMP) restricted to predicates that are "intelligible" in *this* sense becomes totally vacuous. We would in effect just be granting that (COMP) and the original (INST) fail for some predicates that are intelligible by ordinary standards. The pretense that we've *explained* the failures of (COMP) as due to the unintelligibility of the predicates is exposed as a fraud, and we still need an account of which predicates it is for which (COMP) fails.

There is a more interesting version of the view that 'instantiates' is not an intelligible predicate: the **Stratification View**. According to it, we should stop using the predicate 'instantiates', and instead use a hierarchy of more restrictive predicates 'instantiates$_\alpha$', where the subscript is a notation for an ordinal number. This is a radical view: since (INST) and (INST$_w$) involve the "unintelligible" 'instantiates', the view requires that we abandon these principles and replace them by principles that employ only the subscripted predicates. I will eventually be considering this view (or a linguistic analog of it: see note 4), but I would like to defer it for the time being.

Let us for now put the Stratification View aside, and assume that 'instantiates' is a perfectly intelligible predicate (as are predicates built up from it using ordinary logical devices). And let us also put aside the Non-Existence Solution: let us assume that there is a property *doesn't instantiate itself* (the Russell property, which I'll call R). Then (INST$_w$) allows us to argue to the classical contradiction

(*) R instantiates R if and only if R does not instantiate R.

When faced with this, one possibility would be to turn this argument around to argue against (INST$_w$). More specifically, either (i) R instantiates R or (ii) R doesn't instantiate R. Since R is the property of not instantiating itself, case (i) has it that there is an object (viz. R) which instantiates itself and yet instantiates the property of *not* instantiating itself. This conclusion violates (INST$_w$). It also seems highly surprising. Case (ii) is equally surprising: there is an object (viz. R)

which doesn't instantiate itself, but yet doesn't instantiate the property of not instantiating itself. If something isn't a dog, it's hard to see how it can fail to instantiate the property of not being a dog; similarly, if something doesn't instantiate itself, it's hard to see how it can fail to instantiate the property of not instantiating itself. So (i) and (ii) are each counterintuitive; and yet, it follows from classical logic (together with our property-existence assumption) that one of these violations of ($INST_w$) must occur.

So if we put aside the Non-Existence Solution and its variants, classical logic would seem to commit us to one of two solutions; these are

Overspill Solution: For some predicates F, we have: there are objects that aren't F but have the property of being F;

and

Underspill Solution: For some predicates F, we have: there are objects that are F but don't have the property of being F.

Just as there are really many versions of the Non-Existence Solution (differing over *which* predicates have no corresponding properties), so there are many versions of the Underspill and Overspill Solutions: theories of property-instantiation can vary as to how much underspill or overspill there is. At the extreme of Underspill, we could have that no property is ever instantiated by anything: there are red things, and a property of redness, but the red things don't instantiate that property! Similarly, at the extreme of Overspill, we could have that every property is instantiated by everything: the property of redness is instantiated by things that aren't red! Of course no one would go to either extreme, but to get an Underspill or Overspill solution to the paradox one needs to specify precisely how far toward the extreme one is to go.

Actually Underspill and Overspill aren't mutually exclusive: a given theory could have some predicates that underspill and some that overspill. (In fact, if one supposes that there is underspill for one predicate, it is at least somewhat natural to suppose that there is overspill for its negation, and vice versa.)[5] Indeed, a given theory can have a single predicate that both underspills and overspills: it could postulate both an object c_1 that is F but doesn't have the property of being F, and another object c_2 that has the property of being F without being F. But assuming classical logic, it seems we must have either Underspill or Overspill, if there is a property of not instantiating itself.

So unless we follow the Stratified View in abandoning the notion of instantiation, then classical logic commits us to at least one of these three options: either there is no such property as "the property of not instantiating itself"; or there is one, but it's instantiated by some things that "shouldn't" instantiate it, i.e. some

---

[5] It would also be possible to combine property non-existence for some predicates with underspill and/or overspill for others, but I doubt that that route would have much appeal.

things that do instantiate themselves; or there is one, but it isn't instantiated by some things that "should" instantiate it, i.e. things that don't instantiate themselves. None of these seem terribly attractive. Even in the Stratified View, on which there is a variety of restricted instantiation predicates, these three options are the only ones available for any one of them.[6]

Might the problem be the assumption that classical logic applies to the instantiation predicate? That is, might there be a generalization of classical logic that takes the classical rules to be appropriate for dealing with "ordinary" predicates (such as those of standard mathematics and physics) but which allows only weaker rules when dealing with certain "extraordinary" predicates like 'instantiates'? (One obvious rationale for counting this predicate as extraordinary is that it exhibits a kind of circularity: e.g. if U is the predicate 'instantiates itself', then to find out if U instantiates itself it seems *prima facie* that you must first find out whether it instantiates itself.) The most natural way to try to implement this idea of weakening the logic is to argue that (*) isn't really contradictory. In that case, we might be able to simultaneously accept the "naive theory" that there is a property corresponding to every predicate and that such properties satisfy (INST). But is there any plausibility to the claim that (*) isn't really contradictory?

Here is a simple argument that claims of the form $B \leftrightarrow \neg B$ are always contradictory, even for sentences B that contain extraordinary predicates. (Here '$\leftrightarrow$' abbreviates 'if and only if' and '$\neg$' abbreviates 'not'.) For later reference I'll call it the *Central Argument from Equivalence to Contradiction*.

Step One: The claim $B \leftrightarrow \neg B$ and the claim B together imply the claim $B \wedge \neg B$ (where '$\wedge$' means 'and').

This step seems obvious: the two premises $B \leftrightarrow \neg B$ and B together certainly imply $\neg B$, and the second premise by itself trivially implies B, so the two together imply the conjunction $B \wedge \neg B$.

Step Two: The claim $B \leftrightarrow \neg B$ and the claim $\neg B$ together imply the claim $B \wedge \neg B$.

This is similar to Step One: $B \leftrightarrow \neg B$ and $\neg B$ certainly imply B, and the second alone implies $\neg B$, so they imply the conjunction $B \wedge \neg B$.

Step Three: The claim $B \leftrightarrow \neg B$ and the claim $B \vee \neg B$ together imply the claim $B \wedge \neg B$ (where '$\vee$' means 'or').

This follows from Steps One and Two, by the rule of Reasoning by Cases: if assumptions Γ plus A_1 imply C, and those same assumptions Γ plus A_2 imply the same conclusion C, then Γ plus $A_1 \vee A_2$ imply C. And the rule of Reasoning by Cases would seem to be pretty central to the meaning of 'or'.

---

[6] Stratified theories typically adopt the Underspill Option for each instantiation predicate, and argue that the underspill at any one level is made up for at later levels. We will consider this in detail in Chapter 14 (though in the context of truth rather than instantiation).

Step Four: The claim $B \leftrightarrow \neg B$ itself implies $B \wedge \neg B$.

Step Four follows from Step Three, if we assume that $B \vee \neg B$ is a logical truth. That assumption is famously called the law of excluded middle (LEM). It is not only famous, it is famously controversial. There are some (e.g. mathematical intuitionists like the Dutch mathematicians Brouwer and Heyting) who deny its general applicability even within mathematics; indeed some intuitionists (e.g. Michael Dummett) would deny its applicability to any statement that is not "in principle verifiable". But one needn't fall victim to "Dutch LEM disease" to suspect that there might be something suspicious about Step Four: questioning Step Four needn't involve questioning excluded middle in mathematics, physics, etc. but only questioning it in connection with certain applications of "circular" predicates like 'instantiates'.[7]

Without Step Four, it isn't immediately obvious why $B \leftrightarrow \neg B$ should be regarded as contradictory. This suggests the possibility of a fourth solution route:

Paracomplete Solutions: Excluded middle is not generally valid for sentences involving 'instantiates'. In particular, the assumption that the Russell property R *either instantiates itself or doesn't* should be rejected. Indeed, the reasoning of the "paradox" shows that that assumption leads to contradiction.

For this to be an interesting option it must preclude the need for the restrictions on (INST) and (COMP); that is, an interesting Paracomplete Theory must be one in which Naive Property Theory is consistent (where Naive Property Theory is the theory that for every predicate, there is a corresponding property that satisfies the "Instantiation Schema" (INST)). It is far from evident that an interesting Paracomplete Theory meeting this requirement is possible.

Indeed, a precondition of its possibility is that the logic viliate *all* arguments from $B \leftrightarrow \neg B$ to contradiction, not just the Central Argument; and some logics without excluded middle, such as intuitionist logic, invalidate the Central Argument for the contradictoriness of $B \leftrightarrow \neg B$ while leaving other arguments intact. The most obvious route from $B \leftrightarrow \neg B$ to $B \wedge \neg B$ within intuitionism comes from the intuitionist *reductio* rule, which says that if $\neg B$ follows from Γ and B together then it follows from Γ alone. Although intuitionists have reasons of their own for accepting this rule, the most obvious arguments for accepting it assume excluded middle. For instance: $\neg B$ certainly follows from Γ and $\neg B$ together, so if it also follows from Γ and B together then it must follow from Γ and $B \vee \neg B$ together, and hence *assuming excluded middle* it follows from Γ alone.[8]

---

[7] In Chapter 5 I will entertain the possibility of a further bar on excluded middle, to prevent its application to sentences that are crucially vague. But even this further restriction (on which I take no firm stand) would presumably leave the application to mathematics untouched, and wouldn't affect the application to physics in a disturbing way.

[8] An alternative route from $B \leftrightarrow \neg B$ to $B \wedge \neg B$ within intuitionism comes from the so-called "law of non-contradiction", $\neg(B \wedge \neg B)$. Given one of the deMorgan laws, this is equivalent to

There is a class of logics without excluded middle ("deMorgan logics") that don't contain the *reductio* rule and that are in many respects far more natural than intuitionist logic: for instance, intuitionist logic restricts the inference from $\neg\neg A$ to A, and also restricts one of the deMorgan laws (viz., the inference from $\neg(A \wedge B)$ to $\neg A \vee \neg B$), whereas deMorgan logics maintain all the deMorgan laws plus the equivalence of $\neg\neg A$ to A. And in deMorgan logics without excluded middle, $B \leftrightarrow \neg B$ is not contradictory.

A logic in which $B \leftrightarrow \neg B$ is not contradictory is *necessary* for a paracomplete solution, but far from *sufficient*: it remains to be shown that it is possible to consistently maintain the Naive Property Theory ((COMP) and (INST)) in such a logic. Indeed, we really want Naive Property Theory to include a bit more than (COMP) together with the Instantiation Schema (INST); we want it to include an intersubstitutivity claim, according to which

(i) o instantiates the property of being F

is fully equivalent to

(ii) Fo

in the sense that the claims (i) and (ii) can be intersubstituted even in embedded contexts (so long as these contexts are "transparent", that is, don't involve quotation marks, intentional operators, or the like). For instance, we want a principle that guarantees such things as

[It is not the case that o instantiates the property of being F] if and only if [it is not the case that Fo];

[If o instantiates the property of being F then B] if and only if [if Fo then B];

and so forth. Don't these follow from (INST)? They do in classical logic, but we're considering weakening classical logic. Still, I don't myself think a paracomplete solution would be very satisfactory if it required such a weak logic that these no longer followed.

So a good paracomplete solution would involve showing that (COMP) and (INST) can be maintained in a *reasonably strong* paracomplete logic that allows the derivation of the intersubstitutivity of (i) with (ii). Such a solution is in fact possible, as I will demonstrate in due course. In fact, it is a paracomplete solution

---

$\neg B \vee \neg\neg B$, which is a special case of excluded middle—a special case that the intuitionist rejects along with the general principle. But the intuitionist rejects that deMorgan law, and accepts $\neg(B \wedge \neg B)$. Given this latter and the intersubstitutivity of equivalents, $B \leftrightarrow \neg B$ implies $\neg(B \wedge B)$ and hence implies $\neg B$, from which it is easily seen to imply $B \wedge \neg B$.

In the paracomplete solutions I'll consider, $\neg(B \wedge \neg B)$ is equivalent to $B \vee \neg B$, so is not generally accepted, and so this derivation of a contradiction from $B \leftrightarrow \neg B$ is blocked. (As we'll see, calling $\neg(B \wedge \neg B)$ the "law of non-contradiction" is quite misleading. One can reject all contradictions without accepting all instances of that "law". And theorists who accept both B and $\neg B$ will almost certainly accept $\neg(B \wedge \neg B)$ as well as accepting $B \wedge \neg B$. So accepting the "law" is neither necessary nor sufficient for rejecting contradictions.)

within a reasonably strong deMorgan logic that I will eventually be advocating in this book.

The types of solution sketched above do not exhaust the possibilities. For instance, I've noted that one can block the Central Argument at Step Three instead of Step Four:

Semi-classical (*aka* Weakly Classical)[9] **Solutions:** Reasoning by Cases fails for some arguments involving 'instantiates' (but excluded middle is valid). In particular, the claim that R instantiates itself implies a contradiction, and the claim that it doesn't instantiate itself also implies a contradiction. But the claim that it either instantiates itself or doesn't is perfectly consistent, and indeed true! (We must reject Yogi Berra's advice "If you come to a fork in the road, take it.")

This semi-classical route doesn't really block the Russell paradox (not to mention other paradoxes of Naive Property Theory): it blocks the Central Argument for the contradictoriness of $B \leftrightarrow \neg B$ but leaves other arguments intact. It turns out that just as no theory based on full classical logic can consistently accept the Naive Theory of Properties, no semi-classical theory can either (where by a semi-classical theory I mean one that keeps pretty much all of classical logic except Reasoning by Cases and other meta-rules based on it; I'll be more precise in later chapters). But there are ways to develop consistent semi-classical solutions in which the limitations on (INST) are a bit less drastic than on the fully classical solutions. I will devote several chapters to such semi-classical solutions.

The paracomplete approach is not the only one that can be combined with acceptance of the Naive Theory of Properties. Another such approach accepts the conclusion of Step Four: that is, certain explicit contradictions (sentences of form $B \wedge \neg B$) are deemed acceptable. This would be intolerable if, as in classical logic, contradictions were taken to imply everything, but the idea behind this option is to weaken classical logic to a "paraconsistent" logic in which this is not so. So we have

Paraconsistent Dialetheic Solutions: R both instantiates itself and doesn't instantiate itself (but this contradiction is "contained" so as not to imply e.g. that the earth is flat).

I'm not myself a fan of such solutions, but I do think they merit discussion, and they will receive it in this book.

There is a still more radical kind of approach that I shall not consider: it involves revising the structural rules of logic, such as the transitivity of implication, or the principle that the question of whether $A_1, \ldots, A_n$ imply B depends only on B and the formulas in $\{A_1, \ldots, A_n\}$ (that is, not on the ordering of the A_i or on whether any of the A_i occur more than once on the list). I haven't seen sufficient reason to explore this kind of approach (which I find very hard to get my head

---

[9] There is a terminological issue here, of whether to count these solutions as classical. My preference would be not to, but proponents of such solutions tend to regard them as classical; so it seems less prejudicial to use the term 'weakly classical', and this is the policy I have adopted in the main text. But in the rest of the Introduction I have decided to give in to my prejudices.

around), since I believe we can do quite well without it. Throughout the book I will take the standard structural rules for granted.[10]

5. GRELLING AGAIN

I noted at the end of Section 3 that one reaction to Russell's paradox for properties might be: "So much the worse for properties! This just shows that there's no reason to believe in such obscure entities!"[11] Indeed, even one who believed there to be a place for *natural* properties could say that it is *conceptual* properties that lead to paradox, and that there is no reason to believe in *them*. In short, the view would be that if there is an intelligible notion of property at all, it must be one for which the Non-Existence Solution is right: there is simply no such thing as the alleged Russell property.

Rather than taking a stand on this issue, let's go back to the case of predicates, whose existence is much clearer. Because of the evident structural analogy between Russell's paradox for properties and the heterologicality paradox, it is clear that most of the solutions for the former have analogs for the latter. In particular we have the following:

Underspill Solutions (predicate version): For some predicates F, we have: 'F' isn't true of some objects that are F.

Overspill Solutions (predicate version): For some predicates F, we have: 'F' is true of some objects that aren't F.

Paracomplete Solutions (predicate version): Excluded middle fails for some sentences involving 'true of'. In particular, the assumption that 'is not true of itself' is either true of itself or not true of itself is fallacious.[12]

Paraconsistent Dialetheic Solutions (predicate version): 'Is not true of itself' both is true of itself and is not true of itself.

---

[10] I will also take for granted the usual introduction and elimination rules for conjunction. This rules out of consideration "non-adjunctive logics", which can allow the acceptance of contradictory pairs $\{A, \neg A\}$ without going on to accept contradictions in the sense officially defined (single sentences of form $A \wedge \neg A$). Since I assume the conjunction rules, I'll often speak of contradictory pairs as contradictions.

[11] Quine regarded properties as obscure not on grounds of their being "platonic entities" (after all, sets in the standard mathematical sense are "platonic" also), but on the grounds of their being non-extensional: distinct properties can be instantiated by exactly the same things. But note that *this non-extensionality played no role in Russell's paradox*, and anyone who thinks that classical logic must carry over unchanged even when dealing with "circular concepts" must reject a naive theory even of extensional analogs of conceptual properties ("Fregean extensions").

[12] The use of the term 'paracomplete' for solutions that restrict excluded middle was suggested to me by JC Beall, and seems the appropriate dual for 'paraconsistent', which is standardly taken as the term for theories that reject the rule of explosion (explained in the Appendix to Chapter 3). But a warning is in order: the term 'paracomplete' is sometimes used in a very different sense, for "gap theories" on which 'is not true of itself' is neither true of itself nor false of itself. These theories do not restrict excluded middle, but instead posit Underspill; I will discuss this in more detail in Section 3.5.

Semi-classical Solutions (predicate version): It's absurd to suppose that 'is not true of itself' is true of itself, and equally absurd to suppose that it isn't true of itself. Nonetheless, either it is true of itself or it isn't true of itself.

My preference is going to be for a Paracomplete solution without Underspill or Overspill: one which not only validates the schema (TO), but involves a strong enough logic so that this entails the following

Intersubstitutivity Principle: If C and D are alike except that (in some transparent context) one has the formula $A(x)$ where the other has the formula $\langle A \rangle$ *is true of* x, then C implies D and *vice versa*.

(A theory with (TO) and Intersubstitutivity will be called a Naive Theory of truth-of.)

What about a Non-Existence Solution to the heterologicality paradox? The analog of the Non-Existence Solution to Russell's Paradox would seem to be that there's no such thing as the expression 'is not true of itself'. But while this is minimally consistent, it just seems ludicrous: you can see the expression before your eyes, inside quotation marks at the end of the previous sentence. And not only is it an expression, it clearly satisfies the syntactic criteria for being a predicate of English. The schema (TO) from Section 1

(TO)   'F' is true of all and only the things that are F

was supposed to apply to all predicates of English. If we insist on applying full classical logic (including reasoning by cases) to the predicate 'true of', it seems that the Underspill and Overspill options are the only ones that could possibly be maintained.

Are there ways to get around this? One idea would be to insist

(I) that the Schema (TO) should be restricted not just to predicates in the syntactic sense, but to *meaningful* (or *intelligible*) predicates,

and to argue

(II) that 'is not true of itself' isn't a meaningful (or intelligible) predicate.

Then we could with some stretching call this a Non-Existence Solution: what doesn't exist is a *meaningful* predicate.[13]

But in any ordinary sense of 'meaningful', the claim (II) just seems obviously false. (Indeed, in any ordinary sense of 'meaningful', it's hard to see how 'is not true of itself' can fail to be meaningful unless 'true of' fails to be meaningful.) Evidently it must be some special technical sense of 'meaningful' that is intended.

---

[13] I do not mean to include here views on which 'is not true of itself' is *ambiguous* (due to an ambiguity in 'true of'). I will consider such stratified views in later chapters; they are not naturally thought of as "Non-Existence Solutions" to the heterologicality paradox, since they are much more reminiscent of type-theoretic solutions to the set-theoretic paradoxes than of theories like Zermelo-Fraenkel that deny set existence.

The most obvious possibility is that a 'meaningful predicate' in the technical sense is a predicate that expresses a property. If we adopt this line we must rely on a theory of properties that avoids the Russell paradox by the Non-Existence Solution to that. (If only we had an attractive theory of properties of this sort!)

Moreover, the claim in (I) that (TO) holds for "meaningful" predicates (or better, predicates that express properties) doesn't settle the application of 'true of' to "meaningless" predicates (predicates that don't express properties). We can of course settle this by a separate stipulation.

One possible stipulation is that a predicate that doesn't express a property is never true of anything. In that case, 'is not true of itself' isn't true of anything, so it isn't true of itself; but this supposition is just a version of the Underspill solution. (The predicate in question isn't true of itself, but 'isn't true of itself' isn't true of it!) In other words, to handle this possibility we don't need a separate "Non-Existence Solution"; it is already covered in our classification as an "Underspill Solution".

A second possible stipulation (with less *prima facie* appeal) is that a predicate that doesn't express a property is true of everything. That is easily seen, by a parallel argument, to be one version of an Overspill Solution.

A third possible stipulation is that predicates that don't express properties are true of some things and not others, but in a rather unsystematic way; such a view is likely to be committed to both Overspill and Underspill, but again it is already covered in the classification.

Of course, an advocate of the route laid out in (I) and (II) above might well say that the question of whether "meaningless" predicates are true of things is itself "meaningless", at least in some cases: in particular, it is "meaningless" to ask whether the "meaningless" predicate 'is not true of itself' is true of itself. And (especially if we forget for the moment that it is a special technical sense of meaningfulness that is being employed!) this might be taken to imply that we shouldn't assert that it is true of itself, or assert that it isn't, or assert the disjunction of the two. But in that case too, the view is covered in our classification: it is a kind of paracomplete view, one which withholds assent to excluded middle for (some or all) sentences containing predicates that are "meaningless" in the technical sense. Again, there's no need for a separate "Non-Existence Solution" to cover this case.[14]

In short, to say that the predicate 'is not true of itself' is in some sense meaningless is thoroughly unhelpful: it simply disguises the true nature of the solution being proposed.

---

[14] If on the other hand the view asserts that though it is "meaningless" in the technical sense to ask whether 'is not true of itself' is true of itself, still (since it's meaningful in the ordinary sense) we ought to assert

'Isn't true of itself' is either true of itself or not true of itself,

then we will have either Underspill or Overspill or some semi-classical or dialetheic option, despite the attribution of "meaninglessness".

Admittedly, saying that the heterologicality predicate doesn't express a property isn't as unnatural for some solutions to the heterologicality paradox as it is for others. The solutions most naturally described in this way are (1) ones according to which predicates that don't express properties aren't true of anything, and (2) ones according to which atomic sentences containing predicates that don't express properties should be neither asserted nor denied. But even in these cases, the description of the theory as a Non-Existence solution hides crucial details.

Solutions of type (1) are disguised Underspill solutions to the heterologicality paradox; but in order to tell *how much* underspill they posit, we must first find out what they tell us about the extent of the failure of predicates to express properties. Of course, in order to disguise an Underspill solution to the heterologicality paradox in this way, we must adopt a Non-Existence solution to the Russell paradox for properties. That is not my preferred approach to the property paradox. But putting that aside, it seems methodologically preferable to state the solution to the heterologicality paradox without invoking issues of property-existence, for the simple reason that we have clearer intuitions about what predicates are true of than about what properties exist.

Solutions of type (2) are disguised forms of Paracomplete solutions to the heterologicality paradox; but in order to tell *where excluded middle needs restricting* we need to know which predicates fail to express properties.[15] The remarks under (1) then carry over: we'd do better just to present the solution directly as a Paracomplete solution to the heterologicality paradox. For in the first place, it's easier to evaluate theories of truth-of than theories of property-existence. And in the second place, developing the solution directly as a solution to the heterologicality paradox means that we don't need to rely on a Non-Existence solution to the Russell paradox for properties. We might, for instance, want to adopt the same type of solution to the Russell paradox as to the heterologicality paradox: e.g. a Paracomplete theory for both.[16]

I will have more to say about these issues as we proceed.

6. CHANGE OF LOGIC AND CHANGE OF MEANING

There are many other paradoxes closely related to the ones I've discussed. The most well-known is the Liar paradox, which is very similar to the heterologicality

---

[15] Actually some such solutions are disguised semi-classical solutions (see previous footnote); in this case, it is *the extent to which reasoning by cases needs restricting* that depends on the degree to which there's a failure of predicates to express properties.

[16] Moreover, if one thinks that the predicates for which excluded middle is suspect are exactly those that don't express properties, this is likely to prejudice the type of Paracomplete solution one entertains. e.g. one might think that if a predicate doesn't express a property, then no disjunction of that predicate with another could express a property either; but that would force a rather unattractive Paracomplete solution with a very weak logic.

paradox but in some respects simpler to discuss. It will be my starting point. But there are many others, really an infinite variety: these include the rather troublesome Curry paradox (also called Löb's paradox or Henkin's paradox), and the even more troublesome *iterated* Curry paradoxes. There are also paradoxes of denotation and definability. It is important that we not just deal with each paradox piecemeal, but provide a systematic account that can be shown to handle them all. I will be surveying a wide range of options for such an account, and discussing their advantages and disadvantages.

A theme of this book will be that we ought to seriously consider restricting classical logic to deal with all these paradoxes. In particular, we should seriously consider restricting the law of excluded middle (though not in the way intuitionists propose). I say 'restricting' rather than 'abandoning', because there is a wide range of circumstances in which classical logic works fine. Indeed, I take excluded middle to be *clearly* suspect only for certain sentences that have a kind of "inherent circularity" because they contain predicates like 'true'; and most sentences with those predicates can be argued to satisfy excluded middle too. The idea is *not* that we need two distinct logics, classical logic and a paracomplete logic (one without excluded middle). On the contrary, the idea is that we can take the paracomplete logic to be our single all-purpose logic. But we can recognize the truth of all instances of excluded middle in certain domains (e.g. those that don't contain 'true', 'true of', 'instantiates', or other suspect terms). We may not want to count these instances of excluded middle as *logical* truths (though you can if you like—this is a matter for verbal stipulation), but we can recognize them as truths, and truths with something of the high degree of certitude that many logical truths have. So we can reason from them, and reasoning from them will look just like classical reasoning in the domains in question.

Weakening classical logic (whether by restricting excluded middle or in some other way) is not something to be done lightly. There are some obvious advantages to keeping to classical logic even for "circular" predicates: advantages of simplicity, familiarity, and so on. Choosing to forgo these advantages has its costs. But I will argue (primarily in Part II) that the *disadvantages* of keeping classical logic for "circular" predicates are also very great, so that the undoubted cost of weakening the logic is worth bearing.

Perhaps there are some who think that this cost-benefit analysis is inappropriate, that the very idea of tinkering with classical logic is irrational on its face since classical logic is obviously superior. The word 'logicism' would be a natural name for this attitude—in analogy to 'sexism', 'racism', 'species-ism' and so forth. Unfortunately it's already taken, so let's call the view 'Logical Dogmatism'.

One possible defense of such Dogmatism is that if logic is not held fixed then anything goes. As an anonymous referee put it to me, "We didn't weaken the logic as a way of hiding the defects in Ptolemaic astronomy or old quantum theory; why should we modify the logic to hide the blemishes in the naive theory of truth?" The answer to this, I think, is that there is no known way (and little prospect of finding a way) to save either Ptolemaic astronomy or the old quantum theory by a change of logic, and little benefit to so doing since we have far more satisfactory alternatives. The proposal that we save the naive theory of truth by a change of logic is not the cheap non-solution that the objection envisages: it is something that must be earned by working out the details of the logic and of the theory based on it. Once we've worked out such a theory, we must weigh it against competing theories that keep classical logic but restrict the naive principles of truth, using the usual (somewhat vague and subjective) criteria for theory choice. With Ptolemaic astronomy or the old quantum theory, there is no serious prospect for such a theory being worked out that survives such a competition. The reader may think there is little prospect in the case of the theory of truth either, but I invite him to withhold judgement until he has read the book.

A second common defense of Logical Dogmatism is based on the idea that "change of logic requires change of meaning". To this I say, first, that the paradoxes force a change in the basic laws *either* of logic in a narrow sense *or* of the logic of truth, instantiation, etc.; or if you like, it forces a change in opinion about those laws. If change of (opinion about) the basic laws of '¬' and '→' counts as change of meaning, why doesn't change of (opinion about) the basic laws of truth and the basic laws of instantiation? And as we'll see, adhering to the principles of classical logic requires a *huge* change in standard principles about truth and instantiation. The upshot of this is that there is at least as good a case that the classical truth theorist is "changing the meaning of 'true' " as that the defender of the Intersubstitutivity Principle who restricts excluded middle is "changing the meaning of 'not' " (or of 'or').

But second, why make a fetish about whether these things involve a change of meaning? As Putnam 1968 taught us, there is a distinction to be made between change of meaning and *mere* change of meaning. The switch from Euclidean geometry to generalized (variable curvature) Riemannian geometry involved revision of enough basic principles about straight lines that it may be somewhat natural to say that 'straight line' took on a different meaning. But if so, an abandonment of the old meaning and the invention of a new one was required to get a decent physical theory that is observationally adequate: for no reasonably simple observationally adequate theory allows for the existence of "straight lines in the Euclidean sense". We needn't of course have carried over the old term 'straight line' from Euclidean geometry to Riemannian, but there is enough continuity of doctrine to make it natural to do so. This is certainly not a *mere* change of meaning, i.e. a relabelling of terms without alteration of basic theory. The situation with truth is similar: here the "old theory", involving both classical logic and the naive theory of truth, is simply inconsistent. Indeed it's trivial: it implies everything, e.g. that the Earth is flat. If you don't want to be committed to the view that the Earth is flat you need a theory that differs from the naive theory in basic principles, either principles about truth or principles about logical matters more narrowly conceived. If giving up those basic principles involves a "change of meaning", so be it: for then the "old meanings" aren't really coherent, and they *need* changing. This is certainly no *mere* change of meaning, i.e. no mere relabelling.

Any resolution of the paradoxes will involve giving up (or at least restricting) some very firmly held principles: either principles of a narrowly logical sort, or principles central to the ordinary use of truth and instantiation predicates, or both. The principles to be given up are ones to which the average person simply can't conceive of alternatives. That's why the paradoxes are *paradoxes*. In this situation, I think we should be skeptical that asking whether the attempted resolution of the paradoxes "changes the meaning" of the terms involved is a clear question (whether these be ordinary logical terms like 'not' and 'if ... then' or terms like 'true' and 'instantiates'). And I'm even more skeptical that it's a useful question.

The question is *clear* only to the extent that we know how to divide up such firmly held principles into those that are "meaning constitutive" or "analytic" and those which aren't, and this is notoriously difficult. If forced to answer the question in the case of the paradoxes, perhaps the best thing to say is that *all* the principles leading to paradox are "meaning constituting"—logical principles like excluded middle and disjunctive syllogism as well as principles like (TO) and (INST). In that case, the ordinary meanings are jointly incoherent, and a "change of meaning" is required to restore coherence. (Of course, we shouldn't "change meanings" gratuitously, and there are many reasons for trying to keep the new uses of our terms broadly consonant with the old uses.) Perhaps there are subtle techniques of linguistic analysis that would enable us to discover that certain of these principles involved in the paradoxes aren't really constitutive of the "meanings" that English speakers attach to their words in the way that the rest of the principles are, but I am skeptical.

But these linguistic questions, even if deemed clear, strike me as of very little interest. The paradoxes show that there's something wrong with firmly held patterns of reasoning, whether or not these patterns are meaning-constituting. What's of interest is to figure out how best to modify this reasoning: to find a new way of reasoning that we can convince ourselves is intuitively acceptable, and which avoids plainly unacceptable conclusions. Conceivably there's more than one reasonable way to do it, with no non-arbitrary way to choose between them, but we'll be in a better position to judge this after we've investigated the possible solutions. In any case, there is no obvious reason in advance of such an investigation that would rule out the possibility that the best resolution(s) will involve a revision of some general logical principles rather than a revision of the principles of truth and instantiation.

I'm certainly not suggesting that anyone adhering to classical logic is a Dogmatist: one may well think that the benefits of keeping classical logic outweigh the costs. One of the major goals of the book is to provide the materials for an informed decision on this issue.

7. SOME CONNECTIONS TO OTHER ISSUES

I take the resolution of the paradoxes to be a matter that should be of quite general interest, as it has a bearing on many other topics. Obviously it is crucial for our investigations into the nature of truth that we have a consistent theory of truth,[17] and likewise for properties. Moreover, what our consistent theory looks like will affect our answers to general philosophical issues about truth and properties. For instance, in recent years there has been much discussion of what purposes the notion of truth serves. One common answer (particularly among advocates of "deflationary" or "minimal" theories of truth) is that 'true' is primarily a logical device that enables us to make generalizations we would otherwise be unable to make, or unable to make succinctly. According to this viewpoint, even apparently "deep" claims about truth turn out to result from the generalizing function. For instance, the "deep" claim

Truth is distinct from long-run verifiability

is basically just a generalization of

It is possible that either Thales' maternal grandmother ate cabbage on the day she died but there is no way to verify this, or there are now eight neutrinos in the interior of the sun that are arranged precisely in a regular octagon but there is no way to verify this, or … .

For this view of truth to work, we require a quite strong equivalence between claims of form "'p' is true" and the corresponding claims "p"—or so I will argue in Chapter 13. If this is right, then the question of whether this strong equivalence can be maintained in general (without, e.g., analogs of "Underspill" or "Overspill") will turn out to be crucial to these "deflationary" or "minimalist" views.

The paradoxes are also of relevance to metaphysical issues about "indefinite extensibility" of our concepts and/or our ontology. For instance, it is often thought that our concept of truth is indefinitely extensible: there is a simple recipe whereby given any precise theory of truth, we can automatically construct a more extensive one. The general tenor of this book is opposed to that idea. In particular, I will argue against the common view that the semantics of any language can only be given in a broader meta-language; my claim will be that there are languages that are sufficiently powerful to serve as their own meta-languages. This is not to claim that there could be such a thing as a "universal" language capable of expressing any possible concept; only that there are languages comprehensive enough to be "self-sufficient" in that they do not contain within themselves the requirement that they be expanded.

---

[17] Or at least a non-trivial one, i.e. one that doesn't imply everything.

The topics of this book also bear on other issues within mathematical philosophy. One such issue that I will discuss is the nature of logical consequence: some widespread views about this are simply undermined by the paradoxes, or so I will argue. I will also discuss a related issue about Gödel's second incompleteness theorem. The theorem says, very roughly, that no good mathematical theory can prove its own consistency. It is natural to ask: "Why not? Can't it prove that its axioms are true, and that its rules of inference preserve truth? And if so, can't we argue by induction that its theorems are true, and infer from this that it is consistent?" It turns out that different theories of truth have very different things to say about where this reasoning goes wrong. (For many theories of truth, the diagnosis they must give points to highly counterintuitive features of those theories.) This is another topic to which I'll pay considerable attention.

Finally, the topics of this book may well relate to other cases where there seems intuitively to be "no determinate fact of the matter" about the answer to some question. For there is *some* reason to think that the "circularity" of predicates like 'instantiates' and 'true' leads to trouble *because it gives rise to an indeterminacy in the application of these predicates*; if so, it would be natural to extend our account of circular predicates to indeterminacy more generally. One plausible example where indeterminacy may arise is in the application of vague predicates: it is plausible that in some such cases "there is no determinate fact of the matter" as to whether the predicate applies. So there may well be a connection between the truth-theoretic paradoxes and issues of vagueness. (Such a connection has been posited in McGee 1989 and 1991 and Tappenden 1993, though it is by no means generally accepted.) This suggestion raises huge issues, and I won't take a strong stand on it in this book. But I am, on the whole, sympathetic to the suggestion, and in Chapters 5 and 9 I explore some parallels and draw some tentative morals.

PART I

A SELECTIVE BACKGROUND

1
Self-Reference and Tarski's Theorem

In the introduction I focused on the Heterologicality paradox, which involves the notion of a *predicate* being *true of* something. In the next few chapters my focus will be more on the Liar paradox, which involves the notion of a *sentence* being *true*. To get the paradox we first formulate a "Liar sentence" Q that asserts its own untruth. We then argue that if it is true it isn't true, and that if it isn't true it is true; so it is true if and only if it isn't true, which seems contradictory.[1]

Obviously there is a close analogy between these paradoxes. But there are two reasons for initially focusing on a paradox involving truth rather than a paradox involving truth-of. First, truth is a notion of more central interest than truth-of. Second, truth is simpler to discuss than truth-of, since 'true' is a 1-place predicate whereas 'true of' is 2-place.

But achieving simplicity can be slightly complicated: in this case, a clean paradox involving plain old 'true' requires the construction of sentences that directly or indirectly self-refer, and in particular which directly or indirectly assert their own untruth. How does this self-reference work? I will begin this chapter by considering how self-reference is achieved within formalized theories.

But the main focus of the chapter (Sections 1.2 through 1.5) is on how standard mathematical theories manage to block paradox despite having the means for self-reference: namely, by limitations in their expressive capacity. Section 1.6 deals with a certain puzzle that might arise about the Tarski undefinability theorem, but it will play only a small role in what will follow (and experts will find nothing new or controversial in it).

---

[1] What I call the Liar paradox is sometimes called "the Strengthened Liar paradox"; the "Ordinary Liar paradox" is taken to involve a sentence that asserts of itself that it is *false* instead of *not true*. Those who use this terminology typically say that the "Ordinary" paradox is somehow more amenable to solution than the "Strengthened" paradox. That seems wrong: the "Ordinary" Paradox is most directly a paradox of falsity rather than truth, but it is no less paradoxical. Whereas the "Strengthened" paradox assumes the equivalence of True($\langle p \rangle$) to p, the "Ordinary" paradox assumes the equivalence of False($\langle p \rangle$) to $\neg p$. Applying this "falsity schema" to the "Ordinary" Liar sentence, we get "False($\langle p \rangle$) $\leftrightarrow$ ¬False($\langle p \rangle$)", which is inconsistent in classical logic.

'False' is usually taken to be equivalent to 'has a true negation'. Given this definition, the equivalence of False($\langle p \rangle$) to $\neg p$ follows from the equivalence of True($\langle p \rangle$) to p, and any paradox of falsehood is seen to be indirectly a paradox of truth. Still, truth seems the more central notion, and in the case of truth the "Strengthened" Liar sentence leads to paradox more directly, so that is the Liar sentence I'll primarily discuss. Everything I say about it could however be easily adapted to the "Ordinary" Liar sentence.

1.1. SELF-REFERENCE AND GÖDEL–TARSKI DIAGONALIZATION

The simplest and most natural way to achieve self-reference is via empirical description. For instance, suppose someone I think little of is talking, and I say "What is being said by the person in this room with the lowest IQ isn't true." Unfortunately, let us suppose, the person in the room with the lowest IQ is not him but me; so I have inadvertently uttered a sentence that indirectly declares itself untrue. I have uttered what is called a "contingent Liar sentence". (Or imagine a politician, irritated that he can barely make himself heard over the rude insults of a heckling crowd, who complains "Every time I open my mouth, some idiot says something false about me". It's an easy exercise to find assumptions that will make his complaint a contingent Liar sentence.)

This sort of Liar sentence (involving what I'll call *Contingent Self-Reference*) requires a language with empirical predicates, and in formal investigations it is often convenient to consider simpler languages that don't have such predicates. One possibility (which I'll call *Artificial Self-Reference*) is to consider languages within which we can have a name for sentences that contain that very name: we let 'Q' be a name of the sentence 'Q is not true'. But this could well seem suspicious. Fortunately there is a third route to self-reference, which produces the same effect but through much less artificial means. It is due to Kurt Gödel and Alfred Tarski, so I'll call it *Gödel–Tarski Self-Reference*.

The background for Gödel–Tarski self-reference is the observation that any language of sufficient power can express its own syntax; indeed the power required is quite modest. Let us consider two ways in which we might set up a simple language $\mathscr{L}$ that can accomplish this.

The most obvious idea (suggested in Tarski 1931) would be to set up $\mathscr{L}$ so that it has its own expressions as its direct subject matter. If $\mathscr{L}$ is a normal language, its expressions are formed from the letters of a finite alphabet V; so to get direct self-reference we should imagine that among the names in $\mathscr{L}$ (which like all expressions in $\mathscr{L}$ are strings of letters in V) are names of each member of V (just as in English the name 'es' is a name of the letter 's'). We also imagine that $\mathscr{L}$ contains a predicate '$\mathscr{L}$-expression', that holds of precisely the finite strings of alphabet items; and that it contains a 2-place function symbol '$^\frown$' such that '$x^\frown y$' means 'the result of concatenating x and y in that order' (e.g. 'ab'$^\frown$'bc' is 'abbc'). Using this we get, for each $\mathscr{L}$-expression e, a singular term $\langle e \rangle$ that denotes e.[2] And then with a few other devices, we can formulate all the basic syntactic properties of $\mathscr{L}$ within $\mathscr{L}$. (And given any reasonable deductive proof-procedure for $\mathscr{L}$, we can formulate that in $\mathscr{L}$ too.) Moreover, we can formulate a theory in

---

[2] More than one term actually, but there are easy ways to single out one as privileged.

the language (called *concatenation theory* or *protosyntax*)[3] in which we can prove a very comprehensive body of truths about those syntactic (and proof-theoretic) properties.[4] (For a detailed development of this approach, see Quine 1940.)

Rather than proceeding in this direct way, it is easier and more traditional to proceed via number theory. Number theory, on the face value interpretation of it, deals not with its own syntax but with the natural numbers; but by setting up a correlation between the letters in the alphabet of the theory with certain numbers, and between the concatenation relation and a certain relation among numbers, we can set up a secondary interpretation of number theory in which it is in part a theory of its own syntax. This idea is due to Kurt Gödel 1931, and called Gödel numbering. In this case, we get for each expression e of the language a term $\langle e \rangle$ that stands for *the number correlated with e*; but we may as well simply identify the expression with the corresponding number, and say that $\langle e \rangle$ stands for e itself.

There is really little to choose between this arithmetical approach and the more direct syntactic approach: just as syntax can be developed within number theory, so number theory could be developed within syntax (e.g. by identifying the numbers 0, 1, 2, 3, ... with the expressions 'a', 'aa', 'aaa', 'aaaa', ..., for some particular letter 'a' of the alphabet).

Either way we do it, we get a striking result due both to Gödel and Tarski: that for any property expressible in the language, we can find a sentence in the language that in effect attributes that property to itself (or to its own Gödel number, if we want to make that distinction). More precisely:

Gödel–Tarski Diagonalization Lemma (semantic version):[5] For any formula $C(v)$ in the language of arithmetic (or the syntactic language) with v as its only free variable, there is a sentence F in that language such that $F \leftrightarrow C(\langle F \rangle)$ is an arithmetic truth (or on the direct approach, a truth of the syntactic theory).

(More generally: For any formula $C(v; u_1, \ldots, u_k)$ in the language of arithmetic (or the syntactic language), there is a formula $F(u_1, \ldots, u_k)$ in that language with

---

[3] Strictly speaking, we get a different protosyntax for each choice of the finite alphabet V. But if V_1 and V_2 each contain more than one member, the protosyntactic theory for either one is interpretable in the protosyntactic theory for the other; so without loss of generality we can pick a single V with more than one member and confine our attention to its protosyntax.

[4] One could do protosyntax without explicitly introducing a concatenation function, by using quotation mark names: these "self-concatenate", in the sense that the name of the concatenation of two such names is obtained by taking their quotation mark names, deleting the final quotation mark in the first and the initial quotation mark in the second, and concatenating the results. But quotation mark names are unwieldy to use in formal theories, since they generate "opaque contexts" where intersubstitutivity of equivalents fails.

[5] The Diagonalization Lemma is often called the (Gödel–Tarski) Fixed Point Lemma, and I think that label is actually more appropriate. However, we'll be discussing three other kinds of fixed points at various places in this book (Kripke fixed points, Brouwer fixed points, and Yablo fixed points), and adding the phrase "Gödel–Tarski fixed points" to these others would border on the confusing. (To augment the confusion, Kripke fixed points are a special case of a kind of fixed points to which Tarski's name is also attached, viz., Knaster–Tarski fixed points.)

all the same variables other than 'v' free, such that $\forall u_1 \ldots u_k [F(u_1, \ldots, u_k) \leftrightarrow C(\langle F(u_1, \ldots, u_k)\rangle; u_1, \ldots, u_k)]$ is an arithmetic truth (or a truth of the syntactic theory).)

This semantic version of the Diagonalization Lemma uses the notion of arithmetic truth which (it will soon turn out) cannot be formulated in arithmetic language (or the notion of syntactic truth, which cannot be formulated in the syntactic language). For this reason the following version is more useful:

Gödel–Tarski Diagonalization Lemma (proof-theoretic version): For any formula $C(v)$ in the language of arithmetic (or the syntactic language) with 'v' as its only free variable, there is a sentence F in that language such that $F \leftrightarrow C(\langle F \rangle)$ is *provable in the arithmetic (or syntactic) theory*.

(More generally: For any formula $C(v; u_1, \ldots, u_k)$ in the language of arithmetic (or the syntactic language), there is a formula $F(u_1, \ldots, u_k)$ in that language with all the same variables other than 'v' free, such that $\forall u_1 \ldots u_k [F(u_1, \ldots, u_k) \leftrightarrow C(\langle F(u_1, \ldots, u_k)\rangle; u_1, \ldots, u_k)]$ is *provable in the arithmetic (or syntactic) theory*.)[6]

Since the arithmetic (or syntactic) theory is intuitively true, the semantic version is an intuitive consequence of the proof-theoretic, even though it can't be stated in the language.

Proof of Diagonalization Lemma (both versions): (For notational simplicity I'll focus on the less general versions; the extension to the more general versions is routine.) Let the *self-application* of a formula $B(v)$ (with a single free variable v) be the sentence $B(\langle B \rangle)$ that results from substituting the name $\langle B \rangle$ for all free occurrences of v in B. (When the syntax is done in arithmetic, there is a corresponding operation on Gödel numbers that takes the Gödel number of a formula to the Gödel number of its self-application; since it's possible to identify formulas with their Gödel numbers, I'll call this numerical operation 'self-application' as well.) This operation is expressible in the syntactic (or arithmetic) language. Now given the formula $C(v)$, let $D(v)$ be the formula

$$\exists x [x \text{ is the self-application of } v \wedge C(x)].$$

Let F be the self-application of the formula $D(v)$, i.e. the formula

$$\exists x [x \text{ is the self-application of } \langle D(v)\rangle \wedge C(x)].$$

But the claim

$$\langle F \rangle \text{ is the unique self-application of } \langle D(v)\rangle$$

is an obvious truth that is provable by very elementary means available in the arithmetic or syntactic theory. From this and the nature of the formula F, it is clear that

$$F \leftrightarrow \exists x [x = \langle F \rangle \wedge C(x)]$$

---

[6] The arithmetic theory required for the theorem is in fact far weaker than standard first order number theory: "Robinson Arithmetic", which doesn't include mathematical induction and doesn't suffice even to prove such things as the associativity or commutativity of addition, is sufficient.

and hence
$$F \leftrightarrow C(\langle F \rangle)$$
is an obvious truth that is provable by these elementary means. ∎

Minor Observation: F doesn't *literally* say of itself (or even, of its Gödel number) that it has the property C; still, it is *provably equivalent to* a sentence that says that F (or its Gödel number) has property C, and that's all we need. We have achieved something *very like* self-reference by indirect but unquestionably legitimate means. Indeed if the language contained a description operator ι, you *could* get literal self-reference, relative to the Gödel numbering: F could be taken to be $C(\iota x[x$ is the self-application of $\langle D(v) \rangle])$, and the description would refer to (the Gödel number of) F. It is the use of self-reference by descriptions rather than by names that avoids the artificiality of Artificial Self-reference.

Important observation: The Diagonalization Lemma generalizes automatically to apply to richer theories in which arithmetic (or equivalently, protosyntax) can be embedded. The richer theories can contain new vocabulary; $C(v)$ can then be an arbitrary formula in the richer language. **The result even applies when the logic of the richer theory is weaker than classical**, as long as (i) classical logic holds for the arithmetic or protosyntactic subtheory, (ii) a modicum of standard quantifier reasoning is allowed, and (iii) the logic of the biconditional '$\leftrightarrow$' is reasonable; more particularly, (iii-a) $A \leftrightarrow A$ and $\exists x[x = t \wedge C(x)] \leftrightarrow C(t)$ are theorems, and (iii-b) if $A \leftrightarrow B$ is a theorem then intersubstituting B for A preserves theoremhood.

Proof of Important Observation: Let T be a theory in which we can define 'natural number' and the usual predicates of number theory ('is zero', 'is the successor of', 'is the sum of' and 'is the product of'), and in which we can prove (the translations of) the results of restricting the axioms of number theory to the natural numbers. We can then easily introduce names of numbers into T. Then for any formula $C(v)$ in the language of T, define F as above: $\exists x[SA(x, \langle D(v) \rangle) \wedge C(x)]$, where $SA(x, y)$ means 'x is a self-application of y'. Then in the arithmetical portion of T we can certainly prove $\forall x[SA(x, \langle D(v) \rangle) \leftrightarrow x = \langle F \rangle]$, given assumption (i). By the first part of (iii-a), we can prove $\exists x[SA(x, \langle D(v) \rangle) \wedge C(x)] \leftrightarrow \exists x[SA(x, \langle D(v) \rangle) \wedge C(x)]$; by (iii-b) and minimal quantifier reasoning we can infer $\exists x[SA(x, \langle D(v) \rangle) \wedge C(x)] \leftrightarrow \exists x[x = \langle F \rangle \wedge C(x)]$; and using the second part of (iii-a), and (iii-b) again, we get $\exists x[SA(x, \langle D(v) \rangle) \wedge C(x)] \leftrightarrow C(\langle F \rangle)$, which is just $F \leftrightarrow C(\langle F \rangle)$. ∎

1.2. TARSKI'S "UNDEFINABILITY THEOREM"

The Diagonalization Lemma will have many applications in what follows. The first is Tarski's "Undefinability Theorem", which I state first for the arithmetical language, and in a proof-theoretic version. ($\vdash_N A$ means that A is provable in the standard arithmetic theory N. As remarked in an earlier footnote, even a very weak arithmetic theory suffices, but this won't be important in what follows.)

Tarski's theorem for the language of arithmetic (proof-theoretic version): If $B(v)$ is any formula in the language of arithmetic with v the only free variable, then there is a sentence Q in that language such that $\vdash_N \neg[Q \leftrightarrow B(\langle Q \rangle)]$.

Proof of theorem: Apply the Diagonalization Lemma to the negation of B, getting $\vdash_N Q \leftrightarrow \neg B(\langle Q \rangle)$. But in classical logic, $Q \leftrightarrow \neg B(\langle Q \rangle)$ implies $\neg[Q \leftrightarrow B(\langle Q \rangle)]$.

It seems clear that any serious candidate True for a predicate of arithmetic truth should satisfy the condition that for any sentence A of arithmetic, $A \leftrightarrow \text{True}(\langle A \rangle)$. So Tarski's Theorem as just formulated says that no formula definable in the arithmetic language can be a truth-predicate for arithmetic. "Arithmetic truth is not arithmetically definable."[7] (The proof just given then amounts to this: if arithmetic truth were definable in arithmetic, we could construct the Liar paradox within arithmetic, and thus get a contradiction from the uncontroversial assumption that classical logic holds within arithmetic and that *at least when A is arithmetic*, $A \leftrightarrow \text{True}(\langle A \rangle)$. The contradiction shows that arithmetic truth can't be arithmetically definable.)

It is clear from the proof that Tarski's Theorem generalizes to theories in classical logic in which the theory N can be embedded, in the sense discussed in the first part of the "Important Observation" at the end of the previous section. Let's consider several such extensions.

The first extension I will consider I will call $\mathscr{L}_1^{\text{arithm}}$. It is the result of adding to the language $\mathscr{L}_0^{\text{arithm}}$ of arithmetic a primitive predicate of arithmetic truth, '$\text{True}_0^{\text{arithm}}$', meaning intuitively 'is a true sentence of the language $\mathscr{L}_0^{\text{arithm}}$ (the arithmetic language without the truth predicate)'. Assuming that classical logic applies to this predicate (which seems eminently reasonable), the generalized proof of Tarski's theorem tells us that there is a sentence Q such that it is provable in the expanded language that $\neg[Q \leftrightarrow \text{True}_0^{\text{arithm}}(\langle Q \rangle)]$.[8] From the proof of the Diagonalization Lemma, it's clear that this Q will itself contain the predicate '$\text{True}_0^{\text{arithm}}$'. There is obviously no problem in consistently adding as axioms for the expanded language all instances of $A \leftrightarrow \text{True}_0^{\text{arithm}}(\langle A \rangle)$ *for those A in the pure arithmetic language* $\mathscr{L}_0^{\text{arithm}}$ (which, as just remarked, does *not* include Q). We can in fact go beyond this: those instances of the truth schema don't entail any important generalizations, and we can consistently add compositional principles that do entail such generalizations. In this way we can get a good theory

---

[7] **Corollary:** If T is a consistent extension of N, and $B(v)$ is any formula in its language with v the only free variable, then there is a sentence Q in that language such that $\text{not}(\vdash_T [Q \leftrightarrow B(\langle Q \rangle)])$.

Tarski's *Convention T* requires that an adequate truth predicate for a theory be such that for any sentence A of the language, *it is provable in the theory* that $A \leftrightarrow \text{True}(\langle A \rangle)$. The corollary says that no predicate definable in the language can satisfy Convention T *whatever the theory*, unless the theory is inconsistent.

[8] The proof doesn't require any axioms involving the truth predicate, other than logical axioms: it is a proof in pure arithmetic, together with an extension of classical logic to the new predicate.

of pure arithmetic truth—truth for sentences of $\mathscr{L}_0^{\text{arithm}}$—within $\mathscr{L}_1^{\text{arithm}}$. But the theorem shows that we can't consistently extend the interpretation of 'True$_0^{\text{arithm}}$' to make it an adequate truth predicate for sentences of $\mathscr{L}_1^{\text{arithm}}$. $\mathscr{L}_1^{\text{arithm}}$ can't contain its own truth predicate, any more than $\mathscr{L}_0^{\text{arithm}}$ can.

As a second extension, we could consider the language $\mathscr{L}_2^{\text{arithm}}$ obtained by adding to arithmetic not only the predicate True$_0^{\text{arithm}}$ but also a new predicate True$_1^{\text{arithm}}$ meaning 'true sentence of the language of $\mathscr{L}_1^{\text{arithm}}$'. Again, we assume that classical logic applies to this predicate; in which case, the generalized Tarski theorem implies that the language doesn't contain its own truth predicate.

Presumably we can keep on extending this process a very long way (beyond the natural numbers in fact, and for quite a long way through the countable ordinals).[9] I will call this hierarchy (with some historical inaccuracy)[10] *the Tarski hierarchy over arithmetic*.

A more far-reaching extension of arithmetic is to the language of standard set theory, which is a classical-logic theory in which number theory can be embedded. Each of the truth predicates in the Tarski hierarchy over arithmetic can be defined within set theory: extending arithmetic to set theory is far more powerful than extending it by adding a predicate of arithmetic truth. But the generalized theorem implies that the notion of *set-theoretic* truth can't be defined within set theory.

The next extension to consider is to the language of set theory supplemented by a predicate True$_0^{\text{set}}$ of set-theoretic truth, together with appropriate axioms governing it, e.g. compositional axioms that imply all instances of $A \leftrightarrow \text{True}_0^{\text{set}}(\langle A \rangle)$ for A in the pure set-theoretic language. Again, we assume that classical logic applies to this predicate. The generalized theorem then implies that this language can't contain its own truth predicate, and so we are launched on a new hierarchy of truth predicates which might be called *the Tarski hierarchy over set theory*.

Is there some sort of "theory that stands to set theory as set theory stands to arithmetic"? That is, a theory of super-cool entities within which we can define

---

[9] To do this we need some kind of system of notations for an initial segment of the ordinals. Any system of notations is countable, so it can't extend through all of the ordinals, or even all the countable ones.

[10] It is historically inaccurate because the hierarchy that is described in Tarski 1931 doesn't result by considering languages with unrestricted quantifiers but including more and more truth-predicates; it results rather by considering languages none of which contain primitive truth predicates or unrestricted quantifiers, but where the quantifiers become increasingly less restricted. (Tarski was worked in a type-theoretic context, but essentially each of the languages in the hierarchy was one in which all quantifiers were confined to non-sets plus sets of rank less than α for some ordinal α.) So strictly speaking, all levels of Tarski's actual hierarchy (or anyway, all such levels that are hereditarily definable in set theory) are contained in the lowest level of what I'm calling the Tarski hierarchy. Despite this, there are close analogies between Tarski's actual hierarchy and the hierarchy I'm considering (due to the fact that in each level of Tarski's actual hierarchy there is a corresponding *definable* truth predicate); and I think that what I'm considering is what most people have in mind when they speak of "the Tarski hierarchy".

each of the predicates 'True$_a$^{set}'? Maybe, but no one has any idea what it is. And even if there is one, then if it is a classical theory it can't contain its own truth-predicate, and we will just launch a new hierarchy, *the Tarski hierarchy over the theory of super-cool entities*.

It seems that *whatever* mathematical theory we start with, we can successively extend it indefinitely, by going further and further up in a Tarski hierarchy over that mathematical theory. But we need to be careful here, as the next section will show.

1.3. TARSKI'S "UNDEFINABILITY THEOREM" STATES MORE THAN UNDEFINABILITY

Let's consider one last extension of Tarski's theorem: suppose we start with set theory (or the theory of super-cool entities, if we have such a theory) and add a predicate not of set-theoretic truth (or super-cool-entity-theoretic truth) but simply of truth *tout court*, together with some axioms governing this notion that I leave unspecified. I'm not proposing that we try to define this predicate in other terms; just that we add it as a primitive predicate.

But now something weird happens: if we assume that classical logic applies to this predicate, the Tarski theorem implies that there is a "Liar sentence" Q in the language such that we can prove in the resulting theory that $\neg[Q \leftrightarrow \text{True}(\langle Q \rangle)]$. (Other than the extension of classical logic to the predicate 'True', nothing beyond the arithmetic embedded in the set theory is used in the proof.) If one is unwilling to contemplate the idea that the Tarski truth schema

(T) $\langle A \rangle$ is true if and only if A

might have exceptions, then we seem to have proved that what we've added can't really be a truth predicate! So Tarski's Theorem is really far more than an undefinability theorem; it says that full truth can't appear in the language *even as a primitive predicate*, if full truth is assumed to obey both the Tarski schema and classical logic.

Of course, there's something odd about this conclusion: it should lead us to suspect that we don't even understand a concept of full truth that obeys both the Tarski schema and classical logic. There seem to be three possible conclusions:

(1) There's no coherent concept of full truth at all;

(2) There is such a concept, but it violates the Tarski schema;

(3) There is such a concept, but in dealing with it one must generalize the rules of classical logic somehow.

(1) is the standard Tarskian picture of an increasing hierarchy of truth predicates, each more extensive than the previous. (2) and (3) each avoid this, at what may at first seem like a very high cost. However, the cost isn't quite what it seems: if we have a general truth predicate, we can use it to define the restricted Tarskian predicates: for instance, we can define 'is true$_0$' as 'is a true sentence that doesn't contain the truth predicate', and 'is true$_1$' as 'is a true sentence in which "true" is applied only to sentences that don't contain the truth predicate'. Moreover, there is no difficulty within a view of type (2) or (3) of maintaining both classical logic and the appropriate instances of (T) for each of these restrictive predicates (where the appropriate instances of (T) for 'true$_\alpha$' are those in which the sentence A contains no 'true$_\beta$' for $\beta \geq \alpha$).

In short, views of type (2) and type (3) are extensions of views of type (1); their apparently odd behavior occurs only in a domain where view (1) doesn't even venture. So in evaluating view (1), we must compare the cost of not venturing into that domain with the cost of venturing there but saying something in that domain which intuitively seems odd.

The viewpoint underlying this book is that because it is extremely easy to enter the dangerous domain inadvertently, the cost of ensuring that one doesn't enter it is extraordinarily high. This gives a striking advantage to views of type (2) and (3) over views of type (1). And there are in turn striking advantages of views of type (3) over views of type (2), advantages that I will not get into just yet.

It is important to understand why option (3) is not blocked by Tarski's Theorem. A large part of the proof of Tarski's Theorem was the Diagonalization Lemma, and in my "Important Observation" above I remarked that this extends to non-classical logics provided that they meet some fairly minimal conditions. I do *not* propose that we weaken logic to such an extent as to drop any of these conditions; so the Diagonalization Lemma will be accepted even in the weakened logic I will propose. Why then does Tarski's Theorem not generalize to non-classical languages? The reason is that the Diagonalization Lemma yields only the conclusion $Q \leftrightarrow \neg \text{True}(\langle Q \rangle)$; we need an additional step to get from this to $\neg[Q \leftrightarrow \text{True}(\langle Q \rangle)]$, as required by Tarski's Theorem. The inference from $A \leftrightarrow \neg B$ to $\neg(A \leftrightarrow B)$ is valid according to classical logic, and there is no doubt that it can legitimately be assumed in many circumstances; but I think it is contentious to assume that it is valid without restriction. Indeed if $A \leftrightarrow \neg\neg A$ is valid, as it presumably is, then that contentious assumption yields the validity of $\neg(A \leftrightarrow \neg A)$; and in the Introduction I flagged this last as a possible source of the heterologicality paradox and the Russell paradox for properties.

In short: *Tarski's Theorem in the form stated at the start of Section 1.2 (which goes beyond undefinability) need not be valid in a non-classical extension of classical arithmetic, even if the assumptions required for the Diagonalization Lemma are satisfied.*

We do still have that truth is not definable in set-theory, or indeed in any classical language. We can see this in either of two ways: (i) If 'true' were definable in set theory, then the more restrictive predicate 'true sentence of set theory' would also be definable, which conflicts with the extension of Tarski's Theorem to set theory; and since set theory is classical, *that* extension of Tarski's Theorem is valid. An analogous argument can be given for any other classical theory in which arithmetic embeds. (ii) If 'true' were definable in a classical theory like set theory, then it would have to be a classical predicate, so again Tarski's Theorem (in the form stated at the start of Section 1.2) would have to apply.

1.4. ANOTHER FORM OF TARSKI'S THEOREM

Tarski's theorem is often stated in a semantic version; again I start out with the arithmetical language, before considering how it generalizes.

Tarski's theorem for the language of arithmetic (semantic version): No formula $B(v)$ in the language of arithmetic can be true of precisely the true sentences of arithmetic.

The semantic version clearly follows from the proof-theoretic version *in any theory in which we can prove all instances of the schema* $True_0^{arithm}(\langle A \rangle) \leftrightarrow A$ for which 'A' is in the language of pure arithmetic. (For then $\vdash \neg[Q \leftrightarrow B(\langle Q \rangle)]$ yields $\vdash \neg[True_0^{arithm}(\langle Q \rangle) \leftrightarrow B(\langle Q \rangle)]$.) So the semantic version of Tarski's Theorem for arithmetic is certainly a theorem of set theory. But it is not a theorem of arithmetic itself. Indeed, it can't even be *stated* in arithmetic itself, since arithmetic doesn't contain its own truth predicate. (The semantic Tarski theorem can also be proved directly from the semantic Diagonalization Lemma, but that too requires going beyond arithmetic to state.)

What about if we try to generalize the semantic theorem to set theory? For the same reason as for arithmetic, the theorem is not statable, let alone provable, in the language of set theory (though it is statable in the language of set theory with the predicate '$True_0^{set}$' added, and it is provable if sufficiently strong axioms for that predicate are included in one's theory). There are those who think of set theory (without '$True_0^{set}$') as our all-purpose mathematical theory. For them, Tarski's Theorem in its semantic form simply has no analog in the set-theoretic case. The proof-theoretic version is thus of more general applicability.

Like the theorem in its proof-theoretic form, the theorem in the semantic form does not generalize to all non-classical theories. In particular, it doesn't hold for theories in which the inference from $A \leftrightarrow \neg B$ to $\neg(A \leftrightarrow B)$ is restricted, for exactly the reasons we saw in the proof-theoretic case. (Less interestingly, it also doesn't hold for theories in which the logical assumptions required for the Diagonalization Lemma fail.) That is why there is hope for a theory that contains its own truth predicate—indeed, a theory that contains its own truth predicate while still satisfying the Diagonalization Lemma.

(The theorem also doesn't generalize to classical theories according to which the schema $True(\langle A \rangle) \leftrightarrow A$ can have exceptions. As we'll see in detail in Part II,

1.5. CAN SET-THEORETIC TRUTH BE DEFINED?

I've argued that even though Tarski's Theorem in the form stated in Section 1.2 needn't apply when the language is non-classical, still the undefinability claim holds: a general notion of truth, if such a general notion is recognized, can't be definable in any classical sublanguage, such as the language of set-theory. A general notion of truth must be taken as primitive. Some will find this conclusion unappealing. The point of this section is that this does not seem to be unique to general notions of truth: it seems to arise equally for classical notions of truth in the Tarski hierarchy over sufficiently rich mathematical theories. Indeed, it seems to arise even at the lowest level of the Tarski hierarchy, truth$_0$. I say 'seems to' because there is a somewhat controversial philosophical issue involved here, which is what I will be discussing in this section. My discussion will tend to support the view that what seems to be the case is the case.

The issue then will be the definability of truth$_0$—that is, the definability of true-in-$\mathscr{L}$ for languages $\mathscr{L}$ that do not themselves contain 'true' or related notions. In this context, the options of restricting Schema (T) or of weakening the logic seem thoroughly unappealing, so they will receive no mention in this section.

It is sometimes said that Tarski showed that a truth predicate for a language $\mathscr{L}$ is always definable, though only in a more powerful language $\mathscr{L}^*$. But this seems to me an extraordinarily contentious claim. It is also a claim that Tarski quite explicitly *denied*, at least in the original version of his famous article (Tarski 1931). He does begin that article by saying that he will be concerned with defining 'true sentence of $\mathscr{L}$'. But a few paragraphs later he goes on to say that such a definition is possible only when $\mathscr{L}$ is limited in its expressive power. He says that for "richer" languages, definition is impossible, and the goal should be replaced by that of giving an axiomatic theory of truth. (The sort of axiomatic theory he has in mind is what is sometimes called an "inductive definition"; when Tarski speaks of a definition he means explicit definition, i.e. he means that we could introduce the notion of truth as an abbreviation. I will follow him in this usage.) The reason that he gives for why it is impossible to define truth for richer languages is precisely the undefinability theorem we've already discussed.[11]

---

[11] Some of Kripke's remarks on Tarski seem to ignore these very clear statements in Tarski's paper. For instance, Kripke says that the axiomatic or "inductive definition" approach, advocated by Davidson, "has almost become confused with Tarski's original approach" (1976, p. 337). And in his positive paper on truth, Kripke promises to follow Tarski in giving an explicit definition of truth (1975, end of Sec. II). I will argue in Chapter 3 that what Kripke says is thoroughly misleading about his own account as well as about Tarski's.

It does indeed seem that this is the natural conclusion to draw from Tarski's Theorem. It is true that arithmetic truth can be defined in a richer language, the language of set theory. But what about set-theoretic truth? I suppose one could say that it is trivially definable in the language of set theory *plus the notion '$True_0^{set}$' of set theoretic truth*: a sentence x is true-in-the-set-theoretic-language iff $True_0^{set}(x)$! But obviously this sort of trivial definition isn't what Tarski had in mind: he had in mind definition in terms of notions of a "non-semantic" nature.[12] There remains the possibility that we might introduce a theory of super-cool-entities of the sort fantasized about in Section 1.2, and define set-theoretic truth within it; but Tarski doesn't seem to have contemplated the introduction of any such thing. (Certainly not in the original version of his article.)

It might be protested that we already have a theory of super-cool entities, though with a different name: proper classes. (These would have to be the impredicative proper classes of the Morse–Kelley theory of classes; the predicative classes of the Gödel–Bernays theory of classes don't suffice for defining set-theoretic truth.) But if that is the protest, I'd like to change my example: it is now the Morse–Kelley class theory for which truth is undefinable.[13]

A further protest might be that truth-in-Morse–Kelley is likewise definable, by an extension of Morse–Kelley to include "super-classes". Moreover, the protest continues,

(A) this process of introducing more and more powerful entities is never-ending, in a way that precludes the possibility of a single theory governing all of the entities obtainable by the process,

and yet

(B) the powerful entities to be introduced at later stages in the process are available now for defining truth for sentences at earlier stages.

Each of these claims raise huge philosophical issues. Assumption (A) (that "ontology is indefinitely extensible") has been much discussed recently, with little consensus: see for instance Cartwright 1994 and the various essays in Rayo and Uzquiano 2006. But many versions of (A) do not support (B). For instance, one natural way to defend the indefinite extensibility of ontology is to argue

---

[12] This last excludes more than the completely trivial "definition" mentioned in the text. First, it excludes defining true-in-the-set-theoretic-language in terms of a broader truth predicate '$True_\alpha^{set}$' for some α greater than 0: "A sentence x is true-in-the-set-theoretic-language iff $True_\alpha^{set}(x)$ and x employs only the notation of the set-theoretic language." Second, it excludes defining true-in-the-set-theoretic-language in terms of satisfaction-in-the-set-theoretic-language, leaving the latter undefined.

[13] The point would be little changed if instead of introducing proper classes we introduce second order logic, even if that is interpreted as not adding to the ontology but rather as a device of plural quantification as suggested in Boolos 1985. In that case, 'true-in-first-order-set-theory' is definable, but 'true-in-second-order-set-theory' isn't. (The only substantial difference between this and the introduction of proper classes is that since there seems to be no entity-free interpretation of third order logic, the "further protest" considered in the next paragraph would be nipped in the bud.)

that mathematical entities are fictions, and that it's always possible to extend any fiction. But (i) finding a way to fruitfully extend a mathematical fiction is not a routine matter; and (ii) when working within a given fiction of any kind that we know how to clearly articulate, it makes sense to talk unrestrictedly of all mathematical objects. (That is, the claim of indefinite extensibility is external to the fictions: within any fiction that we know how to clearly articulate, there is no indefinite extensibility.) On a view of this sort, we are not able to define an appropriate notion of truth applicable to the total mathematical fiction currently in force, since this would require a non-routine move to a still broader fiction.

Obviously these last remarks don't settle the huge philosophical issues that (A) and (B) together raise. My point is simply that to invoke "indefinite extensibility of ontology", and to declare that it can be used to show that any truth concept is definable, is extraordinarily contentious. Without both the contentious assumptions (A) and (B), we cannot suppose that we can always define a truth predicate for a language $\mathscr{L}$ in non-semantic terms by going to a more powerful language $\mathscr{L}^*$.

What were Tarski's own views on this? As I've said, the original (Polish) version of the article was quite explicit: truth-in-$\mathscr{L}$ simply can't be defined for languages $\mathscr{L}$ that are sufficiently rich in expressive resources; for them, we need an axiomatic theory of truth (one powerful enough to prove not only the instances of the Tarski-schema (T), but a substantial range of important generalizations about truth). However, when the article was translated into German and republished (Tarski 1936a) it contained a new Postscript, and a new footnote referring to that Postscript; these *could* be taken to retract the claim that definition of truth is impossible for sufficiently rich languages, though it is by no means obvious that this is what Tarski intended. If he did intend it, he provided woefully inadequate support.

Let's go through this in somewhat more detail. Tarski was working in the language of type theory, where each variable has a definite ordinal number as its "order"; this means that what that variable ranges over does not include any sets of higher rank than that ordinal. In the original version of the paper, he considered only languages in which all the variables were of finite order. He concluded that in those such languages in which there is a finite bound on the orders of the variables in the language, truth is explicitly definable (in a language where there is no such bound or where the bound is higher); for those for which there is no bound, truth is not explicitly definable (though an axiomatic theory that has the form of an *inductive* definition is possible).

What the footnote and postscript in the later version of the paper do is to remove the restriction that the variables in the language all be of finite order: they are now allowed to be of transfinite order. And the Postscript clearly shows that an obvious generalization holds: if there is an ordinal bound on the orders of the variables in the language, truth is definable (in a language where there is no such bound or where the bound is higher). It is natural to make the further generalization that for those languages for which there isn't even an ordinal bound, truth is undefinable, and we must settle for an axiomatic theory of truth (in the form of an inductive definition). One might, I suppose, suggest that Tarski had an alternative view on which there is simply no such thing as a language for which there is no ordinal bound: if there seems to be such a language, we just "extend the ordinals further". But this, if it can be made clear at all, relies on a conception of the ordinals as "indefinitely extensible" that Tarski does nothing to articulate. Indeed, while the Postscript is not free from ambiguity on this score, nothing is said to prohibit there being a language with variables of all possible orders. In fact, Tarski even says that we need languages with "variables of indefinite order which, so to speak, 'run through' all possible orders" (271). If we take him at his word, it is hard to see how he could have thought explicit definition of truth in accordance with Schema (T) to be possible in such a case.[14]

1.6. INDUCTIVE CHARACTERIZATIONS AND RESTRICTED TRUTH DEFINITIONS

As is well-known, Tarski showed how to characterize truth inductively, for languages that don't themselves contain a truth predicate. (He showed this only for languages that have a very simple structure, and don't contain ambiguous or indexical terms. But these restrictions can be lifted—e.g. in the case of indexicality, by relativizing truth to a context.) In the case of the usual language of arithmetic, where all quantifiers are implicitly restricted to the natural numbers and every object in the restricted domain is denoted by some term in the language, it is very easy to give the inductive definition, for there is no need to go through Tarski's notion of satisfaction or anything similar to it: quantification is treated substitutionally.

---

[14] One complication in any definitive exegesis is that the only place Tarski explicitly considers theories like Zermelo–Fraenkel (ZF), in which the variables are untyped, is in a footnote, and what he says seems an ill thought-out attempt to use extendability of axioms as a surrogate for extendability of ontology. What he says is:

the order of [such a] language is the smallest ordinal number which exceeds the order of all sets whose existence follows from the axioms adopted in the language. (p. 271 n. 1)

This is perhaps not crystal-clear, but presumably the intention is that the order of ZF is to be the first ordinal not in the minimal model of ZF (assuming there to be one). If we minimally extend ZF to postulate such an ordinal, then we can indeed use the extended theory ZF$^+$ to define a truth-predicate for the language of ZF; but this defined truth predicate will be one in which the claim that there is such an ordinal (equivalently, the claim that there is a minimal model) turns out false. But why assume that that is the *right* truth-predicate for the language of those who accept ZF but nothing beyond it? This requires the view that because such an ordinal *isn't provable within their theory*, the claim that it exists is *false in their language*. (But the view also requires that it be *true in the language of those who give the definition of truth*: otherwise, the definition would make every sentence of ZF come out true.) This is not an easily defensible view, and I know of no reason to think Tarski held it beyond this footnote; so I think the footnote was very likely an aberration.

We start with an inductive characterization of denotation:

(i) (The Gödel number of) the name '0' denotes 0 and nothing else;

(ii) for any closed singular terms t_1 and t_2 and any number n, $\ulcorner t_1 + t_2 \urcorner$ denotes n if and only if there are numbers m_1 and m_2 such that t_1 denotes m_1, t_2 denotes m_2, and $n = m_1 + m_2$;

plus similar clauses for the other primitive names and function symbols. ($\ulcorner t_1 + t_2 \urcorner$ is an abbreviation of $t_1{}^\wedge{}'+'{}^\wedge t_2$; that is, it means the result of putting a '+' between t_1 and t_2.) We can then turn this inductive characterization into an explicit definition. This can in fact be done within arithmetic, but it is easier to use a well-known set-theoretic trick (analogous to the trick that Frege used to define 'ancestor of' from 'parent of'):

For any closed singular term t and number n, t denotes n if and only if the pair $<t, n>$ is in every set X that (i) contains the pair $<$'0', $0>$, (ii) contains $<\ulcorner t_1 + t_2 \urcorner, m_1 + m_2>$ whenever it contains $<t_1, m_1>$ and $<t_2, m_2>$, and so on for the other clauses.

We can now inductively define 'true', by first defining a true identity sentence to be one where both terms denote the same thing,[15] and then saying:

For any formula A, its negation is true if and only if A is not true;

For any formulas A and B, their conjunction is true if and only if A and B are both true;

For any variable v and formula A, the result of universally quantifying A with respect to v is true if and only if each sentence that results from A by substituting a term for all free occurrences of v is true;

(Plus similar clauses for disjunction, existential quantification, etc.)

And this too can be turned into an explicit definition within set theory, by essentially the same trick:

A sentence S is true if and only if $<S,1>$ is in every set X that contains

(i) $<A,1>$ for each true identity sentence and $<A,0>$ for each untrue identity sentence;

(ii) $<\neg A,1>$ whenever X contains $<A, 0>$, and $<\neg A, 0>$ whenever X contains $<A, 1>$;

(iii) $<A \wedge B, 1>$ whenever X contains both $<A, 1>$ and $<B, 1>$, and $<A \wedge B, 0>$ whenever X contains either $<A, 0>$ or $<B, 0>$;

(iv) $<\forall v A(v), 1>$ whenever X contains $<A(t), 1>$ for each term t of the language, and $<\forall v A(v), 0>$ whenever X contains $<A(t), 0>$ for some term t of the language.

---

[15] In the usual language of arithmetic, identity is the only primitive predicate. Were there others, we'd generalize this: e.g. if '(evenly) divides' were primitive instead of defined, we'd say that for any singular terms t_1 and t_2, $\ulcorner t_1$ divides $t_2 \urcorner$ is true if and only if there are numbers m_1 and m_2 such that t_1 denotes m_1, t_2 denotes m_2, and m_1 divides m_2.

(Although many inductive definitions can be made explicit *within arithmetic*, this is not so for the inductive definition of arithmetic truth, as Tarski's Theorem shows. An analysis of why we can't make it explicit would pin the blame on the quantifier clause: in particular, on the fact that the truth value of a quantified sentence can depend on the truth value of infinitely many instances. If only suitably restricted quantification were allowed, the problem would not arise.)

Let's consider how this works out for the language of (Zermelo-Fraenkel) set theory. Here there are too many objects to denote in the language, so we must treat quantification in a more complicated way. (To partially compensate, we can take the language not to contain singular terms at all, so there is no need to worry about denotation.) The usual treatment, Tarski's, works via a notion of satisfaction (a generalization of the notion "truth of" used in the Introduction). This involves the use of *assignment functions*, functions which assign objects to the variables of the language; satisfaction is truth relative to an assignment function, and I will use 'A is true$_s$' as a more suggestive version of 's satisfies A'.[16] We inductively characterize truth$_s$ for the language as follows:

⌜$v_1 \in v_2$⌝ is true$_s$ if and only if $s(v_1) \in s(v_2)$

For any formula A, its negation is true$_s$ if and only if A is not true$_s$

...

For any variable v and formula A, the result of universally quantifying A with respect to v is true$_s$ if and only if for each set o, A is true$_{s(v/o)}$; where $s(v/o)$ assigns the set o to the variable v but assigns to each variable u other than v the same set that s assigns to u.

For sentences (formulas without free variables) the assignment function is easily seen to make no difference; so we can regard a sentence as true if it is true$_s$ for all (or equivalently, some) s.

But now, it might seem, we could employ the standard trick and turn the inductive definition of truth$_s$ into an explicit definition within ordinary set theory. We know that to be impossible: if we could, then set-theoretic truth would be definable in set theory, in violation of Tarski's Theorem. Where, though, does the attempt go wrong?

---

[16] It's actually more natural to consider *partial* assignment functions, that assign objects only to *some* variables. We could then take a *fully parameterized formula* to be a pair of an ordinary formula and an assignment function assigning objects to its free variables, and call such a parameterized formula <A, s> true if A is true$_s$, i.e. if s satisfies A. Better yet, we'd take a fully parameterized formula to be an equivalence class of such pairs, where the pair of a formula with v_1 free and a function assigning o to v_1 is equivalent to the pair just like it but with a different free variable. If we picture parameterized formulas as "like formulas, but with objects where the free variables would otherwise be", it is routine to define logical operations such as disjunction on parameterized formulas. Tarski's account could then be recast as a direct inductive definition of truth for fully parameterized formulas. (Truth of a sentence A is identified with truth of <A, ø>, where ø is the "empty partial function".) This is a trivial reformulation of Tarski, but it's convenient because we needn't speak separately of satisfaction, we can speak just of truth—though truth for parameterized formulas, not just for sentences.

If we were to proceed in analogy to what we did in the arithmetical case, here's what we'd get:

A formula F is true$_s$ if and only if $<F, s, 1>$ is in every set X that contains

(i) $<v_1 \in v_2, s^*, 1>$ for all variables v_1, v_2 and assignment functions s^* for which $s^*(v_1) \in s^*(v_2)$, and $<v_1 \in v_2, s^*, 0>$ for all v_1, v_2 and s^* for which $s^*(v_1) \notin s^*(v_2)$;

(ii) $<\neg A, s^*, 1>$ for all A and s^* for which X contains $<A, s^*, 0>$, and for all A and s^* for which X contains $<A, s^*, 1>$;

(iii) $<A \wedge B, s^*, 1>$ for all A, B and s^* for which X contains both $<A, s^*, 1>$ and $<B, s^*, 1>$, and $<A \wedge B, s^*, 0>$ for all A, B and s^* for which X contains either $<A, s^*, 0>$ or $<B, s^*, 0>$;

(iv) $<\forall v A(v), s^*, 1>$ for all v, A and s^* for which X contains $<A(v), s^*(v/o), 1>$ for each set o, and $<\forall v A(v), s^*, 0>$ for all v, A and s^* for which X contains $<A(v), s^*(v/o), 0>$ for some set o.

(Note that the need to vary the assignment function in (iv) forces us to consider assignment functions s^* other than the one s that we may be interested in.) But this gives very bad results! The problem is that there are no sets meeting conditions (i)–(iv), so every formula comes out true$_s$ for every s! Indeed, there's no set X containing even all cases of (i). For if there were such a set, it would have to have a rank α, and so it could contain triples $<v_1 \in v_2, s, 1>$ and $<v_1 \in v_2, s, 0>$ only for s that have lower rank than α, and hence that assign only objects of lower rank than α to all variables. But (i) entails that for each assignment function s no matter how high the ranks assigned, and for any particular variables v_1 and v_2, either $<v_1 \in v_2, s, 1>$ or $<v_1 \in v_2, s, 0>$ is in X; so we have a contradiction. (There is an alternative way to make inductive characterizations explicit that uses existential quantifications over sets rather than universal quantification over sets, but it of course has the opposite problem: instead of making everything true$_s$, it makes nothing true$_s$.)

In the case of arithmetical truth, I remarked parenthetically that we could make the inductive characterization explicit *even in arithmetic* if instead of quantifiers over the natural numbers we had only quantifiers bounded by a specific natural number. The analog holds here: the above attempt at making the definition explicit would work fine if the quantifiers ranged only over sets of rank less than some specific ordinal α, for then there would be sets meeting conditions (i)–(iv). We can now see more clearly why it is that truth is definable in Tarski's languages with variables of bounded order, but not in his languages with variables of unbounded order (let alone his languages with variables of indefinite order).

1.7. FURTHER REMARKS ON EXPLICIT DEFINITION

Even when dealing with a language with unrestricted quantifiers, or a language (like that of set theory) in which the quantifiers aren't *sufficiently* restricted for an explicit truth definition to be possible within set theory, we can define something very like truth: we can define a predicate 'True$^{V_\alpha}$' meaning 'comes out true when all quantifiers are restricted to non-sets and to sets of rank less than α'. The definition is in terms of a corresponding satisfaction predicate 'True$_s^{V_\alpha}$', but *where the assignment function s is required to assign only non-sets and sets of rank less than* α; 'True$_s^{V_\alpha}$' can then be defined in the way attempted in the previous section. The assignment functions s^*, like the assignment function s, are required not to assign sets of rank α or higher; this allows the existence of sets X satisfying the required conditions, and the definition is not anomalous. Of course the defined predicate doesn't satisfy the truth schema (T), but only the modified schema

(T^{V_α})   ⟨A⟩ is true if and only if A^{V_α},

where A^{V_α} is the result of restricting all quantifiers of A to non-sets and sets of rank less than α.

The possibility of explicitly defining 'True$^{V_\alpha}$' (for any ordinal α) is really just a special case of something else: the possibility of defining *truth in a model* (where 'model' is interpreted in its strict sense, according to which the domain is required to be a set). I will discuss this in the next chapter.

There are other limited truth (and satisfaction) predicates that are also explicitly definable within set theory. For instance, it isn't hard to show that for each specific number n, the predicate 'is a true sentence of set theory with no more than n quantifiers' (and the corresponding satisfaction predicate) are explicitly definable in set theory. But the definitions get more and more complicated as n increases, in a way that precludes their being turned into a single definition. I sketch the general idea in a footnote.[17] Given this predicate for a specific n, one can

---

[17] Note first that for arbitrary assignment functions s (with no restriction on the rank assigned), it is easy to modify the definition attempted in Section 1.6 to obtain a definition of 'F is a 0-quantifier formula of the set theoretic language that is true$_s$': simply drop the quantifier clause (iv), *leave the assignment function out of the triples*, and instead of quantifying over assignment functions s^* in (i)–(iii) simply stick to talking about s. (The quantification over s^* in these clauses was needed only so that predicates and truth functional connectives would behave correctly even inside the scope of quantifiers.) In other words, the definition will have the form

A quantifier-free formula F is true$_s$ if and only if $<F,1>$ is in every set X that contains ...

where X is now a set of pairs of form either $<A, 1>$ or $<A, 0>$, A being a formula. Since there is no assignment function in the pairs that are members of X, the problem that arose for explicitly defining the full truth predicate no longer arises.

Now we can easily define truth$_s$ for formulas of the set theoretic language that have form $(\forall v)F$, where F has 0 quantifiers: such a formula is true$_s$ if and only if for all objects o, F is true$_{s(v/o)}$, and we've already defined what it is for a quantifier-free formula to be true$_{s(v/o)}$. Truth$_s$ for formulas of form $(\exists v)F$, where F has 0 quantifiers, is defined similarly.

Of course, 1-quantifier formulas of the set-theoretic language needn't have their quantifiers in the initial position. But they are built up from formulas whose single quantifier is in the initial position by truth-functional operations, so we can now define truth$_s$ for arbitrary 1-quantifier formulas in

of course use the Diagonalization Lemma to construct a sentence that says of itself that it isn't a true sentence with no more than n quantifiers. But that sentence will contain more than n quantifiers, so it is true and in no way paradoxical.

analogy with how we defined truth for 0-quantifier formulas: we can keep the s fixed throughout, because we already know what it is for the 1-quantifier component to be true$_s$.

And we can now use the definition of truth$_s$ for arbitrary 1-quantifier formulas to define truth$_s$ for 2-quantifier formulas one of whose quantifiers is in initial position; then we can use that to extend to a definition of truth$_s$ for arbitrary 2-quantifier formulas. All this is in complete analogy to the 1-quantifier case. Obviously the process can be extended through any finite n.

2
Validity and the Unprovability of Soundness

2.1. VALIDITY AND THE NECESSARY PRESERVATION OF TRUTH

What is it for an argument to be *logically valid*? (Equivalently, for its premises to *logically imply* its conclusion, or for its conclusion to be *a logical consequence of* its premises.) A natural thought is that a valid argument is one that is logically guaranteed to preserve truth. This is sometimes taken as simply what 'valid' *means*: the biconditional

(VAL) The argument from Γ to B is *valid* if and only if $\Box$(if all members of Γ are true then B is true)

is *true by definition of 'valid'*, where $\Box$ indicates logical necessity. (The proposal is that this defines 'valid' in terms of 'logically necessary', not the other way around.) This proposed definition requires both a prior notion of logical necessity and a general notion of truth. Many have been doubtful about the clarity of the notion of logical necessity, or have supposed that it can only be explained in terms of validity rather than the reverse. And we've seen that Tarski doubted the possibility of a general notion of truth as well. His doubts about this did not prevent him from offering a characterization of valid argument (i.e. of logical implication or logical consequence) along lines somewhat similar to (VAL); but the differences will prove to be very important.

Before getting to that, I should mention an alternative approach that would proceed not by trying to specify the meaning of 'valid' but by taking it as a primitive notion that governs our inferential or epistemic practices. (For instance, when we discover that an argument is valid we avoid believing the conclusion less strongly than we believe the conjunction of the premises.) The idea is to specify plausible principles governing validity; these may enable us to deduce (VAL).

To see how this might work, let's use the notation $A_1, \ldots, A_n \models B$ to mean that the argument from the premises $A_1, \ldots, A_n$ to the conclusion B is logically valid. (For simplicity I confine my attention here to the case where the argument has only finitely many premises.) Then assuming that we have a well-behaved general notion of truth, we should have an equivalence between each A_i and the corresponding claim True($\langle A_i \rangle$), and similarly for B. So

(1) $$A_1, \ldots, A_n \models B$$

should be equivalent to

$$\text{True}(\langle A_1 \rangle), \ldots, \text{True}(\langle A_n \rangle) \models \text{True}(\langle B \rangle).$$

That in turn should be equivalent to

$$\text{True}(\langle A_1 \rangle) \wedge \ldots \wedge \text{True}(\langle A_n \rangle) \models \text{True}(\langle B \rangle),$$

by the obvious rules for conjunction built into classical logic and almost every other logic. This in turn should be equivalent to

(2) $$\models \text{True}(\langle A_1 \rangle) \wedge \ldots \wedge \text{True}(\langle A_n \rangle) \rightarrow \text{True}(\langle B \rangle),$$

by the standard rules for the conditional that are also built into classical logic. (2) says that we can validly argue to the claim True($\langle A_1 \rangle$) $\wedge \ldots \wedge$ True($\langle A_n \rangle$) $\rightarrow$ True($\langle B \rangle$) without using any premises: the sentence itself is logically valid. But this seems a fair characterization of what 'logically necessary' means. So letting '$\Box C$' be an abbreviation of $\models C$, we have argued for an equivalence between the claim $A_1, \ldots, A_n \models B$ and the claim $\Box$(True($\langle A_1 \rangle$) $\wedge \ldots \wedge$ True($\langle A_n \rangle$) $\rightarrow$ True($\langle B \rangle$)).[1]

This simple argument, which I will refer to in future chapters as *The Validity Argument*, looks thoroughly convincing at first sight, and seems to offer a rationale for equating validity with necessary truth-preservation that doesn't make it simply a matter of definition. But we'll see in later chapters that *on every possible theory of truth* the argument is problematic, and that the problems with the argument cast considerable doubt on the equation (VAL).

Indeed, it should already be clear that Tarski himself couldn't have accepted either the argument or its conclusion (VAL), since both rely on a general notion of truth that he did not believe in.

2.2. TRUTH IN A MODEL

In order to investigate the nature of logical consequence, Tarski wanted to define logical consequence (that is, valid argument) within the language of set theory. His paper on logical consequence (1936b) raises a few exegetical issues that I'd like to avoid; so what I will really discuss is the modern model-theoretic definition of logical consequence which grew out of Tarski's definition.

---

[1] Strictly speaking, this argument wouldn't quite establish the generalization that an argument is valid if and only if it preserves truth by logical necessity, but only the instances of that generalization. But I take it that anyone who believes each instance will believe the generalization.

We've seen that we can't adequately define truth within set theory, for languages with unrestricted quantifiers. If we thought that validity had to be defined by (VAL), this would mean that in set theory validity too could only be defined for languages with quantifiers restricted to a set. Even then, defining validity within set theory by (VAL) would require first defining a set-theoretic surrogate for the logical necessity operator, and it isn't obvious how to do that: the task of finding such a definition is in effect equivalent to the task of defining validity for single sentences, and this is part of what is at issue.

So in defining validity within set theory, Tarski had two obstacles to overcome: the notion of truth was simply unavailable, and the notion of logical necessity wasn't directly available either. His paper on logical consequence (or at least, the model-theoretic definition to which it gave rise) solved both problems with a single stroke. The definition of consequence is very simple: to say that a sentence B is a *logical consequence* of a set of sentences Γ (that is, to say that the argument from Γ to B is *valid*) is to say that B is true in all models in which Γ is true. This definition is supposed to be applicable not only to restricted languages, but to languages with unrestricted quantifiers, such as the language of set theory itself.

The definition requires the notion of a model, and of truth in a model. If we are defining the consequence relation for a simple classical language $\mathscr{L}$ of the kind under consideration here, we use 2-valued models, defined as follows: a *(2-valued) model* consists of a set (the *domain* of the model) together with an assignment of an object in the domain to each individual constant of $\mathscr{L}$, an n-place operation on the domain to each n-place function symbol of $\mathscr{L}$, and a set of n-tuples of members of $\mathscr{L}$ to each predicate symbol of $\mathscr{L}$. (I impose the additional requirement that the set assigned to the identity predicate is the set of all pairs of form $<o, o>$ for o in the domain, but impose no additional requirements on what is assigned to the predicates.)[2] The inductive definition of truth-in-M where M is (a variable for) a model then mimics the inductive definition of truth for restricted languages: the only difference is that we replace the actual denotations of individual constants by the denotations specified in the model, and similarly for function symbols and predicates; and that we replace the actual range of the quantifiers by the range specified in M (that is, by the domain

---

[2] Since the definition of model doesn't take account of any logical structure beyond quantificational structure plus identity, a definition of "logical consequence" as preservation of truth in all models so understood is really a definition of *consequence in light of quantificational structure plus identity*. But that's too long-winded to keep saying, so I will just speak of 'logical consequence'. This should not be understood as a commitment to a view that only such structure is properly called logical; I hold no such view. (Indeed, later in the book I will switch to a broader interpretation of logical consequence, one which treats the truth predicate as well as the identity predicate as special. I share Tarski's view (Tarski 1936b, pp. 418–20) that which predicates get treated as "special to logic" is largely a matter of convention: one could understand 'logical consequence' in such a way that 'Jones is unmarried' is a "logical consequence" of 'Jones is a bachelor', and if one did so then one should restrict to models where the set assigned to 'bachelor' must be a subset of that assigned to 'unmarried'.)

of M). We can then convert the inductive definition to an explicit definition, just as for truth in a restricted language. (The explicit definition will be of truth in M *for variable M*.)

The idea of defining logical consequence as the preservation of truth *in all (2-valued) models* is that this is a set-theoretically defined surrogate for defining it as *logically necessary* truth-preservation. Models serve as something like "logically possible worlds". The move from possible worlds, whose universes may be too large to be a set, to these surrogates where the quantifiers range only over a set, is essential for carrying out the set-theoretic definition.

There is however a small fly in the ointment: since models have sets as their domains, there is on this explication no possible world that corresponds to the actual world!

The problem is not at all serious when dealing with restricted languages: there we don't need the full actual world to determine what's true, we need only the part of the actual world in the domain of the quantifiers; and there is a model corresponding to that. But in the case of unrestricted languages the problem is more serious. The problem could be put by saying that truth is not a special case of truth in a model; so if to call a sentence valid (or logically true) means that it is true in all models, then there is no obvious bar to a sentence being valid (or logically true) and yet not being true! More generally, if to call an argument valid means that in all models in which the premises are true then so is the conclusion, then it looks like an argument could be valid without preserving *real* truth, but only truth in a model.

We could of course avoid this problem by using the defined concept of validity only in the case of restricted languages, but that is not attractive: we do, apparently, employ an unrestricted language, and have a concept of valid argument for it; and we expect that the extensive body of work that has been done in model theory illuminates the notion of validity for our actual language. But how could it, if logical truth doesn't imply truth, and if a valid argument could have true premises and a false conclusion?

This problem is sometimes papered over in various ways, which are sometimes combined. The first is a vacillation between two senses of 'model': the sense defined above, and a second sense. To avoid confusion on this score, I'll use the term 'interpretation' for the second sense. (It too is used ambiguously: sometimes in the way that follows, but sometimes for models in the sense above.) To *provide an interpretation* of a language $\mathscr{L}$ (of the same sort for which I just defined 'model') is, in part, to specify a formula $U(x)$ for which we then say that the quantifiers of $\mathscr{L}$ range over those things x such that $U(x)$. (We also specify formulas corresponding to the predicates; uniquely satisfied formulas corresponding to the names; and so forth.)[3] Given such an interpretation, we can then inductively define truth in that interpretation. And we can turn the inductive definition into

---

[3] For a rigorous formulation, see Shoenfield 1967, p. 61.

an explicit definition *in the special case where there is a set of all things x such that U(x)*, since in that special case the interpretation specifies a model as defined above.

Another way to paper over the problem is to say that it doesn't arise for "class models", but this brings us to a second linguistic vacillation, between two ways of understanding talk of classes.

First, there are theories which postulate, in addition to sets, additional "set-like entities" called proper classes. (In the usual formulations, sets are a special kind of class: the classes are partitioned into the sets and the proper classes.) According to such theories, although there is no set of all sets, there is still a proper class of all sets; but there is no class of all classes. In such theories we can allow models to be proper classes, and if we do so then there will be a model that contains all sets. Still, no model even in this extended sense can contain all *classes*, and hence we won't have essentially changed the predicament: truth in all models has no obvious bearing on genuine truth.

Second, there is also a standard practice of using the term 'class' informally in theories that don't literally posit proper classes, but only posit sets; talk of classes is viewed as just a dispensable manner of speaking. And in this manner of speaking, it is common to speak of these classes as the domains of "class models". (This is for instance what set theorists usually have in mind when they speak of "class models" of Zermelo–Fraenkel set theory.) But 'class' in this informal sense is just another term for 'interpretation' as understood several paragraphs back; and truth in a "class model" is not explicitly definable in such theories.

(It would be of no help to propose that we define validity not within set theory or class theory but within second order logic, viewing that as a basic logic not explainable in (and more powerful than) the first order theory of sets and classes. Putting aside doubts about the intelligibility of second order logic so conceived, let's grant that it could be used to explain *first order validity*. But the question of interest is defining validity *for the language being employed*, which on the current proposal isn't first order logic but second order logic. And I think it's pretty clear that similar difficulties to those in the first order case would arise for any explicit second order definition of second order validity.)

So however we twist and turn we have a problem to deal with: if validity is defined in a standard way, the claim that a sentence is logically valid doesn't entail that it's true, and the claim that an argument is logically valid doesn't entail that if the premises are true then so is the conclusion. The problem was first adequately addressed by Kreisel (1967).

2.3. THE KREISEL SQUEEZING ARGUMENT

Kreisel's solution to the puzzle introduced in the previous section was essentially this:

1. We should think of the intuitive notion of validity not as literally *defined* by the model theoretic account, or in any other manner; rather, we should think of it as a primitive notion.
2. We then use intuitive principles about validity, together with technical results from model theory, to argue that validity *extensionally coincides with* the technical notion.

This is somewhat similar in spirit to the approach of the Validity Argument in Section 2.1, but considerably different in detail since the idea is to sustain the extensional correctness of the model-theoretic definition rather than of a definition along the lines of (VAL).

To elaborate Kreisel's approach, consider some specific formalization F of (first order) quantification logic (with identity) that employs axioms and rules that seem self-evident. Call an argument *derivable in* F if its conclusion can be derived from its premises together with the axioms of F, using only the rules of F. Then the idea is that intuitive principles about validity guarantee

(Intuitive soundness of F) Any argument that is derivable in F is valid$_{intuitive}$.

Intuitive principles about validity also seem to guarantee

If there is a model in which the premises of an argument are true and the conclusion isn't, then the argument is not valid$_{intuitive}$;

or to put this another way,

(Model assumption) Any argument that is not valid$_{technical}$ is not valid$_{intuitive}$;

So the picture is as shown in Diagram 2.1.

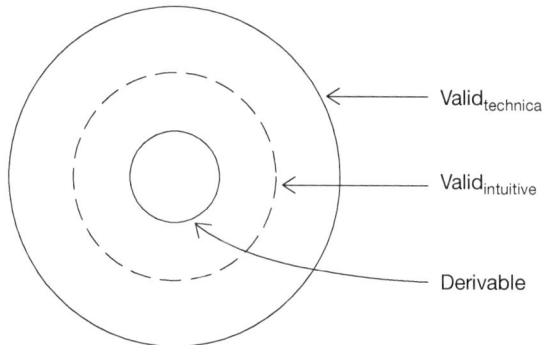

Diagram 2.1.

But now we appeal to the fact that (if the formalization F is properly chosen) we will have a completeness theorem, which says:

(Completeness Theorem for F) Any argument that is valid$_{technical}$ is derivable in F.

And this together with the previous two guarantees that intuitive validity extensionally coincides both with validity in the technical model-theoretic sense and with derivability in F: the outer circle and inner circle are squeezed together, forcing the middle one to line up with both of them.

This analysis (an example of what Kreisel called "informal rigour") seems to me to give quite a convincing reason for accepting the standard model-theoretic "definition" of validity as extensionally adequate for classical (first order) logic, even for unrestricted languages.

An interesting feature of the analysis is that the standard "Soundness Theorem" for F, the converse of the Completeness Theorem, plays no explicit role. (Of course, the Intuitive Soundness Principle and the Model Principle together imply the conclusion of the Soundness Theorem.) This is connected to the issues to be discussed in the following section.

2.4. THE UNPROVABILITY OF SOUNDNESS

In standard metalogic courses we teach a theorem that is billed as showing the soundness of some typical proof procedure for standard predicate logic. This is a bit of a hoax. What this "soundness theorem" actually says is this:

(M)   for any set of sentences Γ and any sentence B, if B is derivable from Γ in the proof procedure then B is true in every model in which all members of Γ are true.

This is "argument soundness". As a corollary, we get the weaker claim of "statement soundness":

(M_w)   for any sentence B, if B is derivable (without assumptions) in the proof procedure then B is true in every model.

But I hope it's clear from the discussion in Section 2.2 that (M) and (M_w) aren't really sufficient for soundness in the intuitive sense. For instance, (M_w) doesn't entail that sentences derivable in this proof procedure are actually true. To what extent can this lacuna be filled?

There are, actually, two quite distinct worries here, only one of which is my immediate concern.

The worry that is *not* my immediate concern (but which is worth mentioning so as to clearly distinguish it from the one that is) is that any argument for the genuine soundness of a logic is obviously going to have to assume that very logic. (I'll call this *the radical worry*, for want of a better term.) For instance, if we are to argue that all instances of excluded middle are true, the obvious way to do it is to say:

(i)   if a sentence x is true, then the disjunction of it with anything else is true; so in particular, the disjunction of x with the negation of x is true;

(ii) if a sentence x is not true, then its negation is true, so the disjunction of anything with the negation of x is true; so again, the disjunction of x with the negation of x is true.

So either way, the disjunction of x with the negation of x is true.

But the "either way" hides the use of excluded middle, the very law being "validated": it assumes that any sentence x is either true or not true. Moreover, anyone who questioned excluded middle would almost certainly question this application of it, leaving the argument with little if any dialectical punch. That all arguments for genuine soundness are circular in this way is widely acknowledged. (The term 'rule-circular' is often used in this or a closely related context, though it may not be quite appropriate here since excluded middle is often thought of as an axiom rather than a rule.)[4]

This radical worry, as I said, is not the worry I am concerned with: I'm worried rather about whether we can prove genuine soundness *even taking classical logic for granted*. But it's worth making a final comment on the radical worry, for it illustrates the import of the difference between real truth and truth in a model. There is good reason why I raised the radical worry only in connection with purported proofs of the *genuine* soundness of first order logic, not in connection with standard proofs of (M) and (M_w). For though those standard proofs do of course employ some logic, and it is typically taken for granted that that logic is classical, one could in fact do those standard proofs in many far weaker logics, including the kind of logic I will eventually recommend. The reason is that those logics, while weakening classical logic in some ways, are "in effect classical" as applied to certain areas of discourse; and *discourse about set-theoretic models is among them*. In such a logic, despite the restrictions on excluded middle, it will still be correct to say

For any sentence x and any (2-valued) model M, either x is true in M or it isn't;

so there is no problem with deducing the claims (M) and (M_w). (I've inserted the term '2-valued', but this is just to indicate that I'm using 'model' *in the same sense used in the classical theorems (M) and (M_w)*.) The advocate of a non-classical logic may well introduce a different though related notion of model, call it '*-model', which is useful in giving a "soundness proof" for their non-classical logic. But the issue of what is true in all *-models is simply a different question from the issue of what is true in all 2-valued models, and (M_w) was intended to deal only with the latter. Given this, advocates of most non-classical logics would agree

---

[4] This raises the question of what the value of soundness proofs is. Certainly part of the answer is that it is easy to make mistakes when formalizing a logic; trying to give a soundness proof often exposes such mistakes, and success in giving one gives a high degree of reassurance that certain kinds of mistakes have been avoided. Dummett 1978 argues that such proofs have additional value: they provide an explanation to those who accept a given logic of why they should accept it over rival logics. I'm inclined to think that these two considerations exhaust the value of soundness proofs, though some authors who acknowledge the rule-circularity claim more: see for instance Boghossian 2000.

that classical logic is sound *in the sense of (M_w)*, but not agree that it is *genuinely* sound; they'd say that classical logic is sound in the sense of (M_w) only because (M_w) deals with models (in the 2-valued sense), and models don't adequately reflect reality.

But to turn finally to the moderate worry, there is still a gap between models and reality *even if we take reasoning within classical logic for granted*. There is a lacuna between using classical reasoning to establish (M_w) and using classical reasoning to establish that classical reasoning is genuinely sound.

It may seem that the Kreisel squeezing argument fills the lacuna: after all, the conclusion of that argument (in the case of sentences, on which for simplicity of formulation I'll now focus) is that logical validity in the intuitive sense coincides with both truth in all models and derivability in F. Logical validity in the intuitive sense would seem to imply truth, so we seem to have an argument that predicate logic is intuitively sound. However, this "argument" would be totally question-begging (not merely "rule-circular"). For one of the premises of the Kreisel argument was that derivability in F suffices for intuitive validity. If we stipulate that one of the requirements on intuitive validity is truth, then we've simply built the conclusion to be proved into the premise.

A route to genuine soundness that might seem more promising would be to try to mimic the standard inductive argument used in "soundness proofs", but using real truth instead of truth in a model.[5] And it seems straightforward to do that, if we have an appropriate truth or satisfaction predicate. If F is a typical Hilbert-style proof procedure, the way to do this, in outline, is first to argue that the axioms of F are all true—or more generally, that all axioms of F are satisfied by everything. The details of this step of the argument will of course have to use classical laws such as excluded middle, but that's OK: we're not addressing the radical worry here, we're taking the use of classical reasoning for granted. And given this, it seems unproblematic to fill in the details. The second step is to argue that all the inference rules of F preserve truth—or more generally, that they preserve the property of being satisfied by everything. Again, it seems unproblematic to fill in the details; and again, the fact that we'll have to use classical logic in the reasoning is unproblematic when pretensions to answer the radical worry are put aside. But given these first two steps, it seems routine to argue by mathematical induction that all theorems are satisfied by everything, and hence that those with no free variables are true.

But we need to ask what kind of truth or satisfaction predicate is required to carry this out. Suppose 'true' here is the lowest truth predicate 'true$_0$' in the Tarski hierarchy of Section 1.2, so that it means "True sentence not containing 'semantic' terms like 'true' or 'satisfies'". Similarly, suppose that 'satisfies' is 'satisfies$_0$'. Then we can give a perfectly good inductive proof, along the lines

---

[5] As stated, this would lose some of the modal force provided by talk of models. To avoid that, one could run the induction on truth *at each possible world*.

just sketched, for the conclusion that any derivation in system F *that uses only sentences without semantic terms in the derivation* results in a formula satisfied$_0$ by everything. Perhaps that's all we expected: we may even have defined the deductive system F so that it only applied to formulas in the "ground language" that has no semantic terms. Even so, one might have hoped to establish (using classical reasoning) that excluded middle, modus ponens, and so forth, are valid *even in expansions of that language*, and the present point is that that would not be established by the proof.

Indeed, the proof doesn't even show that every sentence in the ground language that can be given a derivation in an expansion of the ground language (by the rules of F, as generalized to allow instances in the expanded language) is true: it is only when *the whole derivation* is in the ground language that we can infer that its conclusion is true. Consequently the above version of the soundness proof doesn't show that we can't use modus ponens, excluded middle, and similar rules to derive a clearly false sentence of the ground language.

Obviously just going up in the Tarski hierarchy would change little: it would allow the soundness proof to cover a wider range of arguments, but we would still be left without a proof that there is no way to use ordinary classical logic to derive obvious falsehoods in the ground language. The question of whether we can do better than this using *non-Tarskian* truth predicates, perhaps in non-classical logics, is one that I defer to Chapters 11, 19, and 26.

But what about avoiding these issues about truth, by stating the soundness claim in a more limited way that avoids any truth predicate? What about stating it *schematically*, as consisting of all sentences that result by substituting a sentence of the language for the letter 'C' in the following schema:

(S_w) If $\langle C \rangle$ is derivable (without assumptions) in the proof procedure F then C.

Or more generally,

(S) If $\langle C \rangle$ is derivable from assumptions $\langle A_1 \rangle, \ldots, \langle A_n \rangle$ in the proof procedure F, and if $A_1, \ldots,$ and A_n, then C.

(F is, again, any standard proof procedure for classical predicate logic.) The totality of instances of these schemas wouldn't constitute a full soundness claim, since the latter has a generality that the totality of instances doesn't have; still, it would go a considerable way toward it. So let's ask about the extent of the ability to establish all the instances of (S_w) that are in a language $\mathscr{L}$, without going beyond $\mathscr{L}$ in our reasoning.[6]

---

[6] $\mathscr{L}$ must be rich enough to define the vocabulary used in (S_w), but this requires only the equivalent of number theory. It may be much richer, e.g. it may include standard set theory. And it may contain a truth predicate, but it needn't. Obviously I'm going to allow us to use reasoning that goes far beyond the quantificational proof procedure F: I'll allow number-theoretic reasoning if $\mathscr{L}$ is the language of number theory, set-theoretic reasoning if it is the language of set-theory, and so forth.

I will now argue that we can't in general prove even the limited schematic form of soundness (S_w). Indeed, I'll argue that we can *never* prove all the instances of (S_w) that are in $\mathscr{L}$, when the theory T we use in trying to prove it is a consistent, finitely axiomatized first order theory in the language $\mathscr{L}$. This is really just a simple consequence of Gödel's second incompleteness theorem, but let me lay it out explicitly:

(†) Suppose the axioms of the theory T we are reasoning within are $A_1, \ldots, A_n$. Let $\bot$ be any disprovable sentence of $\mathscr{L}$ (perhaps it's the negation of one of the axioms, or the negation of a tautology). Then an instance of (S_w) is:

(*) If $\langle A_1 \wedge \ldots \wedge A_n \to \bot \rangle$ is derivable in the proof procedure F then $A_1 \wedge \ldots \wedge A_n \to \bot$.

But $A_1, \ldots, A_n$ and $\neg \bot$ are all provable in T, so in T (*) entails

(**) $\langle A_1 \wedge \ldots \wedge A_n \to \bot \rangle$ is not derivable in the proof procedure F.

But F is a standard proof procedure for quantification theory, so this says in effect that $\bot$ is not quantificationally derivable from $A_1, \ldots, A_n$, i.e. from T. (**) is thus a natural formalization of the consistency of T. The second incompleteness theorem tells us however that the consistency of T isn't provable in T, unless T is inconsistent. So assuming T is consistent, it can't prove the instance (*) of (S_w).

Speaking loosely, then, the second incompleteness theorem shows the unprovability of the soundness of classical predicate logic!

This last formulation *is* loose, because it assumes that a proof of soundness would have to be a quantificational derivation from finitely many axioms. The soundness proofs to be considered in Chapter 11 and later will not be quantificational derivations, they will use the logic of a truth predicate that has its own special rules of inference; and we'll see that in some such logics, the soundness of classical predicate logic *is* provable.

Putting that aside for now, the unprovability result (†) is still based on the assumption that the theory in which one is to do the proving is finitely axiomatizable. So the result applies to a set theory like Gödel–Bernays, but not to a set theory like Zermelo–Fraenkel.

However, it isn't clear to me that this last limitation on the unprovability result is all that significant, in light of a theorem proved by Kleene (1952) and generalized by Craig and Vaught (1958), that any recursively axiomatizable theory T_0 with finite non-logical vocabulary all of whose models are infinite has a conservative extension T_c that is finitely axiomatized.

The rough idea (in the Craig and Vaught version) is to let the vocabulary of T_c be that of T_0 plus a truth or satisfaction predicate, and to replace the axioms of T_0 by a rather minimal finite axiomatization of the truth or satisfaction predicate plus the single axiom that all axioms of T_0 are true. A complication is that the notion of truth only has significance within a theory of syntax. So we must also include in T_c a finitely axiomatized syntactic theory, or a finitely axiomatized arithmetic in which it can be encoded. But there is no difficulty adding this background theory in a conservative extension of T_0, using new vocabulary, given that T_0 was stipulated to have only infinite models.

In slightly more detail, the new theory T_c will include

(i) a finitely axiomatized arithmetic adequate to basic syntax,[7] using either vocabulary in T_0 or new vocabulary;

(ii) a finitely axiomatized satisfaction$_0$ predicate (based on a Gödel numbering), where the subscript indicates that it is restricted to formulas *in the original language*. Finitely axiomatizing it is no problem: we follow Tarski's inductive characterization, using the finitely many composition rules plus the finitely many specific rules for the basic vocabulary.

(iii) the further axiom

All objects satisfy$_0$ every axiom of T_0.

(If the axioms of T_0 are all sentences, (iii) just says that every axiom of T_0 is true$_0$.) Note that if T_0 was stated in terms of schemas, we must understand 'axiom of T_0' so as *not* to apply to instances of those schemas containing the new vocabulary: any new instances obviously aren't true$_0$, and the question of whether they are true$_1$ can't be formulated in the new theory.

If we follow this procedure for getting a new theory T_c, then that new theory can easily be seen to be a conservative extension of the original theory; and it is finitely axiomatized. (This has some similarity to the method used to obtain the finitely axiomatized Gödel-Bernays theory from Zermelo-Fraenkel set theory; but that method adds new ontology (the proper classes), whereas this one adds only new ideology as long as the arithmetic ontology is present already.)

In particular, whenever T_0 is consistent, T_c is consistent. And the second incompleteness argument above shows that if T_c is consistent then it can't prove certain instances of (S_w) in its own language:

(††) Some instances of the soundness schema for systems of quantification theory that are in the language of T_c are unprovable in T_c.

What does this show about the original theory T_0, which is weaker than T_c? It *doesn't* show that some instances of the soundness schema for systems of quantification theory that are in the language of T_0 are unprovable in T_0. That is known to be false in the case of some infinitely-axiomatized theories, including Peano arithmetic and Zermelo–Fraenkel set theory. Indeed, it might plausibly be argued that theories like T_c that can't prove all instances of quantificational soundness that are expressible in their language are somehow pathological, in that they won't contain all instances of the induction schema expressible in their language. A more natural expansion of T_0 to include the new vocabulary of

---

[7] Say Robinson's arithmetic, or the far more powerful and tractable theory of the non-negative component of discretely ordered rings (the PA$^-$ of Kaye 1991).

T_c is the theory T_c^+ consisting of T_c *together with all new instances of the schemas of T_0 involving the new vocabulary.* In particular, if T_0 includes an induction schema, T_c^+ will include an induction schema that allows inductions that use the new vocabulary. But then T_c^+ is not finitely axiomatized, so the proof of (††) doesn't go through for T_c^+. Indeed, it isn't hard to show that all instances of the quantificational soundness schema statable in the language of T_c^+ *are* provable in T_c^+. This fact might be thought to undermine my argument.

But it doesn't undermine my argument at all. Remember, the schema (S_w) is far from a full formulation of the claim that the quantificational proof procedure F is sound. It is just that

(AVAIL) The set $(S_w)_\mathscr{L}$ of instances of this schema in a given classical language $\mathscr{L}$ whose only truth predicates are Tarskian is the best surrogate that is available in $\mathscr{L}$ for the full soundness claim.

(AVAIL) applies to each of the following choices of $\mathscr{L}$:

the language of T_0,

the language of its strengthening T_c,

the language of its further strengthening T_c^+,

the language of the further strengthening T_c^* that finitely axiomatizes T_c^+ with still further vocabulary (i.e. that bears the same relation to T_c^+ that T_c bears to T_0),

or any other member of the continuation of this sequence. Presumably the claim that the quantificational proof procedure F is sound has invariant content, independent of the language; $(S_w)_{T_0}$, $(S_w)_{T_c}$, $(S_w)_{T_c^+}$, $(S_w)_{T_c^*}$, ... are successively stronger partial representations of this invariant content. The weakest of these partial representations of soundness, $(S_w)_{T_0}$, will be provable in T_0 (if that is a theory like Peano arithmetic or set theory) and hence in all later theories of the sequence; but the next strongest $(S_w)_{T_c}$ won't be provable in T_c even though it is in the vocabulary of T_c. Because of this, *there can be no reasonable sense in which the full content of quantificational soundness is provable in T_c; and since T_0 is weaker than T_c, there can be no reasonable sense in which the full content of quantificational soundness is provable in T_0, even though the weak surrogate $(S_w)_{T_0}$ is so provable.*

I grant that T_c^+ is in many ways a more natural theory than T_c, but that is irrelevant to the argument since it can't prove full soundness either. To be sure, $(S_w)_{T_c^+}$ will be provable in T_c^+, and hence in all later theories of the sequence. But the next strongest $(S_w)_{T_c^*}$ won't be provable in T_c^* even though it is in the vocabulary of T_c^*. Because of this, *there can be no reasonable sense in which the full content of quantificational soundness is provable in T_c^*; and since T_c^+ is weaker than T_c^*, there can be no reasonable sense in which the full content of quantificational soundness is provable in T_c^+, even though the weak surrogate $(S_w)_{T_c^+}$ is so provable.*

The argument extends to show that there is no member of the chain in which the full content of quantificational soundness is provable.

We see that there is no reasonable sense in which any consistent recursively axiomatized classical theory using Tarskian truth predicates proves the genuine soundness of any standard proof procedure for quantification theory.

3
Kripke's Theory of Truth (Strong Kleene Version)

By far the single most influential paper on truth since Tarski is Saul Kripke's 1975 paper "Outline of a Theory of Truth". This chapter is an introduction to part of it.

The paper begins with a point alluded to in Chapter 1: it is extremely easy to enter the domain of the paradoxes inadvertently, and this seems to make the Tarskian hierarchical approach inadequate to our needs. Kripke considers the example of Jones, who says

(1) Most of Nixon's assertions about Watergate are untrue.

This seems like just the sort of thing people often say. But, Kripke says, suppose that one of the things Nixon said was

(2) Everything Jones says about Watergate is true,

and that everything else Nixon said about Watergate is evenly divided between the unproblematically true and the unproblematically false. Then it looks as if Jones' assertion (1) is true if and only if Nixon's assertion (2) is untrue, and that Nixon's assertion (2) is untrue if and only if Jones' assertion (1) is untrue. So Jones' assertion is true if and only if it is untrue, and we have a contradiction.

To guard against the possibility of paradox, Jones might assert instead

(1_0) Most of Nixon's assertions about Watergate are not true$_0$

(in the Tarskian sense, where a true$_0$ sentence is a true sentence not containing 'true' or other "semantic" terms). This would indeed block the possibility of paradox, but wouldn't be true to what Jones wanted to say: Jones might for instance have known that Nixon made many claims about Watergate that involved the notion of truth unproblematically (e.g. "Ziegler's claim that this was a third rate burglary is true"), and meant to make a far stronger statement than would be made if these were counted as *trivially* untrue. What Jones must do to avoid this problem is to choose a subscript higher than all the subscripts on 'true' employed in Nixon's utterances. (This assumes that Nixon is speaking in accord with Tarski's recommendations!) But Jones might not know which subscripts Nixon employed, and if he chooses one that's too low then his statement would not have the content he wanted it to have.

This shows that if we were to speak in accord with the Tarskian theory, there would be pressure on each of us to choose very high subscripts: if we don't, there will be a high risk that what we say will fall short of what we hope to say. But in raising the subscripts on our own assertions, we make it harder for others to fulfill their intentions. Kripke illustrates this with an example where Nixon and Dean each try to say that nothing the other says is true—each trying to include the other's assertion within the scope of his own. At most one of them can succeed, since success requires using a higher subscript than the other guy uses.

The problem, Kripke observes, is that on the Tarskian theory each utterance has a pre-assigned level. (In a strict Tarskian theory it is determined by the subscripts on the truth predicate in the sentence uttered. But as Kripke notes, the same problem arises if one supposes that the truth predicate isn't explicitly subscripted, but only implicitly subscripted by context together with utterer's intention. If anything the problem is worsened, for it is now harder to know what the levels of other people's utterances are, so it seems harder to carry out the desire to implicitly employ a higher subscript. In any case, the Nixon–Dean problem certainly arises: Nixon and Dean can't both include the other's assertions within the scope of their own.) Kripke memorably suggests that in a proper theory, each utterance should not be pre-assigned a level, but should seek its own level.

One might imagine a theory that does this by taking 'true' to work indexically: a theory on which the Tarskian indices still appear (in the theorist's language at least), but where there is in addition an unsubscripted term 'true' whose "extension" in a given context is always the same as one of the subscripted predicates, but a different one in each context. (I put "extension" in quotes because, as a term in the same ball-park as 'true', it should be governed by a theory similar to the one that governs 'true'; and the use made of it here does not seem to be either replaceable by an explicit subscript or handleable indexically.) Something like this approach is suggested in Burge 1979. One problem with such an approach is filling in precisely how context determines the appropriate subscript. (Indeed, what exactly goes into context? Does it include the speaker's intentions?) I agree with Anil Gupta's comments on this:

> Burge has proposed pragmatic rules which should guide us in assigning levels to the various uses of 'true', but like all pragmatic rules they are (and, I suppose, Burge would argue that they have to be) sloppily stated and do not constitute a theory of levels. [Or rather, of how levels are assigned to tokens of 'true'–HF.] .... [T]he assignment of levels is a pragmatic matter not in the domain of the semantics of 'true'.
>
> It seems to me, *pace* Burge, that if we follow the Tarskian route then the theory of levels [i.e. of how levels are assigned–HF] constitutes the heart of a theory of truth. It does not belong in the garbage dump of informal pragmatics.   (Gupta 1982, pp. 203–4)

The beauty of Kripke's approach is that it avoids any such complaint. Kripke gives a theory that treats 'true' as a single non-indexical term, governed by precise semantic rules; to the extent that the theory contains an analog of Tarski's notion of level, it includes a precise account of how such levels are assigned. And the theory (at least to a large extent) fulfills the intuitive idea that "utterances should seek their own levels".[1]

Actually Kripke gives more than one such theory. In this chapter I will focus on versions based on what is called the *strong Kleene semantics*; and for simplicity I will mostly focus on what are called *minimal fixed points* in such a semantics. Even with these restrictions, there is more than one Kripkean theory, as we shall see.

3.1. THE KRIPKE CONSTRUCTION FOR RESTRICTED LANGUAGES

One of the things Kripke says as a prelude to his own construction is confusing: he says he will follow Tarski in giving a mathematical definition of truth, rather than taking truth to be a primitive notion. As argued in Section 1.5, the goal of explicitly defining truth (or even truth-in-$\mathscr{L}$ for a single $\mathscr{L}$ of sufficient mathematical power) is one that Tarski seems to have explicitly disavowed, for the very good reason that it is impossible to achieve; instead, Tarski seems to have ultimately proposed taking 'true' as a primitive. Moreover, the very good reason that Tarski had for taking truth as a primitive would not seem to be one that Kripke can evade. This gives rise to problems about interpreting what Kripke is up to, problems to which I will return. But we can avoid these problems for a while, by focusing at first on a language $\mathscr{L}$ weak enough that the problem does not arise for it.

More particularly, my focus in this section will be on adding a truth predicate to a language $\mathscr{L}_0$ that is expressively weak enough for Tarskian truth-in-$\mathscr{L}_0$ to be definable in set-theoretic terms. $\mathscr{L}_0$ will be rich enough to express elementary arithmetic, or protosyntax, so that self-referential constructions can be performed within it; for related reasons, it needs to have the means of expressing elementary facts about finite sequences.[2] We can allow it to have the means of expressing

---

[1] The above discussion of Burge could be misleading, since one of the three "constructions" of levels that he considers incorporates something in the spirit of Kripke's Kleene-based fixed point construction. (By a "construction" he means a formal account of what the levels look like; this is needed prior to the pragmatic account of how the levels are assigned.) On the pragmatic theory based on a Kripkean construction, the pragmatic rules come in *after* an initial semantic level-seeking via Kripke's procedure. I'll say a bit about this in Chapter 14. I don't think, though, that this is enough to alter Gupta's verdict: when the pragmatic rules are used in the context of a Kripkean construction they give rise to a "second round of level-seeking" for which we are given an account far hazier than the one employed in the Kripkean construction itself.

[2] This is no additional requirement if $\mathscr{L}_0$ speaks of nothing other than natural numbers or linguistic expressions (or sets).

non-mathematical facts.³ We can also allow it to express more mathematics, such as the theory of real numbers; but we must deny it the ability to speak of arbitrary sets, since that would preclude truth-in-$\mathscr{L}_0$ from being set-theoretically definable. In short: the quantifiers in the language must be restricted so as to range only over the members of some set U.

The idea will be to expand $\mathscr{L}_0$ to a new language $\mathscr{L}_0^+$ just like $\mathscr{L}_0$ except with a new 1-place predicate 'True'. (Actually we ultimately want to add not just the 1-place 'True', but the 2-place 'True of', or a related 2-place predicate like 'Satisfies'; but adding these involves no essentially new ideas, just more notational complexity, so for the moment I'll stick with 'True'.)⁴ Note that 'True' is a primitive of $\mathscr{L}_0^+$; what's going to be explicitly defined isn't this term of $\mathscr{L}_0^+$, but rather a term in the set-theoretic metalanguage ML_0^+ used to describe $\mathscr{L}_0^+$. Kripke uses the term 'True' for that metalinguistic term too, a source of possible confusion; to avoid confusion, I prefer to start out using the colorless term 'has semantic value 1' for the metalinguistic term to be defined. I leave open for now whether we should ultimately identify value 1 with truth: whether to do so involves making a decision on important philosophical issues.

Suppose then that the original $\mathscr{L}_0$ is a first order language with names, predicates and function symbols, and that $\mathscr{L}_0^+$ results from it by adding a new 1-place predicate 'True'. We imagine that the variables range over the members of a set U, that each name names an object in U, and that each n-place function symbol corresponds to an n-place operation on U. Then just as in the original Tarskian theory, these determine a denotation for each singular term relative to each assignment function; where again an assignment function is a function assigning members of U to the variables of $\mathscr{L}_0$.

We also imagine that each n-place predicate *of the original language* $\mathscr{L}_0$ has a set of n-tuples of members of U as its extension. On the other hand, we do not start out by assigning 'True' a permanent extension; instead, we consider various "temporary quasi-extensions" for it. (We will eventually select a "permanent quasi-extension" from among these.) Each temporary quasi-extension X is a subset of U satisfying two conditions:

(i) All the members of X are (Gödel numbers of) sentences
(ii) No sentence and its negation are both in X.

---

³ To keep things simple, it's best to leave quotation marks out of $\mathscr{L}_0$, since they induce opaque contexts; this is no substantive limitation since we can use structural descriptive names instead. I'll also leave other opaque constructions out of $\mathscr{L}_0$, such as propositional attitude constructions; though there's no need to exclude sentential attitude constructions as long as the sentences are ascribed structural-descriptively rather than via quotation marks.

⁴ Sticking with 'True' is no real limitation if for everything in the intended domain U there is a variable-free singular term in the language that denotes it; for in that case, we can easily define 'True of' and 'Satisfies' in terms of 'True'. And we can always artificially imagine an expansion of the original $\mathscr{L}_0$ in which a name is added for everything in U. (If U is uncountable, this involves a language with uncountably many terms, but this raises no serious problems.) But we can also proceed more directly, by means I will sketch in note 7 below.

We let X^{neg} consist of everything in U that is either not a sentence or else the negation of a member of X; by condition (ii), X and X^{neg} are disjoint, though they needn't include all sentences.

We now assign values to formulas of $\mathscr{L}_0^+$, relative to an assignment function s and a temporary quasi-extension X for 'True', as follows:

1. If p is an n-place predicate of $\mathscr{L}_0$ then $p(t_1, \ldots, t_k)$ has value 1 relative to s and X iff there are objects $o_1, \ldots, o_k$ denoted$_s$ by $t_1, \ldots, t_k$ respectively such that $<o_1, \ldots, o_k>$ is in the extension of p; otherwise it has value 0 relative to s and X.

2. True(t) has value 1 relative to s and X iff there is an object o denoted$_s$ by t such that $o \in X$; it has value 0 relative to s and X iff there is an object o denoted$_s$ by t such that $o \in X^{neg}$.[5]

3. $\neg A$ has value 1 relative to s and X iff A has value 0 relative to s and X; and $\neg A$ has value 0 relative to s and X iff A has value 1 relative to s and X.

4. $A \wedge B$ has value 1 relative to s and X iff A and B each have value 1 relative to s and X; and $A \wedge B$ has value 0 relative to s and X iff at least one of A and B have value 0 relative to s and X.

5. $A \vee B$ has value 1 relative to s and X iff at least one of A and B have value 1 relative to s and X; and $A \vee B$ has value 0 relative to s and X iff A and B each have value 0 relative to s and X.

6. $\forall v A$ has value 1 relative to s and X iff for every $o \in U$, A has value 1 relative to $s(v/o)$ and X; where $s(v/o)$ is the assignment that is just like s except that it assigns o to v. $\forall v A$ has value 0 relative to s and X iff for some $o \in U$, A has value 0 relative to $s(v/o)$ and X.

7. $\exists v A$ has value 1 relative to s and X iff for some $o \in U$, A has value 1 relative to $s(v/o)$ and X; and $\exists v A$ has value 0 relative to s and X iff for all $o \in U$, A has value 0 relative to $s(v/o)$ and X.

This is a standard inductive definition; it can be converted to an explicit definition in the standard way discussed in Chapter 1 (relying on the fact that the quantifiers range only over a set). Because X and X^{neg} needn't be exhaustive, formulas sometimes will have neither value 1 nor value 0 relative to a given s and X; it will be convenient to say that such formulas get value $1/2$ relative to s and X. One advantage of this convention is that it would enable us to present the inductive definition in a snappier way: each formula A would get a value $|A|_{s,X}$ relative to any s and X, and the clauses for those values could be stated simply; for instance

3. $|\neg A|_{s,X}$ is $1 - |A|_{s,X}$

and

4. $|A \wedge B|_{s,X}$ is the minimum of $|A|_{s,X}$ and $|B|_{s,X}$.

---

[5] Here I implicitly appeal to the requirement that X and X^{neg} be disjoint: otherwise, we'd be assigning more than one value to some sentences of form 'True(t)'.

In analogy with the Tarskian theory, the assignment function drops out as irrelevant in the case of sentences (formulas with no free variables); that is, a sentence has a given value relative to s_1 and X iff it has the same value relative to s_2 and X. So for sentences, we can speak just of semantic value (1, 0, or $1/2$) relative to X.

Now comes the heart of the Kripke theory: the choice of a permanent quasi-extension. I'll start with the simplest case, where we take this to be "the minimal fixed point". Let X_0 be the empty set. Let X_1 be the set of sentences that have value 1 relative to X_0. More generally, for any ordinal a, let X_{a+1} be the set of sentences that have value 1 relative to X_a. And for a limit ordinal λ, let X_λ be the set of sentences that have value 1 relative to some X_β where $\beta < \lambda$. It is easy to see that if a sentence is in an X_a, it is also in X_β for any $\beta > a$. (The *Roach Motel property*: once a sentence checks in, it never checks out.)[6] But the X_as can't keep growing forever: there is a fixed cardinality C of sentences in the language, so there must be an ordinal β (with no more than C predecessors) for which $X_{\beta+1} = X_\beta$. This is the minimal fixed point.[7]

(The argument can be generalized, by starting the construction not from the empty set but from some larger X_0 that is "sound" in the sense that every sentence in that X_0 gets value 1 relative to that X_0. For instance, the set whose sole member is the sentence that asserts of itself that it is true is sound in this sense. The construction then produces a fixed point that contains every member of the starting set X_0; it contains everything in the minimal fixed point, and may contain more, as it must in this example. I will be concerned almost exclusively with the minimal fixed point, since it suffices for most of my needs, but other fixed points would do as well for my purposes.)

---

[6] To prove this, one first notes that the construction has the Monotonicity Property: if $X \subseteq Y$, then every sentence with value 1 relative to X has value 1 relative to Y, and every sentence with value 0 relative to X has value 0 relative to Y. From this it follows that if $X_a \subseteq X_{a+1}$ then $X_{a+1} \subseteq X_{a+2}$, and by induction (and the definition of X_λ for limit λ as a union) it then follows that if $X_a \subseteq X_{a+1}$ then for all $\gamma > \beta \geq a, X_\beta \subseteq X_\gamma$. And since X_0 is ø, $X_0 \subseteq X_1$; so whenever $\gamma > \beta, X_\beta \subseteq X_\gamma$.

[7] A more general treatment adds, not a 1-place predicate 'True' of sentences, but a 2-place predicate 'True-of', one place of which takes formulas with a single free variable and the other place of which takes arbitrary objects in U. Since the language $\mathscr{L}_0$ can represent finite sequences, this suffices for defining multi-place truth-of: $A(v_1, \ldots, v_n)$ is true of $o_1, \ldots, o_n$ in that order if and only if "$\exists x_1, \ldots, x_n$ (y is an n-tuple whose first component is x_1 and … and whose n^{th} component is x_n)" is true of $< o_1, \ldots, o_n >$. (It also suffices for defining truth: A is true if and only if "$A \wedge y = y$" is true of everything.)

To add 'True of' instead of 'True' to the language, we simply modify clauses (i) and (ii) governing the quasi-extensions in the obvious way: e.g. we replace (i) by the requirement that the members of X are pairs whose first member is a 1-place formula (using the definition of pairing provided in $\mathscr{L}_0$). We also modify clause 2 in the obvious way. Then in the fixed point construction, we let X_{a+1} be the set of pairs $< A, o >$ where A is a formula with one free variable that has value 1 relative to assignment functions that assign o to that variable.

Let's regard a sentence as having value 1 *tout court* if it has value 1 in the minimal (or some other chosen) fixed point; similarly for value 0 and value $1/2$. And by the fixed point property,

(*) The sentences with value 1 in the fixed point are precisely the members of the fixed point. (And the sentences with value 0 in the fixed point are precisely the sentences whose negations are in the fixed point.)

Some sentences clearly will have value $1/2$; an example is any Liar sentence (i.e. any sentence Q for which $\vdash Q \leftrightarrow \neg \text{True}(\langle Q \rangle)$), as the reader can easily check.

Let me note three properties of this construction.

(A) Every true sentence of the ground language $\mathscr{L}_0$ gets value 1; every false sentence of $\mathscr{L}_0$ gets value 0. (The reason: every true sentence of $\mathscr{L}_0$ is already in X_1, and every false sentence of $\mathscr{L}_0$ has its negation already in X_1.)

(B) For any sentence A (of $\mathscr{L}_0^+$), A has value 1 iff $\text{True}(\langle A \rangle)$ has value 1, and analogously for values 0 and $1/2$. (The reason: by clause 2, $\text{True}(\langle A \rangle)$ has value 1 in the fixed point if and only if A is in the fixed point, and has value 0 in the fixed point if and only if $\neg A$ is in the fixed point; so the result follows by (*).)

(C) For any sentences A, W and Z, if A is a subsentence of W and Z is just like W except with an occurrence of A replaced $\text{True}(\langle A \rangle)$, then W has value 1 iff Z has value 1. (This follows from (B), by induction on the complexity of the embedding of the occurrence of A in W.)

Reflection on these properties, and on the fact that clauses 1–7 give *having value 1* compositional features analogous to those we might expect for truth, might tempt one to identify *having value 1* with *being true*, for sentences of $\mathscr{L}_0^+$. This is evidently what Kripke has in mind when he speaks of having *defined* truth for $\mathscr{L}_0^+$.

I think that this identification is a bad one; I will argue for this in Sections 3.2 and 3.4 (with two independent arguments), and propose a different understanding of Kripke's construction.

3.2. THE KRIPKE CONSTRUCTION FOR UNRESTRICTED LANGUAGES

An initial point about Kripke's identification of being true with having semantic value 1 is that it looks quite implausible in the case of languages in which the quantifiers are unrestricted (or aren't *sufficiently* restricted). Let's see why.

In giving the Kripke construction in the previous section, I considered only the case where the range of the quantifiers in the ground language $\mathscr{L}_0$ is a set. This ruled out applying the construction as it stands to the case of set theory: for the quantifiers of set theory range over all sets, and there is no set of all sets.

The reason why I restricted the discussion to the case where the range of the quantifiers in the ground language $\mathscr{L}_0$ is a set is that if I hadn't, I could not have turned the inductive definition of 'A has semantic value 1 relative to s and X' into an explicit definition. (See Section 1.6.) I couldn't have done this even for a single X, e.g. the empty set; thus I couldn't have even defined X_0 in the inductive specification of the minimal fixed point, and so the inductive definition of the minimal fixed point couldn't have gotten off the ground. And since 'has semantic value 1' was taken to mean 'has semantic value 1 in the minimal fixed point', the definition of 'has semantic value 1' couldn't have gotten off the ground. The reliance on the assumption that the quantifiers range over a set is much stronger than in the Tarskian theory; there, we can at least *inductively* define truth (for $\mathscr{L}_0$) within set theory, whereas here even the inductive definition of 'has semantic value 1' is impossible without taking the quantifiers as ranging over a set.

Or rather, it is impossible unless we misinterpret the quantifiers as restricted! But we can easily do that: we can interpret them as ranging only over the members of some set, even when in reality they don't. When we do that, the construction proceeds without a hitch. The cost is that the construction no longer has Property (A) (from the end of the last section): semantic value 1 no longer coincides with truth for sentences in the ground language. (This may seem to deprive the construction of all value, but I will soon argue that this is far from being the case.)

Perhaps a better way to put the matter is this: we now need to introduce an additional variable in our account of semantic value, a variable U for the range of the quantifiers. (We take the allowable values to be sets that contain the denotations of all names in the language and over which the operations given in the function symbols are closed.) We regard U as a free variable throughout the inductive definition: so it is an inductive definition of 'A has semantic value 1 (or 0) relative to s, X *and U*'. (s is required to have only objects in U in its range.) The definition of 'minimal fixed point' then becomes a definition of 'minimal fixed point relative to U', and the definition of 'semantic value' becomes a definition of 'semantic value relative to U'. The key point is that the semantic value of a sentence is always relative to a choice of a set U that restricts the quantifiers. Given this, there should be no temptation to think of having semantic value 1 relative to some given U as necessarily coinciding with truth.

Often we will be able to specify some U for which the impact on Property (A) is fairly minimal. For instance, let us suppose that the background set theory in which we are working is Zermelo–Fraenkel set theory, with the Axiom of Choice[8] plus the postulate of inaccessible cardinals. Let us choose as a value U (the set that we "misinterpret the quantifiers as restricted to") the set of all sets of rank less than the smallest inaccessible cardinal. If we do this, then a great many assertions would be unaffected in truth value were the restriction on the

---

[8] Which I implicitly appealed to in my remarks on cardinality in the previous section.

quantifiers made: in other words, for a great many assertions in the language of set theory, they get semantic value 1 relative to this U if and only if they are true. In particular, all the axioms of Zermelo–Fraenkel set theory with choice get semantic value 1 relative to this U. But the coincidence of truth with semantic value 1 relative to this U is not perfect, for the restriction "falsifies" the postulate of inaccessible cardinals. In other words, that postulate gets semantic value 0 relative to this U, even though it's true. (And so its negation gets semantic value 1 relative to this U, even though it's false.) And note that the postulate in question doesn't itself contain 'true': truth diverges from semantic value 1 (relative to this choice of U) even for the 'true'-free sentences of the language.

This is not an accident of the example: there is simply no way to define a set U for which having semantic value 1 relative to U coincides with truth. This is a consequence of Tarski's undefinability theorem. For if $\mathscr{L}_0$ is the language of set theory and $\mathscr{L}_0^+$ the result of adding 'True sentence of $\mathscr{L}_0^+$' to it, we have defined 'is a sentence of $\mathscr{L}_0^+$ with semantic value 1 relative to U' within set theory. Restricting this to sentences in the ground language $\mathscr{L}_0$, we get a set-theoretic definition of 'is a sentence of $\mathscr{L}_0$ with semantic value 1 relative to U'. But Tarski's theorem tells us that we can't give an extensionally correct definition of 'is a true sentence of $\mathscr{L}_0$' within set theory; so if the set U is definable in the language of set theory, semantic value 1 relative to U can't coincide extensionally with truth *even for sentences in the 'True'-free language*. There's just no way around this.[9]

What then are we to make of Kripke's claim to have shown how to *define* truth for languages with a truth predicate? He does not explicitly confine his claim to languages with only explicitly restricted quantifiers, but perhaps he thought that such a restriction was so obviously needed as to not have to be made explicit.

Or perhaps his line of thought was this: even though you can't define truth for expanded set theory (set theory plus a truth predicate) *within set theory*, still an obvious modification of the procedure would define truth for expanded set theory *within a language C that quantifies over proper classes as well as sets*. But of course that just raises the question of defining truth for the language C (indeed for the expanded C). Well, maybe that can be done in a language C that postulates sets, proper classes, and super-classes? And so on, without end? That we can sensibly talk of such a never-ending hierarchy is the extraordinarily contentious assumption mentioned already in Section 1.5; and if Kripke really intends his remarks to apply without restriction then it seems they must depend on this assumption.

---

[9] I haven't argued that there can't be sets U for which having semantic value 1 relative to U coincides with truth for sentences in the ground language; only that none can be defined in set theory. Hamkins 2003 points out (by means of a compactness argument) that it is *consistent* to suppose that there are such sets (his Lemma 5.4); but his argument (which turns on nonstandard models of syntax) gives no grounds for thinking that the supposition that there are such sets is *true*, and if it is true then the sets U for which it is true are too complicated to be defined in set-theoretic terms and therefore are somewhat unnatural.

3.3. CONSERVATIVENESS

In the next section I will argue that *even in the case of restricted languages where an "absolute" definition of semantic value is possible*, we should not equate semantic value 1 with truth, and so should reject Kripke's claims to have defined truth. But before doing that I address a puzzle: if semantic value 1 *isn't* truth, then of what possible value is his construction?

The answer, I think, is that Kripke's construction implicitly gives a non-classical *model theory* for a language with a truth-predicate; and a large part of the value of this model theory is that it shows the consistency of a certain theory of truth which is "built into the fixed points". The two key features of the theory are (i) that it is based on a certain logic K_3 appropriate to the Kleene semantics (a logic that does not include the law of excluded middle),[10] and (ii) that it contains an inferential rule (*the Intersubstitutivity Principle*) that allows us to substitute occurrences of True($\langle A \rangle$) for occurrences of A, or vice versa, in any non-intensional context, when A is a sentence. (We should also take the theory to include basic principles of syntax, since without a background syntax, discussion of truth makes little sense. This background syntax is assumed to include all instances of the law of excluded middle that are in the syntactic language.) This Kripkean theory is standardly called KFS, and I will use that name.[11] There is room for small variations over exactly what KFS is taken to include: e.g. over exactly how powerful the background syntax we build in, or whether we take it to be part of the theory that non-sentences are never true, or whether certain of its principles are stated as schemas or as generalizations. But for my purposes such variations won't matter. What's crucial for what follows is just that the theory KFS includes (i) and (ii) (and that it not include anything, such as the law of excluded middle, that would prevent the Kripke construction from providing the desired consistency proof).

The idea of the consistency proof is that the inferences allowed in KFS (that is, those of K_3 plus the Intersubstitutivity Principle) never lead from premises in the fixed point to a conclusion not in the fixed point (or what is the same thing, from premises with value 1 to a conclusion with value

---

[10] K_3 is in many ways simpler than a more famous logic without excluded middle, intuitionist logic: intuitionist logic is notable for disallowing both double negation elimination $\neg\neg A \vDash A$ and the deMorgan law $\neg(A \wedge B) \vDash \neg A \vee \neg B$, but these are both allowed in K_3. (Intuitionist logic is of no interest for dealing with the paradoxes: the paradoxes arise in it as much as in classical logic, as noted in Section 4 of the Introduction.) Many formulations of K_3 are available in the literature, but for convenience I give one in an appendix to this chapter. There I also distinguish K_3 from a slightly weaker logic S_3 that is sometimes taken to be the basis for the Kripkean logic of truth (e.g. in Kremer 1988): K_3 is S_3 plus the rule of "disjunctive syllogism", according to which $A \vee B$ and $\neg A$ together imply B.

[11] The name was bestowed in Reinhardt 1986. (Reinhardt's formulation is indirect, in terms of a very different system KF to be mentioned later in this chapter and discussed in Chapter 7, but it amounts to what is given in the text.)

less than 1). Since contradictions can never be in any fixed points, the rules of KFS can never lead to inconsistency.

Kripke's construction actually shows more than consistency: it shows that KFS has an important property of conservativeness (it is "conservative over ω-models").

As background for this, let $\mathscr{L}_0$ be any language in which arithmetic or protosyntax can be developed; its quantifiers needn't be restricted to the members of some set, though they may be. Let M be any classical ω-model of $\mathscr{L}_0$. That is, its arithmetic or protosyntactic portion is an ω-model. This means, in the case of arithmetic, that for each thing n that satisfies 'natural number' in the model, there are only finitely many things in the model that satisfy 'natural number that precedes n'. In the case of protosyntax it means that for each thing e in the model that satisfies 'expression of $\mathscr{L}$' there are only finitely many things in the model that satisfy 'expression that is part of e'. I take it to be evident that our interest in the theory of truth should be focused on ω-models.

Then the conservativeness property is this: If we do the Kripke construction for $\mathscr{L}_0^+$, starting from M, we will get a 3-valued model of the language $\mathscr{L}_0^+$ that validates the theory KFS (in particular, the Kleene logic plus the Intersubstitutivity Principle) *and that is exactly like M in its 'True'-free part.*[12] (It validates KFS in that it takes its rules of inference as preserving the semantic value 1.) This means that we can add that theory of truth to *any theory in $\mathscr{L}_0$ that one likes* and preserve consistency in ω-logic: *if the original 'true'-free theory in $\mathscr{L}_0$ is consistent in ω-logic, so is the theory that results by adding the theory of truth to it.*[13]

Conservativeness (in the ω-logic sense just sketched) is obviously a highly desirable feature of a theory of truth. (Bare consistency isn't enough: a theory of truth might be consistent and yet entail things that no theory of truth should entail, like an answer to how many planets there are in the solar system. Conservativeness entails a very strong consistency property: the theory of truth is not only consistent, but consistent (in ω-logic) with any theory not containing

---

[12] More precisely, when M declares a sentence of $\mathscr{L}_0$ true, the 3-valued model will declare that it has value 1; similarly for false and value 0. Indeed, if for various purposes, e.g. to handle vague terms in $\mathscr{L}_0$, one were to allow 3-valued models of $\mathscr{L}_0$, then the Kripke model based on M would agree with M as to which sentences of $\mathscr{L}_0$ get value $1/2$.

[13] One can in fact get several different conservative theories that include the Intersubstitutivity Principle from Kripke's construction. In addition to KFS, there is the dialetheic theory LP, obtained by taking as valid those inferences that preserve the property of *having value greater than 0* in all models; and the "symmetric" theory (formulated in Kremer 1988) that takes an inference to be valid if it is valid in both KFS and LP, that is, if in every model the value of the conclusion is at least as high as the minimum of the values of the premises. (The logic common to KFS and LP is the logic S_3 mentioned in note 10.) LP will be considered in Part V. I take KFS to be a more useful non-dialetheic theory than the symmetric variant based on S_3: partly because it is slightly stronger, but mainly because its semantics provides a more natural basis for extending the theory to one that contains a well-behaved (modus-ponens-obeying) conditional. Extending the theory in this way is going to be the project of Part III.

'true' that is itself consistent in ω-logic.) Given the difficulties of finding theories of truth that consistently (let alone conservatively) deal with the paradoxes, I think a construction that yields a conservativeness proof is extraordinarily valuable. I am not in fact satisfied with the logic that Kripke's construction shows to be conservative, but his construction will be a paradigm for (and a component of) more complicated constructions that I will give later on in the book for more powerful logics.

Conservativeness, as I've said, is a generalization of consistency: it means, roughly, "can be consistently added to any consistent theory" (taking 'consistent' in each occurrence to mean 'consistent in ω-logic'). In the previous chapter I stressed the conceptual distinction between model-theoretic validity and genuine validity. This generates a distinction between model-theoretic consistency ("comes out true in some model") and genuine consistency: it seems *prima facie conceivable* that a theory that is consistent in the intuitive sense needn't be model-theoretically consistent, since maybe there is no universe *whose domain is a set* that could make it true. We have good informal reasons to think this divergence between model-theoretic consistency and genuine consistency doesn't happen (given, in the case of first order theories, by the Kreisel argument), but there is still this conceptual divergence. The conceptual divergence arises for conservativeness too: in "can be consistently added to any consistent theory", the two occurrences of 'consistent' could be understood either model-theoretically or as genuine consistency. Presumably what we want is the preservation of genuine consistency; however, what Kripke's construction actually proves is the preservation of model-theoretic consistency. I say this not in criticism of Kripke's proof, for I think there is no prospect of doing any better; it is simply a limitation in conservativeness proofs that needs to be noted. When one has a proof of model-theoretic conservativeness, there remains the *possibility* of skepticism about genuine conservativeness, but I see no basis for such skepticism.

Kripke's construction has another value besides proving (model-theoretic) conservativeness: it also provides an easy way to figure out which inferences involving truth are legitimate in the truth theory provided by the construction (the one for which the construction offers a conservativeness proof). This is quite a significant fact. For KFS is a non-classical theory (a *paracomplete* theory, in the terminology of the Introduction: excluded middle is not valid in it). Those of us who have been trained in classical logic find it initially difficult to figure out what reasoning is legitimate in such a non-classical logic and what isn't. By using Kripke's construction, we can use easy classical reasoning to determine the answer.

I don't want to say that the value of Kripke's construction is *exhausted by* its providing a conservativeness proof for a theory and its making it easy to figure out what inferences are legitimate in the theory. It is conceivable that a conservativeness proof could be provided that would seem far less illuminating, even if it was based on a model theory that was as useful as a tool in aiding us to figure out which inferences are legitimate. I wish I had something helpful to say about what makes a construction like Kripke's illuminating, but I don't. I hope I've already made clear, though, that one thing one *can't* easily say is that it is illuminating because it involves the notion of truth. For it involves instead a technical notion of *having semantic value 1* (relative to a set or model), and this cannot in general be identified with truth without commitment to an extraordinarily contentious doctrine.

3.4. DOES TRUTH COINCIDE WITH SEMANTIC VALUE 1 EVEN FOR RESTRICTED LANGUAGES? (KFS *v*. FM)

For restricted languages we can at least define 'has semantic value 1' without relativizing the latter to an unintended domain, so it at least makes sense to contemplate identifying truth with having value 1. But even here, such an identification strikes me as a very bad idea: it would throw away the beauty of the Kripke construction. For the "external" notion of having semantic value 1 is very unlike the "internal" notion used in the language $\mathscr{L}_0^+$, as I will soon explain, and the theory of the external notion (which I will call FM, and discuss in Chapter 7) is very different from the theory KFS of the internal notion. In my view it is the internal notion of truth (which the construction makes no pretense of *defining*) that is primarily important; the "external" notion should be viewed largely as a technical device, used (i) as an aid to help the logician trained in classical logic to figure out what reasoning is valid in the internal theory and (ii) as the basis for a conservativeness proof of the sort discussed in the previous section.

What do I mean by saying that the external notion of having semantic value 1 is very unlike the internal notion of truth? Consider some examples:

1. It is easy to see that in the Kripke construction, a Liar sentence Q can't have value 1 (or value 0 either: it must have value $1/2$). But if it doesn't have value 1, *and value 1 is taken to coincide with truth*, then it isn't true. The claim $\neg \text{True}(\langle Q \rangle)$ that Q isn't true would thus become part of the theory FM that identifies truth with having semantic value 1; but this claim does not appear in the fixed point. There's an unsatisfying divergence between the assertions of the theory FM and the contents of the fixed point.

This is especially disconcerting because the theory FM declares anything not in the fixed point to be untrue. So the claim that the Liar sentence is not true, which is part of the theory FM, is declared untrue by that theory! The theory declares itself untrue! That isn't inconsistent, but it strikes me as a serious anomaly.

2. 'Has semantic value 1' was defined in classical set theory, so it is a classical notion. In particular, every sentence in the language $\mathscr{L}_0^+$ either has value 1 or doesn't have value 1. *If having value 1 is taken to coincide with truth*, as FM supposes, then for every sentence in $\mathscr{L}_0^+$, that sentence is either true or not true. But it is easy to see that claims of form 'Either $\text{True}(\langle A \rangle)$ or not $\text{True}(\langle A \rangle)$' aren't in the fixed point when A has value $1/2$. So

such excluded middle claims, like Liar sentences, are things that the theory FM asserts which aren't in the fixed point. Again, an unsatisfying divergence.

And again, the divergence is especially unsatisfying because for exactly the same reason as above, the theory FM declares these assertions untrue. This is perhaps even more anomalous in the case of excluded middle than in the case of the Liar sentence, for the law of excluded middle is a central part of the theory FM. The theory asserts all instances of the law of excluded middle, but (in the same breath, so to speak) it declares some of those instances that it asserts untrue!

I want to emphasize that these decidedly odd features are not consequences of Kripke's construction. They result, rather, from the identification of truth with having semantic value 1.

A specific version of the theory FM that results from identifying truth with having value 1 in the Kleene-based Kripke theory is often called KF, or the Kripke–Feferman theory. It was first formulated in print in Reinhardt 1986, where it was explicitly contrasted to KFS. I'm using the name FM instead of KF because the similarity in Reinhardt's two acronyms is confusing, and because I think the reference to Kripke possibly misleading; also because, since my focus isn't on proof theory, I won't be concerned with certain technical questions about the precise formulation of the axioms, so it won't be important whether one takes my FM to be precisely KF as traditionally understood. (The 'M' in 'FM' is for Tim Maudlin 2004, an engaging and heroic defense of the view that truth should have the crucial features ascribed to it in this theory.) Theories such as FM that result from identifying truth with having value 1 will be the topic of Chapter 7.

The present chapter is concerned not with FM, but with KFS, and it does *not* have the odd features 1 and 2 just mentioned. KFS consists only of sentences that are in the fixed point—or rather, that are in any fixed point for any ground model that meets the minimal requirements. Since, as we've seen, some instances of excluded middle are not contained in the fixed point, they are not part of the theory: the theory is "paracomplete" in the sense defined in the introduction.

In my opinion, KFS is a far superior theory to FM, though not ultimately adequate. (The first of these claims is also argued in Soames 1999, which would explain the 'S' in 'KFS' if Reinhardt hadn't introduced that name already; also in McGee 1989 and Halbach and Horsten 2006.)[14] One of the main advantages of KFS over FM is that it exploits the *raison d'être* of fixed points rather than throwing it away. What I mean by the *raison d'être* of fixed points is the complete equivalence between True($\langle A \rangle$) and A, for arbitrary sentences A. Not only is it the case that

(+) True($\langle A \rangle$) is in the fixed point whenever A is.

Much more generally, it is the case that

---

[14] The latter two papers indeed accept the second claim as well, but take it in quite a different direction than I will recommend.

(++) If Y results from X by substituting some occurrences of $\text{True}(\langle A \rangle)$ for A or vice versa, then Y is in the fixed point if and only if X is.

Proof: We saw above (point (B) at the end of Section 3.1) that $\text{True}(\langle A \rangle)$ not only has value 1 whenever A does, it always has the same value that A has. And the semantics is value-functional: so if Y results from X by substituting some occurrences of $\text{True}(\langle A \rangle)$ for A or vice versa, then Y has the same value as X does. And finally, the fixed point consists of precisely the sentences with value 1; so Y is in the fixed point if and only if X is.

Now if the theory consists of the contents of the fixed point, then what (++) says is that $\text{True}(\langle A \rangle)$ is completely intersubstitutable for A throughout our theory. The idea that this should be so is what makes the notion of fixed point so appealing.

FM, on the other hand, throws this away. It even throws away the much more limited equivalence between $\text{True}(\langle A \rangle)$ and A in unembedded contexts; that is, it doesn't even regard the assertion of A as equivalent to the assertion of $\text{True}(\langle A \rangle)$, for we saw in 1 and 2 examples where it asserts the former and denies the latter. FM and KFS are about as different as theories can be; and KFS seems far superior.

3.5. GAPS AND GLUTS

An additional difference between FM and KFS is that FM postulates truth value gaps (sentences that are neither true nor false, where 'false' means 'has a true negation'): any sentence that gets value $1/2$ in the minimal fixed point is declared to be neither true nor false. KFS, on the other hand, asserts neither that there are truth value gaps nor that there aren't: for instance, neither

(BIV) $\qquad\qquad\qquad \text{True}(\langle Q \rangle) \vee \text{True}(\langle \neg Q \rangle)$

nor its negation

(GAP) $\qquad\qquad\qquad \neg[\text{True}(\langle Q \rangle) \vee \text{True}(\langle \neg Q \rangle)]$

is in the minimal fixed point, so neither is part of the theory.

This might seem to indicate an unfortunate incompleteness on the part of the theory: it might seem that the advocate of the theory is remaining agnostic on the important question of truth value gaps. I think this would be a mistake. Let's start with a simpler case, the case of the Liar sentence itself. The theory doesn't accept Q and it doesn't accept $\neg Q$. Does that mean the theorist is agnostic as to whether Q? That would be thoroughly misleading: it seems appropriate to say that one is agnostic as to whether A when one accepts $A \vee \neg A$ but is undecided which disjunct to accept, but quite inappropriate to say this when one doesn't accept $A \vee \neg A$. (If one doesn't accept $A \vee \neg A$, one doesn't accept $\text{True}(\langle A \rangle) \vee \neg \text{True}(\langle A \rangle)$; so one doesn't accept that there is a truth of the matter to be agnostic about!) And in the case of the Liar sentence, one doesn't accept that $Q \vee \neg Q$; so it would be wholly misleading to describe the theory's attitude toward Q as a case of agnosticism.

And the same is true about the more complicated case of (BIV) and its negation (GAP). It would be appropriate to call our unwillingness to accept either as due to ignorance only if we accepted the disjunction between them. But that disjunction

$$[\text{True}(\langle Q \rangle) \vee \text{True}(\langle \neg Q \rangle)] \vee \neg [\text{True}(\langle Q \rangle) \vee \text{True}(\langle \neg Q \rangle)]$$

is easily seen to be equivalent in the theory to

$$Q \vee \neg Q,$$

which we've seen not to be acceptable; so the preconditions of ignorance are simply not met.

Surprisingly, some advocates of KFS (e.g. Soames 1999) describe their theory as one on which there are truth value gaps; but it seems to me that the above remarks show this to be a serious mistake. There are "semantic value gaps" (sentences with neither value 1 nor value 0) in the classical semantics for the theory. But failure to have semantic value 1 or 0 is not failure to be true or false.

When I've made this point elsewhere I've heard it charged that I'm introducing a non-standard sense of 'truth-value gap': the charge is that even in KFS, the Liar sense is gappy in the *standard* sense, since it is in neither the extension nor the anti-extension of 'true'. But this is wrong: in the ordinary sense of 'extension', the extension of 'true' comprises the things 'true' is true of; the claim that the Liar sentence isn't in the extension of 'True' is equivalent to the claim that the Liar sentence isn't true, which again is not part of the theory. (And the anti-extension of 'true' comprises the things 'true' is false of, i.e. whose negations 'true' is true of; the claim that the Liar sentence isn't in the anti-extension of 'true' is equivalent to the negation of the Liar sentence, which also isn't part of the theory.) Of course if you took the extension of 'true' to consist in the sentences A for which 'True($\langle A \rangle$)' gets value 1 in the model theory, then the charge would be correct. But that identification is only appropriate if one identifies truth with having value 1; such an identification is part of FM, but is very definitely not part of KFS, since it would undermine the whole point of the theory.

Another misguided view about KFS is that it holds that there are no truth value *gluts*, i.e. sentences that are both true and false. The situation with gluts is just like that with gaps: the theory accepts neither the existence nor the non-existence of gluts, and doesn't regard this as a matter of ignorance because it doesn't accept that there is a truth about the matter. There is simply no asymmetry between truth value gaps and truth value gluts on this theory. One might say that the middle semantic value $1/2$ indicates the *possibility* of a truth value gap, but to the extent that this is right it equally indicates the possibility of a truth value glut.

Any tendency to read the value $1/2$ as more indicative of a gap than of a glut bespeaks a failure to thoroughly distinguish the theory from FM.

Indeed, we can say more: not only is there no asymmetry between gaps and gluts in KFS, the concepts 'gap' and 'glut' are logically equivalent in KFS! The claim that a sentence is a gap is

(GAP) $\qquad\qquad\qquad \neg\text{True}(\langle A \rangle) \wedge \neg\text{True}(\langle \neg A \rangle).$

The claim that it is a glut is

(GLUT) $\qquad\qquad\qquad \text{True}(\langle A \rangle) \wedge \text{True}(\langle \neg A \rangle).$

But by the intersubstitutivity properties of truth, which KFS upholds, these are equivalent to

$$\neg A \wedge \neg\neg A$$

and

$$A \wedge \neg A$$

respectively; and by the equivalence of $\neg\neg A$ to A, plus the commutativity of conjunction (both of which KFS upholds), these amount to the same thing.

What then is the relation between truth value and semantic value, for KFS? In the case of restricted theories (which are the only ones for which we have an unrelativized notion of semantic value), we can say this: having semantic value 1 is sufficient for being true; and having semantic value 0 is sufficient for being false (i.e. having a true negation). For sentences with semantic value $1/2$, we can't say that they're true, or that they aren't, or that they're false, or that they aren't. We can't say whether or not they are "gappy" (neither true nor false), and we can't say whether or not they are "glutty" (both true and false). And our inability to say these things can't be attributed to ignorance, for we don't accept that there is a truth about the matter. This isn't to say that we think there is no truth about the matter: we don't think there is, and we don't think there isn't. And we don't think there either is or isn't. Paracompleteness runs deep.

3.6. THE WEAKNESSES OF KRIPKE'S CONSTRUCTION

Despite what I take to be substantial advantages over FM, KFS does not seem to me an adequate theory. I will mention three reasons.

The first is that the theory is too weak to carry out ordinary reasoning. The most notable weakness is that it does not contain a decent conditional or biconditional. One could of course define a conditional from $\neg$ and $\vee$ in the usual classical manner: take $A \supset B$ to be $\neg A \vee B$. (And once you have a conditional, getting a biconditional is trivial.) But while that does a passable job as a conditional in the presence of excluded middle, it is totally inadequate as a conditional without excluded middle: with ⊃ as one's candidate for →, one wouldn't even get such elementary laws of the conditional as $A \to A, A \to (A \vee B)$, or the inference from $A \to B$ to $(C \to A) \to (C \to B)$. (For instance, $A \to A$ would become an instance of excluded middle, and thus fail to receive the designated value 1 whenever A has value $1/2$.) The lack of a conditional (and also of a biconditional) cripples ordinary reasoning.

The second problem is that though the theory validates the intersubstitutivity of True($\langle A \rangle$) with A, it does not validate the truth schema (nor does it validate either direction of it). This is obvious: each direction of the truth schema is equivalent to $A \to A$, given the intersubstitutivity; and we've already seen that $A \to A$ isn't a law of the theory.

I'm not sure to what extent this second problem is a problem independent of the first: I'm sympathetic with the idea that the need for the truth schema is wholly derivative on our need for the intersubstitutivity together with our need for the law $A \to A$. But this is not a universal view (for instance, in many writings Graham Priest has stressed the importance of maintaining the truth schema even though he thinks the intersubstitutivity principle fails); so it seems worth mentioning the issue of the truth schema separately.

The third problem also involves expressive weakness: there are things that we would apparently like to say about the Liar sentence that we can't express in the language. For instance, although it would be incorrect to say that the Liar sentence is *not true*, in the sense of 'not' used in the Liar sentence, it seems like there ought to be some "weaker form of negation" 'wnot' in which we can correctly say that it is "wnot true". (This seems plausible even if one thinks that 'not' in English is unambiguous, so that the "weaker sense of negation" is not a legitimate reading of the English 'not'.) A natural way to express this in English would be to say that the Liar sentence is *not determinately* true. Here we're in effect defining the weak negation $\neg_w$ as the result of applying ordinary negation to a determinately operator D; so defined, $\neg_w A$ is weaker than $\neg A$ as long as DA is stronger than A. (Equivalently, we could take "weak negation" as primitive and define 'determinately' in terms of it and ordinary negation: as $\neg \neg_w$; but I think taking 'determinately' as the primitive is less likely to engender confusion.) The third problem with KFS, then, is that it has no way to express a determinately operator, so no way to express that the Liar sentence isn't determinately true.

I take these to be serious problems, and one goal of Parts III and IV of the book will be to develop a theory that overcomes them.

3.7. ACCEPTANCE AND REJECTION IN KFS

It is important not to overstate the third of the problems just discussed, for even within the KFS it makes sense to *reject* the Liar sentence: an advocate of KFS can and should distinguish between rejection and acceptance of the negation.

Rejection should be taken to involve, at the very least, a commitment not to accept. Actually I think it should involve more than this: someone who thinks that there can be no possible evidence about some claim (say about the distance past) may be committed to accepting neither that claim nor its negation, but such a person does not reject the claim in the sense that I have in mind. Rather than explaining rejection in terms of acceptance (as in *commitment not to accept*), we should regard acceptance and rejection as dual notions. And how exactly one thinks of rejection will depend on how one thinks of the dual notion of acceptance.

One useful, albeit somewhat crude, notion of acceptance depends on the assumption that we have numerical degrees of belief; acceptance is taken as having a degree of belief over a certain threshold τ. ('Over' could mean either 'greater than' or 'greater than or equal to'. We can allow the threshold to be contextually determined. Of course a consequence of this definition, if τ is less than 1, is that we can accept a bunch of claims without accepting their conjunction; but that seems like a reasonable thing to say given the paradox of the preface.) This notion of acceptance has an obvious dual: rejection is having degree of belief *lower than* the corresponding *co*-threshold $1 - \tau$. (We need to require that τ is at least $1/2$ on the 'greater than' reading of 'over', and strictly greater than $1/2$ on the 'greater than or equal to' reading; otherwise we could simultaneously accept and reject the same claim.)[15] In discussing logic we are mostly concerned with full acceptance and full rejection, where the threshold is 1 and the co-threshold is 0; for that is the only case where acceptance of A and B commits one to acceptance of their conjunction and where rejection of A and B commits one to rejection of their disjunction. But for the moment I will keep the discussion more general.

On classical assumptions about degrees of belief, one's degrees of belief in a sentence and its negation should add to 1. On these classical assumptions, rejection as just defined will coincide with acceptance of the negation: $P(A) \leq 1 - \tau$ iff $1 - P(A) \geq \tau$ iff $P(\neg A) \geq \tau$, where P is the agent's degree of belief ("subjective probability") function. But classical assumptions about degrees of belief clearly need to be abandoned by anyone advocating KFS; after all, classical assumptions also yield that $P(A \vee \neg A) = 1$, which can hardly be acceptable to anyone who doesn't accept all instances of excluded middle. I think that the spirit of KFS requires retaining the prohibition against $P(A) + P(\neg A)$ being greater than 1 but allowing it to be less than 1. In that case, we can have $P(A) \leq 1 - \tau$ without having $P(\neg A) \geq \tau$: we can have rejection without acceptance of the negation. In fact, the degree of belief in a sentence and its negation can both be

---

[15] An irrational agent might, in a sense, accept and reject the same claim simultaneously; but on this picture, that would involve vacillating between more than one assignment of degrees of belief. (Even without such vacillation, an irrational agent could of course accept one claim and reject a logically equivalent claim, even when the equivalence should have been obvious.)

below the co-threshold, indeed can both be 0: that, I submit, is the appropriate view for an advocate of KFS to take of a non-contingent Liar sentence. (With contingent Liar sentences it's a bit more complicated. If I assert 'what the least intelligent person in the room is now saying isn't true', then even if I am in fact the least intelligent person in the room, my degree of belief in the sentence and its negation can be far higher than 0: they should add to nearly $1 - r$, where r is the degree of belief I attach to my being the least intelligent person in the room.)

As I've said, the model of acceptance under consideration in the last two paragraphs was somewhat crude. A slightly less crude model involves interval-valued degrees of belief. On it, acceptance of a claim consists in *the lower bound of the interval* being over a (contextually determined) threshold τ. (Or alternatively, it involves *commitment to taking* the lower bound to be over τ.) But this too has a dual: rejection consists in the *upper* bound of the interval being *below* the *co*-threshold $1 - \tau$ (or commitment to so taking it).

Doubtless there are still less crude models of acceptance. I will not discuss them, but I hope the general moral is clear: whatever the model, a defender of KFS should take acceptance and rejection to be dual notions, and should take rejection not to require acceptance of the negation. By doing so, we can allow for the simultaneous rejection of both a sentence and its negation; even the full rejection of both, i.e. the simultaneous assignment to each of degree of belief 0.

Besides acceptance and rejection, a defender of KFS will probably want to invoke the notions of *conditional* acceptance and *conditional* rejection: the acceptance or rejection of a claim *on certain assumptions*. On the simple model, to accept B conditional on the assumption A is to have one's conditional degree of belief $P(B|A)$ be over the threshold; for conditional rejection it must be under the co-threshold. (One needs to think through how these conditional degrees of belief work when degrees of belief obey the non-standard laws above, but I think that the usual rule $P(A|B) \cdot P(B) = P(A \wedge B)$ is still defensible.) These notions will have to play an important role in KFS. For instance, one of the reasons for the importance of the notion of logical consequence is that if B is a logical consequence of A then we should conditionally accept B on the assumption A; and the above definition of conditional acceptance provides for this.

Indeed, if the advocate of KFS is to explain logical consequence other than in model-theoretic terms, I think it would have to be in terms of laws of conditional belief. It certainly can't be as necessary truth preservation. Let C be the assertion that the first sentence to be uttered in the year 2030 will be true. C is a consequence of itself, or of anything of form $C \wedge D$. But in KFS, the claim that if the premise is true then so is the conclusion must be interpreted as a material conditional, and so amounts to the claim that necessarily either the premise isn't true or the conclusion is true. Because we don't know whether excluded middle will hold for the first sentence uttered in 2030, we're in no position to say this in the case of the inference from C to itself, or in the case of the inference from $C \wedge D$ to C when we're not in a position to deny D.

This shows that on the validity relation of KFS, the Validity Argument of Section 2.1 fails in the step from

$$\text{True}(\langle C \wedge D \rangle) \vDash \text{True}(\langle C \rangle)$$

to

$$\vDash \text{True}(\langle C \wedge D \rangle) \to \text{True}(\langle C \rangle).$$

We can't assume that conjunction-elimination preserves truth. Despite this, the passage from a conjunction to its conjuncts is still valid in the sense that it is legitimate to unqualifiedly believe the conclusion on the assumption of the premise.

3.8. DEFECTIVENESS AGAIN

Let's see if we can put the notions of conditional and unconditional acceptance and rejection to further use. In Section 3.6 I declared it a problem for KFS that it has no way of expressing the claim that the Liar sentence is not determinately true; equivalently, no way to weakly negate it. (Relatedly, there is no way within KFS to say that it is *defective*: neither determinately true nor determinately false.) But is this really a problem? As we've seen, the advocate of KFS can still *reject* the Liar sentence, and reject its ordinary negation too. This isn't the same as introducing weak negation: weak negation is an embeddable operator, whereas rejection is merely an attitude. (We might introduce an artificial symbol N corresponding to rejection, whereby acceptance of NA indicated rejection of A; but there is no reason to think such an "operator" embeddable.) So doesn't this avoid the third problem for Kripke?

I think this does *not* fully avoid the problem: I think that we do still need a notion of determinate truth, or equivalently, of a weakened negation (or of defectiveness). Rejection is inadequate precisely because it doesn't correspond to an embeddable operator: confining ourselves to it would cripple what we can say. Arguing this, however, requires a bit of care.

One way to try to argue this would be by means of a contingent Liar sentence, like my claim that what the least intelligent man in the room is now saying isn't true. We ought to be able to say that *if* I am the least intelligent man in the room *then* my remark was defective (and hence not determinately true); but this involves an embedded attribution of defectiveness or determinate truth, so it looks as if it can't be explained in terms of rejection.

But this example isn't decisive, for it can be handled at least to first approximation by means of the notion of *conditional rejection*.

There are however other examples one might appeal to, which don't seem so easy to handle without an embeddable operator. For instance, consider cases where the notion of defectiveness appears in the antecedent of a conditional rather than the consequent. ("If some of the sentences asserted in this chapter are defective, some reviewer is bound to point this out.") Or cases where the notion of defectiveness appears in a more highly embedded manner. ("There are theories of truth that don't contain defective sentences that are better than all theories that do contain defective sentences.") Debates about what is defective and what isn't would be hard to conduct without embedded defectiveness claims.

There are other possible surrogates for a defectiveness predicate. One possibility would be to go autobiographical: to use the claim that one rejects A and its negation as a surrogate for the claim that A is defective. But this does not seem especially helpful in the examples I've given. A more promising line, perhaps, would be to use as one's surrogate the claim that one *ought* to reject A and reject its negation. (This doesn't do well with "contingently defective" claims, such as the contingent liars, at least without a very special reading of 'ought'; but perhaps one could appeal to conditional oughts, in analogy with conditional rejection.)

I'd be leery of adopting this tack without (i) a clear account of the kind of 'ought' judgements involved, and (ii) a proof that no new paradoxes arise from combining such a normative operator with self-reference and/or a truth predicate (or anyway, a proof that none arise that can't be handled by the means used for handling truth in the non-normative language).

I don't know that there is any *strong* reason to worry about new paradoxes involving normativity: there tend to be more resources for dealing with apparent normative paradoxes than there are for the paradoxes of truth alone. For instance, an obvious analog of a Liar paradox involves a sentence Q^* that asserts that one ought not to accept it. So given naive truth, it is true if and only if one ought not to accept it. Were we to assume excluded middle for 'ought' sentences, we would have

Either Q^* is true but one ought not to accept it, or it is not true but one ought to accept it.

How much of a problem is this?

The first point to make is that accepting either disjunct wouldn't seem to be quite as absurd as accepting the analogous disjuncts in the case of the Liar sentence; but it would be uncomfortable, and I would not recommend it. The second point to make is that because accepting the disjuncts is merely uncomfortable rather than absurd, accepting the disjunction of them doesn't seem so especially worrisome: whereas a disjunction of absurdities seems absurd, a disjunction of uncomfortable alternatives seems more like a fact of life. So in the "normative paradox" case, the analog of "weakly classical" (semi-classical) theories seems far less worrisome than it is for the genuine Liar paradox. The third point to make is that one doesn't need to go this route: the option that KFS takes in the Liar case can be applied to the normative case as well; that is, we could reject excluded middle. I think, myself, that there are considerable grounds to be suspicious of excluded middle for some normative claims. If so, one doesn't need to accept the disjunction of uncomfortable alternatives.

So I see no reason to think that paradoxes of normativity and truth are more difficult than paradoxes of truth alone. But I'd hate to rest much on this: paradoxes have a nasty habit of popping up in unexpected places, and until one has the kind of conservativeness proof that one has governing the addition of a truth predicate to a first-order language, one ought to have something less than total confidence.

Add to this the fact that the discussion of normativity began (several paragraphs back) with the proposal to use normativity as a surrogate for talk of determinateness (or defectiveness). To the extent that it is an *effective* surrogate, any worry one might have had about paradoxes of truth and determinateness together should extend to worries about paradoxes of truth and normativity together. Indeed, the normative notion is one that could apply in many more contexts than as a surrogate for indeterminacy; this, and the fact that it is more logically complicated, suggest that it is *more* likely to breed paradox when combined with truth rather than *less* likely.

However one goes on normativity, we've seen that a language like KFS that contains *neither* normative notions nor the notion of determinateness or defectiveness is inadequate to our needs. We must expand the language to include either a notion of determinateness or a normative notion capable of providing a surrogate for it. To the extent that we need objective normative notions, we should ultimately aim for a theory of truth in a language that can express them. I'm inclined to think, though, that this is simply too hard a task for now, especially since the logic of normative notions isn't well understood even apart from their interactions with a truth predicate. In the meantime we should pursue the more modest step of getting a truth theory for a language with a notion of determinateness (or equivalently, a weak negation). So I stand by my diagnosis of Section 3.6: the inability of KFS to express a notion of determinateness is a crippling limitation.

APPENDIX: KLEENE LOGIC AND OTHER DEMORGAN LOGICS

The Kleene logic referred to in section 3.2 is a special case of what is called a deMorgan logic. The **basic deMorgan logic** (the weakest, barring the qualification in note 2 below) is often called FDE (for "the logic of first-degree entailment"); however, that term is sometimes used differently and also carries some contentious connotations, so I prefer to call it BDM. It can be formulated as a natural deduction system, with the usual structural rules;[1] its non-structural rules consist of "positive and negative introduction and elimination rules" for each connective other than negation, as given below, together with introduction and elimination rules for double negation. (The connectives do not include a conditional. I use $\vDash$ for implication, i.e. consequence. I formulate the rules as implication statements wherever possible; only in the cases where it is necessary to do so do I use the format of a meta-rule, i.e. an inference from one implication statement to another.) I'll focus on the sentential connectives, though I'll mention the extension to quantifiers at the end after considering various ways of extending BDM, including to the desired K_3.

$\wedge$ -rules of BDM:

$(\wedge\text{-Introd})$ $A, B \vDash A \wedge B$

$(\wedge\text{-Elim})$ (i) $A \wedge B \vDash A$; (ii) $A \wedge B \vDash B$

$(\neg \wedge \text{-Introd})$ (i) $\neg A \vDash \neg(A \wedge B)$; (ii) $\neg B \vDash \neg(A \wedge B)$

$(\neg \wedge \text{-Elim})$ $\Gamma, \neg A \vDash C$
                    $\Gamma, \neg B \vDash C$
                    $\overline{\Gamma, \neg(A \wedge B) \vDash C}$

$\vee$ -rules of BDM:

$(\vee\text{-Introd})$ (i) $A \vDash A \vee B$; (ii) $B \vDash A \vee B$

$(\vee\text{-Elim})$ $\Gamma, A \vDash C$
               $\Gamma, B \vDash C$
               $\overline{\Gamma, A \vee B \vDash C}$

$(\neg \vee \text{-Introd})$ $\neg A, \neg B \vDash \neg(A \vee B)$

$(\neg \vee \text{-Elim})$ (i) $\neg(A \vee B) \vDash \neg A$; (ii) $\neg(A \vee B) \vDash \neg B$

---

[1] That is: (i) whether $A_1, \ldots, A_n \vDash B$ depends only on B and on which formulas occur in the list $A_1, \ldots, A_n$ (not on the order in which they occur or the number of times they occur); (ii) if $A_1, \ldots, A_n \vDash B$ then $A_1, \ldots, A_n, C \vDash B$; and (iii) if $A_1, \ldots, A_n \vDash B$ and $A_1, \ldots, A_n, B \vDash C$ then $A_1, \ldots, A_n \vDash C$.

¬¬-rules of BDM:

$$(\neg\neg\text{-Introd}) \quad A \vDash \neg\neg A$$
$$(\neg\neg\text{-Elim}) \quad \neg\neg A \vDash A$$

That's BDM. It gives the core of classical sentential logic, including the distributive laws and the deMorgan laws. We can get from it to classical sentential logic (in a strong sense of that term) by adding two rules:

(LEM) $\qquad\qquad\qquad\qquad \vDash A \vee \neg A$
(EXP) $\qquad\qquad\qquad\qquad A \wedge \neg A \vDash B$

The "explosion rule" (EXP) looks a bit odd, since it may seem to tell us that if we find ourselves accepting a contradiction we should accept everything, which of course would be absurd. In fact the rule does no such thing: in general, a single-premise rule of implication tells us that if we start out accepting the premise but not accepting the conclusion, we should modify our attitudes, either by coming to accept the conclusion or giving up our acceptance of the premise. The point of (EXP) is to tell you not to accept contradictions, since if you do they'll commit you to anything, even obvious absurdities.

If the rule (EXP) still looks odd, we can replace it by the rule of "disjunctive syllogism"

(DS) $\qquad\qquad\qquad\qquad A \vee B, \neg A \vDash B :$

given that $A \wedge \neg A$ implies both A and $\neg A$, and that A implies $A \vee B$, it's clear that from (DS), (EXP) is trivially derived; conversely, (DS) is derivable from (EXP) using ($\vee$-Introd). (And given the negation rules, (DS) just amounts to modus ponens for the material conditional.)

I've said that the addition of (LEM) and (EXP) or (DS) to BDM yields classical logic *in a strong sense*. Why the qualification? Because there is a weaker conception of classical logic that doesn't require commitment to the meta-rules ($\vee$-Elim) and ($\neg\wedge$-Elim); this fact is exploited in the "weakly classical" solutions to the paradoxes that are discussed later on (starting in Chapter 9).[2]

Kleene logic, as I'm understanding the term, is half way between BDM and classical logic (in this strong sense) CL: it accepts (EXP), or equivalently (DS), but doesn't accept (LEM). I'll also call this K_3. The inferences it accepts can be shown to be precisely those that are guaranteed by the strong Kleene truth rules to preserve value 1. Later we'll consider the dual logic that accepts (LEM) but not (EXP) or (DS): this is Priest's "logic of paradox" LP. The inferences accepted in LP can be shown to be precisely those that are guaranteed by the strong Kleene truth rules to preserve the property of having value greater than 0.

---

[2] It is possible to formulate a logic BDM⁻ with the same theorems as BDM but without these meta-rules; it's really BDM⁻ rather than BDM that's the weakest deMorgan logic.

It's also possible to consider the common part of K₃ and LP: this is the set of inferences that preserve both the property of having value 1 and the property of having value greater than 0; in other words, in all valuations by the strong Kleene rules, the value of the conclusion is at least as great as the minimum of the values of the premises. This logic, which I'll call S₃ ('S' for 'symmetric') contains more than BDM: it consists of BDM plus

(S₃-rule) $\qquad\qquad\qquad A \wedge \neg A \vDash B \vee \neg B.$

To summarize, we have five different logics, whose logical relations are as in Diagram 3.1.

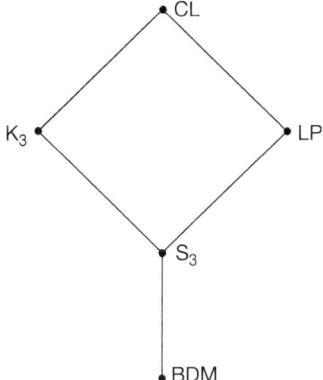

Diagram 3.1.

The main focus late in the book will be on theories of truth preserving all the naive truth rules. Since we will see that we can get such theories both for K₃ and for LP, and indeed for expansions of these to include well-behaved conditionals, there will be little point in looking at theories in the weaker logics S₃ and BDM.[3]

Quantifiers are added to any of these logics in the same way. For instance, for the universal quantifier, we have the obvious

($\forall$-Elim) $\quad \forall x A \vDash A(x/t)$

and

($\neg\forall$-Introd) $\quad \neg A(x/t) \vDash \neg \forall x A,$

---

[3] Really there are not five systems but ten: there is an analogous diagram for the five slightly weaker systems that have the same implications as these ones but which restrict meta-rules like ∨-Elimination. (See previous footnote.) But the only one of these that there will be cause to seriously consider is CL⁻, the weaker version of classical logic. (In Section 25.2 I'll also mention the addition of a new conditional to LP⁻.)

where $A(x/t)$ is the result of substituting t for free occurrences of x in A (and the usual restrictions to prevent variable-occurrences free in t from becoming bound by the substitution are imposed). We also have the meta-rule

($\neg\forall$-Elim) $\quad\dfrac{\Gamma, \neg A \models C}{\Gamma, \neg\forall x A \models C}\quad$ when x is not free in C or in any member of Γ.

For ($\forall$-Introd) there is a slight complication in the current framework (as opposed to the more general sequent calculus framework which allows multiple consequents). One possibility is to use the simplest formulation

($\forall$-Introd) $\quad\dfrac{\Gamma \models A}{\Gamma \models \forall x A}\quad$ when x is not free in Γ,

and then supplement this with the additional rule

(Special) $\quad \forall x[A \vee C] \models \forall x A \vee C \quad$ when x is not free in C.

(One could avoid the need of (Special) by a more cumbersome formulation of ($\forall$-Introd).)

4

Adding a Conditional? Curry and Lukasiewicz

4.1. THE CURRY PARADOX

The discussion at the end of the last chapter suggests that we might go some way toward a more satisfactory theory than KFS by adding a reasonable conditional to the language, and somehow extending Kripke's results to the enlarged language. Unfortunately, this is not as easy as it may sound.

The first difficulty is that Kripke's construction, used to establish the consistency of the Intersubstitutivity of True($\langle A \rangle$) with A in the logic, depended crucially on what I called the Roach Motel Principle; and that in turn depended on the use of a multi-valued semantics (not necessarily 3-valued) in which the connectives are value-functional and a certain monotonicity principle for the connectives holds. And that monotonicity principle rules out any non-trivial conditional '$\rightarrow$' for which $A \rightarrow A$ is a law, at least if the system is non-dialetheic.[1] So if we add a conditional to the language, we will be forced to use quite different methods to show that the system consistently sustains the intersubstitutivity of True($\langle A \rangle$) with A.

---

[1] More carefully, the monotonicity principle is that there is a certain value in the semantics (which Kripke calls 'undefined' and I've called $1/2$) such that for any n-ary connective Φ and any j:

If the value of A_j is $1/2$ but the value of $\Phi(A_1, \ldots, A_n)$ is a value v other than $1/2$, then the value of $\Phi(A_1, \ldots, A_{j-1}, B, A_{j+1}, \ldots, A_n)$ is v for any other B as well.

It easily follows that if Φ is a binary connective in which $\Phi(A_1, A_2)$ has a value v other than $1/2$ when A_1 and A_2 each have value $1/2$, then $\Phi(B, C)$ has value v for every B and C. So unless $B \rightarrow C$ has the same semantic value for every choice of B and C, in which case it is completely trivial, then $A \rightarrow A$ must have value $1/2$, when A has value $1/2$.

This doesn't quite preclude $A \rightarrow A$ being validated by the semantics, because I haven't ruled out $1/2$ being a designated value of the semantics. And it is so, in certain dialetheic systems. But only there: for monotonicity requires that if negation is non-trivial then when A has value $1/2$, so does $\neg A$; and so if $1/2$ is designated then any sentence with this designated value will be such that its negation is designated too.

And the exception for dialetheic systems is not terribly interesting, for it doesn't apply to any non-trivial dialetheic system with modus ponens. Reason: Let A have value $1/2$ and C have a non-designated value (there must be some if the system is non-trivial). Assume $1/2$ is designated. Then if $A \rightarrow C$ has value $1/2$, modus ponens fails. But if $A \rightarrow C$ has a value v other than $1/2$, then monotonicity requires that $B \rightarrow C$ have value v for *every* B. If this v is designated then modus ponens fails whenever B has designated value, and if this v is not designated then $C \rightarrow C$ doesn't have a designated value, contrary to our assumptions.

Another difficulty is that the conditional is going to have to have some unusual properties which require getting used to. This is illustrated by Curry's paradox (*aka* Löb's paradox, *aka* Henkin's paradox), from Curry 1942. Using the Diagonalization Lemma, we construct a sentence K such that K is equivalent to

$$\text{True}(\langle K \rangle) \to \text{The earth is flat.}$$

(Again, we might construct this in innocuous ways: "If the man in this picture is now saying something true then the earth is flat", where unbeknownst to me it is a picture of myself.) Letting '$A \leftrightarrow B$' abbreviate '$(A \to B) \land (B \to A)$', and '$\bot$' abbreviate 'the earth is flat', we now argue as follows:

1. $K \leftrightarrow [\text{True}(\langle K \rangle) \to \bot]$ (By construction of K)
2. $\text{True}(\langle K \rangle) \leftrightarrow [\text{True}(\langle K \rangle) \to \bot]$ (1 and Truth-Intersubstitutivity)
3. $\text{True}(\langle K \rangle) \to [\text{True}(\langle K \rangle) \to \bot]$ (Left to Right of 2)
4. $[\text{True}(\langle K \rangle) \land \text{True}(\langle K \rangle)] \to \bot$ (3, by "Importation": from $A \to (B \to C)$, infer $(A \land B) \to C$)
5. $\text{True}(\langle K \rangle) \to \bot$ (4, by Intersubstitutivity of $A \land A$ with A)
6. $[\text{True}(\langle K \rangle) \to \bot] \to \text{True}(\langle K \rangle)$ (Right to left of 2)
7. $\text{True}(\langle K \rangle)$ (5 and 6, by modus ponens)
8. $\bot$ (5 and 7, by modus ponens).

Something natural has to be given up! Giving up Truth-Intersubstitutivity in favor of the Tarski schema wouldn't help, unless we also abandon transitivity of equivalence: for $\text{True}(\langle K \rangle) \leftrightarrow K$ together with 1 yields 2 by transitivity, without Truth-Intersubstitutivity.

Suppose we put aside the possibility that the problem is with Truth-Intersubstitutivity (or the Tarski schema). In that case, the most obvious culprit is the Importation rule; but if that is abandoned, then the embedding of conditionals is going to have to be more complicated than in classical logic.[2] It will turn out that the usual laws of the conditional can be maintained *for those conditionals for which we have excluded middle for their antecedents and consequents*: the simple embedding laws of classical logic don't need to be completely abandoned, they just need to be restricted in contexts where excluded middle cannot be assumed.

A famous class of logics that restrict the Importation rule in this way are the Lukasiewicz logics (Lukasiewicz and Tarski 1930). Let us see how well they fare with regard to the Curry paradox and related ones.

Let's start with Lukasiewicz 3-valued logic. The semantics of this logic is just like the Kleene semantics, except there is an additional conditional. Taking the

---

[2] Note that if the problem is indeed with Importation, it lies in the special case where A and B are identical. Given the intersubstitutivity of $A \land A$ with A, this amounts to the Contraction Rule: $A \to (A \to C) \vdash A \to C$.

three values to be 1, 0, and ½, with 1 the "designated" value (the one which good inferences are to preserve), the Kleene connectives of the sentential logic were treated as follows:

$|\neg A|$ is $1 - |A|$

$|A \wedge B|$ is the minimum of $|A|$ and $|B|$

$|A \vee B|$ is the maximum of $|A|$ and $|B|$

$|\forall x A|$ is the greatest lower bound of the $|A(o)|$, for all o in the range of the quantifiers[3]

$|\exists x A|$ is the least upper bound of the $|A(o)|$, for all o in the range of the quantifiers.

The Lukasiewicz semantics keeps these, and adds:

$$|A \to B| \text{ is } \begin{array}{ll} 1 & \text{if } |A| \leq |B| \\ 1 - (|A| - |B|) & \text{if } |A| > |B|. \end{array}$$

Note that when we restrict to the two classical values 1 and 0, this reduces to the standard conditional of classical logic; so that in some sense, all of the non-classicality in the conditional results from restrictions on excluded middle. This makes it unobvious that the 3-valued conditional should be regarded as "differing in meaning from" the classical conditional: indeed, a proponent of the Lukasiewicz logic could say that the Lukasiewicz conditional fully represents the ordinary conditional of English, and that the classical conditional is simply the result of restricting to situations in which excluded middle applies. (This involves supposing that the usual "definition" of the conditional in terms of $\neg$ and $\vee$ has no sacrosanct status; but it is a familiar point that laws counted as "definitional" often have no more claim to preservation than other central laws, and I would have thought that giving up such central principles as "if A then A" is more indicative of a "change of meaning" than giving up the equivalence of "if A then B" to "not-A or B". This is not, however, an issue I see any point in pursuing.)

Regarding the Curry paradox, there's good news: In this semantics, we can consistently assign the same value to the Curry sentence K as to $\text{True}(\langle K \rangle)$, even though K is the same as $\text{True}(\langle K \rangle) \to \bot$. Since $|\bot|$ is 0, $|\text{True}(\langle K \rangle) \to \bot|$ is just $1 - |\text{True}(\langle K \rangle)|$, so we just need that $|\text{True}(\langle K \rangle)| = |K| = 1 - |\text{True}(\langle K \rangle)|$; i.e. $|K| = \frac{1}{2}$. (As expected, the semantics diagnoses the failure in the argument for the earth's flatness as residing in the Importation step: if A and B have value ½ and C has value 0, $A \to (B \to C)$ has value 1 but $(A \wedge B) \to C$ only has value ½.)

But there's bad news: a simple modification of the Curry sentence is not evaluable consistently with the requirement that $\text{True}(\langle A \rangle)$ always has the same

---

[3] I hope I will be forgiven for a little sloppiness in writing the quantifier clauses: I wanted to avoid the notational clutter of relativization of all formulas to an assignment function. (Actually the notation $A(o)$ used here, where we "plug an object itself" in for a variable, could be rigorously explained: see the discussion of parameterized formulas in Chapter 1 note 16.)

value as A. Let K_1 be equivalent to $\text{True}(\langle K_1\rangle) \to K$, where K is the ordinary Curry sentence. ("If what the man in the picture is saying is true, so is the ordinary Curry sentence.") The requirement that $|\text{True}(K_1)| = |K_1|$ entails that $|K_1| = |K_1 \to K|$, and since $|K| = 1/2$, the rule for the conditional requires that $|K_1|$ be $3/4$; but that isn't in the value space.

Why not add it to the value space? (And add $1/4$ too, so that we can keep the negation rule.) We can do that, but then we have a problem with the Curry-like sentence K_2 that is equivalent to $\text{True}(\langle K_2\rangle) \to K_1$. Of course we can keep on going with this, getting 2^{n+1}-valued spaces for larger and larger n, but at each stage we find a Curry-like sentence K_n that isn't evaluable in the space in accordance with the the requirement that $|\text{True}(\langle K_n\rangle)| = |K_n|$.

What about going to an infinite valued semantics? Or to be safe, a continuum-valued semantics, in which every real number in the interval [0,1] is allowed as a value? (We keep the algebraic formulations for the values of conditionals, negations, conjunctions and disjunctions given above.)[4]

Here there's very good news to report, which I will develop in the next section. Unfortunately it will turn out not to be quite good enough.

4.2. CONTINUUM-VALUED SEMANTICS

Let S be a quantifier-free first order language with identity—like a sentential language except that instead of sentence letters we have formulas built from predicates (including identity), names, variables and function symbols. (It's important here to disallow definite descriptions, since they are relevantly like quantifiers.) We imagine that it contains names for each symbol in its own alphabet, and a binary function symbol for the concatenation of expressions; so for each expression e of the language there is a "structural-descriptive name" $\langle e \rangle$. We also imagine that it contains a primitive 1-place function symbol NAME, which stands for the function that maps each expression into its structural-descriptive name. (What it does to things that aren't expressions won't matter.) And it contains a primitive 2-place function symbol SUBST, which stands for the function that maps each formula in which a particular variable v_1 occurs and each singular term t into the formula that results by replacing all occurrences of v_1 with t. Take the theory T to include the quantifier-free identity axioms,

---

[4] Adding these extra values has no effect on the $\to$-free part of the logic: precisely the same inferences among $\to$-free sentences are valid in the continuum-valued logic as in the Kleene logic. The effect of the extra values is to slightly weaken the logic of the conditional. (For instance, the problem with K_1 in the 3-valued logic arises from the fact that that semantics validates the rather odd axiom schema: $(A_1 \leftrightarrow A_2) \vee (A_1 \leftrightarrow A_3) \vee (A_1 \leftrightarrow A_4) \vee (A_2 \leftrightarrow A_3) \vee (A_2 \leftrightarrow A_4) \vee (A_3 \leftrightarrow A_4)$. In the other finite-valued systems we weaken the schema by adding more disjuncts, whereas in the continuum-valued logic we just drop the schema entirely.)

the basic true identities and non-identities of the protosyntactic theory for the language, and all true identities of the forms

$$\text{NAME}(e) = f$$

and

$$\text{SUBST}(e, f) = g,$$

where e, f, and g are structural descriptive names. Using this, we can get self-reference even within the quantifier-free language: letting $\text{SA}(e)$ abbreviate $\text{SUBST}(e, \text{NAME}(e))$, then when e and f are structural-descriptive names and what e names is a formula A containing v_1 as its sole variable, we have: $\text{SA}(e) = f$ is true, and a consequence of T, if and only if f names the self application of e, i.e. the result of replacing v_1 in A by $\langle A \rangle$, i.e. by $A(\langle A \rangle)$.[5] So we have a "poor man's self-reference": a minimal sort of self-reference in a quantifier-free language.

The question arises whether such a language can contain a predicate 'True' that satisfies the Tarski schema and the Intersubstitutivity Principle. This isn't as demanding as requiring this for a full language with quantifiers, but it goes a long way toward that. The reason that's so is that our "poor man's self-reference" is all we need to construct most of the standard paradoxes. For instance, $\text{SA}(\langle \neg \text{True}(v_1) \rangle)$ denotes a Liar sentence; $\text{SA}(\langle \text{True}(v_1) \to \bot \rangle)$ a Curry sentence; $\text{SA}(\langle \text{True}(v_1) \to \text{SA}(\langle \text{True}(v_1) \to \bot \rangle) \rangle)$ the modified Curry sentence K_1 mentioned a few paragraphs back; and so forth. So it is clear from what has been said already that if we take the logic of S to be classical, or to be a finite-valued Lukasiewicz logic, then neither the demand of Intersubstitutivity nor that of the truth schema can be met; and that the latter demand also can't be met if we take the logic to be Kleene logic.

But both demands can be met in Lukasiewicz continuum-valued sentential logic. Indeed, we have:

Conservativeness theorem: Let M be any classical ω-model of the 'True'-free part of S. Then there is a continuum-valued model M^+ for the full S in which

(1) $\text{True}(\langle B \rangle)$ and B have the same value in M^+, for any sentence B in the language (including those that contain 'True'),

and

(2) If B is a sentence not containing 'True', it has value 1 in M^+ if it is true in M and 0 if it is false in M.

Indeed, we can strengthen this: we can replace (2) by the stronger requirement that M^+ is just like M in its 'True'-free part: same domain, same assignments to individual constants and function symbols, and effectively the same assignments

---

[5] We can generalize to the case where e names a formula with free variables other than 'v_1', but what's in the text will do for my purposes.

to predicates other than 'True'. (By this last, I mean that M^+ assigns to each n-place predicate p in the 'True'-free language a function f_p which assigns to each n-tuple $<o_1,\ldots,o_n>$ from the domain either 1 or 0, and it assigns 1 if and only if $<o_1,\ldots,o_n>$ is in the M-extension of p.)

The proof of the (strengthened) theorem is in an Appendix to this chapter. In the case of the paradoxical sentences so far mentioned and many more besides, the fact that the corresponding instances of the Tarski schema can be satisfied is a direct consequence of the principle that you can't get from one side of a square to the opposite side in a continuous motion without crossing a given diagonal. (For these examples, we need only the $k=1$ case of what is there called the "Warm-up Result". The proof of the Warm-up Result appeals to what's called the Brouwer fixed point theorem, but in the $k=1$ case only the one dimensional version of that is required, and that's equivalent to the claim about the square.)[6]

It's worth noting that the Conservativeness result covers an immense variety of standard paradoxes. For instance, it covers paradoxes that require "simultaneous solutions": e.g. a sentence A that says that sentence B is true, where B is a sentence that says that A is not true. It also covers many paradoxes of *determinate* truth, as I'll explain in Section 4.4. But first I want to adapt some of the discussion of Sections 3.4 and 3.5 from the context of KFS to the context of continuum-valued semantics.

4.3. WHAT DO THE SEMANTIC VALUES MEAN?

Some people who discuss the continuum-valued semantics think of value 1 as representing truth, value 0 as representing falsehood, and the intermediate values as representing various "degrees of truth" in between them. This would be the analog for the expanded Lukasiewicz language of a view I rejected in the previous chapter for the narrower Kleene language. What should we put in its place?

Since we're really now dealing only with the sentential portion of the language, we can put aside the special problems raised by languages with unrestricted quantifiers, and can regard having semantic value 1 as sufficient for truth and having semantic value 0 as sufficient for falsity. But what can we say about the intermediate values?

The proper answer to this is evident from the Conservativeness theorem together with the semantics of the conditional. Suppose $|A| \leq |B|$. By the semantics of the conditional, $|A \to B| = 1$, and so if truth is introduced in

---

[6] That the Brouwer theorem shows the utility of the continuum-valued semantics for the paradoxes is a fact that seems to have been independently noticed by many people, dating back to long ago. (See for instance Chang 1963, who cites Skolem 1957; though these both concern the set-theoretic "paradoxes".) I suspect that the conservativeness result proved in the Appendix does not go substantially beyond prior work on this topic, though I don't know of a clear prior statement or proof of it.

accordance with the conservativeness theorem, $|\text{True}(\langle A \rangle) \rightarrow \text{True}(\langle B \rangle)| = 1$. But value 1 suffices for truth, and '$\rightarrow$' is just supposed to be a representation of 'if ... then'; so if A is true then B is true. *Just as $|A| = 1$ suffices for the truth of A, $|A| \leq |B|$ suffices for the conditional that if A is true, so is B.* (It also suffices for the contrapositive that if B is not true, neither is A; for conditionals are equivalent to their contrapositives, in continuum-valued logic as in classical.) We have sufficiency only, not necessity: that's inevitable, for claims of form $|A| \leq |B|$ are classical claims, that is, they obey excluded middle, whereas excluded middle does not hold in general for conditionals. In any case, the semantics doesn't commit to any value that represents the division between the true and the untrue; a large part of the "fuzziness" of 'true' can be thought of as a "fuzziness" as to which values are sufficiently high to count as truth.

4.4. DETERMINATE TRUTH IN CONTINUUM-VALUED SEMANTICS

One of the defects noted for the Kripkean theory KFS in the last chapter was that the language it dealt with is too weak to express the idea that the Liar sentence is not determinately true. At first blush it looks as if this expressive deficiency is additional to its not containing a reasonable conditional. It turns out however that in adding a conditional to the language, Lukasiewicz added the means to define a pretty good determinately operator, or equivalently, a pretty good "weak negation" operator 'not determinately'.

First let's look at the conditions we should expect of a determinately operator D in a semantics with values in the interval $[0,1]$. The following seem the most obvious ones:

(ia)   If $|A| = 1$, $|DA|$ should be 1

(ib)   If $|A| = 0$, $|DA|$ should be 0

(ic)   If $0 < |A| < 1$, $|DA|$ should be strictly less than $|A|$

(ii)   If $|A| \leq |B|$, $|DA|$ should be less than or equal to $|DB|$.

Indeed, we should probably strengthen (ib), to

(ib-s) If $|A| \leq 1/2$, $|DA|$ should be 0;

we need (ib-s) to get $|\neg D(\text{True}(\langle Q \rangle))| = 1$, where Q is the Liar sentence. If we define "weak negation" $\neg_w$ by $\neg D$, these correspond to the conditions

(ia*)   If $|A| = 1$, $|\neg_w A|$ should be 0

(ib*)   If $|A| = 0$, $|\neg_w A|$ should be 1

(ic*)   If $0 < |A| < 1$, $|\neg_w A|$ should be strictly more than $1 - |A|$

(ii*)   If $|A| \leq |B|$, $|\neg_w A|$ should be greater than or equal to $|\neg_w B|$

and probably

(ib-s*) $\qquad$ If $|A| \leq 1/2$, $|\neg_w A|$ should be 1.

These conditions are all satisfied in continuum-valued semantics, if we define $\neg_w A$ as $A \to \neg A$ and define D as its ordinary negation, i.e. as $\neg(A \to \neg A)$. For then

$$|\neg_w A| = \begin{array}{ll} 1 & \text{if } |A| \leq 1/2 \\ 2 \cdot (1 - |A|) & \text{otherwise;} \end{array}$$

i.e. it's given in Diagram 4.1. (Ignore the dotted line for the moment.)

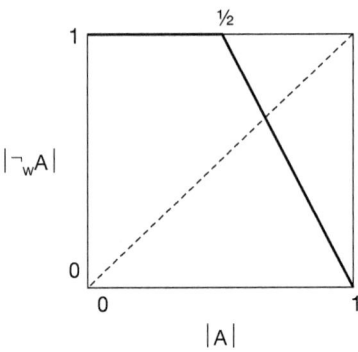

Diagram 4.1.

And

$$|DA| = \begin{array}{ll} 0 & \text{if } |A| \leq 1/2 \\ 2 \cdot |A| - 1 & \text{otherwise;} \end{array}$$

as given in Diagram 4.2.

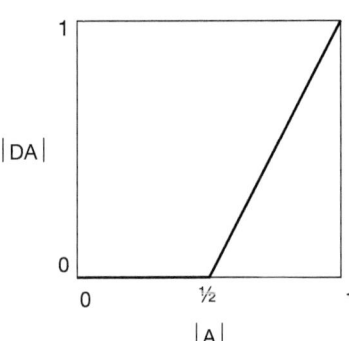

Diagram 4.2.

The required properties (ia), (ia*) etc. are evident from the diagrams.

Given this, it is evident from the Conservativeness Theorem that the continuum-valued semantics consistently handles a Liar-like sentence Q_1 that asserts that it is not *determinately* true; that is, where Q_1 is equivalent to $\neg_w \text{True}(\langle Q_1 \rangle)$ rather than to $\neg \text{True}(\langle Q_1 \rangle)$. Indeed, a look at the graph of $\neg_w$ immediately yields the solution: the graph crosses the dotted diagonal at $2/3$ (and only there), so that is the (unique) value of $\text{True}(\langle Q_1 \rangle)$ for which $|\text{True}(\langle Q_1 \rangle)|$ could equal $|\neg_w \text{True}(\langle Q_1 \rangle)|$, i.e. for which $|\text{True}(\langle Q_1 \rangle)|$ could equal $|Q_1|$.

Since $|Q_1| = 2/3, |DQ_1| = 1/3$. Note that $|DDQ_1| = 0$, so $|\neg DDQ_1| = 1$; so the theory licenses the claim that $\neg DDQ_1$. It does not of course license the claim $\neg DQ_1$: that's equivalent to Q_1, so gets only the value $2/3$.

We see that DD is a stronger operator than D. Its equation is

$$|DDA| = \begin{array}{ll} 0 & \text{if } |A| \leq 3/4 \\ 4 \cdot |A| - 3 & \text{otherwise;} \end{array}$$

and its graph is given as in Diagram 4.3.

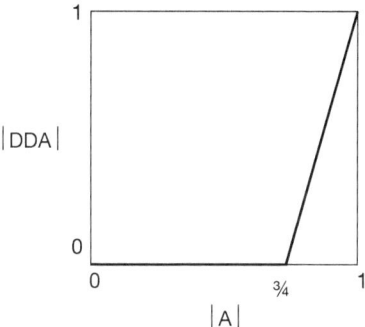

Diagram 4.3.

Clearly it satisfies the conditions of a determinately operator too. Its negation $\neg DD$ is thus a still weaker form of "negation" than $\neg_w$. (Taking $\neg_w$ rather than D as basic, this still weaker form of negation would be written as $\neg_w \neg \neg_w$, with only the middle one unsubscripted. I find that hopelessly confusing, which is why I prefer thinking in terms of D.)

Since DD is in the language, we can formulate in the language a sentence Q_2 that says of itself that it isn't determinately determinately true, and the Conservativeness Theorem shows that there is a value of Q_2 that's consistent with the requirement that $|\text{True}(\langle Q_2 \rangle)| = |Q_2|$. By calculation (or figuring out where the inversion of the graph of DD crosses the diagonal) we see that the value is $4/5$. Obviously we can continue this process through all finite values. As we iterate D more, the graph of the resulting operator stays at 0 for higher and higher values of $|A|$, and so has to rise more steeply to get to the value 1 when $|A|$ is 1. (For the record, the general equation for the nth iteration D^n of D is that $|D^nA|$ is 0 when $|A| \leq (2^n - 1)/2^n$, and $2^n \cdot |A| - (2^n - 1)$ otherwise. And the value of the corresponding Liar sentence Q_n is $2^n/(2^n+1)$.)

So we have a stronger and stronger sequence of determinately operators D^n in the language, each completely unparadoxical.

It seems, though, that if we understand each of the D^n operators, we ought to understand their "infinite conjunction" D^ω. It should be evaluated by the limit of the functions that evaluate the D^ns; in other words, by the function

$$f(x) = 1 \quad \text{if } x = 1$$
$$ 0 \quad \text{otherwise.}$$

This however would be a disaster: the inversion of this function (which would correspond to $\neg D^\omega$) does not intersect the diagonal (which is possible since it is not continuous). So if D^ω were in the language, an "ω^{th} level Liar sentence" that states that it itself is not D^ω true would breed paradox.

The Conservativeness Theorem for the quantifier-free language S shows that D^ω isn't in that language; which is not surprising, since it was explained as an infinite conjunction. But don't we understand it? Doesn't this show that S is simply too limited in expressive powers? I think the answer is clearly 'yes': continuum-valued semantics is ultimately inadequate. This is made precise in the next section. The consideration of this semantics will not have been without point, though: its treatment of the quantifier-free fragment is nice enough that we will want to preserve some of its features in a more adequate account.

4.5. ULTIMATE FAILURE: QUANTIFIERS

It's hard to doubt that if we understand each of the finite iterations D^n of D we also understand their "infinite conjunction" D^ω. And indeed, this *must* be the case if we have a truth predicate that obeys the Intersubstitutivity principle at our disposal, together with quantification and elementary arithmetic (or equivalently, syntax). For we can then use the truth predicate to define the infinite conjunction:

$D^\omega A$ is to be taken as an abbreviation of: For every n, the result of iterating the operator D n times and applying it to A is true.

And then we have the disaster noted at the end of the previous section: if D^ω really is the infinite conjunction of the D^ns and they are evaluated as in the continuum-valued semantics then $|D^\omega A|$ is 1 if $|A|$ is 1 and 0 otherwise; so $|\neg D^\omega A|$ is 0 if $|A|$ is 1 and 1 otherwise; so

(*)   For every sentence A of the language, $|\neg D^\omega A| \neq |A|$.

But by Gödel–Tarski self-reference, there would have to be a sentence Q_ω whose value is the same as $|\neg D^\omega \text{True}(\langle Q_\omega \rangle)|$, and hence (by (*)) different from $|\text{True}(\langle Q_\omega \rangle)|$; that is, $|Q_\omega| \neq |\text{True}(\langle Q_\omega \rangle)|$, contrary to what we wanted.[7]

This is in effect the inadequacy proof for continuum-valued semantics offered in Restall 1992. Restall's discussion highlights a possible reaction to it (not one that Restall advocates): that we might accept the continuum-valued semantics, and the validity of the Tarski equivalences (which require that for every sentence $|\text{True}(\langle A \rangle)| = |A|$), by letting our theory of truth be ω-inconsistent though not actually inconsistent. The reason this seems to be a *possible* way to go, even if not an attractive one, is that if the arithmetic theory is ω-inconsistent, the formalized syntactic theory will be too; so (to put it slightly loosely) $D^\omega A$ as defined above won't actually be forced to hold when each $D^n A$ holds, i.e. $D^\omega A$ as defined will be stronger than an infinite conjunction. (No "genuine infinite conjunction" will be definable in the language.) Indeed, there's no obvious reason why $D^\omega A$ couldn't have value 0 for *all* A, even A with value 1. Given this possibility, (*) won't hold when A has value 1, and the proof will break down.

This is of course not an attractive resolution of the paradox. In the first place, it gives up on the Conservativeness requirement: the 'True'-free part of the language has ω-models for arithmetic and syntax, and the proposed resolution is that we give up on finding a theory of truth that extends them, and accept a theory with no ω-models instead. Moreover, to accept an ω-inconsistent syntax is to accept that there are expressions f of our language that in some sense are not "genuinely finite": for infinitely many expressions e, we accept that e is a proper initial segment of f. We call them 'finite', but we don't really mean *finite*! This seems to border on the incoherent.

The difficulty in talking sensibly about the theory of truth for our own language being ω-inconsistent is due to the fact that such talk involves a failure of the analog of the Tarski schema for 'true of'. More fully, to posit the ω-inconsistency is to say

(?)   For all numbers n, $\langle B(x) \rangle$ is true of n, but $\langle (\forall n \in \text{Number}) B(n) \rangle$ is not true.

Assuming the Tarski schema for truth, this is equivalent to

For all numbers n, $\langle B(x) \rangle$ is true of n, but it is not the case that for all numbers n, $B(n)$.

---

[7] It would be no help to switch from the standard unit interval [0,1] to one with infinitesimals added. The only even *prima facie* promising possibility this adds is to let $\text{True}(\langle Q_\omega \rangle)$ have value within an infinitesimal of 1. But then $D\text{True}(\langle Q_\omega \rangle)$ would also have to have value within an infinitesimal of 1, and so by induction this would hold of each $D^n \text{True}(\langle Q_\omega \rangle)$. That is, each of them has value greater than all real numbers that are strictly less than 1. But then that would hold of $D^\omega \text{True}(\langle Q_\omega \rangle)$ too, since that is an infinite conjunction; so $\neg D^\omega \text{True}(\langle Q_\omega \rangle)$ has value within an infinitesimal of 0. But $\neg D^\omega \text{True}(\langle Q_\omega \rangle)$ is equivalent to Q_ω, so Q_ω has a very different value from $\text{True}(\langle Q_\omega \rangle)$. The problem arises from the fact that the operator D^ω still produces a sharp cut between sentences with nearby values: this time, the cut is between those with values within an infinitesimal of 1 and those with lower values.

94 *Selective Background*

But that is in direct violation of the corresponding schema for 'True of'.

In short: even though it may be in principle possible to "save" the simple theory of truth in continuum-valued semantics by weakening the conservativeness requirement to a consistency requirement and giving up on ω-consistency, this would be giving up on the simple theory of truth-of. It's hard to see that this is of much value.

As if this weren't enough, Hajek, Paris, and Sheperdson (2000) point out that even if we stick to truth as opposed to truth-of, we have a problem for simple consistency as well as for ω-consistency: a theory of truth for continuum-valued logic can't be simply consistent if the theory includes the generalizations that the negation of a sentence x is true if and only if the sentence x is not true, and that a conditional is true if and only if, if the antecedent is true then so is the consequent. (Each instance of both generalizations is already part of the theory; genuine inconsistency as opposed to mere ω-inconsistency results when you include the generalization. So if inconsistency is to be avoided, the theory must be essentially ω-incomplete in a very drastic way, as well as being ω-inconsistent.) For details I refer you to Theorem 3 of their paper.

But the clear inadequacy of the continuum-valued semantics for languages with quantifiers should not blind us to its virtues in a quantifier-free context. Indeed, one might well hope that some simple modification of it would work for languages with quantifiers. In fact, this does not seem to be the case: major revisions in the approach seem to be required. Even so, some of the features of the quantifier-free continuum-valued approach will in fact carry over to more adequate solutions.

4.6. INDETERMINACY AND REJECTION

A key to the success of the continuum-valued semantics in the quantifier-free case is that the attitude of full rejection can't be reduced to the attitude of full acceptance: there is no operator N in the language for which fully rejecting a sentence A coincides with fully accepting the sentence NA. We do have a variety of negation-like operators. For instance, there is the sequence of successively weaker operators

$$\neg, \neg D, \neg DD, \neg DDD, \ldots$$

and the succession of successively stronger operators

$$\neg, D\neg, DD\neg, DDD\neg.$$

(Also other operators that don't fit into the linear order, such as $D\neg D$ and $\neg D\neg D\neg$.) But fully rejecting A doesn't coincide with fully accepting NA, using any of these operators for N. This is the key to the success of the continuum-valued approach in the quantifier-free logic. Indeed, continuum-valued semantics fails in the language with quantifiers precisely because that language allows for the construction of an operator $\neg D^\omega$ such that full acceptance of $\neg D^\omega A$ does coincide with full rejection of A.[8]

This means that one of the weaknesses of KFS is bound to persist *in more limited form* in the quantifier-free continuum-valued semantics, and in any improvement of it that adequately handles the quantifiers. In KFS, we saw, when we reject an instance of excluded middle, there is never anything we accept that "expresses this rejection": we must remain silent. Well, we don't really need to remain silent: we could introduce a speech act that expresses rejection in a way analogous to how assertion expresses acceptance. Utterance of a sentence while holding one's nose might do the job. But the fact is that we tend to be "assertion-oriented": we have a standard convention for expressing what we accept, but no standard convention for expressing what we reject. So it does seem a bit of a defect of KFS that we can never, by expressing what we accept, indirectly express our rejection of instances of excluded middle.

In the Lukasiewicz sentential logic, this defect is partially overcome. For instance, when we reject the ordinary Liar sentence Q, we can make an assertion involving the weak negation operator $\neg D$. Asserting $\neg DQ$ displays our rejection of Q; or at least, it logically commits us to rejecting Q. For the "determinate Liar" sentence Q_1 we cannot express our rejection via acceptance *in this way*, but we can do it in another way, by means of the operator $\neg DD$. In fact the quantifier-free language can be shown to have the feature that for *any* sentence

---

[8] I'm not saying that paradox arises (in any language that permits self-reference and validates the intersubstitutivity of True($\langle A \rangle$) with A) *merely* from the supposition that there is an embeddable operator N by means of which we could reduce rejection to acceptance. To get a paradox, some assumptions about acceptance and rejection would be needed, such as (i) that it is impossible, or at least irrational, to accept and reject the same thing simultaneously; (ii) that we can reason classically about what we accept, or what it is rational to accept; and (iii) that the impossibility of accepting a sentence, or doing so rationally, should lead to its rejection.

With some such assumptions, one might propose a "paradox of acceptance and rejection" of something like this sort:

Given any such operator N and a truth predicate obeying Intersubstitutivity, we can construct a sentence Q_N which is equivalent to NTrue($\langle Q_N \rangle$). But then one should accept Q_N if and only if one should accept NTrue($\langle Q_N \rangle$), hence if and only if one should reject True($\langle Q_N \rangle$), hence if and only if one should reject Q_N. That is, acceptance of Q_N should coincide with rejection of it. But by (i), we can't both accept and reject Q_N; so (using (ii), in particular that excluded middle holds for claims of what we do or should accept) we must neither accept it nor reject it. But then we have a violation of (iii): we've committed ourselves not to accepting it, so we should reject it.

This is loose: I didn't word the assumptions (i)–(iii) carefully, because I wanted to keep an ambiguity between descriptive claims and claims about rationality; and it isn't completely clear how one would word them to get a compelling argument even on the assumption of such an operator N. (For instance, the second disjunct of premise (ii), the part about rationality, seems especially dubious.) Still, it's worth noting that continuum-valued semantics in quantifier-free language seems to avoid even the *prima facie* case for such a "paradox of acceptance and rejection", because it does not contain any such operator. (In a continuum-valued semantics in a language that contains a notion of rejection, we better be sure that 'I reject ($\langle A \rangle$)' isn't itself such an operator; but it is easy enough to resist the strong self-knowledge assumptions required to make it into one.)

that we reject, we can use one of the weak negation operators $\neg D^n$ to express our rejection via acceptance.[9] I take it that that is a substantial improvement over the situation with KFS.

Of course in the full continuum-valued logic, with quantifiers, we *can* fully express the rejection of A with an assertion: we can assert $\neg D^\omega A$. But that is a defect of the full language with quantifiers, not an advantage: it's what gives rise to the paradoxes; and in the next chapter we'll see that it also spoils the application of the semantics to vagueness.

Going back to the quantifier-free logic, it is admittedly awkward not to have a "unified" weak negation operator that when applied to any sentence "expresses rejection" of that sentence. I've mentioned that there are ways of indicating rejection in conversation, such as uttering the sentence while holding one's nose; but a written equivalent of this, such as writing the sentence in a special unattractive font to indicate rejection of it, has obvious disadvantages, and probably would not be acceptable to my publisher. (A satisfactory convention for conveying *conditional* rejection would be even less elegant.) Because of this, it is tempting to indicate one's rejection of a class of sentences either by saying that one is committed not to accepting them, or by saying that it would be inappropriate to accept them. But doing so could raise the worry that one is introducing autobiographical or normative issues into the discussion where they don't belong. (In addition, it has the disadvantage of being in some ways too weak: as noted at the start of Section 3.7, rejection is in many ways stronger than commitment not to accept.) But despite the very real dangers, I will sometimes bow to convenience and speak in this fashion. The reader bothered by this is invited to imagine the autobiographical or normative language replaced by the ugly font.

---

[9] At least, that's so when we use the continuum-valued semantics only for the semantic paradoxes. In the next chapter I will contemplate the use of that semantics to deal with vague discourse, and it is doubtful that the point remains correct in that context.

APPENDIX: THE CONSERVATIVENESS THEOREM

Recall that S is a language without quantifiers or definite descriptions, but has a primitive device of self-reference. The theorem (in the strengthened form mentioned in the text) is:

Conservativeness Theorem: Let M be any classical ω-model of the 'True'-free part of the language S. Then there is a continuum-valued model M^+ for the full S that gives the same value to True($\langle B \rangle$) as to B, for any sentence B in S, and such that M^+ is just like M in its 'True'-free part.

More fully, we first redescribe M (in the manner described in the text) as a degenerate continuum-valued model (for the 'True'-free part of the language S): degenerate in that it employs only the values 0 and 1. To give an extension to the full S that is like M in its 'True' free part is to specify an assignment to 'True'. This will be a function g (which I'll call a *T-function*) that assigns a number in [0,1] to every sentence of S (and assigns 0 to every non-sentence). The model then evaluates each sentence of form 'True($\langle B \rangle$)' (for B in the full S) as having the value g(B), and each other atomic sentence as having whatever value (0 or 1) that it gets in M. This specification of the values for atomic sentences determines a value $|B|_g$ for every sentence of the language, by the rules of continuum-valued semantics. The key requirement that $|\text{True}(\langle B \rangle)|_g = |B|_g$ is equivalent to the requirement

(*) $$|B|_g = g(B).$$

So the task is to show that there is at least one function g that satisfies (*) for each B in S.

Let the *spectrum* of a sentence A be the set of those sentences of the language that are denoted by terms t in subsentences of A with form 'True(t)'. ('True' doesn't appear within any terms, given that we've excluded definite descriptions from the language.) Call a set Σ of sentences *self-sustaining* if the spectra of each of its members is a subset of Σ. (As examples: (i) the singleton whose only member is the Liar sentence is self-sustaining; (ii) so is a set consisting of two sentences A and B, where A says that B is true and B says that A isn't true. The set of all sentences in the language is also self-sustaining.)

I start with a "warm-up result", that directly uses the Brouwer fixed point theorem (that any continuous function on the set of k-tuples of real numbers in [0,1] has a fixed point).

Warm-up result: Let Σ be any finite self-sustaining set of sentences in the full S. Then we can extend the valuation given in M in such a way that $|\text{True}(\langle B \rangle)| = |B|$ for each B in Σ. (That is, for any finite self-sustaining set Σ of sentences, there are functions g that satisfy (*) for each member of Σ.)

Proof of warm-up result: Let Σ be $B_1, \ldots, B_k$. Let Σ^* be the set of sentences whose spectrum is a subset of Σ. (Σ^* is a self-sustaining super-set of Σ, but won't be finite.) The first step is to inductively associate with each member A of Σ^* a $[0,1]$-valued function f_A in k variables (k the cardinality of Σ) each of which range over $[0,1]$: $f_A(x_1,\ldots,x_k)$ is the value that the semantics gives to A when $x_1,\ldots,x_k$ are assigned to $B_1,\ldots,B_k$. The inductive specification is as follows:

> If A is an atomic sentence with predicate letter other than 'True', f_A is a constant function, with value 1 if A is true in M and 0 otherwise;
>
> If A is True(t) for some term t that denotes B_i, f_A is the projection function that maps $<x_1,\ldots,x_k>$ to x_i.
>
> $f_{\neg A}$ is the function defined pointwise as $1 - f_A$. [That is, its value for any $x_1,\ldots,x_k$ is 1 minus $f_A(x_1,\ldots,x_k)$.]
>
> $f_{A\wedge B}$ is the function defined pointwise as min $\{f_A, f_B\}$.
>
> $f_{A\vee B}$ is the function defined pointwise as max $\{f_A, f_B\}$.
>
> $f_{A\to B}$ is the function defined pointwise as min $\{1, 1-(f_A - f_B)\}$.

Given a T-function g that assigns the value x_i to B_i for each i, $|A|_g$ is $f_A(x_1,\ldots,x_k)$, for any A in Σ^*. So what needs to be established is that there is at least one g (i.e. one choice of all the x_is) such that $f_{B_i}(x_1,\ldots,x_k) = x_i$ for each i. To restate this, let $\mathbf{F}_\Sigma$ assign to any k-tuple $<x_1,\ldots,x_k>$ the k-tuple $<f_{B_1}(x_1,\ldots,x_k),\ldots,f_{B_k}(x_1,\ldots,x_k)>$. Then what we want is the existence of a k-tuple $\mathbf{x}$ such that $\mathbf{F}_\Sigma(\mathbf{x})=\mathbf{x}$: in other words, a fixed point for $\mathbf{F}_\Sigma$. But the Brouwer fixed point theorem guarantees this, as long as $\mathbf{F}_\Sigma$ is continuous. And it is continuous, since it is obtained by composition of the obviously continuous operations associated with the connectives. Any g that assigns such a fixed point k-tuple to the x_i will satisfy (*) for every B in Σ. ∎

So for any finite self-sustaining Σ, we can consistently add to S the totality of all sentences of form

(T) $\qquad\qquad\qquad$ True($\langle B \rangle$) $\leftrightarrow$ B

for B in Σ. And the continuum-valued logic is known to be compact, so we get

Corollary to warm-up result: We can consistently add to S the totality of all instances of (T) *for B that are in at least one finite self-sustaining Σ*.

This is enough to show that the usual quantifier-free paradoxes, which involve only finitely many sentences, can consistently be assumed to be jointly handled in accordance with the Tarski schema.

Still, the result is limited in two ways.

First, it doesn't deal with paradoxes that might involve infinitely many sentences together (e.g. an infinite list where each sentence attributes some properties to the next three on the list). While it's hard to find examples *in a quantifier-free language* (where each sentence can refer only to finitely many others) that look especially problematic, it would be nice to have a proof that any such paradox can consistently be solved in accordance with (T).

Second, we're interested in more than consistency, we want conservativeness. We have conservativeness for each of the models given by the warm-up result, but the direct use of the compactness of the logic to get a combined model destroys this.

Fortunately, these two limitations can be overcome with one blow. It involves extending the warm-up result to infinite self-sustaining sets of sentences. This might seem impossible, since it is well-known that there are continuous functions in the real Hilbert space of countably infinite dimension that don't have fixed points. However, if we generalize the above to infinite Σ, the function $\mathbf{F}_\Sigma$ is more than just continuous in this topology, its components are functions that depend on only finitely many values. Because of this, the function is also continuous in the Tychonoff topology on $[0,1]^\omega$ (or equivalently, the Hilbert cube), and it is a consequence of Brouwer's theorem that this space too has the property that every continuous function in it has a fixed point. (See Van Mill 1989, pp. 106–7.)

In more detail:

Proof of Conservativeness theorem: Enumerate the sentences of the language as $B_1, B_2, \ldots$. For each sentence A of the language, associate with it a function f_A from $[0,1]^\omega$ to itself, in obvious analogy to the way done above; in particular,

If A is True(t) for some term t that denotes B_i, f_A is the projection function that maps the infinite sequence $<x_1, x_2, \ldots>$ to x_i.

And let $\mathbf{F}$ assign to the infinite sequence $<x_1, x_2, \ldots>$ the infinite sequence $<f_{B_1}(x_1, x_2, \ldots), f_{B_2}(x_1, x_2, \ldots), \ldots>$. We need only show that $\mathbf{F}$ is continuous in the Tychonoff topology on $[0,1]^\omega$ to conclude that it has at least one fixed point. Once this is established, we assign the ith component of a given fixed point as the value of B_i, for each i, and we have the desired conservative extension of the ground model.

To prove the continuity of $\mathbf{F}$, we need that for any n, if $O_1, \ldots, O_n$ are open subsets of $[0,1]$, then the pre-image of $O_1 \times \ldots \times O_n \times [0,1] \times [0,1] \times \ldots$ under $\mathbf{F}$ is open in the Tychonoff topology. But given the definition of $\mathbf{F}$, this pre-image is just $\{<x_1, x_2, \ldots> \mid f_{B_1}(x_1, x_2, \ldots) \in O_1 \wedge \ldots \wedge f_{B_n}(x_1, x_2, \ldots) \in O_n\}$, and so it is open if and only if for each i, $\{<x_1, x_2, \ldots> \mid f_{B_i}(x_1, x_2, \ldots) \in O_i\}$ is open. But now let $m(i)$ be the smallest m such that the spectrum of B_i is in $\{B_1 \ldots B_{m(i)}\}$. Then $\{<x_1, x_2, \ldots> \mid f_{B_i}(x_1, x_2, \ldots) \in O_i\}$ is just the set of sequences beginning in $<x_1, \ldots, x_{m(i)}>$ such that $f_{B_i}(x_1, .., x_{m(i)}, 0, 0 \ldots) \in O_i$. That is open in the Tychonoff topology if $\{<x_1, \ldots, x_{m(i)}> \mid f_{B_i}(x_1, .., x_{m(i)}, 0, 0 \ldots) \in O_i\}$ is open in $[0,1]^{m(i)}$, and this is so because f_{B_i} is obtained by composition of the obviously continuous operations associated with the connectives. ∎

5
Interlude on Vagueness, and the Paradoxes of König and Berry

There may well be a connection between the paradoxes of vagueness (if they really are paradoxes) and the semantic paradoxes. This chapter will explore the parallels and tentatively draw morals.

5.1. MUST VAGUE PREDICATES HAVE SHARP BOUNDARIES?

Consider the following argument:

(1) Bertrand Russell was old at age 3×10^{18} nanoseconds (that's about 95 years)
(2) He wasn't old at age 0 nanoseconds
(3) So there is a number N such that he was old at N nanoseconds and not old at k nanoseconds for any $k < N$.

Presumably he was old for $k > N$ as well as for $k = N$. Given this, (3) says that there's a sharp boundary between when he was old and when he wasn't.

Many people find this conclusion extremely counterintuitive—perhaps paradoxical. But premises (1) and (2) seem incontrovertible, and (3) follows from them using the least number principle.

Could it be that there's a problem with the unrestricted application of the least number principle to vague or otherwise indeterminate concepts? I take it that there is no question of abandoning the least number principle within ordinary mathematics. But perhaps there is a more general formulation of the principle that would allow its use there but might not in all contexts?

Indeed there is. Here is the usual form of least number principle, the one that legitimizes the argument from (1) and (2) to (3).

(CLNP) $\qquad \exists n F(n)$ implies $\exists N[F(N) \land (\forall k < N)\neg F(k)]$.

(The 'C' here stands for 'classical'.) Here is a slight weakening that allows a substantial amount of least-number reasoning, even when excluded middle isn't assumed across the board:

(GLNP) $\exists n[F(n) \land (\forall k < n)(F(k) \lor \neg F(k))]$ implies
          $\exists N[F(N) \land (\forall k < N)\neg F(k)]$.

('G' is for 'general'.) When the formula F obeys excluded middle, (GLNP) obviously reduces to (CLNP). Presumably excluded middle holds throughout ordinary mathematics, and indeed whenever vagueness or indeterminacy are not at issue. (I'm taking 'indeterminacy' here to include the status of the Liar sentence.) This suffices to explain why in dealing with precise and determinate language (or language that can be taken to be precise and determinate for the practical purposes at hand), (CLNP) can be assumed. But when vagueness is at issue, we could avoid the argument for sharp boundaries by restricting the application of excluded middle for vague concepts, and recognizing that if we do so then the appropriate form of least number principle is (GLNP).[1]

Why exactly is it that we should weaken (CLNP) to (GLNP) if we don't assume excluded middle without restriction? Suppose (to put it in a slightly sloppy but picturesque manner) that for numbers n in a certain range, the claim that Russell was old at n nanoseconds is "fuzzy": it is inappropriate to assume that at that age *he was either old or not old*.[2] (The range where this is fuzzy will *itself* be fuzzy; this is crucial to the plausibility of the approach, and I will discuss it in a moment.) Given this, it's inappropriate to assume that there is a first n at which he was old. For to say of any given n that it is the first is to say that he was old at n nanoseconds of age and not old at $n - 1$, and this will be fuzzy at best: it will be fuzzy if n or $n - 1$ falls into the fuzzy region, false if they both fall outside it. (If it's fuzzy whether one of them falls into the fuzzy region, then it will be fuzzy whether the claim that n is the first one at which Russell was old is fuzzy: we will have higher order fuzziness. But in any case, the claim that n is the first won't be clearly true.)

Supervaluationists argue that even if all claims of form 'n is the first natural number such that Russell was old at n nanoseconds of age' are at best fuzzy, still the existential generalization is clearly true. It seems to me that such a view does not avoid positing sharp boundaries, but I will defer discussion of that until Chapter 9. If I'm right, then if one wants to avoid positing sharp boundaries, one should take an existential generalization of claims that are fuzzy at best to be fuzzy at best. So the view takes it to be inappropriate to assert 'There is a first natural number n such that Russell was old at n nanoseconds of age.'

That doesn't mean one ought to assert that there is no first nanosecond at which he was old. Negations of fuzzy claims are fuzzy too, hence inappropriate

---

[1] Whether we *should* follow this course of restricting excluded middle for vague concepts is a matter I will not take a strong stand on, since it raises many issues that go beyond the scope of this book. My remarks here are intended only to illustrate some consequences of so doing.

[2] Here, and in some other places in this chapter, I slip into speaking as if inappropriateness were an objective matter. My view, actually, is that this is not the case, and when I speak of a claim as inappropriate all I really mean to be doing is rejecting the claim.

to assert. The situation is the same as that of the Liar sentence in KFS, or in the sentential version of continuum-valued semantics: the view of vagueness takes it to be inappropriate to assert that there's a first nanosecond at which he's old, and inappropriate to assert that there isn't such a first nanosecond. That doesn't imply that one is ignorant of whether there is such a first nanosecond; for one could reasonably call oneself ignorant only if one assumed that there either is or isn't such a first nanosecond, and the view takes it to be inappropriate to assume that too.

5.2. PENUMBRAL CONNECTIONS AND HIGHER ORDER VAGUENESS

Views of the sort just sketched obviously raise a huge number of questions, and it is not my purpose here to give a detailed discussion. But I would like to touch on two persistent worries about them.

The first, about which I'll be *very* brief, concerns penumbral connections: we want to be able to express such things as that 'green' and 'blue' are mutually exclusive; but the obvious way of doing that is 'Nothing is both blue and green', and this turns out inappropriate to assert given the existence of borderline cases. But while this would be a genuine problem if the logic used for vagueness did not include a reasonable conditional, it is not a problem when the logic is either Lukasiewicz logic or the logic that I will eventually recommend: there we can express the penumbral connection as 'Anything blue is not green' ($\forall x(Bx \to \neg Gx)$), or equivalently, 'Anything green is not blue.'

A more substantial worry is that an approach like the one I've sketched can avoid a sharp line between the old and the not-old only by introducing other sharp lines, e.g. between what one might call the *determinately* old and the *not determinately* old.

The notion of determinateness is a notion that seems almost certain to arise in discussions of vagueness—especially those that restrict excluded middle.[3] Perhaps it arises even more clearly in the discussion of certain cases of indeterminacy that seem closely related to vagueness: I have in mind the artificially gappy predicates discussed by various authors, such as the predicate 'glub' introduced by the stipulation that natural numbers less than 13 are glub and natural numbers greater than 13 are not glub. (The stipulation is silent about 13.) Here I think we want to say that it is indeterminate whether 13 is glub. In the case of vagueness, one might well suppose that indeterminacy arises in a similar fashion, in "clear borderline cases". But it can intelligibly be doubted that there are clear borderline cases. Certainly trying to get everyone to agree on a clear borderline case of a bald person or of a person who lives near me is unlikely to produce success; that

---

[3] It also tends to arise in discussions of vagueness that assume excluded middle (e.g. supervaluationism), but there it is arguably a bit of a cheat: see the discussion in Chapter 9.

is because 'bald' and 'near' and nearly all other vague terms are context-relative, as well as being "fuzzy" in each context, and it is hard to keep the context sufficiently fixed.

Still, one can plausibly argue that predicates like 'nearby, *as Joe was using that term on such and such occasion*' have clear borderline cases; cases where it is clearly indeterminate whether they apply. And the application of the notion of indeterminacy seems clearer still when we use vague terms to construct complex predicates for which the issue isn't *fuzziness of border*. Consider the predicate 'is a natural number with the same parity (odd or even) as the smallest number n such that Russell was old at n nanoseconds'. Even if one were to decline to accept any examples of

It is indeterminate whether Russell was old at n nanoseconds,

it's plausible that we should accept *every* instance of

It is indeterminate whether k has the same parity as the smallest number n such that Russell was old at n nanoseconds.[4]

I shall take it, then, that the notion of indeterminacy has significant application to sentences in a vague language.

But this brings us to the first version of the higher order vagueness worry: it's that even if the law of excluded middle doesn't apply to the predicate 'old', it must apply to the predicate 'determinately old'. In that case, there would have to be a first nanosecond at which Russell was determinately old. If so, little progress would have been made.

I take it that it's clear what we must say to this: namely, that on any reasonable way of introducing the notion of determinately old, excluded middle cannot be assumed to hold of it.

Consider a few representative attempts at explaining 'determinately':

(A) Russell is determinately old at those nanoseconds for which (i) he's old and (ii) it is true that he's either old or not old;
(B) Russell is determinately old at those nanoseconds for which (i) he's old and (ii) it is appropriate to assume that he's either old or not old;
(C) Russell is determinately old at those nanoseconds for which it is neither the case that he is not old nor that it's "fuzzy" whether he's old.

But on (A), there would be no distinction between 'determinately old' and 'old'. For 'True($\langle p \rangle$)' is equivalent to 'p'; so A(ii) is equivalent to 'he's either old or not old', which is strictly weaker than A(i); so when conjoined with A(i) one just gets A(i), i.e. 'he's old'.

---

[4] Or to avoid a quibble about the singular term:

It is indeterminate whether it is either the case that k is odd and for some odd n Russell was old at n nanoseconds but not at $n-1$ nanoseconds, or the case that k is even and for some even n Russell was old at n nanoseconds but not at $n-1$ nanoseconds.

With (B), adding (ii) does produce a genuine strengthening. But given that 'appropriate' is obviously vague, there's still no reason to think that 'determinately old' has sharp boundaries.

The situation with (C) is similar to that of (B): it's unclear how exactly to explain "fuzzy", but it seems like however one explains it, it's bound to itself be vague.

I might mention another approach to defining 'determinately': use some specific logic, perhaps the Lukasiewicz continuum-valued logic, and define 'determinately' from the connectives in that. For instance, in the last chapter we considered defining 'determinately A' in the continuum-valued logic as $\neg(A \to \neg A)$, though whether this would be plausible outside of the context of that logic is not entirely clear. But if we take this approach, it is again not evident that 'determinately A' obeys excluded middle. Indeed, in the case of continuum-valued logic, it doesn't.

So the first version of the higher order vagueness worry seems to get little support.

5.3. MUST HIGHER ORDER VAGUENESS COLLAPSE?

There are many more sophisticated versions of the higher order vagueness worry. The following is perhaps the most substantial.

The worry is that even if a determinately operator D doesn't itself give rise to sharp borders (e.g. even if excluded middle shouldn't be assumed for 'determinately old'), still it is bound to eventually produce sharp borders upon sufficient iteration. For instance, in the Lukasiewicz continuum-valued logic, we didn't have excluded middle for D, or for DD, or for DDD, or indeed for any D^n where n is finite. But it seemed perfectly intelligible to iterate the determinacy operator into the transfinite. When we did so, we didn't have to go far to produce a clearly bivalent operator (one for which excluded middle clearly holds):[5] this happened already at stage ω.

In my view, this is a serious problem, and in particular, it makes the Lukasiewicz continuum-valued logic totally unsuitable as a logic of vagueness (despite its having been rather widely advocated for just this purpose). For in the Lukasiewicz logic there is a number N such that Russell was determinately$^\omega$ old at nanosecond N but not determinately$^\omega$ old a nanosecond before. But if one is willing to postulate a sharp boundary *there*, there seems no reason not to take it as a sharp boundary for 'old'. Nothing whatever would be gained by going non-classical.

Note that the problem isn't avoided simply by resisting the collapse to bivalence at stage ω; we must resist the collapse *at any ordinal for which the iteration is clearly defined*. And resisting any such eventual collapse is not easy to do. (Indeed, some readers may think they have arguments that resisting it is simply impossible. I will have to ask for their patience: the matter will be discussed in Chapter 22.) I

---

[5] Strictly, we should distinguish between bivalence (being true or false) and excluded middle; but in the context of the Intersubstitutivity Principle the distinction vanishes.

repeat though that unless we can resist eventual collapse, there can be no useful approach to vagueness in a logic without excluded middle.

In any case, we see that the same undesirable collapse that spoils the application of the continuum-valued logic to the semantic paradoxes spoils its application to vagueness as well. Might it even be the case that the proper logics for vagueness and for the paradoxes are the same?

5.4. LINEAR ORDER?

I might mention another less serious worry about using the continuum-valued logic for vagueness: it would require accepting certain principles which, although also accepted in classical logic, seem intuitively doubtful. Here I particularly have in mind the alleged law

(COMPAR) $\qquad\qquad\qquad (A \to B) \vee (B \to A)$

"It is either the case that if Joe is rich then Tim is thin, or that if Tim is thin then Joe is rich". Really? Which one, if both are borderline cases? (Of course it could in some cases be both, but it doesn't seem that this will always be so. And what if it's fuzzy whether one or both cases is borderline?)

It should be clear enough why (COMPAR) arises in Lukasiewicz semantics: it arises because of the fact that the semantic values are linearly ordered. With merely partially ordered semantic values, (COMPAR) would not arise. It turns out that when we try to generalize the continuum-valued semantics to deal with the paradoxes, linear order (and the alleged law (COMPAR)) creates difficulties too. I take this as some small piece of further evidence (far less substantial than the evidence of Section 5.3 or 5.5) that the logic required for the paradoxes and the logic of vagueness are identical (and in both cases, non-classical).

There is, I admit, a worry about this. It's evident that a non-classical logic appropriate to the paradoxes is going to have to be a bit complicated, especially as regards the conditional. And maybe that's OK in the case of the paradoxes, for there it might be thought (at least by those who haven't learned the lesson from Kripke discussed at the beginning of Chapter 3!) that they can be carved off as a matter that needs to be dealt with only in special contexts. But for vagueness (it might be said), the matter is different. Given that almost every term is somewhat vague, and given the complexity of the logic appropriate to the paradoxes, wouldn't applying that logic to the case of vagueness make proper reasoning about ordinary subjects difficult?

I think this worry is greatly exaggerated. It might be useful to compare the case to geometric reasoning. We all know that space is not quite Euclidean, and indeed fails to be Euclidean in a quite complicated way; nonetheless, we are safe in using Euclidean reasoning except in special contexts, because the error involved in doing so is so slight. That seems a reasonable methodology in the case of logic too: reason classically, except for those situations where there is reason to think that the errors induced by such reasoning are significant. Situations where we derive boundaries for vague terms, or where we derive violations of the Tarski schemas, look like just the sort of situation to worry about!

5.5. THE KÖNIG AND BERRY PARADOXES

The worry about 'old' having sharp boundaries seems intimately related to the paradoxes of König and Berry: the natural conclusion of these is that there's something wrong with the supposition that the notion of definability in a given language has sharp boundaries.

Let $\mathscr{L}$ be a given language. Call an object o *definable in* $\mathscr{L}$ if there is a one-place formula of $\mathscr{L}$ that is uniquely true of o, i.e. true of o and not true of anything else. We'll be concerned only with languages in a finite alphabet. Such languages contain only a countable infinity of expressions, and only a finite number of expressions of length less than (say) 1000. (By the length of an expression I mean the number of occurrences of alphabet-items within it.)[6]

The König paradox involves the notion of an ordinal number: all you need to know is that there are uncountably many of them, and that they fall into a natural well-ordering. Since there are uncountably many of them, and only countably many expressions of $\mathscr{L}$, there are ordinal numbers that are not definable in $\mathscr{L}$. So by the "least ordinal principle" (apparently justified by the fact that the ordinals are well ordered), there is a smallest ordinal that is not definable in $\mathscr{L}$, and obviously it is unique. But then doesn't 'x is not definable in $\mathscr{L}$, but all smaller ordinals are' define it?

This is of course not much of a paradox if $\mathscr{L}$ doesn't contain the term 'definable in $\mathscr{L}$', or the term 'true of' from which this was defined. But suppose $\mathscr{L}$ contains 'true of', understood (in analogy with how we want to understand 'true') as applicable to its own expressions? In that case, we have defined 'definable in $\mathscr{L}$' within $\mathscr{L}$, and 'x is not definable in $\mathscr{L}$ but all smaller ordinals are' abbreviates a formula of $\mathscr{L}$. In this case, we do have a paradox: the smallest $\mathscr{L}$-undefinable ordinal isn't undefinable after all.

If one insists on employing classical logic in the context of an unstratified 'true of' predicate and hence an unstratified definability predicate, it is clear what the resolution of the paradox must be: that either there are things not definable in $\mathscr{L}$ but of which 'definable in $\mathscr{L}$' is true ("Overspill"), or there are things definable in $\mathscr{L}$ but of which 'definable in $\mathscr{L}$' is not true ("Underspill").[7] In that case it is simply a fallacy to go from

---

[6] In English we use spaces within expressions, to separate words; we can count the "space symbol" as one of the alphabet items.

[7] I'm reminded of a remark that Bertrand Russell made about Hegel: "… [T]he worse your logic, the more interesting the consequences to which it gives rise." (Russell 1945, p. 746.)

(1) α is an ordinal undefinable in 𝒮 and nothing smaller is, and therefore no smaller ordinal has this property

to

(2) 'x is an ordinal undefinable in 𝒮 and nothing smaller is' is true of α and of nothing smaller.

The paradox, according to the classical logic solution, must be here: the claim that α is the smallest undefinable ordinal is just (1), but the claim that 'x is the smallest undefinable ordinal' defines α is (2).

In my view, this classical-logic resolution is unattractive: I find it hard to see the step from (1) to (2) as fallacious. Instead, I think the problem is with (1). And the problem with (1), I think, is that it assumes the unrestricted form of least ordinal principle: it simply doesn't follow from the well-ordering of the ordinals, any more than the unrestricted form of least number principle follows from the well-ordering of the natural numbers.

Before explaining, let's turn to an almost identical paradox, Berry's, which uses the least number principle rather than the least ordinal principle; to get this simplification, it uses a slightly more complicated notion, *definability by a formula of 𝒮 with length less than 1000*. (Again, we're interested in the case where 𝒮 contains 'true of'.) Call this *restricted 𝒮-definability*. The argument is analogous:

(a) There are natural numbers that aren't restrictedly 𝒮-definable.

(b) So there is a smallest natural number that isn't restrictedly 𝒮-definable.

(c) So 'the smallest natural number that isn't restrictedly 𝒮-definable' defines it (as does the formula that results by replacing the defined term 'restrictedly 𝒮-definable' by its definition).

(d) But by our suppositions this formula (or the formula that it abbreviates) is in 𝒮, and is clearly of length less than 1000; so it restrictedly 𝒮-defines it, which contradicts (b).

Again, the classical-logic resolution is that the step from (b) to (c) is fallacious; whereas the resolution that should be given by an advocate of KFS, or of a logic like KFS but with an added conditional, is that the problematic step is that from (a) to (b).

As remarked in Section 5.1, this does not require entirely giving up the least number principle; that would be absurd. Rather, what is required is simply generalizing it a bit: from (CLNP) to (GLNP). And the same holds for the least ordinal principle used in the König paradox: the proper formulation of this is the (unfortunately acronymed)

(GLOP) $\exists \alpha [F(\alpha) \wedge (\forall \beta < \alpha)(F(\beta) \vee \neg F(\beta))]$ implies $\exists \gamma [F(\gamma) \wedge (\forall \beta < \gamma) \neg F(\beta)]$.

This reduces to the classical least ordinal principle where the formula F can be assumed to satisfy excluded middle. But 'definable in $\mathscr{L}$' can't be assumed to do so, given the way it was defined from 'true of'.

I find the analogy of the König-Berry paradox to the vagueness paradox illuminating. Indeed, if one tried to sharply distinguish them, there would be paradoxes in the same general ballpark that would be hard to classify. Consider the following (which I think I first read of many years ago in Martin Gardner's *Scientific American* column).

It might seem that some natural numbers aren't very interesting. But then there must be a smallest one that isn't very interesting. The smallest one that isn't very interesting! What an interesting number! Contradiction. So every natural number is very interesting.

(In case anyone is tempted to regard the conclusion as correct, it's worth remarking that an analogous "proof" shows that every *ordinal* number is very interesting. Since for any cardinal number C, there are more than C ordinal numbers, this seems *quite* surprising!)

I don't doubt that one can bite the bullet in the face of the vagueness paradoxes, and say that there is indeed a magic moment at which Russell became old. Biting the bullet in the case of the König–Berry paradox, and of the semantic paradoxes more generally, turns out to be considerably more uncomfortable, as I will explore in detail in Part II.

5.6. THE ROLE OF A CLASSICAL META-THEORY FOR A NON-CLASSICAL LANGUAGE

A recurring set of worries, both for non-classical approaches to vagueness and non-classical approaches to the semantic paradoxes, has to do with the fact that these approaches tend to be carried out for logics that are given in a classical meta-theory. There are a number of distinct worries that fall under this heading. Continuum-valued logic seems a reasonable context in which to raise these worries: for though we've seen that it does not adequately handle either vagueness or the semantic paradoxes, still the reasons why this is so are not relevant to the present worries, and the response I will give to the worries can be adapted to other non-classical logics. (There is some overlap among the later objections, but I think that presenting and responding to them separately is heuristically useful.)

First worry: it might seem (a) that the non-classical logician can't accept his or her own model-theoretic explanation of validity, since it is given in a classical theory; and (b) that this is a serious embarrassment.

I think that both the claims in the first worry are dubious. On (a): The non-classical logician needn't doubt that classical logic is "effectively valid" in the part of set theory that doesn't employ the term 'True';[8] and this part of set theory suffices for giving a model-theoretic account of validity for the logic that is at least extensionally correct. (We may well share Kreisel's doubt, raised in Chapter 2, that such model-theoretic definitions of validity are ever *intensionally* correct; but that is no more of a problem for the non-classical logician than for the classical.) We may indeed suppose that the advocate of the non-classical logic explicitly adopts as non-logical axioms all instances of $A \vee \neg A$ for any A in the language of set theory (or at least, in that part of set theory employed in the definition of validity).

This response to (a) would not be available to a non-classical logician such as the intuitionist who rejects classical logic even within elementary mathematics, but such non-classical logicians are not under discussion here. This response would also not be available to a non-classical logician who thought excluded middle dubious even for validity claims: that is, who doubted certain claims of the form

Either inference J is valid or it isn't.

Doubting excluded middle for validity claims is perhaps not totally without motivation. One might even think that it is the proper moral of certain Curry-like paradoxes that employ validity instead of the conditional: "There is a valid inference from this sentence to the claim that the Earth is flat". I doubt this: I will give another treatment of those paradoxes in Chapter 20, and I see no other strong reason for rejecting excluded middle for validity claims. So (a) strikes me as without support.

But even if (a) were accepted, (b) strikes me as dubious: the classical model theory used in explaining validity might (if (a) were accepted) be viewed as a temporary device, useful for explaining the logic to a classical logician. The non-classical logician might hope to eventually come up with a model theory in her own non-classical analog of set theory, or her non-classical property theory. (Or she might argue that validity is a notion that can be made clear without a model-theoretic account: for instance, by developing a theory of the principles governing it, including a theory of what is valid and what isn't, and of how validity is related to conditional belief.)

Second worry: (a) Even if the non-classical logician can accept her own definition of *validity* (as extensionally correct), she can't accept her own definition of *truth*; and (b) *that* is a serious embarrassment.

Here too I reject (a), but for a very different reason: it rests on the false presupposition that the non-classical logician is *offering* a definition of truth.

---

[8] Some have supposed that set theoretic notions like 'ordinal number' have a certain degree of vagueness, in which case on the view under consideration classical logic would not be applicable throughout all of set theory. But even on such a view the point remains: the metatheory required to develop the metalogic of continuum-valued logic requires a rather meager fragment of set theory that is not plausibly regarded as vague.

That, as I argued, would run afoul of Tarski's theorem. Independent of that, it is only plausible if one equates truth with semantic value 1, and such an equation would throw away the virtues of the non-classical approach. The only account of truth that the non-classical logician should offer consists in the instances of the Tarski schema; or better, it consists in a slightly more powerful theory that implies those instances and also implies certain generalizations (such as that in general a disjunction is true if and only if one of its disjuncts is). And once we move from definitions of truth to non-definitional accounts of this sort, it's clear that the non-classical logician can and does accept her own account of truth. (It's actually those who give classical accounts of truth that face a worry on this score. For instance, many stratification theorists introduce defined notions of truth, but they certainly employ notions of truth that go beyond any given one of the defined notions, and face strong pressures to employ a notion of truth that goes beyond all of them collectively.)

Third worry: (a) The non-classical logician defines validity by means of notions that don't closely relate to her notion of truth; and (b) *that* is a serious embarrassment.

Here my main problem is with (b): supposing (a) correct, why is it an embarrassment? The main point of defining validity was to give an account of the notion that aids us in investigating its properties and helps us in ascertaining whether given inferences are valid. (It is especially useful as an aid in establishing invalidity.) An added benefit of defining validity *in (a small fragment of) classical set theory* is that that theory is acceptable to most people whatever logic they assume: it is a theory that even most advocates of non-classical logic (other than intuitionists) regard as "effectively classical". For these purposes, there is no need for the notions employed in the model theory to closely relate to truth.

In addition, I'm not entirely clear what is required for the technical notions of the model theory, such as the ordering of the semantic values and the choice of a designated value, to "closely relate to" the notion of truth. Truth can't possibly be given an extensionally correct definition within the language, whereas validity presumably can; this inevitably creates some divergence between the notions that appear in a definition of validity and truth-theoretic notions. And in the context of restricted languages where truth is definable, the technical notions of the model theory *do* relate to truth: if a sentence A has the designated value 1, that suffices for it being true; and if it has a value less than equal to that of sentence B, that suffices for it being the case that if A is true then so is B. Why ask for anything more?

Fourth worry: The advocate of a non-classical logic for vague language defines validity by means of precise notions, and that is a serious embarrassment.[9]

---

[9] This is really a special case of the third worry, given that in a vague language which respects the equivalence of True($\langle A \rangle$) to A, truth attributions can themselves be vague; but it is worth separate discussion.

This worry is an odd one, for suppose that one were to propose a definition of validity for vague languages in vague terms. Most people would protest at the definition precisely because it was stated in vague terms: they would feel that the vagueness kept them from having a clear understanding of how the definition applied.

Suppose, more particularly, that an advocate of a non-classical logic for vagueness were to propose a definition of validity for vague languages in vague terms. In that case, one would presumably have to use that non-classical logic to apply the definition. Most people who advocated other logics, e.g. classical logic, would protest that they didn't know what to make of the proposed logic: that when *they* employed the definition, using their own classical reasoning, they got different results than those announced by the non-classical logicians who advocated the definition. The point of a definition of validity in an effectively classical set theory that virtually all theorists can agree on is precisely to avoid such an unpleasant situation.

To illustrate this last problem, consider the proposal for a definition of validity mentioned (but not advocated) in Section 2.1:

An inference is valid if, necessarily, if the premises are true then so is the conclusion.

Let us put aside a point to be argued later, that this proposed definition really shouldn't be accepted by either a classical or a non-classical logician (however exactly necessity is understood).[10] And let us put aside any worries about whether the classical and non-classical logicians agree in their readings of the 'necessarily'. The fact is that the classical logician will reach conclusions about what is valid in this sense that the non-classical logician can't accept. A case in point is the inference about Bertrand Russell that began this chapter, using the least number principle: the classical logician will say that if the premises are true then so is the conclusion, whereas the advocate of KFS or Lukasiewicz logic will not agree. (Whether the advocate of the non-classical logic actually declares the inference *in*valid depends on the reading of 'necessarily'. A reading that doesn't license this conclusion is one where 'valid' is not a bivalent notion.)

Indeed, their disagreement will arise even for 0-premise inferences, such as the premise-less inference to sentences of form "Either Russell was old at *n* nanoseconds or he wasn't": classical logicians will regard all claims of this form

---

[10] In the case of classical logic, the proposed definition is correct for inferences not involving the notion of truth (when 'necessarily' is suitably understood); but I will argue that for inferences that do involve truth as conceived in classical theories, the definition would yield very odd results. For the non-classical logics in which the notion of truth behaves more normally than in classical logic, the proposed definition is not quite so odd; but on some readings of 'necessarily' it defines a non-bivalent notion. This non-bivalence creates some difficulties, and tends to undermine the connection we feel exists between valid argument and correct reasoning. We'll see that the proposed definition has two bivalent approximations that are somewhat better in this regard; but I'll argue that the bivalent definition that approximates it *less* well actually gives a more natural notion of validity than the one that approximates it better.

as necessarily true, whereas advocates of KFS or continuum-valued logic will not agree. The account of validity suggested in the previous paragraph is thus useless as a guide to what is valid and what isn't.

Perhaps its very neutrality makes it useful for *some* purposes, e.g. as an account of "what we mean" by 'valid'; I claim only that it is useless as a guide for telling what is and isn't valid. It is this last task that a semantics like the continuum-valued semantics is designed for.

Fifth worry: Classical logic has an account of validity in terms of a notion of truth-in-a-model, which obeys compositional rules very much like the rules for truth. Shouldn't we expect the same for a non-classical logic? (*Truth* in a model, not just *designatedness* in a model.)

This too is a version of the third worry, and in answering that I have raised the question of *why* we should expect a non-classical logic to be like classical in this regard. But I'd like to add a further point, suggested in my answer to the fourth worry: we can in fact give compositional rules for truth in a non-classical logic like the continuum-valued logic, rules such as

A conditional is true if and only if, if its antecedent is true then so is its consequent.

This is perfectly acceptable in the continuum-valued sentential logic, precisely because truth can be assumed to obey the Intersubstitutivity Principle (as the conservativeness proof shows). Of course the 'if...then' that is employed here must be understood to obey only the rules of the logic in question, rather than the full set of classical rules, but that is only to be expected.

The point extends to the quantifiers; or at least it *would* extend, if we could fix up the logic so that Intersubstitutivity could be maintained (for 'True of' as well as for 'True'). For in that case we could give the standard quantifier rule:

A universal quantification of a formula is true if and only if the formula is true of everything.

(We could add the bells and whistles involving assignment functions, which allow for alternations of quantifiers; I omit them only for sake of easy readability.)

These clauses handle *truth*, not *truth in a model*, but it is probably possible to define some non-classical notion of model for which model-relative versions of these clauses could be given; validity could then be taken to be truth-preservation in all models. (Basically it would just seem to involve allowing the quantifiers to be restricted, or demanding that they be, and allowing the names, predicates etc. to take on unintended interpretations. The notion of validity would almost certainly be non-bivalent.) It would of course have the defect of the non-classical definition contemplated under Worry 4: you'd have to already know how to reason in the logic in order to employ this definition of validity.

Sixth worry: A model theory for vague language within set theory will inevitably draw sharp lines; for this reason, it cannot possibly accommodate vagueness of arbitrarily high order. For instance, in any set-theoretically defined model there will have to be a sharp line between those numbers n of which 'Russell was old at x nanoseconds of age' gets the designated value 1 (and hence of which 'It is determinately^a the case that Russell was old at x nanoseconds of age' gets designated value for all a) and those n for which this is not so.

Well, what do you expect? Of course a model-theory for a vague language in a non-vague part of that language won't reflect the vague language as a whole with complete accuracy: it isn't intended to, it is intended rather to get the validity relation right. If you want to "reflect the vague language" with complete accuracy, you can use the truth theory instead of the model theory. That will correctly tell you, for instance, that

'Russell was old at x nanoseconds of age' is either true or false of n if and only if either Russell was old at n nanoseconds of age or he wasn't.

Of course this doesn't settle for which x the left and right hand sides are true, but there's no reason why it should. (We wouldn't expect it to settle for which x the left and right hand sides of the following are true:

'Russell was old at x nanoseconds of age' is true of n if and only if Russell was old at n nanoseconds of age.

But if we don't expect it to settle that, why expect it to settle the previous?) The truth theory will also tell you correctly, for each m, that

'Russell was determinately^m old at x nanoseconds of age' is true of n if and only if Russell was determinately^m old at n nanoseconds of age.

In the case of continuum-valued semantics, we unfortunately can't extend this from finite numerals m to notations for transfinite ordinals, for this would require that the Intersubstitutivity Principle apply to the quantificational language needed for the transfinite extension, and we've already seen that it doesn't. That is a real problem for continuum-valued semantics; but in a fixed up logic that does have a general Intersubstitutivity Principle, the above will generalize to the transfinite case. So the truth theory, unlike the model theory, will completely reflect the higher-order vagueness of reality.

Shouldn't we expect a theory that, like such a truth theory, reflects the vague language with complete accuracy, but which unlike it, also settles validity? It isn't obvious why we should. When I go to a restaurant, I expect a fork and I expect a knife; but it would seem overly demanding to expect something that is both a fork and a knife.

Still, a non-classical model theory of the sort contemplated at the end of my discussion of the Fifth Worry *would* reflect vague language with complete accuracy. And it would in some sense "settle" questions of validity: it would define validity in a way that allows questions about validity to be answered in the logic (except in cases where, due to the failure of bivalence for the notion, no answer is to be expected).

But maybe we should expect a definition of validity that "settles" questions of validity in a stronger sense? Namely, which answers the questions without presupposing the logic? But that would be a demand that can't be met even in the case of classical logic! For to argue, from a classical account of validity, that 'Russell was either old at x nanoseconds of age or he wasn't' is valid, you must assume that for every n, either 'Russell was either old at x nanoseconds of age' is true of n in the model or not.[11]

---

[11] If models are sets, this is less contentious than assuming that for every n, either Russell was either old at n nanoseconds of age or he wasn't; but it is still an application of excluded middle.

PART II

BROADLY CLASSICAL APPROACHES

6
Introduction to the Broadly Classical Options

Let us review the simplest paradox of truth: the Liar paradox (*aka* "the Strengthened Liar": see Chapter 1, note 1). The paradox arises because of our apparent ability to formulate sentences that assert their own untruth: more formally, a sentence (which I abbreviate as 'Q') that is equivalent to $\neg \text{True}(\langle Q \rangle)$. ('$Q$' is an abbreviation of the Liar sentence, not a name of it; its name is '$\langle Q \rangle$'.) The relevant sense of equivalence is at least material equivalence:

(1) $\qquad\qquad Q \leftrightarrow \neg \text{True}(\langle Q \rangle),$

where $\leftrightarrow$ is just 'if and only if'. But the notion of truth seems to be governed by the Tarski schema (T): for arbitrary sentences A,

(T) $\qquad\qquad \text{True}(\langle A \rangle) \leftrightarrow A.$

Instantiating (T) on Q, we have

$\qquad\qquad \text{True}(\langle Q \rangle) \leftrightarrow Q,$

which with (1) yields

(*) $\qquad\qquad \text{True}(\langle Q \rangle) \leftrightarrow \neg \text{True}(\langle Q \rangle).$

This, as we've seen, is contradictory in classical logic, and indeed implies any absurdity you like in classical logic. (It is also contradictory in intuitionist logic, and there too it implies any absurdity you like—or rather, that you don't like. Much of the ensuing discussion in Part II could be extended to intuitionist logic as well as to classical, but I shall not bother to do so.)

There seem to be four broad possibilities for blocking this paradox:

(I) Give up the notion of truth (perhaps replacing it with related notions that don't obey the truth schema)

(II) Keep the notion, but nonetheless prevent the construction of the Liar sentence

(III) Restrict the Tarski schema (T)

(IV) Restrict classical logic so that (*) isn't contradictory; or at the very least, so that it doesn't imply everything.

Most of these possibilities subdivide, often in interesting ways. In this part of the book the focus will be on (I)–(III), especially on (III) and its subdivisions.[1] I will include a separate chapter on (I), but will save it for the end of this Part; my main reason for saving it until last is that the discussion of (III) will bear on it. (That discussion will tell us how close a predicate $B(x)$ can come to satisfying the truth schema, and this will apply to any of the "related notions" referred to parenthetically in (I).)

It used to be often said that (II) is the best solution to the Liar Paradox, but it seems to me to be quite hopeless. In the first place, though some sorts of self-reference can easily be banned (e.g. what I called artificial self-reference in Section 1.2), there are other forms of self-reference that would be very difficult to keep from arising without seriously crippling the expressive capacity of the language: this includes both the "Contingent Self-Reference" and the "Godel–Tarski Self-Reference" of Section 1.2. In the second place, even if we were to come up with some artificial restrictions on the formation rules of a language that would prevent self-referential constructions, it would be of little general use in the theory of the paradoxes: it might block the Liar Paradox, but it wouldn't block (or hint at how to block) other paradoxes that seem superficially quite analogous, such as the Heterologicality Paradox (or paradoxes involving two sentences each referring to the other), for those don't require any such self-referential construction.

More fully, the Heterologicality Paradox involves not Schema (T), but a closely related one:

Schema (TO):   For any object o, $\langle F(v) \rangle$ is true of $o \leftrightarrow F(o)$.

Using this, we get a contradiction in classical logic *without any self-referential construction*, as discussed in the Introduction. And there seems to be virtually no value to retaining (T) if you have to give up (TO). I conclude that line (II) is simply not worth pursuing.

So let us turn to (III).

If we are to keep classical logic, then it isn't enough to restrict which instances of Schema (T) we accept: some instances of (T) lead to contradiction, and classical logic then requires that we not only *not accept them*, but that we *accept their negations*. In particular, it requires that we accept

$$\neg [\text{True}(\langle Q \rangle) \leftrightarrow Q].$$

---

[1] Indeed, the focus will be on those subdivisions of (III) that keep classical logic. Strictly, the theory KFS from Chapter 2 falls under (III) as well as under (IV), if we take the biconditional to be defined from $\neg$, $\wedge$ and $\vee$ as in classical logic; but I'd prefer to count it under (IV). (In any case, KFS will be of no further concern: I'll only be concerned with logics that contain better behaved conditionals so that the Tarski schema can be retained without restriction.)

The biconditional here is the material one, so this amounts to accepting the following disjunction:

(*)   Either [True(⟨Q⟩) ∧ ¬Q], or [Q ∧ ¬True(⟨Q⟩)].

Prima facie, then, we have three options within classical logic: we can accept the first disjunct, we can accept the second disjunct, or we can remain agnostic between them. Perhaps there is a fourth, involving something somewhat like agnosticism but not quite the same thing? I will return to that in a moment.

But first, let's refine the classification slightly, by considering also the possibilities about the claim True(⟨¬Q⟩). From (*) we can derive the following (using excluded middle and other classical principles):

(**)   Either (i)   True(⟨Q⟩) ∧ True(⟨¬Q⟩) ∧ ¬Q
         or   (ii)   True(⟨Q⟩) ∧ ¬True(⟨¬Q⟩) ∧ ¬Q
         or   (iii) ¬True(⟨Q⟩) ∧ True(⟨¬Q⟩) ∧ Q
         or   (iv)   ¬True(⟨Q⟩) ∧ ¬True(⟨¬Q⟩) ∧ Q

So we have four options that don't involve agnosticism or anything akin to it.

Of these four non-agnostic options, the second and third seem to offer few advantages. We seem to have two strong convictions about incoherence:

First Incoherence Principle: For any sentence A, it is incoherent to accept:

   A, but nonetheless ⟨A⟩ isn't true.

Second Incoherence Principle: For any sentence A, it is incoherent to accept:

   ⟨A⟩ is true, but nonetheless ¬A.

Option (i), on which Q is both truth and false, clearly violates the second principle (taking A to be Q). Option (iv), on which Q is neither truth nor false, clearly violates the first principle (taking A to be Q). But (ii) and (iii) violate both principles! Option (ii), on which Q is solely true, violates the first principle with regard to ¬Q and the second with regard to Q. Option (iii), on which Q is solely false, violates the first principle with regard to Q and the second with regard to ¬Q using the fact that Q implies ¬¬Q. Violating *both* seems gratuitous, and for this reason my discussion of the options involving nothing kin to agnosticism will focus on (i) and (iv). (In reverse order: (iv) in the next chapter, (i) in the chapter following that.) But some of what I say will apply to (ii) and (iii) as well.[2]

It remains to consider those options that involve agnosticism between the two disjuncts of (*) (and hence between two or more of the disjuncts (i)–(iv)); or at least, something akin to agnosticism. It may seem that agnosticism has little to offer here, for the following also seems compelling:

---

[2] Examples of views of types (ii) and (iii) are (respectively) Systems C and B in Friedman and Sheard 1987. Both systems are notable by how few of the natural truth rules are valid in them.

Third Incoherence Principle: If one has gotten oneself into a commitment to a disjunction of several options, accepting any of which would be incoherent, one has already gotten oneself into an incoherent position.

But maybe we can reject this third principle? Perhaps there would be an advantage in this, if it enabled us to remain in accord with the first two.

This line could be made more appealing if we could argue that accepting the disjunction while refusing to accept either disjunct isn't a case of agnosticism as ordinarily understood, but rather, is an appropriate response to a kind of indeterminacy as to which disjunct is correct. The position would be analogous to a certain sort of supervaluationist view about borderline cases of vague terms. The supervaluationist view I have in mind is

(a) that we should accept classical logic for vague terms, so that Joe is either bald or not bald even if he is a borderline case;

(b) that in such a borderline case, we can't know whether Joe is bald; but that this is not ignorance of any straightforward sort, because the question of his baldness is somehow "indeterminate". "There's no determinate fact of the matter" for us to be ignorant about.

Supervaluationism in this sense needn't identify truth with "super-truth"; that is, it needn't involve the view that 'indeterminate' implies 'neither true nor false', and the version I have in mind will specifically reject that implication. ('Indeterminate' will of course imply 'neither *determinately* true nor *determinately* false'.)

It is not in the least evident to me that supervaluationism (with or without the identification of truth with supertruth) succeeds in providing an alternative to the ignorance view. Making sense of the claim that it does would require some explanation of indeterminacy that doesn't involve ignorance, and indeed is incompatible with ignorance; and it isn't at all clear what this could involve. This is a matter I will discuss in Chapter 9.

But those who think the view does make sense may think that it helps in understanding a failure of the Third Incoherence Principle. For then a possibility for handling the Liar sentence is to say something like this: "Either Q is true or it isn't true, and we can't decide which; but this inability isn't ignorance exactly, because the matter is indeterminate." The idea is that to accept a disjunction of two absurdities is to commit oneself to an absurdity *unless one regards the question "which disjunct?" as indeterminate*. This may make rejection of the Third Incoherence Principle more palatable. In any case, I will discuss views that adhere to the first two Incoherence principles but reject the third in Chapters 10–13.

7
Truth-Value Gaps in Classical Theories

7.1. GAPS AND (T-OUT)

One natural response to the Liar paradox is to divide up the (classically inconsistent) truth schema into two components, in the obvious way, and retain one of them. The two components are

(T-OUT) $\text{True}(\langle A \rangle) \rightarrow A$

and

(T-IN) $A \rightarrow \text{True}(\langle A \rangle)$.

Which to keep? The most popular choice is to retain (T-OUT), while restricting (T-IN) and adding some additional laws to compensate for the restriction. I'll mention two very different ways of developing this idea in Section 7.2, which I'll call "Kleene-like gap theories" and "supervaluation-style gap theories". The first is exemplified by the Kripke–Feferman theory KF mentioned in Chapter 3, which I'm calling FM ("Feferman–Maudlin");[1] the other is exemplified by gap theories based on supervaluational fixed points, though it has many other exemplifications as well, for instance, gap theories based on revision-rule constructions. Axiomatic theories of this type are the System H of Friedman and Sheard 1987 and the slightly stronger VF of Cantini 1990.

In either the Kleene-like or supervaluation-style variant, it is not enough to keep (T-OUT) and a restricted version of (T-IN), since any reasonable theory will have to imply certain additional schemas such as

(C+) $\text{True}(\langle A \wedge B \rangle) \leftrightarrow \text{True}(\langle A \rangle) \wedge \text{True}(\langle B \rangle)$.

---

[1] Actually the formulation of KF in Reinhardt 1986 doesn't contain (T-OUT) as an axiom schema, but it does contain (in effect) the restriction of this to atomic sentences, and also the "no-glut" axiom "Nothing is both true and has a true negation"; these are easily seen to imply all instances of (T-OUT) given other axioms of the theory, by a routine induction. (Conversely, the *instances of* the no-glut axiom are obviously entailed by (T-OUT).) Occasionally the term KF is used for a system of Feferman's (the system Self-TrAx$_{\mathscr{L}(T,F)}$ in Feferman 1991) that is crucially weaker than Reinhardt's in that it does not contain either the full (T-OUT) or the no-glut axiom: in his discussion of the system, Feferman calls those additions to it intuitively justified, but

That not all instances of (C+) are derivable from (T-OUT) plus a restricted (T-IN) (unless those restrictions are too weak to avoid inconsistency!) should be clear. To get a specific instance of the left to right, we'd need (T-IN) applied to the specific instances A and B (as well as (T-OUT) applied to $A \land B$). And to get a specific instance of the right to left, we'd need (T-IN) applied to the specific instance $A \land B$ (as well as (T-OUT) applied to A and to B).[2] It's clear that with only a *restricted* (T-IN), we can't hope to derive *arbitrary* instances of (C+), i.e. instances of (C+) for *every* choice of A and B.

So any advocate of (T-OUT) in classical logic needs to either adopt (C+) as a primitive schema or else (the more satisfactory course) adopt a universal generalization:

(CONJ+)   For any sentences x and y, True(conj(x, y)) $\leftrightarrow$ True(x) $\land$ True(y),

where of course conj(x, y) represents the conjunction of x and y. This will be part of both Kleene-like and supervaluation-style gap theories. (The most symptomatic difference between those two types of theories will be over the corresponding rule for disjunction.)

A number of other special rules will be needed, if we restrict (T-IN). But let us see what comes simply from retaining (T-OUT).

One immediate consequence of (T-OUT) alone (in classical logic) is that the Liar sentence isn't true. For

$\text{True}(\langle Q \rangle) \to Q$ by (T-OUT)
$Q \to \neg \text{True}(\langle Q \rangle)$ by the construction of Q
So $\text{True}(\langle Q \rangle) \to \neg \text{True}(\langle Q \rangle)$ by transitivity
So $\neg \text{True}(\langle Q \rangle)$

The last step of this uses the rule $A \to \neg A \vdash \neg A$; this is not valid in non-classical logics of the sort we will be discussing (or in the Lukasiewicz logics already discussed), but it is valid in classical logic.

The claim $\neg\text{True}(\langle Q \rangle)$ has a superficial appeal, but the appeal tends to lessen when one reflects that that claim is equivalent to Q itself. So all classical (T-OUT) theories imply the following apparently odd claim:

(1) $\qquad\qquad\qquad Q \land \neg \text{True}(\langle Q \rangle);$

or what amounts to the same thing,

(1*) $\qquad\qquad\qquad \neg\text{True}(\langle Q \rangle) \land \neg\text{True}(\langle \neg\text{True}(\langle Q \rangle)\rangle).$

for technical reasons they are treated separately from what he includes as axioms. When I speak of KF or FM I'll mean a system like Reinhardt's that explicitly includes or implies the instances of (T-OUT), for it is only then that the theory is a gap theory: Self-TrAx$_{\mathscr{L}(T,F)}$ is agnostic between gaps and gluts.

[2] The application of (T-IN) to $A \land B$ doesn't follow from its application to A and to B, unless one already has (C+) at one's disposal.

The first conjunct asserts a claim while the second conjunct asserts that the first conjunct isn't true.³

Before exploring this further, let's look at some more consequences. The next is that Q also isn't false, i.e. its negation isn't true. This proof is easy too:

$\text{True}(\langle \neg Q \rangle) \to \neg Q$ by (T-OUT)
So $Q \to \neg \text{True}(\langle \neg Q \rangle)$ by contraposition
But Q by the previously proved (1)
So $\neg \text{True}(\langle \neg Q \rangle)$ by Modus Ponens

Letting falsehood mean truth of negation, this allows us to expand (1) to

(1**) $Q \land \neg \text{True}(\langle Q \rangle) \land \neg \text{False}(\langle Q \rangle).$

And introducing the term Gappy for "not true and not false", we can rewrite this as

$$Q \land \text{Gappy}(\langle Q \rangle).$$

The fact that we get this last conclusion might be thought to ameliorate the situation with the Liar sentence: maybe it's OK to assert a sentence while declaring in the same breath that it isn't true, if this is because you're willing to also declare in the same breath that it's gappy? There is a sense in which this so: for if Q were declared not just untrue but false, this would be *doubly* odd, in that it would violate the Second Incoherence Principle (Chapter 6) *as well as* the First. But I don't see how it makes the violation of the First Incoherence Principle any less counterintuitive.

It's worth making explicit that according to the theory there are not two kinds of untrue sentences, but three:

(i) false sentences,
(ii) gappy sentences like $\neg Q$ (or $\text{True}(\langle Q \rangle)$) that, like false sentences, it would be objectively wrong to believe;

and

(iii) gappy sentences like Q (or $\neg \text{True}(\langle Q \rangle)$) that are "untrue, but not in the bad way". (As in "morally depraved, but not in the bad way".) Unlike those in (ii), we *should* believe these, despite their being gappy.

---

³ If I had used the "Ordinary Liar" sentence W that declares its own falsehood rather than its own untruth, the same phenomenon would have arisen with its *negation*: the theory declares

$$\neg W \land \neg \text{True}(\langle \neg W \rangle),$$

i.e.

$$\neg \text{True}(\langle \neg W \rangle) \land \neg \text{True}(\langle \neg \text{True}(\langle \neg W \rangle) \rangle).$$

I will discuss these matters further in sections 7.3–7.7. But first, let me quickly sketch the two main types of classical gap theories.[4] The main criticisms of classical gap theories will actually be independent of which type is in question, but I think it helps to get a sense of gap theories if the two are disentangled. (The reader could however skip some of the details in the next section, and start paying more careful attention in Section 7.3.)

While my discussion in this chapter is focused on gap theories that derive gaps from (T-OUT) plus classical logic, much of the discussion would apply equally to any theory in classical logic that declares the Liar sentence gappy. (In any case, though it is easy to construct gap theories in classical logic which impose some restriction on (T-OUT), I doubt that there are examples that are of much interest.)

7.2. KLEENE-STYLE GAPS VERSUS SUPERVALUATION-STYLE GAPS

As remarked, no one could seriously entertain giving up (T-IN) entirely; that would be compatible with nothing being true, or with only sentences containing the word 'zebra' being true.

A. Kleene-style gaps

The most famous theory which keeps (T-OUT) but restricts (T-IN) is the Kripke–Feferman theory KF, mentioned in passing in Chapter 3 but totally different from the theory KFS primarily discussed there. Its prominent features are (a) that it posits truth-value gaps, and (b) that it takes truth to obey the strong Kleene truth rules; and I focus on KF simply as the main exemplar of theories with these features. By far the fullest philosophical defense of taking truth to have these features is in Maudlin 2004: whereas many philosophical defenders of gap theories seem to try to sweep the apparent difficulties of such theories under the carpet (e.g. by moves to be considered in Sections 7.4–7.6), Maudlin emphasizes the *prima facie* difficulties and addresses them head on.[5] In the proof-theoretic contexts where discussions of KF most often occur, the precise details of its formulation matter: it matters, for instance, whether principles

---

[4] By a "gap theory" I shall mean not just any theory that posits gaps, but one that says in particular that *Liar sentences* are gappy (though in fact any other gaps that sufficed for violation of the First Incoherence Principle, or for a specific violation of (T-IN), would do as well). For instance, it is often suggested (e.g. Visser 1984) that Truth-Teller sentences that assert their own *truth* are gappy, but Liar sentences that assert their own *untruth* are both true and false. Such theories are in the scope of the next chapter, not this one.

[5] The one confusing feature of Maudlin's presentation is that he refers to his theory as restricting classical logic, which makes it *sound like* KFS. This is a terminological point that I will soon discuss.

such as the "no-glut" principle of note 1 are stated as single axioms or in weaker schematic form. Such issues won't be of huge relevance in what follows, and in order to focus on what is relevant without the distraction of attention to such details, I will sometimes be a bit cavalier about the distinction. (For the record, the stronger single axiom form is almost always to be preferred, even when the formulations I give are in schematic form.) It is in part to focus away from the precise formal details and instead on the core principles (a) and (b) that I have chosen to call KF the Feferman–Maudlin theory, and abbreviate it as FM.

The distinction between KFS and FM is best seen by concentrating on a given starting ω-model M and a given Kleene-based fixed point based on it, and looking at what I'll call the *internal theory* and the *external theory* of that fixed point. The internal theory is simply the set of sentences in the fixed point. Since no Kleene-based fixed point contains all instances of excluded middle, no such internal theory can possibly be classical. The external theory of a fixed point based on M, by contrast, is the set of sentences that come out true in the classical model obtained from M by letting the extension of 'true' be that fixed point. This is by construction a classical theory. If a sentence A is in the fixed point, then True($\langle A \rangle$) is in both the internal theory and the external theory. If on the other hand A is not in the fixed point, then ¬True($\langle A \rangle$) is in the external theory; but it is in the internal theory only if ¬A is in the fixed point. KFS is just the common part of the internal theories of all the fixed points; or as we might put it, it is the internal theory *of the fixed points collectively*. Similarly, FM is the common part of the external theories of all the fixed points: it is the external theory of the fixed points collectively.[6]

It is clear that in Feferman–Maudlin, ¬True($\langle A \rangle$) doesn't imply True($\langle \neg A \rangle$): consider any sentence that the theory takes to be "gappy", such as Q. Interestingly though, we do have

(COMMUTE) $\quad$ True($\langle \neg \text{True}(\langle A \rangle) \rangle$) $\leftrightarrow$ True($\langle \text{True}(\langle \neg A \rangle) \rangle$).

---

[6] Is what I'm calling the external theory of a fixed point what Kripke had in mind in his brief discussion of the "closed off" truth predicate near the end of his paper (Kripke 1975, pp. 80–1)? Perhaps, but Kripke describes the closed off predicate as one for which the claim that the Liar sentence isn't true comes out as *true* (whereas on the external theory it is correctly assertable but not true). In saying this he appears to be introducing a further predicate (which he calls 'true' but which to avoid confusion should be called 'true*') in a Tarskian metalanguage: we can correctly assert True*($\langle Q \rangle$) and True*($\langle \neg \text{True}(\langle Q \rangle) \rangle$). (Here Q is the ordinary Liar, expressed using 'True' rather than 'True*'; I think the *unasterisked* 'True' is supposed to work in accordance with the external theory.)

If this interpretation is right it immediately raises the question of the status of the Liar sentence Q^* obtained using the True* predicate; and indeed Kripke's discussion suggests that we may need a Tarskian hierarchy at this point. Maudlin 2004 gives the same interpretation to the brief passage where Kripke discusses "closing off", and remarks "It is remarkable to see the main points in favor of a theory abandoned so completely in such an off-hand manner" (p. 28). What Maudlin is objecting to is the introduction of a second truth predicate 'True*' over and above the predicate 'True' of the external theory FM. I agree with him that this is a step down, though my own view is that the main virtues of the fixed point approach had been abandoned earlier, in the move from KFS to FM.

This is valid in the given interpretation since the sentences named in the outer occurrences of each side of the biconditional, viz. $\neg\text{True}(\langle A\rangle)$ and $\text{True}(\langle\neg A\rangle)$, though inequivalent in Feferman–Maudlin, are equivalent *in KFS*; that is, one of these "inner occurrences" is in the fixed point if and only if the other is. This fits with the idea that truth attributions are external commentaries on the fixed point. (I'm speaking of the two "outer" truth attributions that occur in (COMMUTE), that is, the attributions '$\text{True}(\langle\neg\text{True}(\langle A\rangle)\rangle)$' and '$\text{True}(\langle\text{True}(\langle\neg A\rangle)\rangle)$' that are *used as opposed to mentioned*. The two "inner" attributions '$\neg\text{True}(\langle A\rangle)$' and '$\text{True}(\langle\neg A\rangle)$' that are *mentioned as opposed to used* don't seem to be external commentaries on the fixed points, but members of the fixed points that the "outer" attributions comment on.)

It's time to give more details about the Feferman–Maudlin theory (though as remarked above, it is not necessary for my purposes to be totally precise). We want all the instances of (T-OUT) to be at least theorems, and for expository reasons I will for the moment take them to be among the axioms. The axioms should also include the instances of (COMMUTE) (or better, the single-axiom form of it, that for sentences generally equates falsity of truth with truth of falsity), but what else does it have? First, it includes all instances of (T-IN) in which A either

(i) doesn't contain the predicate 'True', or
(ii) is of the form 'True(*t*)'.[7]

More instances of (T-IN) will follow from these, given the axioms to now be specified. (T-IN) clearly does *not* hold in general when A is the *negation of* a sentence of form 'True(*t*)'. For instance,

it is *not* the case that: $\neg\text{True}(\langle Q\rangle) \to \text{True}(\langle\neg\text{True}(\langle Q\rangle)\rangle)$.

This is clear, since $\neg\text{True}(\langle Q\rangle)$ and $\neg\text{True}(\langle\neg\text{True}(\langle Q\rangle)\rangle)$. Indeed, $\text{True}(\langle\neg\text{True}(\langle Q\rangle)\rangle)$ is equivalent, not to $\neg\text{True}(\langle Q\rangle)$ but to the far stronger $\text{True}(\langle\neg Q\rangle)$. (This follows from (COMMUTE), (T-OUT) and (ii).)

The compositional rules for the sentential connectives $\wedge$ and $\neg$ are as follows:

(CONJ+) A conjunction is true if and only if both conjuncts are true;
(CONJ−) The negation of a conjunction is true if and only if the negation of at least one conjunct is true;
(2Neg) The double negation of a sentence *x* is true if and only if *x* itself is true.

(There is no compositional rule for single negation; that's why conjunction requires both a positive and a negative rule.) Defining falsity as truth of negation,

---

[7] These last principles too can and should be strengthened into generalizations rather than schemas. Also, the theory can also be extended from truth to truth-of, in an obvious way; I will make this explicit later in the chapter. (Similar remarks will apply to other theories I'll consider, such as the supervaluation-style gap theories to be considered later in this section; I won't bother to repeat them there.)

(2Neg) says in effect that truth is also falsity of negation, and (CONJ−) says that a conjunction is false iff at least one of the conjuncts is false.

There are obvious dual rules for disjunction:

(DISJ+) A disjunction is true if and only if at least one of the disjuncts is true;

(DISJ−) The negation of a disjunction is true if and only if the negations of both disjuncts are true;

These follow from the previous, if we define disjunction from conjunction and negation in the usual way. Rules for the conditional also follow, e.g.

(IF+) A conditional is true if and only if either its consequent is true or the negation of its antecedent is true;

so conditionals such as $Q \to Q$ or $(Q \wedge Q) \to Q$ are not true.

We need to extend the rules to quantified sentences. For simplicity let's confine our attention to the case where every object in the domain of quantification has a name. In this context, Feferman–Maudlin adopts the obvious generalization of the $\wedge$ rules for the universal quantifier:

(ALL+) A universal quantification is true if and only if all of its instances are true

and

(ALL−) The negation of a universal quantification is true if and only if the negation of at least one of its instances is true.

That's the theory. The Kripke construction of the minimal Kleene fixed point can be used to show that it is consistent, and indeed conservative over ω-models. (So a single construction shows the conservativeness of the non-classical theory KFS and the classical theory FM—and several other theories too, as we shall see. It is in part because Kripke focused more on the construction than on the theory based on it that it is unclear which theory best fits his intentions.) The presence of the compositional rules above, together with the declaration that some sentences are neither true nor false, makes it natural to call FM a "Kleene-style gap theory."

One notable feature of FM, which will distinguish it from the supervaluation-style gap theories to follow, is that not all sentences of form True($\langle A \vee \neg A \rangle$) are part of FM; indeed, FM has theorems of form $\neg$True($\langle A \vee \neg A \rangle$). (The case where A is the Liar sentence is an example.) Nonetheless, all instances of excluded middle are part of the theory: the theory asserts "Either A or not A, but it is not the case that $\langle A$ or not $A \rangle$ is true". We saw in the previous section that the theory asserts the Liar sentence while declaring it untrue; the fact that it does the same for some instances of excluded middle is perhaps a bit more surprising, but not drastically different in kind. (Admittedly, it's odd; and it's because of this odd feature of the theory that I vastly prefer KFS, despite its own limitations.)

Given that the theory asserts instances of excluded middle that it declares untrue, a verbal question arises: should we describe the theory as accepting classical logic? Maudlin says no: the theory is one in which not all instances of excluded middle are true, so it's one in which excluded middle is invalid, so it is not a classical theory. Admittedly, the theory employs classical reasoning, and regards it as fully legitimate to do so (and in some sense incorrect not to do so). But according to Maudlin, this just shows that we need to make a sharp distinction between *permissible* reasoning and *valid* reasoning: employing excluded middle is permissible (and mandatory?), but invalid. I prefer an alternative description: the theory, since it employs classical logic, counts as a classical theory, on which excluded middle is valid; but it takes some valid sentences not to be true. Whether to describe the theory in Maudlin's way or mine seems purely a matter of terminology. But this is my book, so I'll put it my way.

B. Supervaluation-style gaps

Let me now describe what I've called "supervaluation-style gap theories". For readers who don't know what supervaluationism is, you can take this as a mere label. For those who do know what it is, let me just say that the main basis for the label is that like *those versions of supervaluationism that identify truth with super-truth*, the gap theories now to be discussed accept the truth of certain disjunctions when they deny the truth of each disjunct.[8] [A related basis for the name is that Kripke's 1975 paper suggests not only the fixed point constructions we've considered so far, which are based on Kleene's valuation rules; he also considers related fixed point constructions based on alternative valuation rules associated with supervaluationism. I'll discuss these supervaluationist fixed point constructions in some detail in Chapters 10 and 11, where I will be primarily interested in internal theories of the fixed points, theories that bear the same relations to those fixed point constructions that KFS bears to the Kleene-based. By contrast, one can consider *external* theories of supervaluational fixed points. "Supervaluation-style gap theories" include these but also include similar external commentaries on other sorts of constructions, e.g. on the revision-rule constructions to be discussed in Section 11.4. Alternatively, "supervaluation-style gap theories" can be viewed as axiomatic theories in their own right, as they are in Friedman and Sheard 1987 (their System H) and Cantini 1990. Either a supervaluational fixed point construction or a revision-rule construction serves to provide a conservativeness proof for such a theory.]

These gap theories are in many ways similar to the Kleene-based ones: in particular, they contain (T-OUT), and most of them contain (COMMUTE) as

---

[8] The standard reference for supervaluationism is Fine 1975, where it is discussed in its application to vague language. (See also Ch. 9 of this book, for a quick introduction.) "Super-true" is explained in Fine, and means something like "would come out true under any legitimate precisification of the vague terms". For most of the paper, Fine's supervaluationist takes super-truth to be a formal explication of the ordinary notion of truth, but near the end he suggests that super-truth is a better thought of as an explication of a notion of *determinate* truth. It is the former (truth as super-truth) that leads to truth-value gaps.

well.⁹ Their instances of (T-IN) include all those listed for Feferman–Maudlin (i.e. both (i) and (ii)), but more besides: most notably, we also have all instances of (T-IN) in which A is

(iii) a theorem of classical logic.¹⁰

This greatly *reduces* the number of situations where we are forced to violate the First Incoherence Principle, by saying "A, but $\neg\text{True}(\langle A \rangle)$". But it can't eliminate such cases entirely: as we've already seen, the theories must violate the First Incoherence Principle for the Liar sentence; and as we'll see in the next section, it must violate this Incoherence Principle in more important cases as well.

What about compositional rules? These theories will include the compositional rules (2Neg), (CONJ+), and (ALL+) from Feferman–Maudlin (and the dual rules (DISJ−) and (SOME−), to use an obvious notation). But they can't contain the others; for instance, these theories imply

$$\text{True}(\langle Q \vee \neg Q \rangle) \wedge \neg\text{True}(\langle Q \rangle) \wedge \neg\text{True}(\langle \neg Q \rangle),$$

thus entailing the negation of (DISJ+). The loss of (DISJ+) may be disturbing, but in the best such theories¹¹ (including System H and VF) it is partially made up for by the presence of (a generalized form of) the following:

$$\text{True}(\langle \neg A \vee B \rangle) \rightarrow \neg\text{True}(\langle A \rangle) \vee \text{True}(\langle B \rangle).$$

(Note that the negation in the consequent has been moved from "inside" to "outside", and that we have only a conditional rather than a biconditional.) Or to rewrite it:

$$\text{True}(\langle A \rightarrow B \rangle) \rightarrow [\text{True}(\langle A \rangle) \rightarrow \text{True}(\langle B \rangle)].$$

---

⁹ Strictly speaking, not all of the supervaluational fixed point constructions have external theories that include (T-OUT), but I think that those that don't are more mathematical curiosities than defensible theories. Anyway, I will confine my attention to those that do. The VF axioms are "externally correct" only for a more restricted class of supervaluation fixed point constructions than is the case for the axioms of H: for instance (COMMUTE), which is part of VF but not of H, excludes the external theories of some interesting supervaluation constructions, such as that to be considered in note 2 of Chapter 12.

¹⁰ More generally, we have those instances where A is a theorem of the expanded arithmetical language that allows 'True' in the logical axioms and in the induction schema; so in particular, all cases where A is an instance of the Gödel–Tarski Diagonalization Theorem. As a consequence, the theories not only include

$$Q \leftrightarrow \neg\text{True}(\langle Q \rangle),$$

but also

$$\text{True}(\langle Q \leftrightarrow \neg\text{True}(\langle Q \rangle) \rangle).$$

¹¹ Viz., the external theories of supervaluational fixed points under which one "supervaluates over" only deductively closed valuations.

In its generalized form, this says in effect that if a conditional and its antecedent are both true, so is the consequent: that is, modus preserves truth.

Despite their great differences, supervaluation-style theories are quite similar in spirit to Feferman–Maudlin, simply because of the joint presence of (T-OUT) and the violations of the First Incoherence Principle.

7.3. DECLARING ONE'S AXIOMS UNTRUE

A curious consequence of adopting the instances of (T-OUT) as axioms in a classical theory is that this not only results in the theory declaring

A, but $\langle A \rangle$ isn't true

for certain degenerate sentences A like the Liar sentence Q; it results in the theory declaring this for certain instances of (T-OUT) itself! Indeed, in the usual such theories we get this result for the instantiation of (T-OUT) by the Liar sentence: we can prove

(*) $\qquad\qquad\qquad \neg \text{True}[\langle \text{True}(\langle Q \rangle) \to Q \rangle].$

For instance, in a theory based on a reasonable fixed point construction, whether Kleene or supervaluational, $\text{True}(\langle Q \rangle) \to Q$ will never be in a fixed point, and so (*) will be part of the external theory. This result (that we can prove (*)) holds for just about any Kleene-based theory.[12] It also holds in *most* supervaluation-style theories. For some it may not,[13] but something similar does: there is a more

---

[12] Suppose the theory accepts both the compositional rule (IF+) of FM and the equivalence of $\text{True}(\langle \neg \text{True}(\langle Q \rangle) \rangle)$ to $\text{True}(\langle Q \rangle)$. (The latter isn't inevitable in an arithmetic context, despite the equivalence between Q and $\neg \text{True}(\langle Q \rangle)$. However, we're bound to have it in contexts that allow for direct self-reference and where Q is produced by those means, since then the sentence Q will be *identical to* the sentence $\neg \text{True}(\langle Q \rangle)$; and it seems reasonable to think that a theory should handle the indirect self-referential case in the same way it handles direct self-reference.) Then by (IF+), $\text{True}(\langle \text{True}(\langle Q \rangle) \to Q \rangle)$ is equivalent to $\text{True}(\langle \neg \text{True}(\langle Q \rangle) \rangle) \lor \text{True}(\langle Q \rangle)$, hence to $\text{True}(\langle Q \rangle) \lor \text{True}(\langle Q \rangle)$, hence to $\text{True}(\langle Q \rangle)$. So since $\neg \text{True}(\langle Q \rangle)$, we have $\neg \text{True}(\langle \text{True}(\langle Q \rangle) \to Q \rangle)$, as desired.

[13] In Field 2006 (p. 193) I offered an "intuition pump" for the idea that an optimal classical T-OUT theory should assert (*). Letting $(\text{T-OUT})_Q$ be the Q-instance of (T-OUT), I pointed out that such a theory has to take $(\text{T-OUT})_Q$ as equivalent to Q, and so "it is not surprising that" it should take $\text{True}((\text{T-OUT})_Q)$ to be equivalent to $\text{True}(\langle Q \rangle)$. This is suspect as it stands. The principle assumed was that if a theory takes a sentence A to be "equivalent to" Q, then it should take $\text{True}(\langle A \rangle)$ to be equivalent to $\text{True}(\langle Q \rangle)$. But if a theory "taking A to be equivalent to Q" is read in the most obvious way (viz., provability of the biconditional in the theory), no reasonable (T-OUT) theory in classical logic could accept this: Q has got to be a theorem of such a theory, so the theory will take each of its theorems A as equivalent to Q, in which case the principle would require the claim that $\text{True}(\langle A \rangle)$ to be equivalent to $\text{True}(\langle Q \rangle)$ for every theorem A. So we'd have $\neg \text{True}(\langle A \rangle)$, for *every* theorem A! The assumed principle, though it seems very natural, can't be accepted in a classical (T-OUT) theory; which just goes to show how careful one must be in employing such a theory.

That said, the principle does seem plausible for equivalence *of a restricted sort*: equivalence just by logic together with the Gödel–Tarski diagonalization axioms. And $(\text{T-OUT})_Q$ is equivalent to Q by those, so that would be enough to restore the "intuition pump".

complicated sentence Z that yields an instance of (T-OUT) whose untruth we can prove; that is, we can prove

(*) $\qquad \neg\text{True}[\langle\text{True}(\langle Z\rangle) \to Z\rangle].$

That is the content of

Montague's Theorem (Montague 1963): Consider any theory that (i) contains (T-OUT), (ii) proves $\text{True}(\langle A\rangle)$ whenever A is a classical logical truth or a theorem of arithmetic, and (iii) asserts that modus ponens is truth-preserving. Then for a certain sentence Z, the theory proves (*), even though the sentence that (*) asserts not to be true is an axiom of the theory.

I give the proof in a footnote.[14]

It might be protested that it isn't really necessary for a gap theorist to take all the instances of (T-OUT) as *axioms*: if one instead takes just the instances for atomic A together with the "no-glut" schema

(NG) $\qquad \text{True}(\langle\neg A\rangle) \to \neg\text{True}(\langle A\rangle)$

as axiomatic, the other instances of (T-OUT) can be derived by an obvious induction, using the other principles of the theory. (Indeed, the no-glut schema can then be strengthened into a single axiom, so this course is really preferable.) But this doesn't change my underlying point: the theory will still declare some of its axioms untrue. (In Kleene-style gap theories and some supervaluation-style gap theories, the instances of (NG) and the generalization that entails them will be declared untrue; in other supervaluation-style gap theories, instances of

$$\text{True}(\langle A\rangle) \to \text{True}(\langle\text{True}(\langle A\rangle)\rangle)$$

will be declared untrue.) In any case, I think the focus on (T-OUT) is justified since whether or not it is officially an axiom schema, it is central to the intuitive

---

[14] Let R be the conjunction of the axioms of Robinson arithmetic (a finitely axiomatized arithmetic that suffices for self-reference). We get Z from Y, which is a self-referential sentence equivalent to $\text{True}(\langle R \to \neg Y\rangle)$. This equivalence is provable in Robinson arithmetic, so the following is a truth of quantification theory:

$$R \to [Y \leftrightarrow \text{True}(\langle R \to \neg Y\rangle)].$$

But this quantificationally implies

$$[\text{True}(\langle R \to \neg Y\rangle) \to (R \to \neg Y))] \to (R \to \neg Y)$$

Abbreviate $R \to \neg Y$ as Z. Then by (ii), we must have

$$\text{True}(\langle[\text{True}(\langle Z\rangle) \to Z] \to Z\rangle)$$

and so by (iii) we must have

$$\text{True}(\langle[\text{True}(\langle Z\rangle) \to Z]\rangle) \to \text{True}(\langle Z\rangle).$$

So to prove $\neg\text{True}(\langle[\text{True}(\langle Z\rangle) \to Z]\rangle)$, it will suffice to prove $\neg\text{True}(\langle Z\rangle)$.

And proving $\neg\text{True}(\langle Z\rangle)$ is easy: by (T-OUT), $\text{True}(\langle Z\rangle) \to Z$, and given that the theory contains arithmetic, Z is equivalent in the theory to $\neg Y$, so we get $\text{True}(\langle Z\rangle) \to \neg Y$. But Y is provably equivalent to $\text{True}(\langle R \to \neg Y\rangle)$, i.e. to $\text{True}(\langle Z\rangle)$. So we have $\text{True}(\langle Z\rangle) \to \neg\text{True}(\langle Z\rangle)$; hence $\neg\text{True}(\langle Z\rangle)$ as desired.

idea of gap theory; declaring instances of it untrue seems more counterintuitive than declaring an "unintended theorem" like the Liar sentence untrue.

It seems to me highly peculiar to adopt a theory that directly or indirectly postulates all instances of (T-OUT) when one is then going to go on to declare some of these instances untrue.[15] I submit that if (in the context of a non-dialetheic logic—see previous note) we really were forced to declare some of the instances of (T-OUT) untrue, that should lead us to restrict (T-OUT)! (Similarly for (NG), on those versions of gap theory that treat some of its instances as untrue.)

In the next two sections I discuss one attempt to resist this conclusion, and in the one after that I consider one attempt to take the conclusion to heart. Both make use of a very controversial notion of proposition, and I argue that both attempts are misguided and serve mostly to muddy the waters. Neither of these two discussions addresses Tim Maudlin's valiant defense of the idea that a theory should declare itself untrue, which does not turn at all on "propositionalist obscurantism" (though it does get into some very heavy-duty metaphysics!). I cannot do justice to that defense in this book, but in the final section of this chapter I will at least make an effort to buttress the view that we should not accept theories that declare themselves untrue.

7.4. PROPOSITIONS TO THE RESCUE?

Many advocates of (T-OUT) within classical logic try to defuse objections to their theory by saying that the Liar sentence doesn't express a proposition. Their idea is that we can then maintain the following weaker version of (T-IN):

(Weak T-IN)   [There is a proposition *that A*] → [A → True($\langle A \rangle$)]

Of course, for this to be useful we need a theory of what it is for there to be a proposition *that A* (for a given sentence A). And it needs to be a theory which guarantees that for lots of sentences there will be such propositions; otherwise we won't get the instances of (T-IN) that we intuitively need.[16]

Before expressing my main doubts about the helpfulness of this, I would like to point out (what is widely known but still deserves emphasis) that it simply won't

---

[15] At least, this is so in the classical context now under discussion, where calling an axiom untrue precludes calling it true. In the context of the paraconsistent dialetheism to be discussed in Part V, where instances of (T-OUT) could be declared true as well as untrue, the situation might be different.

[16] It's worth noting that if we assume the principle

True($\langle A \rangle$) → there is a proposition *that A*,

then we won't have to worry about whether to keep the full (T-OUT) or only

(Weak T-OUT)   [There is a proposition *that A*] → [True($\langle A \rangle$) → A];

for the two are equivalent given the assumed principle.

work on any ordinary notion of proposition. Consider my remark that what the least intelligent man in the room was saying isn't true. When I said that, I firmly believed it, and had good evidence for so believing it: I firmly believed that Joe Schmoe was the least intelligent man in the room, that he had uttered 'Maine is bigger than Colorado', and that Maine is not bigger than Colorado; and I had good evidence for all these claims. What I said wasn't nonsense. Indeed, had the facts been different—if I hadn't overestimated my own intelligence or underestimated his—what I said would have been clearly true. So if we're going to talk of propositions at all, and talk of sentences and belief-states as expressing propositions, then this would seem to be a clear example: I stood in the belief relation to a perfectly coherent proposition which (like many propositions that are believed) is "conditionally paradoxical" in classical logic. Unfortunately, the conditions for classical paradoxicality were satisfied despite my evidence to the contrary.

That, I submit, is the normal notion of proposition, but it can't be the one assumed by the advocate of (Weak T-IN). So how is the advocate of (Weak T-IN) to develop his theory of propositions? There are several possible routes.

The first possible route is to take 'there is a proposition *that A*' to just be a fancy way of saying '$\langle A \rangle$ is either true or false', i.e. '$\langle A \rangle$ is either true or has a true negation'. In that case, (Weak T-IN) just amounts to

(RT-IN$_1$) $[\text{True}(\langle A \rangle) \vee \text{True}(\langle \neg A \rangle)] \rightarrow [A \rightarrow \text{True}(\langle A \rangle)]$.[17]

But this is completely vacuous, given (T-OUT)! For by (T-OUT) applied to $\neg A$, plus elementary logic, we have

$[\text{True}(\langle A \rangle) \vee \text{True}(\langle \neg A \rangle)] \rightarrow [\text{True}(\langle A \rangle) \vee \neg A]$;

and the consequent of this is equivalent to $A \rightarrow \text{True}(\langle A \rangle)$, so we've derived (RT-IN$_1$) from (T-OUT). This version of (Weak T-IN) thus tells us nothing.

The second route to a theory along these lines is to become less informative: simply replace 'there is a proposition *that A*' by an unstructured operator θA or (probably better) predication $G(\langle A \rangle)$. So we get

(RT-IN$_2$) $G(\langle A \rangle) \rightarrow [A \rightarrow \text{True}(\langle A \rangle)]$.

Of course we'll need some axioms on G to fill this out, but at least this doesn't force vacuity in the way that the previous approach did.

No, it doesn't force vacuity in quite the same sense, but it is also totally unhelpful: the task of axiomatizing G is virtually identical to the task of saying how (T-IN) is to be weakened.

A third route to introducing propositions in a classical (T-OUT) theory is to become more informative rather than less: it is to introduce an autonomous account of propositions. Rather than considering this directly, let's first move to an analogous case: introducing properties into a theory of *truth-of*.

---

[17] Essentially this was proposed in C. Parsons 1974a, p. 234.

7.5. TRUTH-OF, HETEROLOGICALITY, AND PROPERTIES

Corresponding to the schemas (T-OUT) and (T-IN) for truth we have the corresponding schemas for truth-of:

(TO-OUT) $\qquad \forall o[\langle A(v)\rangle \text{ is true of } o \rightarrow A(o)]$

(TO-IN) $\qquad \forall o[A(o) \rightarrow \langle A(v)\rangle \text{ is true of } o]$

Henceforth I will assume that advocates of (T-OUT) accept (TO-OUT) too; indeed, I will use the label (T-OUT) to cover (TO-OUT) as well.

Let's review the Heterologicality paradox (from Section 1 of the Introduction). Let Het(v) abbreviate 'it is not the case that v is true of v'. Then a special case of (TO-OUT) is

$$\forall o[\langle \text{Het}(v)\rangle \text{ is true of } o \rightarrow \text{Het}(o)],$$

that is,

$$\forall o[\langle \text{Het}(v)\rangle \text{ is true of } o \rightarrow \neg(o \text{ is true of } o)].$$

But this implies

$$\langle \text{Het}(v)\rangle \text{ is true of } \langle \text{Het}(v)\rangle \rightarrow \neg(\langle \text{Het}(v)\rangle \text{ is true of } \langle \text{Het}(v)\rangle);$$

which implies

$$\neg(\langle \text{Het}(v)\rangle \text{ is true of } \langle \text{Het}(v)\rangle).$$

In other words,

$$\text{Het}(\langle \text{Het}(v)\rangle).$$

So: there is an object (viz., $\langle$ Het(v)$\rangle$, i.e. 'v is heterological') which is heterological, but which 'heterological' is not true of! That is, we have an explicit counterexample to (TO-IN). This is of course just the analog of what T-OUT says about the Liar sentence. ('Heterological' isn't false of 'heterological' either, on this theory: it is "gappy of it".)

Now let's consider the analog of (Weak T-IN):

(Weak TO-IN) [There is a property $\lambda v A(v)$] $\rightarrow \forall o[A(o) \rightarrow \langle A(v)\rangle \text{ is true of } o]$.

And let's pursue the analog of the "third route" of the previous section: developing an autonomous theory of properties.

Here of course we face a problem: for the naive approach to the theory of properties gives rise to paradoxes too. Indeed, it gives rise to a paradox structurally analogous to the Heterologicality paradox: viz., Russell's Paradox (applied to properties rather than sets). It seems that we must solve a paradox structurally analogous to the heterologicality paradox before we decide how a solution to the heterologicality paradox incorporating (TO-OUT) and a weaker (TO-IN) is to go!

Perhaps this isn't fair: for it is clear that what the proposal to adopt (Weak TO-IN) must amount to is that Russell's paradox for properties must have a certain kind of solution, one on which *there is simply no such property as the alleged property of heterologicality*. And if we adopt a theory of this sort, then the heterologicality paradox isn't to be treated in analogy to the property paradox; for there can be no doubt that the *predicate* 'heterological' exists, there can only be a doubt that there is a property corresponding to it. The proposal, then, is to treat the property paradox as basic, and use a certain kind of solution to it (a non-existence solution) in solving the heterologicality paradox.

Of course, we still need to know the details of the theory of properties, before we have a theory of truth of along these lines. Is there a property of being an electron? If not, then it's compatible with (Weak TO-IN) that electrons exist without 'electron' being true of them. There can't be a property of not being true of itself, on this view, so 'is not true of itself' is not true of itself. But is there a property of being true of itself? Without a theory of properties to rely on, (Weak TO-IN) provides no answer.

Similarly, without a theory of propositions to rely on, (Weak T-IN) provides no theory of truth whatever. It tells us *something about* a theory of truth, namely that the Liar sentence is to be treated as "gappy", but it tells us virtually nothing about where else the alleged gaps occur. And this seems especially uninformative since there is no standard theory of propositions that the advocate of (Weak T-IN) can appeal to. (Insofar as there is a standard theory of propositions, that theory postulates that there is a proposition corresponding to every utterance meaningful by ordinary standards; and that theory would be useless for the purposes at hand, since it would not restrict (T-IN) at all and hence would lead to inconsistency.) Relying on such a totally unspecified theory of propositions amounts to nothing more than the "primitive G predicate" approach dismissed at the end of the previous section.

7.6. RESTRICTED (T-OUT)

Let's return to (T-OUT). I've pointed out that any theory in classical logic that contains this principle must assert certain claims which it then declares untrue (and unfalse as well). I regard this as a serious defect of such theories. The "propositionalist" move was supposed to help with this. Even putting aside everything said so far, it is unobvious that it would do that: after all, (1) (of Section 7.1) in conjunction with (Weak T-IN) entails

$Q \wedge$ there is no proposition *that Q*.

I would have thought that asserting that (when not part of a general denial of the existence of propositions) is as bizarre as what it was supposed to avoid!

At this point, I suspect, some erstwhile advocates of (T-OUT) will want to retrench to a theory that asserts only some instances of (T-OUT): intuitively, to

(Restricted T-OUT) {"True($\langle A \rangle$) → A" | there is a proposition *that A*},

whatever exactly that condition be taken to mean. They may want to combine it with the theory

(Restricted T-IN) {"A → True($\langle A \rangle$)" | there is a proposition *that A*}.

First, let me make clear that adopting (Restricted T-OUT) as one's theory (with or without (Restricted T-IN)) is totally different from adopting the schema

(Weak T-OUT) [There is a proposition *that A*] → [True($\langle A \rangle$) → A]

(with or without (Weak T-IN)). One obvious difference is that as remarked in note 16 of this chapter, (Weak T-OUT) is equivalent to ordinary (T-OUT) given a natural assumption about expressing a proposition; whereas the point of (Restricted T-OUT) is precisely to avoid this.

More fundamentally, a theory with (Weak T-OUT) and (Weak T-IN) is a theory that speaks directly of propositions. In a theory with the restricted axioms, on the other hand, the notion of proposition is used only in the background, to say what the axioms of the theory are. Since the notion of proposition isn't even used within the theory consisting of (Restricted T-OUT) and (Restricted T-IN), there's obviously no hope of deriving within this theory the conclusion that there is no proposition *that Q* when Q is the Liar sentence. (Whereas that is easily derived from (Weak T-OUT) and (Weak T-IN).) The best we can say is that if there is in fact such a proposition, then the Restricted Theory is inconsistent. So the advocate of the Restricted Theory should hope there is no Liar proposition! (A sufficiently convincing theory of propositions according to which there is no such proposition would at least give reason to believe the Restricted Theory consistent.)

Without some theory of propositions, it is of course totally unclear what the content of (Restricted T-OUT) is. But one thing that's clear is that it needn't make for truth value gaps. For instance, on the assumption that there is no proposition corresponding to the Liar sentence, (Restricted T-OUT) says *nothing at all* about the Liar sentence; so it doesn't declare the Liar sentence gappy. Consequently, (Restricted T-OUT) is outside the official scope of this chapter. Indeed, the whole spirit of the theories considered in this chapter was that the problem with the paradoxes was solely in the schema (T-IN); this theory breaks that claimed asymmetry by restricting (T-OUT) as well. And, to repeat, the proposal is to restrict it in a totally unspecified way: the proposal for the theory is in effect "Restrict (T-OUT) somehow, but don't ask me how: that's a matter for the theory of propositions, which I'm not going to tell you about today."

Is this unfair? For surely we have *some* idea what anyone who makes such a proposal has in mind. Clearly they intend there to be a proposition *that snow is white*, and a proposition *that ⟨snow is white⟩ is true*, and so forth; and they intend that there not be a proposition *that Q* where Q abbreviates a Liar sentence. Intuitively, they intend there to be a proposition *that A* when and only when the sentence *A* is "grounded", though the notion of groundedness is one that can be spelled out in more than one way (e.g. in terms of minimal strong Kleene fixed points; or alternatively, in terms of minimal fixed points in any of innumerable supervaluational approaches). But I will now argue that if the proposal is understood in accordance with this intuitive idea, it yields a totally hopeless theory.

For one thing, it doesn't look as if the theory (Restricted T-OUT) can be recursively axiomatized. Let f be any function that is definable in the language and that takes natural numbers to sentences of the language, and consider sentences of form

(S_n) The result of applying _____ to n is not true

where the blank is filled with some definition of f. For each S_n, we have a corresponding instance of (T-OUT):

(U_n) If ⟨The result of applying _____ to n is not true⟩ is true then the result of applying _____ to n is not true.

But on any standard notion of groundedness, S_n is grounded if and only if $f(n)$ is grounded (since S_n just says that $f(n)$ isn't true); so the above suggestion that the theory include all applications of (T-OUT) to grounded sentences requires

Constraint I: If the result of applying f to n is an "unproblematic" sentence like 'Snow is white', then U_n should be one of the axioms of (Restricted T-OUT).

And the following is clearly also part of the suggestion:

Constraint II: If the result of applying f to n is "pathological" (for instance, if it is S_n itself), then U_n should not be one of the axioms.

(Without Constraint II, we wouldn't avoid the problem of the theory asserting the untruth of its axioms.) But now let X be a definable set of natural numbers that isn't recursively enumerable, and f a definable function that assigns "pathological" sentences to all and only those n that are not in X; then the above constraints require that the theory not have a recursively enumerable set of theorems and hence not be recursively axiomatizable.

There is a closely related point to be made, about sentences for which it is an empirical question whether they are pathological: for instance "The first sentence uttered by a member of the NYU Philosophy Department in 2020 will not be true." A theory of truth must tell us whether the corresponding instance of

(T-OUT) is part of the theory. To say that we can't tell whether that instance is part of the theory until 2020 (at earliest) would seem most unsatisfactory.[18]

7.7. DOES DECLARING ONE'S AXIOMS UNTRUE DESTROY THE PURPOSE OF TRUTH?

No theory of truth in classical logic can take 'True($\langle A \rangle$)' to be intersubstitutable with A, and I will give a general argument in Chapter 13 that this is a serious obstacle to the notion of truth serving the purposes we want it to serve in any classical theory. But the point arises in what may seem an especially acute form for classical theories with (T-OUT) (or any other classical theories that declare themselves untrue).

The special form of the problem arises from the oft-noted fact (Ramsey 1927; Strawson 1950; Quine 1970; Grover, Camp, and Belnap 1975; Leeds 1978) that the notion of truth enables us to express agreement and disagreement when that would otherwise be difficult or impossible (as well as conversationally inappropriate). Jones makes some complicated bunch of claims that I agree with, and instead of expressing agreement by repeating the whole thing I say "What he said is true." (Or if I disagree: "What he said isn't true.") Of course, even without a notion of truth one could make the autobiographical assertion that one agrees, or disagrees, with Jones' claims. But what I mean here by *expressing* (as opposed to *asserting*) agreement is saying something which is correct if and only if the claims being assessed are correct. Saying that one agrees with the claims doesn't meet this condition, since this may be a true autobiographical statement even when the claims I agree with are blatantly false. Calling the claims true is the standard way of expressing agreement, in the sense indicated.

There are cases where without a notion of truth, expressing agreement or disagreement would seem impossible. For instance, consider any theory that is not finitely axiomatizable—or rather, which is not finitely axiomatizable *except by using the notion of truth*. How are we to express agreement or disagreement? (Take as an example elementary Euclidean geometry, *conceived as a theory of physical space*; I choose an example of a physical theory to make it easy to imagine

---

[18] Compare theories that weaken (T-OUT) to something of the form

(U*)   If $\langle A \rangle$ satisfies Condition C and True($\langle A \rangle$) then A.

If Condition C were an empirical condition or a computationally complex one, we might not be able to ascertain whether a given sentence A satisfied it; consequently, we couldn't tell whether certain instances of (T-OUT) follow from the theory in conjunction with the empirical or mathematical facts. That would not be a problem, for the content of the theory is quite clear: it consists not of these instances of (T-OUT), but of (U*). In the case of (Restricted T-OUT), by contrast, *which assumptions go into the theory* cannot be ascertained (at least without waiting until 2020 in the one case, or without acquiring super-human computational powers in the other).

a dispute in which participants take opposite sides, and to have an example where merely probabilistic belief is uncontroversially appropriate.) Let's take the case of agreement first. It might at first be thought that to agree with a theory like this is to agree with each of its axioms. But that's too weak: indeed, a quite familiar state of mind is one in which one agrees with each one of a large body of claims individually but suspects that they aren't all correct. If the body of claims is finite (and not unmanageably large), there's no difficulty in expressing this without the notion of truth: I agree with each of $B_1, \ldots, B_n$, but don't agree with $B_1 \wedge \ldots \wedge B_n$. (I take this to be unproblematic. It certainly makes sense on a probabilistic picture in which belief is just degree of belief over some threshold, but there are doubtless more sophisticated models in which it also makes sense.) In the infinite case, though, we can't express it in this way. So what we do is to use the notion of truth to finitely axiomatize, indeed, to axiomatize in a single sentence:[19] to agree with the theory is to agree with the claim "All the statements in the theory are true."

Disagreement with an infinitely axiomatized theory (or a theory with an unmanageably large finite number of axioms) is even more obviously problematic without a notion of truth. For agreement, we can at least get a weak approximation: agreement with each sentence in the theory. For disagreement, the analogous approximation would be that to disagree with a theory is to disagree with at least one of its component claims. But here the inadequacy is more obvious: clearly we often disagree with a theory without being sure where it goes wrong. (The theory consisting of classical logic plus the naive theory of truth might be an example, for many of you.) In the case of a finite body of claims, we can express our disagreement by disjoining the negations of the individual claims. In the case of an infinite theory, the only adequate way to express disagreement is to say: not everything in the theory is true. (Really the point applies to finitely axiomatized theories too, given that it can be an option to reject the theory by keeping the axioms but weakening the underlying logic.)

This point about the utility of a notion of truth for expressing agreement or disagreement is really just a special case of something far more general, implicit in the works cited above and to be discussed in Chapter 13. (Even if one were prepared to bite the bullet and give up on the ability to *express* disagreement in the sense defined, settling instead for autobiographical *statements* of disagreement, that wouldn't be enough to handle the more general point to be discussed there.) But sticking now to the point about agreement and disagreement, it is clear that there's going to be a problem for gap theories. Consider first a simple case: suppose that yesterday Williams hears Jones say

(J)   The Liar sentence is not true,

and hears Smith say

---

[19] Relative to a background theory of (syntax and) truth, anyway.

(S)　The Liar sentence is true.

Williams, let's suppose, is a (T-OUT) theorist, so he agrees with Jones and disagrees with Smith. But in accordance with his (T-OUT) theory, he must hold that neither of their claims is true: in particular, Jones' claim is an equivalent of the Liar sentence, so not true. Similarly, he must hold that neither is false: that *as far as truth and falsity go, (J) and (S) are to be evaluated in exactly the same way in Williams' theory, even though he agrees with (J) and disagrees with (S)*.

Of course if Williams remembers what Jones and Smith said, he can express his agreement by simply repeating Jones' claim. But maybe he doesn't; maybe he just remembers that Jones said something he agreed with having to do with logic, and Smith said something he disagreed with having to do with logic. Williams knows he hasn't changed his mind since yesterday on matters logical, so a natural thing for him to say is

(1)　What Jones said yesterday is true; what Smith said yesterday isn't.

But then his remark fails its purpose. It would equally fail its purpose to say

(2)　What Smith said yesterday is false; what Jones said yesterday isn't.

For Williams, though agreeing with Jones and disagreeing with Smith, should disagree with the first conjuncts of both (1) and (2).

Here's an example that may be more interesting in that it doesn't turn on failure of memory. Suppose this time that Jones utters far more than (J), he puts forward quite an elaborate gap theory involving (T-OUT). And suppose that I disagree with this theory overall, but can't quite decide which specific claims of the theory are problematic. It is natural for me to express my disagreement by saying "Not everything in Jones' theory is true." But this doesn't serve its purpose: since Jones himself, as a gap theorist, believes that important parts of his own theory aren't true, I haven't succeeded in expressing disagreement.

Alternatively, suppose that Jones himself thinks that Brown's theory is wrong, but isn't sure which claims of it are wrong. Then he certainly can't express his disagreement by saying "Not everything in Brown's theory is true", since by his lights that doesn't differentiate Brown's theory from his own.

As far as I know, the only substantial attempt by a gap theorist to deal with this problem is in Tim Maudlin's 2004. What Maudlin says is that the claims the gap theorist makes in elaborating his theory aren't true, but they're *objectively permissible*. Actually he just says 'permissible', but I add 'objective' because it is supposed to be a notion that is not evidence-dependent: e.g. my remark that what the least intelligent man in the room is saying isn't true is objectively impermissible when I am that man, even if I have overwhelming evidence that Joe Schmoe is the least intelligent.[20] Given this view, the way to express agreement

---

[20] Permissibility is actually not *completely* objective on Maudlin's view, for though it doesn't depend on evidence or on norms for how evidence is to be evaluated, it does depend on certain

and disagreement isn't by a truth predicate, but by the objective permissibility predicate. In some circumstances the truth predicate will do the job, but only because in those circumstances truth and permissibility coincide.

This does indeed handle the problem of agreement and disagreement, but only by inventing another notion to do the job that truth has been standardly thought to do. (Indeed, I suspect that many people will regard their own conception of truth as closer to Maudlin's conception of objective permissibility than to Maudlin's conception of truth.) And obviously, if we allow a notion of objective permissibility in addition to truth then it will raise paradoxes of its own: e.g. sentences that assert their own objective impermissibility. Maudlin of course is well aware of this, and proposes a solution. In this case what he proposes is not a (T-OUT) solution (or rather, a (Permissibility-OUT)) solution; instead, he offers a solution of a more standardly Tarskian kind. (This raises the usual worries about Tarskian solutions in that context—e.g. the treatment of examples in which Nixon and Dean try to say of each other's remarks that they are impermissible—but I will not pursue this.) This seems to be a tacit admission, on the part of the most fully developed non-stratified gap theorist, that a non-stratified gap theory just won't work for whatever predicate it is that one uses to express agreement and disagreement.

---

norms for believing claims about truth. He thinks that there could be some rational variation here, though the good norms agree on a lot: for instance, these norms all agree that it is permissible to assert the compositional rules of Maudlin's theory, even though none of those rules is taken to be true; and they all agree that it is permissible to assert all instances of (T-OUT), even the ones declared untrue.

8
Truth-Value Gluts in Classical Theories

8.1. GLUTS AND (T-IN)

To assert the existence of truth-value *gluts* is to assert that some sentences are both true and false; that is, that they and their negations are both true. This might seem to be inconsistent in classical logic (at least if the theory postulates specific examples of "glutty" sentences). The truth behind this thought is that a classical theory that asserts gluts will be inconsistent *if it allows the inference from* $True(\langle A \rangle)$ *to* A. But if, as in the last chapter, we are willing to contemplate views that disallow the inference from A to $True(\langle A \rangle)$, it seems unfair to rule out of consideration views that disallow the converse. The views to be considered, then, will accept both $True(\langle A \rangle)$ and $True(\langle \neg A \rangle)$, for certain A, without accepting both A and $\neg A$; doing the latter would be inconsistent.

I'm tempted to call these "classical glut" views *dialetheic*, for dialetheism is typically defined as the view that some sentences are both true and false. However, the usual practice in discussions of dialetheism is to confine attention to views that do accept the inference from $True(\langle A \rangle)$ to A. Dialetheic views of that kind do indeed embrace classical inconsistencies, and triviality is avoided only by employing a nonclassical logic that disallows the classically valid inference from a sentence and its negation to an arbitrary alternative sentence like 'The Earth is flat.' I'll discuss those "paraconsistent dialetheist" views in Part V. For this chapter, the restriction to classical logic is in force.

Just as the only interesting "gap theories" seem to be the ones that keep the full schema

(T-OUT) $\qquad\qquad\qquad True(\langle A \rangle) \to A$

while restricting the converse schema

(T-IN) $\qquad\qquad\qquad A \to True(\langle A \rangle)$,

similarly the only interesting "glut theories" seem to be the ones that keep the full schema (T-IN) while restricting (T-OUT).

Of course, some specific instances of (T-OUT) are guaranteed just by classical logic, viz., those where A is a theorem of classical logic. The dual of this is that when A is logically contradictory, the instance of (T-IN) is guaranteed. But just as the (T-OUT) theories include the trivial theory that nothing is true, so too the (T-IN) theories include the trivial theory that everything (or rather, every sentence) is true. That theory, though totally uninteresting, deserves a name, because certain claims I'll make will require specifically excluding it; so I'll call it *hyper-dialetheism*. (Since it takes 'true sentence' to be equivalent to 'sentence', I was tempted to call it the redundancy theory of truth, but was afraid that that might cause confusion.) Again, hyper-dialetheism is classically consistent, it just says something strange about truth.

8.2. (T-IN) THEORIES

There is a certain duality between (T-OUT) theories and (T-IN) theories (though one needs to be cautious about this, as we'll see). For instance, one immediate consequence of (T-IN) alone, in classical logic, is that the Liar sentence *is* true. For

$Q \to \text{True}(\langle Q \rangle)$ by (T-IN)
$\neg \text{True}(\langle Q \rangle) \to Q$ by the construction of Q
So $\neg \text{True}(\langle Q \rangle) \to \text{True}(\langle Q \rangle)$ by transitivity
So $\text{True}(\langle Q \rangle)$.

(Again, the last step of this uses a *reductio* rule $\neg A \to A \vdash A$, not valid in the paracomplete logics I'll be recommending but valid classically.)

Of course, $\text{True}(\langle Q \rangle)$ is equivalent to $\neg Q$; so all classical (T-IN) theories imply the following apparently odd claim:

(D1) $\qquad\qquad\qquad \text{True}(\langle Q \rangle) \wedge \neg Q.$

This, to repeat, is classically consistent: for the theory doesn't contain the means to get from $\text{True}(\langle Q \rangle)$ to Q, as would be required to derive the contradiction $Q \wedge \neg Q$. Doubtless it's *odd* (in that it violates the Second Incoherence Principle), but I know of no good argument that it's any *more* odd than the corresponding claim $Q \wedge \neg \text{True}(\langle Q \rangle)$ that one gets in gap theories (and which violates the First Incoherence Principle).

Another consequence is that Q is also false, i.e. its negation is true. This is immediate from the application of (T-IN) to the second conjunct of (D1). So we can expand (D1) to

(D1*) $\qquad\qquad \text{True}(\langle Q \rangle) \wedge \text{False}(\langle Q \rangle) \wedge \neg Q.$

And introducing the term 'Glutty' for "both true and false", we can rewrite this as

$$\neg Q \wedge \text{Glutty}(\langle Q \rangle).$$

Again, I doubt that this expansion should do much to alleviate the discomfort that might be felt by (D1). (I suppose that one might introduce some contrived notion of proposition according to which there is no proposition corresponding to glutty sentences, or (perhaps more likely) according to which there are multiple propositions corresponding to glutty sentences. I don't think this would be any more successful than the corresponding attempts (Sections 7.4–7.6) to defuse worries about (T-OUT) theories, but I will not pause to discuss this.)

As duality considerations might suggest, there are two main types of (T-IN) theories. One is in a sense the dual of Feferman–Maudlin type theories, the other ("subvaluation-style theories") is in a sense the dual of theories like Friedman and Sheard's System H or Cantini's VF. The possibility of these latter theories might escape notice because the Friedman and Sheard paper offers a classification of theories that meet certain basic ground rules (System H is just one of nine theories they discuss), and these ground rules exclude the dual of System H even though allowing System H itself.[1] The duality-breaking ground rules concern the status of modus ponens: I'll explain this in the next section. We'll see that the disallowed subvaluation-style theories actually have some advantages over System H and other classical theories that postulate gaps. (This is not a criticism of the Friedman and Sheard paper: its ground rules weren't intended to allow every system of possible interest.)

The obvious way to get a dual of Feferman–Maudlin is to simply take as true the sentences that Feferman–Maudlin takes not to be false. If you think of the original Feferman–Maudlin theory as based on the minimal Kripke fixed point in a strong-Kleene valuation, you can think of Dual Feferman–Maudlin in the same way. But instead of taking the extension of 'True' to be the set of sentences in the fixed point, you take it to be the set of sentences whose negation isn't in the fixed point; i.e. which get value 1 or $1/2$ in the fixed point.[2] Equivalently, you could take it to be the set of sentences reached by a dual to Kripke's construction, viz. a contracting construction that starts from the set of all sentences and at each stage excludes sentences that get value 0 at prior stages. (Once you're gone, you can never come back.) But such model-theoretic underpinnings aren't really necessary: one can simply start with the Feferman–Maudlin theory, and define within it a predicate $True_{dual}(x)$ to mean

$$Sentence(x) \land \neg True(neg(x));$$

then the consequences of this theory that involve only '$True_{dual}$' and not 'True' constitute the Dual theory. (Or rather, they constitute it when the subscript 'dual' is then dropped.)

---

[1] In the other direction, they allow for hyper-dialetheism, but rule out its dual, the "Nothing is true" view. (They also exclude both Feferman–Maudlin theories and their duals.)

[2] Use of a larger fixed point would result in a weaker theory, raising a terminological issue about the meaning of 'duality': in some ways it might seem more appropriate to use the term 'dual' for the weaker theory that results in this way from what Kripke calls the "maximal intrinsic" fixed point (Kripke 1975, p. 74). The difference won't make a difference for my purposes.

What happens to the truth rules themselves when this transformation is made? They stay the same: taken as a whole they are self dual. For instance, in Feferman–Maudlin we have

$$\text{True}_{\text{dual}}(\langle A \wedge B \rangle) \leftrightarrow \text{True}_{\text{dual}}(\langle A \rangle) \wedge \text{True}_{\text{dual}}(\langle B \rangle).$$

For this can be rewritten as

$$\neg \text{True}(\langle \neg (A \wedge B) \rangle) \leftrightarrow \neg \text{True}(\langle \neg A \rangle) \wedge \neg \text{True}(\langle \neg B \rangle),$$

or equivalently,

$$\text{True}(\langle \neg (A \wedge B) \rangle) \leftrightarrow \text{True}(\langle \neg A \rangle) \vee \text{True}(\langle \neg B \rangle);$$

and this is a law of the theory.

It's *almost* the same for Dual System H (and for duals of supervaluation-style theories more generally). Here too, what's true in the theory is what is not false in System H. If one thinks of system H as based on a fixed point model (this time of a supervaluational sort), one can get Dual H from it in one of the ways mentioned two paragraphs back; alternatively, one could just use the syntactic transformation via 'True$_{\text{dual}}$'. The one cautionary note is that the compositional rules are altered: where System H has (CONJ+) but not (CONJ−), for Dual H it's the other way around, as should be obvious from the derivation just given for Dual Feferman–Maudlin. (Similarly for $\vee$, $\forall$ and $\exists$. $\neg$ is individually self-dual.) This is of course to be expected: the theory will declare both Q and $\neg Q$ true, but declare their conjunction not true.

I don't mean to suggest that the switch from a theory to its dual is insignificant: it may not be, for it may be somehow built into the notion of truth that truth is what we value, and in that case the dual theory will be importantly different from the original. (Switching from a theory to its dual is essentially equivalent to not making the switch but saying that what we should value isn't truth, but non-falsity.)

Actually this argument for there being a more than verbal difference between a theory and its dual is problematic in application to gap theories and glut theories, for it's hard to see how the advocate of either such theory can claim that truth is what we value. After all, gap theorists and glut theorists take Q and $\neg Q$ to be alike as far as truth goes: neither is true on the gap theory, both are true on the glut theory. Yet both theorists differentially value Q and $\neg Q$: the gap theorist asserts Q but rejects $\neg Q$, whereas for the glut theorist it's the other way around.

I leave it to the reader to decide where this leaves us on the question of the significance of the difference between gap theories and their duals. It's still worth saying a bit more about the duals, for they will turn out to have one especially noteworthy feature. (The discussion will also serve as a bit of a warmup to the discussion of paraconsistent dialetheism in Part V.)

8.3. WHAT DO GLUT THEORIES SAY ABOUT THEMSELVES?

We saw that (T-OUT) theories declare some of their own axioms untrue: indeed, Feferman–Maudlin declares all of its composition axioms untrue, and all (T-OUT) theories declare some of the instances of (T-OUT) untrue. But no (T-IN) theory could possibly declare its axioms untrue: if A is an axiom, True($\langle A \rangle$) immediately follows by (T-IN). (And unlike paraconsistent dialetheist theories, these theories are classical, so acceptance of True($\langle A \rangle$) precludes acceptance of $\neg$True($\langle A \rangle$).)

But though (T-IN) theories don't declare any of their own axioms untrue, they have the dual feature: they declare some of their axioms false. False as well as true: they declare themselves to be glutty or dialetheic.

Indeed, Dual Feferman–Maudlin declares *all* of its compositional principles false as well as true.[3] For instance, consider the axiom (CONJ+): "A conjunction is true if and only if both its conjuncts are true". One of the instances of this is

$$\text{True}(\langle Q \wedge Q \rangle) \leftrightarrow \text{True}(\langle Q \rangle) \wedge \text{True}(\langle Q \rangle).$$

This is clearly equivalent to

$$\text{True}(\langle Q \wedge Q \rangle) \leftrightarrow \neg Q$$

and hence to

$$[\text{True}(\langle Q \wedge Q \rangle) \wedge \neg Q] \vee [\neg \text{True}(\langle Q \wedge Q \rangle) \wedge Q];$$

and since True($\langle Q \wedge Q \rangle$) and Q are each both true and false, the whole thing is both true and false. I take it to be a bit of an embarrassment for a theory to assert of itself that it consists almost entirely of dialetheia. But probably it's no worse than the situation for ordinary Feferman–Maudlin, which declares that it has almost nothing true to offer!

Dual System H and similar theories do a lot better in this regard: they declare all of their compositional principles to be solely true. But when we turn to what they say about (T-IN), the matter is different: they declare certain instances of (T-IN) to be dialetheia. In the case of Dual System H itself, just take the instance corresponding to the Liar sentence Q; in the case of the duals of the more general "H-like theories", take the instance corresponding to $\neg Z$, the negation of the Montague sentence Z discussed in 7.3. Whereas in H-like theories we have

$$\neg \text{True}(\langle \text{True}(\langle Z \rangle) \to Z \rangle),$$

in Dual H-like theories we have

$$\text{False}(\langle \neg Z \to \text{True}(\langle \neg Z \rangle) \rangle),$$

---

[3] And all of its logical schemas have instances that it declares to be false as well as true.

as is easily checked.[4] So here too, the theory declares some of its axioms (some of the instances of (T-IN)) to be dialetheia.

Perhaps, you'll say, that's not so bad. "What's important is truth, not failure of falsity; and at least the theorist declares her axioms true."

But wait, there's more! Even if it's only truth that's important, there's still a problem, for these theories also declare modus ponens not to be truth-preserving. (This is why the Friedman–Sheard ground rules exclude these theories.)

To see this, consider the following instance of modus ponens:

(*) $$Q, Q \to 0{=}1 \vdash 0{=}1.$$

Consider any (T-IN) theorist who isn't a hyper-dialetheist: we've seen that such a theorist will hold that $True(\langle Q \rangle)$ and $\neg True(\langle 0{=}1\rangle)$. But $True(\langle Q\rangle)$ is equivalent to $\neg Q$, which entails $Q \to 0{=}1$ in classical logic; so the theorist is committed to $Q \to 0{=}1$, and hence by (T-IN) to $True(\langle Q \to 0{=}1\rangle)$. So the theorist is committed to the premises of (*) being true and the conclusion not being true.[5]

Since presumably hyper-dialetheism is not a serious possibility, the previous paragraph shows that no classical (T-IN) theorist should regard modus ponens as truth-preserving. She can't give up modus ponens, while remaining a classical theorist; so she must hold not only that some of her axioms are false as well as true, but also that some of her rules don't preserve truth.

8.4. EVALUATION OF GLUTS *V*. GAPS

It seems at first blush to be a serious embarrassment to the classical glut theory that it must not only declare some of its axioms to be dialetheia, but also must declare that some of its own rules don't preserve truth. But how does this compare with the predicament of the classical gap theorist? I make five claims.

First, on the particular case of modus ponens, the gap theory seems better if the theories are not regarded as merely notational variants. For the only obvious way to regard them as not notational variants is to privilege truth over non-falsity. So though the gap theorist will say that modus ponens (which he employs as

---

[4] Direct dualizing leads to

$$False(\langle \neg True(\langle \neg Z\rangle) \to Z\rangle),$$

but this is bound to be equivalent to what's in the text, given that $\neg True(\langle \neg Z\rangle) \to Z$ is equivalent to $\neg Z \to True(\langle \neg Z\rangle)$ *in classical logic*. (Because the equivalence is in classical logic rather than depending on the truth rules, the problem mentioned in note 13 of the previous chapter does not arise.)

[5] This result shouldn't be surprising: it's the dual of the fact that in (T-OUT) theories like Feferman–Maudlin and System H, modus ponens doesn't preserve non-falsity: the conclusion of (*) is false in such gap theories but the premises aren't.

part of his theory) doesn't preserve non-falsity, this doesn't seem as bad as the glut theorist's saying that modus ponens (which she also employs as part of her theory) doesn't preserve truth.

But second, the glut theory *overall* fares no worse than the gap theory in this regard: for any objection to holding that some of one's rules don't preserve truth presumably extends at least as much to the claim that some of one's axioms aren't true, which we've seen to be entailed by the gap theory. (Indeed, axioms can be viewed as 0-premise rules, so in a sense the gap theorist too thinks some of her rules don't preserve truth.)

And third, the glut theorist has available a defense that the gap theorist doesn't: that though her rules don't *unrestrictedly* preserve truth, she has no reason to doubt that they do preserve truth *when she employs them in direct contexts*. What I mean here is that the failures of modus ponens to preserve truth, in glut theories, can plausibly be argued to arise only when at least one of the premises is unacceptable. That's certainly so in the example (*) at the end of the previous section: there, one of the premises was the Liar sentence Q, and *though the glut theorist regards this premise as true she does not accept it*. (This is a classical theorist, remember: she will accept some sentences that don't get classical values and reject others. In particular, she will accept $\neg Q$ since she accepts its equivalent $True(\langle Q \rangle)$, and reject Q since she rejects its equivalent $\neg True(\langle Q \rangle)$.) Indeed, *whenever* the glut theorist accepts both A and $A \to B$, she'll accept that modus ponens preserves truth *in that instance*: for A and $A \to B$ commit her to B, and then (T-IN) will commit her to $True(\langle B \rangle)$, which by classical logic implies the instance of truth-preservation

$$True(\langle A \rangle) \wedge True(\langle A \to B \rangle) \to True(\langle B \rangle).$$

To repeat, this argument for truth-preservation is available in each specific case where she accepts both A and $A \to B$. This doesn't entail the generalization that that holds in all cases where she accepts both A and $A \to B$, but it is consistent with it (given that the base syntactic theory is ω-consistent).

So the glut theorist can still consistently hold that modus ponens preserves truth *when it matters*: that is, when she applies it to premises she accepts. The gap theorist has no corresponding defense. Viewing axioms as 0-premise rules is no help: there is obviously no distinction between restricted and unrestricted truth-preservation in that case.

I take this to be a strong advantage of the classical glut theories over the classical gap theories.

Is it enough? My fourth and fifth claims suggest not. The fourth claim (the less substantial of the two) is that it still seems embarrassing to use as axioms claims that one regards as dialetheia. I don't know what to say in defense of this, and realize that glut theorists could easily bite this bullet.

The fifth claim is more substantial: the theorist still has a problem about expressing agreement and disagreement, because here too *agreeing* diverges from *believing true* (though this time in the opposite direction). For instance, recall

Jones, who asserts that the Liar sentence isn't true, and Smith, who asserts that it is true. The glut theorist agrees with Smith and not Jones; but he also thinks that what each of them says is true. And switching to talk of falsity won't help: though the glut theorist thinks that what Jones says is false, she also thinks that what Smith says is false.

On this matter of agreement and disagreement, both gap theories and glut theories seem seriously deficient. This, I think, provides the main motivation for weakly classical theories, which we'll consider next: they have the advantage of retaining classical logic (at least in one important sense), and some of them handle agreement and disagreement as well. (Though as we'll eventually see, they cannot handle a broader phenomenon of which agreement and disagreement is merely a special case.)

9

A Second Interlude on Vagueness

In the last two chapters I have discussed the main views that reject one of the first two Incoherence Principles from Chapter 6. (I have left aside views that reject them both: I know of no interesting view of this sort, and it is hard to see what advantages any such view could be thought to have.) In Chapters 10 through 13 I will consider "essentially disjunctive" classical views that retain the first two Incoherence Principles by rejecting the third. The present chapter provides some background discussion of a possible motivation for such views, by means of classical treatments of vagueness.

9.1. INDETERMINACY IN CLASSICAL THEORIES

As discussed earlier, the application of classical logic to vague expressions results in some conclusions that may seem surprising, such as that there is a first nanosecond at which Russell was old—or to say it more properly, that there is a natural number N such that Russell was old at N nanoseconds of age but not at $N - 1$. Obviously it would be absurd to try to find out the value of this critical number N that marked the magic moment when he became old, or to find out whether N is prime or composite. Why?

The *epistemic theory* (Williamson 1984), at least in its simplest version, says that such questions as whether N is prime are simply beyond our cognitive powers: there are lots of other questions whose answers will forever be unattainable (e.g. very hard questions in mathematics, questions about the detailed arrangements of atoms in the interior of the sun at this moment, and so forth), and these questions about the critical value N are among them. (Which isn't of course to say that the reasons for our inevitable ignorance are precisely the same as in the mathematical case and the case of the interior of the sun; indeed, since the reasons for inevitable ignorance in those two cases are so very different, the reasons for inevitable ignorance in the vagueness case could hardly be the same as both of them.)

This simplest form of epistemic theory strikes many people as highly counter-intuitive, and perhaps one can complicate the theory to make it seem less so: e.g. Horwich 2005 argues that the basic problem isn't that we can't *know* where the boundary is, or whether it's at a prime or composite number, but that we can't even *have a stable belief* about these issues. Perhaps that helps a bit. I won't be concerned with that, but with a different modification of simple epistemicism: one which tries to explain our ignorance, and combat other counterintuitive features of the view, by saying that the questions about the critical value *N have no determinate answer*. I'll call someone who advocates this response to epistemicism, while adhering to classical logic for vague expressions, a *classical indeterminist*.

There are two key questions about classical indeterminism. The first is what it means to call a question indeterminate. The second is how it is supposed to help.

A. On what "indeterminate" means

While it would be nice to have a definition of 'indeterminate' in more primitive terms, I don't think it would be too much of a defeat for the classical indeterminist if he were to say that the term isn't definable and needs to be taken as a primitive.

Still, this can't be the end of the matter: the indeterminist needs to provide principles governing the notion that are incompatible with its being given an epistemicist reading: incompatible, for instance, with reading 'it is indeterminate whether' as 'it would be impossible to find out whether'. And it seems to me that this shouldn't be done simply by specifically postulating that 'it is indeterminate whether' is not equivalent to anything epistemic: what is needed is basic principles about determinacy and indeterminacy from which the non-epistemic nature of the notion follows. If the assumption of the non-epistemic nature of indeterminacy were excisable without loss to basic principles, I don't see why anyone should take it seriously.

The requirement that indeterminacy be shown to be non-epistemic raises no difficulty for the kind of *non*-classical indeterminacy explored in Part I in connection with continuum-valued logic. There are two reasons.

The less important reason is that in continuum-valued logic, indeterminacy turned out to be definable in more basic terms that are not epistemic: 'it is not determinate that *A*' just amounted to '$A \to \neg A$',[1] and so 'it is indeterminate whether *A*' (i.e. $\neg DA \wedge \neg D\neg A$) just amounted to '$A \leftrightarrow \neg A$'. I don't want to rest much on this.[2]

The more important reason is that in continuum-valued logic and other paracomplete logics, a notion of determinacy can be added (whether by definition

---

[1] This is an operator, not a predicate, but of course one can turn an operator into a predicate by use of a truth predicate: '⟨*A*⟩ is not determinately true' is just '$\neg D(\text{True}(\langle A \rangle))$'. (Or '$\neg(\text{True}(\langle DA \rangle))$', but that's equivalent if truth obeys the Intersubstitutivity Principle.)

[2] Reasons: (i) it may seem to be just be an artefact of the use of continuum-valued logic, not generalizable to more satisfactory logics of vagueness; (ii) it might be thought that even in continuum-valued logic, the notion of determinacy defined is intuitively too weak (and hence the notion of indeterminacy defined is intuitively too strong). I'm actually inclined to disagree with both points, but think it is not worth arguing the matter here.

or as a primitive) in a way that guarantees that it can't be read epistemically. The way to do this is to impose as a basic requirement on D that commitment to a disjunction $A \lor B$ requires commitment to $DA \lor DB$. So in paracomplete logics, commitment to $A \lor \neg A$ requires commitment to $DA \lor D\neg A$ (that is, to the claim that it is determinate whether A). And so **the claim that it is indeterminate whether A precludes commitment to $A \lor \neg A$.**

Since the claim that one couldn't know whether A does *not* preclude commitment to $A \lor \neg A$, this enables the advocate of a paracomplete logic to rule out an epistemic interpretation of D from basic principles. The classical theorist is committed to excluded middle, so can't say this. The first challenge to him is to do as well.

B. On why indeterminacy should matter

How does it help remove worries about there being a "magic moment" when Russell moved from being not old to being old to be told that it is "indeterminate" which moment that was? Presumably it matters because if one knows that it is indeterminate whether the first N such that Russell was old at N nanoseconds is prime, then it is irrational to *wonder whether* it's prime, *hope that* it's prime, and so forth. The paracomplete theorist has a clear explanation of *why* this would be irrational. For (to slightly strengthen the point above), it follows from paracomplete views that commitment to it being indeterminate whether A requires *rejection* of $A \lor \neg A$. But presumably it is irrational to reject $A \lor \neg A$ while simultaneously wondering whether A; so on paracomplete views, it is irrational to regard A indeterminate and simultaneously wonder whether A. Essentially the same point goes for hoping.

That's the paracomplete theorist's explanation, but what can the classical theorist say? According to the classical theorist, the critical number N either is prime or it isn't (even if the question is deemed "indeterminate"), so why is it irrational to wonder which?

Another way that indeterminacy would seem to matter is that if it is indeterminate whether A, then (i) it is impossible to know whether A, and (ii) this isn't "ignorance" in any normal sense. A paracomplete theorist has no trouble explaining (i) and (ii). As regards (i), there is an implication from *S knows that A* to A, and hence from *S knows whether A* to $A \lor \neg A$. So, since commitment to it being indeterminate whether A involves rejection of $A \lor \neg A$, it also involves rejection of the claim that someone knows whether A. As regards (ii), when one rejects that S knows whether A because one rejects $A \lor \neg A$, one also rejects $True(\langle A \rangle) \lor \neg True(\langle A \rangle)$; that is, one rejects that there is a truth to be known. That is why the impossibility of knowing is not due to ignorance.

A classical theorist *who is an epistemicist* presumably doesn't agree with (ii), and has no trouble explaining (i): for him, it's part of the meaning of 'indeterminate' that it's impossible to know. But a classical theorist *who is not an epistemicist* seems to have a problem with both (i) and (ii). According to him, the first N such that Russell was old at N nanoseconds either is prime or isn't; the question may be "indeterminate", but not in a sense explained in terms of knowledge. So what reason is there to think we can't know the answer? And when one doesn't know the answer, what reason is there to excuse it as "not really ignorance"? Of course someone could insist that by ignorance he is to mean "not knowing the answer to a question that has a determinate answer". But without an account of why determinacy is important, this is just verbal hocus pocus: it's analogous to my claiming not to be ignorant of matters astronomical by defining ignorance to mean "not knowing the answer to a question with a non-astronomical answer".

9.2. SUPERVALUATIONISM

Supervaluationism is just a special kind of classical indeterminacy theory: one where (at least for restricted languages in which the variables range only over the members of a set U) the notion of determinateness is explained metalinguistically in terms of refinements of the given extensions of the predicates. More fully, the idea is that we associate with each predicate P two non-overlapping sets $E^+(P)$ and $E^-(P)$, which might be called the *determinate extension* and the *determinate anti-extension* of P. The *candidate extensions* of P are taken to be sets X that extend $E^+(P)$ and are disjoint from $E^-(P)$—perhaps all such sets, or perhaps only those sets meeting further conditions. (This latter option is most often employed when there are several vague predicates $P_1, \ldots, P_n$ whose vagueness seems "tied together"; in that case, we impose a condition $\Phi(P_1, \ldots, P_n)$ involving these predicates together, and take the candidate extensions of $< P_1, \ldots, P_n >$ to be those $< X_1, \ldots, X_n >$ such that for each i, $E^+(P_i) \subseteq X_i \subseteq U - E^-(P_i)$ and $\Phi(P_1, \ldots, P_n)$. But even in the single-predicate case, introducing such further conditions can be useful, as will become evident in the next few chapters.) We then use a standard Tarskian definition to define truth *relative to each choice of candidate extensions*; and we regard a sentence as "super-true" if it comes out true relative to each choice of candidate extensions for its predicates. (For simplicity I'm assuming that the only vague terms in the language are 1-place predicates; nothing hangs on this other than ease of presentation.) "Super-truth" is to be a formal explication of determinate truth.

As just described, this applies only to first order indeterminacy. How best to try to extend it to higher order indeterminacy is controversial, but will not be my concern.

Early versions of this approach tended to avoid the term 'determinate truth', and identify *truth itself* with super-truth. ('Indeterminate' was still employed, defined as 'neither true nor false'.) This lessened the options for dealing with higher order indeterminacy; but more to the point here, it meant introducing truth-value gaps, and hence is more in line with theories like System H

(Section 7.2) than with the theories I will consider in the next few chapters. So what I will have in mind by supervaluationism rejects the identification of truth with super-truth; it takes super-truth to be the model-theoretic counterpart not of truth, but of *determinate* truth.

I should remark also that the identification of truth with super-truth would tend to cover over some of the philosophical issues about indeterminacy mentioned in the previous section. For instance, consider the question of why a sentence being indeterminate precludes our knowing it. Calling indeterminateness "lack of truth value" might appear to provide an answer: you can't know what isn't true, and if indeterminate sentences lack truth value then you obviously can't know them! But this is just more verbal hocus pocus: what underlies the claim that you can't know what isn't true is that you can't know that p unless p. You can't know that Russell was old at n nanoseconds unless he was old at n nanoseconds, and you can't know that he wasn't old at n nanoseconds unless he wasn't old at n nanoseconds. But on the supervaluationist view he either was or wasn't, and if you can't know which, that needs an explanation. The use of 'true' to mean super-true just serves to disguise this.

If super-truth is used to define determinate truth rather than truth, what are we to say about truth itself? The best supervaluationist view here is to take 'true' to be a term in the language, not one that is defined metalinguistically; it is itself vague, and "tied to" the other terms in the language. Suppose 'old' and 'true' are both in the language; then the condition Φ on the candidate extensions X_{old} and X_{true} has it that for any object o with name O, $o \in X_{old}$ if and only if $\langle O \text{ is old} \rangle \in X_{true}$. That is, in any joint choice of candidate extensions,

$$O \text{ is old}$$

and

$$\text{True}(\langle O \text{ is old} \rangle)$$

will get the same truth-value. What I've said for 'old' applies to any other predicate *except for those like 'true' that can give rise to paradox*. How to generalize it to "paradoxical predicates" is the task of the next few chapters.

One important fact that supervaluationist claims to *define* determinate truth tend to obscure is that the definitions are available only for restricted languages (in the sense of Chapter 1): languages in which the quantifiers are restricted to a set. For instance, in a language with unrestricted quantifiers, '=' won't have a positive extension: this would have to be the set of pairs $<x,x>$ for all x, and there is no set that big. ('=' won't have a negative extension either.) Similarly, 'old person' won't have a negative extension: that too would have to include all sets. And it does not appear to help to suppose that the term 'set' is itself indeterminate: on this approach, that would seem to mean simply that it has a variety of candidate extensions, *none of which can contain all sets* (since candidate extensions must themselves be sets).

This inability to define determinate truth for an unrestricted language set-theoretically should already have been clear from Tarski's undefinability theorem, given that determinate truth simply coincides with truth for mathematical language. (This last point ignores the possibility that 'set' itself might be indeterminate, but the remark at the end of the previous paragraph suggests that that doctrine couldn't help in the end.)

Even in the case of restricted languages, the supervaluational definition of determinate truth wouldn't seem to help with the first worry of the previous section: the worry about what 'indeterminate' means. For though the supervaluational account does in some sense define 'determinate truth' for restricted languages, it does so only in terms of 'positive determinate extension' and 'negative determinate extension'; which is in effect to say, in terms of 'determinately true of' and 'determinately false of' as applied to atomic predicates. 'Determinately true of' and 'determinately false of' are effectively taken as primitive as applied to atomic predicates. As I said in the previous section, this is not objectionable in itself; but if supervaluationism is supposed to provide an alternative to epistemicism, principles must be assumed about these notions that preclude an epistemic reading: e.g. which preclude taking the positive determinate extension of a predicate as being the set of things for which it is knowable that the predicate applies, on some appropriate reading of 'knowable'. (And these principles should not be *ad hoc* ones, easily excisable from the theory without loss.) I know of no serious supervaluationist attempts to meet this challenge.

As for the second of the worries discussed in the previous section, it is still more obvious that supervaluationism is of no help. The supervaluationist says that at certain stages, Russell was neither in the determinate positive extension nor the determinate negative extension of 'old'. But of what possible interest is this, given that (according to the view) he was at those stages either old or not old? Supervaluationism, like other classical indeterminacy views, seems to be an attempt to talk as if excluded middle were being restricted, without actually restricting it.

Despite this rather negative view of the philosophical underpinnings of supervaluationism and other classical indeterminacy views, I will explore their applications to the paradoxes in the next few chapters. Actually these chapters are somewhat more general: they explore classical views that reject the Third Incoherence Principle of Chapter 6, whether or not they talk of indeterminacy; classical indeterminacy comes in only as a way of trying to make philosophical sense of this. Chapter 13 attempts a general critique that applies to both weakly and strongly classical views.

10

Introduction to Supervaluational Approaches to Paradox

I begin this chapter by outlining the simplest of Kripke's supervaluational fixed point models. (I save the more sophisticated supervaluational models for the next chapter.)

In Chapter 7 I referred to the external theory of certain supervaluational fixed point models. In the external theory we theorize about the fixed points from the outside, and see truth-value gaps. What will be of interest in what follows is the internal theory, which is simply the contents of the fixed point, and includes no claims about the existence of gaps. (Or to be more accurate, the theory we'll be interested in consists of whatever is guaranteed to be in the fixed point, no matter what ω-model for the underlying language we start with.) The internal theory of these models is thus the supervaluationist analog of the paracomplete theory KFS, in the same way that the external theory is the supervaluationist analog of FM (= Feferman–Maudlin). In the supervaluationist context the internal and external theories are easier to confuse, since both are now theories in classical logic (at least in a broad sense of that term—we'll see in Section 2 that there's a sense in which the internal theory isn't *fully* classical). Still, the theories are very different: the internal theory unlike the external does not contain the (T-OUT) schema and the difficulties that that entails; it has some appealing alternative "truth rules" to put in its place.[1]

A main concern of this chapter will be the status of those truth rules. I will introduce a convenient framework for discussing this, that of Boolean-valued semantics. That framework will also be of use in discussing other models for weakly classical theories: not only more sophisticated supervaluation models, but revision rule models as well.

10.1. THE SIMPLEST SUPERVALUATIONAL FIXED POINTS

Let us confine our attention for now to restricted languages (those whose quantifiers are restricted to a set). As noted already, it is not possible to apply the

---

[1] When I speak of supervaluational theories I'll always mean these internal theories; the external theories will be called supervaluational gap theories.

fixed point construction to unrestricted languages, except by in effect pretending that their quantifiers are restricted to a set. This will not prevent us from applying what I'm calling the internal theory to unrestricted languages, as we'll see, but for now the concern is with the fixed point construction itself, so we must restrict.

As in the construction of Strong Kleene fixed points in Section 3.1, we start with a language $\mathscr{L}$ rich enough to contain elementary arithmetic, and which may contain a whole lot more besides, both mathematical and non-mathematical. (But it can't contain all of set theory, since its quantifiers are restricted.) We want to expand it to a language $\mathscr{L}^+$ containing 'True', without altering the semantics of the other terms in the language. Here too, the idea is to start out not by assigning to 'True' an extension, but by considering various "temporary quasi-extensions" for it. We will eventually select a "permanent quasi-extension" from among these; in the language of Chapter 9, this will be its "positive determinate extension".

As in the Strong Kleene case, each temporary quasi-extension X is a subset of the universe U of quantification, satisfying two conditions:

(i) All the members of X are (Gödel numbers of) sentences
(ii) No sentence and its negation are both in X

And again, we let X^{neg} consist of everything in U that is either not a sentence or else the negation of a member of X; by condition (ii), X and X^{neg} are disjoint, though there could be sentences in neither. So far nothing is different from the Strong Kleene case.

Where the difference comes is in the procedure by which we assign values to formulas of $\mathscr{L}^+$, relative to an assignment function s and a temporary quasi-extension X for 'True'. The idea will be to look at "candidate extensions" Y that are supersets of X and disjoint from X^{neg} (and perhaps satisfy additional conditions as well). For each such Y, we look at the classical model in which the extension of 'True' is taken to be Y (and which in other respects is like the ground model). See the discussion at the start of 9.2. We then regard a sentence as having (super-)value 1 according to X (or as being determinately true according to X) if and only if it comes out true in all the candidate extensions Y based on X.

More formally, we define values relative to X as follows:

$|A|_{X,s}$ is 1 if and only if for every Y for which $X \subseteq Y \subseteq U - X^{neg}$, A is true relative to Y and s

$|A|_{X,s}$ is 0 if and only if for every Y for which $X \subseteq Y \subseteq U - X^{neg}$, A is not true relative to Y and s

$|A|_{X,s}$ is ½ otherwise.

(Here I've restricted to the simplest case, where no additional conditions are imposed on the candidate extensions Y besides being a superset of X and disjoint from X^{neg}. The more general case will be considered starting in Section 11.2.)

Note that our condition (ii) amounts to the claim that $X \subseteq U - X^{neg}$. This way of writing it makes evident that there must be some Y satisfying $X \subseteq Y \subseteq U - X^{neg}$ (for instance, Y could be X, or $U - X^{neg}$), so there is no danger that our definition could force $|A|_{X,s}$ to be both 1 and 0.

Except for this altered procedure for assigning values to formulas at each stage, we construct the minimal fixed point as in the Kleene case (Chapter 3). We start out with $X_0 = \emptyset$; for each α, we let $X_{\alpha+1}$ be $\{A \mid A$ has value 1 relative to $X_\alpha\}$; and for limit ordinal λ, we let X_λ be the set of sentences that have value 1 relative to some X_β where $\beta < \lambda$. Again we have the Roach Motel property: once a sentence checks in (is in an X_α), it never checks out (it's in all X_β for $\beta > \alpha$).[2] And then the argument for the minimal fixed point is as before: the X_αs can't keep growing forever, so there must be an ordinal β for which $X_{\beta+1} = X_\beta$. (For more detail, review the argument of Section 3.1.) As in the Kleene case, we can modify the construction by starting with any set X_0 meeting conditions (i) and (ii) that is "sound" in the sense that every member of X_0 is true in all classical models Y for which $X_0 \subseteq Y \subseteq U - X_0^{neg}$; this can produce larger fixed points, but again they will be of little concern here.

By an obvious induction, we see that neither Q (the Liar sentence) nor $\neg Q$ can ever be in any fixed point, even a non-minimal one. (Q can't be in any sound X_0, since it is true relative to X_0 only if it is not a member of X_0; similarly for $\neg Q$. Neither Q nor $\neg Q$ can be in a successor $X_{\alpha+1}$ unless the other was already in X_α; and no sentence can be in a limit stage unless it was in an earlier stage. So there is no stage of the construction where one of Q, $\neg Q$ could enter for the first time.)

The fixed point property also easily gives that if X is a fixed point, then for any sentence A,

(FP) $A \in X$ if and only if for all Y such that $X \subseteq Y \subseteq U - X^{neg}$, A is true in the classical model that assigns Y to 'True' (and is otherwise like the ground model).

(If the fixed point is X_β, use the condition on what it is for A to be in $X_{\beta+1}$, then use the fixed point property to conclude that this is also the condition for A to be in X_β.) So we'll take the fixed point X to be the "positive definite extension" of 'True', and X^{neg} to be the "negative definite extension". The "genuine candidate extensions" will be those Y for which $X \subseteq Y \subseteq U - X^{neg}$.[3] Then we have the standard supervaluationist picture: definite truth (being in the positive definite extension) is just classical truth relative to all candidate extensions, and definite falsity (being in the negative definite extension) is just falsity relative to all candidate extensions.

---

[2] Again this follows from the Monotonicity Property: if $X_1 \subseteq X_2$, then every sentence with value 1 relative to X_1 has value 1 relative to X_2, and every sentence with value 0 relative to X_1 has value 0 relative to X_2. To establish this Monotonicity Property, just note that if $X_1 \subseteq X_2$ then also $X_1^{neg} \subseteq X_2^{neg}$, so $U - X_2^{neg} \subseteq U - X_1^{neg}$, so $\{Y \mid X_2 \subseteq Y \subseteq U - X_2^{neg}\} \subseteq \{Y \mid X_1 \subseteq Y \subseteq U - X_1^{neg}\}$; the Monotonicity is then immediate from the definitions of what it is to have values 1 and 0.

[3] 'Genuine' to contrast with the case of four paragraphs back, where we were considering candidate extensions relative to an X that is not a fixed point.

Note also that when one takes A to have form $\text{True}(\langle B \rangle)$ or $\neg \text{True}(\langle B \rangle)$, we get the following from (FP):

Corollary to (FP): If X is a fixed point then for any sentence B,

(I) $\text{True}(\langle B \rangle) \in X$ if and only if for all Y such that $X \subseteq Y \subseteq U - X^{\text{neg}}$, $B \in Y$;

(II) $\neg \text{True}(\langle B \rangle) \in X$ if and only if for all Y such that $X \subseteq Y \subseteq U - X^{\text{neg}}$, $B \notin Y$.

As a corollary to the corollary, we get

Central Result: If X is a fixed point, then

(I) if $A \in X$, $\text{True}(\langle A \rangle) \in X$

and (II) if $\neg A \in X$, $\neg \text{True}(\langle A \rangle) \in X$.

Proof: (I) if $A \in X$, then for all Y for which $X \subseteq Y$, $A \in Y$; so by (I) of the corollary, $\text{True}(\langle A \rangle) \in X$. (II) if $\neg A \in X$, i.e. $A \in X^{\text{neg}}$, i.e. $A \notin U - X^{\text{neg}}$, then for all Y for which $Y \subseteq U - X^{\text{neg}}$, $A \notin Y$; so by (II) of the corollary, $\neg \text{True}(\langle A \rangle) \in X$. ∎

The converses to (I) and (II) of the Central Result also are evident from (FP). (Whereas (I) and (II) will hold in all the more sophisticated fixed point models to be discussed later, this is not so for the converses. However, the converse to (I) will hold for the only such models that prove to be of interest.) Take the converse to (I):

(c-I) If $\text{True}(\langle A \rangle) \in X$, then $A \in X$.

If $\text{True}(\langle A \rangle) \in X$, then (I) of (FP) gives that for all Y satisfying $X \subseteq Y \subseteq U - X^{\text{neg}}$, $A \in Y$; but X is one such Y, so $A \in X$. Similarly for the converse to (II):

(c-II) If $\neg \text{True}(\langle A \rangle) \in X$, then $\neg A \in X$.

If $\neg \text{True}(\langle A \rangle) \in X$, then (II) of (FP) gives that for all Y satisfying $X \subseteq Y \subseteq U - X^{\text{neg}}$, $A \notin Y$; but $U - X^{\text{neg}}$ is one such Y, so $A \notin U - X^{\text{neg}}$. So $A \in X^{\text{neg}}$, i.e. $\neg A \in X$.

I note that all theorems of classical logic are in every fixed point: indeed, they get into the construction at stage 1. The same is true for the Gödel–Tarski diagonal sentences, such as $Q \leftrightarrow \neg \text{True}(\langle Q \rangle)$. These are both big differences from the Strong Kleene models; and at first blush they may seem to mark a major advantage of the internal theory of the supervaluational model over the internal theory KFS of the Strong Kleene.

The internal theory of the supervaluational model also seems to have big advantages over the gap and glut theories considered in Chapters 7 and 8. In particular, the Central Result guarantees that *the internal fixed point theories don't violate the First or Second Incoherence Conditions of Chapter 6*. This is a huge gain.

In addition, we saw that while glut theories avoid a main pitfall of gap theories, viz. declaring some of their own assertions untrue, they have a somewhat analogous feature that can seem as bad: they declare specific instances of modus ponens to have true premises and an untrue conclusion,[4] even though the theories themselves employ modus ponens as a rule of inference. I tried to put the best face I could on this, by introducing the idea of *restricted* truth-preservation; still, I suspect that many readers will have felt it to be a considerable strike against glut theories.

But we can easily see that this problem doesn't arise for the supervaluationist theory above, or indeed for any consistent theory with the properties (I) and (c-I) (i.e. any consistent theory that contains True($\langle A \rangle$) when and only when it contains A). For suppose that the theory did assert True($\langle A \rangle$), True($\langle A \rightarrow B \rangle$), and ¬True($\langle B \rangle$). By (c-I), it would then assert both A and $A \rightarrow B$; and since it contains modus ponens, it would assert B. So by (I) it would assert True($\langle B \rangle$) as well as ¬True($\langle B \rangle$), contradicting the supposition that it is consistent. So it can't assert True($\langle A \rangle$), True($\langle A \rightarrow B \rangle$), and ¬True($\langle B \rangle$). And the argument generalizes: we can see by analogous reasoning that it can't assert specific counterinstances to the truth-preserving nature of any one of its rules. That seems to be a genuine success for supervaluationism.

I don't want to overstate this last success of supervaluationism: we'll see that supervaluationism has features very close to the presumably undesirable feature of the glut theory. But that's a matter for Chapter 12; savor the success while you can.

10.2. INDETERMINACY, WEAK VALIDITY, AND REASONING BY CASES

The fixed point construction as described in the previous section is possible only when all the quantifiers in the language are restricted to a certain set; and the definition of 'has value 1' (relative to such a fixed point) uses set theoretic resources that are not in the language. This is no surprise: by Tarski's theorem, it couldn't be otherwise (given that for sentences in the ground language, value 1 coincides with truth).

But the construction generalizes, from a definition of *truth* for restricted languages to a definition of *truth in a model* for languages that needn't be restricted. This is in complete analogy with the discussion in Sections 3.2 and 3.3; and the construction then yields a conservativeness result like the one described there. Specifically, it shows that for any ω-model M of the ground language there is a corresponding fixed point model of the enlarged language that is just like M in its 'True'-free part. The inferences which preserve the property of having value 1 in this model will include all the classical inferences together

---

[4] I'm exempting hyper-dialetheism, the view that everything is true, as too silly to consider.

with inferences corresponding to (I), (II), (c-I) and (c-II). I re-label these latter inferences

(T-Introd) $\quad\quad\quad\quad A \models \text{True}(\langle A \rangle)$
(¬T-Introd) $\quad\quad\quad \neg A \models \neg\text{True}(\langle A \rangle)$
(T-Elim) $\quad\quad\quad \text{True}(\langle A \rangle) \models A$
(¬T-Elim) $\quad\quad\quad \neg\text{True}(\langle A \rangle) \models \neg A.$

(In naming these rules, as in my earlier naming of (T-OUT) and (T-IN), I follow the terminology of Friedman and Sheard 1987.)

The use of the double turnstile (read 'implies') in these rules might be thought inappropriate, given that the supervaluationist does not accept the corresponding conditionals ($A \to \text{True}(\langle A \rangle)$, etc.). But there does seem to be a perfectly good sense in which these are rules of implication: *in every allowable model in which the premises have value 1, so does the conclusion.* This is what I will call *weak implication*. Correspondingly, I will call an argument *weakly valid* if its premises weakly imply its conclusion.

A key feature of the logic of supervaluationism is that on this reading of 'implies', certain classical meta-rules must be rejected, including the rule of reasoning by cases (also called ∨-Elimination). For in the above sense of 'implies', both the Liar sentence Q and its negation $\neg Q$ imply contradictions:

(a) Q implies itself. It also implies $\text{True}(\langle Q \rangle)$, which is equivalent to $\neg Q$. So it implies the contradiction $Q \wedge \neg Q$.

(b) $\neg Q$ implies itself. It also is equivalent to $\text{True}(\langle Q \rangle)$, which implies Q. So it too implies the contradiction $Q \wedge \neg Q$.

But according to this logic, $Q \vee \neg Q$ is a logical truth; so *it* had better not imply a contradiction. The only way to keep it from doing so is to restrict the meta-rule of reasoning by cases, viz.,

If A implies C and B implies C then $A \vee B$ implies C.

(I call this a *meta*-rule since it is a rule for inferring from one implication claim to another.)

Two other classical meta-rules need restricting too, though to my mind their restriction is less counter-intuitive.

The first is conditional proof: if $\text{True}(\langle A \rangle)$ and A "imply each other" for every A, this had better not be in a sense in which we can employ conditional proof to get the conditionals $\text{True}(\langle A \rangle) \to A$ and $A \to \text{True}(\langle A \rangle)$ for every A (that is, to get the schemas (T-OUT) and (T-IN)). For those schemas together lead to inconsistency; indeed, *either one* leads to inconsistency given the rules above.

The other classical meta-rule that can't hold without restriction is *reductio*, even in the intuitionistically valid form that if Γ and A jointly imply $\neg A$ then Γ alone implies $\neg A$. For on this view, Q "implies" $\neg Q$ (given the arithmetical background theory Γ), but $\neg Q$ is not valid (or implied by the background theory). Similarly, $\neg Q$ "implies" $\neg\neg Q$, but $\neg\neg Q$ is equivalent to Q in this theory and so is not valid.

The failures of conditional proof and *reductio* in a clear sense depend on the failure of reasoning by cases. To see this for conditional proof, suppose that Γ and A jointly imply B. Then they certainly imply the weaker $A \to B$; and Γ and $\neg A$ also jointly imply $A \to B$ since that follows from $\neg A$ alone. So reasoning by cases would give that Γ and $A \lor \neg A$ jointly imply $A \to B$, which in the presence of excluded middle would mean that Γ alone does. A similar analysis holds for *reductio*. (Were excluded middle not assumed one might have a failure of conditional proof or reductio even if reasoning by cases were regarded as generally legitimate. That is the situation with the Lukasiewicz logics considered in Part I.)

Viewing the supervaluationist as restricting the classical meta-rules is not inevitable—it depends on the weak reading of 'implies'. In Section 10.6 I will introduce a stronger reading of 'implies', with the feature that premises $A_1, \ldots, A_n$ strongly imply a conclusion B if and only if the conditional $A_1 \land \ldots \land A_n \to B$ is a logical truth. (Strong validity will coincide with weak validity when it comes to single sentences; it is only for inferences from premises for which the notions diverge.) But the weak reading has a number of important virtues, two of which I will now discuss (Sections 10.3 and 10.4).

10.3. THE STATUS OF THE TRUTH RULES

Perhaps the main virtue of the weak reading of 'implies' or 'valid' is that (i) this is the reading needed to make the truth rules such as (T-Introd) and (T-Elim) come out valid, and (ii) it seems a virtue of the supervaluational approach that these rules do come out valid.

Point (i) is obvious: because the Tarski conditionals

$$\text{True}(\langle A \rangle) \to A$$

and

$$A \to \text{True}(\langle A \rangle)$$

have exceptions, the rules (T-Introd) and (T-Elim) can't be strongly valid in a supervaluational theory. Similarly for ($\neg$T-Introd) and ($\neg$T-Elim).

But is it important that the rules come out valid? I think it is: anything less seems to understate their status in the theory.

For instance, it is sometimes proposed that the rules (T-Introd), ($\neg$T-Introd), (T-Elim) and ($\neg$T-Elim) are merely rules of theorem-preservation or validity-preservation, like the rule of necessitation in modal logic. I think that this is inadequate to the intentions of the supervaluationist. (A similar remark will apply to the revision theorist, later to be discussed.) For the point of saying that the necessitation rule

$$A/\Box A$$

is merely a rule of theorem-preservation or validity-preservation rather than a rule of implication is precisely that it is inapplicable to sentences that aren't theorems (of an appropriate theory) or that aren't logically valid: we don't, for instance, want to infer '$\Box$(Snow is white)' from 'Snow is white'. In the case of the truth rules, though, we do: *once one is in a position to assert 'Snow is white', then one is in a position to assert 'True(⟨Snow is white⟩)'*. If that *isn't* part of the supervaluationist view, the view has much less value than it seems to at first blush.

Indeed, even the italicized claim above underestimates the import of the truth rules for the supervaluationist: they have application *even to sentences that we are not in a position to assert*. For instance, the supervaluationist presumably thinks that the rules (T-Introd) and (T-Elim) have application to such sentences as

A_1:   Thales' maternal grandmother ate bread the day she died

and

A_2:   Thales' maternal grandmother did not eat bread the day she died:

these rules state an important relation between A_1 and True(⟨A_1⟩), and between A_2 and True(⟨A_2⟩). But on most notions of assertibility neither A_1 nor A_2 is assertible, given the unavailability of the evidence. And even on a highly idealized notion which allows bringing in unavailable evidence, they can't *both* be assertible. So not only is the significance of the rules broader than preserving theoremhood or validity, it is also broader than preserving assertibility.

So it seems hard to explain the significance of rules like (T-Introd) and (T-Elim) other than by saying that they are valid. But can more be said about this notion of weak validity? I explained it above in model-theoretic terms: preservation of value 1 in every model. But I think that this is merely the semantic counterpart of something more fundamental. A proper explanation requires a discussion of conditional assertion.

It's well known that in empirical contexts, conditional assertion is quite different from assertion of the corresponding (material) conditional. Conditional assertion of 'I will be elected President in 2008' given the premise 'I will run for President in 2008' is improper because the conditional probability of the former given the latter is extraordinarily low, whereas assertion of the material conditional 'I will run → I will be elected' is proper (or would be if pragmatic factors could be ignored) since it follows from 'I will not run'. Now, this difference between conditional assertion and assertion of the conditional disappears in a logical context where proper assertion requires logical certainty: if we're logically certain of a material conditional, then we're entitled by logic to make the conditional assertion.[5] For this reason, the notion of conditional assertion tends to disappear in logical contexts.

But it is needed, I think, to represent supervaluationist approaches to the paradoxes. Such approaches, like all classical approaches, must deny that belief in the Tarski conditionals

$$\text{True}(\langle A \rangle) \to A$$

and

$$A \to \text{True}(\langle A \rangle)$$

is legitimate for all A: these are not *valid assertions of conditionals*. But the key idea of supervaluationism, it seems to me—and it will be taken over by revision theories as well—is that nonetheless it is *valid to conditionally assert A* on the basis of $\text{True}(\langle A \rangle)$, or conversely: these conditional assertions are justified by logic alone. The fundamental point to be made about the weak validity of inferences (i.e. the relation of weak implication between premises and conclusion) is that it is the validity relation that governs conditional assertion (as opposed to assertion of the conditional). In standard logic these coincide. But according to supervaluationist solutions to the paradoxes, they do not coincide in the case of the truth rules.[6]

10.4. INDETERMINACY AGAIN

A second virtue of the weak reading of 'implies' or 'valid' is that it is helpful in giving the supervaluationist a non-definitional account of indeterminacy. This is important since a definition of indeterminacy will have to either be outside the language (if the language is restricted) or be simply unavailable (if the language is unrestricted).

What is it for a sentence in the language with 'True' (for instance, a Liar sentence or a Truth-Teller sentence, i.e. a sentence asserting its own truth) to be indeterminate? In the case of restricted languages, where the Kripke construction can be used to define truth, we can think of *having value $1/2$* (i.e. failing to have

---

[5] A proper representation of this using conditional probabilities requires that $P(B|A)$ be defined even when $P(A)$ is 0. This is easily done: a crude way is to take $P(B|A)$ to always be 1 when $P(A)$ is 0; a more sophisticated way was developed in Popper 1959, Appendices iv and v, but it still takes $P(B|A)$ to be 1 whenever $\neg A$ is valid. Either way, $P(B|A)$ will turn out 1 whenever the material conditional $A \to B$ is a logical truth.

[6] When indeterminacy is put aside, *valid* conditional assertion coincides with *valid* assertion of the conditional; the assertion of the material conditional "If I run for President I'll win" is not *valid*, though it is empirically proper. What the Presidency example shows is that (even aside from indeterminacy), *empirically proper* assertion of the conditional is *weaker than* empirically proper conditional assertion. By contrast, when indeterminacy is take into account, *valid* assertion of the conditional is *stronger than* valid conditional assertion; and *empirically proper* assertion of the conditional is then *in some ways weaker and in some ways stronger than* empirically proper conditional assertion.

value 1 or value 0) as *being indeterminate*. But it's important to realize that this doesn't give a definition of indeterminacy within the language, but only in a more extensive metalanguage. In the case of languages with unrestricted quantifiers—which presumably is the case we're really interested in—we don't have a definition of indeterminacy at all because we have no model-independent definition of having value $1/2$. If we define a specific model M for the ground language, the construction shows how to define 'has value $1/2$ in the construction based on M', but this isn't the same as indeterminacy. For instance, consider the sentences

$Q \lor$ There are no inaccessible cardinals

and

$Q \lor$ There are inaccessible cardinals.

Assuming that there are inaccessible cardinals, the first should be indeterminate and the second not (it's determinately true); but in a model with no inaccessible cardinals, it is the second rather than the first that gets value $1/2$. And in any definable model M, there are bound to be such divergences between having value $1/2$ in M and being indeterminate, by Tarski's Theorem. Indeterminacy for unrestricted languages resists definition.

For these reasons, the prospects for *defining* 'indeterminate' in a useful way is unpromising. Is there another way of clarifying what indeterminacy amounts to? I think there is. For a supervaluationist to regard a sentence A as indeterminate is for there to be sentences C for which he rejects the specific meta-inference

A implies C

$\neg A$ implies C

so

C.

Or more generally, it's for there to be Γ and C for which he rejects the specific meta-inference

Γ and A together imply C

Γ and $\neg A$ together imply C

so

Γ implies C.

(By rejecting the *specific* meta-inference I mean: rejecting it for those Γ, A and C.) Rejecting specific meta-inferences of these sorts plays something of the role for the supervaluationist that rejecting specific instances of excluded middle plays for the paracomplete theorist. So this way of looking at what the supervaluationist is doing gives a bit of meat to declarations of indeterminacy: those declarations are simply ways of flagging the rejection of instances of a quasi-logical classical meta-rule.[7] *It is essential for this that 'implies' be used in the weak sense*, for in the strong sense to be introduced in Section 10.6, the classical meta-rules hold without exception.

10.5. BOOLEAN-VALUED SEMANTICS

Supervaluationism is a special case of Boolean-valued semantics. That this is so is nothing new, but thinking of it this way illuminates the viewpoint of the previous section, and will provide a useful point of comparison for the paracomplete theories to be discussed in detail in Parts III and IV.

Boolean algebras are a special case of deMorgan algebras; that more general notion will be of importance in Part III, so to avoid repetition I will explain the more general notion first.

A deMorgan algebra consists of a set V with certain distinguished objects 1 and 0, a 1-place operation $*$ (think 'not'), and two 2-place operations $\sqcap$ and $\sqcup$ (think 'and' and 'or'). They are assumed to obey the following set of laws. (Many of the duals in the right-hand column are redundant, but I think the symmetric presentation is helpful.)

$$x \sqcap 0 = 0 \qquad\qquad x \sqcup 1 = 1$$
$$x \sqcap 1 = x \qquad\qquad x \sqcup 0 = x$$
$$x \sqcap x = x \qquad\qquad x \sqcup x = x$$
$$x \sqcap y = y \sqcap x \qquad\qquad x \sqcup y = y \sqcup x$$
$$x \sqcap (y \sqcap z) = (x \sqcap y) \sqcap z \qquad\qquad x \sqcup (y \sqcup z) = (x \sqcup y) \sqcup z$$
$$x \sqcap (x \sqcup y) = x \qquad\qquad x \sqcup (x \sqcap y) = x$$
$$x \sqcap (y \sqcup z) = (x \sqcap y) \sqcup (x \sqcap z) \qquad\qquad x \sqcup (y \sqcap z) = (x \sqcup y) \sqcap (x \sqcup z)$$
$$0 \neq 1$$
$$x^{**} = x$$
$$0^* = 1 \qquad\qquad 1^* = 0$$
$$(x \sqcap y)^* = x^* \sqcup y^* \qquad\qquad (x \sqcup y)^* = x^* \sqcap y^*$$

A Boolean algebra is a deMorgan algebra with the additional laws

$$x \sqcap x^* = 0 \qquad\qquad x \sqcup x^* = 1.$$

In any deMorgan algebra, and hence in any Boolean algebra, we can define a partial ordering $\leq$: $x \leq y$ is defined as $x \sqcap y = x$, or equivalently as $x \sqcup y = y$. This is provably a partial order, with the property that $x \sqcup y$ is the least upper bound of x and y in the order and $x \sqcap y$ the greatest lower bound; 1 is the

---

[7] If we used the multiple-consequence rules of the sequent calculus, this could be viewed as the rejection of the ground-level rule $A \vee B \vDash A, B$.

maximum, 0 the minimum. * is an order-reversing operation, i.e. x ≤ y entails (indeed, is equivalent to) y* ≤ x*. One can indeed state the laws of deMorgan algebras and Boolean algebras using ≤ and * as the primitives, defining ⊔, ⊓, 1 and 0 from ≤ alone. (Mathematicians then call them deMorgan or Boolean *lattices* rather than *algebras*, but this is a subtlety we needn't concern ourselves with: they are essentially the same objects.) In the Boolean case, * is definable from ≤ also.

The simplest deMorgan algebra is the two-membered set {0, 1}, with 0 < 1 (where x < y means x ≤ y ∧ ¬(y ≤ x)); * flips 0 and 1. This is a Boolean algebra. The linearly ordered sets {0, ½, 1} and [0,1] used in Strong Kleene semantics and continuum-valued semantics respectively are also deMorgan algebras, when they are ordered in the usual way and with x* defined as 1 − x. These are *not* Boolean, and indeed the two-valued Boolean algebra is the only Boolean algebra (up to isomorphism) that is linearly ordered. The simplest deMorgan algebras that are not linearly ordered have four members, and there are two of them: both can be pictured by the partial ordering shown in Diagram 10.1.

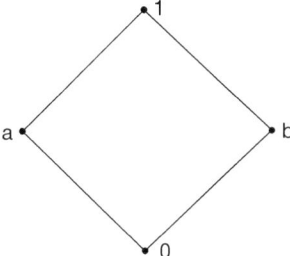

Diagram 10.1.

It is clear from this picture that in both algebras, * must flip 1 and 0. But in one (the Dunn algebra) a* = a and b* = b, so that a ⊔ a* is just a and b ⊔ b* is b, and the algebra is non-Boolean. In the other, a* = b and b* = a, so a ⊔ a* and b ⊔ b* are 1 and the algebra is Boolean. In both cases, a and b are elements smaller than 1 whose "join" a ⊔ b is 1. More generally, no Boolean algebra except the two-valued one has the property that 1 can't be reached by joins of smaller elements; whereas lots of deMorgan algebras have this property. This fact is intimately related to issues about reasoning by cases, for if 1 is taken to be the sole "designated value", using the algebra in a semantics will allow a disjunction to have designated value when neither disjunct does.[8]

---

[8] We could avoid this by taking one of the two values a and b (say b) to be an additional designated value. In the Boolean case this is pointless: there is then no essential difference between b and 1 or between a and 0, so we may as well just use the algebra with the two values {1, b} and

Any deMorgan algebra can be used as a basis for a semantics for a sentential language without a conditional, or for which a conditional can be defined from the other operations; and for a quantificational language too, at least if it is suitably enriched. The basic idea, which generalizes what we did in Strong Kleene semantics and in the $\rightarrow$-free portion of continuum-valued semantics, is that relative to each assignment function we assign a value in the algebra V to each atomic formula; we then let $|\neg A|_s$ be $|A|_s^*$, $|A \wedge B|_s$ be $|A|_s \sqcap |B|_s$, and so forth. The treatment of the quantifiers needs to be analogous: $|\forall x A|_s$ needs to be the greatest lower bound of all the $|A|_{s(x/o)}$. This requires that there be such a greatest lower bound, and when V is infinite, we may need to enrich it to provide a sufficient supply of greatest lower bounds and least upper bounds. There are well-known ways of doing this.[9]

A nice feature of the Boolean case is that if we define a conditional $\rightarrow$ from $\neg$ and $\vee$ in the usual way, we get the highly desirable result

(G) $\qquad |A \rightarrow B|$ is 1 if and only if $|A| \leq |B|$.

This is not so in the case of non-Boolean deMorgan algebras, which is precisely why Lukasiewicz wanted to supplement the deMorgan algebra on [0,1] with a new operator that can be assigned to the conditional to yield (G). (This is also why I will do the same in Part III in connection with a different non-Boolean deMorgan algebra.)

Now let's focus on the relevance of the Boolean case to supervaluational semantics. The key fact is that for any nonempty set X, the set of all subsets of X is a Boolean algebra (of a particularly simple kind): $\sqcap$ and $\sqcup$ are union and intersection; * is complementation; $\leq$ is the subset relation. So if we've defined a set W of classical valuations for a language (each one a legitimate joint choice of candidate extensions of the terms in the language), then the set of all subsets of W is a Boolean algebra (indeed, one that's complete in the sense that greatest lower bounds and least upper bounds exist for arbitrary sets, even infinite ones). In this algebra, the ordering is just the subset relation, and the distinguished elements 1 and 0 are, respectively, the entire set W and the empty set $\emptyset$. Super-truth (truth in all legitimate valuations) is just having the value 1; super-falsehood (falsehood in all legitimate valuations) is having value 0.

One of the virtues of this is that it fine-grains the property of being neither super-true nor super-false: before, we regarded all such sentences as having the same value $^1/_2$ (meaning just: not 1 or 0), but now we've divided this up into

{0, a}. (In the case of theories based on the Dunn algebra the move is significant: b differs essentially from 1 in that b* is designated whereas 1* isn't.)

[9] The usual ways produce *completions of* a given algebra, that is, enrichments of the algebra in which *every* set of elements has a least upper bound. That's a bit of overkill, we really only need *sufficiently many* least upper bounds.

many distinct values. In particular, Q and $\neg Q$ are now regarded as having distinct values, say q and q*. (In the fixed point semantics of Section 10.1, the members of the Boolean algebra are the subsets of $\{Y \mid X \subseteq Y \subseteq X^{neg}\}$, where X is the chosen fixed point; q and q* are $\{Y \mid X \subseteq Y \subseteq X^{neg} \wedge Q \notin Y\}$ and $\{Y \mid X \subseteq Y \subseteq X^{neg} \wedge Q \in Y\}$ respectively.) This allows us to "explain" how $Q \vee \neg Q$ can have value 1 even when $Q \vee Q$ doesn't: q* differs from q, which allows $q \sqcup q*$ to differ from $q \sqcup q$. The point is that we've restored "value-functionality", by fine-graining the value $1/2$.

It's common to distinguish supervaluational approaches to vagueness from degree-theoretic approaches, but this is misleading: supervaluational approaches are in effect degree-theoretic, they use Boolean degrees. The genuine distinction that underlies this way of talking is that standard degree-theoretic approaches use degrees *in which the top value 1 can't be reached by joins*: $a \sqcup b = 1$ implies $a = 1 \vee b = 1$. That, as we've seen, is never true in the supervaluational case (barring the degenerate case where there's only one legitimate valuation to supervaluate over), and this is what marks the big difference between supervaluationism and most other degree-theoretic approaches. It is, for instance, what allows the supervaluationist to give instances of excluded middle value 1 even when the component sentence has value other than 1 or 0.

10.6. STRONG VALIDITY, AND WEAK VALIDITY REVISITED

Given a Boolean-valued semantics (or more generally, a deMorgan-valued one), how are we to use it to give an extensionally correct account of what it is for an inference to be valid (that is, for the premises to jointly imply the conclusion)?

In the case of validity of sentences (or of 0-premise inferences), there's a pretty obvious choice: a sentence is valid if the semantics requires it to have value 1. The choice isn't totally inevitable: we could consider a larger set of "designated values" (values that count as "sufficiently good"); and occasionally (especially in dialetheic theories) there is reason to contemplate this generalization, as hinted in note 8. (The set of designated values will always be a filter, i.e. upwards closed and closed under $\sqcap$.) Usually, though, I will stick to the case where 1 is the sole designated value.

The question of what it is for an *inference* to be valid according to the semantics presents more choice. One obvious idea, which coincides with what I've called *weak validity*, is that an inference is valid (according to the semantics) iff the premises can't get a designated value without the conclusion getting a designated value. Or to stick to the case where 1 is the sole designated value: it's weakly valid if the premises can't get value 1 without the conclusion getting value 1. As I've argued, this is simply a semantic rendering of the intuitive idea of *validity of conditional assertion*: the validity of asserting the conclusion on the assumption of the premises.[10]

But there is also a notion of *strong validity*, in which the semantics calls an inference valid iff the conclusion must have a value that is at least the greatest lower bound of the values of the premises. (The greatest lower bound of the empty set is 1, so this coincides with weak validity in the case of 0-premise inferences, i.e. of sentences.) So strong validity says that the inference can't lead to lower or incomparable values, whereas weak validity says it can never lower the value from 1 (or from out of the set of designated values).

Strong validity is the idea of validity which in the case of the Strong Kleene semantics leads to the relatively weak logic S_3, as opposed to the logic K_3 that I have recommended. (By employing a stronger notion of validity you get a weaker logic, i.e. one where fewer inferences are valid.) In the case of supervaluational theories the distinction between strong and weak is more dramatic. I emphasized in Section 10.2 that the truth rules (T-Introd), (¬T-Introd), (T-Elim) and (¬T-Elim) are weakly valid in simple supervaluationism (and in most other supervaluation theories as well). For instance, if A is any sentence that has value 1 in the model, True($\langle A \rangle$) also has value 1. But none of these rules is strongly valid. For instance, if q is the value of the liar sentence Q, then True($\langle Q \rangle$) has value q*, and it is not the case that q ≤ q* nor that q* ≤ q; so applying either (T-Introd) or (T-Elim) to Q leads to an incomparable value, and the inferences are not strongly valid in the semantics. (The lack of strong validity would become invisible if we threw away the fine-graining and simply regarded Q and True($\langle Q \rangle$) as having value ½; it is essential that we not do so.)

Strong validity is an especially natural idea in the case of a semantics in which the conditional has the property (G) of the previous section, as the Boolean semantics for classical logic does. For in that case, strong validity is the semantic rendering of the intuitive idea of *validity of assertion of the conditional*. For this reason, strong validity keeps the familiar connection between validity and the conditional: the inference from A to B is strongly valid if and only if the sentence $A \to B$ is (strongly or weakly) valid. More generally

$$\Gamma, A \vDash_{str} B \text{ if and only if } \Gamma \vDash_{str} A \to B.$$

With weak validity, as we've seen, only the right to left direction of these hold in general. (But weak validity coincides with strong validity in many contexts,

---

[10] More fully: the model theoretic notion of preserving value 1 in all allowable models can be argued to be extensionally equivalent to the intuitive notion of validity of conditional assertion, by a Kreisel squeezing argument of the sort considered in Section 2.3. (This requires a bit of care about what we count as an allowable model. For instance, it is a presupposition of talk of truth that we have bearers of truth, so we need to restrict to models that contain bearers that meet our specifications. If, as I have been and will continue to be assuming, the bearers are sentences, this involves standard models (ω-models) of syntax.)

e.g. when no terms such as 'True' that need to be treated by supervaluations are involved in the argument.)

It would be a bit of a drag to always have to say 'weakly' or 'strongly'. I choose to use the unadorned term 'valid' for *weakly valid*. Two important advantages of this choice over the opposite one were given in Sections 10.3 and 10.4: it gives appropriate status to the truth rules, and it aids in the explanation of indeterminacy. A third advantage is that one can define strong validity in terms of weak validity, but not conversely, using the conditional and conjunction: we define

(S$_1$) $\quad\quad\quad A_1, \ldots, A_n \vDash_{str} B$ if and only if $\vDash A_1 \wedge \ldots \wedge A_n \to B$,

where $\vDash$ is weak validity. (This requires there to be a reasonable conditional in the language, so it can't be used in the Kleene semantics;[11] it can, though, in continuum-valued semantics, and the other forms of paracomplete semantics to be considered in Part III.)[12]

A limitation of (S$_1$) is that it defines strong validity only for inferences with finitely many premises. One possible way around this would be to simply define $\Gamma \vDash_{str} B$ to mean that there is a finite subset Γ_0 of Γ such that $\Gamma_0 \vDash_{str} B$; but this might not accord with the intended notion, because the intended notion might not be compact. Another way to get around it would be to use a truth predicate to finitely axiomatize Γ: take $\Gamma \vDash_{str} B$ to mean $\vDash \forall x(x \in \Gamma \to \text{True}(x)) \to B$; or, to make it look more symmetrical,

(S$_2$) $\quad\quad\quad \vDash \forall x(x \in \Gamma \to \text{True}(x)) \to \text{True}(\langle B \rangle)$.

This would conform well with the intended notion if the truth predicate behaved reasonably, e.g. if the antecedent behaved as an infinite conjunction of the premises; unfortunately, this isn't so in the broadly classical theories now under consideration. (In them, (S$_2$) isn't equivalent to (S$_1$) when Γ is finite.) This difficulty will be overcome in a paracomplete context in which we have a nice truth predicate: in that context, we can define a general notion of strong validity from weak validity by (S$_2$). For the present, let us avoid this issue by speaking of strong validity only for inferences with finitely many premises, and using (S$_1$).

Getting back to weak validity in Boolean-valued semantics, we clearly have that modus ponens is valid: $A, A \to B \vDash B$. Because of this, we clearly have

If $\Gamma \vDash A \to B$ then $\Gamma, A \vDash B$.

---

[11] But in Kleene semantics there is an alternative explication: $A_1, \ldots, A_n \vDash_{str} B$ if and only if both $A_1, \ldots, A_n \vDash B$ and $\neg B \vDash \neg(A_1 \wedge \ldots \wedge A_n)$. (In typical Boolean or deMorgan algebras this yields a relation intermediate between weak validity and strong validity; it is a special feature of Kleene semantics that it coincides with strong.)

[12] For it to yield the right results in contexts where more values than 1 are designated, (G) needs to be generalized: 'is 1' must be replaced by 'is designated'.

But as we've seen, the converse can't hold in general. For instance, we have the weak validity

$$A \vDash \text{True}(\langle A \rangle)$$

(whatever the A), but we better *not* have

$$\vDash A \to \text{True}(\langle A \rangle);$$

that would say that the (T-IN) axiom is valid, and thus lead (given the classical logic) to the glut theories considered in Chapter 8, that violate the Second Incoherence principle. The classical meta-rule of conditional proof ($\to$-Introduction) thus cannot apply unrestrictedly. (It will hold in special cases: we'll be able to say that if B is proved from Γ and A *in ways that don't use certain rules*, then $A \to B$ can be inferred from Γ.) That the principle of conditional proof requires restriction here should be quite unsurprising, given that proofs are required to preserve only designatedness. More generally, the restriction arises from the fact that weak validity is validity of conditional assertion, which is weaker than validity of the corresponding conditional.

If we do view the supervaluationist implication relation as weak implication, it may not be clear whether supervaluationist views should be regarded as accepting classical logic. On the one hand, they do accept all the ground-level inferences of classical logic (not just the theorems). On the other hand, they reject quite central meta-rules such as reasoning by cases and *reductio*. Let's not fight about the word 'classical': the view in question is at least *broadly* classical, even if not *narrowly* so. From now on 'classical' will mean 'broadly classical' (though I will sometimes add 'broadly' for emphasis); when I mean narrowly classical I will say so. When I want to speak of the broadly classical to the exclusion of the narrowly classical I will say 'weakly classical'.

10.7. YOGI BERRA'S ADVICE AND IGNORANCE INTERPRETATIONS

By virtue of accepting classical logic, the supervaluationist accepts

(D)   Either True($\langle Q \rangle$) but not Q, or Q but not True($\langle Q \rangle$).

At the same time, he tells us not to accept either disjunct, for that would lead to absurdity! Earlier I mentioned Yogi Berra's remark, "If you come to a fork in the road, take it"; the supervaluationist rejects his advice. Can we make sense of this? Most of us think that if you've accepted a disjunction each of whose disjuncts is absurd, you're already committed to an absurdity.

Of course, Yogi's advice as stated can't be correct in general: there's sometimes good reason not to pick either fork, e.g. if you don't know the dangers ahead. The Corrected Berra Principle is: if you come to a fork in the road, and know that neither of the two roads leading from the fork will take you to your desired destination, go back and try a different route! In application to the present context, that means: avoid accepting disjunction (D) in the first place, as the paracomplete theorist does. The supervaluationist advises that you instead stay at the fork and convince yourself that it was your destination.

In Section 10.2 I put this by saying that the supervaluationist restricts the standard meta-rule of ∨-elimination (also called the Rule of Reasoning by Cases):

(∨-Elim) For any sentences x, y and z, if x implies z and y implies z then the disjunction of x and y implies z.

(The relevant case here is when z is an absurdity such as '0 = 1'.) The supervaluationist treatment of the paradoxes allows that the rule might be acceptable when restricted to sentences x and y that don't involve 'True' or related terms; but it can't hold unrestrictedly.

The idea takes some getting used to,[13] but Boolean-valued model theory gives us a good formal grip on how it is supposed to work. In the Boolean-valued representation, what it is for a sentence to imply an absurdity (in the weak sense of 'implies' here at issue) is for it to get a value less than 1 in every Boolean-valued model. So if Q is a non-contingent Liar sentence, it is absurd in this sense, and so is its negation; and yet the disjunction of these has value 1.

In saying that the supervaluationist rejects (∨-Elim) as formulated above, I'm interpreting (∨-Elim) in accordance with the policy of Section 10.6: I'm using 'implies' in the weak sense involving validity of conditional assertion. The supervaluationist doesn't reject the analog of (∨-Elim) for *strong* implication: that would be the principle whose instances are

$$\text{If } X \to Z \text{ and } Y \to Z \text{ are valid then so is } X \vee Y \to Z,$$

which clearly comes out acceptable according to the rules for ∨ and → in Boolean-valued models. One might argue, I suppose, that that's all one ought to mean by ∨-Elim, but I don't think that can be right: ∨-Elim is supposed to allow reasoning by cases, as when one uses the truth rules to get a contradiction from Q and also to get a contradiction from $\neg Q$, and concludes that one can get a contradiction from $Q \vee \neg Q$. Getting contradictions from Q and from $\neg Q$ does not require establishing $Q \to \bot$ and $\neg Q \to \bot$, since we've already seen that the meta-rule of →-Introduction fails in Boolean-valued semantics; indeed, establishing $Q \to \bot$ and $\neg Q \to \bot$ in this classical context would be equivalent to establishing $\neg Q$ and Q, which is clearly impossible.

I believe this is a sympathetic and accurate way to portray the supervaluationist approach to the paradoxes; indeed, the emphasis it puts on restricting ∨-Elim in the presence of indeterminacy may partially answer the skeptical questions raised in the previous chapter about the significance of classical treatments of

---

[13] As does the taste of gasoline.

indeterminacy. But I can imagine a possible protest: that we ought to understand the supervaluationist's point as epistemological or pragmatic, and that once we do so we'll see that the suggestion that it involves abandoning the classical rule of ∨-Elimination is misleading at best.

The basic idea behind this protest would be that we ought to interpret our unwillingness to commit to either of the disjuncts of (D) as epistemological or pragmatic. Here's a first attempt:

> Look, the disjuncts of (D) aren't exactly *absurd*; after all, we've already seen that there are classical gap theories that accept the second disjunct and classical glut theories that accept the first, and these are consistent in first order logic even if they violate common assumptions about truth. So why not just avoid commitment to which is correct about the status of the Liar?

That is a perfectly intelligible view; even, arguably, a rational view. But if that were all the supervaluationist were saying it would be a huge disappointment: it's hardly news that if we have two highly unattractive theories we can remain agnostic between them, but doing so doesn't count as a third theory.

A second way to develop an ignorance interpretation of supervaluationism would be to add to the first a crucial element: that even if the gap theories and glut theories aren't exactly absurd, still *accepting* either of those theories would be absurd. But that seems a very odd view: if you know that one of them is correct, what can be absurd about picking one and learning to live with it? Perhaps the view is that asserting the correct one, whichever it is, would lead to a pragmatic oddity: accepting True($\langle Q \rangle$) while rejecting Q or the other way around? But if True($\langle Q \rangle$) but not Q, then it can hardly be absurd to put pragmatics aside and say so; similarly, if Q but not True($\langle Q \rangle$), then it can hardly be absurd to put pragmatics aside and say that. By (D), these are the only two options, so it seems that not only aren't the options themselves absurd, there must be at least one of them that it can't be absurd to accept.

It seems clear that if the supervaluationist has a serious alternative to offer, it must rest on giving some kind of special status to the four truth rules (T-Introd), (T-Elim), (¬T-Introd) and (¬T-Elim). (Or at least to most of them: as we'll see in the next chapter, there are somewhat attractive supervaluationist views that reject the last.) But what is the special status? I've suggested that *these are valid rules of conditional assertion*. (Not valid in first order logic, of course, but in the logic of truth.) And, I argued in Section 10.3, it is hard to see how else to interpret them that respects their apparent status. (To remind you: the proposal that they are mere rules of validity-preservation demotes their status far below what we expect: 'Snow is white' isn't valid, but we expect (T-Introd) to apply to it. And even the proposal that they are rules of correct assertion is inadequate: we expect the rules to apply to sentences that we can have no evidence for, irrespective of whether they are actually true, as the example about Thales' maternal grandmother indicates.) This view leads directly to the claim that $Q \vDash \bot$ and $\neg Q \vDash \bot$ represent valid conditional assertions, which in combination with the classical rejection of $Q \vee \neg Q \vDash \bot$ requires the rejection of ∨-Elimination.

But maybe there's an alternative epistemic construal that does better? What about saying that what the truth rules do is preserve "idealized knowability", where that is something like the property "would be knowable to someone who knew all the ground facts", where the ground facts are those expressible without the use of 'True'? This needn't lead to the rejection of the Boolean-valued picture, for perhaps the Boolean values themselves could be interpreted epistemically, in a way that allowed having value 1 to coincide with idealized knowability. Then the problem with the non-contingent Liar would be that whatever the ground facts, it couldn't be known; and the problem with the contingent one would be that given the actual ground facts, it couldn't be known. A Liar sentence would "lead to absurdity" only in the sense that *were we to assume we knew it* we could use the truth rules to derive that we knew a contradiction, which would be absurd. In general, "weak implication" would just be preservation of idealized knowability; and since classical logic doesn't concern itself with knowability, giving up (∨-Elim) on this interpretation wouldn't be giving up anything central to classical logic.

Could this be worked into a coherent position? Possibly—though getting the concept of idealized knowability right would require some delicacy. But it seems to me that it would make supervaluationism far less interesting than it seemed to be. Indeed, I'm not clear that we would have advanced all that far beyond the first epistemic interpretation: supervaluationism wouldn't be an alternative to the gap theory or the glut theory, it would only be an alternative to knowable gaps or knowable gluts; gap theories and glut theories would be speculations about the unknowable, but one of them might nonetheless be correct. It seems to me far more in the spirit of supervaluationism to interpret the truth rules as validities of conditional assertion rather than in terms of idealized knowability. In that case, it does indeed give up the classical meta-rule of ∨-Elimination and hence rejects the Corrected Berra Principle (*aka* the Third Incoherence Principle).

11

A Survey of Supervaluational and Revision-Rule Theories

I have two basic worries about the Kripke supervaluational theory that was introduced in the previous chapter:

(I) The theory is exceptionally weak, i.e. it can't prove laws we'd expect;

(II) The theory wouldn't allow the notion of truth to serve the purposes for which we need it, e.g. it wouldn't work as a device of generalization.

(Actually I have another worry: I just find the rejection of the Third Incoherence Principle violates my sense of what disjunction is all about. But there's no point engaging in a contest of incredulous stares.)

I will explain the first of these worries in this chapter, and then go on to consider some other theories (both subtler supervaluational theories and revision-rule theories) which improve upon it in this respect. It will turn out, though, that some of these strengthenings raise a third (or fourth) worry: they make the theory imply *prima facie* unpleasant things about itself. That is the topic of Chapter 12. The more important issue of (II) is the topic of Chapter 13.

11.1. SIMPLE SUPERVALUATIONISM IS VERY WEAK

Here are three laws we might expect in a theory of truth based on classical logic:

(1) For any sentence x, the double negation of x is true if and only if x is true;

(2) For any sentences x and y, their conjunction is true if and only if x and y themselves are both true;

(3) Modus ponens preserves truth: if a conditional and its antecedent are both true then the consequent is true.

Perhaps I should add a dual of (3):

(4) Modus ponens preserves non-falsity: if neither a conditional nor its antecedent is false, then its consequent isn't false.

But the simple supervaluationism of the previous chapter doesn't validate any of these laws. Indeed, it doesn't validate either direction of the biconditionals in (1) and (2); e.g. it doesn't even validate

(2_w) If a conjunction is true then both its conjuncts are true.

The problem isn't in passing from the instances to the generalizations; rather, the problem is with some of the instances. In the model theory, (1)–(4) and (2_w) each have instances that do not have value 1.

Why is this? Consider a simple instance of (2_w):

$$\text{True}(\langle Q \wedge Q \rangle) \to \text{True}(\langle Q \rangle) \wedge \text{True}(\langle Q \rangle);$$

or equivalently,

(?) $$\text{True}(\langle Q \wedge Q \rangle) \to \text{True}(\langle Q \rangle).$$

It's easy to see that this is not in any fixed point of the simple supervaluational theory. For a sentence A to be in a fixed point X, it must have value 1 in that fixed point, which requires this:

For every Y for which $X \subseteq Y \subseteq U - X^{\text{neg}}$, A is true relative to Y (i.e. comes out true in the classical extension of the ground model in which Y is taken as the extension of 'True').

But 'True($\langle Q \wedge Q \rangle$) → True($\langle Q \rangle$)' is true relative to Y if and only if either 'True($\langle Q \wedge Q \rangle$)' is not true relative to Y or 'True($\langle Q \rangle$)' is true relative to Y; that is, if either $Q \wedge Q \notin Y$ or $Q \in Y$. So for (?) to have value 1 in the fixed point X, it would be required that

For every Y for which $X \subseteq Y \subseteq U - X^{\text{neg}}$, either $Q \wedge Q \notin Y$ or $Q \in Y$.

But that can't be true! Let Y be $X \cup \{Q \wedge Q\}$. $\neg(Q \wedge Q)$ is obviously not in X (if it were, $\neg Q$ would have to be since fixed points are closed under consequence, but we've seen that it isn't); so $Q \wedge Q$ isn't in X^{neg}, so it is in $U - X^{\text{neg}}$. So $X \subseteq Y \subseteq U - X^{\text{neg}}$, $Q \wedge Q \in Y$ and $Q \notin Y$.

So we have an instance of (2_w) that isn't in any fixed point of the simple supervaluational theory; and the same idea gives counterinstances to the converse of (2_w), to each direction of (1), to (3) and (4), and to many other laws one might expect to have.

Perhaps we could learn to live with this if we had to; but there's no need, since we can modify simple supervaluationism so as to remove these weaknesses. The idea is obvious: we should restrict the "candidate extensions" Y that we supervaluate over to ones with nice properties. Kripke considers this in his 1975 paper, giving two examples of what these nicer properties might be. In the next section I'll give an initial development of the idea in a general setting, and then specialize.

11.2. GENERAL SUPERVALUATIONAL FIXED POINT THEORIES

What we want to do is to generalize the construction of Section 10.1 by imposing some additional condition Φ on candidate extensions. The basic idea is this:

$|A|_{X,s}$ should be 1 if and only if for every Y for which both $\Phi(Y)$ and $X \subseteq Y \subseteq U - X^{neg}$, A is true relative to Y and s

$|A|_{X,s}$ should be 0 if and only if for every Y for which both $\Phi(Y)$ and $X \subseteq Y \subseteq U - X^{neg}$, A is not true relative to Y and s

$|A|_{X,s}$ should be $\frac{1}{2}$ otherwise.

(Of course this yields the previous case when the condition Φ is vacuous.) However, there is a potential problem: what if none of the Y for which $X \subseteq Y \subseteq U - X^{neg}$ satisfy Φ? In that case, the definition would not assign a unique value to each sentence. We're going to eventually want to restrict ourselves to conditions Φ for which this cannot occur for any X of interest, but in order to get the fixed point construction going it is simplest to allow for such Φ; so let us state the more general supervaluational definition as:

$|A|_{X,s}$ is 1 if and only if there are Y for which both $\Phi(Y)$ and $X \subseteq Y \subseteq U - X^{neg}$, and for each such Y, A is true relative to Y and s

$|A|_{X,s}$ is 0 if and only if there are Y for which both $\Phi(Y)$ and $X \subseteq Y \subseteq U - X^{neg}$, and for each such Y, A is not true relative to Y and s

$|A|_{X,s}$ is $\frac{1}{2}$ there are Y for which both $\Phi(Y)$ and $X \subseteq Y \subseteq U - X^{neg}$, and for some of them A is true relative to Y and s while for others of them A is not true relative to Y and s

$|A|_{X,s}$ has some value @ other than 1, $\frac{1}{2}$ and 0 if there are no Y for which both $\Phi(Y)$ and $X \subseteq Y \subseteq U - X^{neg}$.

With suitable choice of Φ and X the fourth clause will never arise.

Using this, we can now construct the fixed point very much as in Section 10.1, but we need to make a small change to accommodate the value @: we let $X_{\alpha+1}$ be $\{A \mid A \text{ has value 1 or @ relative to } X_\alpha\}$. (And for non-minimal fixed points, we modify the definition of soundness for the starting set X_0, in the obvious way: it is now required that every member of X_0 is true in all classical models Y for which *both* $\Phi(Y)$ *and* $X \subseteq Y \subseteq U - X^{neg}$.) The argument for fixed points then goes through exactly as before. (And it is clear that if Φ_1 entails Φ_2 then the minimal fixed point for Φ_2 is a subset of that for Φ_1.)[1]

However, the generalization allows for some sentences in a fixed point to have value @. Still, it's easy to see that the only way that this can happen is if the fixed point contains every sentence of the language.[2] I'll call this the trivial fixed point. (When dealing with simple supervaluationism I defined 'fixed point' so as to exclude it.) Let's again take *the internal theory of a fixed point* to consist simply of the set of sentences that are in the fixed point. Obviously the internal theory of the trivial fixed point is the inconsistent theory, and is of no interest. (By contrast, the *external* theory of the trivial fixed point—the theory that says that

---

[1] More generally, if X_0 is a suitable starting point for Φ_2 and hence for Φ_1, then the fixed point for Φ_2 generated from X_0 is a subset of the one for Φ_1.

[2] Reason: if A ever gets value @ it must do so first at some successor $\alpha + 1$, but that requires that there be no set Y for which both $\Phi(Y)$ and $X \subseteq Y \subseteq U - X^{neg}$. That in turn requires that every sentence get value @ at $\alpha + 1$ and hence at all later stages; so every sentence will be in the fixed point.

the true sentences are the sentences in the fixed point—is the consistent theory dubbed hyper-dialetheism in Chapter 8.) Conversely, if no sentence ever gets value @, then the internal theory of that fixed point (the set of sentences in the fixed point) is not merely non-trivial, it is classically consistent.[3] And as before, each stage X_α in the construction of the minimal fixed point, and each such stage for $\alpha > 0$ in the construction of any other, is deductively closed in the classical sense (i.e. closed under classical deductive inference).

In an obvious generalization of Section 10.1, we get that if X is a fixed point, then for any sentence A,

(FP) $A \in X$ if and only if for all Y such that $\Phi(Y)$ and $X \subseteq Y \subseteq U - X^{neg}$, A is true in the classical model that assigns Y to 'True' (and is otherwise like the ground model).

(A slight caution is needed about applying standard supervaluationist terminology. Suppose, as in Section 10.1, that we say that the "positive definite extension" of 'True' is the fixed point X, that the "negative definite extension" is X^{neg}, and that the "candidate extensions" are those Y for which $\Phi(Y)$ and $X \subseteq Y \subseteq U - X^{neg}$. Then only if we make the further assumption

(P)   X is the intersection of all Y for which $\Phi(Y)$ and $X \subseteq Y \subseteq U - X^{neg}$

are we able to say that definite truth (being in the positive definite extension of 'True') is just membership in all candidate extensions of 'True'. Nothing rules out the consideration of conditions Φ that don't validate (P), but if we consider them we should be careful not to say that truth in all candidate extensions suffices for definite truth.)

As before, we have the following corollary to (FP), which in turn yields the following Central Result:

Corollary to (FP): If X is a fixed point, then for any sentence B

(I) $\text{True}(\langle B \rangle) \in X$ if and only if for all Y such that $\Phi(Y)$ and $X \subseteq Y \subseteq U - X^{neg}$, $B \in Y$;

(II) $\neg \text{True}(\langle B \rangle) \in X$ if and only if for all Y such that $\Phi(Y)$ and $X \subseteq Y \subseteq U - X^{neg}$, $B \notin Y$.

Central Result: If X is a fixed point, then for any sentence B

(I) if $A \in X$, $\text{True}(\langle A \rangle) \in X$

and

(II) if $\neg A \in X$, $\neg \text{True}(\langle A \rangle) \in X$.

Or to restate the Central Result:

In the internal fixed point theories, the rules (T-Introd) and ($\neg$T-Introd) from Section 10.2 are valid.

---

[3] For if the fixed point X_β is inconsistent then there can be no classical models Y satisfying $X \subseteq Y \subseteq U - X^{neg}$, so $X_{\beta+1}$ contains all sentences, and it is just X_β.

As with the simple supervaluational theory, the "self reference biconditionals" like $Q \leftrightarrow \neg \text{True}(\langle Q \rangle)$ are in any fixed point (they get in at the first stage of the construction). Given this and the Central Result, neither the Liar sentence Q nor its negation can be in any non-trivial fixed point.

Some conditions Φ generate only trivial fixed points, but the following is a useful sufficient condition for non-triviality:

Non-Triviality Lemma: The minimal fixed point of the supervaluational theory based on condition Φ is non-trivial if, for every consistent and deductively closed set of sentences Z not containing Q or $\neg Q$, there is a Y_1 not containing Q and a Y_2 containing Q, each satisfying the condition that $\Phi(Y)$ and $Z \subseteq Y \subseteq U - Z^{\text{neg}}$.

(Proof in footnote 4. The Lemma also holds, and by the same proof, if Q is replaced by a Truth-teller sentence T that asserts its own truth.)[4] This can be used to show the non-triviality of many supervaluational fixed point constructions. For instance, consider the following four candidates for the condition Φ (the first, second and fourth of which are considered by Kripke):

Φ_1: the vacuous condition
Φ_2: the condition that Y must be classically consistent
Φ_3: the condition that Y must be closed under classical deduction
Φ_4: the condition that Y must be maximally consistent.

In all four cases, verifying the sufficient condition of the Non-Triviality Lemma is simple: in all but case Φ_4 we can use Z and the deductive closure of $Z \cup \{Q\}$ as the Y_1 and Y_2, and in case Φ_4 we can use maximal consistent extensions of $Z \cup \{\neg Q\}$ and $Z \cup \{Q\}$.

Let us turn now to the rules (T-Elim) and ($\neg$T-Elim) of Section 10.2; that is, to the converses of (I) and (II) in the Central Result. It turns out that these are not valid for all choices of the condition Φ.

Consider first

(c-I)   If $\text{True}(\langle A \rangle) \in X$, then $A \in X$ (whenever X is a fixed point).

To get a counterexample to this, consider the following (rather bizarre) choice for condition $\Phi(Y)$: $\neg Q \in Y$. This leads to a non-trivial fixed point, because the sufficient condition of the Non-Triviality Lemma is satisfied: e.g. we can take $Z \cup \{\neg Q\}$ for Y_1 and $Z \cup \{Q, \neg Q\}$ for Y_2. But $\text{True}(\langle \neg Q \rangle)$ clearly is in the

---

[4] Proof: If the minimal fixed point is trivial, then there is a smallest α for which either Q or $\neg Q$ is in X_α, and clearly α is a successor $\beta + 1$. X_β is consistent and deductively closed and doesn't contain Q or $\neg Q$, so the proposed sufficient condition guarantees that there is a Y_1 not containing Q and a Y_2 containing Q, each satisfying the condition that $\Phi(Y_i)$ and $X_\beta \subseteq Y_i \subseteq U - X_\beta^{\text{neg}}$. But then $|\text{True}(\langle Q \rangle)|_{X_\beta}$ must be ½, so neither $\text{True}(\langle Q \rangle)$ nor $\neg \text{True}(\langle Q \rangle)$ can be in $X_{\beta+1}$. So since $X_{\beta+1}$ is deductively closed and the self-reference biconditionals are in it, $\neg Q$ and Q can't be in it. Contradiction.

Note that the specific character of the sentence Q comes in only at the end, where the self-reference biconditionals are used; and this would work for the truth-teller T as well.

fixed point; indeed, it already goes in at the first stage of the construction. But $\neg Q$ isn't in any non-trivial fixed point, so we have a counterexample to (c-I).

Consider next

(c-II)   If $\neg \text{True}(\langle A \rangle) \in X$, then $\neg A \in X$ (whenever X is a fixed point).

To get a counterexample to this, consider the following (less bizarre) choice for condition $\Phi(Y)$: $\neg Q \notin Y$. Again, this leads to a non-trivial fixed point, because the sufficient condition of the Non-Triviality Lemma is satisfied: e.g. we can take Z for Y_1 and $Z \cup \{Q\}$ for Y_2. But now $\neg \text{True}(\langle \neg Q \rangle)$ is clearly in the fixed point (indeed, in at the first stage of the construction). But $\neg\neg Q$ isn't, since if it were, Q would be too, and it can't be since the fixed point is non-trivial. We have a counterexample to (c-II).

I would assume that advocates of internal supervaluational theories would want to choose their condition Φ in such a way that at least (c-I), and probably (c-II) as well, is guaranteed for any fixed point X. (The motivation for the Second Incoherence Principle seems to extend to the stronger principle that if one accepts $\text{True}(\langle A \rangle)$ one should accept A, which in the case of fixed point theories amounts to accepting (c-I).) Fortunately, it's easy to see that we do get (c-I) for each condition Φ and corresponding fixed point X for which (P) from earlier in this section holds;[5] this condition is useful for more than justifying standard supervaluationist terminology. And when Φ is any of the conditions I've enumerated, and X any fixed point of it, (P) holds.[6] Also, by a dual argument (c-II) holds whenever the following holds:

(N) $U - X^{\text{neg}}$ is the union of all Y for which $\Phi(Y)$ and $Y \subseteq U - X^{\text{neg}}$;

or equivalently,

X^{neg} is the intersection of all W for which $\Phi(U - W)$ and $X^{\text{neg}} \subseteq W$.

And when Φ is any of the conditions I've enumerated, and X any fixed point of it, (N) holds.[7]

11.3. AVOIDING THE PROBLEMS OF SIMPLE SUPERVALUATIONISM

It turns out that the main weaknesses of the simple supervaluational theory are not overcome by the move from the vacuous condition to Kripke's Φ_2; i.e. by

---

[5] The result is evident from the Corollary to (FP): If $\text{True}(\langle A \rangle)$ is in the fixed point X, then for all Y such that $\Phi(Y)$ and $X \subseteq Y \subseteq U - X^{\text{neg}}$, $A \in Y$; and if (P) holds then X is the intersection of all such Y, so $A \in X$.

[6] If X is a non-trivial fixed point, it itself satisfies Φ_1, Φ_2 and Φ_3; this makes it immediate that (P) and hence (c-I) holds for all non-trivial fixed points of Φ_1, Φ_2 and Φ_3. For Φ_4, X is the intersection of all its maximally consistent extensions that don't include any negations of its members.

[7] If (N) holds for any Φ it must hold for any weaker Φ, so it suffices to establish it for Φ_4. And it holds there since when X is consistent, $U - X^{\text{neg}}$ is the union of the maximally consistent sets that extend X and are disjoint from X^{neg}.

requiring "candidate extensions" to be classically consistent. For instance, the reason that the conditional $\text{True}(\langle Q \wedge Q \rangle) \to \text{True}(\langle Q \rangle)$ was invalid was that there can be candidate extensions that contain $Q \wedge Q$ but don't contain Q; they needn't contain $\neg Q$, so needn't be classically inconsistent. This suggests that the minimal interesting requirement isn't consistency, but closure under classical deductive inference. So from now on I will confine myself to conditions that entail such deductive closure. This leaves only Φ_3 and Φ_4 from the previous list. (One might consider the condition that conjoins consistency with deductive closure, but that yields nothing new: for the only inconsistent deductively closed theory consists of all sentences, and it's already ruled out by the condition $Y \subseteq U - X^{\text{neg}}$. Adding consistency does however produce a notational simplification: $X \subseteq Y$ and Y is consistent entail $Y \subseteq U - X^{\text{neg}}$, so we needn't write $Y \subseteq U - X^{\text{neg}}$ if we require that Y is consistent.) More generally, we have *strong* supervaluational theories entailing Φ_4, and *medium* theories entailing Φ_3 but not Φ_4. *Weak* supervaluational theories that don't even entail Φ_3 will receive little further consideration.

Medium and strong theories have many virtues; in particular, the strong ones overcome all the problems noted for simple supervaluationism in Section 1, and the medium ones all but (4).

- For instance, all medium and strong theories validate claim (3), that modus ponens preserves truth: for in order for

$$\text{True}(\langle A \rangle) \wedge \text{True}(\langle A \to B \rangle) \to \text{True}(\langle B \rangle)$$

to get value 1, all that's needed is that in any *deductively closed* Y for which $X \subseteq Y \subseteq U - X^{\text{neg}}$, B is in Y whenever A and $A \to B$ are; and this is trivial. (Strictly, this shows only that we get each instance of the claim that modus ponens preserves truth; but the argument easily extends to show that we get the generalization.)

- All strong theories validate

(4) $\neg\text{True}(\langle \neg A \rangle) \wedge \neg\text{True}(\langle \neg(A \to B) \rangle) \to \neg\text{True}(\langle \neg B \rangle).$

For to validate this, it suffices to restrict to Y such that when $\neg A$ and $\neg(A \to B)$ aren't in Y, $\neg B$ isn't.[8] But if Y satisfies Φ_4 then the first two conditions imply that A and $A \to B$ are in Y; and since Φ_4 guarantees deductive closure and consistency, $\neg B$ can't be in it, as desired.[9]

---

[8] We won't get this in theories based on Φ_3. Consider the example

$$\neg\text{True}(\langle \neg Q \rangle) \wedge \neg\text{True}(\langle \neg(Q \to \bot) \rangle) \to \neg\text{True}(\langle \neg\bot \rangle),$$

where $\bot$ is some false sentence of the ground language. Let X be the minimal fixed point generated by Φ_3, and let Y simply be X. Then (i) $\neg Q \notin Y$; (ii) $\neg(Q \to \bot) \notin Y$ (given that $Q \notin Y$); and (iii) $\neg\bot \in Y$; so the indented sentence is not classically true relative to Y, and hence is not in X.

[9] Might we, instead of Φ_4, use a condition that directly gets (4), i.e. the condition

For every A and B, if $B \in Y^{\text{neg}}$ then either $A \to B \in Y^{\text{neg}}$ or $A \in Y^{\text{neg}}$?

Yes, but in the presence of deductive closure that condition is equivalent to Φ_4. Reason:

Both sorts of supervaluation theory, especially the strong, thus seem a big step up from simple supervaluationism; and perhaps even more of a step up from classical glut theories, which declare that modus ponens *doesn't* preserve truth.

Which classical compositional rules do we get? In both medium and strong supervaluationism we get the full rule for conjunction, and one direction of the rule for disjunction. In the strong theories we also get the other direction,

$$\text{True}(\langle A \vee B \rangle) \rightarrow \text{True}(\langle A \rangle) \vee \text{True}(\langle B \rangle).$$

Similarly for negation: we get

(T-CONSIS) $\qquad\qquad \text{True}(\langle \neg A \rangle) \rightarrow \neg\text{True}(\langle A \rangle)$

just from deductive closure (or even from Φ_2), since no deductively closed set Y satisfying $X \subseteq Y \subseteq U - X^{\text{neg}}$ can contain inconsistent pairs. The converse

(T-COMPL) $\qquad\qquad \neg\text{True}(\langle A \rangle) \rightarrow \text{True}(\langle \neg A \rangle)$

is easy to get from Φ_4. This shows, incidentally, that strong supervaluation theories that validate (T-Elim) also validate ($\neg$T-Elim).

Strong theories are substantially easier to reason in than medium theories. Are there competing advantages to medium theories over strong ones? Presumably only if there is reason to reject (T-COMPL). Gap theorists take the Liar sentence to provide a counterexample to (T-COMPL), but this is based on their view that the Liar sentence isn't true, a view that is inconsistent in internal supervaluational theories. Indeed, in any internal supervaluation theory that accepts the rule ($\neg$T-Elim), it is inconsistent to suppose that there are *any* counterexamples to (T-COMPL): the supposition that $\neg\text{True}(\langle A \rangle) \wedge \neg\text{True}(\langle \neg A \rangle)$ (for some sentence A) leads, by conjunction rules and ($\neg$T-Elim), to the contradiction $\neg A \wedge \neg\neg A$. So it is at first blush hard to see what could motivate choice of medium supervaluationism over strong. (I will however point to a possible reason in the next chapter.)

In this regard, it's worth remarking that it is also possible to consider a kind of dual to medium supervaluational theories. In the same way that medium theories rule out gluts but are "agnostic" about gaps, the dual theories rule out gaps but are "agnostic" about gluts; and they have the full compositional rule for disjunction but restrict the rule that if both conjuncts are true then so is the

---

$A \rightarrow B \in Y^{\text{neg}}$ means $\neg(A \rightarrow B) \in Y$, which in the presence of deductive closure of Y is equivalent to $(A \in Y) \wedge (\neg B \in Y)$, i.e. $(A \in Y) \wedge (B \in Y^{\text{neg}})$. Given this, the condition simplifies to

For every A and B, if $B \in Y^{\text{neg}}$ then either $A \in Y$ or $A \in Y^{\text{neg}}$.

Since there are $B \in Y^{\text{neg}}$, this is then equivalent to

For every A, either $A \in Y$ or $A \in Y^{\text{neg}}$,

i.e. to Φ_4.

conjunction. Basically, such theories arise by replacing Φ_3 by the condition on Y that if Γ classically implies B, then $B \in Y^{\text{neg}}$ only if some member of Γ is in Y^{neg}. However, in order to get this to be well-behaved, we should add into the dual condition the requirement of *a modicum of* deductive closure, namely closure under addition or deletion of double negation. These theories validate claim (4) from Section 11.1, without validating claim (3). It's easy to see that requiring the conjunction of Φ_3 and its dual is equivalent to requiring Φ_4; indeed, this was in effect proved in note 9. So those who prefer weakening Φ_4 might want to think about whether there is a rationale for choosing Φ_3 over its dual. I will not pursue this issue, or say anything more about dual medium theories.

Enough on the compositional rules for sentential connectives; what about the compositional rules for the quantifiers? Here we must face a bit of a disappointment. In any fixed point theory based on a condition that requires deductive closure, we clearly have both

True($\langle \forall xAx \rangle$) → For any name **c** in the language, True($\langle Ac \rangle$)

and

[For some name **c** in the language, True($\langle Ac \rangle$)] → True($\langle \exists xAx \rangle$).

But what about the converses? Obviously we can't expect the converses to hold when not everything in the domain has a name, but we ought to expect it when everything does have a name—or when the quantifiers are restricted to range over domains like the natural numbers where everything has a name. (Really what's at issue here is a principle about satisfaction that can be stated independent of whether everything has a name, but I want to keep the formulation in the simpler terms of truth.) The principles to be discussed, then, are (in the case of the natural numbers)

(U-Inf) $\forall n(\text{True}(\langle An \rangle)) \to \text{True}(\langle \forall nAn \rangle)$

and

(E-Inf) True($\langle \exists nAn \rangle$) → $\exists n(\text{True}(\langle An \rangle))$.

In each case the quantifiers both range over the natural numbers, and **n** is the numeral for n. I'm assuming that the model on which the supervaluation theory is based is an ω-model, so if these principles fail it isn't because of numbers that don't have names, it is because of a failure of truth (or satisfaction) to commute with the quantifiers.

It's obvious that (E-Inf) implies (T-COMPL). (Let $A(1)$ be $\neg A(0)$ and each other $A(\mathbf{n})$ be vacuous). So we can't have (E-Inf) in weak or medium internal supervaluation theories. But in fact

(i) We can't have (E-Inf) even in a strong internal supervaluation theory based on an ω-model

and

(ii) We can't have (U-Inf) in *any* medium or strong internal supervaluation theory based on an ω-model.

(ii) is the key claim. (i) follows, since any instance of (U-Inf) is implied by an instance of (E-Inf) (with $\neg A$ in place of A), using (T-COMPL) and (T-CONSIS).

Observation (ii) is implicit in McGee 1991 (see note 15 below), and is proved using a sentence G which asserts that it isn't "hyper-true", i.e. that for some natural number n, the result of "iterating True n times and applying it to G" isn't true. (Intuitively, the 0th iterate of a sentence A is just A itself, and if the nth iterate is B then the $(n+1)^{st}$ iterate is True($\langle B \rangle$). The notion *is the nth iterate of* can be precisely formulated in the language.)[10] I'll call G "the McGee sentence". To use somewhat sloppy notation that I hope will make the basic idea clear, let $A(n)$ be "True(the nth iterate of G)"; then $\forall n A(n)$ asserts the hyper-truth of G, and hence is equivalent to $\neg G$.

We can now show, in several steps, that no non-trivial fixed point (whose ground model is an ω-model) can contain this instance of (U-Inf). A proof is sketched in a footnote.[11] Halbach and Horsten 2005 recommend giving up ω-consistency to retain (U-Inf), but this strikes me as a very high price to pay for it.

There are other kinds of conditions it might be natural to build into Φ. For instance, since the fixed point X is going to be closed under T-Introduction

---

[10] Let h be a function that maps any sentence A to the corresponding sentence True(<A>), and let the binary function j (from numbers and sentences to sentences) be defined inductively as follows:

$$j(0, x) = x$$
$$j(n+1, x) = h(j(n, x)).$$

Define Hypertrue(x) as $\forall n[x$ is a natural number $\rightarrow$ True(j(n, x))]. Then by Gödel–Tarski self-reference there is a G such that $G \leftrightarrow \neg \text{Hypertrue}(\langle G \rangle)$, and it will be in each fixed point.

[11] First, non-trivial fixed points (based on an ω-model) are clearly ω-consistent—in particular, if $\neg \forall n A(n)$ is in such a fixed point, there must be an n for which $A(\mathbf{n})$ is *not* in it. But the Central Result implies that if G is in a fixed point, each $A(\mathbf{n})$ is in it too, since $A(\mathbf{n})$ is equivalent to the $(n+1)^{st}$ iterate of G; with the previous, this gives that if G is in a non-trivial fixed point, $\neg \forall n A(n)$ can't be in it; but that is equivalent to G, so G can't be in any non-trivial fixed point.

The claim $\neg \text{True}(\langle G \rangle) \rightarrow G$ is equivalent to the logical truth $\neg A(0) \rightarrow \neg \forall n A(n)$, so it's in any fixed point; so for fixed point theories based on a condition entailing Φ_2 or Φ_3, True($\langle \neg G \rangle) \rightarrow G$ is in the fixed points too.

So $\neg G \rightarrow \text{True}(\langle \neg G \rangle)$ can't be in any non-trivial fixed points: for this with with the previous entail G, which isn't in any.

But $\neg G$ is equivalent to $\forall n A(n)$, and so (in theories based on conditions entailing Φ_3) True($\langle \neg G \rangle$) is equivalent to True($\langle \forall n A(n) \rangle$); so

$$\forall n A(n) \rightarrow \text{True}(\langle \forall n A(n) \rangle)$$

isn't in any non-trivial fixed point either, and so certainly $\forall n A(n+1) \rightarrow \text{True}(\langle \forall n A(n) \rangle)$ (equivalently, $(\forall n > 0)A(n) \rightarrow \text{True}(\langle \forall n A(n) \rangle)$) isn't. But $A(n+1)$ is equivalent to True($\langle A(\mathbf{n}) \rangle$), so we have that

$$\forall n \text{True}(\langle A(\mathbf{n}) \rangle) \rightarrow \text{True}(\langle \forall n A(n) \rangle)$$

can't be in any non-trivial fixed point.

(Central Result (i)), maybe the "candidate extensions" Y should also be closed under T-Introduction? But we must be careful: there is a danger of such strengthening guaranteeing that even the minimal fixed point generated by the condition is the trivial fixed point, so that the theory is inconsistent. The next chapter will illuminate this.

11.4. RULE-OF-REVISION THEORIES

An alternative to theories based on supervaluational models is theories based on revision-rule models; these were developed in the early 1980s by Herzberger, Gupta, and Belnap. These too yield "essentially disjunctive" theories, that assert the disjunction

(D) Either True($\langle Q \rangle$) but not Q, or Q but not True($\langle Q \rangle$)

but refuse to assert either disjunct. But they tend to yield somewhat stronger theories than do supervaluational models. I'm going to be fairly brief about them since the theory of them is more complicated than that of supervaluational models and their added strength is not enough to alter the basic picture of the advantages and disadvantages of weakly classical theories.

These theories involve revision sequences, which are transfinite sequences of 2-valued models, with length some limit ordinal. The part of the 2-valued model not involving 'True' is the same throughout the sequence (it is just the given ground model, which as usual is assumed to be an ω-model so that syntax is standard). So the revision sequence is, in effect, just a transfinite sequence of sets Y_α from the domain of the ground model, each Y_α to serve as the extension of 'True' at the αth stage of the revision process. I'll call a sentence 'true relative to Y_α' if it comes out true in the expansion of the classical ground model obtained by assigning Y_α to 'True'.

Revision sequences are governed by a rule that completely determines the member of the sequence at a successor stage from the member at the immediately prior stage, and another rule that *partially* determines the members of the sequence at a limit stage from the members at "recent" prior stages. The rule for successors is

(Suc) $Y_{\alpha+1} = \{A \mid A \text{ is true relative to } Y_\alpha\}$.

The rule for limit ordinals (that are in the domain of the sequence) is

(Lim) $\{A \mid (\exists \beta < \lambda) \forall \delta [\beta \leq \delta < \lambda \to A \in Y_\delta]\} \subseteq$
$Y_\lambda \subseteq \{A \mid (\forall \beta < \lambda) \exists \delta [\beta \leq \delta < \lambda \land A \in Y_\delta]\}$.

In words: a sentence is in Y_λ if it *is included in* Y_δ for all arbitrarily large predecessors δ of λ; it is not in Y_λ if it *is excluded from* Y_δ for all arbitrarily large predecessors δ of λ. If there are arbitrarily large predecessors for which it's included and arbitrarily large predecessors for which it's excluded, the rule doesn't say whether it's in Y_λ.

Note that (Suc) guarantees that the sets that appear at successor stages in a revision sequence are consistent, complete and deductively closed. Not so for limit stages: for instance, it is compatible with (Lim) that a sentence and its negation both be in Y_λ, or that neither be in Y_λ.

Let a sentence A be *stably included in* a revision sequence if A is in every Y_α in that sequence from some point on. (That is: for some β less than the length of the sequence, A is in all Y_α in the sequence for $\alpha \geq \beta$.)

The simple revision theory (Belnap 1982) consists of all sentences stably included in all sufficiently long revision sequences—that is, for which $\exists \gamma$(it is stably included in all revision sequences of length at least γ). It is easy to see that if a sentence is stably included in a revision sequence of length greater than $\sigma(M)$, it is already stably included in the initial segment of length $\sigma(M)$, where $\sigma(M)$ is the initial ordinal of the first cardinal greater than the cardinality of the starting model M. (One can get a better bound with a bit more trouble, but this one will do.) This allows us to simplify: the theory consists of all sentences stably included in all revision sequences of length $\sigma(M)$.

Revision sequences as defined above are *any* transfinite sequences of sets of sentences governed by (Suc) and (Lim). A *restricted revision sequence* may contain, in addition, some sorts of restrictions on what the initial member Y_0 is like, or on what the limit stages are like, or both.[12] In analogy to what we did in the supervaluational fixed point case, let's treat the situation generally, by letting Ψ be any condition you like on revision sequences. Then corresponding to each such Ψ we obtain a Ψ-revision theory:

T_Ψ consists of $\{A \mid \forall f[f$ is of length $\sigma_M \land \Psi(f) \to A$ is stably included in $f]\}$.[13]

(The simple revision theory is of course just the Ψ-revision theory for which the restriction Ψ is vacuous.) Obviously if Ψ_1 entails Ψ_2 then T_{Ψ_2} is a subset of T_{Ψ_1}. There is no danger of the theory being inconsistent except when Ψ precludes the existence of sufficiently long revision sequences satisfying it.

What properties do Ψ-revision theories have? It's easy to see that they are closed under classical deduction and contain the self-reference biconditionals

---

[12] The most prominent examples in the literature are

Herzberger's restriction (Herzberger 1982), where the values at limits are required to be as small as possible (i.e. $Y_\lambda = \{A \mid (\exists \beta < \lambda) \forall \delta [\beta \leq \delta < \lambda \to A \in Y_\delta]\}$), but where there is no restriction on Y_0;

and

Gupta's restriction (Gupta 1982), where for sentences whose membership in Y_λ isn't settled by (Lim) it is required that they be in Y_λ if and only if they were in Y_0.

I think that other restrictions are probably more interesting: e.g. requiring (Y_0 and) the Y_λ to be deductively closed, or deductively closed and complete.

[13] This could be called the "internal" revision rule theory based on Ψ. The "external" theory would be the strongly classical theory that simply defines 'true' as 'is stably included in all revision sequences satisfying Ψ'; that is a gap theory, and of no concern in this chapter.

188   *Classical Approaches*

such as $Q \leftrightarrow \neg\text{True}(\langle Q \rangle)$: for any such deduction or biconditional is in all Y_α for $\alpha > 0$. Nothing new here. One thing that *is* new is the following, which I prove in a footnote:

Theorem: For any Ψ, T_Ψ is closed under all four rules (T-Introd), (T-Elim), ($\neg$T-Introd) and ($\neg$T-Elim).[14]

Recall that in the supervaluational case the two introduction rules always hold, but there are conditions Φ for which one or both of the elimination rules fail.

The simple revision theory has most of the weaknesses of the simple supervaluation theory: for instance, it can't prove that a true conjunction must have true conjuncts, or that modus ponens preserves truth. For instance, a revision sequence for the vacuous Ψ could throw $Q \wedge Q$ into Y_λ for each limit ordinal λ but not throw in Q; this will keep $\text{True}(\langle Q \wedge Q \rangle) \to \text{True}(\langle Q \rangle)$ from being in stage $\lambda + 1$, so this won't be part of the simple revision theory. Similarly if we throw Q, $Q \to \neg Q$ and $\neg Q$ into each limit, we get a revision sequence that prevents the theory from saying that modus ponens preserves truth.

The remedy is analogous to that for supervaluationism: we move to supervaluational theories that require that the limit stages Y_λ be closed under classical deduction. As before, requiring that the limit stages be consistent as well adds nothing, since the only consistent and classically closed theory is the theory that contains everything, which is already ruled out by the right hand inclusion in (LIM).

When the condition Ψ entails that limit stages are closed under classical deduction (*Closure Requirement*), the situation with the compositional rules is as before:

- We get the full compositional rule for conjunction;

---

[14] **Proof:** Note that by (Suc),

(*) $\text{True}(\langle A \rangle) \in Y_{\alpha+1}$ iff $A \in Y_\alpha$,

(**) $\neg B \in Y_{\alpha+1}$ iff $B \notin Y_{\alpha+1}$,

and (their consequence)

(***) $\neg\text{True}(\langle A \rangle) \in Y_{\alpha+1}$ iff $A \notin Y_\alpha$.

(T-Elim): Suppose $\text{True}(\langle A \rangle)$ is stably included in f. Then it is in all sufficiently late stages of f, so certainly in all sufficiently late successor stages of f. So by (*), A is in all sufficiently late stages of f.
(T-Introd): Suppose A is stably included in f. Then by (*), $\text{True}(\langle A \rangle)$ is in all sufficiently late successor stages of f. An easy induction on limit stages (using the left hand inclusion in (Lim)) shows that it must then be in all arbitrarily late limit stages too.
($\neg$ T-Elim): Suppose $\neg\text{True}(\langle A \rangle)$ is stably included in f. Then it is in all sufficiently late stages of f and hence all sufficiently late successor stages of f; so by (***), A is not in any stage after a certain point. So by (**), $\neg A$ is in all arbitrarily late successor stages. An easy induction on limit stages, using the left hand inclusion in (Lim), shows that $\neg A$ must then be in all arbitrarily late limit stages too.
($\neg$ T-Introd): Suppose $\neg A$ is stably included in f. Then by (**), A doesn't appear in any sufficiently late successor stage. An induction on limit stages (using the right hand inclusion of (Lim)) shows that A can't appear in any sufficiently late limit stages either, so by (***) $\neg\text{True}(\langle A \rangle)$ appears in all sufficiently late successor stages, and then by another induction on limits (using left hand inclusion of (Lim)) $\neg\text{True}(\langle A \rangle)$ appears in all sufficiently late limit stages too.

- We get at least one direction of the rule for disjunction; we get the other direction if, but only if, we build into Ψ the *Completeness Requirement*, that limit stages must contain either A or $\neg A$ for each A.
- For negation, we get

(T-CONSIS) $\text{True}(\langle \neg A \rangle) \to \neg \text{True}(\langle A \rangle)$,

but we get the converse only if we have the Completeness Requirement.

So we can introduce the same weak/medium/strong dichotomy as we used with supervaluational theories. *Strong revision theories* (where both Closure and Completeness Requirements are in place) give the full sentential compositional rules. *Medium revision theories* (where Closure but not Completeness is required) give the partial ones mentioned. Weak theories, where not even Closure is required, don't even give those. (There are also *dual medium theories*, which give partial rules for conjunction instead of for disjunction and which give the converse to (T-CONSIS) instead of (T-CONSIS) itself.)

Finally, in neither medium nor strong revision theories can we get the non-obvious direction of the universal quantifier rule (even when everything is assumed to have a name): the argument based on the McGee sentence goes through substantially as before.[15]

From the point of view of the basic shape of the theory, then, there is little difference between the revision theories and the supervaluational theories: the main difference is that revision theories can't deal with the possibility of disallowing the rule ($\neg$T-Elim),[16] whereas supervaluation theories can do so if they desire, by an appropriate choice of Φ.

Even as regards model theory, there is a fundamental similarity between supervaluation and revision theories: both can be viewed as involving Boolean-valued semantics.

- In the case of the supervaluational fixed point theories, we use the Boolean algebra consisting of the set of subsets of $V_1 = \{Y \mid \Phi(Y) \wedge X \subseteq Y \subseteq U - X^{\text{neg}}\}$, where X is a non-trivial fixed point generated by Φ from the underlying ground model. The "semantic values" are subsets of this algebra; and a sentence is regarded as "determinately true" in the model if its value is the maximum, i.e. V_1 itself, and "determinately false" if its value is ∅.
- In the case of the revision theory, we can regard two revision sequences (of length σ_M) as "essentially equivalent" if there is some point (less than σ_M)

---

[15] Indeed, the argument I gave in note 11 was just an application to supervaluationism of a general theorem of McGee's (1991, p. 29), that if T is an ω-consistent classical theory (with a modicum of arithmetic) that is closed under T-Introduction and contains (T-CONSIS) and (the instances of) the truth-preservingness of modus ponens, then T can't contain the rule that for a universal quantification over numbers to be true it suffices that all its instances be true.

[16] Or, for that matter, (T-Elim); I omitted mention of this only because I don't think anyone would want to disallow it.

after which they agree. Let V_2 be the set of equivalence classes of revision sequences under this equivalence relation; then we use the Boolean algebra consisting of the set of subsets of V_2. Here too "semantic values" are subsets of this algebra. And here too, a sentence is regarded as "determinately true" (or "categorically true", as revision theorists prefer to say) in the model if its value is the full V_2, and "determinately false" (or "categorically false") if its value is $\emptyset$.

This isn't to say that the differences of how the Boolean algebra is generated can have no interest. For instance, Gupta and Belnap attach considerable importance to the idea that revision sequences somehow explain the pattern of ordinary reactions to the Liar sentence (Gupta 1982, p. 233): they regard their theory as incorporating some of the contextualist ideas of Burge and others (mentioned early in Chapter 3 and to be looked at further in Sections 14.1 and 14.2), but in a rigorous model-theoretic framework. Perhaps so (though actually I'm not sure I fully understand the claim; see L. Shapiro 2006 for an interesting discussion). But it's worth reiterating yet again that in the case of unrestricted languages, the notions that appear in the model theory won't exactly match any ordinary notion of determinate (or categorical) truth: there will be a divergence between the two even for sentences in the ground language.[17] This fact seems to me to lessen the value of having a model-theory closely tied to the pattern of ordinary reactions to the Liar sentence.

But I leave it to the reader to decide on the respective merits of revision-rule semantics and supervaluational semantics; for my purposes, where what's of primary importance is the theories of truth they generate, they come to very much the same thing.[18]

11.5. SOUNDNESS PROOFS REVISITED

In Chapter 2 I argued that despite what we tell our students, there is no way to prove the soundness of classical logic within classical set theory (even by a rule-circular proof): we can only prove a weak surrogate. This is in large part because we can't even *state* a genuine soundness claim: doing so would require a truth predicate. And a definable truth-predicate, or a stratified truth-predicate, is inadequate for stating the soundness of classical logic, and even less adequate for proving it. With a predicate 'true$_\alpha$' we can *state* that when the premises of a classical argument are true$_\alpha$ then so is the conclusion. This isn't satisfactory as a statement of soundness since it doesn't cover arguments whose premises contain

---

[17] At least, there will be a divergence if the model is definable in the language; and there is no reason to think there are even undefinable models for which there is no divergence. See note 9 of Chapter 3.

[18] Putting aside the added flexibility of supervaluational accounts with respect to ($\neg$T-Elim).

'true$_\beta$' for some $\beta \geq \alpha$. But worse, we can't *prove* it with only stratified truth predicates, since to prove it we would need to consider all ways of getting from the premises to the conclusion, with no bound on the predicates that can appear along the way.

The problem of *stating* the soundness of classical logic is overcome in theories that have a generally applicable truth predicate—that is, in all the theories considered in this part of the book, barring those to be considered in Chapter 14. But what about *proving* it, by the obvious inductive proof? Such a soundness proof for classical logic can be carried out in medium and strong supervaluation and revision theories (in which the truth predicate is allowed in the arithmetical induction axioms), and also in *supervaluation-style* gap theories (such as H and VF, Section 7.2). But it cannot be carried out in any of the other theories we've considered (excluding hyper-dialetheism). This should be evident: what is required for the proof is that the axioms of classical logic are all true and that the rules preserve truth; and it is well-known that modus ponens can be taken to be the sole rule (e.g. Hunter 1971). Theories such as FM deny the truth of some of the classical axioms (e.g. some instances of excluded middle); glut theories (other than hyper-dialetheism) imply that modus ponens is not truth-preserving; and weak supervaluation and weak revision theories fail to imply that modus ponens is truth-preserving. So none of those theories can carry out a soundness proof for classical logic.[19]

How significant is this? The value of such a soundness proof for classical logic can be questioned, on two grounds. The most obvious ground is that, as discussed in Chapter 2, any such proof is "rule-circular", and begs the question against proponents of alternative logics.

But the ground I'd like to emphasize here is that anyone giving such a soundness proof is employing a notion of truth subject to rules which themselves have a claim to logical status. The question of the soundness of classical logic is really just part of the question of the soundness of the overall "logic" employed in the theory, including the "logic of truth". If the theories that allow a proof of the soundness of classical logic don't allow a proof of the soundness of their own logic of truth, it is not so obvious that they have a dramatic advantage over those that don't allow a proof of the soundness of logic narrowly conceived.

We've already seen that gap theories can't allow a proof of the soundness of their logic of truth: indeed, they imply that that logic is not sound (Montague's Theorem). Do the moderate and strong supervaluation and revision theories do better? That is the subject of the next chapter.

---

[19] Supervaluation-style glut theories can prove the "dual soundness" of classical logic: it preserves non-falsity. Strong (and dual-medium) supervaluation and revision theories can prove this too, but the other theories can't.

12

Are Supervaluational and Revision Theories Self-Undermining?

We've seen that one substantial worry about simple supervaluationism is its excessive weakness: it doesn't include such rules as that a true conjunction must have true conjuncts, or that modus ponens must preserve truth. And we've seen that the best supervaluational and revision theories go a long way toward escaping this particular worry.

But there are other substantial worries about supervaluationism. I'll save the most important one for the next chapter. In the present chapter I deal with a less central (but still significant) issue, of what the strengthened theories say about themselves and whether they should be viewed as somehow "self-undermining".

12.1. WHAT DO STRONG SUPERVALUATIONAL AND STRONG REVISION THEORIES SAY ABOUT THEMSELVES?

Classical gap theories, we've seen, declare some of their own axioms untrue. Classical glut theories, we've seen, declare that modus ponens doesn't preserve truth. (Well, this isn't so for hyper-dialetheism, the view that *everything* is true; but hyperdialetheism is too silly to consider.)

Strong supervaluational and revision theories are far from having these problems: they assert all their axioms to be true, and they declare modus ponens and all other inference rules of classical logic to preserve truth. Nonetheless, they do have a feature analogous to the feature of classical glut theories: they declare that of their four central truth rules (T-Introd), (T-Elim), (¬T-Introd) and (¬T-Elim), *none* of them is truth-preserving.

How can this be? I noted in Section 10.1 that we can't possibly cite a specific instance of the application of a rule where a supervaluational or revision theory will imply that the premises are true and the conclusion isn't. For instance, to cite a specific such instance for (T-Introd) would be to cite an A where the theory implies both True($\langle A \rangle$) and ¬True($\langle$True($\langle A \rangle$)$\rangle$). But that would clearly be inconsistent in the theory, since the assertion of True($\langle A \rangle$) in fact licenses True(⟨True(⟨A⟩)⟩); and we know from the models that the theory is not inconsistent.

Still, this doesn't preclude the next worst thing: that we will be able to pick *two* instances of the application of the rule, such that the theory implies that *in at least one of the two instances* the premises are true and the conclusion isn't. The above shows that it would be inconsistent to assert a failure of truth preservation in the first instance, and also inconsistent to assert a failure of truth preservation in the second instance. This might lead one who endorsed the "fallacy" of reasoning by cases to assume that it was inconsistent to assert that *in one case or the other* there was a failure of truth preservation. But according to supervaluation and revision theories, that *is* a fallacy. So there is no obvious bar to the theory asserting the failure of truth-preservation in *one or the other* of two applications of its rules.

And exactly that happens in the strong supervaluational and revision theories. First I pause to state a general lemma and two applications of it.

Lemma: In all *medium or strong* supervaluation or revision theories, if $A \to B$ is a theorem then so is True(⟨A⟩) $\to$ True(⟨B⟩). So if $A \leftrightarrow B$ is a theorem, so is True(⟨A⟩) $\leftrightarrow$ True(⟨B⟩).

(To prove this, simply apply (T-Introd) to the theorem $A \to B$, getting True(⟨$A \to B$⟩); then the truth-preservingness of modus ponens gives True(⟨A⟩) $\to$ True(⟨B⟩). Similarly reversing A and B; so $A \leftrightarrow B \vdash$ True(⟨A⟩) $\leftrightarrow$ True(⟨B⟩).)

Applications: since $Q \leftrightarrow \neg$True(⟨Q⟩) and its contrapositive True(⟨Q⟩) $\leftrightarrow \neg Q$ are theorems in all these theories, we get in particular the following theorems, in any medium or strong theory:

(I) True(⟨Q⟩) $\leftrightarrow$ True(⟨¬True(⟨Q⟩)⟩)

and

(II) True(⟨True(⟨Q⟩)⟩) $\leftrightarrow$ True ⟨¬Q⟩).

If we now specialize to strong theories (where True(⟨¬A⟩) is equivalent to ¬True(⟨A⟩)), we can use either of these to get

(*) $\qquad\qquad$ True(⟨True(⟨Q⟩)⟩) $\leftrightarrow \neg$True(⟨Q⟩).

(Or to put it another way, True(⟨True(⟨Q⟩)⟩) $\leftrightarrow Q$.) And from (*) and the equivalence of its right hand side to Q, we get

(i) $Q \leftrightarrow$ [True(⟨True(⟨Q⟩)⟩) $\land \neg$True(⟨Q⟩)]

and

(ii) $\neg Q \leftrightarrow$ [True(⟨Q⟩) $\land \neg$True (⟨True(⟨Q⟩)⟩)]

Since $Q \lor \neg Q$ is a theorem, this gives us

[True(⟨True(⟨Q⟩)⟩) $\land \neg$True(⟨Q⟩)] $\lor$ [True(⟨Q⟩) $\land \neg$True(⟨True(⟨Q⟩)⟩)].

So we have

First negative result: It is a theorem of any strong supervaluational or revision theory that either (T-Introd) or (T-Elim) fails to preserve truth when applied to the Liar sentence.

Of course the theory can't consistently say *which* rule fails to preserve truth when applied to Q: that would require deciding between Q and $\neg Q$, and the theory is precluded from deciding between those on pain of inconsistency.

It should be clearly noted that (i) and (ii) don't merely say that we can infer a failure of (T-Elim) to preserve truth from the assumption Q, and that we can infer a failure of (T-Introd) to preserve truth from the assumption $\neg Q$. Such weak implication claims wouldn't allow for the first result, since we don't have reasoning by cases in these theories. No, (i) and (ii) involve assertion of conditionals, not merely conditional assertions; they say that the failures of truth preservation are *strongly* implied by Q and by $\neg Q$ respectively.

Let's go a bit further, bringing in the other two rules:

Expanded first result: It is a theorem of any strong supervaluational or revision theory that either (T-Introd) and (¬T-Elim) both fail to preserve truth when applied to the Liar sentence, or else (¬T-Introd) and (T-Elim) both fail to preserve truth when applied to the Liar sentence.

Proof: Using (I) in connection with (T-CONSIS) and (T-COMPL), we get

(**) $\qquad \text{True}(\langle \neg\text{True}(\langle Q \rangle)\rangle) \leftrightarrow \neg\text{True}(\langle \neg Q\rangle),$

with both sides holding when $\text{True}(\langle Q\rangle)$, i.e. when $\neg Q$, and neither side holding when $\neg\text{True}(\langle Q\rangle)$, i.e. when Q. So we get not only (i) and (ii) above, but also

(i*) $\qquad Q \leftrightarrow [\text{True}(\langle \neg Q\rangle) \wedge \neg\text{True}(\langle \neg\text{True}(\langle Q\rangle)\rangle)]$

and

(ii*) $\qquad \neg Q \leftrightarrow [\text{True}(\langle \neg\text{True}(\langle Q\rangle)\rangle) \wedge \neg\text{True}(\langle \neg Q\rangle)]$

So if Q, then (¬T-Introd) as well as (T-Elim) fails to preserve truth when applied to Q; and if $\neg Q$, then (¬T-Elim) as well as (T-Introd) fails to preserve truth when applied to Q. ∎

Even this expanded first result isn't yet quite what I announced, which is that each rule fails to preserve truth. (So far we only have that two of them do, and can't even say which two.) To get what I announced, let's see what happens when we apply the rules to $\neg Q$. First, note that in strong theories we have

$$Q \leftrightarrow \neg\text{True}(\langle Q\rangle) \leftrightarrow \text{True}(\langle \neg Q\rangle);$$

applying the Lemma, this gives

$$\text{True}(\langle Q\rangle) \leftrightarrow \text{True}(\langle \text{True}(\langle \neg Q\rangle)\rangle),$$

and so by the negation rule for strong theories again,

$$\neg\text{True}(\langle \neg Q\rangle) \leftrightarrow \text{True}(\langle \text{True}(\langle \neg Q\rangle)\rangle).$$

Both sides hold if $\text{True}(\langle Q\rangle)$, i.e. if $\neg Q$; neither side holds if Q. So

(i**) $\qquad Q \leftrightarrow [\text{True}(\langle \neg Q\rangle) \wedge \neg\text{True}(\langle\text{True}(\langle\neg Q\rangle)\rangle)]$

(ii**) $\qquad \neg Q \leftrightarrow [\text{True}(\langle\text{True}(\langle\neg Q\rangle)\rangle) \wedge \neg\text{True}(\langle\neg Q\rangle)]$

But putting these together with (i) and (ii), we get

(i) $\qquad Q \leftrightarrow [\text{True}(\langle\text{True}(\langle Q\rangle)\rangle) \wedge \neg\text{True}(\langle Q\rangle) \wedge \text{True}(\langle\neg Q\rangle) \wedge$
$\qquad\qquad \neg\text{True}(\langle\text{True}(\langle\neg Q\rangle)\rangle)]$

and

(ii) $\qquad \neg Q \leftrightarrow [\text{True}(\langle Q\rangle) \wedge \neg\text{True}(\langle\text{True}(\langle Q\rangle)\rangle) \wedge \text{True}(\langle\text{True}(\langle\neg Q\rangle)\rangle)$
$\qquad\qquad \wedge \neg\text{True}(\langle\neg Q\rangle)]$

So

Second negative result: It is a theorem of any strong supervaluational or revision theory that (T-Introd) and (T-Elim) each fail to preserve truth. If Q, then (T-Introd) fails to preserve truth when applied to $\neg Q$; if $\neg Q$, then (T-Introd) fails to preserve truth when applied to Q. We can't say which failure it is that occurs, but either way, we have a truth-preservation failure for (T-Introd). Similarly for (T-Elim), but the other way around: if Q, then (T-Elim) fails to preserve truth when applied to Q; if $\neg Q$, then (T-Elim) fails to preserve truth when applied to $\neg Q$.

We can also expand the second result to incorporate the other two rules. For the discussion above gives $Q \leftrightarrow \text{True}(\langle\neg Q\rangle)$. Contraposing and applying the Lemma, we get

$\qquad \text{True}(\langle\neg Q\rangle)$ if and only if $\text{True}(\langle\neg\text{True}(\langle\neg Q\rangle)\rangle)$;

and so using the strong negation rules,

$\qquad \neg\text{True}(\langle\neg\neg Q\rangle)$ if and only if $\text{True}(\langle\neg\text{True}(\langle\neg Q\rangle)\rangle)$.

Both sides hold if Q, fail if $\neg Q$; so this gives a counterinstance to ($\neg$T-Elim) if Q, and to ($\neg$T-Introd) if $\neg Q$. Combining with the previous we have:

Expanded second result: It is a theorem of any strong supervaluational or revision theory that each of the four rules fails to preserve truth. If Q, then (T-Elim) and ($\neg$T-Introd) fail to preserve truth when applied to Q, and (T-Introd) and ($\neg$T-Elim) fail to preserve truth when applied to $\neg Q$; so all four fail to preserve truth. If $\neg Q$, then (T-Introd) and ($\neg$T-Elim) fail to preserve truth when applied to Q, and (T-Elim) and ($\neg$T-Introd) fail to preserve truth when applied to $\neg Q$; so in this case too all four fail to preserve truth.

These results—especially the expanded second—could be thought to make the strong supervaluation and revision theories "self-undermining". I'll discuss this in Section 3, but first let's take a look at the situation for medium-strength supervaluation and revision theories.

12.2. WHAT DO MEDIUM SUPERVALUATIONAL AND MEDIUM REVISION THEORIES SAY ABOUT THEMSELVES?[1]

It shouldn't be a surprise that one can weaken strong supervaluational and revision theories so that they no longer state that their own rules don't preserve truth. The weakening to medium theories seems sufficient to do this; that is the main burden of this section. But we'll see that even here, the theories say something about themselves that is *prima facie* self-undermining.

First the good news: some medium supervaluation theories declare that at least one of their central truth rules *does* preserve truth (though no revision theories have this feature).

Positive Result: Some medium supervaluation theories consistently declare that (T-Elim) preserves truth.

To prove this, we need a fixed point model. The obvious choice is to take the condition $\Phi(Y)$ to be "Y is deductively closed, and also closed under (T-Elim)". Obviously the instances of $True(\langle True(\langle A \rangle) \rangle) \to True(\langle A \rangle)$ are in the fixed points generated by this condition; and the generalization must then be too, since the minimal fixed point is ω-complete. Since deductive closure was built in, we have a medium theory. The only issue is whether the fixed point is non-trivial. I demonstrate its nontriviality in a footnote.[2]

The positive result depends on the fact that supervaluation theories, unlike revision theories, needn't include the rule ($\neg$T-Elim). The following result makes this clear:

Third negative result: Medium revision theories, and medium supervaluation theories with ($\neg$T-Elim), can't consistently declare that (T-Elim) preserves truth, or that ($\neg$T-Introd) does.

Proof: For (T-Elim) to preserve truth we need $True(\langle True(\langle Q \rangle) \rangle) \to True(\langle Q \rangle)$, which by (II) of Section 12.1 is equivalent to $True(\langle \neg Q \rangle) \to True(\langle Q \rangle)$. But these theories also entail $True(\langle \neg Q \rangle) \to \neg True(\langle Q \rangle)$. Putting these together, we get $\neg True(\langle \neg Q \rangle)$. But

---

[1] The discussion here will correct some overstatements made in the section on weakly classical theories in Field 2006.

[2] To show its non-triviality, we first establish inductively that every stage in the construction of the minimal fixed point under the condition Φ obeys the condition Φ. The key step of the induction is the successor step, and it works because for $True(\langle A \rangle)$ to be in X_{a+1}, A must be in Y for every Y satisfying both $\Phi(Y)$ and $X_a \subseteq Y \subseteq U - X_a^{neg}$, and by the induction hypothesis that includes X_a; so A must be in X_a and therefore (Roach Motel) in X_{a+1}.

Using this, we can easily prove inductively that a sentence T asserting its own truth never gets in at any stage of the construction (which establishes non-triviality). Again the key is the successor step: for T to be in X_{a+1}, it must be in Y for every Y satisfying both $\Phi(Y)$ and $X_a \subseteq Y \subseteq U - X_a^{neg}$; but by the above, that includes X_a. So T couldn't get in for the first time at a successor stage, and it obviously couldn't get in for the first time at the 0 stage or a limit stage either.

then (¬T-Elim) gives ¬¬Q, hence Q, and we know that the theories can't consistently entail that.
For (¬T-Introd) to preserve truth we need True (⟨¬Q⟩) → True(⟨¬True(⟨Q⟩)⟩). But by (I) of Section 12.1 this is equivalent to True(⟨¬Q⟩) → True(⟨Q⟩). From there the reasoning is the same as for (T-Elim). ∎

Incidentally, a theory without (¬T-Elim) but which has (T-Elim) obviously can't have (T-COMPL). Given this, our results answer a question left unanswered in Section 11.3: the question of how a supervaluationist could possibly be motivated to reject (T-COMPL), given that he can't offer a counterexample to it. For if a supervaluationist has strong reason to accept (T-Elim), and also accept that it is truth-preserving, then it would be inconsistent for him to accept (¬T-Elim) or (T-COMPL), even though he can't point to any specific example where either must fail. (The question of what could motivate a *revision theorist* not to accept (T-COMPL) remains unanswered.) This might in fact provide a substantial motivation for choosing a moderate supervaluational theory without (¬T-Elim) over a strong one, if the positive result for (T-Elim) could be extended to the rules (T-Introd) and (¬T-Introd).

And it might seem that what was done for (T-Elim) in the Positive Result could be done for any of the other rules: simply build the truth-preservation claim for those rules into the Fixed Point construction. But that's too quick: one needs to prove that the resulting fixed point is non-trivial. Indeed, it turns out that for at least two of the rules[3] no analog of the Positive Result is possible:

Fourth negative result: No medium supervaluational or revision theories can consistently declare that (T-Introd) preserves truth, or that (¬T-Elim) does.

Proof: For (T-Introd) to preserve truth we need True(⟨Q⟩) → True(⟨True(⟨Q⟩)⟩), which by (II) of Section 12.1 is equivalent to True(⟨Q⟩) → True(⟨¬Q⟩). But these theories also entail True(⟨¬Q⟩) → ¬True(⟨Q⟩); putting these together, we get True(⟨Q⟩) → ¬True(⟨Q⟩), hence ¬True(⟨Q⟩). But we know that the theories can't consistently entail that.
For (¬T-Elim) to preserve truth, we need True(⟨¬True(⟨Q⟩)⟩) → True(⟨¬Q⟩). By (I) of Section 12.1, this is equivalent to True(⟨Q⟩) → True(⟨¬Q⟩). From there the reasoning is as for (T-Introd). ∎

These two rules must be in any revision theory, and at least (T-Introd) must be in any supervaluation theory. So in medium theories of each kind as well as strong ones, the assumption that certain rules of the theory preserve truth leads to contradiction.

If classical *reductio* reasoning were available, we could conclude from this that in medium theories as well as strong ones, rules of the theory such as (T-Introd)

---

[3] The situation with the remaining rule, ¬T-Introduction, is not entirely clear to me. One can dualize the argument of note 2 to get a non-trivial fixed point model validating the truth preservation of (¬T-Introduction), but it yields not a medium supervaluation theory but a *dual-medium* one. Whether a model for a medium supervaluation theory in which (¬T-Introd) preserves truth can be obtained by other means, I do not know.

don't preserve truth. But we've seen that though these theories are in some sense classical, they don't validate standard classical meta-rules like *reductio*; so there is no obvious reason why the medium theories can't just remain in some sense "agnostic" on whether the rules (T-Introd) and (¬T-Elim) preserve truth.

To clarify the situation, note that the proof of the fourth result can be converted to a proof (in any medium theory) that *if True(⟨Q⟩) then* the rules (T-Introd) and (¬T-Elim) fail to preserve truth.[4] The reason that the truth-preservation claim can't be consistently added is that there's no way to rule out True(⟨Q⟩), i.e. to prove ¬True(⟨Q⟩). But this fourth result doesn't tell us that the rules also fail to preserve truth if ¬True(⟨Q⟩). We did get that from the second result, but only on the assumption of (T-COMPL), which is justified only by the strong theories.

If we were to give a similar analysis of the third result, would we get (in any medium theory *with* (¬T-Elim)) that *if ¬True(⟨Q⟩) then* the rules (T-Elim) and (¬T-Introd) fail to preserve truth? If so, we could argue for an extension of the first result to medium theories with (¬T-Elim): that either (T-Introd) and (¬T-Elim) or (T-Elim) and (¬T-Introd) must fail to preserve truth, though we can't say which. But analysis of the proof of the third result doesn't give a result quite so strong: only that *if True(⟨¬Q⟩) then* the rules fail to preserve truth.[5] So it isn't clear that medium theories must assert that some of their rules fail to preserve truth.

Is this a big advantage for medium theories over strong ones? Only if one takes the fact that strong theories declare their own rules not to be truth-preserving as showing that they "undermine themselves", and as we'll soon see, there is reason to doubt this. In addition, it might be argued that the medium theories come close to saying what the strong ones do: for instance, since their conditional is just the material one, we can restate the result two paragraphs back as:

(*) Either ¬True(⟨Q⟩) or the rules (T-Introd) and (¬T-Elim) fail to preserve truth;

and the one about (T-Elim) and (¬T-Introd) as

Either ¬True(⟨¬Q⟩) or the rules (T-Elim) and (¬T-Introd) fail to preserve truth.

But the first disjuncts of both, according to medium theories with (¬T-Elim), are absurd! (And the first disjunct of the first is absurd according to *all* medium theories.) If it's self undermining to declare one's own rules not truth-preserving, isn't it almost as self-undermining to declare that *barring some absurdity* they fail to preserve truth?

I admit to less than total conviction about the force of this rhetorical question. A full discussion would involve going back to the issues of Section 10.7,

---

[4] For (T-Introd) it goes like this: True(⟨Q⟩) → ¬True(⟨¬Q⟩); so by (II), True(⟨Q⟩) → ¬True(⟨True(⟨Q⟩)⟩). That is, True(⟨Q⟩) → [True(⟨Q⟩) ∧ ¬True(⟨True(⟨Q⟩)⟩)].

[5] For (T-Elim) it goes like this: True(⟨¬Q⟩) → ¬True(⟨Q⟩); so by (II), True(⟨¬Q⟩) → [True(⟨True(⟨Q⟩)⟩) ∧ ¬True(⟨Q⟩)]. (This derivation doesn't involve (¬T-Elim); it's just that without (¬T-Elim) one can't derive a contradiction from the antecedent.)

concerning just how one interprets the "absurdity" of claims like Q. On a "pure ignorance" interpretation, it's really a misnomer to say that Q (or equivalently, $\neg\text{True}(\langle Q\rangle)$) is absurd: it would just be absurd to *assert* it. In that case, what (*) reflects is simply that we are inevitably agnostic about whether rules like (T-Introd) preserve truth. Would this help? If a theorist shouldn't employ rules he knows don't preserve truth, it might be wondered whether he ought to employ rules that he thinks might very well not preserve truth.

On an alternative interpretation, where Q has some kind of "objectively indeterminate" status, there is a kind of genuine absurdity in asserting $\neg\text{True}(\langle Q\rangle)$. On the other hand, the force of the rhetorical question seems to depend on the thought that asserting

Barring an absurdity, p

is almost tantamount to asserting p; and that seems to depend on reasoning by cases, which the theory rejects.

I'll leave the matter there; the issue won't make much difference, if one doesn't take seriously the charge against strong theories that they are "self-undermining".

12.3. ARE EVEN THE STRONG THEORIES REALLY "SELF-UNDERMINING"?

The situation of theories declaring their own rules not to be truth-preserving is one we've seen already, in the case of (non-hyper-dialetheic) glut theories. In those theories, the rule declared not to be truth-preserving was modus ponens. In the strong supervaluation and revision theories, modus ponens is declared truth-preserving; but these theories say about their truth rules what glut theories said about modus ponens. So *if* one supposes that a theory that declares some of its own rules not to be truth-preserving is somehow "self-undermining", then the move from glut theories to strong supervaluational or revision theories brings no relief.

It might even be said that in moving from glut theories we've made the situation worse. In the case of typical glut theories, we can point to specific examples of where the "offending" rule fails to preserve truth: e.g. the inference from Q and $Q \to 0=1$ to $0=1$. In the case of the strong supervaluational and strong revision theories, on the other hand, the theory is unable to say for which instance the failure occurs. Indeed, it would be *inconsistent* to say, for any given rule, that the failure occurred when the rule is applied to Q, and also inconsistent to say that it occurs when the rule is applied to $\neg Q$; at the same time, the theory says that there must be a failure either when the rule is applied to Q or to $\neg Q$. Once again, the theory escapes downright inconsistency only because it disallows reasoning by cases. This may seem like mystery-mongering. On the other hand, we already knew that the theory mongers mysteries in this way, so it's probably unfair to say that the situation is worse than for glut theories. Still, it's hard to see how we can declare it any better as regards this issue.

Recall, though, that the glut theorist is quite a bit better off than the gap theorist. While the glut theorist is forced to declare that her rules don't *unrestrictedly* preserve truth, she has no reason to doubt that they do preserve truth in the contexts *where it matters*, viz., when the premises are not pathological. And it doesn't seem entirely fair to call a theory "self-undermining" if it merely says that its rules wouldn't preserve truth when applied to pathological sentences that one doesn't accept. (The gap theorist, who is forced to say that even some of his basic principles aren't true, has no corresponding defense.)

And the strong supervaluationist or strong revision theorist can take exactly the same line as the glut theorist:

> Sure, the truth rules employed in my theory don't *unrestrictedly* preserve truth, but the counterexamples to truth-preservation all involve pathological sentences like Q and $\neg Q$. I have no reason to doubt that my rules preserve truth *in the situations where I directly employ them*, i.e. to premises I accept. Why ask for anything more?

Indeed, I think this is not too bad a defense. So I think that while the strong supervaluationist or revision theorist has no advantage over the glut theorist on the question of "self-undermining", he enjoys the same advantages that the glut theorist enjoys over the gap theorist. And the moderate theorist can take the same line: that though the only way to maintain that his rule (T-Introd) *unrestrictedly* preserves truth would be to maintain that the Liar sentence is untrue, which would be inconsistent, still it is perfectly possible to believe without contradiction that the rule preserves truth "where it counts". In particular, there is no reason to doubt that the rules lead only to true theorems.

Of course the issue of "self-undermining" isn't the only issue relevant to debates between supervaluational/revision theories, glut theories, and gap theories. For instance, there are issues surrounding the intrinsic unpalatability of violations of each of the three Incoherence Principles of Chapter 6. Whether one takes those considerations to favor the supervaluationist over the glut theorist or gap theorist, or the other way around, depends on just how counterintuitive one takes violating the Third Incoherence Principle to be.

12.4. GÖDEL'S SECOND INCOMPLETENESS THEOREM

So far, we've seen, classical gap theories declare some of their axioms untrue; classical glut theories other than hyper-dialetheism declare that some of their rules fail to preserve truth; and strong supervaluationist and revision theorists are like classical glut theories in this regard. Medium strength supervaluational and revision theories don't declare that some of their rules don't preserve truth, but they also don't declare that they do preserve truth. Indeed, they "come close to" doing the former: they declare that the only way for their rule T-Introd to preserve truth is for the Liar sentence to be untrue, while taking the claim that the Liar sentence is untrue to be inconsistent.

This situation is illuminated by a consideration of Gödel's Second Incompleteness Theorem, which says that no remotely adequate mathematical theory can prove its own consistency.[6]

A natural initial thought is that the Second Incompleteness Theorem is slightly puzzling for languages that contain their own truth predicate: we ought to be able to prove the consistency of a mathematical theory T within T by

(A) inductively proving within T that T is sound, i.e. that all its theorems are true,

and

(B) arguing from the soundness of T to the claim that T is consistent.

Where does this fail?

In the context of classical logic in which we're now working, the claim that T is consistent is equivalent to the claim that not all its sentences are theorems. So the claim of (A) that all the theorems of T are true, i.e. that everything that isn't true isn't a theorem, implies consistency given only the premise that there are sentences of the language that aren't true. Of course, hyper-dialetheism rejects that, and does so consistently; but hyper-dialetheism aside, any other classical theory with its own truth predicate must diagnose the problem with the purported consistency proof as residing in (A).

Let's set out the argument alluded to under (A) in more detail. To simplify the discussion, imagine that we're working in a formulation of logic where reasoning is done only at the level of sentences: formulas with free variables are never axioms, and the rules of inference don't apply to them.[7] In that case, the reasoning alluded to under (A) is this:

(1) Each axiom of T is true
(2) Each rule of inference of T preserves truth. (That is, whenever the premises of the rule are true, so is the conclusion.)

Since a theorem of T is just a sentence that results from the axioms by successive application of rules of inference, a simple mathematical induction yields

(3) All theorems of T are true; i.e. T is sound.

---

[6] Here a "remotely adequate" theory is one that is (i) recursively axiomatized, (ii) powerful enough to include a certain minimum of arithmetic, and (iii) nontrivial in the sense that not every sentence in the language of the theory is provable. I assume that consistency is defined using a standard provability predicate.

[7] Such a formalization can be found in Quine 1940. But I appeal to such a formalization only for simplicity: if one uses a more standard formalization of logic, the inductive argument is that all theorems (which now may have free variables) are satisfied by all objects.

Unless one were to suppose that mathematical induction on the truth predicate isn't allowed—a wholly unappealing supposition, it seems to me—one has to fault either (1) or (2). Classical gap theories fault (1); classical glut theories and supervaluation and revision theories fault (2).

There are, to be sure, ways of faulting (1) or (2) other than declaring that some of one's axioms aren't true or that some of one's rules of inference aren't truth preserving. That is, to fault (1) or (2) needn't involve asserting its negation, it could simply involve not asserting it.

In the case of (1), I don't think the option of refusing to assert without actually denying is of much interest, when the theory contains a general truth predicate. First, note that when the theory T contains a general truth predicate, it has the resources to *express* that each of its axioms is true.[8] It may not *imply* this, but if it doesn't, that is of little interest if it can be consistently extended so that it implies it, without restricting the inference rules of the theory. In the case of theories like gap theories that are forced to explicitly deny (1), there is obviously no way to get such a consistent strengthening. But in other cases, there is no obvious bar to consistently strengthening the theory so that it asserts (1). I won't try to rigorously argue that this is possible in every conceivable case, but a method that will usually work mimics the Craig–Vaught strategy of Section 2.4 but now without expanding the language.

More fully: given a recursively axiomatized theory T with a general truth predicate (and the language of number theory), consider a theory T^* in the same language whose axioms are those of a finitely axiomatized arithmetic plus the assertion "All axioms of T are true"; take the rules of T^* to be all the rules of T, plus the rule of universal instantiation and (T-Elim) and (T-Introd) if they aren't included in T. (Unlike in Section 2.4, there's no need for compositional truth rules.) T^* will imply that all of its own axioms are true: for since it contains (T-Introd), it implies True($\langle A \rangle$) for each of its own axioms A (including the axiom "All axioms of T are true"); and since there are only finitely many of these, there is no worry about getting to the generalization. T^* will also imply everything T does.[9] It may well imply more: indeed, in the case of theories like gap theories that explicitly deny (1), it will clearly be inconsistent. But for theories that don't deny (1), it's *hard to see* why the passage from T to T^* should lead to inconsistency; this is especially so in the case of supervaluational and revision theories, which already contain the rules (T-Introd) and (T-Elim). In that case, the failure of the theory to assert (1) is just a case of unnecessary reticence.

If this is right, then the only interesting way for a theory that doesn't imply the negation of (1) *not* to prove its own consistency (other than by being

---

[8] This requires that 'axiom of T' be definable in the language, but this follows from assumptions already made, viz. that the theory is recursively axiomatized and includes the language of arithmetic.

[9] From "All axioms of T are true" and universal instantiation and (T-Elim), we get each axiom of T; and each rule of T is also a rule of T^*.

hyper-dialetheic), and hence the only interesting way for it to actually be consistent, is for (2) not to be provable. And typically there are only finitely many rules of inference in T and hence T^*, so the only way for that to happen is for there to be some rule of inference R such that the claim

($*_R$) R is truth-preserving

isn't provable in T^*. This can happen because the theory asserts the negation of ($*_R$), as in the case of strong supervaluation and revision theories; or because it takes it to be in some sense "indeterminate" whether ($*_R$), as in the case of moderate theories.

So the situation that we've seen for supervaluation and revision theories is really quite inevitable. It in itself could hardly be viewed as a criticism of those theories; especially since, as noted before, advocates of these theories have no reason to doubt that their rules preserve truth *when applied to sentences that the theory accepts or is committed to accepting*.

This last point might be thought to re-raise the question of how these views escape the Second Incompleteness Theorem. To inductively establish the soundness of the theory, why do we need more than (i) that the axioms are true and (ii) that the rules preserve truth *when applied to sentences that the theory accepts or is committed to accepting*? The answer is that claim (ii) can't possibly be a consequence of the theory: the advocate of the theory may reasonably believe it, but this belief must depend on the belief that the theory isn't committed to accepting sentences like Q as theorems and thus on the view that the system is consistent. The point of my defense of glut theories, supervaluation theories and revision theories against the charge that they are "self-undermining" is that an advocate of such a theory who believes his theory consistent (as presumably all such advocates do) can *use this belief* in arguing that while the rules of the theory do not preserve truth unrestrictedly they do so restrictedly. The belief that is used is not part of the theory.[10]

---

[10] If the theorist believes it, why not take it to be part of his theory? One can do that, passing from an original theory T to the theory T^* that includes the consistency of T; but of course this won't entail the consistency of T^*, one needs a still more expansive theory T^{**} to get that. One can iterate this process well into the transfinite. (See Feferman 1962.) But at each stage of iteration, the theory is slightly less secure: the new consistency claim is supported only by a more extensive soundness assumption than the earlier theory can supply.

We can crudely picture the situation in terms of degrees of belief: if we start off with a theory T consisting of ZF with an expansion of its schemas to incorporate some weakly classical truth predicate, then our degree of belief in its consistency will be quite high, and our degree of belief in the consistency of $T^* = T + \text{Con}(T)$ will be less by only a minuscule amount. In general, as we move up the "Feferman hierarchy" of more and more powerful theories, our degree of belief should drop gradually. There is doubtless some arbitrariness in deciding at which point the degree of belief has become low enough so that the iteration no longer counts as part of our overall theory, but the location doesn't matter: wherever one takes the location to be, we will have a theory T_α which is believed to sufficient degree to count as part of our theory whereas the addition of $\text{Con}(T_\alpha)$ would lower the degree of belief to below the required threshold. (We can make the threshold vague, in which case it's vague where this point is.)

12.5. CONCLUSION

I've been defending supervaluation and revision theories against the charge that they are self-undermining. I do myself find it disquieting that these theories not merely *don't prove (*$_R$)* for some of their rules R, they *do* prove either

R *doesn't* preserve truth

(in the case of the strong theories) or (in the case of moderate theories)

Either R doesn't preserve truth, or Q (where the theory takes Q to imply a contradiction).

But though this strikes me as disquieting, it's hard to use it as the basis for a compelling argument against these theories. In sum, there does not seem to be a legitimate charge of "self-undermining" independent of other worries.

13
Intersubstitutivity and the Purpose of Truth

I observed in Chapter 7 that one purpose of the notion of truth is to enable us to express agreement when that would be otherwise difficult or impossible. For instance, I can express agreement with a certain theory (perhaps not finitely axiomatized, but the set of whose axioms is definable) by saying "Everything entailed by the theory is true". I noted there and in Chapter 8 that both gap theories and (classical) glut theories are forced to impose severe limits on the ability of truth to serve this purpose, for they both force a distinction between agreeing with something and believing it true. In gap theories, you can agree with claims you don't believe true, and in glut theories you can believe claims true even while not agreeing with them.

Supervaluational and revision theories are better in this regard. All revision theories, and all supervaluation theories worth taking seriously, accept both the rules (T-Introd) and (T-Elim); so an advocate of such a theory believes a claim if and only if he believes it true. This looks at first blush like a huge gain over gap and glut theories.

In Chapters 7 and 8 I discussed not only the issue of expressing agreement, but the related and (I claimed) somewhat more pressing issue of expressing disagreement. Here too, gap and glut theories do very badly, while revision theories and at least some supervaluation theories seem to do much better. All revision and supervaluation theories accept the rule (¬T-Introd), allowing passage from ¬A to ¬True($\langle A \rangle$); so if an advocate of such a theory disagrees with A, he will disagree with the claim that A is true. And all revision theories, and some supervaluation theories, accept the rule (¬T-Elim), allowing passage from ¬True($\langle A \rangle$) to ¬A; so if an advocate of such a theory disagrees with the claim that A is true, he will disagree with A. This seems at first blush to strongly favor versions of supervaluationism that keep (¬T-Elim) over those that don't, as well as over classical gap and glut theories.[1]

This point about disagreement requires a bit more discussion, for two reasons. First, there are ways of advocating truth-value gaps, or otherwise abandoning

---

[1] Recall that early in Section 12.2 we saw what looked at first like a strong advantage in the other direction: a supervaluationist who doesn't accept the rule (¬T-Elim) can consistently declare her rule (T-Elim) to be truth-preserving. But this advantage looked less striking by the end of the section, where it turned out that even if a supervaluational theory can declare (T-Elim) truth-preserving, it can't declare some of its other rules truth preserving.

the rule (¬T-Elim), that wouldn't be too disruptive of our abilities to use 'true' to express disagreement. In Section 13.1 I will discuss this, but argue that it is of no help to those who advocate rejecting (¬T-Elim) to treat the paradoxes (whether in a gap theory or a supervaluational context). Second, there is an issue about whether revision theories and supervaluation theories with (¬T-Elim) do as well on disagreement as the above would suggest: I discuss this in Section 13.2.

I keep those two discussions brief, because in Section 13.3 I argue that the matter of expressing agreement and disagreement is just the tip of an iceberg, and that there's little point debating the subtleties of which theories evade the tip when they are equally affected by the rest of the iceberg.

13.1. HARMLESS GAPS

Are there sentences that are neither true nor false? Sure: there are sentences in non-indicative moods (questions, commands, and so forth), and there are sentences that are by ordinary criteria meaningless. (Also orthographic sentence-types that are ambiguous or require a context to fix what they say on a given occasion.) If the rule ¬T-Elim were taken to apply to sentences like these, it would yield absurd results: we can hardly argue from the fact that 'Potrzebie ferschlugginer' isn't true to the "conclusion" 'It is not the case that potrzebie ferschlugginer'. But of course the gap theories of Chapter 7 and the supervaluation theories that abandon ¬T-Elim aren't at all like this: they posit gaps, or at least abandon ¬T-Elim, for indicative sentences that they treat as having a perfectly clear content. (The sentences in question are non-indexical, and built up by ordinary compositional rules from terms that these theorists understand; and the theorists employ these sentences, and logical compounds of them, in their own reasoning.)

A truth-value gap view that is superficially more similar to the gap theories of Chapter 7 is the view (espoused e.g. by Frege 1892) that many or all sentences with non-denoting singular terms are neither true nor false. In my opinion there is little reason to believe this view: the intuitions that seem at first to support it are best explained pragmatically (Stalnaker 1974), and by far the simplest systematic theory governing all sentences with non-denoting terms (including, e.g. negative existentials) is one that takes those sentences to have exactly one of the two standard truth values (putting aside the special issues about certain sentences containing predicates like 'true'). Which of these truth-values a given such sentence has is determined by (i) the standard compositional rules for negation, conjunction and so forth, together with (ii) a rule for the atomic predicates. There is some room for variation over (ii), but at least for *typical* predicates, the appropriate view is presumably that atomic sentences involving that predicate are false when any of the terms in them fail to denote. A theory of this sort is, I think, by far the best theory, but I don't want to rest my claims in this book on this issue; so for purposes of this book I would like to treat the Frege view as a case of "(more or less) harmless gaps".

I'll now argue that these cases of "harmless gaps" pose little problem for the use of a truth predicate to express disagreement; but also that this is of no help to those who advocate abandoning (¬T-Elim) for reasons connected with the paradoxes. (I'll focus on disagreement. The gap theories of Chapter 7 also have a problem with agreement, due to their rejection of (T-Introd); this issue doesn't arise for harmless gap theories, since they accept (T-Introd).)

Let's begin with the *really* harmless gaps, those arising for meaningless sentences, non-indicatives, and so forth. Here the inability to pass from ¬True($\langle A \rangle$) to ¬A is of course completely unsurprising: the conclusion doesn't even make an assertion. But is there a problem of using the truth predicate to express disagreement? I don't think so, but we have to distinguish broader and narrower senses of disagreement. In the narrowest sense, we disagree with someone only if we think he has expressed an intelligible indicative content that we disagree with, while in broader senses we count ourselves as disagreeing with him in some or all of the cases where we think he hasn't expressed an intelligible content even though he may think he has. In order to figure out how to use a truth predicate to express disagreement, we need to make up our minds which "strength" of disagreement we want to express. We can for instance say:

(i) One of the sentences Jones uttered yesterday was meaningful, indicative, and unambiguous (or contextually disambiguated), but not true;

or

(ii) One of the sentences Jones uttered yesterday was indicative but not true;

or

(iii) One of the sentences Jones uttered yesterday was not true.

(i) expresses disagreement in a narrow sense; (ii) expresses disagreement in a broad sense; (iii) expresses "disagreement" in such a broad sense that it shouldn't really count as disagreement. (I don't disagree with someone merely because he asks a question.) If you make up your mind what "strength" of disagreement you want to express, you can accurately express it using a truth predicate. Of course, here as so often elsewhere, accuracy would require being pedantic: usually we'd settle for something something closer to (iii) than to (i) or (ii), even though it isn't quite what we intend.

The point is really little different in the case of Fregean gaps, under the pretense that they really are harmless—though here we have to be careful not to let evidence that they aren't harmless interfere with our judgements. Suppose Smith says 'The angel Moroni has appeared to me and ordered me to take three twelve-year old wives', and Jones says 'The angel Moroni has never appeared to me nor ordered me to do anything'. The Fregean who doesn't believe in the angel Moroni presumably must say that these both have the same status:

neither one is either true or false. And it is hard to see how such a Fregean could disagree with Smith but not with Jones, on any sense of disagreement that didn't involve a heavy use of pragmatic reinterpretation. This consequence strikes me as counterintuitive, but given that that's the view, then the Fregean has the same options as discussed in the last paragraph: he has available both a wide sense of disagreement in which he disagrees with both Smith and Jones, and a narrow sense in which he disagrees with neither, and there is no problem expressing either sense using a truth predicate.

The situation with the gap theories of Chapter 7, and with supervaluation theories that reject (¬T-Elim), is not in this way harmless. In the case of the gap theories of Chapter 7, the reason is that the theory discriminates between sentences it regards as untrue: it agrees with some of them (e.g. the Liar sentence Q, or the axiom True($\langle Q \rangle$) → Q), and disagrees with others (e.g. True($\langle Q \rangle$), or True($\langle$True($\langle Q \rangle$) → $Q\rangle$)). This isn't a vacillation about what 'disagrees' means: Q and True($\langle Q \rangle$) → Q follow from the gap theory, and True($\langle Q \rangle$) and True($\langle$True($\langle Q \rangle$) → $Q\rangle$) are incompatible with it, even though the theory declares all four of them untrue. Given this, there is simply no way to express disagreement via a truth predicate.

The situation with supervaluational theories that reject ¬T-Elim for reasons having to do with the paradoxes is similar. I'll focus on the case considered in Section 11.2: medium strength theories that reject ¬T-Elim in order to be able to assert that T-Elim preserves truth. As the proof of the "Third Result" in that section makes clear, such a theorist will accept ¬True($\langle\neg Q\rangle$); but like all (internal) supervaluationists he won't accept ¬True($\langle Q \rangle$), and will regard Q and ¬Q as each unacceptable since both lead to contradictions. It seems clear that in whatever sense the theorist disagrees with ¬Q, he equally disagrees with Q; and yet he accepts that the first is not true but doesn't accept that the second is not true. Again, there seems to be no way to use judgements of non-truth to express disagreement.

13.2. ACCEPTANCE AND REJECTION IN WEAKLY CLASSICAL THEORIES

In my introductory remarks to this chapter I suggested an argument that revision theories, and supervaluational theories with (¬T-Elim), do better than classical gap and glut theories as regards disagreement. But this argument assumed that to 'disagree with' a claim is to accept its negation. A more natural interpretation of 'disagree with' is 'reject'. In general, that's different, as we saw in Section 3.7. If we adopt the simple picture that accepting a claim involves having a degree of belief over some threshold τ, then rejecting it should involve having a degree of belief lower than the corresponding co-threshold $1 - \tau$.

For strongly classical theories, the degree of belief in a sentence and its negation should add to 1. In that case, rejection does coincide with acceptance of negation, so the argument that strongly classical theories do badly with regard to disagreement needs no modification. But we saw that for paracomplete theories like KFS, one's degrees of belief in A and in $\neg A$ should only add up to one's degree of belief in $A \vee \neg A$; this allows for rejecting A while not accepting its negation when one doesn't fully accept $A \vee \neg A$. It is arguable that something rather like this holds in weakly classical theories as well.

More fully: we've seen that many advocates of such theories operate with the idea that when disjunction elimination is suspect for a sentence A, that is because A is not assumed to have "determinate truth value". If that is one's picture, then the degree of belief in A is plausibly taken to be the degree to which one believes it determinately true; in which case one's degrees of belief in A and in $\neg A$ can add to less than 1, much as in the case of paracomplete theories like KFS. (*Much* as, not *exactly* as, because the laws that the weakly classical theorist would take to govern these non-standard degrees of belief would have to differ from those that the paracomplete theorist assumes, given the different attitudes these two theorists take to excluded middle.)[2] This is the position that a weakly classical theorist would need to take if she wanted to maintain that since the Liar sentence and its negation each lead to contradiction they should each be believed to degree 0. I think this is the most plausible position for a weakly classical theorist to take.

On this position, rejection does not coincide with belief in the negation. But in that case, showing that one can believe $\neg True(\langle A \rangle)$ when and only when one believes $\neg A$ doesn't seem relevant to establishing that one can reject $True(\langle A \rangle)$ when and only when one rejects A. But rather than discuss this and its implications further, I would now like to pass on from the matter of handling agreement and disagreement to a broader consideration.

13.3. THE REST OF THE ICEBERG

Talk of truth isn't *just* a means of expressing agreement and disagreement, for the same reason that talk of goodness isn't *just* a means of expressing approval and disapproval: 'true', like 'good', occurs in embedded contexts (contexts embedded more deeply than a negation).

In particular, 'true' is used inside conditionals. And in order for it to serve its purpose, it needs to be well-behaved there: inside conditionals as in unembedded

---

[2] The paracomplete theorist will accept the classical law $P(A) + P(\neg A) = P(A \vee \neg A)$; when $P(A) + P(\neg A) < 1$, that's because $P(A \vee \neg A) < 1$. The weakly classical theorist regards $P(A \vee \neg A)$ as always 1, so the classical law would have to be weakened to $P(A) + P(\neg A) \leq P(A \vee \neg A)$. More generally, the weakly classical theorist could adopt the laws of Shafer 1976; for an adaptation to the context of a supervaluationist view of vagueness, see Field 2000.

contexts, 'true' needs to serve as a device of infinite conjunction or disjunction (or more accurately, a device of quantification). Suppose I can't remember exactly what was in the Conyers report on the 2004 election, but say

(1) If everything that the Conyers report says is true then the 2004 election was stolen.

Suppose that what the Conyers report says is $A_1, \ldots, A_n$. Then relative to this last supposition, (1) better be equivalent to

(2) If A_1 and ... and A_n then the 2004 election was stolen.

And this requires $\text{True}(\langle A \rangle)$ to be intersubstitutable with A even when A is the antecedent of a conditional.[3]

The point clearly generalizes to more complex constructions: in order for the notion of truth to serve its purposes, we need what I've been calling the *Intersubstitutivity Principle*:

If C and D are alike except that (in some transparent context) one has a sentence "A" where the other has "$\langle A \rangle$ is true", then one can legitimately infer D from C and C from D.

And supervaluation and revision theories, like other classical theories (gap and glut), have to reject this. Indeed, since such theories accept $A \leftrightarrow A$, Intersubstitutivity would lead to $\text{True}(\langle A \rangle) \leftrightarrow A$, which we know that no classical theorist can consistently accept.

So, though revision theorists and supervaluation theorists that keep (T-Elim) may handle the problem of agreement and disagreement, the significance of this is open to question: the Titanic avoided the tip of the iceberg too.

---

[3] This and other points made in this chapter extend from 'true' to 'true of'. For instance, "If there are objects satisfying all the predicates Joe mentioned then ____ " should be equivalent to "If there are objects x such that $F_1(x)$ and ... and $F_n(x)$ then ____ ", relative to the assumption that the predicates Joe mentioned were exactly $F_1, \ldots, F_n$. This requires the intersubstitutivity of "$<F>$ is true of x" with "$F(x)$" even inside conditionals.

14
Stratified and Contextual Theories

14.1. CONTEXTUAL THEORIES AND "STRENGTHENED LIAR REASONING"

There are two ideas about how to treat the paradoxes that often go hand in hand, though they are separable. The first is stratification, the second is contextualization.

By a *stratified*, or *hierarchical*, theory of truth I mean a theory which says that there is no general truth predicate, but instead a hierarchy of predicates '$true_0$', '$true_1$', and so on, extending at least through the natural numbers and more typically through a substantial segment of the countable ordinals.

By a *contextual*, or *indexical*, theory of truth I mean one according to which the content of any individual sentence-token involving 'true' depends upon the context of utterance, where this includes what others have recently said in the conversation, and may perhaps include also the speaker's intentions.

A contextual (indexical) theory of 'here' requires a prior non-contextual account of what places are, so that context can attach such a place to a given token of 'here'. Similarly, a contextual theory of 'true' requires a prior non-contextual account of what the available "extensions" are for the predicate on any given occasion of use. On some but not all versions of contextualism, this prior non-contextual account is hierarchical: the "extensions" of 'true' on any occasion are the "extensions" of the different '$true_\alpha$' predicates (if I may informally use 'extension' in a way that does not appear to be licensed by the theory).[1]

A main motivation for contextual theories has been the thought that reflection on a given Liar sentence requires a use of 'true' different from the one involved in that Liar sentence. This has often been discussed under the heading "Strengthened Liar reasoning". Suppose I utter a sentence not realizing it to be a contingent Liar: for instance, I say

(1) What the guy on the department store TV screen is saying isn't true,

---

[1] For a non-hierarchical version of contextualism, see Simmons 1993. For hierarchical versions, see C. Parsons 1974a, Burge 1979, and Glanzberg 2004.

unaware that the TV is showing me as I speak. A bystander (call him Tim) who overhears me and knows the situation might be inclined, if he were a gap theorist, to say

(2) What the guy on the department store TV screen said isn't true (and isn't false either: it's defective).

A third person (call him Charles), who also knows the situation and overhears Tim and thinks there's something right about Tim's gap theory, might be inclined to say

(3) What Tim said is true.

Of course, neither a weakly classical theorist nor an advocate of (KFS) will agree with Tim, or with Charles either. But what would a gap theorist of the sort discussed in Chapter 7 say? According to such a theorist, Tim is right but Charles isn't: Charles should have expressed his agreement with Tim not by saying (3), but by repeating (2) (perhaps with the addition of "As Tim said"). The reason is that the non-parenthetical part of (2) appears to be identical in all relevant respects to (1): it's a different token of course, but the singular term refers to the same person in each case (viz., me), and the same apparently unambiguous predicate is applied. So what Tim said, viz., (2), is semantically equivalent to what I (the guy on the TV screen) said: if that isn't true, then what Tim said isn't true either. And so the proper conclusion for a gap theorist is of form

A, but ⟨*A*⟩ isn't true;

'*A*' is to be replaced here by the sentence (2) (or equivalently, the sentence (1)). That's what Tim himself should say if he's a gap theorist (and what Tim Maudlin 2004 *does* say); and Charles is contradicting this if he utters (3).

There is doubtless something counterintuitive about this feature of the gap theory, and a main motivation of contextualism is to do better. The contextualist thinks that the gap theorist of Chapter 7 fails to take account of a contextual shift in the meaning of 'true', either between (1) and (2) or between (2) and (3) or both.[2]

Perhaps the initially more plausible place to put the shift is between (1) and (2). On this view, it is only appropriate to call (1) "not true" after a contextual shift in 'true'. (There is then no obvious need for a shift from (2) to (3), since what Tim said isn't the same as what the guy on the TV screen said.) This however would leave unsettled what to say about the truth status of (1) *in the sense of 'true' used in (1)*. If one were to say that (1) isn't true in that sense either, that would undermine the rationale for saying that there has been a conceptual shift in the move from (1) to (2). Perhaps the view is that it is somehow illegitimate to ask the truth status of (1) in the sense of 'true' used in (1)? I'm not sure how

---

[2] Skyrms 1970 tried to do better without a contextual shift, by restricting the substitutivity of identity, but this strikes me as an act of desperation.

this could be argued. Thus if one sees a contextual shift between (1) and (2) it is probably best to hold either a weakly classical view or a paracomplete view of how the truth predicate works prior to the contextual shift.

An alternative place to put the contextual shift, which accords more with gap theory, is in the step from (2) to (3). In this view (quite explicit in Burge 1979 and 1982), the use of 'true' in (2) accords with a gap theory, but when Charles comments on (2) in the manner of (3) he has switched to a broader use of 'true' (perhaps still gappy, but with fewer gaps). This view would I think have to agree that (2) isn't true *in the sense of 'true' used in (2)*; but perhaps the contextual pressures on our ordinary use of 'true' make it difficult to say so.

There is another major division among contextual theorists: between those like Burge and Simmons who think that the context-dependence resides primarily in 'true' (and related terms like 'satisfies'), and those like C. Parsons (1974a) and Glanzberg (2004) who think that it resides primarily in the quantifiers and only derivatively in 'true'. The latter two take sentential truth to be explained in terms of propositional truth plus quantification: a sentence is true if and only if there is a true proposition that it expresses. They think that there is a kind of context-dependence in the use of quantifiers, even by those who intend their quantifiers to be unrestricted: context sometimes requires the introduction of new propositions that simply weren't in the old ontology, and this expansion of the range of propositions leads to a weakening of the truth predicate.

This view raises huge issues: both (i) the issues about indefinite extensibility of ontology mentioned in Section 1.5, and (ii) the issues of "propositionalist obscurantism" mentioned in Chapter 7. With regard to the latter, let me just say that since *propositional* truth is treated as non-contextual on this view, the view would either need to provide an account of contingent Liar *propositions* or say that there can't be any. Parsons and Glanzberg clearly take the latter route. But this raises the question: what is someone believing when she believes that the person on the TV screen is saying something untrue when (unbeknownst to her) she is the one on the screen? There appear to be two possible answers: (a) that she won't believe a proposition at all in this situation; (b) that she will believe one, but it won't be the obvious analog of the one she would have believed had it been someone else on the screen. As far as I know neither Parsons nor Glanzberg address the question of (a) *versus* (b), but I think that Glanzberg's discussion of how context works commits him to the former option. In the case of Parsons I'm less sure.

All these contextualist views are doubtless worthy of detailed discussion, but I'm going to have to forgo the detail. In the case of Parsons and Glanzberg, the issues raised (indefinite extensibility, belief, etc.) are simply too big for an already big book. And in all of the cases there is the worry voiced by Gupta in the quotation early in Chapter 3, that the pragmatic rules for context-shift in these theories are just too vaguely stated for the theories to be easily evaluable. This is much less so of Glanzberg's theory than of the others: his paper develops an extremely elaborate theory of context, which may well settle issues that other theories leave vague. But this account too is too big to deal with here; and besides, it is beyond my expertise.

In the rest of the chapter, then, I will primarily focus on stratified or hierarchical theories that have no contextual elements. I will however point to places where there is some reason to think that a contextualized version of the theory might do better, and to other places where there is reason to think it would not. Section 14.2 will deal with stratified theories that, if contextualized, locate the primary context shift between (2) and (3); 14.3 with stratified theories whose contextualized versions locate it in the shift from (1) to (2). These two ways of stratifying turn out to be extremely different, as will become especially clear in 14.4.

14.2. STRATIFIED GAP AND GLUT THEORIES

The simplest stratified gap theory is Tarski's: for each ordinal α in the hierarchy, 'true$_\alpha$' is true only of sentences that contain no truth predicates with subscripts of α or greater. (The hierarchy can extend only through a proper initial segment of the countable ordinals—indeed, probably only through a proper initial segment of the recursive ordinals—for reasons I confine to a footnote.[3] Details of the theory, and of the fact that it is a proper part of the Kripkean theory KFS, can be

---

[3] The subscripts are pieces of notation, not ordinal numbers themselves, and so the extent of the hierarchy is going to depend on the extent of a system of notations for the ordinals. Assuming the language to be countable, only countably many ordinals will have notations. I'll only be interested in notation-systems in which an ordinal gets a notation only if every predecessor gets a notation, so that a notation system can only extend part way through the countable ordinals.

There is a well-known theory of systems of ordinal notations due to Church and Kleene, which because of certain recursiveness requirements must limit the ordinals that have notations far more severely, to the recursive ordinals. In fact, if we assume that the notation system is "recursively related", i.e. that there is a mechanical method for deciding if one notation is a notation for a smaller ordinal than is another notation, then the system can't cover even all of the recursive ordinals, though it can be chosen so as to go through any given one. (For a clear presentation of the Church–Kleene requirements and the results I've mentioned here, see Rogers 1967, secs. 11.7–11.8.)

In the present context, where the notations are subscripts of primitive truth predicates and hence must be treated in the syntactic theory of the language, it seems reasonable to impose the Church–Kleene requirements—plus the requirement of "recursive relatedness", since information about whether the ordinal notations in a sentence to which 'True$_\alpha$' are ascribed are for lower ordinals than those 'α' denotes is needed to determine whether a (T-IN) axiom applies. (Halbach 1997 may seem to differ on this, since he speaks of a theory using a notation system that goes through all the recursive ordinals; however, I think this is intended merely as a convenient manner of speaking, and that he regards the legitimate theories as just the fragments that go through proper segments.) In Chapter 22 I'll discuss a broader kind of ordinal notation, for use in a situation where the notations are not part of the primitive syntax; in that context there will be no reason to think that even the Church–Kleene requirements apply, and the hierarchy of notations will extend far beyond the recursive ordinals. In the present chapter I will be careless about the distinction between ordinals and their notations.

found in Halbach 1997.) Defining 'false$_\alpha$' as 'has a true$_\alpha$ negation', we see that sentences that contain truth predicates with subscripts of α or greater are neither true$_\alpha$ nor false$_\alpha$—they are "α-gappy". But any such sentence will be either true$_\beta$ or false$_\beta$ whenever β is greater than all the subscripts in the sentence.

Kripke's critique of the Tarskian theory was given in the opening paragraphs of Chapter 3, and it seems to me thoroughly convincing. But there are subtler stratified gap theories, which by using a far coarser stratification can deflect some of Kripke's critique. To see what I mean, note that the Tarskian stratified theory has as its "ground floor" the theory of truth for sentences not containing any truth or satisfaction predicate; in this theory, any sentence containing a truth predicate is "0-gappy". But we saw in Chapter 7 that there are much more extensive gap-theories, which declare only sentences that seem slightly pathological to be gappy; why not take one of these theories as the ground floor of a stratified theory? That is, why not take one of these theories (whether FM or a supervaluation-style gap theory) as a theory of a basic predicate true$_0$?

If we do so, what should our theory of truth$_1$ be like? Or more generally, what should our theory of truth$_\beta$ be like, once we have our theory of truth$_\alpha$ for each $\alpha < \beta$? The basic idea is that in constructing the theory of truth$_\beta$ we should proceed just like for truth$_0$ except that we treat the terms 'true$_\alpha$' for $\alpha < \beta$ just like non-semantic terms: they are ordinary classical predicates, and so the construction will yield the biconditional

(i$_\beta$) $$\text{True}_\beta(\langle A \rangle) \leftrightarrow A$$

for any sentence A containing no truth predicates beyond these. Since the ways we constructed gap theories in Chapter 7 all guaranteed (T-OUT), we will also get

(ii$_\beta$) $$\text{True}_\beta(\langle A \rangle) \rightarrow A$$

even for sentences that contain 'True$_\beta$'. And since no predicate 'True$_\gamma$' for $\gamma > \beta$ is in the language at the time we do the construction for truth$_\beta$, it will yield

(iii$_\beta$) $$\neg \text{True}_\beta(\langle A \rangle)$$

for sentences containing such True$_\gamma$ (and hence (ii$_\beta$) will hold in these cases too, and so hold without restriction). In summary, (ii$_\beta$) holds unrestrictedly; (i$_\beta$) holds whenever the only truth predicates in A have subscripts strictly lower than β; and (iii$_\beta$) holds whenever A contains a truth predicate with a subscript strictly greater than β. (When A contains 'True$_\beta$' but no truth predicate with a subscript strictly greater than β, things are more complicated, and pretty much analogous to the situation with the unsubscripted truth predicate in the gap theories of Chapter 7.) This holds for each β.

We can now show, whenever $\alpha < \beta$, that

(M) $$\text{True}_\alpha(\langle A \rangle) \rightarrow \text{True}_\beta(\langle A \rangle).$$

(For if A contains 'True$_\gamma$' for some $\gamma > \alpha$, (iii$_\alpha$) yields $\neg\text{True}_\alpha(\langle A \rangle)$, which implies (M). And if A doesn't contain such a 'True$_\gamma$', (ii$_\alpha$) yields $\text{True}_\alpha(\langle A \rangle) \to A$ and (since $\beta > \alpha$) (i$_\beta$) yields $\text{True}_\beta(\langle A \rangle) \leftrightarrow A$, and these together imply (M).)[4] Since falsehood is just truth of negation (or more accurately, falsehood$_\sigma$ is truth$_\sigma$ of the negation, whatever the σ), it follows, when $\alpha < \beta$, that

(M∗) $\qquad\qquad\qquad \text{False}_\alpha(\langle A \rangle) \to \text{False}_\beta(\langle A \rangle).$

We *won't* have that whenever $\alpha < \beta$,

(X) $\qquad\qquad\qquad \neg\text{True}_\alpha(\langle A \rangle) \to \text{False}_\beta(\langle A \rangle);$

this can fail if A contains predicates with subscript α or higher.

So the effect of the added weakness of the predicates with higher subscripts is that some gaps get closed. For instance, if Q_0 is a sentence that asserts $\neg\text{True}_0(\langle Q_0 \rangle)$, then though the gap theory for truth$_0$ asserts

$$Q_0 \land \neg\text{True}_0(\langle Q_0 \rangle),$$

the gap theory for truth$_1$ allows us to expand this to

$$Q_0 \land \neg\text{True}_0(\langle Q_0 \rangle) \land \text{True}_1(\langle Q_0 \rangle).$$

The new truth predicate 'True$_1$' now allows us to construct a modified sentence Q_1 that asserts its own lack of truth$_1$, so we'll also have

$$Q_1 \land \neg\text{True}_1(\langle Q_1 \rangle) \land \text{True}_2(\langle Q_1 \rangle);$$

and so forth. Call such theories *coarsely stratified* gap theories.

There is a dual construction for glut theories based on (T-IN), which is like the above except that (ii$_\beta$) is replaced by its converse and the negation in (iii$_\beta$) is dropped. Then reasoning as above, we can derive the converse of (M). This time, the effect of raising the subscript is to *strengthen* the truth predicate, in such a way that some gluts get eliminated. (This dual approach may be somewhat less attractive: the modified (iii$_\beta$) seems somewhat unnatural.) I don't think the stratification of glut theories raises any issues beyond those raised by the stratification of gap theories, so from now on I'll stick to the case of gaps.

In what follows, I will discuss (A) an apparent advantage of coarsely stratified gap theories over Tarski's stratified theory, and (B) how coarsely stratified gap theories deal with two of the worrisome features of the unstratified gap theories of Chapter 7. In each case, I will start out discussing coarsely stratified theories that are not contextualized, but then say something about how contextualization is likely to affect the issue.

---

[4] I have done this instance-wise for notational simplicity, but we could develop the theory in a more general way so as to imply $\forall x[\text{True}_\alpha(x) \to \text{True}_\beta(x)]$ whenever β is a notation for an ordinal greater than the ordinal for which α is a notation.

A. Coarse *v*. Fine Stratification

Coarsely stratified gap theories have a huge *prima facie* advantage over Tarski's stratified theory: use of coarsely stratified truth predicates (as our sole truth predicates) would seem to be far less crippling to ordinary discourse than the use of Tarski's would. Indeed, even were everyone to stick to the predicate 'true$_0$' of the coarsely stratified gap theory, we would have all the advantages that the unstratified theories of Chapter 7 had over Tarski. (Trivially: the theory of truth$_0$ in the coarsely stratified theory *just is* one of the theories of Chapter 7.) For instance, suppose Smith admires Nixon, and says

(*) All of Nixon's assertions about Watergate are true$_0$.

And suppose Nixon said

(**) Ziegler's claim that Watergate was a third rate burglary is true$_0$.

If 'true$_0$' were used in the Tarskian sense, then Nixon's saying (**) would refute (*) *even under the supposition that Watergate was a third rate burglary*, which is obviously not what Smith intends. But if 'true$_0$' is used in the sense of the coarsely stratified theory, there's no such problem. In short, the advantage over the Tarskian approach is that in the coarsely stratified theory, the lowest level predicate 'true$_0$' has some claim to sufficing for ordinary purposes.

Of course to the extent that 'true$_0$' suffices, the coarse stratification plays no role. Indeed I will now argue that to the extent that higher 'true$_\alpha$' predicates were used in ordinary discourse, the problems with the cruder Tarskian stratification would tend to recur.

The problem is that the use of the truth predicates with subscripts higher than 0 brings back pressure to raise the subscripts of one's assertions. Consider again Nixon and Dean: Nixon wants to make a claim of the form

(N$_\alpha$) Everything Dean ever has said, is saying, or will say about Watergate is false$_\alpha$,

and Dean wants to make a claim of the form

(D$_\beta$) Everything Nixon ever has said, is saying, or will say about Watergate is false$_\beta$.

Suppose for the sake of argument that everything else either of these guys ever said was false$_0$. Then even on the new theory, for one guy to succeed in saying what he intended he must pick a strictly higher subscript than the other.[5] Because of this, there is pressure for Nixon and Dean to get into a subscript contest.

---

[5] For instance, if β is strictly greater than α, then (D$_\beta$) isn't even in the language on which truth$_\alpha$ and falsity$_\alpha$ are defined, so (D$_\beta$) isn't false$_\alpha$; and if $\alpha = \beta$, then we have the analog of the situation in the unstratified theory where we have two sentences each declaring the other false. Neither assertion is correct, assuming the minimal fixed point (or any other "intrinsic" fixed point) is used in the evaluation.

And this is more of a problem than one might initially think, for it means that there is pressure for others who want to comment on Nixon's or Dean's utterances to use high subscripts too. For instance, for Smith's remark

($*_\gamma$)   All of Nixon's assertions about Watergate are true$_\gamma$

to be correct, γ must be at least as high as any truth predicate used in any of Nixon's assertions about Watergate. So because Nixon was led to use a high subscript in commenting on Dean, Smith is indirectly pressured into using a high subscript in ($*_\gamma$) as well.

Typically of course the subscripts aren't made explicit; the theory, if intended to correspond to actual behavior, would have to be that they are implicitly intended. But that makes the problem worse! Since we don't typically know the subscripts intended by others, and know only that others are under constant pressure to intend high ones, this will give us pressure to intend high ones too, in quite ordinary remarks.

Once this is realized, the advantages of coarsely stratified theories over Tarski's don't look as large. What I said before remains true: *if everyone were to stick to the predicate 'true$_0$' of the new stratified gap theory*, we would have all the advantages that the gap theories of Chapter 7 had over Tarski. But why *should* everyone stick to the predicate 'true$_0$' of the coarsely stratified theory? We've seen that there is considerable pressure not to, pressure that is fueled by the fact that the ground level theory (one of the theories from Chapter 7) declares so many of its own assertions untrue. To the extent that there is such pressure, even the coarsely stratified gap theories have quite substantial *dis*advantages over the unstratified theories of Chapter 7.

This however is before contextualization, and at first blush that seems bound to improve the situation: to the extent that the assignment of subscripts to an indexical term is done by external context rather than by the speaker's intentions, it is difficult to engage in subscript contests with such a term.[6] The idea is to use contextual principles to get utterances containing 'true' to "seek their own levels"—not levels in the Tarskian hierarchy, but levels in the hierarchy of coarsely stratified gap theories. This brings back the worry voiced early in Chapter 3: we don't really have a precise account of how sentences "seek their own levels" in this sense, we are now operating with imprecise pragmatic principles. But perhaps these principles are clear enough to get us the results we want?

Let's look at how this plays out in a familiar case. Suppose Nixon and Dean are ordinary speakers that have only the indexical truth predicate, and utter (N) and (D) (the analogs of (N$_\alpha$) and (D$_\beta$) but without the specific subscripts).

---

[6] Perhaps not impossible: by saying other things, refraining from saying other things, and provoking Dean to say other things, Nixon might indirectly affect the subscripts in his and Dean's assertions of (N) and (D) [the analogs of (N$_\alpha$) and (D$_\beta$), except with subscripts removed]. And if his intentions as well as external context play a role in determining the subscript, there is still more opportunity to try to outdo Dean. I will ignore these points in what follows.

And assume, as before, that everything else each of them said was clearly false. Assume also that each of them has reached the same level in their other Watergate utterances (that is, for some a, each has made Watergate-utterances of level a but none of higher level). If context determines subscript in any remotely reasonable way that is independent of their intentions, it must assign their utterances the same subscript (a or $a + 1$, depending on the nature of the other utterances), by the symmetry of the situation. (Burge 1979 and 1982 calls the appeal to symmetry the Principle of Justice.) So there is no significant raising of prior subscripts, and we reproduce the result of the classical gap theories of Chapter 7 for this example: neither Nixon's nor Dean's remark is true.

What about if we alter the example slightly, by supposing that Dean has made other Watergate utterances of level 3, but that Nixon has made none of level higher than 1? (We still imagine that all these other Watergate-remarks were clearly false.) Burge seems to claim (1982, p. 360) that even then, the symmetry or Justice principle requires that the implicit subscripts of (D) and (N) must be the same—both at least 3, for (D) as well as (N)—but I don't see how his principles yield this: it seems to me that his principles yield instead that (N) should get a higher subscript than (D). If that's right, then Nixon's remark (N) comes out true on Burge's theory while (D) comes out false.

This seems grossly counterintuitive. It also seems to re-open the way for subscript contests, if not on the part of Nixon and Dean (though see n. 6) then at least on the part of more sophisticated agents who know the contextual theory. Imagine two logicians who hate each other and want to warn anyone who will listen about the other's views. One of them, D, worries that he may have used the indexical 'true' with a higher implicit subscript than N has ever done, and so if he says an analog of (D) while N says an analog of (N), then his rival N will have won out. To avoid this, he decides to use an explicit subscript in (D)—a quite high one. N on the other hand is clever enough to realize that D will have done this, so he too uses a high explicit subscript. The war is on. I don't see how the use of such explicit subscripts could be prohibited: they are, after all, part of the theory, even though the ordinary speaker is not assumed to know about them.

If I'm right about this, then the contextualized theory isn't that much of an improvement over the uncontextualized stratified theory as regards Nixon–Dean situations; indeed, if the counterintuitive consequences mentioned two paragraphs back can't be avoided by subtler pragmatic principles, it may be worse.

As for the uncontextualized theory, the problems I've been discussing may not be so severe if one can find pragmatic reasons for sticking to 'true$_0$' except in special circumstances. But to the extent that one does so, the theory becomes much closer to the unstratified gap theories of Chapter 7.

B. Stratified *v.* Unstratified

Are there advantages to the stratified gap theories over the unstratified ones? I don't see a lot. A small positive for the uncontextualized stratified theory is that we can't say that the theory declares itself untrue. But that's only because it can't declare *anything* untrue, since that would be to use an unsubscripted truth predicate which the theory doesn't allow. It is still the case that for each α, the theory declares itself not to be true$_\alpha$: for it contains the axiom schema

$$\text{True}_\alpha(\langle A \rangle) \to A,$$

some instances of which are not true$_\alpha$ but only true$_{\alpha+1}$ even on a course-grained stratification. (See the discussion of Montague's Theorem in Chapter 7.)

Admittedly, for each axiom of the theory, there is a subscript β such that we can say that that axiom is true$_\beta$; but it is not clear to me that this is of great significance. It may seem of more significance than it is, because we have a tendency to quantify over the subscripts: to treat "There is a β such that x is true$_\beta$" as an intelligible predicate. But of course such a predicate *isn't* intelligible, according to this theory: (i) the subscripts are ordinal notations, not ordinals, and so direct quantification over them is impossible; and (ii) the strategy of getting the effect of quantification indirectly, by saying "There is an ordinal notation such that the truth predicate with that notation as a subscript is true of x" is unavailable, since it requires an unsubscripted truth-of predicate. Given this, the theory allows no adequate surrogate of the generalization that for each axiom of the theory, there is a sufficiently large subscript β such that that axiom is true$_\beta$.

On this point the contextualized theory seems to fare no better, and may fare worse. In the Postscript to his paper (pp. 115–16), Burge recognizes a second use of the unsubscripted 'true' beyond the indexical: the schematic use. In what I believe is the intended construal of this, an utterance involving 'true' is interpreted as a systematically ambiguous assertion of every claim that results from it by substituting the same subscripted predicate for each occurrence of 'true'. If that is indeed the intended reading, then the principle

$$\text{True}(\langle \text{True}(\langle A \rangle) \to A \rangle)$$

fails; indeed, for each subscript, there are sentences A for which the negation holds. Perhaps there is a way to interpret the schematic reading so that in cases like this different subscripts will be used for different occurrences of 'true', but it isn't clear exactly how this would work.

Let's turn to a different issue. Perhaps the most crucial defect of the gap theories of Chapter 7 was their inability to express agreement and disagreement (though as noted in the previous chapter, this is really just part of a bigger problem). Does stratification help with this? Not in any significant way.

Let's consider the uncontextualized theory first. Suppose I disagree with someone's overall theory of something, but haven't decided *which part* is wrong.

The usual way of expressing my disagreement would be to say "Not all of the claims of his theory are true", but this requires a general truth predicate. Without one, the only recourse is to pick some large α, and say "Not all of the claims of his theory are true$_\alpha$".

One problem with this is that I may not know how large an α I need; this problem is especially severe since as already noted, everyone is under strong pressure to use very high subscripts α even in fairly ordinary circumstances.

But there is an additional problem. Suppose that I want to express disagreement with a stratified truth theorist's overall "theory of truth" (i.e. the theory he expresses with all of his 'true$_\alpha$' predicates), but haven't decided which part of it is wrong. Here the problem isn't just with knowing how high an α to pick; rather, no α that I pick could serve its purpose. The reason is that whatever α I pick, it's *already part of the stratified theory* that some of its claims aren't true$_\alpha$, namely, the principles about truth$_\alpha$; that's why the theorist introduced the notion of truth$_{\alpha+1}$. So I haven't succeeded in expressing our disagreement.

And on this point contextualization seems to offer no help: I'm not clear what directions the pragmatic picture would offer about how high an index to pick in this case, but it doesn't matter, given that whatever index they pick, it is already part of the stratified theory that not all of its claims are true$_\alpha$.

There is one issue on which stratified gap theories do seem a bit better than the unstratified gap theories of Chapter 7: the issue of Strengthened Liar reflections, from Section 14.1. Recall the situation: gap theorist Tim declares a Liar sentence untrue, and Charles wants to express his agreement with Tim. It is natural for him to do so by calling Tim's declaration true, but this makes sense only if there has been a shift in the "extension" of 'true' between Tim's remark and Charles's. (For this advantage, it may not be completely essential that the shift be fully contextual: we would get much the same effect by just imagining that 'true' is ambiguous and that Charles intended his use of 'true' to be broader than Tim's, though perhaps this is less psychologically plausible.) But I take this to be less a favorable remark about stratified gap theories than an unfavorable one about unstratified gap theories.

I've already mentioned that one way to avoid Strengthened Liar reasoning is simply to not make Tim's claim in the first place: that's what the theories we've considered so far that aren't gap theories do, and what the theories to be considered in Part III of the book do as well. But there is another option too: we can stratify one of these *non*-gap theories, so as to justify Strengthened Liar reasoning in a different way than the one considered so far. This alternative will also invoke a shift of extension in 'true' (perhaps contextual, perhaps not). But the shift won't be between Tim's remark and Charles's; rather, it will be between the paradoxical utterance and Tim's. This alternative form of stratification will be the focus of the next section.

14.3. "THE GHOST OF THE TARSKI HIERARCHY": STRATIFIED INTERNAL FIXED POINT THEORIES

Near the end of Kripke's 1975 paper, he speaks of "the ghost of the Tarski hierarchy". This phrase may be misleading for what Kripke intends. Tarski's theory, and stratified gap theories generally, involve hierarchies of truth predicates *each weaker than the previous*; but there is some reason to interpret Kripke as suggesting a hierarchy of truth predicates *each in some ways stronger than* the previous. If that is Kripke's idea, it might be better to call it a proposal for a *reverse* Tarski hierarchy. (That term isn't quite appropriate either, since there is weakening as well as strengthening as one goes up. Still, the most salient change as one goes up is a strengthening.)

Let's look at what Kripke says. Kripke introduces his remarks about "the ghost of the Tarski hierarchy" by saying that "many who have worked on the truth-gap approaches to the semantic paradoxes have hoped for a universal language, one in which everything that can be stated at all can be expressed" (p. 79). This is a bit of a straw man if taken literally: why saddle the proponents of these theories with the ideal of a language in which, among other things, every possible physical theory could be expressed? But for purposes of Kripke's discussion what seems relevant isn't a universal language but a *self-sufficient* language: a language that there is no reason to go beyond *simply to say what we want to say about truth and related concepts*. Kripke goes on to express doubts about whether the goal of a universal language (or a self-sufficient language, I think) can be achieved.

His first doubt is that when one defines truth for a number-theoretic object language, one needs a broader metalanguage. That of course is true, but its relevance to universality or self-sufficiency is unclear at best: the obvious moral is that if there is a universal/self-sufficient language it won't *define* truth, but take it as a primitive notion that obeys certain rules, perhaps the rules validated in one's favorite internal or external fixed point theory. (Kripke seems to have in mind the different view that I discussed at the end of Section 1.5 and which Parsons and Glanzberg advocate, on which we have available a sequence of more and more powerful set theories with no upper bound. But that view is at best contentious, and clearly not one that anyone drawn to a universal or self-sufficient language would find obvious.)

But the second reason Kripke gives for his doubts about universal or self-sufficient languages is more to the present point. The second reason is that

> there are assertions we can make about the object language that we cannot make in the object language. For example, Liar sentences are *not true* in the object language, in the sense that the inductive process never makes them true; but we are precluded from saying this in the object language. (pp. 79–80)

This passage takes "the theory of the object language" to be what I've called the *internal* theory of a fixed point: it does not license the claim that the Liar sentence isn't true. So "the theory of the object language" is either KFS or a weakly classical theory, depending on which valuation scheme one uses. But the passage also says that this internal theory is inadequate precisely because it doesn't license that claim. This initially seems to suggest that we should move to the external theory.

But there is a problem about interpreting Kripke as suggesting a move to the external theory: his remarks here are supposed to buttress doubts about the possibility of a universal language; and the suggestion that we move to an external theory does not do that. For suppose that the advocate of a universal or self-sufficient language were to adopt one of the external theories discussed in Chapter 7—a classical gap theory. Were he to do so, the indented quotation would have no force whatever, since it would already be a theorem of the proposed language that the Liar sentence isn't true; there would be no need of an ascent to a higher language to get that result.

Is there another way to interpret Kripke? One possibility—which I am not at all sure reflects what he intended, but which seems in any case interesting—is that he is suggesting a hierarchy of truth predicates that involves a strengthening at each stage (as opposed to the hierarchies of weaker and weaker ones used in the Tarski hierarchy and in the approach of Section 14.2). These will be given by a transfinite sequence of fixed point constructions. At each level β that appears in the hierarchy, let $\mathscr{L}_\beta^+$ be the result of expanding the ground language to include subscripted truth predicates with subscripts no higher than β. (The '+' is for consistency with the notation in the earlier chapters, but it may be confusing in this context; if so, ignore it.) Take the theory of truth$_0$ to be an *internal* fixed point theory (either Kleene-based or supervaluational) in the language $\mathscr{L}_0^+$, constructed much as in Chapters 3, 10, or 11, but using 'True$_0$' instead of 'True'. For $\beta > 0$, we likewise use an internal fixed point construction for 'True$_\beta$'; but instead of constructing *the minimal* fixed point by using the empty set as our starting set, we choose a starting set that "closes off at β" the fixed points F_α for the languages $\mathscr{L}_\alpha^+$ where $\alpha < \beta$. More fully, in constructing the fixed point F_β we take as our starting set X_0 the union of all $S_{\alpha\beta}$ for $\alpha < \beta$, where $S_{\alpha\beta}$ is the following:

$$F_\alpha \cup \{\neg \text{True}_\beta(\langle A \rangle) \mid A \text{ is in the language } \mathscr{L}_\alpha^+ \wedge A \notin F_\alpha\}.$$

We need a small and obvious modification of the fixed point construction, to ensure monotonicity; I will discuss this in a moment. But the key characteristic should be evident already: when $\alpha < \beta$ and A is in the language $\mathscr{L}_\alpha^+$ but neither A nor $\neg A$ is in the fixed point F_α, $\neg \text{True}_\beta(\langle A \rangle)$ isn't in F_α but is in F_β. Since a *negated* truth predication goes in at later stages, this involves a strengthening at the later stages. (There is also a weakening at the later stages, somewhat analogous to that in the Tarski hierarchy, due to the fact that no sentence containing 'True$_\beta$' is in the extension of any 'True$_\alpha$' for $\alpha < \beta$.)

Here is how the modified fixed point construction for the fixed point F$_\beta$ works, in more detail. The 0th stage X$_0$ was given above. At each stage X$_\gamma$, we evaluate sentences in the language $\mathscr{L}_\beta^+$ by using X$_\gamma$ and X$_\gamma^{neg}$ to evaluate 'True$_\beta$', while using F$_\alpha$ and F$_\alpha^{neg}$ (F$_\alpha$ being a previously constructed fixed point) to evaluate 'True$_\alpha$' for $\alpha < \beta$. Then each successor stage X$_{\gamma+1}$ is to be *the union of X$_\gamma$ with the set of sentences that get value 1 relative to X$_\gamma$*. This ensures monotonicity. At limits we take unions.

Clearly, if A is in $\mathscr{L}_\alpha^+$, True$_{\alpha+1}(\langle A \rangle)$ will be in F$_{\alpha+1}$ if and only if True$_\alpha(\langle A \rangle)$ is in F$_\alpha$; but ¬True$_{\alpha+1}(\langle A \rangle)$ will be in F$_{\alpha+1}$ not only when ¬True$_\alpha(\langle A \rangle)$ is in F$_\alpha$, but more generally when True$_\alpha(\langle A \rangle)$ is not in F$_\alpha$. Negative truth claims become easier to assert as the subscript increases: that is the sense in which 'True$_{\alpha+1}$' strengthens 'True$_\alpha$'. For sentences in $\mathscr{L}_\alpha^+$ the added strength "maxes out with True$_{\alpha+1}$": if A is in $\mathscr{L}_\alpha^+$ and $\beta > \alpha$, ¬True$_\beta(\langle A \rangle)$ is in F$_\beta$ if and only if ¬True$_{\alpha+1}(\langle A \rangle)$ is in F$_{\alpha+1}$. Still, for each α there are sentences B in $\mathscr{L}_\alpha^+$ for which we are unable to assert ¬True$_\alpha(\langle B \rangle)$ but can assert ¬True$_{\alpha+1}(\langle B \rangle)$: the Liar sentence Q_α that asserts that it is not true$_\alpha$ is an obvious example.[7] So in some sense the strengthening continues indefinitely.

If we were to follow this approach then we could take the theory based on this construction to consist of the union of all the fixed points. What is this theory like? Observe that in the construction of F$_\beta$, True$_\beta(\langle A \rangle)$ goes into the initial stage only when A itself goes in at that stage, so there will be no violations of (T$_\beta$-Elim) at stage 0; it is fairly evident that there won't be at later stages either, in the Kleene-based construction or in the supervaluational for reasonable Φ. And of course (T$_\beta$-Introd) and (¬T$_\beta$-Introd) are bound to be validated, since they are validated in all fixed point constructions. What about (¬T$_\beta$-Elim)? Clearly it's *not* going to hold, for $\beta > 0$. For instance, if Q_0 is a "0-level Liar"—a sentence asserting that it is not true$_0$—then ¬Q_0 will never appear in the iterated fixed point construction, but ¬True$_\beta(\langle Q_0 \rangle)$ is built into the fixed point construction from the start for each $\beta > 0$.[8]

Note the sharp contrast to the stratified gap theory of Section 14.2:

(i) Here Q_α is neither declared true$_\alpha$ nor declared not true$_\alpha$, whereas there it was declared not true$_\alpha$;
(ii) Here Q_α is declared *not* true$_{\alpha+1}$; there it was declared true$_{\alpha+1}$.

---

[7] I hope it's clear that the Q_α mentioned here are merely analogous to, not identical to, the Q_α discussed in Chapter 4: these involve stratified truth predicates, those involved iterations of an operator D.

[8] This doesn't mean that we are limited to those versions of supervaluationism whose minimal fixed points don't satisfy (¬T-Elim). Rather, the point is that even for those whose minimal fixed points satisfy (¬T-Elim), the non-minimal ones under consideration here will not.

This is a sharp illustration of how the present proposal "reverses the Tarski hierarchy" by proposing strengthening in the successive truth predicates rather than just a weakening.

It seems to me that for those who share the standard contextualist intuitions about Strengthened Liar reflections, this "reverse Tarski hierarchy" is the best way to make sense of those intuitions. On this view, a plausible construal of the remark I made while looking at myself on the TV screen was that what the person on the screen was saying isn't $true_0$. Tim's remark about me can be construed as the correct remark that what I said isn't $true_1$; and there is no need of a further contextual shift from Tim to Charles, because it is $true_1$ that my remark was not $true_1$.[9] (We could imagine that 'true' is an indexical predicate in which these shifts are made automatically, independent of our intentions; but I'm not sure there would be a great deal of advantage to doing so.)

14.4. STRATIFIED DETERMINACY PREDICATES FOR WEAKLY CLASSICAL THEORIES

The stratified theory of the previous section strikes me as a good bit more appealing than that of Section 14.2, and it would become more appealing still if we made a notational change. Instead of thinking of it as invoking a hierarchy of truth predicates, why not take '$true_0$' as the sole truth predicate, and think of the other predicates in the hierarchy as a sequence of stronger and stronger notions of *determinate* truth? So in the Strengthened Liar scenario, Tim isn't really shifting from one notion of truth to another, but from a notion of truth to a notion of determinate truth. We'd do better to relabel '$true_\alpha$' as '$dtrue_\alpha$' whenever $\alpha > 0$, and perhaps drop the subscript in '$true_0$'. (However, this truth predicate '$true_0$' is limited in scope: it doesn't apply to sentences containing any '$dtrue_\alpha$' predicates. And there are analogous limitations in scope in the '$dtrue_\alpha$' predicates: they don't apply to any sentences containing '$dtrue_\beta$' for $\beta > \alpha$. This is why the "reverse hierarchy" doesn't strictly involve stronger and stronger truth predicates as the subscript increases, but a combination of strengthening and weakening.)

Those who can remember back to Section 3.6 will recall that one of the *prima facie* weaknesses of Kripke's internal Kleene-based theory was that it has no notion of determinate truth. In a sense this was remedied in Lukasiewicz continuum-valued semantics, but not really, since outside the narrow range of sentential logic the Lukasiewicz notion of determinateness led to paradox. If we had a notion of determinateness, we could declare the Liar sentence to be defective (neither determinately true nor determinately false); but in the Kleene-based theory KFS, which lacks such a notion, there is no way to do this.

---

[9] Could Charles have meant that Tim's claim isn't $true_0$? No: '$true_1$' isn't in the language on which '$true_0$' has been defined.

Indeed, the issue isn't just what one can *publicly* declare, it is what one can "declare to oneself"; or rather, it is what one can believe. For in KFS, it would be as inconsistent to believe that the Liar sentence isn't true as to believe that it is true. What one must do, in KFS, is simply withhold belief from both, and indeed, withhold belief from the claim that it either is true or isn't. And one also can't consistently believe that it neither is true nor isn't; that, after all, implies that it isn't, which as already remarked is inconsistent. It might seem, then, that we are stuck in the ineffable.

As I went on to say in Section 3.8, this worry is slightly overstated: the problem is lessened if we broaden our focus to include not just *acceptance* but also *rejection*, and introduce some means for publicly expressing rejection. But as also noted there, allowing for rejection and its public expression doesn't fully handle the problem: for instance, it doesn't enable us to engage in debates about what is defective and what isn't. For that, we need a defectiveness predicate. We don't have one in the Kleene-based theory.

And though I didn't raise this point in connection with supervaluational and revision theories, they too have a similar difficulty: no reasonable predicate of determinate truth or defectiveness seems to be definable in such theories.[10] This is a very significant problem, for the same reason as it is in the case of KFS.

Because of this, the stratified theories of the previous section, reconstrued as theories that involve a hierarchy of determinacy predicates, seem to me a bit of an advance over the simple internal theories we've considered so far. The advance is somewhat limited, in that the resultant theory would be syntactically restricted: we couldn't meaningfully (or at least, truly) predicate 'true' of sentences containing any 'dtrue$_\alpha$', nor predicate 'dtrue$_\alpha$' of any containing 'dtrue$_\beta$' for $\beta > \alpha$. (This, as I've remarked, is why the hierarchy involves weakening as well as strengthening as the subscript increases.) Still, it's something.

Let us see how this would work in the context of internal supervaluation and revision theories. The idea would be to have a single such theory as one's unstratified theory of truth. (In my opinion the best choices for this would be the theories that validate (T-COMPL), but there's no need to insist on this.) We then add a hierarchy of predicates of determinate truth, viz. dtruth$_1$, dtruth$_2$, ...,

---

[10] One obvious attempt to do so would be to let 'A is determinately true' mean 'True($\langle A \rangle$) ∧ True($\langle$True($\langle A \rangle$)$\rangle$)'. But though the determinate truth predicate would then strengthen the truth predicate, it would not strengthen it enough to guarantee the law

$$\text{Determinately true}(\langle A \rangle) \to A.$$

(Further "iterations" of the truth predicate wouldn't help.) Alternatively, we might might let 'A is determinately true' mean '$\langle$True($\langle A \rangle$)$\rangle$ is provable in such and such a theory'. But unless the theory in question is so weak that hardly anything is determinately true in this sense, then determinate truth in this sense wouldn't imply truth, by the second incompleteness theorem.

extending a good way into the countable ordinals; each is applicable to the language that contains itself but no later predicates on the list, and each one has a theory formally like an internal supervaluation or revision theory. This means that we should *not* expect the analog of the (T-OUT) axiom (dtrue$_\alpha$($\langle A \rangle$) → A): that would be inconsistent for certain choices of A, for instance the αth level Liar sentence that asserts that it is not dtrue$_\alpha$.[11] Indeed, for the same reason, the analog of (¬T-Elim) must be abandoned.

Instead of the analog of (T-OUT), we will have the analogs of (T-Introd), (T-Elim) and (¬T-Introd). We obviously won't have the analog of (T-COMPL) for any of the dtrue$_\alpha$: for we will in fact have ¬(dtrue$_\alpha$($\langle Q_0 \rangle$)) ∧ ¬(dtrue$_\alpha$ ($\langle \neg Q_0 \rangle$)), where Q_0 is the ordinary liar that uses the truth predicate rather than the determinacy predicates. This absence of a completeness law is not only compelled by the construction, it seems central to any reasonable notion of determinate truth. Note that since we're taking there to be a big intuitive difference between truth and each of the dtrue$_\alpha$ predicates, there is no especial oddity if we decide to keep (T-COMPL) while rejecting its analog for the determinacy predicates.

Expanding a supervaluational or revision theory in this way is somewhat tempting. It wouldn't overcome the main problem with such a theory, over Intersubstitutivity. Nor would it obviate the need to reject reasoning by cases.[12] Nor, if the original supervaluation or revision theory is deemed objectionable as regards "self-undermining", would it improve the theory's situation with regard to that. Still, it does in a limited way address the problem of the absence of a defectiveness predicate.

Even this success is limited, for two reasons. The less important limitation is that each dtrue$_\alpha$ predicate needs to be taken as a separate primitive. This may not seem like such a big deal, since all obey formally analogous rules. However, it raises the following difficulty. Since each predicate 'dtrue$_\alpha$' is a primitive of the theory, the advocate of the theory seems forced to talk schematically about all of them; but then there's a problem attributing determinate truth of any sort to parts of the theory given by schemas. For instance, the stratified theory includes all sentences of form dtrue$_\alpha$($\langle A \rangle$) for which A is a truth of the ground language, for all ordinal notations α. Suppose we want to say that this part of the stratified theory is determinately true, or something to roughly that effect. We can't do it, for lack of an ordinal notation great enough. The best we can do is pick a

---

[11] We would get a restricted form of the axiom: it would hold when A doesn't contain the predicate 'dtrue$_\alpha$'. It might seem that if we can get a contradiction by instantiating with the αth level liar, we could also get one by instantiating with the claim that the αth level liar is true (i.e. true$_0$); but this reasoning is blocked by the fact that 'true' ('true$_0$') doesn't apply to sentences containing the 'dtrue$_\beta$' predicates.

[12] And related to this, it wouldn't undercut the worry expressed in Chapter 9, that the claim $A \vee \neg A$ undermines the claim that it isn't determinate whether A, or shows that the notion of determinateness being employed lacks philosophical interest.

very large ordinal notation β, and say that whenever A is a truth of the ground language then for any α less than or equal to β, $dtrue_\alpha(\langle A \rangle)$ is $dtrue_\beta$.

The more substantial limitation on our "success" in introducing defectiveness predicates is that the predicates we've introduced are heavily stratified: the normal truth predicate ($true_0$) can't be applied to sentences containing any '$dtrue_\alpha$', and a given '$dtrue_\alpha$' predicate can't be applied to sentences containing higher '$dtrue_\alpha$' predicates. This seems to me quite serious: it would mean, for instance, that the use of truth as a device of generalization would not apply to sentences containing the $dtrue_\alpha$ predicates.

In short, this stratification of internal supervaluation theories brings only a small improvement over the unstratified theories as regards a defectiveness predicate (and it doesn't address the major issues facing internal supervaluation theories, the ones discussed in earlier chapters).

We could apply this stratification idea not just to supervaluation theories, but to Kleene-based theories. I think, though, that there is little reason to do so: we will see in Parts III and IV that there is a nice way to develop determinateness predicates within paracomplete extensions of KFS, without the severe limitations that stratification imposes.

PART III

PARACOMPLETENESS

15

What Is To Be Done?

15.1. A FRAMEWORK FOR GENERALIZING CONTINUUM-VALUED SEMANTICS

In some ways the most successful theory we've considered so far is the Lukasiewicz continuum-valued logic for the quantifier-free fragment of the language (but with self-reference allowed by non-quantificational means). Like the Kripkean theory KFS in Kleene logic, but unlike all the broadly classical theories, it allows the full Intersubstitutivity Principle: True($\langle A \rangle$) is everywhere intersubstitutable with A (and the analogous principle for 'true of' holds as well).[1] But unlike KFS, it has a reasonable conditional; in particular, this allows it to contain all instances of the Tarski schema

$$\text{(T)} \qquad \text{True}(\langle A \rangle) \leftrightarrow A$$

(and the analogous schema for 'true of'). The logic comes with a pleasing model-theoretic semantics, in which all connectives including the '$\rightarrow$' are treated "value-functionally"—that is, sentences are assigned values merely on the basis of the values of their immediate components. True($\langle A \rangle$) always gets assigned the same value as A, which explains why the two sentences are intersubstitutable. Also, the values are ordered, with a conditional getting value 1 if and only if the value of the antecedent is less than or equal to that of the consequent; this together with the fact that $|\text{True}(\langle A \rangle)| = |A|$ explains why all instances of Schema (T) hold. I've been speaking of 'true', but the point extends to 'true of' and related notions. In short, the naive theory of truth, truth-of, etc. in a sentential logic based on continuum-valued semantics would be a very nice theory, if only it could be generalized to apply to the full quantificational language without generating inconsistencies, or ω-inconsistencies, or non-conservativeness (in the sense of conservativeness employed in Section 3.3), or anything similarly unpleasant.

Let's abstract from many of the details of continuum-valued semantics, in order to give a semantic framework in which to find a theory that, even in the

---

[1] Obviously intersubstitutivity would need restriction within quotation marks and within sentential attitude contexts like 'believes that' and 'hopes that', but we've excluded them from the language for simplicity.

presence of quantifiers, accords with the naive theory of truth, truth-of, and so forth. (Also the naive theory of properties, though I won't mention that again until Chapter 20.) My ultimate interest is less in the semantics than in the logic that the semantics validates, but the easiest way to find a logic that accords with the naive theory of truth is to look for a semantics in which for any sentence A, $|\text{True}(<A>)| = |A|$ (the "Model-Theoretic Intersubstitutivity Condition").

The key to generalizing continuum-valued semantics will be to find a suitable set V of semantic values, with a suitable partial ordering on them. (The set will be infinite.) We will take the value of a conjunction to be the greatest lower bound of the values of the conjuncts, and the value of the disjunction to be the least upper bound of the values of the disjuncts; this requires of course that any two elements of V have a greatest lower bound and a least upper bound, so let us require that the space $<V, \preceq>$ have this feature. (In technical terminology, it must be a *lattice*.) In order to make the logic of $\wedge$ and $\vee$ standard, we'll require that it be *distributive*:

$$a \sqcup (b \sqcap c) = (a \sqcup b) \sqcap (a \sqcup c)$$

and

$$a \sqcap (b \sqcup c) = (a \sqcap b) \sqcup (a \sqcap c),$$

where $\sqcap$ and $\sqcup$ are greatest lower bound and least upper bound respectively. We'll also require that it be *bounded*, i.e. have a greatest element 1 and a least element 0; 1 will serve as the sole designated value. Finally, since I want to allow reasoning by cases to be legitimate, I'll insist that that the designated value 1 not be the least upper bound of any two strictly smaller members. ("1 is *join-irreducible*.") All these conditions are of course met in both the Kleene value space $\{0, 1/2, 1\}$ and the continuum-valued space $[0,1]$, so we are simply generalizing.

We also suppose that corresponding to negation there is an "up-down symmetry" operator $*$ on the space: that is, an operator that reverses order ($a^* \preceq b^*$ iff $b \preceq a$) and whose double application is just the identity operator. From these it follows that 1^* is 0 and 0^* is 1, and that the deMorgan laws

$$(a \sqcup b)^* = a^* \sqcap b^*$$

and

$$(a \sqcap b)^* = a^* \sqcup b^*$$

hold. In the terminology of Section 10.5, the space is a deMorgan lattice (or deMorgan algebra), one with the added requirement that 1 is join-irreducible. This last requirement rules out all Boolean algebras other than the 2-valued one (since $a \sqcup a^*$ being 1 violates join irreducibility when a is neither 0 nor 1), and it rules out many non-Boolean ones besides. We'll also add one more condition, to rule out the 2-valued algebra: that there be an element $1/2$ that the operation * leaves fixed: $(1/2)^* = 1/2$.[2]

Extending these ideas to quantifiers is straightforward: the value of $\forall x Ax$ should be the greatest lower bound of the values of the "parameterized formulas" $A(o)$ (i.e., the values that $A(x)$ takes on relative to each assignment of an object o to the variable x), and similarly for existential quantification except with least upper bound. This means that the lattice must be "sufficiently complete" for these greatest lower bounds and least upper bounds to exist in it; I'll hold off a bit before stating this precisely. In analogy with the deMorgan laws, we get the usual laws about the relations between the quantifiers and negation: $\forall$ is equivalent to $\neg \exists \neg$ and $\exists$ to $\neg \forall \neg$. To make for reasonable quantifier laws we also need weak infinite distributivity assumptions, viz., $a \sqcup (\sqcap_a b_a) = \sqcap_a (a \sqcup b_a)$ and its dual $a \sqcap (\sqcup_a \{b_a\}) = \sqcup_a \{a \sqcap b_a\}$ (whenever those greatest lower bounds and least upper bounds exist).

Finally, we need an operation $\Rightarrow$ on V corresponding to the conditional. For now I impose only three requirements:

(I) $a \Rightarrow b$ is 1 if and only if $a \preceq b$
(IIa)   if $b_1 \preceq b_2$, then $(a \Rightarrow b_1) \preceq (a \Rightarrow b_2)$
(IIb)   if $a_1 \preceq a_2$, then $(a_2 \Rightarrow b) \preceq (a_1 \Rightarrow b)$
(III) $1 \Rightarrow 0$ is 0.

I'm tempted to add a fourth, viz.

(IV) $(a^* \Rightarrow b^*) = (b \Rightarrow a)$,

but for reasons of generality will keep that optional for a bit.[3] All of these requirements are met in continuum-valued semantics. ((I) is not met by the "conditional" $a^* \sqcup b$ of Kleene semantics.) Note that (I) and (III) imply that on the 2-valued subspace $\{0, 1\}$, $\Rightarrow$ behaves just like the material conditional of classical logic; all the other operators clearly behave like their classical counterparts on this subspace as well. So the semantics will be a genuine generalization of classical 2-valued semantics: it generalizes that semantics by allowing for extra values. The extra values will be the ones used for sentences in which $A \vee \neg A$ does not get the designated value 1. Because we allow sentences in which $A \vee \neg A$ doesn't get a designated value, the logic is "paracomplete".

It is within a semantics with this general structure that I propose to add a truth predicate; or more generally, a true-of or satisfaction predicate. (By "adding"

---

[2] Another structural feature of the Kleene and continuum-valued spaces is that for any $a \in V$, $a \sqcap a^* \preceq 1/2 \preceq a \sqcup a^*$. (From this it follows that $1/2$ is the *only* element that the operation * leaves fixed.) DeMorgan algebras with an element $1/2$ with this property are sometimes called *Kleene algebras* (though that term is also used in a different sense). The value spaces I'll consider will all be Kleene algebras.

[3] (I) and our assumptions about * already imply a weak version of (IV): that $(a^* \Rightarrow b^*) = 1$ if and only if $(b \Rightarrow a) = 1$.

such a predicate I mean: adding it to a rich ground language, of the sort described in Section 3.1.) Of course, not just any semantics with this general structure will do: neither 2-valued semantics nor continuum-valued semantics is adequate. What an adequate semantics has to do is meet the conservativeness requirement already discussed in connection with KFS, where this requirement is extended in the obvious way to accomodate the operation $\Rightarrow$.

Let's be a bit more precise about this. (The reader who finds the technical formulation obscure may want to review Section 3.3.) Let a *V-valued model* for a language $\mathscr{L}$ consist of

(i) a domain U for the quantifiers to range over;

(ii) an assignment of an object in this domain to each individual constant of $\mathscr{L}$;

(iii) an assignment of an n-place operation on the domain to each n-place function symbol of $\mathscr{L}$

and

(iv) an assignment, to each n-place predicate of $\mathscr{L}$, of a function that maps n-tuples of members of U into V.

A classical model is, in effect, a V-valued model in which only the values 1 and 0 are employed (the extension of a predicate being the set of n-tuples mapped into 1). If $\mathscr{L}^+$ is the expansion of $\mathscr{L}$ to include the terms 'True' and 'True of', and M and M^+ are V-valued models for $\mathscr{L}$ and $\mathscr{L}^+$, then call M the *reduct* of M^+ if it is just like M^+ except for not assigning anything to the extra predicates that are in $\mathscr{L}^+$ but not $\mathscr{L}$. (That is, the models have the same domains, and the same assignments to all individual constants, function symbols, and predicates of $\mathscr{L}$. When M is a classical model, it can be a reduct of M^+ only if M^+ is classical except with regard to the extra vocabulary such as 'True'.) Given a V-valued model for a language, we assign values in V to formulas of the language relative to assignments of objects in the domain to the variables in the familiar way.

Then an initial statement of the conservativeness requirement is as follows:

Conservativeness Requirement—First Stab: If M is any classical ω-model of the ground language $\mathscr{L}$, then there is a V-valued model M^+ of the expanded language $\mathscr{L}^+$ which has M as its reduct, and which satisfies these conditions:

(Ai) For any sentence A of $\mathscr{L}^+$, $|\text{True}(\langle A \rangle)| = |A|$

(Aii) For any assignment function s, if $|\text{Sentence}(v)|_s = 0$ then $|\text{True}(v)|_s = 0$

More generally,

(Bi) For any formula A of $\mathscr{L}^+$ with only one free variable, and any assignment function s, $|\text{True-of}(\langle A \rangle, v)|_s = |A^*|_s$, where A^* is the result of substituting v for the free occurrences of the free variable of A.[4]

---

[4] I assume that no occurrences of the free variable of A are in the scope of a quantifier associated with the particular variable v.

(Bii) For any assignment function s, if $|\text{Formula-with-only-one-free-variable}(v)|_s = 0$ then $|\text{True-of}(v, w)|_s = 0$.

(Note that since M^+ has M as its reduct, then the value that M^+ assigns to a sentence of the ground language, or to a formula of the ground language relative to an assignment function, is the same as the value that M assigns it.)

Here 'Sentence(v)' and 'Formula-with-one-free-variable(v)' are formulas of the ground language $\mathscr{L}$ (which of course we're assuming to be adequate to expressing syntax); since M is classical, these only take on values 0 and 1. (In formulating (Ai) I have made use of the fact that in ω-models the objects satisfying 'Sentence' are precisely the denotations of terms of form '$\langle A \rangle$'; analogously for (Bi).)

[Notes: (a) Although the notion of truth-of that I've added applies only to 1-place formulas, this is no real limitation when the ground language contains the means to construct ordered n-tuples, as it will in cases of interest (e.g. when it includes the language of set theory with urelements, or alternatively when it is the language of pure arithmetic). See Chapter 3, note 7. (b) We don't really need to add 'True' if we're adding 'True of', given that a sentence is true if and only if it (or the conjunction of it with '$x = x$') is true of everything. My reason for formulating the conditions on 'True' separately is just that they look simpler, and that in order to achieve readability I will often formulate my claims just for 'True' and tacitly leave the obvious extensions to 'True-of' for the reader.]

This first stab at the Conservativeness Requirement will need a very small correction later, but it should convey the spirit of what is needed. We will see how to achieve it (or rather, the corrected version of it) in Sections 16.2 and 17.1.

15.2. DETERMINATENESS AND THE LIAR HIERARCHY

One of the striking features of continuum-valued semantics noted in Chapter 4 was that it contains the means for defining a determinately operator. This carries over to the more general framework introduced in the previous section: indeed, almost the very same definition will do.

Recall the conditions there imposed on a determinacy operator. (I add a subscript for assignment functions, since we're now letting A contain free variables.)

(ia) If $|A|_s = 1$, $|DA|_s$ should be 1
(ib) If $|A|_s = 0$, $|DA|_s$ should be 0
(ic) If $0 \prec |A|_s \prec 1$, $|DA|_s$ should be strictly less than $|A|_s$
(ii) If $|A|_s \preceq |B|_s$, $|DA|_s$ should be less than or equal to $|DB|_s$.

As I remarked there, we should probably strengthen (ib), to

If $|A|_s \preceq 1/2$, $|DA|_s$ should be 0;

I'll actually strengthen it slightly further, to

(ib-s)   If $|A|_s \preceq |\neg A|_s$, $|DA|_s$ should be 0.[5]

For expository purposes it will also be useful to consider a weakening of (ic), viz.

(ic-w)   If $0 \prec |A|_s \prec 1$, $|DA|_s \preceq |A|_s$.

In these clauses, D is an operator on formulas of the language. In the semantics, it will correspond to an operator ∂ on the value space, and we can restate these conditions as conditions on ∂:[6] e.g. (ic) becomes "If $0 \prec a \prec 1$ then $\partial a \prec a$".

These conditions on D are not only natural algebraically, they correspond to the following natural inferential laws:

(1) $\vDash DA \to A$
(2) $A \vDash DA$
(3)   If $\vDash A \to DA$ then $\vDash A \vee \neg A$
(4)   If $\vDash A \to \neg A$, then $\vDash \neg DA$.
                     (So in particular
                          (i) if $\vDash \neg A$ then $\vDash \neg DA$;
                     and (ii) $\vDash \neg DQ$.)
(5)   If $\vDash A \to B$ then $\vDash DA \to DB$.

(1) is guaranteed by (ib) and (ic-w), and (2) by (ia). (3) is guaranteed by (ic), (4) by (ib-s), and (5) by (ii).

It is easy to see that if we define DA as $A \wedge \neg(A \to \neg A)$ (or pretty much equivalently, define ∂a as $a \sqcap (a \Rightarrow a^*)^*$), all these algebraic conditions *except for the full (ic)* are guaranteed by our assumptions about conditionals (together with our assumption about the operators corresponding to negation and conjunction). More particularly, (ia) comes from (III), (ib), and (ic-w) are immediate from the properties of $\sqcap$, (ib-s) comes from (I), and (ii) from (IIa) and (IIb). The full (ic) requires the assumption that $(b^* \Rightarrow b) \preceq b$ only if b is 0 or 1. This assumption will hold in the particular spaces I'll consider, though it doesn't have the immediate naturalness of the other conditions; that's why I'm temporarily weakening (ic) to (ic-w). So from now on, let's let a *weak determinacy operator* be one satisfying (ia), (ib-s) and hence (ib), (ic-w), and (ii); and a *determinacy operator* be a weak determinacy operator that in addition satisfies the full (ic).

It turns out that most of the striking features of determinacy operators in continuum-valued semantics turn only on their being weak determinacy

---

[5] $|A|_s \preceq 1/2$ implies $(1/2)^* \preceq |A|_s^*$, i.e. $1/2 \preceq |\neg A|_s$, and so $|A|_s \preceq |\neg A|_s$. So (ib-s) entails the preceding claim, that $|DA|_s$ is 0 when $|A|_s \preceq 1/2$.

[6] Strictly speaking, the formulation involving an operation on the value space is stronger, since there is no requirement that for every member of the value space, there is a formula that takes on that value relative to some assignment function; but the difference in strength won't matter to anything that follows.

operators, and thus will extend to the current framework. In particular, that is so of the Liar hierarchy. Recall the following sequence of Liar-like sentences:

$$Q_0 : \neg \text{True}(\langle Q_0 \rangle)$$
$$Q_1 : \neg D\text{True}(\langle Q_1 \rangle)$$
$$Q_2 : \neg DD\text{True}(\langle Q_2 \rangle)$$

and so on. Now, assume for the moment that we have a semantics of the sort I've outlined that licences a conservativeness claim, and hence allows us to interpret 'True' so that the Intersubstitutivity Condition holds (i.e. $|\text{True}(\langle A \rangle)| = |A|$ for every sentence A). Then we have

$$|Q_0| = |\neg Q_0|$$
$$|Q_1| = |\neg DQ_1|$$
$$|Q_2| = |\neg DDQ_2|$$

and so on. From these we can show the following (where $D^n A$ is the result of prefixing A with n occurrences of D):

Hierarchy Theorem (finite case): For any n, $|D^{n+1}Q_n| = 0$ but $|D^n Q_n| \neq 0$, and hence D^{n+1} is in some sense a strictly stronger operator than D^n.[7]

Proof: $|D^n Q_n|$ can't be 0, for if it were then the equation for Q_n would yield $|Q_n| = 1$ and we'd have a contradiction with the n-fold iteration of (ia). But $|D^{n+1}Q_n|$ must be 0: for by n-fold iteration of (ic-w), $|D^n Q_n| \preceq |Q_n|$, so by the equation for Q_n, $|D^n Q_n| \preceq |\neg D^n Q_n|$, so by (ib-s), $|D^{n+1}Q_n| = 0$. ∎

(Of course, this theorem is derived only on the assumption of a semantics in which the Intersubstitutivity Condition holds. I have yet to focus on a particular version of the semantics for which this assumption is justified.)

Moreover, further use of the assumption that we have a truth predicate for which Intersubstitutivity holds enables us to extend the sequence $D, D^2, D^3, \ldots$ into the transfinite and to generalize the hierarchy theorem to that case. The rough idea is that for a limit ordinal λ, we should take $D^\lambda A$ to be in effect the infinite conjunction of the $D^\alpha A$ for $\alpha < \lambda$. But the language doesn't contain a primitive device of infinite conjunction, so how are we to achieve this? The answer, of course, is by a truth predicate: roughly speaking, if we've defined the αth iteration of D for each $\alpha < \lambda$, we'll define the λth iteration of D as the operator which, applied to a sentence A, yields "For all $\alpha < \lambda$, the result of prefixing the αth iteration of D to A is true". (Of course, for this to be equivalent to the infinite conjunction, the predicate 'True' used in the definition needs to behave in accord with the Intersubstitutivity Principle.) The above sketch of the definition is quite imprecise: it fails to respect the distinction between ordinals and their notations. And when I make it precise in Chapter 22, it will

---

[7] In any case, $\neg D^{n+1}$ is a weaker operator than $\neg D^n$. (In the terminology of Chapter 10: $\neg D^{n+1}A$ doesn't in general *even weakly* imply $\neg D^n A$: the former can have value 1 when the latter doesn't. And $D^n A$ doesn't in general *strongly* imply $D^{n+1}A$.)

become clear that the hierarchy of D^β operators can't continue forever (if each is satisfactorily defined, i.e. defined in a way that takes $D^\lambda A$ for any limit $\lambda \leq \beta$ to be in effect the infinite conjunction of the $D^\alpha A$ for $\alpha < \lambda$). But it will continue for a long way through the countable ordinals. And whenever D^α is satisfactorily defined, we will be able to formulate a new Liar-like sentence Q_α (asserting that it is not D^α-true). This enables us to extend the hierarchy theorem into the transfinite, showing that we have a stronger and stronger sequence of operators:

Hierarchy Theorem (general case): Suppose that D^β is satisfactorily defined. Then for any $\alpha < \beta$:

(i) For every A, $|D^\beta A| \preceq |D^\alpha A|$
(ii) For some A, $|D^\beta A| \prec |D^\alpha A|$; in particular, $|D^\beta Q_\alpha| = 0$ but $|D^\alpha Q_\alpha| \succ 0$.

Proof: (i) An obvious induction on β, using (ic-w) at successor stages and the definition of the operator as "an infinite conjunction of its predecessors" at limits.

(ii) First we show, by an obvious induction analogous to that in (i), that if $|A| = 1$ then for every α, $|D^\alpha A| = 1$. So if $|A| = 1$, $|\neg D^\alpha A| = 0$ and hence $|\neg D^\alpha A| \neq |A|$. So the equation for Q_α precludes $|Q_\alpha|$ from being 1 and hence forces $|D^\alpha Q_\alpha| > 0$.

To complete (ii), we must show that if $\alpha < \beta$ then $|D^\beta Q_\alpha| = 0$. This is done by induction on β. If β is a successor $\gamma + 1$, it suffices to show that $|D^{\gamma+1} Q_\gamma| = 0$. (For if $\alpha < \gamma$, the induction hypothesis tells us that $|D^\gamma Q_\alpha| = 0$, and then $|D^{\gamma+1} Q_\alpha| = 0$ is immediate.) Proof of that: (i) gives $|D^\gamma Q_\gamma| \preceq |Q_\gamma|$, which with the equation for Q_γ gives $|D^\gamma Q_\gamma| \preceq |\neg D^\gamma Q_\gamma|$, which with (ib-s) gives $|D^{\gamma+1} Q_\gamma| = 0$. Finally, if β is a limit, then $\beta > \alpha + 1$; the induction hypothesis yields $|D^{\alpha+1} Q_\alpha| = 0$, so $|D^\beta Q_\alpha| = 0$ by (i).

A noteworthy consequence of the Hierarchy Theorem is that for any ordinal β for which D^β is well-defined, "excluded middle for D^β" is not generally valid: that is,

Corollary: For any β for which D^β is well-defined, there are sentences A for which

$$D^\beta A \vee \neg D^\beta A$$

has value less than 1.

Indeed, any sentence A for which $|D^{\beta+1} A| \prec |D^\beta A|$ clearly must have this feature; the sentence Q_β used in the proof of the main theorem is merely one example.

I repeat that the Hierarchy Theorem assumes that we have a truth predicate for which the Intersubstitutivity Principle holds. That assumption fails in continuum-valued semantics, which is why the hierarchy breaks down there after the finite stages. We have yet to see that there is any semantics in the current framework that validates the Intersubstitutivity Principle; if there isn't, the Hierarchy Theorem will prove to be empty. But we'll see in Sections 16.2 and 17.1 that there are indeed ways to validate the Intersubstitutivity Principle in a semantics falling under this framework; so what we've shown is that in any such "good semantics", the Hierarchy Theorem is inevitable.

I've been a bit vague on just how far the above hierarchy extends. Clearly it extends as far as D^λ can be satisfactorily defined; but how far is that? It is clear that in any countable language, the process of defining the D^λ has to break down somewhere in the countable ordinals; but exactly how and where the process breaks down is complicated, and can't be addressed without more precision about the definition of D^λ for limit λ. Making the definition precise and discussing why, how, and where it breaks down for large countable ordinals is a matter I defer until Chapter 22. The nature of the breakdown is a matter of some philosophical interest, as we'll see.

15.3. MORE ON THE NEVER-COLLAPSING HIERARCHY OF DETERMINATELY OPERATORS

It would be misleading to call the hierarchy of determinately operators "unending", since for sufficiently large countable ordinals it can't be satisfactorily defined (that is, defined in such a way that at every limit λ, D^λ behaves as the infinite conjunction of the D^α for $\alpha < \lambda$); but we can say that it "never collapses", meaning that insofar as it can be satisfactorily defined, the operators become stronger and stronger. That is what the hierarchy theorem tells us. (Again, I'm jumping the gun by assuming the result of Section 16.2, that it is possible to have a truth predicate that obeys Intersubstitutivity and thus makes the Hierarchy Theorem applicable.)

We've seen that the existence of such a never-collapsing hierarchy is an inevitable consequence of a paracomplete theory in the framework of Section 15.1 that allows for a truth predicate satisfying Intersubstitutivity. But it seems to me that it is, in addition, an attractive feature in a solution to the paradoxes. If one allows a determinately operator into one's language at all, then a sentence Q_1 that asserts its own lack of determinate truth is virtually inevitable. It would seem awkward to say that Q_1 isn't determinately true: for since that's equivalent to asserting Q_1, we'd be saying

Q_1, but Q_1 isn't determinately true,

which has the ring of incoherence. It would seem even more awkward to say that Q_1 *is* determinately true: for since that's equivalent to asserting $\neg Q_1$, we'd be saying

Q_1 is determinately true, but $\neg Q_1$.

How then can we express the somewhat "quasi-defective" status of Q_1? Saying that it isn't determinately determinately true seems the most initially promising way to do this, and that's what our framework provides.[8]

A second point to note is that if we're attracted to the idea of using the theory for vagueness (as was tentatively suggested in Chapter 5), then the Corollary to the Hierarchy Theorem seems required. Suppose we think that we should avoid assuming that there is a first natural number n such that Russell was old at n nanoseconds; to do this, we must avoid assuming that for every number n Russell *either was or wasn't* old at n nanoseconds. I tentatively suggested in Chapter 5 that this might be an attractive approach to vagueness. But the approach would be totally spoiled if for some β, we had to assume that for every number n, Russell either was or wasn't determinately$^\beta$ old at n nanoseconds, for then there would have to be a first natural number n such that Russell was determinately$^\beta$ old at n nanoseconds. In other words, 'determinately$^\beta$ old' would have to have sharp boundaries, and if you're willing to swallow that then there is little point in not saying the same about 'old'. This is of course a standard worry about higher order vagueness in paracomplete logics; but the worry is shown unfounded if the paracomplete logic obeys the Corollary to the Hierarchy Theorem. (If anyone thinks that the worry is justified anyway, because of the fact that in any given model M there's a sharp boundary between those n for which 'Russell was old at n nanoseconds' has value 1 and those for which it doesn't, I refer them back to the discussion of models *versus* reality in Section 5.6.)

It's worth pointing out that applying the sort of paracomplete logic under consideration to vagueness wouldn't require that for each β there be a sentence in ordinary vague language (without 'true') with the feature of the sentence Q_β: viz., the feature that one is in a position to assert $\neg D^{\beta+1} A$ but not in a position to assert $\neg D^\beta A$. The logic *allows* that there be such sentences, but doesn't *demand* that there be such, other than certain peculiar sentences containing 'true'. Indeed in ordinary discussions of vagueness, where we are considering applying a single vague predicate to finitely many objects, it would be absurd to suppose the existence of such a sentence for more than finitely many β. It isn't obviously absurd to suppose this for some infinite β, since it could hold for a given β without holding for all its predecessors, but in these cases there must be a β past which it never holds. (That isn't to say that for sufficiently large β we should take all instances of "If $D^\beta A$ then $D^{\beta+1} A$" to be obvious: the conditional can be unobvious even if one isn't prepared to assert the negation of its consequent.) Indeed, I'd regard it as highly doubtful that one is ever in a position, in ordinary vagueness cases, to assert $\neg DDA$ when one is not in a position to assert $\neg DA$;[9]

---

[8] If 'defective' means 'neither determinately true nor determinately false', we can't really say that Q_1 is defective (nor that it isn't). Hence "quasi-defective": the claim that it is non-defective is itself defective.

[9] Again, that isn't to say that $\neg DDA \to \neg DA$ is obvious.

and it isn't even *completely* obvious that in ordinary vagueness cases one is ever in a position to assert $\neg DA$ when one is not in a position to assert $\neg A$. This in no way rules out using the logic for ordinary vagueness, it just means that not all of its potentialities are exploited in the vagueness case. What *would* rule out use of a paracomplete logic for vagueness is if, contrary to the Corollary, iteration of the determinately operator eventually collapsed to a bivalent operator. That is what *does* happen in continuum-valued semantics, and is the main reason cited in Chapter 5 for why that semantics is unsuited to handle vagueness.

The hierarchy of determinately operators in "good" paracomplete theories may be reminiscent of the hierarchy of determinately operators contemplated for weakly classical theories in Section 14.4, and also of the Tarskian hierarchy of truth predicates and the improved Tarskian hierarchy discussed in Section 14.2. In fact, though, the differences are huge, as I will discuss in detail in Chapter 23.

16
Fixed Points and Revision Rules for Conditionals

The goal, then, is to find a semantics that fits the framework of Section 15.1 and that will support (the Model-Theoretic Intersubstitutivity Condition and hence) the Intersubstitutivity Principle. But rather than plunging into this directly, I'd like to build up the motivation slowly. This will require ignoring the infinite-valued framework for the space of this chapter, and returning to a 3-valued framework in which distinctions among sentences that don't get value 1 or 0 are blurred.

I begin with a rather trivial observation, but one which will prove useful. Let $\mathscr{L}$ be a ground language (no truth predicate) of the sort described in the second paragraph of Section 3.1. Assume that it contains a primitive notation for a conditional (as well as the usual $\neg$, $\wedge$, $\vee$, $\forall$ and $\exists$, none defined in terms of the conditional). Let M be an ω-model for $\mathscr{L}$. Let $\mathscr{L}^+$ be the result of adding 'True' to $\mathscr{L}$. (Or better, 'True of', but I'll illustrate with 'True' to keep the notation simple.) Let Z be the set of all conditionals in $\mathscr{L}^+$, including those with other conditionals embedded inside them. Let a *generalized atomic formula* of $\mathscr{L}^+$ be a formula that is either atomic or a member of Z. The ground model M determines semantic values for the normal atomic formulas, relative to an assignment function s of objects in the domain of M to the variables.

Let us now imagine that we have available a *valuation for conditionals*: a function **v** that assigns a value in $\{0, 1/2, 1\}$ to each $<C, s>$ for which $C \in Z$ (subject to the condition that if $<C, s_1>$ and $<C, s_2>$ get different values then s_1 and s_2 differ in what they assign to some variable that is free in C). Then it is clear that Kripke's Kleene-based fixed point construction from Chapter 3 can be applied (proceeding this time from *generalized* atomic formulas). The minimal fixed point X gives us a 3-valued model (where $|A|_s = 1$ if $<A, s> \in X$, $|A|_s = 0$ if $<A, s> \in X^{neg}$, $|A|_s = 1/2$ otherwise), obeying the Kleene rules for the connectives other than $\to$, which has M as its reduct and in which

(i) for any sentence A, $|\text{True}(\langle A \rangle)| = |A|$
(ii) for any $C \in Z$, $|C|_s$ is as given by the valuation for conditionals.

If **v** is the valuation for conditionals, I'll call this *the minimal Kripke fixed point over* **v** (relative to the ground model M). We can also get *non-minimal* fixed points over **v**, by similar means. They too give conditionals the value assigned them by

v, so they agree with the minimal fixed point in the evaluation of conditionals. But they can give value 1 or 0 to non-conditionals (with or without conditionals embedded in them) to which the minimal fixed point over **v** gives value $1/2$.

The construction of fixed points over a valuation for conditionals isn't by itself very interesting, because there need be no connection whatever between the semantic values of the conditionals (or their membership in the fixed point X) and the semantic values of their antecedents and consequents (or their membership in X). Indeed, even though (i) is guaranteed, the 3-valued model needn't even license the Intersubstitutivity Principle: it only need license intersubstitutivity *outside the scope of the conditionals*.

We can remedy this last failing by starting from a special sort of valuation for conditionals. Call a valuation for a set Y of formulas *transparent* if for any $B \in Y$ and any s, if $B^@$ is the result of replacing some subsentence A of B with True($\langle A \rangle$) then $<B,s>$ and $<B^@,s>$ get the same value. A simple induction shows that the minimal fixed point over a transparent valuation for conditionals will itself be transparent.[1] (This isn't in general so for *non*-minimal fixed points over transparent valuations; however, each transparent valuation will have lots of transparent non-minimal fixed points.) This gives us the following

Trivial Observation: If we start from a transparent valuation for conditionals and construct the minimal Kripkean fixed point in the way just discussed, the internal theory of that fixed point obeys the Intersubstitutivity Principle.

But we are left with two related problems. The first is that transparent valuations of conditionals can be baroque and unappealing; there's no reason, for instance, why they can't include $A \to B$ but not $(A \wedge A) \to B$, or why they can't include $0 = 0 \to \neg(0 = 0)$. Getting a decent theory would require starting from a "nice" transparent valuation, and it is not immediately clear what this should be taken to involve.

The second problem is that on almost any decision about what "niceness" is taken to involve, it isn't clear how to obtain it. Suppose for instance that we think that a "nice" valuation should satisfy a certain compositional principle for conditionals. It would be easy enough to stipulate that a starting valuation satisfies this compositional principle *as applied to formulas not containing 'True'*. But a valuation for conditionals must assign values even to conditionals that contain 'True'. Consider a conditional of form 'True(t_1) $\to$ True(t_2)'. How are we to ensure that the assignment of a value to this accords *both* with a given compositionality principle *and* with the transparency requirement? The transparency requirement compels us to take the value of that conditional to be the same as the value of $A \to B$, when t_1 names the sentence A and t_2

---

[1] By a transparent fixed point I mean, of course, one whose corresponding 3-valued valuation is transparent. Equivalently, it is transparent if, whenever B and C are alike up to substitution of A with True($\langle A \rangle$) for subsentences A, then B is in the fixed point if and only if C is.

names the sentence B. But A and B can both be very complicated sentences (possibly containing 'True' and '$\rightarrow$') whose truth value is determined by the Kripke fixed point construction over **v**, and thus doesn't seem available in the specification of **v**. Indeed, A and/or B could itself be the very conditional 'True(t_1) $\rightarrow$ True(t_2)', or have this conditional as a subformula, in which case there seems to be no reasonable sense in which its value is available prior to the specification of **v**. Given this, how are we to ensure that **v** obeys the chosen composition principle? It is not initially obvious how this circularity problem can be overcome.

Despite the obstacles, we are not without resources. I will consider two approaches to getting a transparent valuation to employ in connection with the Trivial Observation. One, suggested in Yablo 2003, has an appealing simplicity. Unfortunately, as it stands it has some highly undesirable properties, and I have not been able to find a way to fix it up. I don't totally despair of there being a way to fix it, though, and so discuss the approach and its problems at some length in Section 16.1. 16.2 is devoted to an approach of my own which I think is less problematic. Some of Yablo's ideas can be used to produce a variation on this, to be discussed in the next chapter.

16.1. YABLO FIXED POINTS

Yablo's approach involves using a fixed point construction to get a particular transparent valuation for conditionals (the *minimal Yablo fixed point*); this is then used as the basis for a Kripkean fixed point, in line with the Trivial Observation. (Actually the dependence on Kripke fixed points is much deeper than this might suggest: not only is the Kripke construction applied to the Yablo fixed point, but in addition it is applied infinitely many times in the process of constructing the Yablo fixed point.) The version of this that Yablo gives uses a 4-valued semantics, but I'm going to simplify things by using a 3-valued analog. All the virtues of his account that Yablo cites survive this simplification; and the problems I'll note for his account would arise for the 4-valued version as well.[2]

Here's the idea. For any transparent valuation **v** (of conditionals), let S[**v**] be the set of transparent valuations that *extend* **v**, in the sense that they assign 1 to every conditional to which **v** assigns 1 and 0 to every conditional to which **v** assigns 0. S[**v**] can't be empty, since **v** belongs to it and is transparent. For any nonempty set S of valuations, let **w**[S] be the valuation (of conditionals) given as follows: for any A and B,

---

[2] Besides simplification, the use of the 3-valued semantics leads to a more powerful logic for the connectives other than the conditional: with a 4-valued semantics one must apparently sacrifice either the rule of disjunctive syllogism or the meta-rule of reasoning by cases, whereas these can be jointly maintained on a 3-valued semantics.

$\mathbf{w}[S](A \rightarrow B)$ is 1 if $(\forall \mathbf{v})(\forall T)$[if $\mathbf{v} \in S$ and T is a transparent Kripke fixed point over $\mathbf{v}$ then $|A|_T \leq |B|_T$],

0 if $(\forall \mathbf{v})(\forall T)$[if $\mathbf{v} \in S$ and T is a transparent Kripke fixed point over $\mathbf{v}$ then $|A|_T > |B|_T$],

$1/2$ otherwise.[3]

Clearly $\mathbf{w}[S]$ is transparent if all members of S are. Moreover if $\mathbf{v}_1$ extends $\mathbf{v}_2$ then $S[\mathbf{v}_1] \subseteq S[\mathbf{v}_2]$, and if $S_1 \subseteq S_2$ then $\mathbf{w}[S_1]$ extends $\mathbf{w}[S_2]$; consequently, if $\mathbf{v}_1$ extends $\mathbf{v}_2$ then $\mathbf{w}[S[\mathbf{v}_1]]$ extends $\mathbf{w}[S[\mathbf{v}_2]]$.

Let a *Yablo fixed point* be a valuation $\mathbf{v}$ for which $\mathbf{v}$ is identical to $\mathbf{w}[S[\mathbf{v}]]$; that is, a valuation $\mathbf{v}$ such that for any A and B,

(Y) $\mathbf{v}(A \rightarrow B)$ is 1 if $(\forall \mathbf{u})(\forall T)$[if $\mathbf{u}$ is a transparent extension of $\mathbf{v}$ and T is a transparent Kripke fixed point over $\mathbf{u}$ then $|A|_T \leq |B|_T$],

0 if $(\forall \mathbf{u})(\forall T)$[if $\mathbf{u}$ is a transparent extension of $\mathbf{v}$ and T is a transparent Kripke fixed point over $\mathbf{u}$ then $|A|_T > |B|_T$],

$1/2$ otherwise.

It is easy to show that there are Yablo fixed points; indeed, there is a natural Kripke-like construction of the smallest one. We define a transfinite sequence of transparent valuations, as follows:

$\mathbf{v}_0$ assigns each conditional the value $1/2$;

$\mathbf{v}_{\alpha+1}$ is $\mathbf{w}[S[\mathbf{v}_\alpha]]$;[4]

$\mathbf{v}_\lambda$ is the minimal extension of each $\mathbf{v}_\beta$ for $\beta < \lambda$, when λ is a limit ordinal.

A trivial inductive argument shows that if $\alpha < \beta$ then $\mathbf{v}_\beta$ extends $\mathbf{v}_\alpha$; so by a standard fixed point argument analogous to Kripke's, there must be an ordinal ξ such that $(\forall \alpha \geq \xi)(\mathbf{v}_\alpha = \mathbf{v}_\xi)$. $\mathbf{v}_\xi$ is *the minimal Yablo fixed point*. In effect what we've done is started from the set S_0 of all transparent valuations, and for each α letting $S_{\alpha+1}$ be $S[\mathbf{w}[S_\alpha]]$, taking intersections at limits; this has a nonempty intersection S_∞, and $\mathbf{v}_\xi$ is $\mathbf{w}[S_\infty]$.

Yablo's suggestion (modified to fit 3-valued semantics) was to use this minimal Yablo fixed point $\mathbf{v}_\xi$ as the valuation for conditionals, and the minimal Kripke fixed point over $\mathbf{v}_\xi$ (call it Z_ξ) as the assignment to the truth predicate. He says that evaluating the conditional by (what I'm calling) a Yablo fixed point

---

[3] One could consider variations in which one considered only the minimal fixed points over transparent extensions, rather than all transparent fixed points, in the 0 clause and/or the 1 clause. The problems I will note don't turn on which choice is made on this.

[4] That is: $\mathbf{v}_{\alpha+1}(A \rightarrow B)$ is

1 if $(\forall \mathbf{u})(\forall T)$[if $\mathbf{u}$ is a transparent extension of $\mathbf{v}_\alpha$ and T is a transparent Kripke fixed point over $\mathbf{u}$ then $|A|_T \leq |B|_T$],

0 if $(\forall \mathbf{u})(\forall T)$[if $\mathbf{u}$ is a transparent extension of $\mathbf{v}_\alpha$ and T is a transparent Kripke fixed point over $\mathbf{u}$ then $|A|_T > |B|_T$],

$1/2$ otherwise.

gives it an appealing modal-like semantics: if $\mathbf{v}$ is a Yablo fixed point then each $<M,\mathbf{u},T>$ for which $\mathbf{u}$ is a transparent extension of $\mathbf{v}$ and T is a transparent fixed point over $\mathbf{u}$ can be viewed as a possible world accessible from $\mathbf{v}$.

The suggestion has virtues, among them that it validates some desirable laws (i.e. gives all instances of them value 1, in the case of sentences; preserves value 1, in case of inferences).

- For a *very* simple illustration, consider $A \wedge B \rightarrow A$. For any fixed point T over any valuation at all, $|A \wedge B|_T \leq |A|_T$, so the construction gives the conditional value 1 at $\mathbf{v}_1$ and hence at every valuation thereafter.

- Somewhat more interesting is the inference from $(A \rightarrow B) \wedge (A \rightarrow C)$ to $A \rightarrow (B \wedge C)$. If the premise gets value 1 at $\mathbf{v}_\xi$ then by the fixed point property, $|A|_T \leq |B|_T$ whenever $\mathbf{v}_T$ is a transparent extension of $\mathbf{v}_\xi$, and also $|A|_T \leq |C|_T$ in the same circumstances; from which it follows that $|A|_T \leq |B \wedge C|_T$ in those circumstances, and hence that $A \rightarrow (B \wedge C)$ has value 1 at $\mathbf{v}_\xi$.

- Modus ponens is validated as well: if $A \rightarrow B$ has value 1 at $\mathbf{v}_\xi$, then for any fixed point T over a transparent extension of $\mathbf{v}_\xi$, $|A|_T \leq |B|_T$; so in particular when Z_ξ is the minimal Kripke fixed point over $\mathbf{v}_\xi$, $|A|_{Z_\xi} \leq |B|_{Z_\xi}$; so if A has value 1 at Z_ξ, so does B.

A list of some other laws that are validated in the theory is given in [12]. (The list is of things validated in the 4-valued semantics; but anything validated in the 4-valued is validated in the 3-valued as well.)

The bad news is that the account does terribly on conditionals that have other conditionals embedded within them. For instance, one thing we would certainly hope for is the intersubstitutivity of equivalents (the inference from $A \leftrightarrow B$ to $X_A \leftrightarrow X_B$, where X_B is the result of substituting B for one or more occurrences of A in X_A). But this fails in the Yablo semantics, in dramatic ways.

- For instance, though $A \leftrightarrow (A \vee A)$ is valid, $[A \rightarrow C] \leftrightarrow [(A \vee A) \rightarrow C]$ isn't. Suppose for instance that in $\mathbf{v}_\xi$, $A \rightarrow C$ (and hence $A \vee A \rightarrow C$) gets value $1/2$. Then in some extensions of $\mathbf{v}_\xi$ one of $A \rightarrow C$ and $A \vee A \rightarrow C$ will get value 0 while the other one gets a value different from 0, and this means that $[A \rightarrow C] \leftrightarrow [(A \vee A) \rightarrow C]$ will get value $1/2$.

Clearly this situation arises because the extensions of $\mathbf{v}_\xi$ that one quantifies over in the truth conditions at $\mathbf{v}_\xi$ can be extraordinarily badly behaved; we will consider in a moment whether this can be fixed.

A related point is that Yablo's claims to have given the '$\rightarrow$' a modal semantics seem considerably overstated, for when a conditional is embedded inside another conditional, the "modal semantics" applies only to the outer conditional, not to the occurrence of the conditional embedded inside it. The analogs of "possible worlds" on the Yablo semantics are the transparent Kripke fixed points over extensions of the Yablo fixed point $\mathbf{v}_\xi$; in an embedded conditional, the inner conditionals are thus evaluated at extensions of $\mathbf{v}_\xi$. But these extensions of $\mathbf{v}_\xi$ are, for the most part, not themselves Yablo fixed points, and the evaluation of conditionals at them does not proceed by considering the values of their antecedents and consequents at other worlds. Rather, the evaluation of conditionals at them is just built in by brute force, it's built into the specification of which extension of $\mathbf{v}_\xi$ is in question.

This makes it tempting to try to restrict the class of worlds quantified over to more well-behaved worlds, but I have been unable to find a way to do this that yields satisfactory results. One natural suggestion along these lines would be to iterate Yablo's construction, so that the extensions of $\mathbf{v}_\xi$ that we quantify over in evaluating conditionals at $\mathbf{v}_\xi$ are themselves Yablo fixed points. To carry this out, let's introduce a new sequence of sets starting with the set S^1_0 of all Yablo fixed points, with its corresponding valuation $\mathbf{v}^1_0 = \mathbf{w}[S^1_0]$, and successively decrease the former and build up the latter until a new "second level Yablo fixed point" is reached. This seems to have a similar motivation to Yablo's: we start from a set of valuations (in this case, the Yablo fixed points) from which we want to draw our final valuation, and construct further valuations from it successively: the valuation at stage $\alpha + 1$ is obtained by quantifying only over what remains at stage α. It is natural to hope that if we do this, we will get something closer to a truly modal semantics, and that the problems over intersubstitutivity of equivalents within conditionals might disappear.

But such hopes are dashed: the iterated version breaks down right at the start. To see this, consider the Curry sentence K, which says $\text{True}(\langle K \rangle) \to 0 = 1$. This has value $1/2$ not only in $\mathbf{v}_\xi$ but in every ("first level") Yablo fixed point.

Proof: If K has value 1 at a valuation $\mathbf{v}$, then it has value 1 in every extension of $\mathbf{v}$ and so in every Kripke fixed point over such an extension; but then the evaluation rules for $\text{True}(\langle K \rangle) \to 0 = 1$ yield that it has value 0 at $\mathbf{w}[S[\mathbf{v}]]$, so $\mathbf{v}$ can't be a Yablo fixed point. Similarly, if K has value 0 at a valuation $\mathbf{v}$, then it has value 0 in every extension of $\mathbf{v}$ and so in every Kripke fixed point over such an extension; but then the evaluation rules for $\text{True}(\langle K \rangle) \to 0 = 1$ yield that it has value 1 at $\mathbf{w}[S[\mathbf{v}]]$, so $\mathbf{v}$ can't be a Yablo fixed point.

So defining S^1_0 and $\mathbf{v}^1_0$ as above, every member of S^1_0 gives K the value $1/2$; so by the valuation rules for the conditional, $\mathbf{v}^1_0$ gives K the value 0, and hence is not even a first level Yablo fixed point, i.e. not a member of S^1_0. We no longer get a monotonic construction, and thus a fundamental feature of Yablo's account would be destroyed.

Even if iteration is a bad idea, one might still hope that the (uniterated) Yablo account could be given a genuine modal semantics, by finding some accessibility relation on the set $S[\mathbf{v}_\xi]$ (the set of Kripke fixed points over transparent extensions of $\mathbf{v}_\xi$) such that for each T in $S[\mathbf{v}_\xi]$,

$\mathbf{v}_T(A \to B)$ is 1 if $(\forall U \in S[\mathbf{v}_\xi])$[if U is accessible from T then $|A|_U \leq |B|_U$]

0 if $(\forall U \in S[\mathbf{v}_\xi])$[if U is accessible from T then $|A|_U > |B|_U$], and there are U accessible from T

$1/2$ otherwise.

I don't think this is at all promising. First, note that for every T, there must be U accessible from it: otherwise every conditional would have value 1 at T, which can't happen since $0 = 0 \to 0 = 1$ clearly gets value 0 in every member of $S[v_\xi]$. (So the second conjunct of the clause for value 0 can be dropped.) Now consider the Curry sentence K (which is equivalent to $K \to 0 = 1$); using that equivalence, the above yields

$v_T(K)$ is 1 if $(\forall U \in S[v_\xi])[$if U is accessible from T then $|K|_U = 0]$

0 if $(\forall U \in S[v_\xi])[$if U is accessible from T then $|K|_U > 0]$

½ otherwise.

And since K is a conditional, $|K|_U$ is just $v_U(K)$. We know that there are in $S[v_\xi]$ plenty of valuations where K has value 1; so in all nodes accessible from such a node (and there are some accessible from it), K has value 0. Clearly then the accessibility relation can't be reflexive, and can't be connected in any nice way with the extendability relation. It also can't be transitive. For consider a node s_2 where K has value 0 that is accessible from a node s_1 where K has value 1. Since K has value 0 at s_2, it must be that in all nodes s_3 accessible from s_2 (and there are some), K has value greater than 0; so such nodes s_3 can't be accessible from s_1 given that K has value 1 at s_1. I suspect that one could prove that there is no accessibility relation whatever that would work, but the above makes pretty clear that at the very least any one that did work would have to be extraordinarily unnatural.

The lack of a specifically modal semantics isn't particularly troubling, but what does seem to me a bit troubling is that the Yablo account comes with no compositional semantics at all: no semantics where the value of a sentence is determined from the values of its basic parts. Of course we can't expect a semantics which is compositional with respect to the assignment of the coarse-grained values 0, ½ and 1 to the sentence: we already know that the conditional is not a three-valued truth function. What we *can* reasonably expect is a semantics which is compositional with respect to more fine grained semantic values. Such a fine-grained semantics might be given either in the algebraic style of the previous chapter, but it needn't: a 3-valued (or 4-valued) modal semantics is a reasonable alternative. In a 3-valued modal semantics, the fine-grained value of a sentence would consist of the set of worlds at which it has value 1 together with the set of worlds at which it has value 0. In the simplest cases of modal semantics, we would then use an accessibility relation to determine fine-grained values for complex sentences from fine-grained values for simple ones. I have no objection to the use of a modal version of compositional semantics instead of an algebraic version, and indeed I will consider one in the next chapter. But the blindness toward the properties of embedded conditionals on Yablo's account appears to rule out any compositional semantics at all.

I take these to be clear deficiencies in Yablo's account as it now stands; there may conceivably be ways to fix the problems without altering its spirit, though my own efforts in this regard haven't been successful. But despite the defects, Yablo's account has virtues that I haven't yet discussed: in particular, its quantification over non-minimal Kripke fixed points (in the definition of the **w** operator and hence in (Y) on p. 245) produces very intuitive results for conditionals in which the antecedent and consequent could consistently be assigned values in more than one way. This is a matter I'll defer until a later chapter, when I'll consider adapting features of Yablo's account to a different context.

16.2. REVISIONISM

If we can't construct a reasonable valuation for conditionals by using a fixed point construction, what about using a revision-rule construction? Not a revision-rule for truth directly (we've seen that that leads to a broadly classical theory that violates intersubstitutivity), but rather for the conditional.[5] And while the usual revision rule approach to truth proceeds in a 2-valued context, the idea here is to use a revision rule for conditionals in a 3-valued context. This idea can be developed in a number of different ways, to produce a number of somewhat different theories. In my view, these are the best theories of truth currently available. Let's look first at one of the simplest.

Suppose we start out with a simple transparent valuation for conditionals v_0; it doesn't make a whole lot of difference which one (though it does make a little bit of difference), but for definiteness take it to be the valuation that assigns every conditional the value $1/2$. We know from the Trivial Observation at the start of the chapter that we can extend this valuation for conditionals to a transparent valuation for the whole language including 'True': the simplest choice is the minimal Kripke fixed point over v_0. The internal theory of this fixed point (i.e. the set of sentences that comprise it) will validate the Kleene rules and have the intersubstitutivity property, but it will be quite unsatisfactory because the valuation for conditionals that it incorporates is unsatisfactory. (In the case of my particular choice for v_0, no conditionals, not even those of form $A \to A$, will be part of the theory.)

But now let's initiate a revision sequence, as follows: given v_α and the Kripke fixed point X_α that it generates, we construct a new valuation for conditionals as follows:

$$|A \to B|_{s,\alpha+1} = 1 \text{ if } |A|_{s,\alpha} \leq |B|_{s,\alpha}$$
$$0 \text{ if } |A|_{s,\alpha} > |B|_{s,\alpha}$$

(No use of the value $1/2$.) By and large, this new valuation for conditionals is an improvement on the old.

---

[5] It might count as indirectly a revision-rule theory for truth, since it is those conditionals that contain the truth predicate that create the main difficulty and that force the valuations at one stage to be re-evaluated at the next. But its approach to the truth predicate itself involves a Kripkean fixed point construction (iterated infinitely many times, as in the Yablo approach) rather than revision rules.

Illustrations

(i) At any successor ordinal, $A \to B$ will get value 1 whenever B is a consequence of A in Kleene logic; once the limit rule (to be given immediately below) is in place, we'll see that in fact this holds at all ordinal stages from 1 on.

(ii) At any double-successor ordinal (successor of a successor, e.g. 2, 3, 4, ...; $\omega + 2, \omega + 3, ...$), $C \to (A \to B)$ will get value 1 whenever B is a consequence of A in Kleene logic; once we have the limit rule in place, it will be clear that in fact this holds at all ordinal stages from 2 on.

(iii) Unlike the revision theories in Chapter 11, the Liar sentence will get value $1/2$ at every ordinal stage.

What about ω and other limit stages? Here I propose the following: If α is a limit then

(*) $\quad |A \to B|_{s,\alpha} = 1$ if $(\exists \beta < \alpha)(\forall \gamma)[\beta \leq \gamma < \alpha \to |A|_{s,\gamma} \leq |B|_{s,\gamma}]$
$\qquad\qquad\qquad\;\; 0$ if $(\exists \beta < \alpha)(\forall \gamma)[\beta \leq \gamma < \alpha \to |A|_{s,\gamma} > |B|_{s,\gamma}]$
$\qquad\qquad\qquad\;\; 1/2$ otherwise.

I've said that this is the rule for limit stages, but when applied to successors it yields the same result as the rule above (since then there is no loss of generality in taking β to be the immediate predecessor of α). Indeed, it also yields our choice of $\mathbf{v_0}$ as a special case, though of course if we wanted a different $\mathbf{v_0}$ we could confine the application of (*) to the case where $\alpha > 0$. It's easy to see that the application of (*) to limit ordinals is effectively the same as the following "continuity principle":

(CONT) $\qquad$ If λ is a limit ordinal then

$|A \to B|_{s,\lambda} = 1$ if $(\exists \beta < \lambda)(\forall \gamma)[\beta \leq \gamma < \lambda \to |A \to B|_{s,\gamma} = 1]$
$\qquad\qquad\quad\; 0$ if $(\exists \beta < \lambda)(\forall \gamma)[\beta \leq \gamma < \lambda \to |A \to B|_{s,\gamma} = 0]$
$\qquad\qquad\quad\; 1/2$ otherwise.

(CONT), unlike (*), works *only* for limit ordinals; and it applies only to conditionals. (Note that if $|A \to B|_{s,\lambda}$ is 1 or 0 by this rule, there is no reason in general why $|A \to B|_{s,\lambda+1}$ couldn't have a different value. Even if the roaches that are conditionals are in at all finite stages from a certain point on, they can eventually check out; just not at the limit. And roaches that aren't conditionals needn't obey even this constraint.)

We can keep this revision process going on forever. At each stage we have not only a valuation $\mathbf{v}$ for conditionals, but a valuation for arbitrary formulas (relative to assignment functions), obtained from the minimal fixed point over $\mathbf{v}$. A crude categorization of possible outcomes of the revision process (for arbitrary formulas, not just conditionals) is this:

$<A, s>$ could have ultimate value 1: that is, there could be a β such that for all $\gamma \geq \beta, |A|_{s,\gamma} = 1$

$<A,s>$ could have ultimate value 0: that is, there could be a β such that for all $\gamma \geq \beta, |A|_{s,\gamma} = 0$

Neither of the above.

The "neither" category includes many different possibilities. One is that there is a point β after which $|A|_{s,\gamma} = 1/2$; obviously that can't be so if A is a conditional, since conditionals can't get value $1/2$ at successor ordinals, but it can be true for other sentences (including sentences that contain conditionals). The other possibilities are ones where however far one goes on, the formula continues to oscillate in value, either between all three values, or between $1/2$ and 1, or between $1/2$ and 0. (From all that's been said so far it looks as if eventual oscillation between 1 and 0 without $1/2$ should be a possibility too, though it is a consequence of the strong form of the Fundamental Theorem below that that can't happen.)

This gives a three valued semantics for the language with 'True' and a conditional: we take $|||A|||_s$ to be 1 if $<A,s>$ has ultimate value 1, $|||A|||_s$ to be 0 if $<A,s>$ has ultimate value 0, and $|||A|||_s$ to be $1/2$ in all these other cases. (I'll call $|||A|||_s$ the ultimate value of $<A,s>$, even when $<A,s>$ doesn't settle on value $1/2$ but oscillates.) It is clear by induction that the valuation at each stage of the construction is transparent, so that the Intersubstitutivity Condition holds at each stage of the construction.

But there's a worry: it isn't immediately obvious that this semantics will validate the Kleene rules, or be otherwise attractive. There is no problem about it validating the Kleene rule for negation, but there is for conjunction and disjunction, and also the quantifiers.

In the case of disjunction, it's clear that if either $|||A||| = 1$ or $|||B||| = 1$ then $|||A \vee B||| = 1$. (If $|||A||| = 1$ then for some β, $(\forall \gamma \geq \beta)(|A|_\gamma = 1)$, and since the Kleene rules hold at each stage by the fixed point construction, $(\forall \gamma \geq \beta)(|A \vee B|_\gamma = 1)$; so $|||A \vee B||| = 1$. Similarly if $|||B||| = 1$.) But the converse is not so clear: if $|||A \vee B||| = 1$, then for some β, $(\forall \gamma \geq \beta)(|A \vee B|_\gamma = 1)$, so by the Kleene rule for stages, $(\forall \gamma \geq \beta)(|A|_\gamma = 1 \vee |B|_\gamma = 1)$; but what is to preclude A and B from each oscillating between 1 and other values, in such a way that one of them is always 1? As a matter of fact this can't happen, but this is not at all obvious. If it *could* happen, then reasoning by cases would not be validated, which I think would be a major strike against the proposal.

Analogously for the existential quantifier: if $|||\exists v A||| = 1$, it doesn't *obviously* follow that there is an object o such that $|||A|||_{s(v/o)} = 1$. Were there actually cases where this fails, then we'd have a failure of the classical meta-rule of $\exists$-elimination (that something follows from an existential quantification if it follows from an arbitrary instance of it). This too would be highly unattractive.

In order to rule out such problems we need a theorem:

Fundamental Theorem: There are ordinals Δ such that for every formula A and every assignment function s, $|A|_{s,\Delta} = |||A|||_s$.

I call such ordinals Δ *acceptable ordinals*; they are ordinals that accurately represent ultimate values. Once we establish this theorem, we'll know that the Kleene evaluation rules hold for ultimate values, since it is built into the Kripke fixed point construction over the various $\mathbf{v}_\alpha$ that they hold at each ordinal stage α and hence in particular at stage Δ. I'll sketch the proof of the Fundamental Theorem in the Appendix to this chapter. The proof given there actually establishes the theorem in the following strong form:

Strong form of Fundamental Theorem: For any ordinal μ, there are ordinals $\Delta > \mu$ such that for every formula A and every assignment function s, $|A|_{s,\Delta} = |||A|||_s$.

I defer the main discussion of this "revision theory for conditionals" until the next chapter, but here are two initial points about it.

A

The first concerns the extent to which the ultimate value of a conditional is determined by the ultimate values of its antecedent and consequent.

1. It's clear that when $|||A|||_s = 0$ or $|||B|||_s = 1$ then $|||A \to B|||_s = 1$. (In other words, $|||A \to B|||_s = 1$ whenever $|||A \supset B|||_s = 1$, where $\supset$ is defined from $\neg$ and $\vee$ in the usual way.)
2. It's clear that when $|||A|||_s = 1$ and $|||B|||_s = 0$ then $|||A \to B|||_s = 0$. (In other words, $|||A \to B|||_s = 0$ whenever $|||A \supset B|||_s = 0$.)
3. What about when $|||A \supset B|||_s = 1/2$, i.e. when either

     (i) $|||A|||_s = 1$ and $|||B|||_s = 1/2$

or (ii) $|||A|||_s = 1/2$ and $|||B|||_s = 0$

or (iii) $|||A|||_s = 1/2$ and $|||B|||_s = 1/2$?

In cases (i) and (ii) we clearly can't have $|||A \to B|||_s = 1$, for the latter obviously requires that $|||A|||_s \leq |||B|||_s$; but $|||A \to B|||_s$ can be either $1/2$ or 0 in these cases. (For instance, in case (i) $|||A \to B|||_s$ will be 0 if there is a stage after which $|B|_s$ never assumes value 1, and will be $1/2$ otherwise.) In case (iii), it is clear that $|||A \to B|||_s$ could assume either the value 1 or the value $1/2$. (For instance, it has value 1 when B is just A; it has value $1/2$ in lots of other cases, e.g. in any case where B is $\neg A$ and A assumes the value 1 arbitrarily late.) Can $|||A \to B|||_s$ ever have value 0 in case (iii)? No: for a consequence of the strong form of the Fundamental Theorem is that in case (iii) there are arbitrarily large Δ for which $|A|_{s,\Delta}$ and $|B|_{s,\Delta}$ are both $1/2$; but then the valuation rule for $\to$ tells us that $|A \to B|_{s,\Delta+1}$ is 1. Since this happens arbitrarily late, $|||A \to B|||_s$ can't be 0.

B

The second point concerns substitution inside conditionals. The present approach avoids the striking defect of the fixed point approach of section 16.1: we have the following

Theorem on Intersubstitutivity of Equivalents: Suppose A and B are any formulas with the same free variables, and X_A is any formula with A as a subformula, and X_B results from X_A by substituting B for one or more occurrences of A. Suppose also that for all s, $|||A \leftrightarrow B|||_s = 1$. Then for all s, $|||X_A \leftrightarrow X_B|||_s = 1$.

[More generally, if X_B results from X_A by substituting B for one or more *positive* occurrences of A, and for all s, $|||A \to B|||_s = 1$, then for all s, $|||X_A \to X_B|||_s = 1$; and if X_B results from X_A by substituting B for one or more *negative* occurrences of A, and for all s, $|||A \to B|||_s = 1$, then for all s, $|||X_B \to X_A|||_s = 1$.]

The basis for establishing this is the following facts, each of which is easily checked:[6]

(Neg) If $|||A \to B|||_s = 1$ then $|||\neg B \to \neg A|||_s = 1$

(Conj) If $|||A \to B|||_s = 1$ then $|||A \wedge C \to B \wedge C|||_s = 1$ and $|||C \wedge A \to C \wedge B|||_s = 1$

(Disj) If $|||A \to B|||_s = 1$ then $|||A \vee C \to B \vee C|||_s = 1$ and $|||C \vee A \to C \vee B|||_s = 1$

(Cond) If $|||A \to B|||_s = 1$ then $|||(B \to C) \to (A \to C)|||_s = 1$ and $|||(C \to A) \to (C \to B)|||_s = 1$

(Univ) If for all o, $|||A \to B|||_{s(v/o)} = 1$ then $|||\forall v A \to \forall v B|||_s = 1$

(Exis) If for all o, $|||A \to B|||_{s(v/o)} = 1$ then $|||\exists v A \to \exists v B|||_s = 1$

Given these, the Intersubstitutivity of Equivalents follows by an easy induction. (On the Yablo fixed point approach, each half of the rule (Cond) fails, so the induction is blocked.) Thus I keep a promise made long ago, of getting a logic for the conditional strong enough so that the Intersubstitutivity Principle for truth follows from the Tarski schema as well as entailing it.

16.3. THE TRANSFINITE LIAR HIERARCHY AND OTHER EXAMPLES

I'd like to give a feel for how the semantics deals with specific examples. Let's look first at the Liar hierarchy: the transfinite hierarchy of sentences Q_σ, where each Q_σ is equivalent to $\neg D^\sigma \text{True}(\langle Q_\sigma \rangle)$. Here the D^σ are defined,

---

[6] Indeed, the first three of these rules hold in stronger form:

(Neg$^+$) $|||(A \to B) \to (\neg B \to \neg A)|||_s = 1$

(Conj$^+$) $|||(A \to B) \to (A \wedge C \to B \wedge C)|||_s = 1$ and $|||(A \to B) \to (C \wedge A \to C \wedge B)|||_s = 1$

(Disj$^+$) $|||(A \to B) \to (A \vee C \to B \vee C)|||_s = 1$ and $|||(A \to B) \to (C \vee A \to C \vee B)|||_s = 1$.

as explained in Section 15.2, by transfinitely iterating an operator D, where DA is $A \wedge \neg(A \to \neg A)$. (It's easy to see that in this particular semantics, DA is equivalent to $A \wedge (\top \to A)$, where $\top$ is any sentence getting value 1 at every stage, say $0 = 0$. This equivalence seems to be special to this semantics. The definition $A \wedge \neg(A \to \neg A)$ seems to be useful in a wider variety of semantics.)

For the basic operator D, the following is immediate:

(i) If there is a $\beta < \alpha$ such that $(\forall \gamma)[\beta \leq \gamma < \alpha \to |A|_{s,\gamma} = 1]$, then $|DA|_{s,\alpha} = |A|_{s,\alpha}$;
(ii) If there is a $\beta < \alpha$ such that $(\forall \gamma)[\beta \leq \gamma < \alpha \to |A|_{s,\gamma} < 1]$, then $|DA|_{s,\alpha} = 0$;
(iii) If the antecedents of (i) and (ii) both fail, then $|DA|_{s,\alpha}$ is $1/2$ or $|A|_{s,\alpha}$, whichever is less.

(Note that $|DA|_{s,\alpha}$ can be 0 or $1/2$ in case (i) as well as in cases (ii) and (iii) respectively.) In particular,

(i-suc) $|DA|_{s,\alpha+1} = |A|_{s,\alpha+1}$ whenever $|A|_{s,\alpha} = 1$
(ii-suc) $|DA|_{s,\alpha+1} = 0$ whenever $|A|_{s,\alpha} < 1$ (as well as when $|A|_{s,\alpha+1} = 0$).

(DA can thus have value $1/2$ at a successor stage only when A itself has value $1/2$ at that stage; this is not so for limit stages.) Also

$$|DA|_{s,0} = 0 \text{ if } |A|_{s,0} = 0$$
$$1/2 \text{ otherwise.}$$

Now let's look at the transfinite hierarchy of sentences Q_σ. Since Q_σ is equivalent to $\neg D^\sigma \text{True}(\langle Q_\sigma \rangle)$,[7] and the Intersubstitutivity Principle holds at each stage of the construction, we must have that for all α

(*) $$|Q_\sigma|_\alpha = 1 - |D^\sigma Q_\sigma|_\alpha.$$

For all α and all A, $|D^\sigma A|_\alpha \leq |A|_\alpha$, so it follows from (*) that for every σ and α, either

(I) $$|Q_\sigma|_\alpha = |D^\sigma Q_\sigma|_\alpha = 1/2$$

or

(II) $$|Q_\sigma|_\alpha = 1 \text{ and } |D^\sigma Q_\sigma|_\alpha = 0.$$

Moreover, (i) and (*) imply that if there is a σ-interval immediately preceding α where Q_σ takes on only the value 1 then $|D^\alpha Q_\sigma|_\alpha = |Q_\sigma|_\alpha$, so $|Q_\sigma|_\alpha$ must be $1/2$. And (ii) and (iii) imply that if there is a σ-interval immediately preceding α where Q_σ takes on the value $1/2$ at any point then $|D^\alpha Q_\sigma|_\alpha = 0$, and so by (*), $|Q_\sigma|_\alpha$ must be 1. Eventually, then, the sentence will cycle in values, each cycle

---

[7] And since this equivalence is provable in the arithmetic theory (expanded to include the new vocabulary); this guarantees that *at each stage of the construction*, Q_α has the same value as $\neg D^\sigma \text{True}(\langle Q_\sigma \rangle)$.

consisting of a ½ followed by σ 1's. (Indeed, it turns out that it cycles in this way right from the start: there is no need of a correction process in this case. Reason: It obviously has value ½ at 0; and it is easy to see that if $0 < α < σ$ then $|D^α A|_α$ is 0 for any A; so $|\neg D^α Q_0|_α$ is ½ at $α = 0$, and is 1 for the next σ values of α, and then the cycle starts again.) Q_0 is just the normal Liar sentence, with the value ½ at every stage.

Let's look in more detail at how this works. Suppose we start with $Q_σ$, with cycles of ½ followed by σ 1's, where σ is a large finite or infinite number. We then apply a single D to it; what we'll get still has cycles of the same length $1 + σ$, but this time it is ½, then 0, then 1 at remaining values. If we apply D again (i.e. consider $D^2 Q_σ$), we'll get cycles of the same length, but with ½ followed by two 0's followed by all 1's. If σ is a finite number N, then when D is applied $N − 1$ times we get ½ followed by $N − 1$ 0's followed by a 1 (and then cycling again); and when D is applied N times we get ½ followed by N 0's, with no 1's. This is the negation of Q_N, as desired. When we apply D one more time, we get ½ followed by 0's forever.

Similarly if σ is infinite. In this case, each $D^k Q_σ$ for finite k has ½ at stage 0, 0 at stages $1, \ldots, k$, and 1 thereafter—until stage σ (which is identical to $1 + σ$ in the infinite case), where the cycle begins again. So $D^ω Q_σ$, which is the intersection of all $D^k Q_σ$ for finite k, has value ½ at stage 0, 0 at all finite stages; if σ is just ω, it will then have value ½ at ω (since application of $D^ω$ won't lower the value of stages with an immediate ω-sequence of predecessors); on the other hand if $σ > ω$, then $D^ω Q_σ$ will have value 0 at stage ω, and we will need to wait until stage σ to get back to ½.

I think this is quite an appealing picture.[8]

I've paid a lot of attention to the transfinite hierarchy of Liar sentences, but there are plenty of paradoxes other than the Liar. The construction in the previous section guarantees a treatment of all of them that's consistent with Intersubstitutivity (a fact I'll state more carefully in the next chapter); let me consider as an example the Curry paradox from Chapter 4. That involved a sentence K which is provably equivalent to

$$\text{True}(\langle K \rangle) \rightarrow \bot,$$

where $\bot$ is some absurdity. Since the Intersubstitutivity Condition holds at each stage, it must be the case that for each α,

(1) $\qquad\qquad\qquad |K|_α = |K \rightarrow \bot|_α.$

Given that $\bot$ will get value 0, what must K be like for (1) to hold?

---

[8] What about if α is larger than the first acceptable ordinal? The answer is that it can't be; any remotely adequate system of iterating D must break down long before we get there. As we'll see in Chapter 22, it is possible to extend the hierarchy of iterations a very long way: to include every ordinal that's hereditarily definable in the 'True'-free fragment of the language, and indeed in higher fragments as well. But acceptable ordinals are bigger than that.

From our assumption about the starting valuation v_0, the right hand side of (1) gets value $1/2$ at stage 0; so by (1), $|K|_0$ is $1/2$. The evaluation rules then tell us that $|K \to \bot|_1 = 0$ (since $1/2 > 0$); so $|K|_1 = 0$. The evaluation rules then tell us that $|K \to \bot|_2 = 1$ (since $0 \leq 0$); so $|K|_2 = 1$. Continuing in this way, we see that the value of K must alternate between 0 and 1 through the positive integers. Applying (CONT) to the right hand side of (1) and employing (1), this means that $|K|_\omega = 1/2$. We then apply the same argument as before to get $|K|_{\omega+1} = 0, |K|_{\omega+2} = 1$, and so on. It's easy to see that $|K|_\alpha = 1/2$ whenever α is a limit λ, $|K|_\alpha = 0$ whenever α is an odd ordinal, and $|K|_\alpha = 1$ whenever α is an even successor.[9]

Now consider the sentence K_1 that is provably equivalent to

$$D\text{True}(\langle K_1 \rangle) \to \bot,$$

i.e. in effect to

$$DK_1 \to \bot$$

A similar analysis to the above yields that $|K_1|_0 = 1/2, |K_1|_1 = 0, |K_1|_2 = 1, |K_1|_3 = 1$, and then we continue to have cycles of 0,1,1 throughout the positive integers. At limits we go back to $1/2$, and the whole thing keeps repeating in the same way.

As you might guess, we get similar results with the sentence K_n that asserts that if it is D^nTrue then the earth is flat: its value at 0 and limits is $1/2$, and after this value it goes through cycles of a 0 followed by $n+1$ 1's.

What about a sentence K_ω that asserts that if it's D^ωTrue then the Earth is flat? The reader who takes the trouble can easily check that this is $1/2$ at stage 0, 0 at stage 1, and 1 at all other finite stages. By (CONT), it must then be 1 at stage ω, and $D^\omega K_\omega$ is easily seen to be 1 here too, so K_ω has value 0 at $\omega + 1$; and then by repeating the above, it has value 1 at $\omega + n$ for all finite $n > 1$ and also at $\omega + \omega$. Does it ever get value $1/2$ again? Yes, but not until stage $\omega \cdot \omega$; after that, the whole cycle repeats itself.

I invite the reader to work through this and other examples.[10]

---

[9] The argument is easily generalized so as not to rely on the assumption about the starting valuation: whatever the starting valuation, K will be evaluated as described from stage ω on.

[10] In addition to considering sentences that assert that if they're D^α True then the Earth is flat, for large α, it's illuminating to consider sentences with nested conditionals, e.g. a sentence K^* that asserts

$$\text{True}(\langle K^* \rangle) \to [\text{True}(\langle K^* \rangle) \to \bot].$$

(Recall from the discussion of continuum-valued semantics that there's no reason to think that this will be equivalent to the result of "importing" the outer conditional, so as to get $[\text{True}(\langle K^* \rangle) \wedge \text{True}(\langle K^* \rangle)] \to \bot$; the latter is obviously equivalent to $\text{True}(\langle K^* \rangle) \to \bot$, but there's no reason to expect the former to be, and it isn't.) There is in fact a complicated multi-dimensional hierarchy of Curry-like sentences, which any theory of the paradoxes needs to be able to handle. (There is a partial discussion in Section 5 of Field 2003a.) Their solution on this theory strikes me as rather elegant even if complex; and its hard to see how it could fail to be complex on any adequate theory.

APPENDIX: THE FUNDAMENTAL THEOREM

The theorem, in its strong form, is:

Fundamental Theorem: For any ordinal μ, there are ordinals $\Delta > \mu$ such that for every formula A and every assignment function s, $|A|_{s,\Delta} = |||A|||_s$.

Here's a detailed sketch of the proof.

For each ordinal α, let H_α be the function that assigns to each pair of a formula A and an assignment function s the value $|A|_{s,\alpha}$ that the revision procedure assigns.[1] Let $\Im$ be the set of functions f such that $\exists \alpha(f = H_\alpha)$. The domain of any given H_α has the same cardinality as the starting model—call it $\mathfrak{C}$—so there are at most $2^\mathfrak{C}$ functions in $\Im$. ($3^\mathfrak{C} = 2^\mathfrak{C}$, since $\mathfrak{C}$ is infinite.) From this it follows that some members of $\Im$ must occur arbitrarily late in the sequence of H_αs; call such members of $\Im$ *repeating*. Call an ordinal α *repeating* if H_α is repeating. Clearly if α is repeating and $\beta > \alpha$ then β is repeating (for β will be $\alpha + \delta$ for some δ, and then if H_{α^*} is H_α then $H_{\alpha^*+\delta}$ will be H_β).

The hard part is showing that among these repeating ordinals are some that assign to every parameterized formula (i.e. each pair $<A,s>$ of a formula and assignment function) its ultimate value. (These ordinals I've dubbed the acceptable ones.) First, note that if a parameterized formula $<A,s>$ has ultimate value 1 or 0, then it has this value at every repeating ordinal. (If it has value 1 or 0 after some stage, then this prevents any valuation that doesn't give it this value from repeating.) *So a repeating ordinal can fail to be acceptable only by assigning 1 or 0 where it ought to assign* $1/2$. The task, then, is to show that there are repeating ordinals that assign the value $1/2$ whenever they ought to.

Let τ be some repeating ordinal. Since there are at most $2^\mathfrak{C}$ repeating members of $\Im$, there must be an ordinal ς such that all of them occur in $\{H_\sigma \mid \tau \leq \sigma < \tau + \varsigma\}$. Since τ is repeating, there must be a ρ such that (i) $H_\tau = H_{\tau+\rho}$ and (ii) $\varsigma \leq \rho$, so that all repeating members of $\Im$ are included in $\{H_\sigma \mid \tau \leq \sigma < \tau + \rho\}$. We will let Δ be $\tau + \rho \cdot \omega$, and show that Δ assigns the value $1/2$ to $<A,s>$ whenever it ought to, and hence (since it's repeating) is acceptable. (It then follows that an acceptable ordinal will already have appeared earlier, somewhere in $\{H_\sigma \mid \tau \leq \sigma < \tau + \rho\}$. Also, since Δ is repeating it follows that there are acceptable ordinals bigger than any given μ.)

The first step is to show that *when A is a conditional* and $<A,s>$ has ultimate value $1/2$, Δ assigns the value $1/2$ to $<A,s>$. For this, we first note an easy consequence of (ii): that for all finite n, all repeating members of $\Im$ are included in $\{H_\sigma \mid \tau + \rho \cdot n \leq \sigma < \tau + \rho \cdot (n+1)\}$. Given this, we argue that if $<A,s>$ has ultimate value $1/2$, then for each n it gets that value at some H_σ for which $\tau + \rho \cdot n \leq \sigma < \tau + \rho \cdot (n+1)$; so by (CONT), it gets that value at $\tau + \rho \cdot \omega$, i.e. at Δ.

---

[1] This of course depends on the starting model M. The assignment functions in question assign only objects in the domain of M to variables. If the language we're starting with contains unrestricted quantifiers, then of course M can't be an intended model—there is then no intended model, as I've discussed several times. But as I've also discussed, the model-theoretic semantics is useful for consistency proofs even in the case of unrestricted languages.

The final step is to extend this to all formulas A. This can be done by an inductive proof, though one must be careful to set up the induction correctly. The claim to be proved is that for any parameterized formulas $<A,s>$, if it has ultimate value $1/2$ then it has value $1/2$ at Δ; in other words, if it has value $1/2$ then at each stage σ of the Kripke fixed point construction over $\mathbf{v}_\Delta$, it has value $1/2$ at that stage. Reversing quantifiers, this says that for each σ,

(I_σ) for any parameterized formulas $<A,s>$, if it has ultimate value $1/2$ then it has value $1/2$ at the σth stage of the Kripke fixed point construction over $\mathbf{v}_\Delta$.

To prove this inductively, we need to prove (I_σ) on the assumption of (I_β) for all $\beta < \sigma$.

For this, we do a sub-induction on the complexity of A, counting conditionals as of complexity 0, as in the Kripke construction for the Trivial Observation, where they were decreed "generalized atomic". Then the complexity 0 case comprises only (i) the conditionals, where the claim has already been proved; (ii) the genuine atomic A for predicates in the ground language, for which the claim is vacuous; and (iii) formulas of form True(t). So suppose $|||\text{True}(t)|||_s = 1/2$; then t denotes some sentence C relative to s, and $|||C|||_s = 1/2$; but then by the induction hypothesis, C gets value $1/2$ relative to s at all stages $\beta < \sigma$ in the Kripke construction; and therefore $|||\text{True}(t)|||_s$ has value $1/2$ at stage σ.

The cases of higher complexity, i.e. where the main connective is one of the usual Kleene connectives or quantifiers, are now routine. ∎

17

More on Revision-Theoretic Conditionals

17.1. ALGEBRAIC SEMANTICS

The first task of this chapter is to fit the material of Section 16.2 into the framework of Chapter 15. In Section 16.2 I use only three semantic values: 1, 0, and $1/2$. But the latter value (when used as an "ultimate value") hid a great many distinctions. To use the framework of Chapter 15, we need to fine-grain the ultimate value $1/2$ of the three-valued semantics into an infinity of different values. One of these will have a special role, and will be called $\mathbf{1/2}$, using boldface to avoid confusion with the more generic $1/2$ used in the 3-valued framework; I will also use boldface $\mathbf{1}$ and $\mathbf{0}$ for the largest and smallest values of the fine-grained framework.

There is more than one way to do the fine-grained semantics, but all are variations on the same idea: that the semantic value of A relative to s, which I will denote $||A||_s$, is to be a function that assigns to each ordinal in its domain the value $|A|_{\Delta_0 + \alpha}$, where Δ_0 is the smallest acceptable ordinal. In other words, the idea is to throw out the early "single-bar" values of the revision process, before the valuation process stabilized into a fixed cycle; and in addition, to make sure we start the "official counting" at a particularly nice ordinal (an acceptable one). The effect of the latter is that every $f_{A,s}$ that isn't either constantly 1 or constantly 0 will begin with $1/2$ (i.e. it will assign the value $1/2$ to 0).

More fully, let Π be some acceptable ordinal bigger than Δ_0; write it as $\Delta_0 + \Sigma$. Let V_Σ^+ be the set of functions f from $\{\alpha | \alpha < \Sigma\}$ to $\{0, 1/2, 1\}$. I'll use Pred_Σ to abbreviate $\{\alpha | \alpha < \Sigma\}$; but for present purposes it is best to think of Pred_Σ not as having the linear order of the ordinals, but a circular order: after you go through all the ordinals less than Σ you come back to 0 again.

Let $\preccurlyeq$ be defined on V_Σ^+ pointwise; that is, $f \preccurlyeq g$ if and only if $(\forall \alpha < \Sigma)$ $(f(\alpha) \leq g(\alpha))$. So the function $\mathbf{1}$ that assigns 1 to every ordinal less than Σ is greatest in the order, and the function $\mathbf{0}$ that assigns 0 to every ordinal is least. The operations corresponding to the connectives and quantifiers are defined pointwise too, e.g. f^* is the function given by $f^*(\alpha) = 1 - f(\alpha)$, and $f \sqcap g$ is the function defined by $(f \sqcap g)(\alpha) = \min\{f(\alpha), g(\alpha)\}$. And $f \Rightarrow g$ is defined by two conditions. First, when $\alpha > 0$,

$(f \Rightarrow g)(\alpha)$ is
- 1 if $(\exists \beta < \alpha)(\forall \gamma)(\beta \leq \gamma < \alpha \to f(\gamma) \leq g(\gamma))$
- 0 if $(\exists \beta < \alpha)(\forall \gamma)(\beta \leq \gamma < \alpha \to f(\gamma) > g(\gamma))$
- $1/2$ otherwise.

Second,

$(f \Rightarrow g)(0)$ is
- 1 if $(\exists \beta < \Sigma)(\forall \gamma)(\beta \leq \gamma < \Sigma \to f(\gamma) \leq g(\gamma))$
- 0 if $(\exists \beta < \Sigma)(\forall \gamma)(\beta \leq \gamma < \Sigma \to f(\gamma) > g(\gamma))$
- $1/2$ otherwise;

that is, (as befits the idea that the appropriate order on Pred_Σ is circular) it "has the value it would have at Σ were that in the domain of the function". The space is a (complete) deMorgan algebra with the additional operation $\Rightarrow$.

So far we haven't satisfied the condition that **1** be join-irreducible. We do have that whenever $f \sqcup g = \mathbf{1}$ *and f and g are assigned to parameterized formulas*, then $f = \mathbf{1}$ or $g = \mathbf{1}$; this is because $f(0) = 1$ or $g(0) = 1$, and I've noted that when a function h is assigned to a parameterized formula, $h(0)$ won't be 1 unless h is the constant function **1**. So the values actually assigned to parameterized formulas will belong to some subspace V_Σ of V_Σ^+ in which **1** is join-irreducible. We can choose the V_Σ to be such that for any f in it other than **0** and **1**, $f(0) = 1/2$, but we then need further restrictions so that V_Σ will be closed under $\Rightarrow$.

As I've hinted, there is more than one choice for Σ (or equivalently, for $\Pi =_{df} \Delta_0 + \Sigma$). The most obvious is to let $\Delta_0 + \Sigma$ be the first acceptable ordinal after Δ_0 (in which case I use the notation Σ_0). The Fundamental Theorem of the previous chapter guarantees that there is a subspace V_{Σ_0} of $V_{\Sigma_0}^+$ that is closed under $\Rightarrow$ and all the other operations (including the least upper bounds and greatest lower bounds required for the quantifiers), and is sufficiently comprehensive to contain a value for every parameterized formula of the language in a valuation that accords with the Intersubstitutivity Principle. But a downside of this choice is that it is hard to find an explicit representation of such a subspace V_{Σ_0}: we know only that there is one.

For this reason it may be appealing to use a larger Σ. Perhaps the simplest choice is to let Σ be the smallest initial ordinal of cardinality greater than that of Σ_0; I'll call this Σ^*. Then Σ^* will be a multiple[1] of Σ_0 and so $\Delta_0 + \Sigma^*$, which will be identical to Σ^*, will be acceptable. With this choice of Σ we can explicitly represent V_Σ as the set of all functions from $\text{Pred}(\Sigma)$ to $\{0, 1/2, 1\}$ meeting the following conditions:

(i) If $f(0) = 1$ then $\forall \alpha (f(\alpha) = 1)$;

(ii) If $f(0) = 0$ then $\forall \alpha (f(\alpha) = 0)$;

(iii) If $f(0) = 1/2$ then there is some $\rho < \Sigma$, of which Σ is a multiple, such that f is *ρ-cyclic*; that is, $(\forall \alpha)(\forall \beta)[\rho \cdot \alpha + \beta < \Sigma \to f(\rho \cdot \alpha + \beta) = f(\beta)]$.

---

[1] By 'multiple' here and in what follows I mean right-multiple: that is, there is a δ such that $\Sigma_0 \cdot \delta = \Sigma$.

The Fundamental Theorem of the previous chapter shows that every function assigned to a parameterized formula $<A,s>$ meets this condition, for it is Σ_0-cyclic. And it is easy to see that the space is closed under $\Rightarrow$, and also closed under greatest lower bounds and least upper bounds of sets of cardinality no greater than $\mathfrak{C}$ (the cardinality of the model M); this ensures that it is adequate for dealing with the quantifiers as well as the conditional.[2] (The infinite distributivity laws mentioned in Chapter 15 are also easily checked.) I think this ability to explicitly represent the space V is appealing, and some supplementary considerations point in the same direction.[3]

One's choice on the issue of big space versus small does not affect the basic picture of what the space looks like. At the top is the point **1** (the function that assigns 1 to every ordinal in Pred(Σ)); this is the value that will be assigned to the sentences that are true in the ground model for the base language, and to the "clear truths" of the expanded language (logical truths, sentences of form 'True($\langle A \rangle$)' for A true in the ground model, etc.). At the bottom there is the point **0**, which will be assigned to the sentences that are false in the ground model and the "clear falsehoods" of the expanded language. In the middle there is the value $1/2$ (the function that assigns $1/2$ to every ordinal in Pred(Σ)), which is the value that will be assigned to the Liar sentence. There are also many other values: those in the "upper portion" strictly between $1/2$ and **1**; those in the "lower portion" strictly between **0** and $1/2$; and those "on the sides" that are incomparable with $1/2$. The latter are the ones that assign 0 to some ordinals and 1 to others (as well as $1/2$ to still others). These "side values" play a crucial role in the theory. For instance, any conditional that doesn't have value **1** or **0** must clearly have a side value.[4] The sentences Q_α of the transfinite Liar hierarchy have values in the upper portion of the space, but the application of D to one of them (other than Q_0) results in a side value, and the further application of D to them results in a sequence of lower and lower side values until we've "applied D α times", at which point we reach a value in the lower portion; then the $(\alpha + 1)^{st}$ application of D brings the value down to **0**.

---

[2] See Field 2004, pp. 86–7. If the reader is confused about how expanding the domain of the functions past Σ_0 can help to make the space of allowable functions easier to represent, the key to the answer is that many of the functions on the larger domain aren't Σ_0-cyclic, but only ρ-cyclic for larger ρ. (As a result, they won't be assigned to any pair $<A,s>$ for which A is a formula of the language and s is an assignment function for the model M.)

[3] The larger space is required if we generalize the requirement of join-irreducibility to $\mathfrak{C}$-*join-irreducibility*: if S is a subset of the space and S has cardinality no greater than $\mathfrak{C}$ (the cardinality of the starting model), then the least upper bound of S isn't **1** unless one of the members of S is **1**. This is the natural algebraic analog of $\exists$-Elimination, just as ordinary join-irreducibility is the natural analog of $\vee$-Elimination (reasoning by cases). However, we don't strictly need the algebraic analog, for $\exists$-Elimination to be legitimate: such reason is legitimate as long as an existential quantification never takes on value 1 unless one of its instances does, and that is guaranteed by the Fundamental Theorem.

[4] Its value is a function that assigns only 1 and 0 to successor ordinals. And if it assigns the same value to all successor ordinals, it would have to assign that same value to every ordinal (by (CONT) and the effective identification of 0 with Σ).

More generally, the operator ∂ corresponding to D obeys all the principles of Section 15.2, including (ib-s) and the full (ii). The only values brought to **0** by the operator ∂ are $1/2$ and the "lower portion" values strictly below it. "Upper portion" values other than **1** are all mapped by ∂ into "side values", and application of ∂ to side values typically results in lower side values, though once the values get low enough a further application brings you to a value in the lower portion and a still further application brings you to **0**.

17.2. CONSERVATIVENESS AND SCHEMAS

In previous chapters I have belabored the point that any model-theoretic semantics for a language is based on treating the quantifiers of the language as if they were restricted to a set. This is as true of the semantics offered in the previous section as of any other. Indeed, the whole construction of acceptable ordinals in Section 16.2 was based on the assumption that the quantifiers range only over the members of a fixed set. Since the quantifiers of our language presumably range over all sets, not just the members of a given one, this means that we have given no sense to any "absolute" assignment of values to the sentences of our language; the semantics assigns them values only relative to a set for the quantifiers to range over. That's the way it has to be, by Tarski's Undefinability Theorem. This does not prevent use of the semantics for defining logical consequence, even for unrestricted languages: this point was discussed in the context of classical logic in Chapter 2, and I will come back to it in the non-classical context at the end of Chapter 20.

There is however a minor complication that arises in the current context. It arises because the value space itself depends on the cardinality of the ground model for the base language: the bigger the cardinality of the model, the bigger the value space that we need. This slightly complicates the definition of consequence: instead of there being a fixed space of values, and consequence involving preservation of the designated value **1** of this fixed space whatever the underlying model, we need to proceed in a slightly different manner. The simplest procedure is to define, for each infinite cardinal $\mathfrak{C}$, a notion of $\mathfrak{C}$-validity, using the "big" space $V_{\Sigma_\mathfrak{C}}$ of the previous section. More fully: an argument is $\mathfrak{C}$-*valid* if in all models of cardinality no greater than $\mathfrak{C}$ in which the premises get value **1** in $V_{\Sigma_\mathfrak{C}}$, the conclusion also gets value **1** in $V_{\Sigma_\mathfrak{C}}$. Then an argument is *valid* if it is $\mathfrak{C}$-valid for every $\mathfrak{C}$. (The need for this roundabout approach arises in any semantics in which the size of the value space depends on the cardinality of the model. For instance, although I didn't bother to comment on it in Chapter 10, it arises for Boolean-valued treatments of supervaluationism: there too the Boolean algebra one employs needs to be bigger for large-cardinality ground models than for small-cardinality ones. Even in 2-valued semantics, we *could* proceed in this roundabout way, and it would be equivalent to the usual more direct definition;

it's just that with a common value space for models of every cardinality, there is no need to do so.)

With this clarified, I can now properly state the Conservativeness Requirement (which I gave a first stab at in Section 15.1):

Conservativeness Requirement: If M is any classical ω-model of the ground language $\mathscr{L}$, with cardinality $\mathfrak{C}$, then there is a $V_{\Sigma_{\mathfrak{C}}}$-valued model M^+ of the expanded language $\mathscr{L}^+$ which has M as its reduct, and which satisfies these conditions:

(Ai) For any sentence A of $\mathscr{L}$, $|\text{True}(\langle A \rangle)| = |A|$

(Aii) For any assignment function s, if $|\text{Sentence}(v)|_s = 0$ then $|\text{True}(v)|_s = 0$

(Bi) For any formula A of $\mathscr{L}$ with only one free variable, and any assignment function s, $|\text{True-of}(\langle A \rangle, v)|_s = |A^*|_s$, where A^* is the result of substituting v for the free occurrences of the free variable of A

(Bii) For any assignment function s, if $|\text{Formula-with-only-one-free-variable}(v)|_s = 0$ then $|\text{True-of}(v, w)|_s = 0$.

(Since M^+ has M as its reduct, then M^+ agrees with M in its assignment of values to formulas of the ground language.)

The construction of Section 16.2, in conjunction with the remarks in the previous Section, shows that this conservativeness requirement is satisfied. It thus gives precise sense to the claim that a truth predicate obeying the intersubstitutivity principle can be added to any ω-model of a language without that truth predicate, without disrupting the underlying model. The price is that even if the logic of the underlying language is classical, the logic of the expanded language will be weaker: it will include only inferences declared valid by this semantics.

A word of caution is needed about how this result is to be interpreted. Theories in the ground language $\mathscr{L}$ are often formulated using schemas: for instance, induction schemas for arithmetic, and schemas of separation and replacement for set theory. The conservativeness result guarantees that when one extends the model M of the ground language to a non-classical model M^+ of the expanded language, every sentence true in the ground model will get value 1 in the enlarged model; but it does *not* automatically guarantee that *schemas* valid in the ground language will remain valid in the expanded language. If a schema is valid in the ground language, in the sense that all ground-language instances of it are true in the ground model, then conservativeness guarantees that all *ground-level instances of it* will get value 1 in the expanded model; but it does not automatically guarantee that all the *new instances in the expanded language* get value 1. For certain schemas, there will be a way of arguing this—for instance, since the conservativeness proof produces an ω-model, it obviously legitimizes extending both the standard induction rule

$$A(0) \wedge \forall n[A(n) \to A(n+1)] \vDash \forall n A(n)$$

and the course of values induction rule

$$\forall n[(\forall m < n)A(m) \to A(n)] \vDash \forall n A(n)$$

to formulas A that involve 'True'. But it is not something that is licensed in general. (Indeed, it isn't even licensed for all formulations of induction: the failure of the contrapositive rules such as $\neg \forall n A(n) \vDash \neg \forall n[(\forall m < n)A(m) \to A(n)]$ has already been remarked on.)

17.3. MODAL SEMANTICS

Some philosophers may find a modal-like semantics more natural than an algebraic one. It is the purpose of this section to point out that what was offered in Section 16.2 is in effect a modal-like semantics, indeed one that could be generalized in natural ways that might be useful if one wanted a combined theory that applies to vague discourse as well as to the semantic paradoxes. More specifically, we get a semantics on which '$\to$' is what Lewis (1973) called a *variably strict conditional*, though not one of quite the sort Lewis employed in his theory of counterfactuals.

To give a modal-like semantics for a variably strict conditional one must posit

(i) a system of *worlds*, one of which is singled out as special ("the actual world")

and

(ii) a system of *neighborhoods* around each world.

(The worlds are usually called *possible worlds*, though that label seems inappropriate when the modal-like semantics is used for something with no immediately obvious connection to possibility and necessity. The term 'actual world' is similarly inappropriate here, but I'll use it anyway. Lewis called the neighborhoods *spheres of similarity*, which is of doubtful appropriateness even in his semantics of counterfactuals, and is less so here. The word 'neighborhood' is better, but I caution that it is not being used in its topological sense.) In the case of the language $\mathscr{L}^+$ obtained by adding 'True' to the ground language $\mathscr{L}$, we can suppose that the worlds correspond to ordinal numbers up to and including some acceptable ordinal Δ (say the smallest one); the actual world is (the world corresponding to) Δ. The neighborhoods around a world α are the semi-open intervals of form $[\beta, \alpha)$ (that is, $\{\gamma \mid \beta \leq \gamma < \alpha\}$), for $\beta < \alpha$. The semantics of Section 16.2 is one on which each sentence (or formula relative to an assignment of objects in the domain) is assigned one of the three values 0, $\frac{1}{2}$ and 1 at each world. The values of the atomic predications of the ground language is the same at each world, as is the domain of the quantifiers: both are determined by the starting model M on which the whole construction is based. Only 'True' is treated differently from world to world. The value of each compound formula whose main connective isn't a conditional, at a world α, is determined from the values of its immediate constituents at the world, in the usual way. And the conditional is treated according to the following recipe:

The value of $A \to B$ at world α is

1 iff there is a neighborhood around α throughout which the value of A is less than or equal to that of B;

0 iff there is a neighborhood around α throughout which the value of A is greater than that of B;

$1/2$ otherwise.

This is just what was offered in Section 16.2, restated in terms of worlds. It was noted that (by use of the Kripke fixed point construction) we could guarantee that at each world, True($\langle A \rangle$) always has the same value as A (for any sentence A).

A somewhat unexpected feature of this semantics is that none of the neighborhoods around any world α include that world. To some extent this can be remedied: it is a consequence of the notion of an acceptable ordinal that the values of all formulas would be the same if we took the neighborhoods around such an ordinal α to be not the semi-open intervals but the closed intervals of form [β,α] (that is, $\{\gamma \mid \beta \leq \gamma \leq \alpha\}$), for β < α. Calling a world *normal* if the neighborhoods around it contain it, this makes acceptable ordinals normal; and in particular, it makes the actual world normal.

I'm not going to make any use of the modal semantics in what follows, but I should mention that part of its appeal may be in giving a unified treatment of the semantic paradoxes and vagueness. (The worlds would not then be identified with ordinals.) If we do that we should of course give up the assumption that all atomic predications for predicates other than 'True' get the same value at each world: the only requirement we impose on the values of atomic predications is that if some such predication gets the value 1 or 0 at @ then it gets that value throughout some neighborhood around @. (That requirement is satisfied for predications involving 'True', by the Fundamental Theorem.) In the context of a semantics for vagueness, it seems quite restrictive to suppose that the neighborhoods around each world are linearly ordered by inclusion; it would be more natural to allow two neighborhoods to overlap without either including the other. It turns out that allowing for this has little impact on the mathematical development or on which laws are valid, as long as the system of neighborhoods around each world satisfies the following "directedness" condition:

If U_1 and U_2 are neighborhoods of world w, then there is a neighborhood of w that is a subset of both.

A few other structural features of the system of neighborhoods used in the ordinal space can be built into the general framework, and with them, nearly all of the laws of the conditional that are derivable in the algebraic framework of

Section 17.1 (where predicates other than 'True' were assumed classical) carry over to the general modal semantics for vagueness. More details can be found in Field 2003b.

17.4. LAWS AND NON-LAWS

I'd like to give a sense of which claims and inferences the semantics validates and which ones it doesn't. (I mean primarily the algebraic semantics of Section 17.1, or the modal semantics prior to the generalization to vagueness. I exclude the generalized modal semantics only because I haven't supplied all the details of it; when the details are filled in, it yields pretty much the same laws.) The laws that I will mention all result from rather central features of the semantics: they *don't* turn, for instance, on the choice of minimal fixed points at the various stages of the construction, or on the fact that I started the revision-procedure by giving all conditionals value $1/2$.

First, the obvious laws from classical logic involving only unembedded conditionals hold in the semantics, for instance these:

$\vDash A \to A$
$\vDash A \land B \to A$ and $\vDash A \land B \to B$
$\vDash A \to A \lor B$ and $\vDash B \to A \lor B$
$\vDash A \to \neg\neg A$ and its converse
$\vDash A \land (B \lor C) \to (A \land B) \lor (A \land C)$ and its converse
$\vDash \neg(A \land B) \to \neg A \lor \neg B$ and its converse; also $\vDash \neg(A \lor B) \to \neg A \land \neg B$
  and its converse
$\vDash \forall x A \to A(x/t)$ and $\vDash A(x/t) \to \exists x A$
$\vDash \forall x A \to \neg \exists x \neg A$ and its converse; also $\vDash \exists x A \to \neg \forall x \neg A$ and its converse
$\vDash \forall x(A \lor Bx) \to A \lor \forall x Bx$ and its converse, when x is not free in A

Also the following obvious rules involving unembedded conditionals:

$A \to B, B \to C \vDash A \to C$ (Transitivity)
$A, A \to B \vDash B$ (Modus Ponens)
$\neg A \to \neg B \vDash B \to A$ and its converse (Weak Contraposition)
$A \to B \vDash A \land C \to B \land C$ and $A \to B \vDash C \land A \to C \land B$
$A \to B \vDash A \lor C \to B \lor C$ and $A \to B \vDash C \lor A \to C \lor B$
$\forall x(A \to B) \vDash \forall x A \to \forall x B$
$\forall x(A \to B) \vDash \exists x A \to \exists x B$
$A \to B, A \to C \vDash A \to B \land C$
$A \to C, B \to C \vDash A \lor B \to C$
$\forall x(A \to Bx) \vDash A \to \forall x Bx$ when x isn't free in A
$\forall x(Ax \to B) \vDash \exists x Ax \to B$ when x isn't free in B
$A, \neg B \vDash \neg(A \to B)$ [which I will call "the Negative Horseshoe Rule"
  since it can be restated as $\neg(A \supset B) \vDash \neg(A \to B)$]

$\neg A \vee B \vDash A \rightarrow B$ ["the Positive Horseshoe Rule", $A \supset B \vDash A \rightarrow B$]
$\neg(A \rightarrow B) \vDash A \vee \neg B$

which together with the previous yields

$$\neg(A \rightarrow B) \vDash B \rightarrow A.$$

The rules are to be understood as weak validities, in the sense of Chapter 10: they are validities of conditional assertion. (This is the kind of validity that is modeled by the relation *preserves designated value in all models*.) In addition to these obvious ones, I note a couple of others that are less obvious since they are rather trivial in a 2-valued framework:

$$\vDash (A \wedge \neg A) \rightarrow (B \vee \neg B)$$
$$\forall x(\neg Ax \rightarrow Ax) \vDash \neg \forall x Ax \rightarrow \forall x Ax$$

If we introduce a special symbol Q for a Liar sentence, the first of these could be broken up into two parts: $\vDash (A \wedge \neg A) \rightarrow Q$ and $\vDash Q \rightarrow (B \vee \neg B)$.

We also get the usual laws of Kleene semantics. Most of these follow from conditionals given above, by applying modus ponens. (One that doesn't follow in quite this way is the rule that contradictions (weakly) imply everything: $A, \neg A \vDash B$. But this one too needn't be posited separately: from "the Positive Horseshoe Rule" and rules for disjunction we get $\neg A \vDash A \rightarrow B$, from which we get $A, \neg A \vDash B$ using Modus Ponens.) The semantics also validates the two meta-rules typically taken to be implicit in Kleene semantics, viz. ∨-Elimination and ∃-Elimination. (On the latter, see note 3 of Section 17.1.)

When it comes to conditionals embedded inside other conditionals, the situation is more complicated. There are some positive results to report, the most important of which is probably Intersubstitutivity of Equivalents:

$$A \leftrightarrow B \vDash X_A \leftrightarrow X_B,$$

where X_B results from X_A by substituting B for one or more occurrences of A: this holds in complete generality, even when A and B are conditionals or have conditionals embedded within them. The crucial claims used in establishing this that go beyond the list above are the following strengthenings of Transitivity,

$$A \rightarrow B \vDash (C \rightarrow A) \rightarrow (C \rightarrow B)$$

and

$$A \rightarrow B \vDash (B \rightarrow C) \rightarrow (A \rightarrow C).$$

These are easily verified to hold in the semantics, and the Intersubstitutivity of Equivalents is then proved as sketched in Section 16.2. This is a key point where other attempts to add a conditional to Kleene logic often fail; we've already seen this for the Yablo semantics of Section 16.1.

We also have valid statements and rules that involve conditionals embedded inside conditionals. For instance, Weak Contraposition strengthens to Strong Contraposition:

$$\vDash (\neg A \to \neg B) \to (B \to A)$$

and its converse. (In the terminology of Chapter 10, this means that contraposition is strongly valid, not just weakly valid.) Some of the other rules cited above have conditional strengthenings; for instance, we have

$$\vDash (A \to B) \to (A \land C \to B \land C)$$
$$\vDash (A \to B) \to (A \lor C \to B \lor C)$$
$$\vDash \neg(A \to B) \to (B \to A).$$

I now turn to laws one might expect to hold, but that don't. One principle that we've already seen must fail, in any system with Intersubstitutivity and modus ponens and intersubstitutivity of logical equivalents, is the "Importation Rule"

$$A \to (B \to C) \vDash_? A \land B \to C;$$

it must fail because of the Curry Paradox (Section 4.1). Indeed, it must fail even in the special case where B is A; this case (given the equivalence of $A \land A$ to A and intersubstitutivity of equivalents) is in effect the "Contraction Rule"

$$A \to (A \to C) \vDash_? A \to C.$$

To see that these fail in the semantics, take A and B to be the Curry sentence K, whose values we've seen to be repetitions of ω-cycles $< 1/2, 0,1,0,1,0,1,\ldots >$, and take C to be a clear falsehood. Then $A \to C$ is equivalent to A; so the premise has value **1** whereas the conclusion has the value of K.

We also have a failure of the converse of Importation, i.e. of the "Exportation Rule"

$$A \land B \to C \vDash_? A \to (B \to C).$$

Taking C to be A, this yields as a special case (since $A \land B \to A$ is logically true) the following:

$$\vDash_? A \to (B \to A).$$

If this fails it must fail in the special case where B is a clear truth (since lowering the value of B can only raise the value of $A \to (B \to A)$), but it does fail there, as the reader can easily check taking A to be the Curry sentence (or its negation).

Another failure (not really surprising given the failures of Importation and Exportation) is the "Permutation Rule"

$$A \to (B \to C) \vDash_? B \to (A \to C).$$

Taking A to be $B \to C$, this yields as a special case

$$\vDash_? B \to ((B \to C) \to C);$$

this too fails when B is a clear truth and C is the Curry sentence or its negation.

It should also be clear that as with weakly classical theories, conditional proof (the meta-rule that if $\Gamma, A \models B$ then $\Gamma \models A \to B$) must fail. It is indeed an immediate lesson of the Curry paradox that one can't have conditional proof together with modus ponens and the Intersubstitutivity Principle, as I will discuss in Chapter 19. The restricted version of conditional proof that's valid is

$$\frac{\Gamma, A \models B}{\Gamma, A \vee \neg A \models A \to B}$$

which yields the usual form when excluded middle is assumed for A.

Because of the need to restrict conditional proof, it is not surprising that for many of the valid rules stated above, their conditional strengthening is not valid (unless appropriate instances of excluded middle are added as additional premises); these rules represent *merely weak* validities, i.e. weak validities that aren't strong. One example is the conditional strengthening of the "Positive Horseshoe Rule": that would be

$$\models_? (A \supset B) \to (A \to B),$$

and in the discussion of Exportation we've already seen that even in the weakened form $B \to (A \to B)$, this is invalid. (We do of course have

$$A \vee \neg A, B \vee \neg B \models (A \supset B) \to (A \to B).)$$

A second example is the explosion rule $A, \neg A \models B$; its conditional strengthening would be

$$\models_? A \wedge \neg A \to B,$$

which clearly fails (take A to be a Liar sentence or Curry sentence and B a clear falsehood). A third example is modus ponens: its conditional strengthening is

$$\models_? A \wedge (A \to B) \to B,$$

which can be seen to fail by taking A to be the Curry sentence and B to be a clear falsehood.[5] (Of course, we do get

$$A \vee \neg A, B \vee \neg B \models A \wedge (A \to B) \to B.)$$

In short, the Positive Horseshoe Rule, Explosion, and Modus Ponens are all *merely* weakly valid; and this is true also of quite a few other rules on the list.

The fact that quite a few standard "laws" that involve conditionals embedded within other conditionals turn out invalid in their unrestricted form is, I think,

---

[5] Indeed, it is well known that the conditional strengthening of modus ponens implies the non-structural Contraction Rule. For from $A \to (A \to B)$ we can easily derive $A \to [A \wedge (A \to B)]$; and if the conditional strengthening of modus ponens were valid, we could then derive $A \to B$.

an unpleasant feature of the current theory. In the case of many of these "laws", they *must* fail to be unrestrictedly valid if *anything like* the current theory is correct: for instance, if the Intersubstitutivity Principle and modus ponens are valid then the conditional strengthening of modus ponens is bound to require restrictions, because of the Curry paradox. In some other cases, it might be possible to retain the law without restriction by altering the details of the current theory. However, it is a familiar feature of variably strict conditionals that the embedding of conditionals inside other conditionals doesn't work smoothly, and so it seems unlikely that one will get major improvements without altering that aspect of the theory. Are there satisfactory ways of treating conditionals other than as variably restrict while retaining the Intersubstitutivity Principle? I don't know: the Yablo approach in Section 16.1 initially seemed a promising attempt, but it turned out to have far worse problems, even with regard to the embedding of operators like conjunction inside conditionals. But I do not rule out the possibility of a better theory, perhaps even one along similar lines to Yablo's.

Among the principles that will fail in any theory like this are versions of induction stated as conditionals, e.g. $\forall n[(\forall m < n)A(m) \to A(n)] \to \forall nA(n)$. One way to see that this has to fail is to note that were it to hold it would contrapose, yielding $\neg \forall nA(n) \to \neg \forall n[(\forall m < n)A(m) \to A(n)]$; then by Modus Ponens we would get the least number principle, and could reproduce the Berry paradox. A more direct way to see that it fails is to take all the $A(m)$ for $m \geq 1$ to be equivalent to each other; in this case the antecedent reduces to $[\top \to A(0)] \wedge [A(0) \to A(1)]$ and the consequent to $A(0) \wedge A(1)$, so the claim implies $[\top \to A(0)] \wedge [[A(0) \to A(1)]] \to A(1)$; this conditional fails when $A(0)$ is the Curry sentence and $A(1)$ a clear falsehood. In practice, it is the rule forms of induction (positive and negative) which we employ, so there is little impact of the failure of the conditional form beyond the failure of the negative rule form, i.e. the least number principle. As we've seen, the positive rule forms are quite unproblematic.

I should mention one non-law involving the defined determinacy operator:

(DIST) $\hspace{4em} \vDash_? DA \wedge DB \to D(A \wedge B).$

The weaker rule form obviously holds, but this conditional form doesn't: taking A to be K and B to be $\neg K$, the antecedent has value $1/2$ at limits whereas the consequent has value 0 everywhere. This example is important, due to an argument that Williamson 1994 (p. 160) uses against higher order vagueness. (Williamson's argument is given in the context of classical logic, but in conversation I have heard others employ it for non-classical theories.) Williamson's argument employs an infinitistic strengthening of (DIST) to conclude that any iteration of a determinacy operator must collapse by stage ω, i.e. $D^\omega A \to D^{\omega+1}A$ should be a law. That result would of course be a disaster—the disaster that beset continuum-valued logic—but it is avoided here because (DIST) and its infinitistic strengthening fail. (For further remarks on this, see Field 2007, note 35.)

I should reiterate that the current theory validates full classical logic in many contexts, viz. any context where excluded middle can be assumed. (And the current theory takes that to include any context where the usual "paradoxes", and related phenomena such as Truth-teller sentences, do not arise.) In particular, the conditional behaves just like the material conditional in such contexts: this is because it is a law of the logic that

$$A \vee \neg A, B \vee \neg B \vDash (A \supset B) \leftrightarrow (A \to B).$$

The theory also validates the full Tarski theory of truth, in the sense that restricted Tarskian predicates are definable in the theory, and behave in a completely classical fashion. The restriction on excluded middle, and resultant restrictions on certain natural principles involving conditionals, is needed only when one ventures into a domain that the classical Tarskian theory does not cover.

17.5. VARIATIONS

I know of several ways to vary the details of the current approach, without altering its fundamental character: in particular, without altering the reliance on a revision procedure. I'll mention two of them; both involve slight alterations in the treatment of the conditional.

The first variant, which I will not discuss in any detail, makes it harder for conditionals to get value 0 at any ordinal stage. We modify (*) of Section 16.2 (for all α, not just limits) as follows:

$$(*_{mod}) \quad |A \to B|_{s,\alpha} = 1 \text{ if } (\exists \beta < \alpha)(\forall \gamma)[\beta \leq \gamma < \alpha \to |A|_{s,\gamma} \leq |B|_{s,\gamma}]$$
$$0 \text{ if } (\exists \beta < \alpha)(\forall \gamma)[\beta \leq \gamma < \alpha \to (|A|_{s,\gamma} = 1 \wedge |B|_{s,\gamma} = 0]$$
$$1/2 \text{ otherwise.}$$

The development with this altered conditional is not hugely different than with the conditional of Section 16.2; in particular, one can still prove the Fundamental Theorem, with little variation in details. In some ways this modification simplifies the account: now when A has ultimate value $1/2$ and B has ultimate value 0, $A \to B$ inevitably has ultimate value $1/2$ (as opposed to the Official Theory of Section 16.2, where it might have ultimate value $1/2$ or ultimate value 0); similarly when A has ultimate value 1 and B has ultimate value $1/2$. The Curry sentence turns out to have the same valuation as the Liar: at each ordinal it gets value $1/2$. But I don't think there is in the end any real simplification: it's just that in this theory, you need a slightly more complicated sentence to behave in the way that the Curry sentence behaves in the Official Theory.[6] I personally find the Official Theory more natural, but this may be just that I discovered it earlier and have used it more.

The second variant was inspired by a complaint that Steve Yablo made against the Official Theory, in the paper already cited. Yablo's complaint[7] against the Official Theory is that it produces unintuitive results for conditionals in which the antecedent and consequent could consistently be assigned values in more than one way. Consider for instance the conditionals $Q \to T$ and $T \to Q$, where Q is a Liar sentence and T is a Truth-Teller (a sentence that asserts its own truth). The Official Theory gives these conditionals the value **1**, since Q and T have precisely the same value in the algebraic semantics, viz., the function that assigns $1/2$ to each ordinal. Yablo regards this as counterintuitive, and I have some sympathy with that. As he puts it, my conditional isn't sufficiently strict.

Yablo gives two other examples of the insufficient strictness. One involves the sentence $T \to \neg T$ and its converse: again, these get value **1** on the Official Theory, and this too may seem counterintuitive. It is an inevitable feature of accounts like the one I've considered that $Q \to \neg Q$ and its converse get value **1**, and this has a strong intuitive basis since Q asserts its own untruth. But there is no corresponding intuitive basis for the corresponding conditionals that involve T instead of Q.

Yablo's final example of "insufficient strictness" is this: Suppose Jones and Smith each say that what the other says is not true. Any account that respects the naive theory of truth (the Equivalence Principle plus the Tarski biconditionals) will yield that $J \to \neg S$ and $S \to \neg J$ have value **1**; and the symmetry of the situation seems to rule out giving one of J and S the value **0** and the other the value **1**, so both must get some sort of intermediate value. But the Official Theory yields that J and S have exactly the same intermediate value, and hence will yield that the conditionals $J \to S$ and $S \to J$ also have value **1**; and this may seem somewhat undesirable.

Recall that both the Official Theory and Yablo's own theory (the one considered in Section 16.1) make use of Kripkean fixed points; his theory differs from the Official Theory primarily in his using Yablo fixed points for conditionals as well, whereas the Official Theory uses a revision theory for conditionals. But an analysis of how his theory comes to different verdicts on the three examples above reveals that this isn't due to his use of Yablo fixed points rather than a revision procedure; rather, it is due to the fact that he takes into account Kripke fixed

---

[6] Let Q_{-1} be the sentence that asserts that it is definitely not true (defining DA as $A \wedge \neg(A \to \neg A)$; the alternative definition $A \wedge (\top \to A)$ is not equivalent on this theory, and won't serve the purpose of a definitely operator). As in the Official Theory, this takes on value $1/2$ at even ordinals and 0 at odd ordinals. Now consider the sentence K_* that asserts that if it is true then so is Q_{-1}; in the variant theory (and in the Official Theory too for that matter), it takes on value $1/2$ at 0 and limits, 1 at odd ordinals, and 0 at odd successors; so its negation has the same sequence of values that the Curry sentence has in the Official Theory.

[7] Actually this is one of three complaints against the Official Theory that he makes in that paper; all three are discussed in Field 2005b, but here I discuss only the one that interests me most.

points other than the minimal one, whereas the Official Theory took account only of the minimal Kripke fixed point. This suggests that we might modify the Official Theory to take account of non-minimal Kripke fixed points.

As in the construction of 15.2, we start with a transparent valuation of conditionals, v_0. But then instead of simply considering the value that every sentence (or more generally, parameterized formula) gets at the minimal fixed point over v_0, we consider the value that every sentence gets at *each* transparent fixed point over v_0; all these values are used in determining the next valuation of conditionals, v_1, by the following rule:

$v_1(A \to B)$ is

    1 if $\forall T[T$ is a transparent Kripke fixed point over $v_0 \to |A|_T \leq |B|_T]$;

    0 if $|A|_{Z_0} > |B|_{Z_0}$, where Z_0 is the minimal fixed point over v_0;

    $1/2$ otherwise.

(We could, if we liked, quantify over non-minimal fixed points in the 0 clause as well as in the 1 clause, but this is not needed to get the verdicts that Yablo wants in the three examples above, and I think it would probably be undesirable.) More generally, we construct a transfinite sequence of valuations of conditionals, $\{v_\alpha\}$, as follows:

$v_\alpha(A \to B)$ is

    1 if $(\exists \beta < \alpha) \forall \gamma \forall T[\beta \leq \gamma < \alpha \wedge$ T is a transparent Kripke fixed point over $v_\gamma \to |A|_T \leq |B|_T]$;

    0 if $(\exists \beta < \alpha) \forall \gamma [\beta \leq \gamma < \alpha \to |A|_{Z_\gamma} > |B|_{Z_\gamma}]$, where Z_γ is the minimal Kripke fixed point over v_γ;

    $1/2$ otherwise.

We then take the ultimate value of a sentence to be 1 if $\exists \beta (\forall \gamma \geq \beta) \forall T[T$ is a transparent Kripke fixed point over $v_\gamma \to |A|_T = 1]$; equivalently, if $\exists \beta (\forall \gamma \geq \beta)[|A|_{Z_\gamma} = 1]$. Analogously for 0. If neither of these hold, its ultimate value is $1/2$. We define an acceptable ordinal as an ordinal Δ such that every parameterized formula gets its ultimate value at Z_Δ. The proof that there are ultimate ordinals is essentially as before.

This alteration of the Official Theory removes Yablo's worries about "insufficient strictness", while leaving the main features of the Official Theory intact. For instance, what distinguishes the Truth-teller T from the Liar Q is that while Q gets value $1/2$ in every fixed point, T gets value $1/2$ in some, 1 in others, and 0 in still others. That is so whatever the valuation of conditionals v_γ on which the fixed point is based; because of this, the revised clause for conditionals having value 1 guarantees that $T \to Q, Q \to T, T \to \neg T$ and $\neg T \to T$ will never get value 1; they will have value $1/2$ at every ordinal stage. ($Q \to \neg Q$ and $\neg Q \to Q$ will still have value 1.) Similarly in the third example: $J \to \neg S$ and

$S \to \neg J$ will still have value 1 at each ordinal, as desired, but now $J \to S$ and $S \to J$ will have value $1/2$ at each ordinal.

I'm inclined to think that this modification of the original semantics does give slightly more intuitive results in these cases of conditionals whose antecedent and consequent could consistently be assigned values in more than one way. The only downside I see to it is that it is slightly more complicated. (I should remark that the algebraic and modal semantics used for the Official Theory could easily be extended to the variant theory.)[8] But we need not decide between them: the central core of the inferences validated in one semantics will be validated in the other as well.

---

[8] For the modal semantics, take the worlds to be transparent fixed points over valuations of conditionals that appear in the cycle from one acceptable ordinal Δ to the next one $\Delta + \Sigma_0$. Each world is thus associated with a particular valuation of conditionals. Imagine those valuations arranged in order (say "clockwise") on a transfinite circle obtained by identifying Δ with $\Delta + \Sigma_0$. Imagine that at each valuation **v** on the transfinite circle, there is a "tangent space" attached; on it reside the worlds associated with **v** (i.e. the transparent fixed points over **v**), with the minimal fixed point over **v** right on the circle and the other fixed points further away. For any world attached to a point α of the transfinite circle other than Δ, we get a neighborhood of it by picking another point β on the transfinite circle and considering all worlds attached to points in the semi-open interval from β to α in the clockwise order, including β but excluding α. For any world attached to Δ it is the same, except that this time we include Z_Δ in the neighborhoods. Then the general semantics given before applies, except that in the case of the 0 clause we confine quantification to those worlds in the neighborhoods that are distinguished by being right on the transfinite circle—i.e. to the minimal fixed points.

The modification of the algebraic semantics is similar: whereas the members of the algebra for the Official Theory were functions mapping a certain transfinite circle of ordinals into $\{0, 1/2, 1\}$, the members of the algebra for the modified theory will be functions mapping a certain "hairy transfinite circle" of ordinals into $\{0, 1/2, 1\}$, where the hairy circle consists of the transfinite circle plus its various tangent "hairs". The reader can easily supply the details.

18
What Has Been Done

The previous chapter was concerned with a lot of messy details, and I hope that they have not obscured the basic picture. The basic picture is that we have done what we set out to do back in Part I: we have generalized the Kripkean theory KFS (the internal strong-Kleene-based Kripkean theory), in a way that solves the problems for that theory that were set out in Chapter 3; and we have done so in a way that accords with the general spirit though not the details of the continuum-valued semantics discussed in Chapters 4 and 5.

More fully, we have shown how for any reasonable classical model of the ground language, there is a non-classical model of the language that extends it by adding 'True', which is exactly like the ground model except where 'True' is concerned. In particular, it is classical except where 'True' is concerned. This non-classical model fully validates the Intersubstitutivity Principle: the sentence True($\langle A \rangle$) is fully equivalent to the sentence A, in the sense that if you substitute True($\langle A \rangle$) for A in any sentence B, the resultant sentence B^* is logically equivalent to the sentence B you started with.

Moreover, though 'True' is nonclassical, this theory contains the classical Tarskian theory as a part: for within this theory one can define the stratified Tarskian predicates, and it follows from this theory that those predicates are classical. More fully, define

$True_0(x)$ as: $True(x) \land x$ is a sentence not containing 'True';

$True_1(x)$ as: $True(x) \land x$ is a sentence whose only occurrences of 'True' are in definitional abbreviations of '$True_0$';

and in general

$True_\alpha(x)$ as: $True(x) \land x$ is a sentence whose only occurrences of 'True' are in definitional abbreviations of '$True_\beta$' for $\beta < \alpha$.

(Here the α and β are ordinal notations, in some system of notations that assigns a unique notation to each member of an initial segment of the ordinals.) An obvious induction shows that each predicate '$True_\alpha$' obeys excluded middle, and hence behaves in an entirely classical manner. It is only insofar as the unsubscripted predicate 'True' transcends the Tarskian hierarchy that it is nonclassical.

All this extends straightforwardly to 'true of', or to 'satisfies'.

Everything in the previous three paragraphs holds also for the Kripkean theory KFS. But KFS is a theory in a logically impoverished language, with no reasonable conditional and no means of expressing the "defectiveness" of sentences like the Liar sentence. What Chapters 16 and 17 do is the same *sort* of thing, but in a language that does have a reasonable conditional. This has three advantages.

1. It enables us to come much closer to carrying out ordinary reasoning. (Of course, to the extent that ordinary reasoning involves classical logic as well as a naive truth predicate, it leads to contradiction; so we better not be able to carry out *all* ordinary reasoning!)
2. It enables us to validate the Tarski biconditionals

$$\text{True}(\langle A \rangle) \leftrightarrow A.$$

   KFS, you'll recall, didn't validate them despite validating the Intersubstitutivity Principle.
3. It enables us to define a notion of defectiveness (via a definition of a notion of determinateness), which does not generate paradoxes: indeed, defectiveness and determinateness are defined from the conditional in almost exactly the way done in continuum-valued semantics (and the definition used here is equivalent in continuum-valued semantics to the one used there). But in continuum-valued semantics the definitions had a crippling defect, viz., the collapse of determinateness upon iteration: this spoiled the application of continuum-valued semantics both to the semantic paradoxes and to vagueness. In this semantics, that defect in the definition of determinateness is completely overcome: I discussed this in Chapter 15, and will return to it in Part IV.

Despite the difference with continuum-valued logic mentioned under 3, the logic of this theory is in many ways like that of continuum-valued logic: for instance, each can be given a model-theoretic semantics based on adding an additional operator to a deMorgan algebra, and quite a few of the same laws hold of each (though each obeys laws that the other doesn't). One of the things that both conditionals have in common is that they each reduce to the classical conditional on the assumption of excluded middle for their antecedent and consequent: they are simply *generalizations of* the classical conditional. I have heard it charged that the claim to have validated the Tarski biconditionals is an illusion, since the conditional employed "differs in meaning from" the conditional that Tarski employed. The charge seems to me to have no bite, given that in the presence of excluded middle the conditional behaves just like classical logic says a conditional should behave.

One issue I haven't discussed is *how many* of the inferences that preserve value 1 really ought to be declared logically valid *tout court* (as opposed to, validated by the formal semantics). If one says that they *all* should, then one will need to make a decision on some seemingly arbitrary features of the semantics, such as the choice of a starting valuation for conditionals[1] (and the special role of *minimal* Kripke fixed points at each stage of the construction, even in the Yablo variation), in order to decide what is "logically valid". In addition, the set of "logically valid inferences" will have an extremely high degree of non-computability: see Welch (forthcoming) for details. It might be better to adopt the view that what is validated by a given version of the formal semantics outruns "real validity": that the genuine logical validities are some effectively generable subset of those inferences that preserve value 1 in the given semantics. If one adopts this viewpoint then there would doubtless be some arbitrariness in which effectively generable subset to choose, but that seems perfectly acceptable unless one wants to put high (and I think unreasonable) demands on the significance of the distinction between those inferences that are logically valid and those that aren't. (The very fact that it is controversial which inferences are valid is enough to destroy some overblown views of the significance of the distinction.) Whatever subset of those inferences is chosen, the semantics of Section 16.2 offers a proof that one won't get into trouble operating with the inferences in it.

---

[1] One example of how the starting valuation for conditionals affects what preserves value 1 in the model theory is given by a "determinate truth-teller" T_1: a sentence that asserts its own determinate truth. On the starting valuation I've chosen, T_1 gets value 0; but if the starting valuation had assigned $\top \to T_1$ the value 1, T_1 would have gotten value 1. I myself would be disinclined to regard either $\neg T_1$ or T_1 as a "logical law"; or if it is one, it is one that we are free to adopt or deny by a convention with little effect on the rest of our logical theory. (Another example of dependence on the starting valuation, one where the starting valuation I've officially adopted yields odd results, was noted in Yablo 2003 (p. 319) and discussed in Section 5 of Field 2005b.)

PART IV

MORE ON PARACOMPLETE SOLUTIONS

19

Validity, Truth-Preservation, and the Second Incompleteness Theorem

19.1. ANOTHER FORM OF CURRY'S PARADOX

In Chapter 4 I presented Curry's paradox in a slightly unusual form; here is a more traditional formulation of the paradox, which will be useful for drawing morals about validity. This version does not employ the full Intersubstitutivity Principle, but only the rules (T-Introd) and (T-Elim) employed in weakly classical theories.

As in Chapter 4, let K be a sentence that is equivalent to

$$\text{True}(\langle K \rangle) \to \text{The earth is flat.}$$

We now reason as follows: Assume $\text{True}(\langle K \rangle)$ for the sake of argument. By the rule (T-Elim), we can conclude K, which is equivalent to the displayed sentence above; and since we've assumed $\text{True}(\langle K \rangle)$, we can conclude by modus ponens that the earth is flat. This, of course, depends on the assumption $\text{True}(\langle K \rangle)$; that is, what's been established is that

$$\text{True}(\langle K \rangle) \vDash \text{The earth is flat.}$$

So far the reasoning is fairly uncontroversial. But now, using $\to$-Introd, this yields

(1) $\qquad \vDash \text{True}(\langle K \rangle) \to \text{The earth is flat,}$

hence (by the equivalence "defining" K)

$$\vDash K.$$

By the rule (T-Introd), this yields

(2) $\qquad \vDash \text{True}(\langle K \rangle);$

and from this and (1) we have

$$\vDash \text{The earth is flat,}$$

by Modus Ponens.

Where does the reasoning go wrong? I think by far the most intuitive diagnosis is that the bad step is the $\to$-Introduction. This is the step where every non-philosopher whom I have ever tried to convince of the seriousness of Curry's Paradox balks. And it is the diagnosis not only of the paracomplete theorist, but of the weakly classical theorist. Both hold that the meta-rule

$$\frac{\Gamma, A \vDash B}{\Gamma \vDash A \to B}$$

is not validity-preserving (even in the special case where Γ is empty); to infer the conclusion we need the additional assumption $\vDash A \vee \neg A$.

In discussing weakly classical theories I suggested a rationale for the failure of $\to$-Introduction: it involves distinguishing *conditional assertion* from *assertion of a conditional*, and takes the implication relation $\vDash$ to mark the validity of a conditional assertion. I think the paracomplete theorist should adopt this proposal as well. On this understanding, the conclusion $\Gamma \vDash A \to B$ is not immediate from the premise $\Gamma, A \vDash B$. The premise $\Gamma, A \vDash B$ does license $\Gamma, A \vDash A \to B$ (since one can conditionally assert $A \to B$ on the assumption B; that is, $B \vDash A \to B$). In addition, we have $\Gamma, \neg A \vDash A \to B$ (since one can conditionally assert $A \to B$ on the assumption $\neg A$ alone; that is, $\neg A \vDash A \to B$). So if we allow reasoning by cases (as the paracomplete theorist does), we have

$$\frac{\Gamma, A \vDash B}{\Gamma, A \vee \neg A \vDash A \to B}$$

and hence

$$\frac{\Gamma, A \vDash B \qquad \vDash A \vee \neg A}{\Gamma \vDash A \to B.}$$

But these are the closest we get to $\to$-Introduction, from the perspective that $\vDash$ marks the validity of conditional assertion. This seems to me a quite natural explanation of where and why the Curry reasoning goes wrong.

The view that the fault in the Curry reasoning is in the $\to$-Introduction step is not completely inevitable. For instance, the classical gap theorist will accept that step, and fault the later step where (T-Introd) is applied: this theorist believes K but disbelieves $True(\langle K \rangle)$. And the classical glut theorist holds that the argument erred before the $\to$-Introduction, in the use of (T-Elim) in the "fairly uncontroversial" part of the argument: this theorist believes $True(\langle K \rangle)$ but disbelieves K.

Two other views on which the argument erred before the $\to$-Introduction locate the error in the structural rules. As announced earlier, I'm not going to seriously discuss "substructural logics" in this book, but for completeness I give the basic idea in a footnote.[1]

Another possible diagnosis is that the argument fails in one or both of the Modus Ponens steps (either the one in the "fairly uncontroversial" part of the argument, or the one at the very end of the argument, or both). Interestingly, the model-theoretic semantics of Section 16.2 (or 17.1 or 17.3) shows one way that this diagnosis could be consistently developed; we could use the same basic model theory, but understand validity differently. Instead of saying that an argument is valid if, in all models, when the premises have value **1** then so does the conclusion, we say instead that an argument is valid if, in all models, the value of the conclusion is at least the greatest lower bound of the values of the premises. In the terminology of Chapter 10, this is the switch from "weak validity" to "strong validity". In this altered sense of validity, modus ponens is not valid (according to paracomplete theories). And in this sense of validity, →-Introduction *is* validity-preserving in the special case where Γ is empty, or more generally, where excluded middle holds for each instance of Γ. (No assumption that excluded middle holds *for A* is required.) Only that special case of →-Introduction is needed in the above version of the Curry argument, so on this altered account of validity, the blame in that version of the paradox would be put entirely on the Modus Ponens steps.

In Chapter 10 I argued that weak validity and strong validity are the semantic analogs of two different informal notions: weak validity corresponds to validity of conditional assertion, strong validity to validity of the assertion of the conditional. These are both perfectly good notions, and it is a matter of convention which

---

[1] One of the "substructuralist" diagnoses points out that the argument from 'True($\langle K \rangle$)' to 'The earth is flat' used the assumption 'True($\langle K \rangle$)' *twice*, and claims that because of this, the reasoning only establishes

(*) $\quad\quad\quad\quad\quad\quad$ True($\langle K \rangle$), True($\langle K \rangle$) ⊨ The earth is flat.

To get from this to

$\quad\quad\quad\quad\quad\quad$ True($\langle K \rangle$) ⊨ The earth is flat

one uses "structural contraction" (the meta-rule that if B follows from Γ, A, A then it follows from Γ, A). The view in question is that this rule is invalid. (Structural contraction is not to be confused with the (non-structural) contraction rule of Chapter 4, that $A \to (A \to B) \vDash A \to B$; that rule must in any case be rejected if True($\langle K \rangle$) is to be intersubstitutable with K, as discussed in Chapter 4.)

The other "substructuralist" diagnosis, advocated in Weir 2005, locates the problem even earlier, in the argument to (*) from

$\quad\quad\quad\quad\quad\quad$ True($<K>$), True($<K>$) → the earth is flat ⊨ The earth is flat

and

$\quad\quad\quad\quad\quad\quad$ True($<K>$) ⊨ True($<K>$) → the earth is flat.

We get from these to (*) by the generalized transitivity rule "Cut" (from X,Y ⊨ Z and W ⊨ Y infer X,W ⊨ Z), but Weir proposes that Cut needs restrictions.

one the unadorned term 'validity' is used for. Does it follow that the question of whether it is Modus Ponens or →-Introduction that is to blame in the Curry argument is just a verbal question? Not quite. If one party places the blame exclusively on the →-Introduction step and another party exclusively on Modus Ponens, it does seem *quite likely* that the difference is verbal: that both agree that it is fine to conditionally assert B on the basis of A and $A \to B$ but not to assert the conditional $A \wedge (A \to B) \to B$, and they differ only on how to describe this in terms of validity. But it is conceivable that the difference isn't verbal, that the second party means to deny that one can legitimately assert B on the assumption of A and $A \to B$. In this case, though, it seems to me that the second party is suggesting a radical change in our ordinary reasoning, one with little to recommend it.

We've seen four possible diagnoses of where the Curry argument fails: either in the rule T-Elim, or the rule T-Introd, or the rule →-Elim (Modus ponens), or the rule →-Introd. And unless one is prepared to mess with the structural rules (e.g. transitivity of entailment, or structural contraction), these seem to be the only possible diagnoses, for the four rules mentioned are the only non-structural rules used in the argument. Restricting →-Introd seems to me (as to the weakly classical theorist) by far the least disruptive way to accommodate the paradox.

19.2. THE VALIDITY ARGUMENT

At the beginning of Chapter 2 I mentioned an obvious argument for the view that an inference is valid if and only if it is logically necessary that it preserves truth. To spell it out slightly:

'*Only if*' *direction:* Suppose $A_1, \ldots, A_n \vDash B$. Then by (T-Elim), $\text{True}(\langle A_1 \rangle), \ldots, \text{True}(\langle A_n \rangle) \vDash B$; and by (T-Introd), $\text{True}(\langle A_1 \rangle), \ldots, \text{True}(\langle A_n \rangle) \vDash \text{True}(\langle B \rangle)$. By ∧-Elim, $\text{True}(\langle A_1 \rangle) \wedge \ldots \wedge \text{True}(\langle A_n \rangle) \vDash \text{True}(\langle B \rangle)$. So by →-Introd,

$$\vDash \text{True}(\langle A_1 \rangle) \wedge \ldots \wedge \text{True}(\langle A_n \rangle) \to \text{True}(\langle B \rangle).$$

That is, the claim that if the premises $A_1, \ldots, A_n$ are true, so is the conclusion, is valid, i.e. holds of logical necessity.

'*If*' *direction:* Suppose $\vDash \text{True}(\langle A_1 \rangle) \wedge \ldots \wedge \text{True}(\langle A_n \rangle) \to \text{True}(\langle B \rangle)$. By Modus ponens, $\text{True}(\langle A_1 \rangle) \wedge \ldots \wedge \text{True}(\langle A_n \rangle) \vDash \text{True}(\langle B \rangle)$. So by ∧-Introd, $\text{True}(\langle A_1 \rangle), \ldots, \text{True}(\langle A_n \rangle) \vDash \text{True}(\langle B \rangle)$. So by T-Introd, $A_1, \ldots, A_n \vDash \text{True}(\langle B \rangle)$; and by T-Elim, $A_1, \ldots, A_n \vDash B$.

This is a compelling argument. Its only problem is that it relies on all four of the logical principles T-Introd, T-Elim, →-Introd, and →-Elim, which the Curry paradox shows to be jointly inconsistent.[2]

---

[2] Again I put aside solutions that turn on rejection of the usual structural rules.

An advocate of full classical logic (or full intuitionist logic) including reasoning by cases can't accept *either* direction of the argument in full generality, since each direction relies on both the rules T-Introd and T-Elim, which are inconsistent in such a logic.

Of course, an advocate of such a logic can accept special cases of the reasoning. One special case is where none of the sentences $A_1, \ldots A_n, B$ involved in the argument contain 'True' or related terms. Application of (T-Introd) to such sentences, and of (T-Elim) to sentences that attribute truth to such sentences, is unproblematic, and so the reasoning above goes through, in both directions.

But this special case is quite limited. Can the advocate of full classical or intuitionistic logic accept the reasoning of the 'only if' part in the slightly less special case where $A_1, \ldots A_n, B$ may contain 'True' *but where none of the reasoning involved in the argument exploits the logic of those terms*? No! In fact, we've seen that some fully classical theories reject that valid arguments of this sort always preserve truth (even actually, let alone of necessity). For instance, classical glut theories (other than hyper-dialetheism) deny that modus ponens always preserves truth, though (being classical) they take modus ponens to be valid. And many classical gap theories, such as the external theories of Kleene-based fixed points, take any inference to $Q \vee \neg Q$ to be valid, but they don't regard the inference as truth-preserving when the premises are true, since they don't regard the conclusion true.

There are, to be sure, fully classical theories that do accept that when there is a valid argument from $A_1, \ldots A_n$ to B that employs no principles involving 'True' or related terms, then the argument preserves truth: external theories of certain supervaluational fixed points are an example. But even for these, that conclusion cannot be established by applying the reasoning of the Validity Argument to that special case; it must be established by other means.

To repeat, an advocate of full classical (or full intuitionist) logic can accept *neither* direction of the Validity Argument, because each direction relies on both of the minimal truth rules (T-Introd) and (T-Elim).

By contrast, an advocate of a typical paracomplete solution or weakly classical solution (or paraconsistent dialetheist solution, as will be discussed in Part V) will accept the 'If' direction of that argument, since it relies only on these minimal truth rules plus modus ponens. On these views, any inference that by logical necessity preserves truth must be valid. The 'Only if' direction must however be rejected, just as on the fully classical theory. It still holds in the special case where none of the sentences $A_1, \ldots A_n, B$ involved in the argument contain 'True' or related terms: application of $\rightarrow$-Introd to sentences that attribute truth to such sentences is unproblematic. (On the dual view which keeps $\rightarrow$-Introd but restricts Modus Ponens, it is the 'Only if' direction that holds generally, and the 'If' direction that holds only in special cases.)

Of course, none of this precludes an advocate of any of these logics from simply defining 'valid' to mean 'necessarily truth-preserving', thus obviating the need for the Validity Argument. But to do so is to divorce "validity" from acceptable reasoning. I remarked on this possibility in Chapter 7, in connection with Tim Maudlin: he's a gap theorist who regards all classical reasoning as *legitimate*, but says that some of it is *invalid* since it doesn't preserve truth. As I said then, this just seems a notational variant of the view that such reasoning is valid but doesn't preserve truth. Similarly, the classical glut theories in which modus ponens doesn't preserve truth could have been presented as holding that reasoning by modus ponens is perfectly legitimate, but invalid because not truth-preserving; again, this would just seem to be a notational variant of the view as I presented it. I prefer to let 'valid' go with legitimate reasoning rather than with truth-preservation, but nothing hangs on this choice of terminology.

If we use 'valid' in the legitimate reasoning sense, then the above discussion makes clear not only that none of the theories that have been seriously discussed can accept the Validity Argument, but that none can accept the 'Only if' direction of its conclusion. Indeed, none of these can accept even that valid arguments all *actually* preserve truth, let alone that they do so of necessity.[3] This is a situation that we have already come to grips with for the fully and weakly classical theories, in the context of the second incompleteness theorem. Let us now look at how paracomplete theories diagnose the second incompleteness theorem.

19.3. THE SECOND INCOMPLETENESS THEOREM

By Gödel's Second Incompleteness Theorem, no remotely adequate mathematical theory can prove its own consistency.[4] As observed in Chapter 12, this theorem can seem slightly puzzling for languages that contain their own truth predicate, because it seems as if in an acceptable theory T for such a language we ought to be able to both

(A) inductively prove within T that T is sound, i.e. that all its theorems are true,

and

(B) argue from the soundness of T to the claim that T is consistent.

Where does this fail, in the case where the theory of truth is the sort of paracomplete theory discussed in the previous two chapters?

The problem can't be in (B): these theories certainly imply $\neg \text{True}(\langle 0 = 1 \rangle)$, so the soundness of T would imply that '$0 = 1$' isn't a theorem of T; and this implies that T is consistent (since in these theories inconsistencies imply

---

[3] I've mentioned two sorts of theories to which this last does not apply: hyper-dialetheism, according to which every inference preserves truth; and the "dual" paracomplete theories that accept →-Introduction but give up Modus Ponens instead. For these it is the 'If' direction of the conclusion that must be abandoned.

[4] See note 6 of Chapter 12.

everything). The problem must, then, be with (A). But as in the case of classical theories, the intuitive reasoning looks straightforward. If, again, we assume for simplicity a formulation of logic in which reasoning takes place among sentences only, then the argument is

(1) Each axiom of T is true
(2) Each rule of inference of T preserves truth (that is, whenever the premises of the rule are true, so is the conclusion)

Since a theorem of T is just a sentence that results from the axioms by successive application of rules of inference, a simple mathematical induction yields

(3) All theorems of T are true; i.e. T is sound.

And as in the case of classical theories, the problem can't in general be traced to the gap between asserting of each single axiom that it is true and asserting that all of them are true: for we can use the truth predicate to finitely axiomatize. Nor can the problem be in the use of the truth predicate in induction: all that is required is a positive induction rule, which we've seen to extend unproblematically to formulas involving 'True'. The only place that the argument can conceivably go wrong is where it went wrong for classical glut theories and weakly classical theories: in (2).

A substantial similarity among nearly all theories that diagnose the failure of the argument as residing in (2) is that a distinction is made between restricted and unrestricted truth preservation. Let's review how this distinction applies in the case both of glut theories and of the "strong supervaluational theories" and "strong revision theories" of 11.3, 11.4, and 12.1. These theories not only don't declare all their own rules to be unrestrictedly truth-preserving, they actually declare some of them not to be unrestrictedly truth-preserving. But as I argued in Part II, this is not as clear a defect as one might initially think: for it is perfectly possible for the advocate of such a theory to believe that the rules preserve truth *in the circumstances in which they are directly applied*. For instance, a strong supervaluational theory will hold that the rules (T-Introd) and (T-Elim) each fail to unrestrictedly preserve truth: either (T-Introd) fails to preserve truth when applied to Q and (T-Elim) fails to preserve truth when applied to $\neg Q$, or the other way around. But Q and $\neg Q$ aren't the kind of sentences that we are committed to, or so we hope. If we're not committed to them, there's no reason to doubt that the rules preserve truth when applied to the sentences we're committed to.

As we'll see, paracomplete theories of the sort considered in Part III are a bit different: they don't declare that their rules fail to unrestrictedly preserve truth. Indeed, they declare that their *truth rules* all *do* unrestrictedly preserve truth. Still, there will be other rules (the explosion rule and some rules involving the conditional) that are part of the paracomplete theory even though the theory doesn't declare that they preserve truth unrestrictedly. (It does "come close to" doing so, in that the claim that these rules don't unrestrictedly preserve truth would lead to inconsistency.) But the paracomplete theorist can and should take the same line as the weakly classical theorist as regards restricted truth-preservation: there is no reason to doubt that these rules preserve truth *when applied to sentences we're committed to*. As a result, there is no reason to doubt the conclusion (3), that T is sound, even though the inductive "proof" of this is unacceptable.

Indeed, we can say more: in any specific case where premises (say $A_1,\ldots,A_n$) entail a conclusion (say B) in the logic, commitment to the premises requires commitment to the entailment being truth-preserving in that instance. For accepting $A_1,\ldots,A_n$ commits one to B, which in turn commits one to $\text{True}(\langle B \rangle)$; and this commits one to $\text{True}(\langle A_1 \rangle) \wedge \ldots \wedge \text{True}(\langle A_n \rangle) \to \text{True}(\langle B \rangle)$, by the rule $B \vDash A \to B$ that is built into the logic, as part of the "Positive Horseshoe Rule" of Section 17.4. (This argument holds for classical glut theories and weakly classical theories too, since truth-introduction and $B \vDash A \to B$ are part of these logics as well.)

There is another similarity between the paracomplete theorist's diagnosis of the failure of (2) and something we've seen before. According to the "strong" and "medium strength" supervaluational and revision theories from Chapters 11 and 12, the illegitimacy of step (2) of the inductive argument is due to the failure of $\to$-Introduction: in particular, the rule-instances that are accepted but not declared to be truth-preserving are precisely the rule-instances whose corresponding conditional is not accepted. Paracomplete theories agree that failure of $\to$-Introduction is the "culprit".[5] Indeed, it is clear that a paracomplete theorist must accept this diagnosis: since paracomplete theories accept the Intersubstitutivity Principle, the claim that if the premises of $A_1,\ldots,A_n \vDash B$ are true then so is the conclusion is equivalent to the claim $A_1 \wedge \ldots \wedge A_n \to B$.[6] The diagnosis, then, is that *the illegitimacy of step (2) is an inevitable consequence of the gap between conditional assertion and the assertion of the conditional.*

I've mentioned in passing that unlike classical glut theories and "strong" supervaluation and revision theories, paracomplete theories don't actually declare that any of their rules *don't* preserve truth unrestrictedly; they just fail to declare that they do. Let's pursue this, by means of two examples.

First, explosion, i.e. the rule $A \wedge \neg A \vDash \bot$ (for arbitrary A). Paracomplete theories accept this as a rule of conditional assertion: accepting $A \wedge \neg A$ commits you to everything. (Of course, this doesn't mean that if you find yourself accepting $A \wedge \neg A$, you should accept everything; rather, you should question what led you to accept $A \wedge \neg A$.) These theories don't accept the corresponding conditional $A \wedge \neg A \to \bot$, for arbitrary A: indeed, on those versions where the

---

[5] But to repeat, paracomplete theories differ from the others over which rules it is for which the gap between conditional assertion and the assertion of the conditional arises. For the strong and medium strength supervaluation or revision theorist, the gap arises for the truth-rules but not the rules for the conditional or explosion; for the paracomplete theory it is the other way around.

[6] For strong and medium strength classical theories, which don't accept Intersubstitutivity, one can give an alternative argument using the premise that modus ponens preserves truth: see the Lemma of Section 12.1.

conditional contraposes, this implies excluded middle for A (it is equivalent to $\neg\bot \to A \vee \neg A$, which yields $A \vee \neg A$ by Modus Ponens). Since we don't have $A \wedge \neg A \to \bot$ in general, and truth obeys Intersubstitutivity, we shouldn't expect to have True($\langle A \wedge \neg A\rangle$) $\to$ True($\langle\bot\rangle$) in general; i.e. we shouldn't expect Explosion to be a rule that unrestrictedly preserves truth. But *we also don't accept any counterinstances, or any disjunction of counterinstances, or the claim that there are counterinstances*. There are no sentences A, even paradoxical ones, for which we accept True($\langle A \wedge \neg A\rangle$) but don't accept True($\langle\bot\rangle$); for we don't accept anything of form True($\langle A \wedge \neg A\rangle$). (Nor do we accept the existential generalization, that there are sentences A for which the corresponding sentence $A \wedge \neg A$ is true.) By contrast, a classical glut theory will identify a specific instance of modus ponens which the theory takes to be legitimate but not truth-preserving; and "strong" supervaluation and revision theories will say, for each of its truth rules, that though that rule is legitimate it either fails to preserve truth when applied to Q or fails to preserve truth when applied to $\neg Q$.

Next, consider the rule of Modus Ponens, $A \wedge (A \to B) \vDash B$. Again, this seems like a good rule of conditional assertion: if you accept the antecedent, you're committed to the consequent. But we've seen that some instances of the corresponding conditional breed paradox (e.g. when B is an absurdity and A the corresponding Curry sentence). So we shouldn't expect the claim that the rule unrestrictedly preserves truth to be acceptable. On the other hand, in paracomplete theories

(a) we don't get specific counterinstances to truth-preservation, of the sort we have in classical glut theories;

(b) nor do we get disjunctions of counterinstances, of the sort we have in strong supervaluation theories;

(c) nor do we get even the claim that there are counterinstances.

And to repeat: in paracomplete theories as in weakly classical ones, we should expect this and each other rule of the theory to preserve truth in those situations where we directly apply it (though to expect this involves expecting our theory to be consistent, and thus goes beyond the theory).

The reader may recall that "moderate strength" supervaluation and revision theories also refuse to declare their own rules unrestrictedly truth-preserving while not quite declaring them not to be unrestrictedly truth-preserving. (They say only "Either my rule R isn't unrestrictedly truth preserving or B", where B is something they regard as absurd to accept.) This is the closest classical analog of what the paracomplete theorist says about his own rules. But it really isn't that close. For though the moderate strength supervaluation or revision theorist avoids saying that her rules don't unrestrictedly preserve truth, she shares the basic presupposition that they either unrestrictedly preserve truth or they don't. This is the basic presupposition that the paracomplete theorist rejects.

Look again at Explosion. For the paracomplete theorist, the question of whether Explosion unrestrictedly preserves truth is the question of whether any sentences of form $A \wedge \neg A$ are ever true. And that question is simply indeterminate:

$$\neg D(\exists x[\text{True}(\text{conj}(x, \text{neg}(x)))]) \wedge \neg D\neg(\exists x[\text{True}(\text{conj}(x, \text{neg}(x))))]).$$

(The fine-grained value of any sentence of form $A \wedge \neg A$ is less than or equal to that of the Liar sentence, and in the case of the Liar it is equal; so the displayed sentence has the same value as $\neg DQ \wedge \neg D\neg Q$, which is 1.) And the claim that it is indeterminate whether the rule unrestrictedly preserves truth is incompatible with the claim that either it unrestrictedly preserves truth or doesn't: accepting the indeterminacy forces the rejection of excluded middle for the unrestricted truth preservation claim.

Much the same is true of Modus Ponens. Strictly, we can't say that it isn't determinate whether it unrestrictedly preserves truth. But (because of the fact that $\neg D^2\text{True}(\langle K \rangle)$) we can say that it isn't *determinately determinate* whether it unrestrictedly preserves truth. And that is enough to force rejection of the claim that modus ponens either unrestrictedly preserves truth or doesn't unrestrictedly preserve truth. (For any β, $A \vee \neg A$ weakly implies $D^\beta A \vee D^\beta \neg A$, so accepting the negation of the latter requires rejecting the former.)

Our inability to prove certain of our rules to be unrestrictedly truth-preserving is thus not due to ignorance about whether they unrestrictedly preserve truth, it is due to a "fuzziness" in the question.[7] And the "fuzziness" arises because of a "fuzziness" in the assertion of a conditional, in a context where a mere *conditional assertion* is unproblematic.

I have heard it argued that the failure of paracomplete theories to declare their own rules (unrestrictedly) truth-preserving is a grave defect in those theories. We've seen that because of the second incompleteness theorem, it is virtually inevitable for *any* theory, not just a paracomplete one, that it either not declare some of its axioms to be true or that it not declare some of its rules to be truth-preserving. Either way, non-trivial theories can't prove their own soundness. Graham Priest has claimed (1987, 2006) that paraconsistent dialetheic theories do better: that there are non-trivial such theories that can prove their own soundness. We shall see.

---

[7] The "moderate strength" supervaluation or revision theorist may also be able to find a sense of indeterminacy in which it is indeterminate whether her rules preserve truth; but the force of this is less clear in her case, since far from forcing the rejection of excluded middle, it is held in the face of the claim that the rules either preserve truth or don't.

20
Other Paradoxes

20.1. PARADOXES OF DENOTATION

There are a number of semantic paradoxes that, as standardly presented, involve definite descriptions or other complex singular terms, together with a notion (e.g. 'definable' or 'denotes') that can be explained using 'true of'. The most famous of these paradoxes are the definability paradoxes of König, Berry, and Richard. I've already discussed versions of these paradoxes in Chapter 5 (at least, versions of König and Berry; and Richard's adds nothing new). But the versions I discussed avoided the use of complex singular terms: I presented them as paradoxes of definability alone, not as paradoxes of denotation. Priest (2005) has argued that by presenting them in this way I have left out something important to these paradoxes: we need a treatment of the paradoxes applicable to a language with a description operator. In this section I fill the lacuna, and argue that there are no new paradoxes specifically of denotation.

There is actually more than one way to fill the lacuna—the choice depends on one's views on how to treat non-denoting descriptions (and non-denoting singular terms more generally) in languages *without* 'True'. It would take us far afield to discuss the various options on this, so I'll mostly confine discussion to a very simple, common, and quite natural approach. On this approach,

(i) A description ιxFx denotes an object o (relative to an assignment of objects to any free variables in F other than x) if and only if Fx is true of o and nothing else (relative to that assignment of objects to the other free free variables).

(ii) An atomic formula $P(t_1, \ldots, t_n)$ is false (relative to an assignment) if any of the terms t_i fail to denote anything (relative to that assignment). If each of them denote something (relative to that assignment), the truth value of the formula (relative to that assignment) is determined in the usual way from the semantics of the predicate.

Claim (ii) could easily be liberalized, to allow for atomic predicates (say 'nonexistent') that "take gaps in certain positions into truths": we could simply build into the semantics of each predicate how to treat gaps at each of its positions.[1] Allowing

---

[1] Let a *generalized n-tuple* of objects in U be a partial function from $\{1, \ldots, n\}$ to U. Then in the 2-valued case, we assign to each predicate a set of generalized n-tuples; this is essentially the approach of Scott 1967. In the V-valued case we make the obvious generalization: we assign to each predicate a function from the generalized n-tuples to members of V.

for this would complicate the discussion below without changing it in any essential way. But if we stick to (ii) as stated, then an *atomic* sentence existentially commits to the unique satisfaction of the conditions in any definite description that occurs directly in it.[2] Whether the use of a definite description in a *non-atomic* sentence S is existentially committing will depend on whether the atomic subformula in which it occurs is in a positive or negative occurrence within S: for instance, in the negation of an atomic sentence it is not existentially committing.[3]

Claims (i) and (ii) can be carried over to the enlarged language with 'True of' in it; of course, in that case we cannot assume excluded middle for claims about denotation.[4] It's easy to see that $P(\iota x F x)$ is then equivalent to $\exists x[F x \wedge \neg \exists y(F y \wedge y \neq x) \wedge P x]$ when P is a 1-place atomic formula. More generally, if P is an n-place atomic formula, k of whose places are filled with descriptions (say the first k, for notational simplicity), then

(1) $$P(\iota x F_1 x, \ldots, \iota x F_k x, t_{k+1}, \ldots, t_n)$$

is equivalent to

(2) $$\exists x_1 \ldots \exists x_k [F_1 x_1 \wedge \ldots \wedge F_k x_k \wedge \neg \exists z(F_1 z \wedge z \neq x_1) \wedge \ldots \wedge \neg \exists z(F_k z \wedge z \neq x_k) \wedge P(x_1, \ldots x_k, t_{k+1}, \ldots, t_n)].[5]$$

(On the more liberalized approach that doesn't commit to (ii) holding generally, there might be predicates P for which the equivalent to (1) isn't (2) but something without existential commitments or with fewer of them.) Each sentence involving definite descriptions is thus equivalent to a sentence not containing descriptions, by successive applications of the equivalence between (1) and (2) (or in the liberalized approach, between (1) and the analogs of (2) corresponding to the atomic predicates in whose immediate scope the descriptions appear). In a sense, then, definite descriptions are eliminable, even though syntactically they are genuine singular terms.

This equivalence between sentences with definite descriptions and sentences without them makes it evident that a solution to the paradoxes in a description-free language $\mathscr{L}^+$ carries over to a solution in an expanded language $\mathscr{L}^{++}$ with a description operator: the semantic value of any sentence of $\mathscr{L}^{++}$, in the deMorgan algebra used for $\mathscr{L}^+$, will be the same as the semantic value of its description-free transform in $\mathscr{L}^+$.

So far we've added descriptions but not 'denotes'. But we can take 't denotes o' as an abbreviation of 't is a closed singular term, and the identity formula with

---

[2] By 'occurs directly' here I mean 'occurs not as part of another definite description'.

[3] Allowing for non-denoting terms obviously requires a minor adjustment of the predicate calculus: e.g. $\forall x F x$ doesn't entail $F t$ without the additional premise $\exists x(x = t)$.

[4] In (i) I interpret '$\langle F x \rangle$ is true of nothing other than o' as '$\neg \exists z(\langle F x \rangle$ is true of z and $z \neq o)$'; that is, if put in conditional form the claim should involve '$\supset$' rather than '$\rightarrow$', so that its value is the greatest lower bound of the values of the $F o^*$ for o^* distinct from o.

[5] The F_i may contain anonymous free variables.

it on the left and a variable on the right is uniquely true of o'. (When t is 'ιxFx', this is equivalent to '$\langle Fx \rangle$ is uniquely true of o'.)

It can easily be checked that these conventions are such that

$$\langle \iota xFx \rangle \text{ denotes } \iota xFx$$

has the same value as

$$\exists y(y = \iota xFx).$$

That is,

$$\langle \iota xFx \rangle \text{ denotes } \iota xFx \leftrightarrow \exists y(y = \iota xFx)$$

is valid. This is exactly what the "naive theory of denotation" demands.[6]

In application to versions of König's paradox stated in terms of descriptions, this yields that

'The smallest ordinal not definable in $\mathscr{L}^{++}$' denotes the smallest ordinal not definable in $\mathscr{L}^{++}$

has the same semantic value as

There is a smallest ordinal not definable in $\mathscr{L}^{++}$;

and from the discussion in Chapter 5, it is clear that this value is between **0** and **1**.[7]

---

[6] Because of policy (ii), one must in general be careful in introducing primitive predicates by definition and using them in descriptions: policy (ii) couldn't be carried over to the defined predicate unless the definition makes it existentially committing in all places (which is one reason why Scott's liberalization of (ii) is attractive). But there is no problem in the case of 'denotes': the first conjunct in the definition ensures that it is existentially committing.

[7] There is another paradox of denotation worth mentioning, due to Keith Simmons (2003). As a warm-up to it, I'll mention a less puzzling paradox. Suppose I write down on an otherwise empty blackboard 'the sum of 3 and the number denoted by the singly-embedded description on the first blackboard manufactured in 2005'. As luck would have it, the blackboard I wrote it on was the first manufactured in 2005; so the embedded description appears to denote 3 more than whatever it denotes!

The obvious possibilities for resolving this paradox are that the description doesn't denote anything and that it is indeterminate whether (and if so, what) it denotes. (That is, either we can assert that it doesn't denote anything, or we can't assert that it either does or doesn't.) Which of these the account in the text yields depends on how 'number' is construed. Most construals (e.g. integers, or reals, or positive reals) will yield the second diagnosis. But if we take 'number' as 'natural number' then the claim that the term denotes 0, 1 or 2 clearly has value 0; from which it follows that the claim that it denotes 3, 4 or 5 has value 0; and so on, from which it follows that the term does not denote. (The paradox is equivalent to a paradox involving 'true of' instead of 'denotes', involving a predicate F defined by

$F(n) \leftrightarrow (n$ and $n - 3$ are numbers and $\langle F \rangle$ is uniquely true of $n - 3$).)

The actual Simmons paradox is more interesting. Suppose this time I write down two terms on the board: '3' and 'the sum of all numbers denoted by expressions on the first blackboard manufactured in 2005'. If 'number' is taken to include only natural numbers, can't we argue as

20.2. THE NAIVE THEORY OF PROPERTIES, RELATIONS, AND PROPOSITIONS

I return at last to a main topic of the Introduction: the Naive Theory of (Conceptual) Properties. This involves the naive comprehension schema, which I state now in a slightly more general form:

(NC) $\forall u_1 \ldots u_n \exists y [\text{Property}(y) \wedge \forall x(x \text{ instantiates } y \leftrightarrow \Theta(x, u_1, \ldots, u_n)]$.

(Also

(0) $\forall x \forall y [x \text{ instantiates } y \rightarrow \text{Property }(y)]$.)

As with the naive theories of truth, truth of, and denotation, this is inconsistent in classical logic, because of many paradoxes including Russell's. But it is perfectly consistent in the paracomplete logic I've been advocating.

Indeed, we have a conservativeness theorem analogous to the one in Section 17.2: for any classical ω-model M of the ground language $\mathscr{L}$, there is a V-valued model M^+ of the sort discussed there that satisfies (NC) and has M as its reduct. 'Reduct' here has to be defined slightly differently: instead of merely eliminating the ideology 'true', 'true of' etc., the reduct now eliminates both the ideology 'instantiates' and the ontology of properties. So the theorem goes as follows:

If M is any classical ω-model of the ground language $\mathscr{L}$, with cardinality $\complement$, then there is a $V_{\Sigma_\complement}$-valued model M^+ of the expanded language $\mathscr{L}^+$ that adds 'property' and 'instantiates', such that

(i) M^+ validates the naive theory of properties ((NC) and (0));

(ii) the domain of M is the set of things in the domain of M^+ that don't satisfy 'property' in M^+;

(iii) names have the same denotation in M^+ as in M; the operation assigned by M^+ to any function symbol agrees with the operation that M assigns to it on the domain of M, and analogously for predicates other than 'property' and 'instantiates'.

---

before that the description doesn't denote 0, 1 or 2, and then by induction that it doesn't denote anything? But then we still have a paradox, for then the term should denote 3!

The resolution to this paradox depends on how exactly we formalize the description written on the board. The only obvious way to do so within the language $\mathscr{L}^{++}$ is as 'the sum of all members of the set of numbers denoted by terms on the board'; in this case, the paradox arises in the first instance because as we'll see later in the chapter, it is illegitimate to assert the existence of sets defined by conditions for which we have no license to assume excluded middle. We needn't decide whether it's legitimate to assert the *non*-existence of the set in question: if it is legitimate to assert non-existence, then the sum doesn't exist and so the description doesn't denote anything, in which case the argument that it denotes 3 is fallacious; if (as is actually the case) it isn't legitimate to assert non-existence, then it's illegitimate to assert one way or the other whether the description denotes and again paradox is avoided. I think that any reasonable way to expand the resources of $\mathscr{L}^{++}$ to allow other formalizations of the description will avoid paradox in one of these ways.

It follows that if A is any sentence of $\mathscr{L}$ and $A^{\neg \text{Prop}}$ is the sentence of $\mathscr{L}^+$ that results from A by restricting all quantifiers by the condition $\neg \text{Property}(x)$, then $A^{\neg \text{Prop}}$ is true in M^+ if and only if A is true in M. Adding properties in accordance with the naive theory yields what is, in a natural sense, a conservative extension of the original language (conservative over ω-models anyway).

Of course the logic for the property theory can't be classical: excluded middle can't be assumed for the predicate 'instantiates'. Excluded middle is however assumed of 'Property': everything either is a property or isn't. It is also assumed of identity, even among properties: if p_1 and p_2 are properties, they are either the same property or not the same property.

We can prove this conservativeness theorem either directly or as a corollary of the conservativeness theorem for truth-of. The idea of the latter approach is to model properties by "partially parameterized formulas": pairs of formulas together with assignments of objects to all but a certain one of their free variables, say 'v_1'. We then model instantiation by truth-of: more fully, the "property" $<A, s>$ is "instantiated" by o if A is true relative to an assignment of o to 'v_1' and the assignments given by s to the other free variables. The conservativeness proof for the naive theory of truth-of then carries directly over to naive property theory. Relying on such an approach does not, of course, require that one thinks that properties "really are" partially parameterized formulas. Nor does it require the view that the only properties there are are those definable from parameters in some given language. The invocation of partially parameterized formulas serves only to show that the naive theory of properties is strongly consistent (i.e. conservative in the sense explained before).

The above construction obviously can be extended from properties in the usual sense to their multi-place analogs: *relations* (in the pre-set-theoretic sense, in which there can be different relations with the same extension, and in which there can also be "proper-class-like" relations that can't exist within the set-theoretic hierarchy because they relate too many things). We thus get a naive theory of properties and relations together, that avoids inconsistencies by its restrictions on classical logic.

Just as in the case of truth, these restrictions make little difference in normal contexts: e.g. we can apply classical logic without restriction when reasoning with the property of being square, or the property of not being a snail, or even the property of being a property; for in all these cases, any x either instantiates the property or doesn't, and this is enough to guarantee that classical logic will work. It is only properties specified via the notion of instantiation that require care, and many of them behave classically too. We can reason classically, for instance, with the property of being a property instantiated only by horses, or the property of being a property instantiated by infinitely many physical objects. Classical logic doesn't apply in reasoning about "weird" properties like the property of being a property that doesn't instantiate itself; but we knew from Russell that *something* had to give in reasoning about such properties, and as in the case of truth I think the least disruption to reasoning occurs by making excluded middle and some consequent reasoning about conditionals be what gives.

Just as we can generalize the account from ordinary 1-place properties to include multi-place properties, otherwise known as relations, we can also generalize it to include 0-place properties, otherwise known as propositions. Propositions as normally construed are the objects of belief, desire and so forth. Beliefs can be paradoxical in classical logic, just as sentences can: I might *believe* that what the least intelligent man in the room is saying is untrue, on the mistaken assumption that the least intelligent man is someone other than me; in this case, *the proposition believed* is paradoxical in classical logic. And the solution I've offered to the paradoxes of sentential truth carry over to the paradoxes of propositional truth: the naive theory of truth is preserved, and without the counter-intuitive step of denying that there are the propositions that there seem to be in cases like the one just rehearsed. The easiest way to prove the consistency of the naive theory is to model propositions as sentences; but again, this is quite compatible with thinking that the propositions far outrun what can be expressed in any given language.

20.3. SET THEORY

The most famous paradoxes of set theory, such as Russell's, don't turn on any difference between sets and properties, and so it might well be thought that a solution to the paradoxes for property theory could be applied to set theory as well. Even if this is so, there is no obvious reason to *want* to apply it: the notion of set is primarily a mathematical notion, and the familiar hierarchical conception of sets has served mathematics just fine. (There may be dissent from the category theorists here, but I won't get into that discussion.) Still, it is an interesting question whether one *could* carry over the solution of the property-theoretic paradoxes to set theory.

I don't have a definitive answer here, but I can say that there is a serious obstacle. It comes from a central axiom of set theory, the axiom of extensionality, which has no analog for properties. The axiom is normally stated as: if sets x and y have the same members, they are the same set. And the usual laws of identity tell us that if x and y are the same set, then x is a member of exactly the same sets that y is a member of. Putting these two together, we get the following version of extensionality:

(Ext)   If $Set(x)$ and $Set(y)$ and $\forall z(z \in x \leftrightarrow z \in y)$ then $\forall w(x \in w \leftrightarrow y \in w)$.

The problem of proving the consistency of a naive set theory is to find a way to guarantee this or something like it. It is unobvious how to modify the proof sketched in Sections 16.2 and 17.1 so as to yield any such thing.

One of the problems in investigating this is deciding how close one needs to come to (Ext), to count as being successful. For instance, we know that in paracomplete logics, conditional formulations of laws are stronger than rule formulations; perhaps one ought to weaken (Ext) to

(Ext_w)   Set(x) and Set(y) and $\forall z(z \in x \leftrightarrow z \in y) \vDash \forall w(x \in w \leftrightarrow y \in w)$.

But it is not obvious how to prove the consistency even of this plus Naive Comprehension. (There is a way to show the consistency of (Ext_w) plus a stripped-down version of Naive Comprehension, which postulates the existence of $\{x \mid A(x)\}$ for every condition $A(x)$, but which replaces one direction of the biconditional

$$y \in \{x|A(x)\} \leftrightarrow A(y)$$

by a rule (leaving the other direction intact). But I take it that the retreat to such a stripped-down version of Naive Comprehension would be a big step down.) Some more details on these matters can be found in the final section of Field 2004. It's also worth pointing out that if one takes the left hand side of (Ext_w) as defining identity between sets, then one needs to postulate that identity between sets is indeterminate: see Field 2005a, n. 18. By contrast, there is no need for indeterminate identity in the case of naive property theory.

I think it not worth going into these matters in detail because I see no need for a naive set theory. (Recall Gödel's remark, quoted in the Introduction, that the only serious paradoxes are in property theory rather than set theory.)

There is, to be sure, a justified dissatisfaction with Zermelo–Fraenkel set theory taken by itself: the non-existence of "collections" too big to be sets forces one to frame natural talk (e.g. about "the constructible universe") in awkward linguistic terms, or else to talk loosely (e.g. by speaking of "proper classes" even though the theory posits no such thing). This dissatisfaction with Zermelo–Fraenkel set theory sometimes leads people to advocate theories like Gödel–Bernays or Morse–Kelley that do literally postulate proper classes, but this also seems philosophically problematic: at least without some special story, the "proper classes" seem just like another level in the set theoretic hierarchy, which then makes it curious that they aren't allowed to appear as members of anything.

But there is a better course: instead of using set-like proper classes to avoid the awkwardness of ZF, use properties instead: for instance, one can speak of the property of being a constructible set. Properties are completely different from sets, in being not only non-extensional but also non-hierarchical: e.g. some properties instantiate themselves. Because they are so fundamentally different, this doesn't have the disadvantages of proper classes as normally construed: one can invoke something beyond sets while thinking that sets are the only *hierarchical* entities that there are.

The picture I'm suggesting is not really so different from that of some recent defenders of proper classes (C. Parsons 1974b; Maddy 1983); they argue for a conception of classes that makes them quasi-linguistic and very different from sets, so that even when there is a set corresponding to a predicate there is also a class, and it is different from the set. But their classes differ from properties: first, they don't postulate classes corresponding to *every* predicate (e.g. the predicate 'class', or the predicate 'doesn't belong to itself'); and second, they do assume that classes are extensional. To my knowledge, the assumption of extensionality does not play a significant role in the application of classes (as distinct from sets), so I suspect that properties would do as well for whatever purposes proper classes have been thought to serve. But I should also say that one can always get a limited extensionality. Suppose one is interested only in those properties that fall into a certain hierarchy: "first level" properties that apply only to non-properties; "second level" properties that apply only to non-properties and first level properties; and so on. Among *these* properties, the relation of *being instantiated by the same things* is a bivalent congruence relation, and so one can always "divide out by" this relation to get the effect of an extensional theory. Using this procedure, one in effect recovers the extensional proper classes that Parsons and Maddy talk about, and more, within the universe of properties. This way of doing things further emphasizes the very fundamental difference between proper classes and sets.

20.4. PARADOXES OF TRUTH AND VALIDITY

I will now discuss paradoxes that involve the notions of truth and validity taken together. Of course it should be clear from the start that there are no genuinely new paradoxes here, at least if we continue with the assumption tacitly made so far, that the notion of validity is to be literally defined in set theory. I'll discuss that assumption in the next section, where I will argue that the conclusions of this section are unlikely to ultimately depend on it. (To suppose that validity is definable in set-theoretic terms leaves the form of the definition unspecified—it might be given model-theoretically, or in terms of some effectively generable subset of what is validated in a model theory, or in some other way. For ease of illustration I will for the moment take it to be explained model-theoretically.) Given this assumption that 'valid' is set-theoretically definable, the strong consistency proof from Chapter 16 is already enough to show that we can keep the truth schema intact even for sentences that employ both validity and the truth or satisfaction predicates. Still, there are some *prima facie* paradoxes here, and it will be useful to see how the theory handles a representative one.

The "paradox" I'll choose for my illustration is most naturally presented in terms of the notion of inconsistency, which can be defined from validity in one of the following ways:

(D-i) Γ is inconsistent iff the argument from Γ to $\bot$ is valid

or

(D-ii)   Γ is inconsistent iff for some contradiction C, the argument from Γ to C is valid.

If 'valid' is used in the weak sense (requiring preservation of value **1** in all models, or all decent models), it makes no difference which of (D-i) and (D-ii) we use to define inconsistency: either way, we get

(W-Inc)   A set of sentences is inconsistent if and only if there is no decent model in which its members all get value **1**.

If 'valid' is used in the strong sense (requiring that the value of the conclusion is at least as high as the greatest lower bound of the values of the premises), (D-i) and (D-ii) diverge.[8] To avoid this complexity—and because it is in any case more natural—let us stipulate that 'valid' shall be used in its weak sense. (I've added the term 'decent' to allow the defender of paradoxicality some wiggle room: a paradox requires only that *some* notion of decency give rise to trouble.)

The "paradox" involves a sentence Y (constructed for instance by Gödel–Tarski diagonalization) that is equivalent to

(1) $\exists x(x$ is a true sentence of $\mathscr{L}^+$ that is inconsistent with $\langle Y \rangle)$.

("x is inconsistent with y" means the same as "$\{x, y\}$ is (weakly) inconsistent".) We now argue as follows:
Consider any sentence B. The triad

B,
Y,
$\langle B \rangle$ is inconsistent with $\langle Y \rangle$

is surely inconsistent. The inconsistency survives if one replaces the first member by True($\langle B \rangle$) and then conjoins it with the third. So by ∃-Elimination, we get that the following pair is inconsistent:

Y
$\exists x(\text{True}(x) \wedge x$ is inconsistent with $\langle Y \rangle)$.

But the second member of this pair is equivalent to Y, given how Y has been defined; so Y is itself inconsistent. As a result, any sentence is inconsistent with Y; in particular the true sentence '$0 = 0$' is inconsistent with Y. But given how Y has been defined; this means that Y is true. And surely this (or the fact that we've *shown* this) shows that Y is *not* inconsistent, contrary to the above.

---

[8] The strongest notion of inconsistency is the one we get using strong validity in (D-i). In the algebra of ch. 17, the greatest lower bound of a countable set is **0** if and only if one of the members is **0**, so (D-i) yields

A set Γ of sentences is *strongly inconsistent* if for every decent model M, some member of Γ gets value **0** in M.

(D-ii), on the other hand, yields (the somewhat unnatural)

A sct Γ of sentences is *medium-strength inconsistent* if for every decent model M, the greatest lower bound of the values of the members is less than or equal to $1/2$.

This argument has two holes, or so I claim; I've done you the courtesy of clearly labeling them (by the standard means of labeling holes in arguments, viz. the word 'surely'). I claim that these are *demonstrable* holes, *having nothing to do with the theory of truth*. That is what the rest of the section will argue. It will also address the question of which hole is "the crucial one", that is, the question: is Y consistent, or isn't it? (It has to be one or the other, since we're assuming that validity and hence inconsistency satisfy excluded middle.) To discuss that will require discussing standards of decency.

But before analyzing this apparent paradox further, let's look at a somewhat analogous pseudo-paradox that arises for the notion of validity or inconsistency alone, *without truth*, and on the assumption that "validity" and "inconsistency" mean *classical* validity and *classical* inconsistency. The "paradox" I'm about to mention is broadly Gödelian in nature, and has a quite uncontroversial resolution within classical logic. It arises in the first instance for the meta-theory of classical logic. It is actually not a single puzzle, but a whole family of them—one for each specification of the "standards of decency" used in defining validity. So I will make the dependence on those standards explicit.

Classical validity is definable in classical set theory, in a way that certainly seems extensionally correct: that was the moral of the Kreisel squeezing argument. That argument concerned purely logical validity; but if we're dealing with the "validity" of sentences in the language of set theory, it is natural to employ weaker notions of validity (i.e. notions that make more sentences valid). There are a bunch of related notions of validity to choose from: among them are

truth in all models *in which the axioms of a specific theory (say ZFC) are true*;

truth in all *ω-models* in which the axioms of ZFC are true;

truth in all *well-founded* models in which the axioms of ZFC are true;

truth in all *natural* models (i.e. in any model V_κ that results from cutting off the set-theoretic universe at a certain height κ in a way that makes the axioms of ZFC true);

truth in all natural models V_κ for which κ is an inaccessible ordinal;

and many more. To handle the matter generally, let Ψ be any condition on models formulated in the language of standard set theory (no truth predicate); and let a Ψ-*model* be a model satisfying this condition. A choice of Ψ is simply a way of explicating what counts as a *decent* model. Then we can call an argument in this language Ψ-*valid* if for all classical Ψ-models M, if the premises are all true in M then so is the conclusion.

If we now define Ψ-inconsistency from Ψ-validity in either of the two equivalent ways above, we get that a set of sentences Γ is Ψ-inconsistent if and only if there is no Ψ-model in which all members of Γ are true. It must be emphasized that the notions of Ψ-validity and Ψ-consistency involve only the notion of truth *in M*, not genuine truth, so they are definable in the standard language of set theory without a truth predicate (given that Ψ is so defined, as I've demanded).

But for any choice of Ψ, we can use Gödel–Tarski diagonalization to find a sentence W_Ψ equivalent to

$$\langle W_\Psi \rangle \text{ is } \Psi\text{-inconsistent.}$$

(By 'equivalent to' I mean equivalent in a minimal arithmetical theory, which can of course be developed within set theory; I'll mostly be interested in conditions $\Psi(M)$ that entail that the axioms of ZFC are true in M, so use of the unadorned term 'equivalent' seems harmless.) Such sentences can't of course ever be paradoxical in any serious sense: we're in the domain of classical set theory, which virtually everyone agrees to be paradox-free; and classical logic applies.

But there is a *prima facie* argument for paradox in the case of W_Ψ that almost exactly parallels the argument that the sentence Y is paradoxical. Dropping the Ψ for the moment, the argument for paradox based on W goes as follows:

The triad

$0 = 0$

W,

$\langle 0 = 0 \rangle$ is inconsistent with $\langle W \rangle$

is *surely* inconsistent. But the last member is equivalent to

$\langle W \rangle$ is inconsistent,

which in turn is equivalent to W; and the first member is valid and so can be dropped; so W is inconsistent. But that claim is just W! This proves W, so *surely* we can infer that $\langle W \rangle$ is consistent; so we have that it is both consistent and inconsistent.

This piece of reasoning has to be fallacious, since it argues for an inconsistency in the domain of classical set theory; but the analogy of it to the previous reasoning involving Y is so close as to make clear that the original "paradox" is nothing of the kind, it is simply a piece of uncontroversially invalid reasoning.

Which of the two steps that I've flagged is the crucial error? Answering that requires a more subtle analysis, since it depends on the standards of decency in place, i.e. on the condition Ψ. (The choice of Ψ affects not only whether the sentence Y or W is Ψ-consistent, it affects which sentence Y or W is in question: we need to talk not of Y and W, but of Y_Ψ and W_Ψ.) In the case of W_Ψ, classical logic applies, and we can show that one of the following is the case:

W_Ψ, but $\langle W_\Psi \rangle$ is Ψ-inconsistent;

or

$\neg W_\Psi$, but $\langle W_\Psi \rangle$ is Ψ-consistent.

Or to put it in a way that goes very slightly beyond classical set theory in employing a truth predicate in a very minimal way:

(DISJ) Either W_Ψ is true but Ψ-inconsistent, or else it is false but Ψ-consistent.

In the special case where $\Psi(M)$ says only that M is a model of standard set theory (say ZFC), Ψ-inconsistency coincides with disprovability in ZFC (disprovability being provability of the negation); so in this case, W_Ψ is in effect a Gödel-like sentence that asserts its own *dis*provability in ZFC. Unlike the usual Gödel sentence for ZFC, which asserts its own *un*provability and which we normally take to be true but not provable in ZFC, this one is normally taken to be false but not disprovable in ZFC: it is thus very much like the negation of the usual Gödel sentence.

So in this special case, the normal view of the matter is that it is the second disjunct of (DISJ) that's correct. (Indeed, this normal view of the matter, though not provable in ZFC, is easily proved in the theory that extends ZFC by adding a truth predicate to the language and using it in the induction rules.) And whenever Ψ is chosen so that the second disjunct is correct, the above argument clearly fails at the first 'surely'. For W_Ψ is equivalent to the conjunction of all members of the triad

$$0 = 0$$
$$W_\Psi$$
$$\langle 0 = 0 \rangle \text{ is } \Psi\text{-inconsistent with} \langle W_\Psi \rangle;$$

and by the second disjunct of (DISJ), this is perfectly Ψ-consistent even though the conjunction is false. And if the argument fails at this step for W_Ψ, even in the classical case, then the analogous argument fails at this step in the case of Y_Ψ.

But what about if we choose different decency standards, ones that make the first disjunct of (DISJ) the correct one? We can certainly find unnatural Ψ for which this is so, and *natural* Ψ for which *it isn't absurd to suppose* that it's so. (That we can find natural Ψ for which it's *plausible* to suppose that it's so is less obvious.) For instance, it is immediate that the first disjunct is the right one when Ψ is a condition true of no models, so that every set of sentences is Ψ-inconsistent. That's a pretty trivial example when it is *provable in ZFC* that Ψ is true of no models, but the situation can arise elsewhere too. For example, consider the last choice of Ψ on the list above, where $\Psi(M)$ is "M has form V_κ for some inaccessible κ". In that case, on the assumption that there are no inaccessible ordinals, there are no Ψ-models (since the full universe can't constitute a model); so *at least on this assumption*, W_Ψ is true but Ψ-inconsistent.

It isn't just for vacuous Ψ that something can be true without being Ψ-consistent. Indeed, it's clear that in any case where Ψ holds of at most one model, then there have to be cases of true sentences in the language of set theory that are Ψ-inconsistent. For since 'Ψ-consistent' is definable in the language of set theory, it can't extensionally coincide with truth; and if A is Ψ-consistent but not true then (given that Ψ holds of at most one model) $\neg A$ is true but not Ψ-consistent. For such Ψ—and also for many Ψ which hold of more than one model, or for which it is not provable whether they hold of more than one model—ascertaining which disjunct of (DISJ) holds may be quite non-trivial.

When the first disjunct of (DISJ) holds, or more generally when Ψ is chosen in such a way that it is possible for truths to be Ψ-inconsistent, then it is clear that the argument for paradox in the case of W_Ψ is fallacious in its final step, the second 'surely': for that step consisted precisely in inferring from the truth of W_Ψ to its Ψ-consistency. And for Ψ for which that step of the argument involving W_Ψ is invalid, the corresponding step of the argument involving Y_Ψ is invalid too. (In these cases, the argument also looks suspect at the first 'surely' as well, though I will not go into this.)[9]

In short: whatever the choice of Ψ, the argument at the start of this section fails in at least one of the two steps noted; and this has nothing whatever to do with truth or any other notion that is plausibly thought paradoxical.

20.5. "NON-BIVALENT" VALIDITY?

The previous section took model-theoretic definitions of validity at face value. But there is a complication that needs to be addressed: in Section 2.3 I recommended Kreisel's analysis of model theoretic accounts of classical validity, according to which model theory doesn't supply an *intensionally correct* definition. This in itself is not a problem: the analysis of the previous section would go through just as well if the model-theoretic definition were merely *extensionally correct*. But the complication concerns whether we can assume even extensional correctness. In the classical context, Kreisel gave a plausible argument that validity coincides extensionally with a model-theoretic notion. Can this argument be carried over to the paracomplete context? If not, does that affect the conclusions of the previous section about paradoxes of truth and validity?

A. Kreisel Revisited

The move from classical logic to a paracomplete logic does force us to distinguish between two intuitive notions of validity (validity of conditional assertion and validity of assertion of conditional): these correspond to two different model-theoretic notions. (See Sections 10.2 and 10.6.) But aside from this, the move to a paracomplete logic does not in itself alter anything in Kreisel's analysis:

---

[9] The initial plausibility of the first 'surely' turns on the thought that not all members of the triad

$0 = 0$
Y_Ψ
$\langle 0 = 0 \rangle$ is Ψ-inconsistent with $\langle Y_\Psi \rangle$

can be true; and that thought is incorrect for these choices of Ψ. However, the first 'surely' step didn't actually say that they couldn't all be true, it said that the triad is Ψ-inconsistent. And at least in the case of Ψ that hold of no model, the triad is Ψ-inconsistent even though all its members are true, so we don't actually have a counterexample to the first 'surely' step.

indeed, that analysis carries over *completely* to each of the validity concepts *in the →-free sublanguage* of the paracomplete language $\mathscr{L}$.

To recapitulate Kreisel's argument for this modified context, let F be a standard proof procedure for quantified Kleene logic (which is the logic of the →-free language). Take 'valid$_{\text{intuitive}}$' to be a primitive notion, not explained in model-theoretic terms or in terms of truth. Then the argument (in the case of validity of conditional assertion) is this:

(A) Intuitive principles about validity guarantee

If B is provable from Γ in F, then the argument from Γ to B is valid$_{\text{intuitive}}$,

in other words

(**Intuitive soundness of F**) Any argument that is valid$_{\text{proof-theoretic}}$ is valid$_{\text{intuitive}}$.

(B) Other intuitive principles about validity guarantee

If there is a model in which all members of Γ have value 1 and B has smaller value, then the argument from Γ to B is not valid$_{\text{intuitive}}$;

in other words,

Any argument that is not valid$_{\text{model-theoretic}}$ is not valid$_{\text{intuitive}}$;

or contraposing,

(**Model assumption**) Any argument that is valid$_{\text{intuitive}}$ is valid$_{\text{model-theoretic}}$.

(C) But now we invoke a

(**Completeness Theorem for F**) Any argument that is valid$_{\text{model-theoretic}}$ is valid$_{\text{proof-theoretic}}$.

This in conjunction with the intuitive soundness assumption and the model assumption guarantees that all three notions of validity coincide.[10]

(We could make the argument more compelling by breaking (A) down into a set of simpler intuitive assumptions, though Kreisel himself didn't do this: the set would contain, for each primitive rule of F, the assumption that that rule preserves validity$_{\text{intuitive}}$.[11] Breaking (A) down in this way would require extending the induction rule to validity$_{\text{intuitive}}$, but that seems unproblematic.)[12]

This Kreiselian analysis works fine for Kleene logic, but what happens if we try to extend this analysis to the full paracomplete logic that includes '→'?

A minor obstacle is that it might be doubted that we even have an intuitive notion of validity in this case: the principles that we have to give up to make

---

[10] As in the previous section, one could distinguish different model-theoretic notions, by considering restrictions Ψ on the kinds of models involved; but the distinctions wouldn't matter in the present context.

[11] I say nothing about axioms since in the case of Kleene logic there are none, but in a somewhat larger logic a claim about axioms would need to be added.

[12] A small complication is that some natural formulations of paracomplete logics employ meta-rules such as disjunction elimination. There are various ways around this, of which the best may be to reformulate in terms of a multiple-consequent sequent calculus; but it is not worth taking the space to pursue this.

'→' consistent with naive truth theory are ones that we find so natural that talk of "intuitive validity" seems inappropriate. This obstacle is not so serious, since anyone who has played around with the logic a bit does have tutored validity judgements, and the question is whether there is an argument that "validity in the tutored sense" should strictly coincide with model-theoretic validity. That it should isn't entirely obvious, for the tutored notion too seems to have a bearing not just on interpretations in which the quantifiers range only over the members of a set, but on interpretations where they are unrestricted. It would be nice if we had an analog of the Kreisel argument that made plausible that this restriction on domain doesn't make an extensional difference.

But there's a serious obstacle to that, regarding the issue of a completeness theorem: I haven't given such a theorem, and indeed Welch (forthcoming) observes that none is possible on the semantics I've given. This doesn't rule out that "validity$_{\text{intuitive}}$" (or "validity to the tutored intuition") might coincide with validity$_{\text{model-theoretic}}$, but it removes the neat argument for coincidence.

The situation is similar to one that arises for the notion of validity in second-order logic. Second-order logic also lacks a complete proof-procedure on the standard semantics for it, so that there is no neat argument for the extensional equivalence of the intuitive notion (or the tutored notion) to the model-theoretic. Still, many people think that the model-theoretic notion of second-order validity does extensionally coincide with the intuitive notion, despite the lack of intuitive guarantee. To the extent that this is plausible, I don't see why this wouldn't be plausible in the case of the full paracomplete logic as well. But this is not a matter I'm inclined to take a strong line on.

B. Arguments for Non-Bivalent Validity

The most interesting question raised by the possibility that the appropriate "tutored intuitive" notion of logical validity may not correspond to the model-theoretic is that the former might not obey excluded middle (whereas the latter clearly does). It might seem, at first, as if certain paradoxes of validity tend to support this. Consider a sentence that asserts of itself that it is not logically valid—abbreviate it as *IN*. If validity is classical, then either

(i) *IN* is true but not logically valid,

or

(ii) *IN* is logically valid but not true.

Or to put it without the inessential term 'true': either

(i*) $\qquad\qquad IN \wedge \neg \text{Valid}(\langle IN \rangle)$, or

(ii*) $\quad\quad\quad\quad\quad\quad\quad$ Valid($\langle IN \rangle$) $\wedge \neg IN$.

Presumably we don't want to accept (ii)/(ii*), so we should accept (i)/(i*). But don't we then have a logical argument for (the truth of) *IN*, making *IN* in some clear sense logically valid?

I don't think that this argument is particularly compelling. It's true that (ii)/(ii*) is repugnant, and I'm prepared to agree that we ought to accept (i)/(i*). But to get to the conclusion that (i) or (i*) is in some sense logically valid (not in classical logic, of course, but in an appropriate logic for the notion of validity), we need not only that we should reject (ii) and (ii*), but that we should reject them *on logical grounds*. This seems unobvious: why not regard *IN* as like the Gödel sentence, where our reasons for rejecting the analog of (ii)/(ii*) are generally taken to go beyond logic proper?

And even if it is agreed that we should reject (ii)/(ii*) on logical grounds, the case for (i)/(i*) being a logical truth is shaky. To get from the rejection of (ii)/(ii*) to the acceptance of (i)/(i*) requires an instance of excluded middle. And to get from the rejection of (ii)/(ii*) on logical grounds to the acceptance of (i)/(i*) on logical grounds requires that this instance of excluded middle be accepted *as a logical truth*. Given that we don't accept excluded middle in general, we might well accept all instances of excluded middle that involve 'valid' (as long as they don't involve 'true' or similar terms), but regard them as *non-logical* truths. If so, one could accept excluded middle for validity claims and think that a proper "logic of validity" licenses the rejection of (ii)/(ii*), without thinking that *that logic* licenses the acceptance of (i)/(i*). (This second option would allow us to accept all instances of excluded middle for validity claims, though not to accept them as logical truths. The option of the previous paragraph, by contrast, allows their acceptance even as logical truths.)

Another way one might try to argue against excluded middle for validity claims would be

(i) to argue that valid arguments are those that necessarily preserve a property *P* of "intuitive designatedness" which itself needn't obey excluded middle (see the discussions of "non-classical notion of model" in Section 5.6, under the First, Fifth and Sixth Worries);

and

(ii) to argue that if we don't assume excluded middle for this property *P*, then we shouldn't assume excluded middle for the property *P** of *necessarily* preserving property *P*.

But even granting (i), I think that (ii) is highly unobvious. The kind of necessity involved in (ii) couldn't be taken to be "metaphysical necessity", if the account of validity is to have any plausibility; it must, rather, be logical necessity, i.e. a matter of *what logic requires*. But in that case, (ii) just begs the question: if validity obeys excluded middle, then in cases where it is indeterminate whether a claim is designated, logic doesn't require it to be designated, and there is no worry about excluded middle for the logical necessity claim.

C. Conclusions Regarding Paradox

So far I've argued that there is no obvious problem with assuming excluded middle for validity claims. To this I'd add

(a) that assuming excluded middle for validity claims leads to simpler reasoning about validity;

and

(b) that it would seem to be somewhat detrimental to the role of logic as regulator of reasoning if we were unable to say that any given piece of reasoning is either valid or not valid.

These considerations together seem to me to make the assumption that validity claims obey excluded middle a reasonable working hypothesis. And any notion that obeys excluded middle and is not of truly exorbitant computational complexity can be extensionally captured within standard set theory; since it would also seem detrimental to the role of logic as regulator of reasoning if validity claims had truly exorbitant computational complexity, there is a case to be made for strengthening the working hypothesis slightly, to the hypothesis that validity is set-theoretically definable in this extensional sense of definition. And that would justify the conclusion of Section 20.4: since we have a theory that handles the addition of truth to set theory, there can be no new paradoxes of truth and validity.

But I wouldn't want to rest my claims to have resolved the apparent paradoxes of truth and validity on the working hypothesis. Fortunately, I don't have to. The solutions one gets for any such alleged paradox, from a given set-theoretic explication of 'valid', are forced on one by that explication of 'valid' together with the theory of truth offered in Section 16.2. Such a solution will *not* be *forced* on us if we decline to explicate 'valid' in that way, but it will still be a possible solution to the apparent paradox—a solution that accords with the naive view of truth and with the proposed logic of the conditional. And the existence of at least one possible solution is all that is needed to show that an apparent paradox is only apparent. The possibility that 'valid' isn't extensionally equivalent to any set-theoretic notion tends to make for *more* possible solutions to any apparent paradoxes, not fewer.

In particular, the most plausible reason for questioning that 'valid' is set-theoretically definable (on extensional standards of definition) involves questioning that it obeys excluded middle. But it seems clear that questioning this just allows for *more* ways that any given paradox of truth and validity could be handled.

Consider for instance the sentence W from Section 20.4, which asserts its own inconsistency; reasoning classically, we were led to

(DISJ)   Either W is true but inconsistent, or else it is false but consistent,

and then had to argue for one disjunct or the other depending on the details of the definition of consistency (i.e. on which restrictions on the notion of model are in force). But if excluded middle isn't assumed for 'valid' and hence for 'consistent', (DISJ) will not be forced on us. A solution in this case *may* involve accepting one or the other of the disjuncts of (DISJ)—more likely the second—but there is now another option as well. What Section 20.4 does is to show how such paradoxes are to be handled *even under the most demanding assumption*, viz. that 'valid' is a bivalent notion.

21

Do Paracomplete Solutions Depend on Expressive Limitations?

It is sometimes argued that paracomplete solutions to the paradoxes rest on expressive limitations in the language in which they are couched. In this chapter and the next two, I try to rebut such arguments.

21.1. BOOLEAN NEGATION AND "EXCLUSION NEGATION"

The language $\mathscr{L}$ to which the notions of truth and satisfaction have been added is sometimes said "not to contain Boolean negation". This is a bit misleading, since it contains a notion of negation which behaves according to the usual Boolean laws *within* $\mathscr{L}$. In expanding $\mathscr{L}$ we have restricted one of the Boolean laws (excluded middle) so that it does not apply throughout the full expanded language $\mathscr{L}^+$, but it still applies to large fragments of it, including (but extending far beyond) the full original language $\mathscr{L}$. To say that we've abandoned "Boolean negation" is a bit like saying that theories that allow for radioactive decay, in contradiction to Dalton's assumptions about how elements behave, abandon the notion of "Daltonian elementhood". (Or like saying that when Cantor extended the theory of cardinality to infinite sets he was abandoning the notion of "pre-Cantorian cardinality", according to which the cardinality of a set is always strictly greater than the cardinality of any proper subset.)

That said, I of course agree that according to the logic I've advocated for the language $\mathscr{L}^+$, there is no negation that obeys all the Boolean laws without restriction: if there were, it would be impossible to have a truth predicate that obeys the Intersubstitutivity Principle. The question is whether this is a defect. There is no good theory according to which the notion of element obeys all of Dalton's assumptions, or the notion of cardinality obeys all of the pre-Cantorian ones; if one wants to argue that a good theory *should* posit a notion of negation that obeys all of Boole's, that needs an argument.[1]

---

[1] I've heard it argued that even if no *good* theory posits a Boolean negation, we haven't solved the paradoxes until we've given an account of how to apply the term 'true' to the sentences of

One old argument (Hahn 1933) starts from the idea that we can stipulate that an operator NEG obeys the following truth rule: for any sentence x, NEG(x) is true if and only if x is not true. From this stipulation (the argument goes) we can logically derive that exactly one of x and NEG(x) is true (as well as that NEG(NEG(x)) is true if and only if x is true, and so forth); and this (when combined with similar stipulations for the other connectives) will make the usual Boolean laws such as excluded middle come out true. Here the proper response is not to deny the legitimacy of the stipulation; rather, the proper response is that from the stipulation, one can derive such claims as that exactly one of x and NEG(x) is true *only if we assume Boolean laws for the 'not' used in making the stipulation*. If, for instance, one doesn't assume excluded middle for 'not', then there is no way to derive from the stipulation that either x or NEG(x) is true.

This reply to Hahn's argument is familiar, and I know of no rebuttal; but one still hears the argument frequently, especially in the literature on truth value gaps. Here a distinction is often made between "choice negation" and "exclusion negation". "Choice negation" is defined as taking truths into falsehoods, falsehoods into truths, *and gaps into gaps*; it is thought to raise no problems for the paradoxes. "Exclusion negation", by contrast, takes truths into falsehoods, falsehoods into truths, *and gaps into truths*; and it is alleged to be incompatible with the naive truth schema.

If this were correct it would be serious: for by the above definitions, exclusion negation obeys the natural law given above for 'NEG', viz.,

(E) $\neg_E A$ is true iff A is not true,

whereas choice negation obeys the much less natural law

(C) $\neg_C A$ is true iff A is not true and not gappy.

Abandoning exclusion negation in this sense in favor of choice negation would seem to simply be abandoning negation as we normally understand it, and putting some pale surrogate in its place.

---

someone who has a *bad* theory according to which the word 'not' obeys all of Boole's assumptions. (Or at least, to the sentences of someone for whom this bad theory plays such a central role in his linguistic practices that it determines what 'not' means for him.) But I don't think that this raises an interesting challenge. There is bound to be a certain arbitrariness in how we attribute truth-values to sentences that contain concepts we find defective (e.g. 'tonk' (Prior 1960) or 'Boche' (Dummett 1973, p. 454)). We can't, for instance, regard both 'All Germans are Boche' and 'All Boche are prone to cruelty' as true, unless we share the racist beliefs of those who possess the concept; but a decision as to which (if either) should count as true, in the language of the racist for whom both beliefs enter into his practices in a "meaning-constitutive" way, seems both pointless and unlikely to have a principled answer. Similarly for the use of 'not' by someone with a defective theory. Probably the simplest course is to translate his 'not' with our 'not', in which case his claims to the validity of excluded middle will come out false even though they were "meaning-constitutive"; but there's no reason to take a stand on this translation, or to think that there's a determinate fact of the matter as to whether it's correct.

But the claim that we have abandoned (E) for (C) simply isn't true. The charge would be correct against theorists that *postulate* gaps: the classical theorists considered in Chapter 7. But the paracomplete theories considered in Part III—which *allow for* gaps, even though they don't posit them—obey the natural rule (E), not the unnatural rule (C). The arguments that exclusion negation as defined via (E) leads to inconsistency with naive truth all turn, like Hahn's, on assuming that the 'not' used on the right hand side of (E) obeys excluded middle. While classical gap theorists make this assumption, it is by no means inevitable, and the blame for inconsistency with the naive truth theory is based on that assumption rather than the adoption of a negation that accords with (E).

Another famous argument for the legitimacy of a notion that obeys the Boolean assumptions was given by Belnap (1962). He argued that we can stipulate the legitimacy of a set of connectives satisfying all classical deductive laws, including the Boolean laws for negation, since these laws conservatively extend the "prior" deducibility relation that holds among sentences not containing these connectives. The main problem with this argument is that the claim that the extension is conservative is simply false, if the "prior" deducibility relation contains the usual truth rules.[2]

Another way to try to argue for a kind of Boolean negation would be to try to read it off the model-theoretic semantics. In the model-theoretic semantics we have defined a notion of a sentence having value 1 in a model M. So we also have the notion of a sentence not having value 1 in M. The model-theoretic semantics was developed in a part of the language, classical set theory, for which excluded middle holds; so each sentence either has value 1 in M or it doesn't have value 1 in M (and not both). Shouldn't we be able to introduce a notion of negation into the language that corresponds to *not having value 1 in M*, and won't it obey the Boolean laws? (The idea is to collapse the lattice employed in the model theory to the 2-valued Boolean algebra, by ignoring any distinction between values other than 1.)

In response, one might ask what is meant by a notion of negation that "corresponds to" not having value 1 in M. The language already contains the notion '⟨doesn't have value 1 in M' (where 'M' is either a variable or a description of a specific model); if identity is a special case of correspondence, then there's no need to expand the language to get a "negation" corresponding to this. But if we define NA as '⟨A⟩ doesn't have value 1 in M' (say for some specific M, given by a description), then N will *not* obey the Boolean laws such as excluded middle. It would do so only if A and '⟨A⟩ has value 1 in M' were equivalent, for all A. But that can't be so, by Tarski's undefinability theorem; indeed, it can't be so even for sentences A that don't contain 'True' or related terms, but contain unrestricted quantifiers. Recall the discussion from Section 3.2. (Exactly which

---

[2] i.e. the general intersubstitutivity principle; or just the rules (T-Introd) and (T-Elim), if the classical laws one is adding include ∨-Elimination.

instances of "excluded middle for N" fail to be true depends on the choice of M. In the example from earlier where M is the set of sets of rank less than the first inaccessible cardinal, 'Either there are no inaccessibles or N(there are no inaccessible cardinals)' won't be true, since 'There are no inaccessible cardinals' has value 1 in M but is not true.)

That earlier discussion depended, of course, on taking models to be sets, and therefore to not contain everything in their domain. But we've seen that it's possible to make sense of a naive notion of property, on which there can be a universal property; might we be able to construct a non-standard notion of model where the quantifiers range not over the members of some set but over the things instantiated by some property? Mightn't we still introduce a notion of having value 1 in such a model? Mightn't we then single out as special the model M_{spec} where the quantifiers range over the things instantiated by the universal property, and where the names, predicates etc. are treated as they ought to be? If we can do these things, then '$\langle A \rangle$ has value 1 in M_{spec}' ought to be equivalent to A, for sentences without 'True' or related terms; and it should be a sufficient condition of truth more generally. So now shouldn't '$\langle A \rangle$ doesn't have value 1 in M_{spec}' define a Boolean negation, one that coincides with $\neg$ on the ground language? I think that this or something like it is what some advocates of "exclusion negation" really intend.

But the suggestion that this will lead to Boolean laws like excluded middle has no basis. (I think we can say this with confidence, despite the dangers of speculating about an undeveloped "property-based model theory".) For the imagined negation to obey excluded middle, we would have to assume that the following is a law:

(*) Either A has value 1 in M_{spec} or it doesn't.

When model theory is developed within set theory, excluded middle is obviously guaranteed for claims about the values of sentences. But in the imagined development of a property-based model theory, in a naive theory of properties that escapes contradiction by restricting excluded middle, there is no reason whatever to suppose that (*) would hold, and in fact it clearly couldn't.

21.2. INTUITIONIST NEGATION AND THE INTUITIONIST CONDITIONAL

Just as $\mathscr{L}^+$ doesn't contain any negation that obeys all the Boolean laws, it doesn't contain any negation that obeys all the intuitionist laws. In particular, it contains no operator N that obeys the standard introduction and elimination laws

(N-Elim) $\qquad\qquad\qquad A, NA \vDash \bot$

and

(N-Introd) $$\frac{\Gamma, A \vDash \bot}{\Gamma \vDash NA}.$$

The Conservativeness Theorem shows that it can't contain any such operator N, for these laws lead to contradiction (not just with full Intersubstitutivity, but even with the weaker laws (T-Introd) and (T-Elim)). For consider the Liar-like sentence Q_N that asserts $N[\text{True}(\langle Q_N \rangle)]$. $\text{True}(\langle Q_N \rangle)$ implies Q_N by (T-Elim), which is equivalent to $N(\text{True}(\langle Q_N \rangle))$; so by (N-Elim), $\text{True}(\langle Q_N \rangle)$ implies $\bot$. So by (N-Introd), $N[\text{True}(\langle Q_N \rangle)]$ is valid; so Q_N is valid. So by (T-Introd), $\text{True}(\langle Q_N \rangle)$ is valid; but we've already seen that it implies $\bot$, so $\bot$ is valid.

This is really just the Curry paradox argument all over again. For "intuitionist negation" NA is typically defined as $A \to \bot$; given this definition, (N-Elim) and (N-Introd) are just special cases of ($\to$-Elim) and ($\to$-Introd), and they are the special cases used in the version of the Curry paradox in Section 19.1. So the argument for paradox just given is a transcription of the Curry argument given there.

In the next two sections I consider two arguments for the intelligibility of intuitionist negation—or more generally, of the intuitionist conditional—and hence for the conclusion that the language $\mathscr{L}^+$ escapes paradox only because it doesn't have the means to express a perfectly intelligible notion. Each of the two arguments attempts to show that for any A and B, there is a weakest proposition which together with A implies B; hence in particular, a weakest proposition that is inconsistent with A, in the sense that it together with A implies $\bot$. (For simplicity I'm confining attention to the case where A contains no free variables.) Once this is established, the case for the intuitionist rules is straightforward:

For the conditional: Take $A \to B$ to be the weakest proposition which together with A implies B. Then

(a) By definition it together with A implies B, so modus ponens is justified for $\to$.

(b) But now suppose that Γ together with A implies B. Since $A \to B$ is *the weakest* proposition that together with A implies B, then $A \to B$ is at least as weak as "the conjunction of all members of Γ"; that is, Γ implies $A \to B$. So $\to$-Introduction is justified.

For negation: As a special case of the above, take NA to be the weakest proposition that is inconsistent with A, in the sense that it together with A implies $\bot$. Then

(a) By definition it is inconsistent with A, i.e. (N-Elim) holds.

(b) If Γ is inconsistent with A, then since NA is *the weakest* proposition that is inconsistent with A, NA is at least as weak as the "conjunction of all members of Γ"; that is, Γ implies NA. So (N-Introd) is justified.

314   *More on Paracompleteness*

Given the assumption that for each A there is a weakest proposition inconsistent with A, or the more general assumption that for each A and B there is a weakest proposition that together with A implies B, these arguments are unexceptionable.[3] But why make that assumption? The next section considers two closely related arguments for the assumption. For simplicity I focus on the more limited assumption for negation, though the discussion extends straightforwardly to the more general assumption for the conditional.

21.3. WRIGHT'S ARGUMENT

The first attempt to argue that for each A there is a weakest proposition inconsistent with A is one I haven't seen in print; I first heard it from Crispin Wright, in a seminar, and I don't know if he was actually advocating the argument or merely suggesting it as one worth thinking about—as it is.

Let $N_{Wright}A$ be the proposition that there is a true proposition that is inconsistent with A. Then taking N to be N_{Wright}, the idea is to argue

(1) that NA is inconsistent with A, and

(2) that anything that is inconsistent with A implies NA.

I've stipulated that 'A is inconsistent with B' is to means '$A, B \models \bot$'; given this stipulation, (1) suffices for (N-Elim) and (2) suffices for (N-Introd), as we saw in the previous section.

But how exactly are we to argue for (1) and (2)? Wright didn't say, but a natural initial thought would be to do so along the lines of the purported "paradox of truth and validity" considered in Section 20.4. (Indeed, I first came up with that fallacious argument in thinking about how one might try to argue for (1) and (2).)

The argument for (1) would turn on the principle

(I) $A, B, \langle B \rangle$ is inconsistent with $\langle A \rangle \models \bot$,

and might go something like this:

Apply (T-Elim) and $\wedge$-Elim to (I), getting

$$A, \text{True}(\langle B \rangle) \wedge (\langle B \rangle \text{ is inconsistent with } \langle A \rangle) \models \bot,$$

for arbitrary B. But since this holds for arbitrary B, something on the order of $\exists$-Elim should yield

$$A, \exists x[\text{True}(x) \wedge x \text{ is inconsistent with } \langle A \rangle] \models \bot.$$

But this is just (1), on the proposed definition N_{Wright} of N.

---

[3] At least for finite Γ, where the existence of a "conjunction of all members of Γ" is uncontroversial; and the result for finite Γ would be enough to reinstate the Curry paradox.

The argument for (2) needs to be a bit more general than the one in Section 20.4, but here's a natural shot at one, based on the assumption

(II) If $\langle B \rangle$ is inconsistent with $\langle A \rangle$ then $\vDash [\langle B \rangle$ is inconsistent with $\langle A \rangle]$.

The argument might go something like this:

Consider any $\langle B \rangle$ that is inconsistent with $\langle A \rangle$. By (II), we have

$$\vDash [\langle B \rangle \text{ is inconsistent with } \langle A \rangle]$$

and so $\quad\quad\quad\quad B \vDash [\langle B \rangle \text{ is inconsistent with } \langle A \rangle].$

But by (T-Introd),

$$B \vDash [\langle B \rangle \text{ is true}],$$

so $\quad\quad\quad\quad B \vDash \exists x[\text{True}(x) \wedge x \text{ is inconsistent with } \langle A \rangle],$

that is $\quad\quad\quad\quad B \vDash N_{\text{Wright}} A.$

This holds for any B inconsistent with A. Something like universal generalization then should yield (2).

There are some questionable transitions in these, indicated by my cautious formulations ('something on the order of' and 'something like'). But the main question is, why believe that there is any intelligible understanding of $\vDash$ for which, when 'A is inconsistent with B' is defined from it as '$A, B \vDash \bot$', both (I) and (II are correct? We can show, as was in effect done in Section 20.4, that there is no such notion of $\vDash$ for classical logic, as well as no such notion for $\mathscr{L}^+$; the supposition that there are intelligible languages for which there is such a notion seems highly contentious.

I want to make clear that I'm not charging Wright's argument with the fallacy discussed in Section 20.4. The argument Wright offered for consideration was an argument for expanding the language $\mathscr{L}^+$ to include intuitionist negation. We can't simply assume that since in classical logic and in $\mathscr{L}^+$ there is no notion satisfying his assumptions, the same must be true in an expanded language. Still, the point remains that arguing for intuitionist negation on the basis of assumptions that don't hold for other logics seems highly contentious. (This is especially so given that the use of intuitionist negation breeds semantic paradox!)

I should add that the argument for (1) and (2) is one that no intuitionist should accept, even if he did accept [I] and [II]! The reason is that the argument for (1) depends not only on (I), but on (T-Elim); and the argument for (2) depends not only on (II), but on (T-Introd). But as we've seen, these two truth rules can't consistently be accepted by anyone who adheres to the rules (N-Elim) and (N-Introd) that are being argued for.

An intuitionist should say, then, that though the arguments for (1) and (2) have a correct conclusion, at least one is faulty, because it uses an unacceptable truth rule. I think that this is far less plausible than my diagnosis, which is that at least one of the conclusions [I] and [II] is faulty.[4] That diagnosis seems far more plausible since even classical notions of implication, defined model-theoretically in the general framework of Section 20.4, all fail to satisfy at least one of [I] and [II].

21.4. RESTALL'S ARGUMENT

Another very interesting attempt to argue that for each A there is a weakest proposition inconsistent with A (and hence that we ought to allow the addition of intuitionist negation to the language) is given in Restall 2007. It is similar to Wright's argument, but relies on adding to the language a primitive notion of infinite disjunction, one which allows disjunctions over sets (of formulas or sentences) *that aren't definable in the language*. And this seems at first blush to evade the problem with Wright's argument.

Here is the argument in more detail. (Restall gives it for the intuitionist conditional instead of intuitionist negation; but as above, I will focus on the special case of conditionals with absurd consequents, which is how the intuitionist understands negations. And again I focus on the application of the operator to sentences only.) Let $N_{Restall}A$ be the infinite disjunction of all sentences that are (weakly) inconsistent with A. (*Not* the infinite disjunction of all sentences of form $S \wedge (\langle S \rangle$ is inconsistent with $\langle A \rangle)$, which was essentially Wright's proposal, but the infinite disjunction of all sentences S that *really are* inconsistent with A.) Then it seems that

(1) $N_{Restall}A$ is at least as weak as anything inconsistent with A. For suppose B is inconsistent with A; then B is one of the disjuncts of $N_{Restall}A$, in which case B implies $N_{Restall}A$.

This would justify $N_{Restall}$-Introduction. In addition,

(2) $N_{Restall}A$ is inconsistent with A; i.e. $A \wedge N_{Restall}A \vDash \bot$. For take any B that is inconsistent with A; by definition (plus $\wedge$-rules), $A \wedge B \vDash \bot$. But presumably we have a generalized rule of disjunction elimination, even for infinite disjunctions. If so then $\bigvee \{A \wedge B \mid B \text{ is inconsistent with } A\} \vDash \bot$. And presumably we also have an infinitary distribution law, that takes $A \wedge \bigvee \{B \mid B \in X\}$ to imply $\bigvee \{A \wedge B \mid B \in X\}$. If so, we have $A \wedge \bigvee \{B \mid B \text{ is inconsistent with } A\} \vDash \bot$. This is just the desired result $A \wedge N_{Restall}A \vDash \bot$.

---

[4] Which one is faulty depends on exactly how implication is explained (e.g., exactly what kinds of models one quantifies over in the definition), but [I] is the more likely culprit.

Expressive Limitations? 317

So we have $N_{Restall}$-Elimination.

An initial reaction might be that the infinitary distributive law invoked in (2) is suspicious: it's well known that the infinitary distribution law fails in many complete distributive lattices (i.e. complete lattices that are *finitely* distributive, which is the normal meaning of 'distributive').[5] But I don't think the problem can plausibly be blamed on this, especially given that the argument in (2) doesn't require that there is more than a weak implication from $A \wedge \bigvee \{B \mid B \in X\}$ to $\bigvee \{A \wedge B \mid B \in X\}$ (i.e. it requires only that if the first has value 1 then so does the second).[6] It may now seem that there is nothing left in Restall's argument to challenge!

But there is. To get at the real problems with the combination of (1) and (2), let's first be explicit about the apparent structure of Restall's overall argument. The argument seems to be this:

Construal 1: We start out with a general notion of implication among propositions (propositions that needn't be expressible in our initial language). We then use this general notion of implication to define a notion of infinitary disjunction, by means of introduction and elimination rules. This notion of infinitary disjunction is explainable in this way *prior* to a notion of truth (or at least, prior to a notion of truth on the full language $\mathscr{L}_\infty$ that includes infinitary disjunction); that's how it avoids the problems of the Wright argument considered in the previous section. And we can see, *independent of bringing in truth*, that the behavior of this infinitary disjunction allows us to define intuitionist negation (and more generally, an intuitionist conditional). And this prevents adding a truth predicate that accords with the Intersubstitutivity Principle, or even one that accords with just the pair of principles (T-Introd) and (T-Elim).

Perhaps Restall didn't really intend the overall argument to be as in Construal 1; but before turning to an alternative construal, it is important to see the chief defect of the argument under this construal of it. (The key point of Construal 1 that will be dropped in Construal 2 is this: on Construal 1, the goal of the argument (1) and (2) is to show that the logic justifies the intuitionist connectives, *independent of bringing in self-referential constructions involving a truth predicate*.)

There is another interpretive issue, of just how Restall is understanding the infinite disjunction in the definition of $N_{Restall}$. On its face, the definition has a highly impredicative character, in that $N_{Restall}A$ is stipulated to be the infinite disjunction of all propositions inconsistent with A, including those that can only be expressed using infinitary disjunction—indeed, *possibly including the*

---

[5] Example: the lattice of closed subsets of almost any topological space. Here the join of a set of closed sets X_α is the *closure of* their union; so any limit point of the union that isn't in any of the X_α will nonetheless be in their infinite join.

[6] It's also worth noting that the deMorgan algebra of Section 17.1 obeys the infinite distributive law even in the form corresponding to strong implication, for infinite disjunctions of cardinality no greater than that of the underlying model. (But this is of only indirect relevance to the present discussion since Restall is discussing a proposed expansion of the language to include a device of infinitary disjunction not representable in it; and it isn't obvious that the model theory would carry over unchanged to that expanded language.)

very proposition $N_{Restall}A$ itself, and others built up out of it. If so, then under Construal 1 this impredicativity is brought about not by the use of Gödel–Tarski diagonalization using a truth predicate; it is conceived of as there prior to the introduction of the truth predicate. Indeed it is what makes the introduction of a well-behaved truth predicate (which would allow only for a more controlled impredicativity) impossible.

But this kind of impredicativity would be highly suspicious. Let's begin with ordinary disjunction (finite, in fact binary). This is introduced into the language in a predicative fashion. If we call a disjunction-free sentence (or formula) one of *level 0*, we first allow disjunctions of level 0 sentences; these and sentences constructed from them by operations other than disjunction have *level 1*. Then disjunctions of level 1 sentences with level 0 or 1 sentences have *level 2* (as do sentences constructed from them without disjunction); and so on, through all finite levels. What we *don't* do is say: there is a set of all propositions, and for any pair of propositions from this set there is a proposition that is their disjunction. That would be bizarre: it would allow for a disjunction D one of whose disjuncts is D itself (or one of whose disjuncts is the conjunction of D and something else). We disallow this in the case of finite disjunctions. (We may be able to eventually simulate impredicative finite disjunctions, using a truth predicate and Gödel–Tarski diagonalization; but I'm speaking now of disjunction unaided by a truth predicate.) If we didn't disallow it, we would have paradoxes independent of truth. For instance, let D be the disjunction whose first disjunct is the negation of D and whose second disjunct is '0 = 1'; clearly it is equivalent, in the 'True'-free language, to its own negation. At the very least we'd have to say that the 'True'-free language of finite but impredicative disjunctions is non-classical, but I think a better thing to say is that the idea of impredicative disjunctions, even finite ones, just isn't coherent.

I take it, then, that if we are going to generalize finite disjunction to infinite disjunction, we should disallow impredicativity in the infinite case as we do in the finite. We should say that there are 0-level propositions, expressible without infinitary disjunction; and for each a up to a certain point there are a-level infinitary disjunctions, none of whose disjuncts contain infinitary disjunctions of level a or higher (but such that for any $\beta < a$, there are disjuncts containing infinitary disjunctions of level at least β).[7] (Rigorous treatments of infinitary languages also impose cardinality restrictions on the size of the infinitary disjunctions—this is required if the sentences of the language are to form a set. If they don't form a set we have a further problem: the infinitary disjunction of *all* sentences meeting certain conditions will have length greater than every ordinal! But rather than trying to impose rigor here, I will follow Restall in ignoring the cardinality problem. Taking it into account wouldn't improve the prospects of Restall's argument, and might make them worse.)

[7] Since these formulas may have infinite length, the levels will go into the transfinite.

Expressive Limitations? 319

But the introduction of a predicativity requirement would be devastating for Restall's argument under Construal 1: it would mean that $N_{Restall}$ is simply ill-defined. The best we could do is define, for each $\alpha > 0$, an operator $N^\alpha{}_{Restall}$, by the stipulation that $N^\alpha{}_{Restall}A$ is the infinite disjunction of all sentences *of level less than* α that are inconsistent with A. But then there's no reason to think that $N^\alpha{}_{Restall}A$ is the weakest proposition inconsistent with A; $N^{\alpha+1}{}_{Restall}A$ is *prima facie* weaker. Put another way, the argument in (1) breaks down: if B is a proposition of level α or higher that is inconsistent with A, then it is not one of the disjuncts of $N^\alpha{}_{Restall}A$; so there's no reason to think that B implies $N^\alpha{}_{Restall}A$.

So contrary to Restall under Construal 1, there is no difficulty in adding a reasonable (i.e. predicative) infinitary disjunction to the language while avoiding the intuitionistic laws.

But this is just a prelude to the second construal of Restall's argument, under which he concedes this but argues that we cannot add a truth predicate to the language in accordance with the Intersubstitutivity Principle or even the weaker pair of laws (T-Introd) and (T-Elim). Of course there's no question that adding such a truth predicate would require restricting excluded middle, since we need to do that when adding a truth predicate even without infinitary disjunction; Restall's claim, under Construal 2, is that we can't add such a truth predicate satisfying Intersubstitutivity *even with excluded middle restricted*.

It looks at first blush as if this claim must be right, for the truth predicate destroys the hierarchy of levels: whatever level a sentence B has, True($\langle B \rangle$) has level 0. So using just the lowest level infinite disjunction, we can infinitely disjoin all sentences of form True($\langle B \rangle$) for B in X, for any set X, and assuming Intersubstitutivity (or even just (T-Introd) and (T-Elim)) this should be equivalent to infinitely disjoining all members of X.

Let's be more explicit about how the argument so construed would have to go. Let N^*A be the infinite disjunction of all *level 0* sentences incompatible with A, *including those of form True($\langle B \rangle$) when B is of higher level*. For the argument to go through we'll have to take 'inconsistent' here to mean not just 'inconsistent in the infinitary non-classical logic without the truth predicate', but 'inconsistent in a given infinitary non-classical logic of truth'. Then if we assume that this logic obeys infinitary ∨-Elim and infinite distributivity, we can easily modify the argument in (2) to get the conclusion that N^*A is inconsistent with A: simply confine the B in the argument to level 0 sentences. No assumption about truth is required in this argument, which I will call (2*).

The above analog of argument (2) does not seem to depend on the details of the logic of truth used in defining N^*A (though exactly what N^*A means depends on this). But if we assume that this logic obeys at least the rules (T-Introd) and (T-Elim), we can now also get an analog of the argument for (1):

(1*) Suppose B is a (not necessarily level 0) sentence that is inconsistent with A; then by (T-Elim), True($\langle B \rangle$) is inconsistent with A, and since it has level 0 it is one of the disjuncts of N^*A. So True($\langle B \rangle$) implies N^*A, and so by (T-Introd), B implies N^*A.

Given (2*) and (1*), the second construal is as follows:

Construal 2: Take N*A to be the infinite disjunction of all level 0 sentences incompatible with A in the appropriate logic, including those sentences of form True($\langle B \rangle$) where B is of higher level. Then N*A is incompatible with A; and *if we were to assume that the logic satisfies (T-Introd) and (T-Elim)* it would follow that it is the weakest sentence incompatible with A and thus would give rise to the intuitionist reductio law as well. But its satisfying both these intuitionist negation laws is in turn incompatible with (T-Introd) and (T-Elim). So the assumption of (T-Introd) and (T-Elim) is self-refuting, in the presence of even a predicative infinite disjunction.

This is an apparently compelling argument. It seems to pose a challenge to weakly classical as well as to paracomplete approaches to the paradoxes.

I'll suggest a way around this argument in a moment, but first I note that even if it were unanswerable, the most it would show is that we'd need to restrict the application of naive truth (or weakly classical truth) to infinitary sentences, so as not to be able to define an intuitionist negation or intuitionist conditional. This might not be so hard to live with: it seems to me that restricting the application of naive truth to infinitary sentences wouldn't drastically affect our ordinary practices! If a need to so restrict the application of naive truth to infinitary sentences really could be shown, that might well be taken as a reason for thinking that infinitary sentences in general are at best "second rate" (though the ones that can be simulated by means of a truth predicate and quantification could still be allowed to be OK). This is very different than Restall's apparent conclusion, the one given under Construal 1. Far from wanting to restrict the application of the usual laws of truth to infinitary sentences so as to preclude defining connectives obeying intuitionist laws, Restall's view under Construal 1 was that such connectives make sense already, prior to introducing truth; on that view, all that could be in question is whether truth obeys the usual laws for sentences that involve these unproblematic connectives.

But I don't think we should concede to Restall even that there is a problem in adding a truth predicate to an infinitary language. I've remarked that to introduce infinitary disjunction in an intelligible fashion, it should be done predicatively; but I think that there is another constraint on intelligibility as well, which is that for any infinitary disjunction D it should be determinate what the disjuncts are. That of course is always satisfied in the case of ordinary finite disjunction. For the infinitary case, the appropriate principle on the existence of infinitary disjunctions would then seem to be that *on the assumption that every sentence (of level less than α) either satisfies condition ϕ or doesn't satisfy it*, there is a disjunction of all sentences (of level less than α) that meet condition(ϕ).[8]

---

[8] This actually was already built into how I characterized infinitary disjunction above (albeit not very saliently). For I said that there were infinitary disjunctions for *sets* of sentences (of level less than α); and as Section 20.3 argued, it is only reasonable to postulate a set corresponding to condition ϕ on the assumption of excluded middle for ϕ.

To illustrate the need for such a restriction, suppose D were the infinite disjunction of all level 0 sentences *that are not true*. Since it is indeterminate whether the Liar sentence is true, it is indeterminate whether the Liar sentence is one of the disjuncts. Granting the intelligibility of such a disjunction would lead to all sorts of anomalies. For instance, does the Liar sentence strongly imply D? It does if the Liar sentence is not true, for then the Liar sentence is one of the disjuncts of D. But if the Liar sentence is true, it presumably does not strongly imply any untruths, and D is untrue since it is a disjunction of untruths. Given that it's "fuzzy" whether the Liar sentence is true, it's "fuzzy" what the disjuncts of D are and hence "fuzzy" what logical relations D enters into. Put more soberly: the conclusion would be that we shouldn't assume that either Q strongly implies D or Q doesn't strongly imply D; i.e. we shouldn't assume that $Q \to D$ is either valid or not valid. This conclusion would be very disruptive to the whole point of logic.

The problem here isn't the infinitariness of D: we would have an equal problem with a finite (predicative) "disjunction" in which the disjuncts are the members of the "set" that

(i) includes 'Snow is white' and 'Grass is green',
(ii) includes the Liar sentence if and only if it is true,

and

(iii) doesn't include any sentences other than these.

It seems to me that the best thing to say is that there is no such finite disjunction as this. The disjunctions

D_1 Snow is white ∨ Grass is green ∨ Q

and

D_2 Snow is white ∨ Grass is green

exist, but the idea of a "disjunction" that is *either D_1 or D_2 but it's indeterminate which* simply makes no sense. If so, we should say that in the infinitary case too.

If we do say this, then the argument in Construal 2 needs to be buttressed to include an argument that the disjunction N^*A exists. At first blush this may seem easy: the condition used in defining N^*A is "sentence of level 0 *that is inconsistent with A*" (where 'inconsistency' means 'weak inconsistency'), and I argued in Section 20.5 that even for languages that contain predicates like 'True' and 'Satisfies' for which excluded middle can't be assumed in general, we *can* assume excluded middle for the notions of validity and inconsistency. In that discussion I was talking about ordinary languages, without infinitary disjunction (except insofar as that is simulated by the truth predicate); but I'd be prepared to extend it to infinite disjunctions too, provided that we restrict to infinite disjunctions where it is determinate what the disjuncts are. (If we don't make such a restriction, it is *inevitable* that excluded middle must be restricted for implication claims, as just argued.)

But *is the condition that it be determinate what the disjuncts are satisfied in the current case, where the disjuncts are specified via the notion of inconsistency*? It is met if inconsistency in the required sense obeys excluded middle, but not otherwise. So there is a circularity involved in establishing its legitimacy. And its legitimacy must be established if Restall's argument is to proceed.

Formally, what the legitimacy requirement of several paragraphs back imposes is that the existence of N^*A can't be assumed outright, it can only be assumed conditionally on the assumption of excluded middle for claims of implication in the infinitary logic with the truth predicate. Without an argument for that assumption, Restall's argument simply wouldn't get off the ground.

The difficulty doesn't actually depend on the use of *infinite* disjunctions, it depends only on the use of disjunctions that are specified by means of a condition involving an underspecified notion of implication. Suppose I define $N^{**}A$ as the finite disjunction of all sentences that are either the sentence '$0 = 1$' or a sentence that is both equivalent to $N^{**}A$ (say in number theory) and implies the Liar sentence in this logic. Then it is determinate what the disjuncts are only if we can somehow argue that were we to take it to be a legitimate definition we could take it to be determinate whether it implies the Liar sentence. But establishing the latter would require a determinacy in the disjuncts, so we have a similar kind of circularity.

A natural way to avoid such circularity is to introduce a new kind of predicativity requirement on our specifications of the disjuncts of a disjunction: it must use only a stratified notion of inconsistency.

Let us first consider an infinitary language, without a truth predicate, that allows infinite disjunctions defined by conditions φ that clearly obey excluded middle *and do not include any notion of implication*.[9] (Call this infinitary language IL_0. I will not define it rigorously, but trust that the intent is clear.) Call the implication relation of such an infinitary language implication$_0$, and call the corresponding inconsistency relation inconsistency$_0$. This language doesn't allow for the formulation of anything like the definition of N^*A, so Restall's argument doesn't arise. Consequently, we have no reason to doubt that a truth predicate can be conservatively added to the infinitary logic of implication$_0$, in accord with the Intersubstitutivity Principle, resulting in a language IL_0^+. (Of course I haven't established that adding a truth predicate in this way is possible, which would require much more precision about the infinitary logic; but the game isn't to do that, but to undermine Restall's argument that it is not possible.) This gives us a notion of implication$_{0+}$: implication in the full logic of truth in the language IL_0^+.

---

[9] Given the deplorable frequency with which people pronounce '$\rightarrow$' as 'implies', I should add that IL_0 does not in any way restrict the use of '$\rightarrow$' in infinite disjunctions.

Implication$_{0+}$ presumably obeys excluded middle, so we should be able to use it together with other conditions obeying excluded middle to legitimately define infinite disjunctions. Let IL$_1$ be the infinitary language that extends IL$_0^+$ by adding such infinite disjunctions. (So far, we haven't added a truth predicate that applies to sentences of IL$_1$ that aren't also in IL$_0$.) In particular, we can unproblematically define N$_1^*A$ to be the infinite disjunction of all level 0 sentences of IL$_1$ that are inconsistent$_{0+}$ with A. ('Level 0' here has the same meaning as before: free of infinite disjunctions. But the level 0 sentences of IL$_1$ include those of form True($\langle B \rangle$) where B is a higher level sentence of IL$_0^+$.) We can plausibly argue as in (2*) that N$_1^*A$ is inconsistent$_1$ with A in the infinitary logic (where inconsistency$_1$ is defined in the usual way from the implication relation of IL$_1$). But we cannot argue as in (1*) that N$_1^*A$ is implied$_1$ by every sentence that is inconsistent$_1$ with A, but only that it is implied$_1$ by every sentence *of IL$_{0+}$* that is inconsistent$_1$ with A. This is not enough for paradox, since a paradoxical sentence would have to be built from N$_1^*$, and hence not be in the language IL$_0$. So we have no reason to doubt that a truth predicate can be conservatively added to IL$_1$ in accordance with the Intersubstitutivity Principle, getting a new language IL$_1^+$. Its validity and inconsistency relations presumably obey excluded middle, and can be used to define still further infinite disjunctions, yielding language IL$_2$. And so on. (The truth predicate for any IL$_n^+$ will extend that for any IL$_m^+$ where $m < n$.)

Two points about this proposed stratification deserve emphasis. First, it is not at all *ad hoc*: it arises out of the need to ensure that we only talk about disjunctions for which it is determinate what the disjuncts are. And second, it is not fundamentally a stratification in the notion of truth, but in the notion of infinite disjunction—or more generally, in the notion of any disjunction, finite or infinite, that is specified not by listing the disjuncts but by defining them by some condition.[10] If some kind of stratification isn't imposed on the condition used in defining the disjunction, we cannot non-circularly establish that it is determinate what the disjuncts are. But once we have a language in which the notion of infinite disjunction has been intelligibly introduced, there is no obstacle to adding to the language a truth predicate that is completely unstratified—or at any rate, that has no further stratification than what is inherited from any sentences with infinite disjunctions (with disjuncts specified via a notion of implication) to which the truth predicate applies.

We see, then, that while Restall's argument makes vivid the need for considerable care in dealing with infinite disjunctions—and more generally, with any disjunctions specified by conditions on the disjuncts rather than by listing

---

[10] Indeed, the stratification isn't even *secondarily* in the notion of truth: it is primarily in the notion of infinite disjunction, secondarily in the notion of implication that governs it, and only tertiarily in the notion of truth applied to infinite disjunctions whose disjuncts are specified using the notion of implication.

the members—it does not succeed in showing that intuitionist negation or the intuitionist conditional must be a legitimate notion.

So far, then, we've seen no remotely compelling reason to think that paracomplete solutions to the paradoxes turn on expressive limitations in the language $\mathscr{L}^+$. In the next chapter I turn to another argument that the solutions turn on expressive limitations—an argument that will take more work to answer.

22
Determinateness, Hyper-Determinateness, and Super-Determinateness

In Chapter 15 I argued that in paracomplete theories of a quite general sort one can define a notion of determinateness, obeying very natural laws, in which one can say of certain sentences like the Liar that they are neither determinately true nor determinately not true. And saying this isn't just saying that their truth value is unknowable, it has real import about "non-factuality": to say that a sentence A isn't determinately true or determinately untrue commits one to *not* accepting the corresponding instance of excluded middle $A \vee \neg A$. We saw in Section 16.2 that it is possible to develop paracomplete theories of this sort which contain the truth schema and Intersubstitutivity Principle and are strongly consistent, i.e. conservative in the sense of Section 3.3. This shows that there can be no genuine paradoxes of determinateness in such a theory.

How is it that a sentence Q_1 that asserts that it itself is not determinately true escapes paradox? The secret, we saw, was that excluded middle can't be assumed for 'determinately true' (or for the bare operator 'determinately'):

$$DA \vee \neg DA$$

is *not* a logical law. In particular, we can't assume $DQ_1 \vee \neg DQ_1$. *A fortiori*, we can't assume $\neg DQ_1$. It turns out, though, that we can prove $\neg DDQ_1$. So DD is, in a sense, a stronger operator than D: DA does not, in general, strongly imply DDA (and $\neg DDA$ doesn't even weakly imply $\neg DA$).

Moreover, this situation generalizes to iterations of D, even to "transfinite iterations": given any operator D^α formed by "iterating D α times", we will be able to form a Liar sentence Q_α asserting that it itself is not D^α-True. Paradox is avoided by rejecting

$$D^\alpha Q_\alpha \vee \neg D^\alpha Q_\alpha,$$

and *a fortiori* by rejecting $\neg D^\alpha Q_\alpha$; but we will always be able to prove $\neg D^{\alpha+1} Q_\alpha$. So for any α, $D^{\alpha+1}$ is a genuine strengthening of D^α.

There are various worries this might raise.

- One of them is that we seem able to use the truth predicate to "infinitely conjoin" all the determinateness predicates, thereby getting a hyper-determinateness predicate. And such a predicate seems bound to lead to paradoxes in paracomplete theories, or at least render the discussion of the "ordinary" D and its iterations pointless.

- A second worry is that even if no reasonable hyper-determinateness predicate is *definable in the language*, still a hyper-determinateness predicate is *intelligible*, and results in paradox; so that paracomplete theories avoid paradox only by being expressively limited.

- A third is that the objections against classical theories that stratify the truth predicate will carry over to paracomplete theories.

It is these and similar worries with which the present chapter and the next are concerned. (The first is a main topic of this chapter, the third is discussed in the next, and the second is a topic of both.)

22.1. TRANSFINITE ITERATION MADE RIGOROUS

In order to treat these worries properly, it is necessary to be more precise about how the hierarchy of iterations of D is defined and how far it can be extended.

The hierarchy of iterations of D is, obviously, unending, in the sense that it has no last member. Indeed, once D^α is defined, it is obvious how to define $D^{\alpha+1}$: it is just $D(D^\alpha)$. But this leaves open the crucial question of how D^λ is to be defined when λ is a limit ordinal, and indeed for which limit ordinals it can be defined at all. The general idea for defining D^λ is clear: we want D^λ to be the intersection of all D^α for $\alpha < \lambda$. So why not define it as follows: '$D^\lambda A$' abbreviates '$(\forall \alpha < \lambda)\text{True}(\langle D^\alpha A\rangle)$'?

The general idea here is fine, but there are two problems. A minor one is that it handles the application of iterations of D only to sentences, whereas we really want to do it for formulas. It's clear enough how to fix this: e.g. if A contains a single free variable v, we alter the above definition of '$D^\lambda A$' to '$(\forall \alpha < \lambda)(\langle D^\alpha A\rangle$ is true of $v)$'. Generalizing this to formulas with arbitrarily many free variables is routine, but involves a notational complexity I'd like to avoid here; in order to do so, I'll confine the application of determinately operators in this chapter to sentences. This is purely a matter of simplifying the discussion: the more rigorous treatment in Field 2007 handles the matter in a more general fashion.

The far more serious problem with the proposed definition of '$D^\lambda A$' involves use and mention; the need to set it right substantially affects the shape of the overall theory. The problem is that we need to distinguish ordinals from their notations.[1] $D^\lambda A$ is to be a formula—or in the simplification adopted here, a

---

[1] Here 'ordinal notation' is not used in the specific technical sense due to Church and Kleene (see Rogers 1967, secs. 11.7-8) but simply for a linguistic item denoting an ordinal—either a singular term referring to an ordinal, or a formula true of one and only one ordinal. Since the language may

sentence. So the superscript must be a piece of notation for the ordinal λ, not the ordinal λ itself. (The notation needn't actually be in $\mathscr{L}^+$, it could be in a definitional expansion of $\mathscr{L}^+$, but this doesn't alter the point that it is linguistic.)

Because of this, the most straightforward way to define the notation D^λ corresponding to a particular ordinal λ is to choose a particular definition ❶ of λ, and use that definition in defining D^λ. We will also need a definition ❷ of a function that assigns, to each ordinal α prior to λ, a definition of an operator D^α corresponding to α. Given these, we could define '$D^\lambda A$' as an abbreviation of something like

($\forall \alpha <$ ❶)($\forall$O)[(O is the operator that results by applying the function ❷ to α) → (the result of prefixing O to ⟨A⟩ is true)].

However, the function that assigns operators D^α to ordinals α will in turn depend on definitions "already chosen" for limit ordinals prior to λ; so doing all this properly will require a very careful inductive definition.

A reader interested in the details of how this is done should consult the later parts of Field 2007 (specifically, Sections 14–18 plus the Appendix). The following outline will be enough for what follows. (Since even the outline is somewhat technical, let me say that the basic moral of the discussion is contained in the last paragraph of this section; the reader could just skim the rest for now, returning to the details only as needed in Section 3.)

First, let an $\mathscr{L}$-*path of length* λ be a function that assigns, to each ordinal α < λ, some formula of $\mathscr{L}$ that is true of α and of nothing else, to serve as a notation for α. ($\mathscr{L}$ is here the ground language, i.e. the set-theoretic language without 'True'. I'll soon generalize to paths for larger languages.)[2] Note that $\mathscr{L}$-paths can have any limit length up to but not including the first ordinal that is not definable in $\mathscr{L}$.[3]

Second, it is possible to define in $\mathscr{L}$ a function Φ that maps any $\mathscr{L}$-path p of length λ into an $\mathscr{L}$-*hierarchy of length* λ, that is, into a function that assigns to each ordinal α < λ a sequence $D^\alpha{}_{(p)}$ of operations on sentences meeting the obvious three constraints:

(Zer) $D^0{}_{(p)}$ is the identity operation, i.e. it assigns any sentence of $\mathscr{L}^+$ to itself;

(Suc) $D^{\alpha+1}{}_{(p)}$ is the operator that assigns to each sentence A of $\mathscr{L}^+$ the result of applying D to $D^\alpha{}_{(p)}$;

---

not contain sufficiently many singular terms, it is convenient to take the notations to be formulas uniquely true of ordinals.

[2] The $\mathscr{L}$-path itself (the function that assigns formulas of $\mathscr{L}$ to ordinals) needn't be definable in $\mathscr{L}$, or even in $\mathscr{L}^+$. (Indeed there are uncountably many $\mathscr{L}$-paths, only countably many of which are definable even in $\mathscr{L}^+$.)

[3] Readers familiar with the Church–Kleene systems of ordinal notations will note an obvious similarity to the notion of path used there; however, Church–Kleene systems of notations include strong recursiveness constraints that I have not imposed, and as a result of those constraints, paths in Church–Kleene systems can have length no greater than the first non-recursive ordinal. That is far shorter than the paths allowed here. (In addition, the path-independent hierarchies introduced later in this section have no analog in the Church–Kleene theory, since they would violate the recursiveness constraints that are the rationale for that theory.)

(Lim) $D^\lambda{}_{(p)}$ is an operator (*which* operator depends on p) which assigns to each sentence A of $\mathscr{L}^+$ a sentence that is true if and only if for each $\alpha < \lambda$ the result of applying $D^\alpha{}_{(p)}$ to A is true.

The hierarchy $D^\alpha{}_{(p)}$ defined in this way from $\mathscr{L}$-path p is called a *path-dependent hierarchy*. (To say that it is definable *from the $\mathscr{L}$-path p* does not imply that it is definable, even in $\mathscr{L}^+$; and it won't be, when p itself isn't definable in $\mathscr{L}^+$. See note 2.)

We could also consider more general hierarchies, not generated in this way from $\mathscr{L}$-paths; however, the study of them would need extreme care. The reason that such care would be required for a general notion of hierarchy is that, because of the use of 'true' in (Lim), we couldn't assume that the predicate 'is a hierarchy' obeys excluded middle. That difficulty is avoided for hierarchies generated from $\mathscr{L}$-paths: 'is an $\mathscr{L}$-path' is bivalent since it applies truth-like terms only to $\mathscr{L}$-formulas, and the application of the hierarchy-generating function Φ is bivalent since it is definable in $\mathscr{L}$.

The procedure just outlined, besides producing hierarchies that are path-dependent, defines separate operators for each ordinal: it does not define $D^\alpha{}_{(p)}$ for variable α. But both of these defects can be overcome, by using the truth predicate to generalize:

Third step of outline: we can use the definition of path-dependent hierarchies to define (in $\mathscr{L}^+$) a *path-independent hierarchy*, in which 'α' *is a variable*: $D^\alpha{}_{[\mathscr{L}]}A$ is defined as $\exists p(p$ is an $\mathscr{L}$-path of length greater than $\alpha \wedge$ the result of applying $[\Phi(p)](\alpha)$ to $\langle A\rangle$ is true).

It's clear that this path-independent hierarchy is quite well-behaved for ordinals that are hereditarily definable in the ground language $\mathscr{L}$ (i.e. such that they and all their predecessors are definable in $\mathscr{L}$): analogs of the constraints (Zer), (Suc) and (Lim) are clearly satisfied. As already observed, $\mathscr{L}$-paths needn't be definable, even in $\mathscr{L}^+$; and in the definition of $D^\alpha{}_{[\mathscr{L}]}$ we quantify over *all* $\mathscr{L}$-paths, not just the definable ones.

Note that in this path-independent hierarchy, $D^\alpha{}_{[\mathscr{L}]}A$ is false for any α not hereditarily definable in $\mathscr{L}$, *even when A is a clear truth*. In other words, the operator $D^\alpha{}_{[\mathscr{L}]}$ is *useful* only for ordinals α that are hereditarily definable in the ground language $\mathscr{L}$. Indeed, only for such ordinals α should $D^\alpha{}_{[\mathscr{L}]}$ count as the αth iteration of D: for bigger α, it isn't an iteration of D at all, it is unwanted garbage.

Can we get more extensive hierarchies (both path-dependent and path-independent)? Yes. Our full language $\mathscr{L}^+$ goes beyond $\mathscr{L}$, in that it contains a truth predicate, indeed, a satisfaction predicate. With a satisfaction predicate we can define 'definable in the ground language $\mathscr{L}$': an object o is definable in $\mathscr{L}$ if and only if there is a formula of $\mathscr{L}$ that is true of o and of nothing else. This enables us to define more ordinals: for instance, we can certainly define the smallest ordinal that is not definable in the ground language $\mathscr{L}$. And we can use this to extend the notion of path, and thereby extend the possible path-dependent hierarchies, and thereby extend the path-independent hierarchy.

This development is entirely routine and unsurprising, up to a certain point. Let $\mathscr{L}_R$ be any fragment of $\mathscr{L}^+$ for which bivalence can be assumed. ($\mathscr{L}$ itself is such a fragment, of course. So is the fragment obtained by adding to $\mathscr{L}$ the predicate 'is a true sentence *of* $\mathscr{L}$', or '*s* is an assignment function and A is a formula *of* $\mathscr{L}$ that s satisfies'.) Then everything said above for $\mathscr{L}$ extends to $\mathscr{L}_R$: in the extended language $\mathscr{L}^+$,

(i) we can define a notion of $\mathscr{L}_R$-path, which allows $\mathscr{L}_R$-paths to have any length smaller than the first $\mathscr{L}_R$-undefinable ordinal;

(ii) we can apply the function Φ to $\mathscr{L}_R$-paths, getting path-dependent hierarchies of the same lengths as the paths;

and

(iii) we can then define a path-independent hierarchy, with variable superscript, which behaves very nicely as long as the superscript is restricted to hereditarily $\mathscr{L}_R$-definable ordinals but is useless for larger ones.

Moreover, it is not hard to show that if an ordinal α is in the "range of good behavior" of the path-independent hierarchies for two such fragments $\mathscr{L}_{R_1}$ and $\mathscr{L}_{R_2}$, then the operators $D^\alpha{}_{[\mathscr{L}_{R_1}]}$ and $D^\alpha{}_{[\mathscr{L}_{R_2}]}$ are equivalent; the only significant difference between the path-independent hierarchies for different bivalent fragments is how far they extend.

Given any syntactically specifiable fragment $\mathscr{L}_R$ for which bivalence can be assumed, we can easily get a larger fragment $\mathscr{L}_{R*}$, by allowing 'true' or 'satisfies' to appear as long as they are restricted to $\mathscr{L}_R$-formulas. So the hierarchy $\{D^\alpha{}_{[\mathscr{L}_{R*}]}\}$ is well-behaved for longer than the hierarchy $\{D^\alpha{}_{[\mathscr{L}]}\}$: it produces more genuine iterations of D, before turning to garbage. Since each fragment for which bivalence can be assumed can be extended in this way, we have a sequence of longer and longer path-independent hierarchies, each well-behaved until one reaches the "critical length" for that hierarchy.

But why restrict to fragments that can be assumed bivalent? Can't we extend the treatment to allow paths that assign definitions in the full $\mathscr{L}^+$? Indeed we can. However, here we need to tread with extreme care, because we are in the realm where classical reasoning is no longer appropriate; in particular, we are in the realm of König's paradox.

More fully, suppose we define $\mathscr{L}^+$-*path* in analogy with how we defined $\mathscr{L}$-*path* and $\mathscr{L}_R$-*path*. The definition is perfectly fine; however, it uses the notion of definability in $\mathscr{L}^+$, which is defined in terms of an unrestricted notion of truth-of; as a result, there is no reason to think that we can consistently assume excluded middle for claims of form 'p is an $\mathscr{L}^+$-path'. (Indeed, it is easily seen that the assumption of excluded middle would lead to König's paradox.) Given an arbitrary function p, we can also apply the same generating function Φ (which is definable in the 'true'-free fragment $\mathscr{L}$) to p, and we can show that

p is an $\mathscr{L}^+$-path ⊨ Φ(p) is a (path-dependent) hierarchy.[4]

And we can define a path-independent $\mathscr{L}^+$-hierarchy, analogously to our definitions of the path-independent $\mathscr{L}$-hierarchy and the path-independent $\mathscr{L}_R$-hierarchies for fragments $\mathscr{L}_R$. But we can't say that the path-independent $\mathscr{L}^+$-hierarchy goes up to "the smallest ordinal not definable in $\mathscr{L}^+$", because we saw back in Chapter 5 that it is inconsistent to assume that there is such an ordinal, and that the apparent argument for one turns on an illicit use of excluded middle. What we can say is that the path-independent $\mathscr{L}^+$-hierarchy is well-behaved only for ordinals that are hereditarily definable in $\mathscr{L}^+$. These are all countable, since $\mathscr{L}^+$ is; and of course any ordinal hereditarily definable in $\mathscr{L}$, or in the language that results by adding to $\mathscr{L}$ a truth or satisfaction predicate in the Tarski hierarchy, is also hereditarily definable in $\mathscr{L}^+$. But the question of exactly how far this $\mathscr{L}^+$-hierarchy is well-behaved is "fuzzy".

To put this without the impressionistic term 'fuzzy', call the $\mathscr{L}^+$-hierarchy *well-behaved at α* (or *non-trivial at α*) if True($\langle D^\alpha_{[\mathscr{L}^+]}(0=0)\rangle$) (or for sticklers about use and mention, if $\langle D^v_{[\mathscr{L}^+]}(0=0)\rangle$ is true of α). Then

⊨ ∀α(α is uncountable → ¬(the $\mathscr{L}^+$-hierarchy is well-behaved at α));

⊨ ∀α(α is hereditarily $\mathscr{L}$-definable → the $\mathscr{L}^+$-hierarchy is well-behaved at α);[5]

and

α is hereditarily $\mathscr{L}^+$-definable ⊨ the $\mathscr{L}^+$-hierarchy is well-behaved at α.

But it is *not* the case that

⊨ (the $\mathscr{L}^+$-hierarchy is well-behaved at α) ∨ ¬(the $\mathscr{L}^+$-hierarchy is well-behaved at α).

Indeed, the assumption of excluded middle for well-behavedness claims can be shown to lead to contradiction. Because of this, it makes no sense to talk of "the maximal segment of the ordinals throughout which $D^\alpha_{[\mathscr{L}^+]}$ is well-behaved"; that would enable us to define the first α for which it is

---

[4] Note that this is not in conditional form: it is a weak implication, not a strong one. For certain p, it may be "fuzzy" whether p is an $\mathscr{L}^+$-path (because of the dependence of this on questions of $\mathscr{L}^+$-definability), and "fuzzy" whether Φ(p) is a genuine hierarchy (because of the use of 'true' in the clause (Lim) in the definition of a hierarchy); and there is no reason to think that these "fuzzinesses" are sufficiently related for the conditional to hold.

[5] More generally,

$\mathscr{L}_R$ is a bivalent fragment of $\mathscr{L}^+$ ⊨ ∀α(α is hereditarily $\mathscr{L}_R$-definable → the $\mathscr{L}^+$-hierarchy is well-behaved at α).

22.2. HYPER-DETERMINATENESS: THE PROBLEM

Let us ignore the niceties of the previous section for a while, and speak loosely. Speaking in this loose fashion, the sequence of operators D^α gets stronger and stronger as α increases. This suggests defining a *hyper-determinately* operator: HA is to mean "Each sentence of form $D^\alpha A$ is true". And it would seem that this should obey the following two laws:

(1) $$\vDash HA \to A$$

(2) $$A \vDash HA.$$

The justification for (1) is clear: HA as defined includes $\text{True}(\langle DA\rangle)$ as an instance, and $\text{True}(\langle DA\rangle) \to A$ by Intersubstitutivity plus $DA \to A$. (Indeed, HA as defined has $\text{True}(\langle A\rangle)$ as an instance, so we don't even need $DA \to A$.) The justificaton for (2) seems almost as clear: HA is in effect the infinite conjunction of all the $D^\alpha A$, and we should be able to establish inductively that $A \vDash D^\alpha A$ holds for each α, and thus get $A \vDash HA$ by an infinite conjunction rule.

(1) and (2) would lead to paradox if we could assume "Excluded middle for H" (that is, $\vDash HA \lor \neg HA$); the argument for that should by now be familiar.[7] But that is perhaps not so big a deal, since it is not immediately obvious that "Excluded middle for H" should hold.

But there is an apparently weaker condition than "Excluded middle for H" that may well seem more compelling: the condition

(3) $$\vDash HA \to DHA.$$

The intuitive idea here is that H iterates D as far as it can be iterated; iterating it one more time should produce nothing new. But then we're in trouble, for (3) leads to paradox in combination with (1) and (2). Indeed, one doesn't even need the full strength of (3), one gets the paradox using only the still weaker

(3_w) $$\neg DHA \vDash \neg HA.$$

---

[6] For similar reasons, we can't talk of "the first ordinal not in any hierarchy of form $D_{[\mathscr{L}_R]}$ for some classical fragment $\mathscr{L}_R$ of $\mathscr{L}^+$", taking a classical fragment to be one throughout which excluded middle holds. For the claim that excluded middle holds throughout a given fragment $\mathscr{L}_R$ does not in general obey excluded middle (though of course it does in many special cases, such as when $\mathscr{L}_R$ is just $\mathscr{L}$, or is any member of the Tarski hierarchy over $\mathscr{L}$). The assumption of a first ordinal not in any such hierarchy in fact leads to contradiction, because it would enable us to include it in such a hierarchy.

[7] Let Q_H be the "Hyper-Liar", equivalent to $\neg HQ_H$. We have $\vDash HQ_H \to Q_H$ by (1), so $\vDash HQ_H \to \neg HQ_H$; so Excluded Middle for H would yield $\vDash \neg HQ_H$, hence $\vDash Q_H$, from which (2) yields $\vDash HQ_H$ and thus an inconsistency.

The argument: Let Q_H be the "Hyper-Liar", equivalent to $\neg HQ_H$. We have $\vDash HQ_H \to Q_H$ by (1), so $\vDash HQ_H \to \neg HQ_H$. (So far just like the argument using excluded middle, given in the preceding note.) But now by the laws for D, we have $\vDash \neg DHQ_H$. (3) or (3_w) then yields $\vDash \neg HQ_H$, from which we get $\vDash Q_H$; (2) then yields $\vDash HQ_H$, so $\vDash HQ_H \wedge \neg HQ_H$.

Actually, this argument doesn't even need to use the full strength of (2), but only the weaker principle

(2_w) $\quad\quad\quad\quad\quad\quad\quad A, \neg HA \vDash \bot;$

for prior to the step invoking (2) we'd established $\vDash \neg HQ_H$ and $\vDash Q_H$.

What's gone wrong? A preliminary point: in the logic of D I've adopted, (3) *isn't* weaker than excluded middle for H: since D always strictly lowers values other than **0** and **1**, we have $\vDash A \vee \neg A$ whenever we have $\vDash A \to DA$. I take this to show that the intuitive argument for (3) is suspect, though I suppose one might think that it shows that a failure of excluded middle for H is especially surprising. In any case, (3_w) genuinely is weaker than excluded middle, and the paradox uses only that; so (assuming for the moment that (1) and (2) or at least (2_w) are indeed unproblematic) we need only consider whether the intuitive argument makes a good case for (3_w).

How exactly is the intuitive argument for (3_w) to be spelled out? HA is the "infinite conjunction" of the $D^\alpha A$; how exactly are we supposed to get from $\neg D[\bigwedge_\alpha D^\alpha A]$ to $\neg \bigwedge_\alpha D^\alpha A$?

We might try to argue that (for any A) $\neg D[\bigwedge_\alpha D^\alpha A]$ should entail $\neg \bigwedge_\alpha DD^\alpha A$, i.e. $\neg \bigwedge_\alpha D^{\alpha+1} A$; this last is the negation of the "infinite conjunction" of the $D^\alpha A$ for *successor* α, which certainly entails the negation of the "infinite conjunction" of *all* the $D^\alpha A$. But why should $\neg D[\bigwedge_\alpha D^\alpha A]$ entail $\neg \bigwedge_\alpha DD^\alpha A$ (for arbitrary A)? This fails when α is restricted to the finite ordinals: $\neg D[\bigwedge_{\text{finite } \alpha} D^\alpha A]$ is $\neg D^{\omega+1} A$ and $\neg \bigwedge_{\text{finite } \alpha} DD^\alpha A$ is $\neg D^\omega A$, and we know that the former doesn't entail the latter. So why, exactly, should the inference hold when the restriction to the finite is removed?

Another way to try to spell out the argument for (3_w) is model-theoretic. Suppose $|||\neg DHA||| = \mathbf{1}$, i.e. $|||DHA||| = \mathbf{0}$. Then $|||HA||| \leq \mathbf{1/2}$. To get the conclusion, we need that $|||HA||| = \mathbf{0}$. So to argue for (3_w), we'd need that the "infinite conjunction" of the sentences $D^\alpha A$ (for all α and fixed A) can't have a non-zero value less than or equal to $\mathbf{1/2}$. But why should this be?

Despite these questions about the intuitive basis for (3_w), it turns out that on the definition of H suggested above, H *does* obey (3_w); it also obeys (3), and Excluded Middle for H. But it does these things only because on this definition, H is a trivial operator, whose application to any sentence at all yields a clear falsehood: we have $\vDash \neg HA$ for every A! (This doesn't lead to inconsistency, because (2) and (2_w) fail, despite the apparent argument above.) The reason that H as defined above leads to trouble, and the obvious attempt to revise the definition to cure the problem, will be given in the next section. It will turn out though that the cure is rather limited: in versions of the cure that are drastic enough to preserve (2) or even (2_w), any intuitive case for (3_w) is totally destroyed.

22.3. HYPER-DETERMINATENESS: THE SOLUTION

What the attempt at paradox in the previous section failed to take into account is that the process of trying to iterate D in a path-independent way eventually collapses; and collapses in a bad way. By saying that the process *collapses* I mean that past a certain point, all the D^α are equivalent to each other; that is certainly true, for instance, in the uncountable ordinals, given that there are only countably many sentences. By saying that it collapses *in a bad way* I mean that by the time that α is big enough for $D^{\alpha+1}$ to be equivalent to D^α, D^α is useless: it takes even clear truths into falsehoods. That is, for such large α, $\models \neg D^\alpha(0 = 0)$, and similarly for any other truth substituted for '0 = 0'. I explained why this "bad collapse" is inevitable in Section 22.1. So if we really were to define HA as an infinite conjunction of *all* the D^α, including those that don't correspond to genuine iterations of D, then it would be the trivial operator, turning every sentence to a clear falsehood.

The obvious attempt to restore paradox is to take HA not as the infinite conjunction of *all* the $D^\alpha A$, but as the infinite conjunction of all those *that correspond to genuine iterations of D*; that is, all those *for which the definition of D^α is well-behaved (non-trivial)*. In the rest of this section I will argue that there is no way to restore paradox by this route.

A. Warm-Up Arguments

I will first give two non-rigorous arguments, designed to incline you to be suspicious about any claim that such a re-defined H could breed paradox.

The first non-rigorous argument is supposed to show that if we re-define H as the conjunction of all the *well-behaved* iterations of D, then it is not itself a well-behaved iteration of D and so it is of no interest (and won't breed paradox since it doesn't satisfy (2_w)). The argument runs as follows:

> For any well-behaved iteration D^α, the successor $D^{\alpha+1}$ (i.e. DD^α) is certainly also a well-behaved iteration that strengthens D^α. So it seems that the conjunction of all the well-behaved iterations must be a limit "iteration" D^λ that occurs strictly *after* all the well-behaved ones. But then H, defined as the conjunction of all the well-behaved iterations, would not be a genuine iteration of D.

As I say, this argument is intended only as an intuitive warm-up to the serious discussion. It can't be taken entirely seriously, because it treats 'genuine iteration of D' as if it obeyed excluded middle, and the moral of Section 22.1 is that it can't be so treated—at least, not if the iterations of D are those given by the hierarchy $D_{[\mathscr{S}+]}$. Nonetheless, when we get to the serious discussion, we'll see that this intuitive argument isn't far off the mark: the proper conclusion will be not that the supposition that the conjunction of all the well-behaved iterations is itself well-behaved is *false*, but that it *leads to inconsistency*. (Without *reductio*, the latter does not entail the former.)

The second non-rigorous argument comes into play only if we assume, contrary to the first argument, that revising the definition of H to quantify over only the well-behaved ordinals results in a well-behaved (i.e. non-trivial) operator. The claim of the second argument is that this destroys whatever intuitive case there was for (3) and (3_w), and thus removes the paradox. The argument runs like this:

> The intuitive case was based on the thought that H iterates D as far as it can be iterated, so iterating it one more time should produce nothing new. But on the revised definition, H doesn't iterate D as far as it can be iterated, precisely because iterating it further would lead to triviality! Indeed, it seems that if DH is such a further iteration beyond those that don't lead to triviality, it is bound to be trivial. So on our assumption (contrary to the first argument) that H itself is non-trivial, DH is bound to be strictly stronger than H.

So much for the intuitive warm-up; let's now be more precise.

B. The Easy Case

We've seen that path-independent hierarchies are defined by quantifying over path-dependent hierarchies, and that they collapse to triviality for any ordinal for which there are no path-dependent hierarchies of that length. Where this collapse occurs depends on the resources allowed for defining the paths in the hierarchy.

The situation is clearest when we use only a clearly classical fragment $\mathscr{L}_R$ of $\mathscr{L}^+$ to define paths. In Section 22.1 I denoted the operators of the resultant path-independent hierarchy (obtained by quantifying over such paths) as $D^\alpha_{[\mathscr{L}_R]}$. We saw that these operators are well-behaved whenever α is less than the first ordinal not definable in $\mathscr{L}_R$ (which I'll call $\alpha_{\mathscr{L}_R}$); but that for α greater than or equal to $\alpha_{\mathscr{L}_R}$, $D^\alpha_{[\mathscr{L}_R]}$ maps every sentence into a clear falsehood. Suppose now that we define $H_{[\mathscr{L}_R]}A$ as "For all α less than $\alpha_{\mathscr{L}_R}$, $D^\alpha_{[\mathscr{L}_R]}$ is true". In this case, $H_{[\mathscr{L}_R]}$ is not a trivial predicate, nor is $DH_{[\mathscr{L}_R]}$: both satisfy (2), as well as (1). The "intuitive warm-up" arguments don't apply to $H_{[\mathscr{L}_R]}$, because $H_{[\mathscr{L}_R]}$ is not in the hierarchy $\{D^\alpha_{[\mathscr{L}_R]}\}$.

$H_{[\mathscr{L}_R]}$ is however equivalent to an operator in a longer hierarchy, that obtained by quantifying over paths defined in the classical fragment $\mathscr{L}_{R*}$ (in which 'true' or 'satisfies' can appear as long as they are restricted to $\mathscr{L}_R$-formulas). That hierarchy is well-behaved for longer, viz. up to the first ordinal not definable *in* $\mathscr{L}_{R*}$; and in it, the operator $D^{\alpha_{\mathscr{L}_R}}_{[\mathscr{L}_{R*}]}$ assigned to $\alpha_{\mathscr{L}_R}$ is just $H_{[\mathscr{L}_R]}$. The operator $D^{\alpha_{\mathscr{L}_R}+1}_{[\mathscr{L}_{R*}]}$ assigned to the successor of $\alpha_{\mathscr{L}_R}$ is $DH_{[\mathscr{L}_R]}$. Since the hierarchy $\{D^\alpha_{[\mathscr{L}_{R*}]}\}$ is well-behaved for ordinals that are hereditarily definable in $\mathscr{L}_{R*}$, this means that $DH_{[\mathscr{L}_R]}$ is strictly stronger than $H_{[\mathscr{L}_R]}$: (3_w) definitively fails for $H_{[\mathscr{L}_R]}$.

The failure of $H_{[\mathscr{L}_R]}$ to satisfy (3_w), for any clearly classical fragment $\mathscr{L}_R$, isn't at all surprising: it depends on the fact that the hierarchies based on classical fragments don't go as far as they can go, that is, on the fact that the classical fragment can be extended so as to accommodate new ordinals in a well-behaved manner.

C. The Hard Case

Now let's look at what happens when one allows use of the full language $\mathscr{L}^+$ in defining the paths that the path-independent hierarchy quantifies over.

This is the case that the warm-up arguments were intended for, and it seems at first blush that the first one, for the triviality of $H_{[\mathscr{L}^+]}$, is intuitively compelling. (The second warm-up argument assumed the failure of the first, so the issue of it doesn't even arise.) How could the hyper-determinately operator $H_{[\mathscr{L}^+]}$ fail to be trivial? After all, shouldn't it coincide with an iteration of D of length longer than all those definable in $\mathscr{L}^+$? If so, then since there are no $\mathscr{L}^+$-paths that long, such an iteration is bound to be trivial. Again, though, the reasoning is somewhat suspect: it is in the vicinity of the reasoning that leads to König's paradox. So let us be more careful.

A more careful presentation requires us to distinguish two different formulations of $H_{[\mathscr{L}^+]}$. The most natural is $H_\to$: $H_\to A$ is defined as

$$\forall \alpha[\text{the } \mathscr{L}^+\text{-hierarchy is well-behaved at } \alpha \to \text{True}(\langle D^\alpha_{[\mathscr{L}^+]}A\rangle)];$$

or more rigorously,

$$\forall \alpha[\text{the } \mathscr{L}^+\text{-hierarchy is well-behaved at } \alpha \to \langle D^v_{[\mathscr{L}^+]}A\rangle \text{ is true of } \alpha].$$

This is, unfortunately, an extremely complicated operator to rigorously analyze, given the complexity of the definition of the $\mathscr{L}^+$-hierarchy. (Much of the complexity stems from issues discussed in Field 2007 but skipped over here, such as the precise definition of the function Φ.) It will be useful to begin with a similar operator $H_\supset$, which is just like $H_\to$ except for having $\supset$ instead of $\to$ as the main connective inside the quantifier. (Obviously the complexity of the antecedent and consequent are the same as with $H_\to$, but we don't need as much detail about their behavior to figure out how $H_\supset$ will behave.) Because of the fact that $\supset$ is such a poor surrogate for 'if ... then' outside of the context of excluded middle, the situation is not quite what we'd intuitively expect: $H_\supset$ is not a trivial operator in quite the sense I've defined. But it is almost as bad.

More fully, I will first argue that (2) fails very badly for $H_\supset$: for any sentence whatever, even one that is clearly valid, $H_\supset A$ is "at best fuzzy". The reason is clear: $H_\supset A$ is

$$\forall \alpha[\text{the } \mathscr{L}^+\text{-hierarchy is well-behaved at } \alpha \supset \langle D^v_{[\mathscr{L}^+]}A\rangle \text{ is true of } \alpha];$$

that is,

$$\forall \alpha[\text{the } \mathscr{L}^+\text{-hierarchy is not well-behaved at } \alpha \vee \langle D^v_{[\mathscr{L}^+]}A\rangle \text{ is true of } \alpha].$$

But consider any α for which it's "fuzzy" whether the $\mathscr{L}^+$-hierarchy is well-behaved at α; or to be more precise, for which the claim 'the $\mathscr{L}^+$-hierarchy is well-behaved at α' has value other than **0** and **1** in a given model. For such α, '$\langle D^v_{[\mathscr{L}+]}A\rangle$ is true of α' can't have value **1**, since obviously

$\langle D^v_{[\mathscr{L}+]}A\rangle$ is true of $\alpha \vDash$ the $\mathscr{L}^+$-hierarchy is well-behaved at α.

So the universal quantification must have value less than **1**; that is, for *every* sentence A, even '$0 = 0$', $|||H_\supset A||| < \mathbf{1}$.

It's clear, then, that $H_\supset$ is not a useful hyper-determinateness operator. But if its gross violation of (2) weren't enough, it also fails to serve the purpose for which hyper-determinateness was wanted, viz. to ensure that $DH_\supset$ is no stronger than $H_\supset$! We can see this by considering the $H_\supset$-Liar: a sentence $Q_{H_\supset}$ equivalent to $\neg H_\supset (\text{True}(\langle Q_{H_\supset}\rangle))$. In other words, $Q_{H_\supset}$ says:

$\neg\forall\alpha$[the $\mathscr{L}^+$-hierarchy is well-behaved at $\alpha \supset \langle D^v_{[\mathscr{L}+]}Q_{H_\supset}\rangle$ is true of α],

that is,

$\exists\alpha$[the $\mathscr{L}^+$-hierarchy is well-behaved at $\alpha \wedge \langle D^v_{[\mathscr{L}+]}Q_{H_\supset}\rangle$ is not true of α].

The first thing to note is that $Q_{H_\supset}$ can't be valid: if it were, then there would have to be a specific α for which it is valid; but this would mean that there would have to be some α for which both the claim that the hierarchy is well-behaved at α and the $D_{[\mathscr{L}+]}$ formalization of the claim $\neg D^\alpha Q_{H_\supset}$ are both valid; and these two claims together are clearly incompatible with $Q_{H_\supset}$ being valid.

But if $Q_{H_\supset}$ isn't valid, neither is $\neg H_\supset Q_{H_\supset}$: they are equivalent. And yet $\neg DH_\supset Q_{H_\supset}$ *is* valid: by the basic laws for D, it follows from $H_\supset Q_{H_\supset} \to \neg H_\supset Q_{H_\supset}$, which is equivalent to $H_\supset Q_{H_\supset} \to Q_{H_\supset}$, which is beyond doubt. So $DH_\supset$ is strictly stronger than $H_\supset$. To put it model-theoretically, we've found a sentence A for which $|||DH_\supset A||| = \mathbf{0}$ and yet $|||H_\supset A||| > \mathbf{0}$. (This accords with the second intuitive warm-up argument.)

We see then that $H_\supset$ fails its intended purpose *doubly*: it does not preclude strengthening by D, and it is useless in that it is illegitimate to assert even of clear truths that they are "hyper-determinately true" in the given sense.

Let's now turn to $H_\to$. As I've said, this is much harder to analyze, but I think it has the main defect of $H_\supset$: $|||H_\to A||| < \mathbf{1}$ for every A, even clear truths. I think it may well even be the case that $|||H_\to A|||$ is **0** for every A. (In that case, of course, there would be no problem with (3_w), or with Excluded Middle for $H_\to$!)

I have to admit that I don't have a rigorous argument that $|||H_\to A||| < \mathbf{1}$ for every A, but I sketch what I take to be reason to think so in a footnote.[8] One

---

[8] Why do I think that $|||H_\to A||| < \mathbf{1}$ for every A? Suppose this weren't so; then for *every* ordinal α, including those for which

(FUZ) $\mathbf{0} < |||$the $\mathscr{L}^+$-hierarchy is well-behaved at $\alpha||| < \mathbf{1}$,

thing can be said with complete certainty though: *if* there are any A at all for which $|||H_\to A|||$ is 1, then $DH_\to$ is a genuine strengthening of $H_\to$. Why is that? First, (1) clearly holds, so if $|||H_\to A|||$ is 1 then A is 1. Second, $H_\to$ is a defined operator in the language, and is thus value functional; together with the first point, this means that if there are any A for which $|||H_\to A|||$ is 1, then $|||H_\to A|||$ is 1 whenever $|||A|||$ is 1. That is, (2) holds. But we've already seen that in this semantics (1) and (2) are incompatible with (3) and (3_w), given the strong consistency proof. So:

Either $H_\to$ is a quasi-trivial operator, one for which $|||H_\to A||| < 1$ for every A, or else it fails to achieve the aim of getting an "unstrengthenable" determinateness operator. (It may have *both* defects, as $H_\neg$ does.)

---

we'd have to have that for clear truths A

$|||\text{the } \mathscr{L}^+\text{-hierarchy is well-behaved at } \alpha||| \leq |||\langle D^\nu_{[\mathscr{L}^+]}A\rangle \text{ is true of } \alpha|||.$

Given the method of defining the path-independent $D^\nu_{[\mathscr{L}^+]}$, this says that for *every* α,

$|||\text{the } \mathscr{L}^+\text{-hierarchy is well-behaved at } \alpha||| \leq |||\exists p(p \text{ is an } \mathscr{L}^+\text{-path of length greater than } \alpha \wedge \text{ the result of applying } [\Phi(p)](\alpha) \text{ to } \langle A\rangle \text{ is true})|||,$

i.e.

(*) $|||\text{the } \mathscr{L}^+\text{-hierarchy is well-behaved at } \alpha||| \leq \bigsqcup_p\{|||p \text{ is an } \mathscr{L}^+\text{-path of length greater than } \alpha||| \sqcap |||D^\alpha_{(p)}A|||\}.$

I'll now argue, somewhat impressionistically I'm afraid, that this is implausible.

Consider for instance the smallest α for which $|||\text{the } \mathscr{L}^+\text{-hierarchy is well-behaved at } \alpha||| < 1$. (Model-theoretic claims obey excluded middle, so this is unproblematic.) Call this α_0. Then for any function p on an initial segment of ordinals (with limit length) that includes α_0, it is "at best fuzzy" (i.e., "fuzzy" or clearly false) whether p is an $\mathscr{L}^+$-path, and hence whether the restriction of p to the smallest limit after α_0 is an $\mathscr{L}^+$-path. It is clear that any such p must assign to α_0 a formula $B(u)$ that does not clearly define α_0; either

(i) $\qquad\qquad\qquad\qquad\qquad |||B(\alpha_0)||| < 1,$

or

(ii) $\qquad\qquad\qquad$ for some β other than α_0, $|||B(\beta)||| > 0$,

or both. (We can't rule out (ii) by restricting to paths which assign formulas with "uniqueness conditions", i.e. "$\Theta(v) \wedge (\forall u \neq v)\neg\Theta(u)$": for these paths exploit the full resources of $\mathscr{L}^+$, where we don't have excluded middle; and without excluded middle, "uniqueness clauses" have little effect.) It's also clear that if $|||B(\beta)||| > 0$ for some $\beta < \alpha_0$, then $|||\text{ p is an }\mathscr{L}^+\text{-path}|||$ would be 0; such p wouldn't contribute to the value of the right hand side of (*). So in the cases that matter, either (i) or

(ii*) $\qquad\qquad\qquad |||B(\alpha_0)||| < 1$, or for some $\beta > \alpha_0$, $|||B(\beta)||| > 0$,

or both. I suspect it will be hard to find formulas $B(u)$ for which (i) holds without (ii*). And when (ii*) holds (with or without (i)), the claim $D^\alpha_{(p)}A$ (that the result of applying $[\Phi(p)](\alpha)$ to $\langle A\rangle$ is true) "says to non-zero degree that $D^\beta A$"; but since $\beta > \alpha_0$, this claim presumably has a very low value, either less than or incomparable to $|||\text{the } \mathscr{L}^+\text{-hierarchy is well-behaved at } \alpha|||$.

That's just the case for α_0. For $|||H_\to A|||$ to be 1, we'd need (*) to hold for *every* ordinal satisfying (FUZ); and as α increases beyond α_0 but is still "in the lower part of the fuzzy region", it seems to become harder and harder for this to be so.

I'm virtually certain that the first disjunct is correct (and probably the second as well); but suppose for the sake of argument that *only* the second disjunct is the case, i.e. that $|||H_\to A|||$ is **1** for every A but $DH_\to$ strengthens $H_\to$. In that case, $DH_\to$ is perfectly well-behaved too, and we can continue to a new hierarchy $\{D^\alpha H_\to\}$, continuing as long as this is well-behaved (and using the truth predicate to define the limit iterations by paths of definitions, using the same tricks as before). By the same argument as before, this new hierarchy never reaches a fixed point until it trivializes, and the question of where it does that is "fuzzy". So now we have a "doubly fuzzy" hierarchy: after the initial region of fuzziness in which the D^αs trivialize, we achieve the clarity of $H_\to$, $DH_\to$, $DDH_\to$, ..., but eventually we reach a region where it's fuzzy whether the $D^\alpha H_\to$ are trivial. Perhaps we could go further, and at this point define a non-trivial notion of "hyper-hyper-determinateness". And so on.

So *even if $H_\to$ is well-behaved* (i.e. $|||H_\to A|||$ can have the value **1**), it wouldn't affect anything important. The crucial point would survive: no amount of iteration, or conjunction or quantification over what has been iterated, can achieve a useful operator that is immune to further strengthening by D.

22.4. EXPANDING THE LANGUAGE?

The preceding sections have been largely devoted to understanding what happens when you define hyper-determinateness in the language $\mathscr{L}^+$. The discussion in those sections is also indirectly relevant to another issue: whether we could *expand the language* to include a "super-determinateness predicate" that behaves as we might have *hoped* 'hyper-determinate truth' would behave.

I don't really think that this is a promising suggestion: it's something like suggesting that because the ordinary notion of natural numbers has a surprising property (say having an essentially incomplete theory), we should add a new notion of natural numbers that avoids that defect. The "defect" comes not from an expressive limitation of the language, it is intrinsic to the notion. But let's look at the suggestion in more detail: in general terms in this section, and in specific form in the next two.

I should emphasize at the start that I do not contend that the language $\mathscr{L}^+$, or any other language, is "expressively complete" in the sense of being able to define every notion that could ever be made intelligible. Even if (as I've imagined) the full resources of present mathematics were encoded into $\mathscr{L}^+$ (and present physics, chemistry, psychology, etc. too), there is always room for people to invent new concepts not definable in the pre-existing language. Conceivably there could be additions to the language that would make more ordinals hereditarily definable than are hereditarily definable now, which would expand the extent of the hierarchy of D^α operators. Or rather, it would enable us to define a modified hierarchy that is well-behaved for longer.⁹ But this would affect nothing substantial: the hyper-determinateness operator ($H_\supset$ or $H_\to$) defined from that extended hierarchy would have all the features of the one defined in $\mathscr{L}^+$: it would not be the well-behaved non-extendable operator that the proponent of hyper-determinateness was hoping for.

But can't we imagine a maximal possible language, in which all possible iterations of D are expressible, and a hyper-determinateness operator defined from that? I'm not sure we can coherently imagine this, but suppose we can. It still wouldn't affect the basic point: even there, the hyper-determinateness operator would be ill-behaved. For its ill-behavedness results from the following facts:

1. Any version of the process of iterating D eventually becomes ill-behaved.

2. If we use only clearly bivalent resources to define the iteration process, there will be a clear point at which the process gives out; we can always go beyond that point by using broader clearly bivalent resources.

3. If we try to talk about "the maximal extent reachable by an iteration process defined from clearly bivalent resources" we are going beyond clearly bivalent resources: we must be, since otherwise by 2 we could introduce still broader clearly bivalent resources than the allegedly maximal ones.

4. While use of such not clearly bivalent resources (e.g. a general truth or satisfaction predicate) in defining the iteration process is perfectly legitimate, it results in its being "fuzzy" exactly where the breakdown in the iteration process defined by such resources occurs.

5. If one naively defines 'hyper-determinately' in terms of *iterating forever*, it is bound to be completely trivial, whatever the iteration process, because of 1 above. If one, more reasonably, defines it in terms of *iterating for as long as iteration is well-behaved*, then the result depends on the nature of the iteration process employed:

   (a) If one uses only clearly bivalent resources in the iteration process, then by quantifying over the well-behaved members of the process one gets a perfectly well-behaved notion of hyper-determinateness, one that is more powerful than any of the D^α *defined by that process*. But it won't be a "maximal determinateness operator", it will still be strengthenable by D, because that process itself wasn't maximal (by 3 above). This is true not just in $\mathscr{L}^+$, but in any expansion of it; it depends not on the vocabulary of the language but on the nature of the iteration process.

   (b) If one goes beyond clearly bivalent resources in the iteration process, such as an unrestricted truth or satisfaction predicate, then because of the "fuzziness" in 4 above, quantifying over the well-behaved members of the process

---

⁹ An alternative kind of expansion, that doesn't work in quite the way here contemplated, will be discussed in Section 22.5

is ill-behaved. Again this is true not just in $\mathscr{L}^+$, but in any expansion of it; it depends not on the vocabulary of the language but on a quantification over an "intrinsically fuzzy" domain. (Quantification is something like infinite conjunction; so quantification over an "intrinsically fuzzy" domain is something like conjunction in which it's "intrinsically fuzzy" what the conjuncts are. It's hardly surprising that this sometimes produces anomalous results! Indeed, we saw such anomalies earlier, in Section 21.4)

In short, the fact that none of the defined notions of hyper-determinacy meet the joint expectations of well-behavedness and maximality isn't due to a limitation of the language $\mathscr{L}^+$, it is due to the nature of the notion ("remains true when prefixed by any well-behaved iteration of 'determinately'"). The problem was with the expectations: they result from a failure to think through the consequences of the definition. (Part of the point of the "intuitive warm-up arguments" in the previous section was to make clear that these expectations were suspect independent of the details of the paracomplete theory.)

22.5. HIGHER-ORDER RESOURCES

In a recent paper, Rayo and Welch (2007) suggest expanding the language to include higher order resources. (Their explicit goal isn't to define a limit to the iterations of D, but one of the things I will look at is whether their proposal would serve that goal.)

The centerpiece of the Rayo and Welch paper is a technical result: that one can use higher order resources, that are intelligible but are not available in the ground language $\mathscr{L}$, to carry out an analog of the model-theoretic construction of Section 16.2. This analog construction involves not ordinary models with sets as their domains, but a kind of extended model defined using the higher order resources; so "the real universe" can be a model in the extended sense. And taking it to be the intended model, their construction defines what it is for a sentence of $\mathscr{L}^+$ ($\mathscr{L}$ with 'true' added) to have "real world value **1**", as opposed to value **1** relative to a model that interprets the quantifiers as restricted.

Rayo and Welch are concerned that their higher order quantifiers not be understood as ranging over special entities not in the range of the first order quantifiers. (Any such entities would have to be set-like in nature but not in the range of the first-order quantifiers; and yet the first-order quantifiers were supposed to range over *all* sets and set-like entities.) To this end, they insist that no resources beyond second order logic are needed to carry out the construction, and appeal to Boolos's (1985) well-known view that second order logic is to be interpreted as not quantifying over special entities but in terms of plural quantification. While I'm not fully clear on the details of how the construction is to be done without going beyond the second order, I'll take it for granted that they are right.

What exactly is the philosophical significance of their technical result? Before turning to this question, I'd like to emphasize that in a sense, the language $\mathscr{L}^+$ already contains higher order resources that go beyond what is available in first order set theory. The *ground* language $\mathscr{L}$ doesn't contain higher order resources (only first order set theory). But in adding a 'true of' predicate one in effect adds a certain kind of property quantification (as is evident from Section 20.2): for the claim that the parameterized formula $A(x; o_1, \ldots, o_n)$ is true of o serves the same purposes as the claim that the property $\lambda x A(x; o_1, \ldots, o_n)$ is instantiated by o. (The effective equivalence between higher order resources and truth-of or satisfaction predicates has been frequently noted by Charles Parsons: e.g. in Parsons 1974b.) As in the case of plural quantification, this involves no addition to the ontology, but now for a different reason: this time, it's because instead of actually adding properties one uses property-surrogates (viz., parameterized formulas), and these were already in the ontology of $\mathscr{L}$. (One also employs no new ideology beyond the 'true of' predicate of $\mathscr{L}^+$.)

The kind of higher order resources one gets from a 'true of' predicate depends of course on the laws governing that predicate; for instance, a stratified classical truth predicate yields a predicative higher order logic (i.e. ramified type theory). In the case of the truth predicate employed in the theory of Parts III and IV, the "property theory" we get isn't divided into orders (e.g. we have a property of being a property); still, it would be possible to develop within it a sub-theory postulating only second-order properties that are instantiated only by non-properties, third-order properties instantiated only by second-order properties, and so on. If we do this, we get what might be called a *quasi-impredicative higher order logic*: there are no predicativity restrictions on the comprehension schema, but properties that are defined predicatively have special status. Their special status is that claims about which such properties there are and what instantiates them are guaranteed to obey excluded middle, whereas this is not in general so for impredicatively defined properties.[10] (The higher-order logic we get by this means does not obey extensionality, but it is obvious how to define an equivalence relation that behaves like identity for second order properties; indeed this can to some extent be carried over to properties that can coherently be ascribed higher levels.)

So the higher order apparatus that Rayo and Welch are employing goes beyond $\mathscr{L}^+$ only if it includes impredicative comprehension *and employs bivalence in connection with it*. Rayo and Welch do implicitly take their apparatus to go beyond $\mathscr{L}^+$ in this way: in order to mimic the inductive construction of Section 16.2 at the "real world" level to get a notion of "real world value 1", they must assume

---

[10] In Chapter 20 I pointed out that in the full property theory, *being a property* can be assumed to obey excluded middle. But excluded middle is illegitimate for *being a property of a given order*, as I've defined that: consider the property Z of *either being a horse or being such that the Russell property instantiates itself.*

impredicative comprehension;[11] and so in taking for granted that every sentence either has "real world value 1" or doesn't, they go beyond what is available in $\mathscr{L}^+$. Since they don't go beyond bivalent impredicative constructions of second order, and they interpret these as plural quantifications, one might call what is being assumed Bivalent Impredicative Pluralese.

I myself am inclined to be suspicious of Bivalent Impredicative Pluralese when applied to "pluralities" unrestricted in rank. (When applied to "pluralities" of bounded rank it is harmless since it can then be interpreted as quantification over a set, and hence as not really going beyond $\mathscr{L}^+$.) There is no reason to think that impredicative plural quantifiers might engender contradictions; but we've already seen cases where excluded middle is somewhat suspect independent of any worry about contradictions. (For instance, I argued in Part I that there is a certain appeal to restricting excluded middle for the predicate 'Russell was old at N nanoseconds of age'; but there was no worry that adhering to excluded middle in this case would engender contradictions. Perhaps more to the present point, there is no worry about getting into contradiction by assuming that either the Truth-Teller is true or it isn't; but few who would restrict excluded middle for the Liar sentence would assume it for the Truth-Teller.) In the case of impredicative "pluralities", the worry about excluded middle is somewhat similar to the worry in the case of the Truth-Teller: answering such questions as whether a given object is part of the plurality can get one into a vicious circle. (If "pluralities" or properties were just *sets*, such circularity would not be worrisome, on either a platonist view of sets or a fictionalist view that accepts the platonist picture as a good fiction. But "pluralities" or properties are supposed to be very different from sets: this is what justifies their not being in the range of the first order quantifiers.)

These brief remarks are obviously not intended as an adequate discussion of a big issue, so let me put my doubts about Bivalent Impredicative Pluralese aside. What would be the consequence of recognizing as legitimate a kind of impredicative plural quantification that obeys excluded middle unrestrictedly? The consequence would be that the construction alluded to in Section 16.2 would only be a warm-up exercise to what we really need, since it applies only to what is by hypothesis an expressively limited language. What we'd really need, on this hypothesis, is to show that a truth predicate could be added to the language of *(bivalent impredicative) second order* set theory in a conservative fashion. My hunch is that the kind of construction I give might be somehow generalized to

---

[11] In particular, it is used in the theory of the "long well-orderings" discussed in Section 5 of their paper. (These are pluralities of ordered pairs, and their length can be much longer than the order type of all ordinals. The simplest such "well-orderings" can be defined from ordinary sets by predicative second order formulas, but Rayo and Welch require the use of much more complicated ones definable only by impredicative second order formulas, and they employ full classical reasoning in connection with these.)

the second order context (using plural quantifiers in the metalinguistic part of the object language), but I'll leave it to those who favor Bivalent Impredicative Pluralese to confirm or refute this.[12]

What would the effect be on the hierarchy of determinateness operators? We would still have a hierarchy, it's just that it would extend slightly further before collapsing, in almost exactly the way that the addition of new large cardinal axioms would result in its extension. It would extend because the higher order apparatus would allow more countable ordinals to be (clearly) definable. As a result, certain sentences in $\mathscr{L}^+$ that can never be declared $\neg D^\alpha$-True for any α in the $\mathscr{L}^+$-hierarchy might be declared $\neg D^\beta$-True for a β in the expanded Pluralese-hierarchy. But the expanded Pluralese hierarchy would still have no ultimate member: there is no more a hyper-determinateness predicate if Pluralese is the ground language than there is if $\mathscr{L}^+$ is. As far as I can see, recognizing (Bivalent Impredicative) Pluralese would change nothing of significance.[13]

22.6. SUPER-DETERMINATENESS

Suppose that we forget about trying to define a notion of hyper-determinateness in terms of the iteration of D, even in an expansion of $\mathscr{L}^+$; instead, let's consider introducing a primitive predicate S of super-determinate truth.[14] The idea is to

---

[12] The Rayo–Welch paper has little bearing one way or other on this: they are talking only about using a metalanguage with plural quantifiers to give a meta-theory for a *narrower* language that doesn't contain them.

[13] The Rayo–Welch paper raises other interesting issues. For instance, they assume (i) that a set theoretic definition of 'has value 1' for sentences in the language $\mathscr{L}_a^+$ obtained by adding a truth predicate to an arithmetic ground language would define a genuine designatedness predicate for $\mathscr{L}_a^+$; and that by analogy, (ii) a Pluralese definition of 'has value 1' for sentences in the full language $\mathscr{L}^+$ would define a genuine designatedness predicate for $\mathscr{L}^+$, one which is bivalent. Obviously the bivalence claim turns on the assumed bivalence of Impredicative Pluralese, about which I'm skeptical. But I'm also skeptical of (i), and of the part of (ii) not involving bivalence. It isn't as if the *only* obstacle to thinking of a model-theoretic construction within set theory as representing "genuine designatedness" for a language is that models of the sort discussed in set theory have their quantifiers restricted to a proper part of reality. That may be the only obstacle when the language is classical; but there is an independent and more important obstacle when the language is non-classical, which is that (as argued in Chapter 5) no model explained in classical terms can faithfully represent a non-classical reality. To put it picturesquely, a model explained in classical terms (even if many-valued) inevitably draws lines; whereas the central idea of the nonclassical picture I've been presenting is that in the case of many predicates, plausibly including 'old' and certainly including 'true', there are no lines to be drawn.

Of course, even if their claims (i) and (ii) were correct, there would still be no "real world designatedness" predicate for the language that results from adding 'true' to Pluralese.

[14] Why a predicate instead of an operator? An operator Ω would do as well, *if we assume that the truth predicate continues to behave naively when applied to sentences containing* Ω, for in that case we can define a predicate S from Ω and 'True' that is guaranteed to obey laws corresponding to those we impose on the operator. (S($\langle A \rangle$) would just be Ω(True($\langle A \rangle$)), or equivalently, True($\langle \Omega A \rangle$).) But depending on what laws are proposed for the added operator Ω, the proof that naive truth can be added in a conservative fashion may not carry over to a language with S; it is to avoid having to worry about this that I proposed adding the predicate directly.

simply take it as part of the concept of super-determinate truth that it obeys the main laws for determinate truth, but also is a maximal notion:

(1) $\vDash S(\langle A \rangle) \to A$
(2) $A \vDash S(\langle A \rangle)$
(or at least(2_w), $A, \neg S(\langle A \rangle) \vDash \bot$)
(3) $\vDash S(\langle A \rangle) \to DA$
(or at least(3_w), $\neg DA \vDash \neg S(\langle A \rangle)$; or to restate it without using D, $A \to \neg A \vDash \neg S(\langle A \rangle)$)[15]
(4) $\vDash S(\langle A \rangle) \to S(\langle S(\langle A \rangle) \rangle)$
(or at least(4_w), $\neg S(\langle S(\langle A \rangle) \rangle) \vDash \neg S(\langle A \rangle)$).

Well, we can postulate these things all we like, just as we can postulate the naive truth theory together with classical logic; postulation is no guarantee against inconsistency. And it is easy to see that these postulates *are* inconsistent, *quite independent of any assumptions about truth*: applying (3_w) to $S(\langle A \rangle)$ and then applying (4_w), we get $\neg DS(\langle A \rangle) \vDash \neg S(\langle A \rangle)$; and from this and (1) and (2) we get essentially the same inconsistency noted for hyper-determinateness in Section 22.2. To set out the inconsistency more explicitly, let Q_S be equivalent to $\neg S(\langle Q_S \rangle)$. Using (1) and this equivalence, $\vDash S(\langle Q_S \rangle) \to \neg S(\langle Q_S \rangle)$; so by ($3_w$), $\vDash \neg S(\langle S(\langle Q_S \rangle) \rangle)$; so by ($4_w$), $\vDash \neg S(\langle Q_S \rangle)$, and so by the equivalence again, $\vDash Q_S$; and the last two lead to absurdity by (2_w).

The argument, I repeat, doesn't use the notion of truth: the "truth-like" assumptions needed for paradox are built into the intuitive postulates for the predicate S. I don't doubt that these postulates might be so central to someone's intuitive understanding of super-determinate truth as to be "part of his concept"; but if so then his concept is defective and needs to be replaced. And any attempt to justify the postulates in terms of iteration (or well-behaved iteration) of a decently behaved determinately operator fails: it either fails to meet (2_w) or it fails to meet (4_w).

My preferred route would be to live with a notion of determinate truth that violates (4_w). In that case, the prefix 'super-' is inappropriate, and nothing much is gained over the notions of determinate truth available in the language.[16] But let's see if there are attractive alternatives that would restore consistency while keeping (4_w).

I don't think that a proposal to weaken (1) or to weaken (3_w) would have any appeal: a concept of super-determinate truth that doesn't entail determinate

---

[15] (1) is redundant given the full (3), but not given (3_w).
[16] Indeed, as it stands we could then take S to just be the ordinary determinate truth predicate: determinate truth satisfies (1)–(3). We could remedy this by buttressing (3), to say $\vDash S(\langle A \rangle) \to D^\alpha A$ *for a for which the iteration is legitimate*. Whether the italicized clause could be made precise in a way that would force S to be stronger than all the legitimate iterations and yet not to collapse is a question I will not pursue; but even if the answer is positive, S would not be a predicate of an essentially different nature than the D^α.

truth seems of little interest! (It's worth noting that completely abandoning (3_w) would be especially uninteresting, since (1), (2) and (4) are compatible with S being just the truth predicate, which is already in the language. To avoid such trivialization, we'd need a weakened form of (3_w), such as the restriction of (3_w) or (3) to sentences not containing S. But it seems unlikely that we'd want to make such a restriction: if for instance the idea were that no sentence containing 'S' can be super-determinately true, there would be no need to weaken (1) or (3), since they would hold vacuously for sentences containing 'S', as well as continuing to hold for sentences not containing 'S'.) I conclude that the only initially appealing alternative to restricting (4_w) is restricting (2_w).

Restricting (2_w) would be intolerable if the "determinately true" predicate S were defined in $\mathscr{L}^+$ in the obvious way, from a determinateness operator Ω and a truth predicate. (See note 14.) For operators in $\mathscr{L}^+$ must be value-functional in the semantics of Section 17.1, and so the predicate S would have to be as well; and so any failure of (2_w) and hence of (2) would mean that even clear truths failed to be super-determinate. But since we're considering a predicate S that isn't defined in $\mathscr{L}^+$, we can simply say that the semantics of Section 17.1 doesn't apply to it.

What would the proposal to weaken (2_w) but keep the remaining principles amount to? If we look at the argument at the end of the paragraph that began this section, we see that keeping the principles other than (2_w) would require saying that the "super-Liar sentence" Q_S is both provable and not super-determinately true: we have Q_S and $\neg S(\langle Q_S\rangle)$ together. There is no obvious inconsistency here, if we give up (2_w). Doing this has a bit of the flavor of the gap theories of Chapter 7, but instead of truth value gaps we have "super-determinateness gaps": sentences neither super-determinately true nor super-determinately false. One key defect of the theories of Chapter 7 is avoided or at least lessened: the proposed theory doesn't assert its own untruth, but merely its own lack of super-determinate truth, which seems less bad. Moreover, the theory contains a truth-predicate that obeys the full Intersubstitutivity Principle, at least as applied to sentences not containing 'super-determinately true'; and perhaps this Intersubstitutivity proof could be extended to the full language with S.

However, I doubt that this approach is ultimately attractive.

First, the fact that for some sentences that we believe, we also believe that they aren't super-determinately true seems to indicate that super-determinateness isn't a goal of belief, so why is it of any interest? Indeed, not enough has been said about the concept of super-determinateness to make it clear what is intended. For instance, (1), (3) and (4) are compatible with S being false of everything, or of everything not containing the name 'Dick Cheney'. Such obviously unwanted interpretations could be ruled out by requiring some restricted form of (2_w) or (2): for instance, requiring that they hold for sentences that don't contain the predicate S.[17] But even so, it isn't clear that we have a clear grasp of the intended notion. And to repeat, the fact that the proposal requires that we believe sentences that we believe not to be super-determinately true seems to suggest that whatever super-determinate truth means, it isn't a notion that we should care that much about.

Second, from what has been said so far there is no obvious guarantee that application of the notion of truth to sentences containing 'super-determinate' won't breed new paradoxes of truth, given that those sentences aren't in the language $\mathscr{L}^+$ for which the conservativeness proof applies. Unless we can prove that 'True' can be made to satisfy Intersubstitutivity *even as applied to sentences containing the new predicate S*, we may be forced back into one of the theories from Part II that we'd thought we'd gotten beyond.

Third, the behavior of the super-determinateness predicate seems in any case odd. We've already seen that the "super-Liar" Q_S is going to be derivable, along with the claim that it isn't superdeterminately true. But if Q_S is derivable, so are DQ_S, DDQ_S, and so on. (This assumes that the rule of D-Introduction still applies to sentences containing 'S', but it's hard to see why that shouldn't be so given how D was defined: it just amounts to the claim that from A we can validly infer $\neg(A \to \neg A)$.) So "for each legitimate iteration" we have $\vDash D^\alpha Q_S$; but we also have $\vDash \neg S(\langle Q_S \rangle)$? It looks as if S can't mean what it was intuitively supposed to mean.

Fourth, the motivation for a notion of super-determinateness was supposed to be that it would put an end to those annoying hierarchies that have no limit. But the example just given shows that it doesn't really do so: since for each legitimate iteration, $\vDash D^\alpha Q_S$, but also $\vDash \neg S(\langle Q_S \rangle)$, we have a never-ending hierarchy that can't be broken by S. The same line of thinking that led to the super-determinateness predicate S thus leads to a notion S* according to which $\vDash S^*(\langle Q_S \rangle)$. I won't pursue the question of what kind of laws might be proposed for this new S*, nor what should be said about the Liar-like sentence Q_{S^*} that it leads to. Besides the laws for S* alone, there would be questions about how it interacts with S; and we'd need to consider paradoxes involving both notions together. Already the situation looks very complicated; and I'm not sure that in the end we could rest with just these two predicates S and S*, we might need an infinite battery of them. Each would need to be a primitive predicate, and the whole thing seems as if it is bound to be far less appealing than the much simpler hierarchy of iterations of the single determinacy operator.

The upshot of all this is that while it is initially tempting to expand the language to include a super-determinateness predicate, it is far harder to live with one than to live without one. We should just say 'no'.

---

[17] Actually this particular restriction is unavailable if the goal is to avoid restricting (4) and (4_w): for those, together with the claim that sentences containing 'S' are never superdeterminately true, imply that *nothing* is superdeterminately true.

23
Determinateness, Stratification, and Revenge

23.1. STRATIFIED TRUTH V. ITERATED DETERMINACY

I've been arguing that we can't make sense of a notion of super-determinateness. But is it possible to live with just a hierarchy of ever-stronger operators D^α, without any notion of super-determinateness?

It might be thought that a hierarchy of ever-stronger operators D^α gives rise to all the problems of stratified theories of truth and satisfaction in classical logic. But there are at least three reasons why this isn't so.

1. What we have for Determinacy isn't Stratification

There are two sub-points to be made here.

1A. No Need of Separate Primitives

The less important point about why iteration isn't stratification is that in classical truth theories that involve stratification, the stratification consists of there being a whole hierarchy of primitive truth predicates 'True$_\alpha$': later ones are not definable from earlier ones. But in the case of the paracomplete theories considered in this part of the book, there is no such need for a hierarchy of primitives. Rather, there is a single primitive notion of truth, and a single notion of determinateness;[1] the other notions are all defined by iterating the basic notion of determinateness, using the truth predicate to define the transfinite iterations.

It's worth remarking that in some of the *non-stratified* weakly classical theories we could have introduced something more analogous to what we have here with determinateness—though it would have been of little interest. For instance, we might have introduced a sequence of stronger and stronger "truth predicates", by taking $\text{True}^1(\langle A \rangle)$ to be just $\text{True}(\langle A \rangle)$, $\text{True}^2(\langle A \rangle)$ to be $\text{True}(\langle A \rangle) \wedge \text{True}(\langle \text{True}(\langle A \rangle) \rangle)$, and so forth. $\text{True}^\omega(\langle A \rangle)$ would say that for all $n \geq 1$, the nth member of the sequence is true, $\text{True}^{\omega+1}(\langle A \rangle)$ will be $\text{True}^\omega(\langle A \rangle) \wedge \text{True}(\langle \text{True}^\omega(\langle A \rangle) \rangle)$, and we can iterate a reasonable way through

---

[1] Not itself primitive, as a matter of fact, though I don't think much hangs on this.

transfinite more or less as we did for D.[2] Such a sequence of truth predicates is of no great interest in the context of weakly classical theories, because these predicates are not very well-behaved. For instance, none of the predicates in this sequence satisfy such basic axioms as

$$\text{True}^\alpha(\langle A \rangle) \to A.$$

Moreover, the claim to "transfinite iteration" is hollow: because of the failure of the basic truth predicate to be intersubstitutable, the predicate defined at level ω fails to be a genuine infinite conjunction of the preceding ones, and there will be analogous failures at every other limit ordinal. This problem is especially dramatic in the case of weak supervaluation theories (see previous footnote), but even in medium and strong ones the "truth predicate" produced at limits can be inappropriately strong.

I don't want to discuss such a system of truth predicates or its defects in any detail. My point in mentioning it is simply that whatever its defects, it is not stratification in the sense understood in Sections 14.2 and 14.3, since the "truth predicates" described in the last paragraph are all built from a single primitive truth predicate. The sequence of determinately operators is broadly analogous to this system of *non-stratified* truth predicates—except that it yields far nicer results, in that we *do* have $D^\alpha A \to A$, and we *do* have that $D^\omega A$ is the infinite conjunction of the $D^n A$. It is not at all like the hierarchies of primitive truth predicates considered in Chapter 14.

The above is all an elaboration of the *less* important reason why what we have in the case of an iterable determinacy operator isn't really stratification. But I attach more weight to the following:

1B. No Restriction on Significant Application

The main reason why iteration isn't stratification is that in the case of an iterable determinacy operator there is no restriction on significantly applying predicates of form 'D^αTrue' to sentences containing 'D^βTrue' for β greater than α. Many sentences containing 'D^{17}True' are D^αTrue for α much lower than 17; indeed, many are D^0True, i.e. just plain true. This is completely different from stratification, and much less restrictive.

2. Peripherality of the Notion

Besides the fact that no real stratification is involved (and for two reasons), another important point is that the "quasi-stratification" is applied only to

---

[2] Actually the claim that these predicates get stronger and stronger requires qualification: it presupposes that if a conjunction is true then so are its conjuncts, and this fails in weak supervaluation theories. Truth$^\omega$ is equivalent to the notion called "hyper-truth" in Section 11.3, in the discussion of the McGee sentence.

the relatively peripheral notion of determinateness, not to the crucial notion of truth. On the views considered here, we do have a unified notion of truth (and of satisfaction too). It is the notions of truth and satisfaction, not of determinate truth, that we need to use as devices of generalization. We've seen that stratifying the truth predicate would seriously cripple our ability to make generalizations; this is so not only for the crude Tarski stratification, but also for the more coarsely stratified theories considered in Chapter 14.[3] But the ability to use truth as a device of generalization isn't affected at all in the paracomplete theories now under discussion, since the truth predicate isn't even quasi-stratified.

Of course, to say that a quasi-stratification of determinateness doesn't cripple us *in the way that stratifying truth would* isn't to say that it doesn't cripple us in other ways. The question of whether it does is one I'll return to shortly.

3. No Undermining

The third disanalogy between what we have for determinateness and what we have in classical stratified truth theories is that we can reasonably hope, for each α, that our overall theory of truth and determinateness is D^αTrue. This is in marked contrast to stratified classical truth theories. Indeed, in the standard such theories, those discussed in Section 14.2, 'True$_\alpha(\langle A \rangle) \rightarrow A$' is an important part of the theory, but it is not true$_\alpha$ (but only true$_{\alpha+1}$). As a result, there is no α such that we should believe that *even that part of our overall theory that uses only the predicate 'True$_\alpha$'* is true$_\alpha$. (For those theories discussed in Section 14.3 we avoid this strong form of the problem, but we still have the problem that the part of our theory that involves predicates 'True$_\beta$' for $\beta > \alpha$ doesn't come out true$_\alpha$; so there is still no α for which our entire theory is true$_\alpha$.) This was one of the central objections that I raised against stratified theories, and it simply doesn't arise against the current theory.

4. Disanalogy

In addition to **1–3** there is a fourth disanalogy between what we have for determinacy and what we had for truth in stratified theories, though probably it is of no great interest. This difference is that we can actually define "unified determinately operators" in the current theory, e.g. as $H_\supset$ or $H_\rightarrow$; it's simply that the results turn out to be either ill-behaved, or not genuinely maximal in the way we might have hoped, or both.

---

[3] I have primarily in mind the accounts of Section 14.2. Those in 14.3 are probably better viewed as involving a stratification of determinateness, not of truth (as argued in 14.4); but even there, there is a real limitation in expressing generalizations, since no 'True$_\alpha$' applies to sentences containing 'True$_\beta$' for $\beta > \alpha$.

23.2. GENUINE COSTS

I now return to the question raised at the end of point 2 from the previous section: even if the lack of a well-behaved "unified determinateness predicate" doesn't have all the costs of the lack of a unified truth predicate in stratified classical theories, mightn't it have some of those costs, and mightn't these suffice for rejecting the theory?

There is of course no question that the lack of a unified determinateness predicate has some costs—costs *reminiscent of* some of the problems with coarsely stratified classical theories, even though (for reasons 1–3) far less severe. You can't consistently have everything. (You can't even *inconsistently* have everything, as we'll see in Part V.) I'll look at two such problems.

A.

The first such problem concerns Nixon–Dean cases. There is no difficulty here as long as Nixon and Dean each stick to talking about truth: if each says that what the other guy says is false (or equivalently, isn't true), then neither utters a determinate truth, and that's all there is to be said about the matter. But what about if they start talking in terms of determinate truth, including iterations of that? Then we have a situation reminiscent to that discussed under **A** of Section 14.2: if one of them iterates 'determinately' more times in making his negative comment on the other, then what he says is determinately true while what the other guy says is determinately false. So they can engage in "superscript contests".

I don't see any way around this. (One might try going contextual, by invoking pragmatic principles that will ensure that under normal circumstances all agents use the same implicit subscript; but I don't think this would be any more successful than the corresponding attempt considered in Section 14.2.) How big a problem is it? I'd say it is less of a problem than the problem for coarsely stratified gap theories, for two reasons.

The most obvious reason is that mentioned under **2** of the previous section: it would take a fairly fanciful story to make it natural for Nixon and Dean to be interested in the *determinate* truth of each other's remarks as opposed to their truth, especially given that the ordinary notion of truth is now totally well-behaved.

Less obvious, but probably more important, is that in the present case the pressure to raise superscripts is less contagious. The reason for that is the one mentioned under **1B** of the previous section: there is a non-trivial division between those sentences involving 'determinately$^\beta$' that are determinately$^\alpha$ true and those that aren't, even when α is far less than β. One doesn't need to go to β or higher to comment on the status of sentences involving 'determinately$^\beta$'.

In addition to these two points, I remind the reader that in Chapter 14 I did not say that Nixon–Dean problems are a clear problem for (non-contextual) coarsely stratified gap theories: I was at pains to point out that *as long as we can confine normal discourse to a discussion of truth$_0$* there is little problem, and I concluded my discussion by holding out some possibility that coarsely stratified theories (unlike Tarskian theories) would have the means for so confining it.

My main claims against coarsely stratified gap theories didn't concern these issues, but instead concerned whether those theories can overcome the problems of unstratified gap theories like those discussed in Chapter 7: in particular, the problem about theories declaring themselves untrue and the problem about expressing disagreement. My conclusion (argued under **B** of Section 14.2) was that they cannot overcome these problems.

In this there is a very sharp contrast with the situation with iterated determinateness operators: these operators are defined in a theory in which truth behaves in a fully adequate manner: it obeys the Intersubstitutivity Principle, and does so in the full language that contains the iterations of the determinacy operator as well as containing 'true'. Whereas the stratification of gap-theoretic truth seems to be an unsuccessful attempt to overcome the defect that gap theories declare themselves untrue, there is no analogous defect to overcome in the case of the paracomplete theories in which the iterable determinately operators appear.

B.

Let's turn to a second problem raised by the lack of a unified determinateness predicate. Suppose I heard Brown speak yesterday, and remember that he said something that was "defective at some level"; but I can't remember how high that level was. To speak sensibly, I must pick an ordinal α, and say that what he said was defective at level no greater than α. But there is a risk that I won't have picked a high enough α.

Well, there is a bit of risk here, but it doesn't strike me as unacceptably high.[4] The fact is that people rarely iterate determinately operators very far or use highly embedded conditionals (that is, conditionals that contain conditionals that contain conditionals that ...); given this, the chance of someone's uttering a sentence that is defective$_\beta$ but not defective$_\alpha$ for any lower α strikes me as small, when β is bigger than 2 or 3. (And in the unlikely event that Brown did produce such a sentence, his doing so would probably be quite memorable, and one would know one needed to go high in that case!) I suspect, for instance, that even in a book like this, where iterations of 'determinately' are a prime topic,

---

[4] Conversation is full of risks as to the strict and literal truth of what is said. I often say "There's no beer in the fridge" when the purposes of the remark would be fulfilled by the claim that there's no *drinkable* beer in the fridge, only stuff that's been open for a month, or Bud Lite, or drops that have spilled onto the bottom shelf, or that is part of the sauce of a beef stew, or .... If I say that Brown's remark isn't determinately true when strictly speaking I should have said that the remark isn't *determinately* determinately true, well, that's life: in most contexts the distinction is too subtle to care about.

it is unlikely that there are "inadvertently defective" sentences that are defective at a level more than (say) 3 but not at any smaller level. This is in contrast at least to the situation with Tarskian versions of stratified gap theories, where in quantifying over other people's remarks (or speaking of single remarks that are themselves so quantified) there is a substantial risk that the subscript we choose will be too low. (It may well also be in contrast to the case of coarsely stratified truth theories. This is especially so because of the problem mentioned near the end of Chapter 14 (pp. 227–8), about attributions of determinate truth to all instances of a schema; but I will not press that point here.)

It's worth noting that problem **B** (two paragraphs back) really wasn't even intelligibly formulated. It isn't that on my theory, I can remember that Brown said something that was "defective at some level", but for some reason am not allowed to say this. Rather, the situation is that there is no well-behaved thought that what he said was "defective at some level". (By 'no *well-behaved* thought', I mean that while we can have the thought that what he said was "defective at some level", this thought doesn't have the critical power one wanted it to have: because of the collapse of the hyper-determinately operator, *everything* turns out "defective at some level".) I say this not to dismiss the second problem: indeed, it in some way makes the problem more acute, because I think there is a powerful impulse to regard the thought as well-behaved. But it is hard to see how to free the theory of this feature without giving up most of the virtues of the theory as well.

It might be thought that I could ameliorate the situation by going autobiographical or normative, but there are related problems with any such move. For instance, consider the sequence of Liar sentences Q_α. Instead of saying that each of them is "defective at some level" (which has the problem noted in the previous paragraph), suppose I instead simply say that I do or should reject each of them? But that won't work either, for I don't and shouldn't: if the ordinal is past where the breakdown occurs, then the corresponding Liar sentence is trivially true, so I should and do accept it! And if I want to fix this by restricting to ordinals prior to the breakdown, then for reasons we've seen, I must make the restriction severe enough to exclude some ordinals that could have been included. As this illustrates, the limitations of what I can properly say with defectiveness predicates aren't substantially lessened by the use of statements about what I can or should reject.

This is undoubtedly slightly awkward. Is it debilitating? I don't think so: for instance, for each ordinal that I know how to name and for which I'm confident that I could name each of its predecessors too, I can reject the Liar sentence Q_α obtained from using the name for that ordinal in its formulation. Indeed, there's no need to put this in terms of rejection: for each such sentence α, I can say that the sentence is defective$_{\alpha+1}$ (i.e., neither $D^{\alpha+1}$-true nor $D^{\alpha+1}$-false). During the course of the book I have indulged from time to time in claims such as "All the Q_α are defective", but this was simply to get the idea of the theory across

23.3. TRYING TO GET REVENGE

I close by considering a group of objections raised in sections 3 and (especially) 4 of Priest 2005. Priest says that any theory of truth other than the paraconsistent dialetheic theories that he favors will lead to "revenge paradoxes":

> There is a certain notion the intelligibility of which the theory presupposes which, if it is included in the language in question, can be used to refashion the paradox. Hence consistency can be maintained only at the cost of [expressive] incompleteness—which naturally gives rise to a hierarchy of metalanguages, and so to familiar problems of the same kind. (p. 44)

And, he claims, the theory of Part III is no exception: he says that despite my protestations to the contrary, it presupposes the notion of super-determinacy. The claim here is not merely the one considered in the previous section, that the notion of super-determinacy seems to make intuitive sense and that a theory that can't make sense of it is thereby suspect; the claim, rather, is that *this notion is presupposed by the theory of Section 16.2.*

Priest puts the claim very strongly:

> Field's metatheory cannot be expressed in the object language any more than that of ZF can be expressed in ZF, and for exactly the same reason. If it could be, the theory would be able to establish its own consistency, which is impossible, by Gödel's second incompleteness theorem. Consistency, then, is maintained only by the usual trade-off with expressiveness. (p. 45)

The central premise here is that any *expressively* complete theory can prove its own consistency (independent of any further claim of deductive completeness). I take it that this is intended to apply not just to theories that are "expressively complete" in the sense of being able to express everything (which would be uninteresting, since few would claim to have a theory that is expressively complete in that sense), but to theories that are "expressively complete" in the sense of being able to express *their own meta-theoretic notions*. But in any case, why should expressive completeness require the ability to prove consistency? I don't think that Priest adequately answers this question.[5] (And as we'll see in Chapter 26,

---

[5] In his 1987 he does say

> if a theory is to give an account of its own semantics, it must give an interpretation of some kind for the language of the theory. Then, to show that it is a semantics of the theory, it must be able to give a soundness proof of the theory with repect to the interpretation. (Priest 1987, p. 24)

But the second sentence seems doubly false. Even if we assume that a theory must *be* sound with respect to a correct semantics for it (which itself seems false), still providing a correct semantics is the suggestion that an adequate theory needs to be able to establish its own consistency, or even its own non-triviality, is a suggestion that would rule out Priest's own proposals for solving the paradoxes.)

Still, Priest's general point (given in the first and third sentence of the last quote) is of interest independent of the claim about the relevance of consistency proofs. To investigate it, let's clarify 'meta-theory'. That can mean at least three different things: proof theory, model theory, and theory of truth. The first is obviously not what Priest intends: there is no difficulty in doing proof theory (whether the proof theory of ZF or of a broader theory ZF_{true} that adds 'True' to the language in accord with my theory and allows its use in a positive induction rule) within ZF and hence within ZF_{true}. But it doesn't look as if Priest could mean either of the other two either. If he meant truth theory, then he would be right about ZF: it doesn't contain its own truth predicate, by Tarski's Theorem. But he would obviously be wrong about ZF_{true}: it contains its own truth predicate, and that predicate obeys all the laws anyone could ask for: in particular, it obeys the Intersubstitutivity Principle. (It also contains obvious generalizations about truth, such as that a disjunction is true if and only if one of its disjuncts is; and it contains instances of the induction rule that involve 'true'.) Perhaps then Priest means model theory? But then he would be wrong both about ZF and about ZF_{true}: the model theory of both is included in ZF and hence in ZF_{true}.

I suppose that Priest or someone else *might* respond to this by objecting that the truth theory I'm advocating for ZF_{true} is unsatisfactory because uninformative. The objector would point out that a person presented with just the formation rules of ZF_{true} plus the Intersubstitutivity Principle, the compositional principles, and the instances of induction involving 'true' would be in no position to understand ZF_{true}. That of course is correct, but it's only an objection if you think that it's a goal of a theory of truth for a language to serve as a potential basis for understanding the language. And that should never have been anyone's goal for a theory of truth.

It has often been pointed out, for instance, that one is never going to learn to understand 'and' by being told what a theory of truth tells us, viz.,

⟨A and B⟩ is true iff ⟨A⟩ is true and ⟨B⟩ is true,

for that explanation uses the very word 'and'. What's involved in coming to understand 'and', rather, must involve learning to use it in accordance with certain inferential rules. (If the truth theory were in German one could learn to understand 'and' from it, but only because the theory employed a corresponding word 'und' that had to be learned by learning inferential rules.) Understanding ordinary words has nothing to do with truth. Of course, once we understand

---

one thing and proving that the semantics one has provided is correct (according to that assumed standard) is something else again.

'true', then in coming to understand a sentence S we come to understand the claim that S is true; but this is just because our understanding of 'true' is such that the claim that S is true is equivalent to S. A theory of truth need only justify this equivalence, together with the legitimacy of using truth in the induction schema etc. (Of course, doing "only this" is no small task, because of the paradoxes.)

But I think Priest would respond to my objection of three paragraphs back in another way: not that there's a problem with my truth theory, but that there's a problem with my model theory. The model theories I mentioned for ZF and ZF_{true} are inadequate (according to Priest) because they don't include the real universe as a model.

The fact that the standard model theories of ZF and ZF_{true} don't allow the real world to be a model is, of course, something that I too have repeatedly emphasized (following Kreisel): it's why we have no intuitive *guarantee* that the model-theoretic explications of validity are extensionally correct, though we may have a reasonable conviction that they are. (The fact that the real world is excluded from being a model could only affect the validity of sentences with unrestricted quantifiers, so the impact of a possible extensional failure is limited. Still, it's there.) A guarantee against extensional failure would be nice, but it's a mean old world, and I doubt that there are any prospects for a model theory that provides such a guarantee without having offsetting problems. For instance, if the real world is automatically a model of our theory, and we explain consistency of the theory as the existence of a model, then model theoretic consistency in this sense is easily provable; whereas its irrefutability better not be, by the second incompleteness theorem. So a model-theoretic soundness theorem, according to which model-theoretic consistency implies irrefutability, would then seem to be precluded. Priest thinks that his dialetheic logic allows an escape from this argument, but I believe that this view is based on a mistake about how his logic deals with the second incompleteness theorem; I will defer that issue until Chapter 26.

In any case, Priest's view that even ZF without a truth predicate has a problem developing its own model theory is highly idiosyncratic. A more common view, I'd imagine, is that a perfectly adequate model theory for ZF can be given in ZF, but that ZF_{true} is different in this regard. The strong form of the claim is that no adequate model theory for ZF_{true} can be given even in ZF_{true}; the weak form is that no adequate model theory for ZF_{true} can be given in its classical subtheory ZF.

Even the weak form seems to me dubious: if the goal of an adequate model theory for a logic ℓ is to give an account of ℓ-validity that is both (i) extensionally correct and (ii) stated in terms that are neutral enough so that we can investigate questions about ℓ-validity without pre-judging the correctness of ℓ, then the model theory of Section 17.1 for ZF_{true} in ZF seems to me quite adequate. Some may feel that there is no hope for an adequate model theory for a non-classical logic in a classical metalanguage, but I have addressed this view at length in Section 5.6 and will not repeat the discussion here. Suffice it to remind the reader that I grant that you can't give an adequate *truth theory* for a non-classical logic in a classical metalanguage; but we have an adequate truth theory for ZF_{true} within ZF_{true}, and there is no obvious reason why a model theory for ZF_{true} should do the work of that truth theory as well as the work of aiding investigations of validity.

But are there special worries about super-determinateness? I can imagine two worries: (1) that the model theory of Section 17.1 *doesn't* allow me to make sense of a notion of super-determinateness meeting intuitive preconceptions, but *ought to*; (2) that that model theory *does* allow me to make sense of such a notion, but *ought not*.

Let me address the latter worry first. I agree, of course, that the model theory ought not make sense of a notion of super-determinateness meeting intuitive preconceptions: my claim is that the notion is ultimately unintelligible. The worry is that it seems to: the value space contains the values **1** and **0** as well as many other values, and it is a classical space with an identity predicate, so there is an operation on the space that maps **1** into itself and everything else into **0**. Why isn't this a perfectly intelligible operator?

I've given part of the answer to this already: the model theory is primarily just a model theory, used for explaining validity; no sense has been given to an assignment of values to sentences in an absolute sense, independent of a model. I now add that *a value space itself* has no significance for the real world, for it is of use only for models of cardinality no greater than a given cardinal **C**; for higher cardinality models you need a bigger value space, and the real world has higher "cardinality" than *any* **C**. Given that the value space has no significance for the real world, we shouldn't be disturbed by any "monsters" that it contains.

I don't think that Priest would be satisfied by this, and I can see some intuitive pull to his resistance. Shouldn't we have a model theory that employs a value space with values that are intimately connected with how the sentences are properly used? So let me be concessive: I think there may well be a place for a theory that postulates a model-independent space of values with some analogy to the space employed in the model theory of Section 17.1. However, the only hope for carrying out this idea is to make such a space of values reflect non-classical reality in a way that no construction given in classical set theory could ever do; this would require a restriction of excluded middle in developing the theory of such a space, at least as applied to the relation assigning values to sentences and probably even as applied to the relation of identity among the values of the space. In particular, *we could not assume that a given sentence either has value* **1** *or doesn't have value* **1**, *and so there would be no basis for constructing a "revenge paradox"*.

This is all speculative: I haven't developed such a non-classical theory of values that would be appropriate to model-independent assignments of values to sentences,[6] and don't think it's *obvious* that there's a need for one. Still, I do see

---

[6] Some suggestions in this direction can be found in Leitgeb 2007. It is also possible that the Rayo–Welch construction or something akin to it might be used for these purposes, interpreting their higher order quantifiers in the quasi-impredicative manner discussed in Section 22.5.

some intuitive pull for the demand for one, and this is the direction I'd want to go in were I to give in to that pull.

Turning now to the opposite worry (1), the claim that I dispute is that the model theory *ought* to allow for a super-determinateness operator meeting intuitive preconceptions. I've argued that this is not so, that in fact such an operator doesn't really make sense (though I grant that this is initially quite surprising); but Priest's view seems to be that this position is one I can't coherently hold, because (he thinks) the notion is presupposed by my own theory, or by the motivation for it.

But why? The motivation of the theory does require that the ordinary Liar sentence Q_0 is in some sense defective, but I can say that: it is defective in the most straightforward sense of being neither determinately true nor determinately false. (It is defective$_1$.) The motivation also requires that the "next level Liar" Q_1 is in some sense defective. It needn't be defective in quite the same sense: perhaps it is "defective" only in the extended sense that the claim that it isn't defective (in the first sense) is defective (in the first sense). That's what the theory yields: $\neg DDQ_1$, so defective$_1$($\langle \neg$defective$_1(\langle Q_1 \rangle)\rangle$). But we can introduce a broader sense of defectiveness, defectiveness$_2$, that includes both this "second order defectiveness" and defectiveness$_1$; in this broader sense, Q_0 and Q_1 are both defective. Similarly as we go higher. If I want to say that there is a kind of defectiveness of such high order that $Q_0, Q_1, Q_2, \ldots, Q_\omega, \ldots, Q_{\omega \cdot \omega}, \ldots Q_{\omega^\omega}, \ldots, Q_{\epsilon_0}, \ldots, Q_{\omega_{1_{CK}}}, \ldots$ are all defective ($\omega_{1_{CK}}$ being the first non-recursive ordinal), I can say that too. Of course, the content depends on how the dots are filled in. If the claim were understood as a claim about all ordinals whatever it would be false: Q_{ω_1} (where ω_1 is the first uncountable ordinal) turns out to be straightforwardly true, because it says that it isn't D^{ω_1}-true, and even clear truths aren't D^{ω_1}-true. So in order to make the claim with the dots at the end true, it must be understood in such a way that there is an implicit limit on how far the extension goes: say, the first ordinal λ_0 not definable in the 'true'-free part of the language. But once the claim is clarified in this way, the defectiveness claim is truly statable: all of the claims on the intended list are defective$_{\lambda_0}$. The theory may be slightly awkward because of the inability to neatly quantify over "vague totalities", but it isn't ineffable. So the charge that it leads to "revenge paradoxes" seems to me mistaken.[7]

---

[7] It seems appropriate to end a discussion of revenge problems with a quotation chosen from the rich literature of revenge songs. An undeservedly neglected one from the 1960s, in which a woman is addressing an ex-boyfriend who rudely dumped her for another woman who has now betrayed him, ends with the lines:

> Yeah, and my hurting's just about over,
> But baby, it's *just starting* for *you*.

("Whatsa Matter Baby, Is it Hurting You?", by one Timi Yuro.) Unfortunately, the philosophy doesn't really fit the song lyrics: while Part V will take a critical look at Priest's own theory, its appraisal of it will be far less negative than would be required for giving these lyrics a more prominent place.

PART V

PARACONSISTENT DIALETHEISM

24

An Introduction to Paraconsistent Dialetheism

24.1. DIALETHEISM, THE TRUTH SCHEMA, AND INTERSUBSTITUTIVITY

Dialetheism is the view that some sentences are both true and false; that is, both they and their negations are true. Or alternatively, that some contradictions (sentences of form $A \wedge \neg A$) are true: this isn't very different, since it is usually taken for granted that a conjunction is true if and only if both conjuncts are true.

Dialetheism in this sense comes in two fundamentally different types. We've already met one of them, in Chapter 8: classical glut theories. These theories accept that some contradictions are true; indeed, there are specific contradictions that they take to be true, such as $Q \wedge \neg Q$ (where Q is the Liar sentence). And yet these theories don't accept any contradictions. Getting from True($\langle Q \wedge \neg Q \rangle$) to $Q \wedge \neg Q$ might seem a trivial step, but it is a step that classical glut theorists reject. But let us now turn to *paraconsistent dialetheism*, which accepts this further step: it accepts some contradictions, not merely that some are true. It is the kind of dialetheism that will be the focus of Part V.

In classical logic, contradictions imply everything: we have the explosion rule

(EXP) $\qquad A, \neg A \vDash B$

(or equivalently given the standard rules of conjunction, $A \wedge \neg A \vDash B$). Obviously a paraconsistent dialetheist won't accept this: then the acceptance of a contradiction would commit one to accepting everything. It is the rejection of the classical rule (EXP) that makes the view "paraconsistent". (EXP) is a trivial consequence of a more intuitive-looking inference called "disjunctive syllogism"; this is the inference

(DS) $\qquad A \vee B, \neg A \vDash B.$

So the paraconsistent dialetheist rejects disjunctive syllogism as well.

Paraconsistent dialetheism has been promoted in recent years, by Graham Priest and others, as the best way of dealing with the semantic paradoxes and related paradoxes such as Russell's. (Priest cites other motivations as well, but few have found these persuasive and I will not discuss them.) According to Priest, the key to the resolution of the Liar paradox is to recognize that the Liar sentence is both true and false—indeed, as both true and also not true. This idea initially strikes most philosophers as a desperate measure, to be tried only if all else fails. Indeed, some philosophers seem to have the attitude that it shouldn't even be tried then! But it seems to me that if the view really does handle the paradoxes better than other approaches do, then it deserves to be taken seriously.[1] I am, however, skeptical that it does as well as its proponents advertise.

The advantage of paraconsistent dialetheism as a solution to the paradoxes is that it can accept some naive principles about truth that no (strongly or weakly) classical theory can accept. We've seen that there are two natural ways to formulate "the Naive Theory of Truth". The first is that the Naive Theory accepts all instances of the Tarski schema

(T) $\qquad\qquad\qquad\text{True}(\langle A\rangle) \leftrightarrow A.$

The second is that the Naive Theory accepts the Intersubstitutivity Principle:

(IP) If C and D are alike except that (in some transparent context) one has "A" where the other has "$\langle A\rangle$ is true", then one can legitimately infer D from C and C from D.

These two formulations are equivalent in classical logic; and classical theories are forced to reject both of them. The formulations are also equivalent in paracomplete and paraconsistent logics, given some natural principles governing the biconditional '$\leftrightarrow$' (or governing the conditional, from which the biconditional is defined in the obvious way). The paracomplete theory considered in Parts III and IV accepted those principles for the conditional and biconditional (see the Theorem on the Intersubstitutivity of Equivalents in Section 16.2), and managed to satisfy both (T) and (IP). There are paraconsistent dialetheic theories that do this also.

Priest himself, however, rejects (IP); he accepts (T) only for a conditional that violates some of the natural assumptions required for the equivalence proof. In particular, his theory rejects contraposition *even in rule form*: it not only declares the conditional $(A \to B) \to (\neg B \to \neg A)$ invalid, it rejects the rule

$$A \to B \vDash \neg B \to \neg A.$$

Indeed, it rejects even the still weaker rule of modus tollens

$$A \to B, \neg B \vDash \neg A,$$

---

[1] A main worry that many people have about paraconsistent dialetheism is that once someone allows the acceptance of contradictions they can never be rationally persuaded to reject anything: if the person starts out believing that there were weapons of mass destruction in Iraq and you present evidence to the contrary, the person can agree that there weren't while retaining his belief that there were. I'm embarrassed to admit that I once tentatively voiced this worry in print, but as Priest 2006a (ch. 7) argues convincingly, it is misguided: it rests on ignoring all rationality considerations besides the purely logical. In any case, we can take someone who advocates paraconsistent dialetheism solely on the grounds of the paradoxes to reject any contradiction in the "ground language" (the language without 'true', 'instantiates', etc.), and to accept explosion within this ground language; this is the analog of what the paracomplete theorist says about excluded middle in the ground language.

thus allowing that even though $\vDash \text{True}(\langle B \rangle) \to B$, it is impossible to infer

$$\neg B \vDash \neg \text{True}(\langle B \rangle).$$

This is to abandon not only (IP) but even the much weaker rule (¬T-Introd).

To my mind, this rejection of (IP) limits the interest of Priest's proposal. Indeed it seems to me that the primary motivation for naive truth involves the fact that 'true' serves as a device of generalization, and this motivation is a direct motivation not for (T) but for (IP); (T) is plausible mainly because it is an immediate consequence of (IP), given the obvious logical principle $A \leftrightarrow A$. To save "naivety" by validating (T) without (IP) would, I think, be a big disappointment. (Suppose I say "I think everything Jones said is true. But if not, then we're in trouble". It's a blow to the purposes of a truth predicate if the last part isn't equivalent to "If $\neg(A_1 \wedge \ldots \wedge A_n)$ then we're in trouble", relative to the assumption that what he said was $A_1, \ldots, A_n$.)

Still, Priest does abandon (IP), and he is the most prominent defender of paraconsistent dialetheism; it wouldn't do to leave him out of the discussion. So my focus will be on versions of paraconsistent dialetheism that accept *at least* (T), but I will regard with special interest those which accept (IP) as well. (One such full-Intersubstitutivity version of paraconsistent dialetheism is suggested in Beall 2005, though without a full working out of the logical details. Others will be mentioned in Section 24.2.)[2]

I will assume that even paraconsistent dialetheists who don't accept (IP) do accept the weak classicist's rules (T-Elim) and (T-Introd). (The former is the rule required to get from accepting the truth of some contradictions to accepting some contradictions.) These indeed follow from (T), if it is assumed that the conditional for which (T) holds obeys modus ponens; and Priest does assume this. Priest also accepts (¬T-Elim). But as mentioned, he does not accept (¬T-Introd). In some ways then he is further from the naive theory of truth than are most versions of weakly classical theories, on which all four of these inferential rules are accepted.

24.2. ACCEPTANCE, REJECTION, AND DEGREE OF BELIEF

Classical glut theories are easy to understand, even if hard to accept; for we can reason within them in familiar classical ways. Paraconsistent dialetheism is much harder to understand, for we have to resist the strong inclination to pass

---

[2] Beall differs with Priest not only over Intersubstitutivity but also over the Law of Excluded Middle: Priest assumes excluded middle, Beall doesn't. These two differences are mostly independent: one could weaken Priest's system by restricting excluded middle, and the theories to be discussed in Section 24.2 contain both Intersubstitutivity and excluded middle.

automatically from accepting $\neg A$ to rejecting A (e.g. from accepting the claim that the Liar is not true to rejecting the claim that the Liar is true). But the fact that the view is hard to understand doesn't mean that it is incoherent. It isn't; it just requires getting used to.

Indeed, the idea that accepting $\neg A$ needn't be the same thing as rejecting A should by now be familiar: we've seen it already in the case of paracomplete theories, starting with KFS in Chapter 3, and also in the case of weakly classical theories. In both those cases, the view was that one could reject A without accepting $\neg A$; this was possible because one's degrees of belief in A and $\neg A$ could add to less than 1 and hence both could be low. What's new in the case of paraconsistent dialetheism, and needs getting used to, is that we can have the dual situation: we need to allow that the degrees of belief in A and its negation can add to more than one, so that both can be high. It's easy enough to get a non-standard theory of degrees of belief that does this: it's one very similar to the one that the paracomplete theorist uses, in that it retains the general law from classical subjective probability theory

$$P(A \vee B) = P(A) + P(B) - P(A \wedge B).$$

When B is $\neg A$, this gives

$$P(A) + P(\neg A) = P(A \vee \neg A) + P(A \wedge \neg A).$$

The paracomplete theorist (who I assumed not to also be a dialetheist) takes $P(A \wedge \neg A)$ to be 0 but allows $P(A \vee \neg A)$ to be less than 1, so $P(A) + P(\neg A)$ must be less than or equal to 1. The paraconsistent dialetheist, if he accepts excluded middle as Priest does, takes $P(A \vee \neg A)$ to be 1 but allows $P(A \wedge \neg A)$ to be greater than 0, so $P(A) + P(\neg A)$ must be greater than or equal to 1. In that case, rejecting A (having degree of belief below $1 - \tau$, where τ is the threshold for acceptance) requires acceptance of $\neg A$, but the converse fails.

Note the contrast to the classical glut theorist. As an advocate of strongly classical logic, the classical glut theorist will accept the usual laws of probability for degrees of belief: $P(A) + P(\neg A)$ will always be 1. This does not preclude having $P(\text{True}(\langle A \rangle)) + P(\text{True}(\langle \neg A \rangle))$ be greater than 1, for part of the classical glut theorist's position is that $P(\text{True}(\langle A \rangle))$ can be higher than $P(A)$ (and analogously for $\neg A$). The paraconsistent dialetheist, by contrast, accepts the rules T-Introd and T-Elim, and hence takes $P(\text{True}(\langle A \rangle))$ to be equal to $P(A)$ (and analogously for $\neg A$); so the only way for him to allow $P(\text{True}(\langle A \rangle)) + P(\text{True}(\langle \neg A \rangle))$ to be greater than 1 is to allow $P(A) + P(\neg A)$ to be greater than 1.

24.3. GLUTS, GAPS, AND INTERSUBSTITUTIVITY AGAIN

As I've mentioned, Priest himself wants to reject the Intersubstitituivity Principle (IP), and indeed, to reject even the far weaker rule ($\neg$T-Introd). One reason is that he wants to accept that certain claims are truth value gluts while rejecting that they are gaps. That of course is the position of the classical glut theorist (Chapter 8); the question is whether the paraconsistent dialetheist should go along with it.

It may seem obvious that one should: after all, saying that a sentence such as the Liar sentence is a glut obviously implies that it is *not* a gap. That's a good reason for a classical glut theorist not to accept of a sentence that it is both a glut and a gap: doing so would be contradictory. But the whole point of paraconsistent dialetheism is to accept contradictions, so this is no reason for a paraconsistent dialetheist not to accept that some or all gluts are gaps as well as not being gaps.

Indeed, any dialetheist who accepts the Intersubstitutivity Principle must say that *all* gluts are also gaps. From the point of view of the Intersubstitutivity Principle, there is simply no distinction to be made between gaps and gluts: a common name should be given to both, perhaps the name 'weird'. (I'm assuming that the person who accepts Intersubstitutivity also accepts some kind of deMorgan logic, as Priest does.) The reason (to repeat from Chapter 3): the claims that A are "gappy" and "glutty" are, respectively,

(GAP) $\qquad\qquad \neg \text{True}(\langle A \rangle) \wedge \neg \text{True}(\langle \neg A \rangle)$

(GLUT) $\qquad\qquad \text{True}(\langle A \rangle) \wedge \text{True}(\langle \neg A \rangle).$

But by (IP), these are equivalent, respectively, to

$$\neg A \wedge \neg \neg A$$

and

$$A \wedge \neg A;$$

and by the equivalence between $\neg\neg A$ and A, plus the commutativity of conjunction, these amount to the same thing. So no one who accepts the Intersubstitutivity Principle can accept the claim that a sentence is "glutty" without also accepting that that very sentence is "gappy", and conversely. If this is surprising, I think that is because of a common tendency to confuse paraconsistent dialetheism with classical glut theory (in analogy with another common confusion, between paracomplete theories and classical gap theories).

Priest, as I've said, wants to be able to say of a sentence A that it is both true and false without concluding from this that it is neither true nor false. Indeed, he doesn't want to be able to conclude either that it is not true or that it is not false. Given (T-Elim), which he clearly accepts, (GLUT) implies A, which in turn implies $\neg\neg A$; it also implies $\neg A$. So we could get to $\neg \text{True}(\neg A)$ and to $\neg \text{True}(\langle A \rangle)$ if we had the rule

($\neg$T-Introd) $\qquad\qquad \neg B \models \neg \text{True}(\langle B \rangle).$

So clearly Priest rejects this rule. The rule follows by modus tollens from one half of the Tarski biconditional,

$$\text{True}(\langle B \rangle) \to B;$$

this is the reason why, as remarked above, Priest needs to reject modus tollens (for the conditional that he uses to formulate the Tarski biconditional).

It might be objected that the above discussion of the relation between gaps and gluts turns on the equation of falsehood with truth of negation. Priest himself accepts this equation (Priest 1987, p. 64), but perhaps it will be thought that he shouldn't. In that case, we should formulate the claims that A is gappy and glutty as

(GAP*) $\quad\quad\quad\quad\quad\quad \neg\text{True}(\langle A \rangle) \wedge \neg\text{False}(\langle A \rangle)$

and

(GLUT*) $\quad\quad\quad\quad\quad\quad \text{True}(\langle A \rangle) \wedge \text{False}(\langle A \rangle),$

taking falsehood as a primitive notion rather than equating it with truth of negation.

This would change the picture a little bit, but not very much. For if we take falsehood as a primitive notion, we need some rules governing it. Presumably one rule is an analog of (T-Elim):

(F-Elim) $\quad\quad\quad\quad\quad\quad \text{False}(\langle A \rangle) \vDash \neg A.$

And this plus (¬T-Introd) is enough to get at least *half* of the argument from accepting (GLUT*) to accepting (GAP*): it plus (¬T-Introd) gives

(1) $\quad\quad\quad\quad\quad\quad \text{False}(\langle A \rangle) \vDash \neg\text{True}(\langle A \rangle).$

And that suffices for getting from the claim that A is a glut to the claim that it is not a glut; and also (given excluded middle, which Priest accepts) for getting from the claim that A is a glut to the claim that it is either a gap or solely false. So if one wants to say of some sentences that they are gluts, without saying that they are either gaps or solely false, then even taking False as primitive does not obviate the need to restrict (¬T-Introd) and hence restrict Intersubstitutivity for truth.

It would of course be a lot less confusing if, once we had accepted that a sentence is a glut, we could reject the claim that it is not a glut: accepting of a sentence that it both is and is not a glut is difficult for someone with an unrefined and sluggish mind to get his head around. But even on Priest's theory, one must accept of *some* sentences both that they are gluts and that they are not gluts: indeed, he clearly must say of the Liar sentence Q that though it's a glut, it also isn't true and hence isn't a glut. (Recall that the Liar sentence as I'm understanding it asserts of itself that it is not true, rather than that it is false. So if it's a glut it's true, and by (T-Elim) it's not true and hence not a glut. But something similar happens with a modified Liar that asserts its own falsity: it too is a glut and hence false, and from this we can argue that it is not false and hence not a glut.)

The conclusion that some or all gluts are also not gluts is of course perfectly coherent in paraconsistent logic, even if difficult for those of a more classical bent to understand. But if one is going to accept it for the Liar sentence (and the modified Liar too), it is unclear to me why one shouldn't accept it for all sentences one regards as gluts, if one can get the full Intersubstitutivity Principle by so doing. For as argued in Chapter 13, the full Intersubstitutivity Principle seems crucial to truth serving its role as a device of generalization.

25

Some Dialetheic Theories

25.1. PRIEST'S LP

The simplest dialetheic treatment of the paradoxes, which Priest often mentions but does not advocate, is based on a dual of the strong Kleene logic; Priest has dubbed this logic LP (for "logic of paradox"). Kripke's fixed point construction can be used (or alternatively, dualized) to show the consistency of the Naive Theory of Truth (the full Intersubstitutivity Principle plus the truth schema) within this logic.

In more detail: the Kripke construction offered in Section 3 yields, for any classical ω-model of the ground language, a corresponding 3-valued model based on the strong Kleene valuation in which for any sentence A, the value of True($\langle A \rangle$) is always the same as the value of A. We can use this construction to form a variety of different theories of truth. Here are four of them, three of which we've seen before:

Kleene gap theory for the model: The strongly classical theory in which the extension of 'True' is the set of sentences with value 1 in the model.

Internal Kleene paracomplete theory for the model: The theory consisting of all sentences with value 1 in the model.

Kleene glut theory for the model: The strongly classical theory in which the extension of 'True' is the set of sentences with value other than 0 in the model.

Internal Kleene dialetheic theory for the model: The theory consisting of all sentences with value other than 0 in the model.

In each case, we can abstract from the particular model, by looking at what is bound to be in the theory whatever the ground model (provided that it is an ω-model). In the first and third cases we get classical gap and glut theories considered in Chapters 7 and 8. In the second case we get the simple paracomplete theory KFS, whose underlying logic is K_3. In the fourth, we get the truth theory based on LP. LP can thus be viewed as a logic based on the strong Kleene tables, but with the designated values including not just 1 but also $1/2$.

The weakness of the truth theory for LP is like the weakness of KFS: the theory contains no reasonable conditional. Here, as in KFS, the "conditional" $\supset$, where $A \supset B$ is defined to be $\neg A \vee B$, simply doesn't behave in a reasonable way. But here the reasons are different. Unlike in KFS, $A \supset A$ is a law, since given the definition of $\supset$ this is just an equivalent of excluded middle. But we don't have "modus ponens for $\supset$": that's an equivalent of disjunctive syllogism, and hence of the explosion rule (EXP). The absence of a conditional with modus ponens is enough to prevent any semblance of ordinary reasoning. (Among many other things, it precludes reasoning by mathematical induction: a theory that invalidates modus ponens will clearly invalidate induction as well.)[1] But if the absence of modus ponens isn't enough, we also have a failure of transitivity: $A \supset B$ and $B \supset C$ don't entail $A \supset C$. (Take A to have value 1, B to have value $1/2$, and C to have value 0.)

On the positive side, the Kripke construction guarantees that the Intersubstitutivity Principle for truth does not lead to contradiction within LP. And since LP unlike K_3 contains $A \equiv A$ as a law (where $\equiv$ is defined from $\supset$ in the obvious way), the Intersubstitutivity Principle implies a version of the truth schema in this logic (the version where $\equiv$ is used as the biconditional).

But even if getting a truth schema is viewed as an important goal separate from that of the Intersubstitutivity Principle, this way of getting one seems a rather hollow victory. For in this theory, the instance of $\text{True}(\langle A \rangle) \equiv A$ where A is a paradoxical sentence has the same pathological status as A itself: it's only because the theory adopts such low standards of assertibility as to allow for the assertion of pathological sentences like the Liar and its negation that it allows for the assertion of $\text{True}(\langle Q \rangle) \equiv Q$.

I'm inclined to the view that the only satisfactory way of validating a truth schema within a dialetheic logic is to reject that the instances of the schema are dialetheias. That is, not only should all instances of

(T) $\qquad\qquad\qquad\text{True}(\langle A \rangle) \leftrightarrow A$

be validated, but *no instance of the negation should be validated*. This is a goal that can be met, as we'll see in the next section; but it is not met in LP, even on the reading of $\leftrightarrow$ as $\equiv$.

25.2. DUALIZING PARACOMPLETE THEORIES

Just as one can use the Kripke model of Chapter 3 to get a dialetheic theory instead of a paracomplete one, one can do the same using other models for paracomplete theories. For instance, take Lukasiewicz continuum-valued models for sentential logic. In Chapter 5, the valid sentences of such models were taken as the sentences with value 1. But suppose we took the valid sentences to be

---

[1] Suppose A and B are such that both A and $A \supset B$ have designated value but B doesn't. Let $A(0)$ be A, and for each $n > 0$ let $A(n)$ be B. Then $A(0) \land \forall n[A(n) \supset A(n+1)]$ is equivalent to $A \land (A \supset B)$, hence has designated value, while $\forall n A(n)$ is equivalent to $A \land B$ and hence entails the undesignated B.

those with value greater than 0? Or alternatively, those with value $1/2$ or greater? In either case, we would get dialetheic logics (in which excluded middle holds): both the Liar sentence and its negation would be valid.

Moreover, these theories would do better than LP as regards the truth schema: all instances would still be true, but now non-dialetheically so; that is, no negation of an instance of the truth schema would be true. (The construction of Chapter 4 shows that instances of Schema (T) get value 1, so the negations get value 0.)

Of course, such continuum-valued models aren't ultimately adequate: we saw in Chapter 4 that the models break down when we try to extend them past sentential logic to quantificational logic. That not only rules out successful paracomplete theories based on such models, it rules out successful dialetheic theories based on them as well.

But can't we use dialetheic theories based on the model theory of Section 17.1? We can indeed. There are two notable such theories, one which takes the valid sentences to be those with value greater than **0** (whatever the underlying ground model) and the other that takes the valid sentences to be those with value greater than or equal to $1/2$ (whatever the underlying ground model). I'll call these the "Weak-Standards Theory" and the "Medium-Standards Theory" respectively. In both theories, the Liar sentence Q and its negation are each valid, since their value is $1/2$ in any model. In the Weak-Standards Theory, the Curry sentence K and its negation are valid, since their values are never **0**; in the Medium-Standards Theory, neither is valid, since their values are incomparable with $1/2$. Both theories validate the Intersubstitutivity Principle. And both not only validate the truth schema, they don't validate the negation of any instance of it: negations of instances of the truth schema always have value **0**. So we've found two fairly successful paraconsistent dialetheic theories.[2] Both theories validate excluded middle: $A \vee \neg A$ always gets a value of at least $1/2$.

Both theories, however, have some disadvantages. The most obvious disadvantage of the Weak-Standards Theory is that it doesn't validate modus ponens. For as we've seen, the Curry sentence K is valid in it. Since K is equivalent to '$K \rightarrow$ The earth is flat', the latter is valid too. But these two valid sentences lead by modus ponens to 'The earth is flat', which obviously is not valid: so modus ponens is not a valid rule of inference in the Weak-Standards Theory.

This problem is avoided in the Medium-Standards Theory: if A and $A \rightarrow B$ each have value greater than or equal to $1/2$ in the semantics of 17.1, B does too, as the reader can easily check.[3] The main disadvantage of the Medium-Standards Theory is that it doesn't validate disjunction elimination: a disjunction can take

---

[2] And of course for each of the variant paracomplete theories considered in Section 17.5, one could get two corresponding dialetheic theories in the same way.

[3] Despite the section heading, the Medium-Standards Theory is not really a dual of the theory in 17.1, or of any other paracomplete theory with modus ponens. In Chapter 8 I observed that modus ponens breaks the duality between classical glut and classical gap theories. So too it breaks the duality between paraconsistent dialetheic and paracomplete theories.

on a designated value even though neither disjunct does. For instance, when K is the Curry sentence, $K \vee \neg K$ takes on a designated value (greater than $1/2$ but less than 1) in *every* model, but there is *no* model in which either disjunct does. Indeed, given that the logic validates modus ponens and Intersubstitutivity, K leads to contradiction. So, though in every model $\neg K$ has a non-designated value, the disjunction of it with something that leads to contradiction has a designated value. (Similar points arise for $\exists$-elimination.)

The Medium-Standards Theory, then, has something of the flavor of weakly classical theories (though of course it avoids their main defect, by licensing full Intersubstitutivity). This is probably not enough to rule the Medium-Standards Theory out of consideration; but the fact that the theory of Section 17.1 validates $\vee$-Elimination and $\exists$-elimination seems to me to give it a striking advantage over the Medium-Standards Theory.

25.3. PRIEST'S CONDITIONALS

Priest has made a number of different suggestions over the years for supplementing LP with conditionals. He has offered a non-triviality proof for the truth schema in one of them, and suggested that it can be adapted to some of the others.

The theory for which he's actually offered the non-triviality proof (in Priest 2002, section 8.2)[4] employs a contraposable conditional, hence is not really to Priest's liking because the Tarski schema based on such a conditional does not allow for a distinction between gluts and gaps. Moreover, the non-triviality proof works by a construction using iterated Kripke fixed points over transparent valuations for conditionals, as in Chapter 16, so that even if it can be adapted to non-contraposable conditionals (and ones not supporting modus tollens) it is hard to see how to adapt it to a theory that allows for violations of Intersubstititivity (as is required to allow for a glut-gap distinction).

Admittedly, a system that includes Intersubstitutivity is strictly stronger than one without it, so any non-triviality proof for the former proves the non-triviality of the latter. But this is uninteresting if the non-triviality proof doesn't allow for a failure of Intersubstitutivity, since the whole point of the weaker system was to allow for such a failure.[5]

Indeed, the situation is really worse than that: the theories allowing for violations of Intersubstitutivity don't seem to have been clearly set out.

---

[4] This is based on a proof for a different system given in Brady 1989.
[5] Indeed, while the standard way of talking about logical systems specifies only what the system accepts, it would be natural to introduce an expanded conception of logical system in which it is also specified what the system *rejects*. In that case, a system that rejects the claim that all gluts are gaps isn't a subsystem of one with Intersubstitutivity, it is incompatible with it, and so it is even more straightforward that the non-triviality proof that Priest offers does not apply to the systems of interest to him.

The treatments of non-contraposable conditionals are clear: for the simplest, see Sections 6.5 and 9.2 of Priest 1987, which has been reprinted with new commentary as Priest 2006b; for a modified version with improved chance of allowing a non-trivial truth theory, see the new commentary on those sections in Sections 19.8 and 19.11 of Priest 2006b. As required for theories that distinguish gluts from gaps while keeping the truth schema, these conditionals are such as to invalidate modus tollens. The invalidity has an intuitive explanation in these theories. The motivation is simplest to explain for the Priest 1987 version: here the conditional is treated in a fairly standard modal fashion, except using the three LP values in the valuations at each world; $A \to B$ has a designated value at the ground world unless there is a world accessible from the ground world in which A has a designated value and B doesn't. If Q is a Liar sentence, it and its negation are designated in all worlds (as is $0 = 0$); so $0 = 0 \to Q$ is designated at the ground world, and so is $\neg Q$, but $\neg(0 = 0)$ obviously isn't, and so modus tollens fails.[6] So far everything is clear.

But to allow for a distinction between gluts and gaps while keeping the truth schema, Priest needs not only to allow violations of modus tollens but to allow them in some cases where the conditional is of form $\text{True}(\langle A \rangle) \to A$. And the problem is that Priest doesn't actually tell us how to evaluate sentences of form '$\text{True}(t)$' in these logics, so it isn't obvious that we will get failures of this form. That requires a valuation in which $\text{True}(\langle A \rangle)$ has a different value from A (even at the ground world of the model), but Priest gives no account of when that happens.

The issue is over cases when A has value $1/2$. In cases where A has value $1/2$, $\text{True}(\langle A \rangle)$ must have value $1/2$ or 1 to maintain the truth schema, but we need to know in which of these cases it's 1 and in which $1/2$,[7] and Priest doesn't tell us. (It has to be $1/2$ in some of these cases, such as the Liar; and for Intersubstitutivity to fail it also has to be 1 in some of these cases.) In a personal communication, Priest tells me that he wants $|\text{True}(\langle A \rangle)|$ to be 1 *in typical cases* in which $|A|$ is $1/2$, in line with the view that *typically*, gluts are not also gaps. But we need more precision than this before the issue of non-triviality can be investigated; and as noted, an interesting proof of non-triviality would obviously have to be on very different lines from that used for theories that always give $\text{True}(\langle A \rangle)$ the same value as A.

Let's put these worries aside: we do have at least one clear theory here, that of Priest 2002, and it is known to be non-trivial; and there may well be non-trivial theories using the conditionals Priest suggests in Priest 1987 and Priest 2002b. But there are two reasons why I'm unhappy about all such actual and possible theories. A minor reason is that in all such theories, the negations of some

---

[6] In Priest 2006b the semantics is modified by the use of a three-valued accessibility relation (of the sort familiar from relevance logic) instead of the two-valued one: in it, $A \to B$ has a designated value at the ground world unless for some pair $<x, y>$ of worlds that is accessible from the ground world, A has a designated value at x and B doesn't have a designated value at y. Modus tollens still fails for essentially the same reason.

[7] I'm naming the values as I did for LP: 1, $1/2$ and 0, corresponding to Priest's $\{1\}$, $\{1, 0\}$ and $\{0\}$.

instances of the truth schema will be validated, as they are in LP. Of course, this doesn't preclude the instances from being validated as well, so it doesn't undermine Priest's claims to have validated the truth schema; still, I think it would be far more desirable to validate it in a way that makes all instances of the truth schema come out "solely true" rather than being dialetheias. (We saw in the previous section that this further demand can be met.)

But my main reason for being unhappy about Priest's dialetheic theories (both those with Intersubstitutivity and those without) is that conditionals of form $A \to B$ behave very oddly *even when A and B are in the ground language* (the language not containing 'True', 'instantiates', etc.).

Part of the point here is that these conditionals do not reduce to the classical conditional when the antecedent and the consequent are in the ground language. For instance, A and B can be truths of the ground language (hence not dialetheic), and yet $A \to B$ not be true. That is to be expected if, like Priest,[8] one treats $A \to B$ as having a kind of modal force which the conditional of classical logic does not have: Priest's arrows, restricted to the ground language, are closer to $\Box(A \supset B)$ than to $A \supset B$. There's nothing wrong with having a modalized conditional in the language, but it seems to me that one wants an unmodalized conditional as well, one that obeys modus ponens and validates the truth schema. Priest doesn't supply one.

But a more important part of the point about the odd behavior of Priest's conditionals is that they behave very differently *even from the classical modalized conditional* $\Box(A \supset B)$, and *even in the ground language*. The problem arises because of embedded conditionals. For instance, with Priest conditionals, not all sentences of form $A \to (B \to B)$ will be true, even when A and B are in the ground language. The basic reason is that the truth of such a conditional at the actual world requires preservation of designatedness at all accessible worlds *including impossible ones*; in these impossible worlds, conditionals are evaluated in very weird ways while non-conditionals are evaluated according to the usual rules. So when A is a necessary truth of the ground language whose main connective isn't the $\to$ (e.g. when it is an instance of excluded middle), there will be an impossible world accessible from the actual world in which A is true and $B \to B$ isn't (even when B is also in the ground language). $A \to (B \to B)$ will then fail. This strikes me as quite different from any prior conception I had of a conditional; so different that I'm not sure of the significance of a consistency proof for a version of the Tarski schema formulated in terms of such a conditional.

Priest argues that deviation from the classical conditional even within the ground language is a *good* thing: in defense of it, he cites the well-known oddities of the material conditional even for 'True'-free sentences, such as the fact that "If I run for President in 2008 I'll win" comes out true since its antecedent is

---

[8] In the 2002 account as well as the 1987 and 2006b ones.

false. This raises big issues, on which I have no confident opinion. One issue is whether such oddities call for a new conditional connective at all. There are two ways to resist the claim that it does. One of them (Jackson 1979; Lewis 1986) is to try to handle examples like the above as involving the material conditional, but to invoke pragmatic rules for why such obviously true material conditionals are inappropriate to assert. I'm a bit skeptical of this, but more inclined to an alternative view, according to which the 'if... then' of English is ambiguous. The simplest version of this (to which one can add epicycles) has it that *embedded* conditionals in the ground language always behave in accordance with classical logic; but that in a typical utterance of an *unembedded* conditional "If A then B", the 'if... then' isn't really an operator at all. Instead, the unembedded conditional is to be evaluated accorded to the Ramsey test: the assertion is legitimate if and only if the conditional probability of B given A is high.[9]

I'm inclined to think that some such view of indicative conditionals is the best available, but there are other views, according to which typical 'if... then' statements of English in the ground language are to be handled by special connectives, such as the Stalnaker connective (Stalnaker 1968). This connective '$\rightarrow$' obeys radically different laws from the material conditional: in addition to being non-contraposable, it is not transitive ($A \rightarrow B$ and $B \rightarrow C$ don't imply $A \rightarrow C$) and strengthening of the antecedent is invalid ($A \rightarrow C$ doesn't imply $A \wedge B \rightarrow C$). In fact, the laws it obeys are the same as those of the counterfactual conditional. I think it would be desirable to show that a ground language that contained the Stalnaker connective in addition to a classical conditional can be conservatively extended to one containing a truth predicate, in accordance with the Intersubstitutivity Principle. To do this one would presumably have to generalize the Stalnaker connective a bit to contexts where excluded middle isn't assumed, just as one has to generalize the classical connective a bit. This would be a worthy project, which I have not undertaken. If Priest's point were that it would be nice to have such an account, I'd fully agree.

But what does this have to do with the conditionals Priest proposes? To anyone who thinks that the "paradoxes of material implication" show that indicative conditionals of English require a non-classical conditional, Priest's conditionals won't serve the purpose. First, Priest's conditionals obey strengthening of the antecedent, so that we can infer from "If that's a cockroach, it has six legs" to "If that's a cockroach that has had a leg amputated, it has six legs"—which is just the kind of inference that those worried about "paradoxes of material implication" will declare invalid. Second, Priest's conditionals obey transitivity: this implies strengthening of the antecedent, and so gives rise to a variant of the above example (use as the additional premise "If that's a cockroach that has had a leg amputated, it's a cockroach").

---

[9] This is similar to the view of Adams 1975 and Edgington 1995, though instead of saying that 'if... then' is ambiguous they restrict it to the unembedded use.

In addition, it's hard to believe that the indicative conditional of ordinary English doesn't license "If $0 = 0$ then if snow is white then snow is white", which as we've seen is invalid for Priest's conditional.

It seems to me that the conditional Priest uses in his validation of the truth schema is nothing like *any* ordinary conditional, even within the ground language; so the "truth schema" that he's validated has only a vague resemblance to the kind of truth schema we really want.[10]

These doubts do not at all cut against the heart of Priest's program: the idea of extending LP by adding a reasonable conditional and validating the Tarski schema for it (and preferably, (IP) as well) is still an attractive prospect, and I know of no reason to think that it can't be carried out with a more attractive conditional than the ones that Priest has offered. Indeed, the Medium-Standards Theory of the previous section seems to me to embody a far more attractive conditional than Priest's, so I take that theory to be some indication of the promise of Priest's program. As noted there, it does have a substantial defect that the analogous paracomplete theory offered in Chapter 17 does not share (viz., the absence of ∨-Elim); and *I don't know of* any form of paraconsistent dialetheism that avoids its problem without having other grave defects. But I have no reason to doubt that there are better forms of paraconsistent dialetheism not yet invented (and better forms of paracomplete theories too).

---

[10] A similar complaint could be made against my earliest attempt to save the truth schema in a paracomplete logic, that in Field 2002. But the ones developed in my later papers, and discussed in this book, are immune to the objection because in them the conditional reduces to the classical conditional within the ground language.

26
Paraconsistent Dialetheism and Soundness

None of the theories of truth considered in earlier parts of the book (other than hyper-dialetheism) declare themselves sound: some declare their own axioms untrue; many declare their rules not to be unrestrictedly truth-preserving; and even the theories that avoid those defects, notably the paracomplete theories, refrain from declaring their own rules unrestrictedly truth-preserving (though they don't actually declare them not to be).

It might be thought that paraconsistent dialetheism does better in this regard. Indeed, Priest argues that it does. I will argue that it does not, and indeed that the standard versions of it do worse.

26.1. THE FIRST INCOMPLETENESS THEOREM, CURRY'S PARADOX, AND TRUTH-PRESERVATION

It is clear that Priest thinks that our naive proof procedures declare themselves unsound: these proof procedures lead from premises that they declare true to the Liar sentence, which they declare untrue. But Priest thinks that what's important isn't whether they declare themselves *un*sound, but whether they declare themselves *sound*; and he claimed, in Chapter 3 of Priest 1987, that our naive proof procedures can *prove* their own soundness, as well as proving their own unsoundness.

Priest also argued that these naive proof procedures are recursive. So the notion of naive proof has an extensionally adequate definition in arithmetic, and so we can formulate a Gödel sentence that asserts in effect that it is not provable by the naive proof procedures. Then either (i) it is true and unprovable or (ii) it is false and provable. But if provable, it's also true, by the soundness of our naive proof procedures, which Priest claims to be naively provable. So in case (ii) as well as case (i), the Gödel sentence is true. This proves that it's true, hence proves the Gödel sentence itself; so it's provable, by a naive proof. And since it asserts it is not provable, it's false. Finally, it is unprovable, since it's true and says it's unprovable. So both (i) and (ii) hold: it's both true and false, and both provable and unprovable. And the Gödel sentence is a purely arithmetic sentence: we've "established" an inconsistency within arithmetic! "In this context (viz., of naive proof procedures) the Gödel sentence becomes a recognizably paradoxical sentence", and is a dialetheia. (Priest 1987, p. 46; pagination here and below is that of the 2006b reprinting.) This conclusion is not withdrawn in the commentary on the chapter in the new edition (2006b), and indeed is re-emphasized in the new Chapter 17.

I think this conclusion that there are dialetheias within arithmetic defies belief, and I don't think insisting on it will bring many converts to dialetheism. (As John Lennon put it: "If you go carrying pictures of chairman Mao, you ain't going to make it with anyone anyhow.") And insisting on it is unnecessary: the argument that dialetheism implies it fails. Why? Some may feel the problem lies in the claim that we can sensibly talk of naive proof procedures or that such naive proof procedures are recursive, but I share Priest's view that both assumptions are plausible. (The second seems *highly* plausible, given the first.) What is questionable, rather, is the assumption that naive proof procedures can prove their own soundness.

Priest's defense of that claim (Priest 1987, pp. 49–50) is that we can give the obvious inductive proof: the axioms are true, the rules of inference preserve truth, so by induction the theorems are all true. I now want to argue that this is incorrect: even in Priest's paraconsistent dialetheic context, it is impossible to argue that all the rules preserve truth.[1]

The dialetheic systems of naive proof that Priest thinks prove their own soundness go beyond LP, in that they contain a conditional that obeys modus ponens. I will argue that it is impossible for such a system (if non-trivial) to prove that modus ponens preserves truth. In fact, I will argue that in such a system we can show that modus ponens doesn't preserve truth. But before arguing this, it's worth remarking that a system based on LP could also not prove its own soundness, though for a different reason. The problem with proving soundness within LP is that the only obvious method for trying to prove soundness is via mathematical induction, and (as noted in 25.1) this is not a valid rule in LP or any other system that invalidates modus ponens.

Returning to paraconsistent dialetheic systems with a modus-ponens-supporting conditional, why can't we prove within them that modus ponens preserves truth? Because of Curry's paradox. The claim that modus ponens preserves truth is the claim

(1) $\forall x \forall y \forall z [(x$ and z are sentences$) \land (y$ is the conditional with antecedent x and consequent $z) \land (x$ and y are true$) \to z$ is true$]$.

For any particular sentences A and B, this entails

$$\text{True}(\langle A \rangle) \land \text{True}(\langle A \to B \rangle) \to \text{True}(\langle B \rangle).$$

But let A be the Curry sentence K, equivalent to $K \to$ The Earth is flat; and let B be 'The Earth is flat'. Then in particular, the claim that modus ponens preserves truth implies

---

[1] Here I'm assuming that "Priest's dialetheic context" is not trivial, i.e. that it can't prove everything.

(*) $\text{True}(\langle K \rangle) \wedge \text{True}(\langle K \rightarrow \text{The Earth is flat} \rangle) \rightarrow \text{True}(\langle \text{The Earth is flat} \rangle)$.

But since "$K \rightarrow$ The Earth is flat" is equivalent to K, the second conjunct is equivalent to $\text{True}(\langle K \rangle)$. So (*) is equivalent to

$$\text{True}(\langle K \rangle) \rightarrow \text{True}(\langle \text{The Earth is flat} \rangle),$$

which in turn is equivalent to

$$\text{True}(\langle K \rangle) \rightarrow \text{The Earth is flat},$$

and hence to K. In short, the claim that modus ponens preserves truth entails the Curry sentence. But accepting the Curry sentence would commit one to accepting that the Earth is flat (given modus ponens and (T-Introd), both of which Priest accepts). So for the same reason that paracomplete theories can't accept that modus ponens preserves truth, paraconsistent dialetheic theories can't either: the claim leads to triviality.

If the claim that modus ponens preserves truth leads to triviality, does that show that modus ponens *doesn't* preserve truth? According to paracomplete theories, no; but according to any theory that accepts both excluded middle and ∨-Elimination, and hence the reductio rule, yes. (See the discussion of how to get from excluded middle and ∨-Elimination to the reductio rule in Section 4 of the Introduction.) Priest does accept excluded middle and ∨-Elimination and hence reductio. And so even though he accepts modus ponens, he must both

(i) accept that modus ponens does not preserve truth,

and

(ii) refuse to accept that it does preserve truth.

The claim that modus ponens preserves truth comes out not a dialetheia, but "solely false".

Part (i) of this is not, I think, essential to paraconsistent dialetheism: a view could be both a form of paraconsistent dialetheism and be paracomplete (and Beall 2005 suggests such a theory). On such a view, there would be no obvious argument from the inconsistency of the supposition that modus ponens preserves truth to the claim that it does not preserve truth. But if one is going to restrict excluded middle, it is unobvious what the advantages are of going dialetheic, given that non-dialetheic views without excluded middle are already adequate to preserving the naive theory of truth (and of property-instantiation etc.) So I think that Priest's view on this is probably the better one for a dialetheist to take, and it does commit its proponent to holding that modus ponens fails to preserve truth (as well as to rejecting the claim that it does preserve truth).

It may be complained that this depends on using (1) as the reading of the claim that modus ponens preserves truth. Aren't other readings possible? Yes, but they won't serve for purposes of a soundness proof.

The first reading is the one that Priest implicitly gives in arguing that modus ponens preserves truth:

(2) $\forall x \forall y \forall z[(x \text{ and } z \text{ are sentences}) \wedge (y \text{ is the conditional with antecedent } x \text{ and consequent } z) \wedge (y \text{ is true}) \rightarrow (x \text{ is true} \rightarrow z \text{ is true})]$.

On this reading, modus ponens does preserve truth: that's because on Priest's theory we have the "Conditional Intersubstitutivity Principle"

(CI) $\text{True}(\langle A \rightarrow B \rangle) \leftrightarrow [\text{True}(\langle A \rangle) \rightarrow \text{True}(\langle B \rangle)]$.

(The ordering of the embedding of the conditionals is very important: if you reverse the formulas 'y is true' and 'x is true' in (2), or '$\text{True}(\langle A \rightarrow B \rangle)$' and '$\text{True}(\langle A \rangle)$' in (CI), you no longer have a law.)

There is something about the suggestion that we read 'truth-preservation' in this way that looks suspicious: it makes a lot depend on the fact that we have formulated modus ponens as the two-premise rule $A, A \rightarrow B \vDash B$ rather than as the single-premise rule $A \wedge (A \rightarrow B) \vDash B$, which is equivalent using the usual conjunction rules. Had we used the latter, there would seem to be no alternative to rendering the truth-preservation of modus ponens as implying each instance of $\text{True}(\langle A \wedge (A \rightarrow B) \rangle) \rightarrow \text{True}(\langle B \rangle)$, which like (1) would generate triviality.

But what exactly is the problem with the suggestion that we define 'truth-preservation' by (2)? The problem is that (2) is not enough for a soundness proof: the induction step in such a proof requires (1). This point requires comment, given Priest's discussion of the format for an inductive soundness proof: Priest seems to formulate what's required in the induction step not as a conditional but as a rule.

Now suppose that A is inferred from $A_1, \ldots, A_n$ by rule R, and that we have established that $\langle A_1 \rangle, \ldots, \langle A_n \rangle$ are true. Then we infer that $\langle A \rangle$ is true by, essentially, rule R.... (1987, pp. 49–50; notation altered to the notation used in this book.)

But this is *not* all that's involved in the induction step. It's true that if the aim were only to establish that a particular theorem A is true, this is all we'd need; but if that were all we wanted to do we wouldn't need an inductive soundness proof, we'd just derive A and then derive $\text{True}(\langle A \rangle)$ from it by the truth schema plus modus ponens. What a soundness proof requires is more than the proof of $\text{True}(\langle A \rangle)$ for each theorem A, it requires proof of a generalization: for all sentences x, if x is a theorem then x is true. And certainly the standard format for such a proof is to prove an induction step of form (1). It might perhaps be thought that an alternative format might be possible, using an induction step of form (2), but I think the reader tempted by this thought will not be able to work it out satisfactorily (in a system where (2) doesn't imply (1)). It's true that one can get to any specific conclusion of form $\text{True}(\langle B \rangle)$ from the premises $\text{True}(\langle A \rightarrow B \rangle)$ and $\text{True}(\langle A \rangle)$, but again, getting the specific instances isn't the issue, the issue is getting the generalization. (A quick and incomplete answer to the question of why one can't use (2) for an induction step in Priest's systems is that in the semantics, (2) evaluates the conditional *y* and its antecedent *x* at different worlds.)

A second alternative suggestion for how to understand the soundness of modus ponens would be like (1) but with '→' replaced by '⊃' (where $A \supset B$ is defined as $\neg A \vee B$):

(3) $\forall x \forall y \forall z[(x$ and z are sentences$) \wedge (y$ is the conditional with antecedent x and consequent $z) \wedge (x$ and y are true$) \supset z$ is true].

(By a conditional is still meant a formula of form $A \to B$, not one of form $A \supset B$.) (3) is valid in the theories based on the Priest conditionals of Section 14.3 (though not in the Medium-Standards Theory of Section 14.2). But this is no help in the soundness proof, for the shift to the ⊃ prevents the use of mathematical induction, which as I've noted several times is not valid for ⊃.

The fact that paraconsistent dialetheic theories *can't* prove their own soundness is, I think, a virtue: it means that a dialetheist needn't conclude that there are dialetheia even within ordinary arithmetic.[2]

26.2. CAN WE GET EVEN RESTRICTED TRUTH-PRESERVATION?

I've argued that Priest should accept that in the most important sense of truth-preservation (and the only one that could be used in a soundness proof), modus ponens fails to preserve truth in a dialetheic theory. And it isn't that it both preserves truth and fails to preserve it: a dialetheist must reject the claim that modus ponens preserves truth, on pain of triviality.

That needn't prevent a dialetheist from accepting modus ponens, of course: he can employ it, while accepting that it doesn't preserve truth. Indeed, in considering other theories that hold that their own rules don't preserve truth (classical glut theories and strong versions of supervaluation and revision theories), we've seen a way to make pretty good sense of this: by means of the distinction between restricted and unrestricted truth preservation. Can the paraconsistent dialetheist employ the same defense?

From the example so far, it certainly looks as if this is possible. So far, the only example given where a paraconsistent dialetheist declares one of her own rules not to be truth preserving is modus ponens; and the counterexample to its preserving truth (in the sense of (1), not (2) or (3)) involves the premises K and $K \to \bot$, where K is the Curry sentence. And these are sentences that the dialetheist doesn't accept. (Although dialetheists sometimes suggest that all

---

[2] S. Shapiro 2002 shares Priest's assumption that a dialetheic theory can prove its own soundness and hence its own Gödel sentence, and from this draws consequences for dialetheism that would not be at all easy to swallow.

paradoxical sentences are dialetheias, this can't be so of the Curry sentence. To treat it as a dialetheia would be to accept both it and its negation. But accepting K would require accepting the absurdity that is its consequent, by the dialetheist's truth rules plus modus ponens. Acceptance of its negation as well would do nothing to change this. So the dialetheist rejects K. If, like Priest, she accepts excluded middle, she will hold that K is "solely false"; more accurately, she will hold it false without also holding that it is true.) So the example above is no counterexample to *restricted* truth preservation—to the claim that her rules preserve truth *where it matters*, viz., when applied to theorems or to other sentences that the dialetheist accepts.[3]

Can the paraconsistent dialetheist maintain that *all* her rules are restrictedly truth-preserving (even though not including this as part of her theory)?

She could if her theory included the rule $B \vDash A \to B$ (which in addition to being part of classical logic is part of the paracomplete logics considered in Parts III and IV, as part of the "Positive Horseshoe Rule"). For then she could adapt an argument from Section 19.3 that is available to other theorists (classical glut theorists, weakly classical theorists, and paracomplete theorists) whose theories don't imply that their rules are unrestrictedly truth-preserving. The argument is that in any specific case where premises (say $A_1, \ldots, A_n$) entail a conclusion (say B) in the logic, commitment to $A_1, \ldots, A_n$ commits one to B, which in turn commits one to $\text{True}(\langle B \rangle)$, which by the aforementioned rule commits one to $\text{True}(\langle A_1 \rangle) \wedge \ldots \wedge \text{True}(\langle A_n \rangle) \to \text{True}(\langle B \rangle)$. So commitment to the premises requires commitment to the entailment being truth-preserving in that instance. And there would then be no obvious bar to accepting the universal generalization that it preserves truth in all instances where we are committed to the premises; which isn't to say that the theorist would be in a position to prove such a generalization.

Actually this argument doesn't really require the full rule $B \vDash A \to B$: the weaker rule

(*) $\qquad\qquad\qquad A, B \vDash A \to B$

would do as well for the argument. This rule is acceptable on some readings of the conditional for which the rule $B \vDash A \to B$ is not acceptable: notably, for the Stalnaker conditional and the Lewis counterfactual conditional. (I don't know of a satisfactory truth theory incorporating such conditionals, but expect that such theories are possible.)

But to argue in this way, the paraconsistent dialetheist would seem to need at least the rule $A, B \vDash A \to B$ if not the stronger rule $B \vDash A \to B$. Are these rules dialetheically acceptable? They certainly aren't for the dialetheic conditionals considered in Section 25.2: although these theories are based on the same algebra

---

[3] Of course this couldn't be used to restore a soundness proof, for reasons we've discussed in connection with other theories.

as used for paracomplete theories that have both rules, the switch in "threshold for designatedness" invalidates the rules.

More generally, the rules can't be acceptable for *any* contraposable dialetheic conditional (that supports modus ponens). For by contraposition, the stronger rule would yield $B \vDash \neg B \to \neg A$, which would then yield explosion by modus ponens (plus double-negation elimination). Similarly, the weaker rule would yield $A, B, \neg B \vDash \neg A$, which is close enough to explosion to be clearly unacceptable to a dialetheist (and which indeed leads to explosion given excluded middle and ∨-Elimination).

Priest, as we've seen, favors uncontraposable conditionals, thereby removing the most obvious bar to his accepting (*). Indeed, like the uncontraposable Lewis and Stalnaker conditionals, the Priest conditionals have a kind of modal force; and as noted, the Lewis and Stalnaker conditionals support (*). However, the modal force that the Priest conditionals have is quite unlike that which the Stalnaker and Lewis conditionals have: in order for $A \to B$ to be true (or designated) at the actual world, it doesn't suffice that A and B both be true (or designated) at the actual world; we also need something about other worlds (or pairs of worlds) accessible from the actual world. As a result, (*) is invalid for the Priest conditional. This makes it *unobvious* that a dialetheism based on such a conditional can maintain that its own rules are even restrictedly truth preserving.

And in fact it is worse than unobvious: it is false. (At least, that's so if for each axiom B, we count it as a rule that we can infer B from any sentence.) For let B be any axiom with a conditional as its main connective: say one of form $C \to C$. Then the inference to B from any validity not containing a conditional is valid: e.g. $0 = 0 \vDash C \to C$. But in all these theories, $0 = 0 \to (C \to C)$ and hence $\text{True}(\langle 0 = 0 \rangle) \to \text{True}(\langle C \to C \rangle)$ will be false, because of "impossible worlds" where the conditional $C \to C$ behaves badly though non-conditionals are well-behaved.

So these theories deem the inference from $0 = 0$ to $C \to C$ a valid inference *with a true premise*, but they also declare the inference not to preserve truth in this instance (in the sense of truth preservation that would be required for a soundness proof). This seems a far worse situation than we had for either classical glut theories or weakly classical theories or paracomplete theories.

Indeed, the situation is worse still. For in this example, the premise $0 = 0$ is not only true but "solely true": the dialetheist rejects its negation. So we have a failure of even *super-restricted* truth preservation, that is, truth-preservation of the inference when applied to solely true premises. And indeed, it is a failure where the conclusion as well as the premise is in no way paradoxical. Of course, this only serves to illustrate how very strange Priest's conditional is.

The situation is *less* bad for certain other dialetheic conditionals, for instance, that of the Medium-Standards Theory of Section 25.2: there we get no counterexamples to restricted truth preservation in which the premise has maximum semantic value. But the Medium-Standards Theory is not very satisfactory since it violates ∨-Elimination.

A severe version of the problem of the last four paragraphs is inevitable for any non-trivial paraconsistent dialetheic theory that validates the truth schema, modus ponens, and Conditional Intersubstitutivity and that meets the following other natural constraints:

(i) it obeys ∨-Elimination
(ii) it obeys excluded middle
(iii) the conditional obeys a contraposition rule.

The reason: Using (i) and (ii), $\neg K$ must be a theorem; so $\neg(0 = 1) \models \neg K$. If restricted (or even super-restricted) truth-preservation holds, $\models \text{True}(\langle \neg(0 = 1) \rangle) \to \text{True}(\langle \neg K \rangle)$, which by Conditional Intersubstitutivity is equivalent to $\models \neg(0 = 1) \to \neg K$. But given (iii) this yields $K \to 0 = 1$, hence K, hence $0 = 1$; so a non-trivial theory with (i)–(iii) can't allow for even a restricted (or indeed even a super-restricted) truth-preservation claim.

Moreover, the latter part of the proof shows that if we have (iii) we can derive a contradiction from $\text{True}(\langle \neg(0 = 1) \rangle) \to \text{True}(\langle \neg K \rangle)$; so with (i) and (ii) in addition, we can derive

$$\neg[\text{True}(\langle \neg(0 = 1) \rangle) \to \text{True}(\langle \neg K \rangle)].$$

Since by (i) and (ii) alone we have $\neg(0 = 1) \models \neg K$, this means that (i)–(iii) allow us to assert that our theory is *not* restrictedly (or even super-restrictedly) truth-preserving. In short: we can declare restricted (and even super-restricted) truth-preservation false *and* we can't declare it true.

The conclusion is that if a paraconsistent dialetheist wants restricted truth-preservation, as I think he should, he can't have all of (i)–(iii).

Perhaps the road most in the spirit of Priest would be to come up with a theory that (like Priest's) satisfies (i) and (ii) but not (iii), but that is restrictedly truth-preserving (and provably non-trivial). Such a theory might still validate full Intersubstitutivity (the failure of that doesn't follow from the failure of contraposition, the implication between the two is in the other direction); or one might follow Priest in restricting Intersubstitutivity, though to my mind the cost is high.

If one wants to keep (iii), one has a choice between (i) and (ii); and giving up reasoning by cases strikes me as a high cost, so I think there is something to be said for giving up excluded middle even in a dialetheic context. But of course if we do this, it is unobvious what the dialetheism gains us, since we've already seen *non-dialetheic* theories without excluded middle but with (i) and (iii) that keep the Tarski schema and the Intersubstitutivity of $\text{True}(\langle A \rangle)$ with A. I don't say that it's inconceivable that allowing for dialetheias in such a context could bring some advantages; but I have no clear idea what the advantages would be.

27

Hyper-Determinacy and Revenge

Priest believes that paraconsistent dialetheic theories are not subject to genuine revenge problems, and I am (somewhat tentatively) inclined to agree with him about this. However, I also think (and far less tentatively) that any *apparent* revenge problem for the paracomplete theory of Part III arises *with at least equal force* for paraconsistent dialetheic theories: there is no possible advantage of paraconsistent dialetheic theories over paracomplete theories with regard to revenge.

To the extent that revenge worries are based on the inability of paracomplete theories to prove their own soundness, it should already be clear from the previous chapter that going dialetheic offers no advantage. (Putting aside the possibility of declaring that there are dialetheias within classical set theory, anyway.) So the focus in this chapter will be on other matters: primarily

The (paraconsistent) dialetheist's view of his own metatheory,

and

Issues of expressive incompleteness.

27.1. MODEL THEORY, DESIGNATED VALUES AND TRUTH

Each of Priest's various suggestions for a dialetheic logic are given by providing a classical metatheory in which the proposed validity relation is explained. Validity is taken to involve *preservation of designated value*. In the modal semantics that Priest prefers, there are three possible values at each world in the model structure; I've called these 1, $1/2$, and 0, but to use a notation more like Priest's we can instead call them {1}, {1,0} and {0}. An inference is taken to be *valid* if in every model, whenever the premises have value {1} or {1,0} in the ground world of the model, the conclusion has one of these values there as well.

This model theory could be offered in either of two spirits. The obvious way of understanding it is that it is supposed to be strictly correct: not necessarily as giving the *meaning* of 'valid', but as literally extensionally adequate. If we put aside the possibility that we should take a dialetheic attitude toward set theory itself—a possibility that Priest takes seriously but I suspect few of his readers will, and which in any case I am unwilling to—then this requires that validity is an effectively classical notion. In particular, the notion of validity would be non-dialetheic: any claim that an inference is *both valid and not valid* would have to be rejected. This is certainly the easiest way to understand Priest's theory. And it seems unobjectionable: there are plenty of areas of discourse that are effectively classical, and standard set theory is presumably one of them; what can be wrong with holding that discourse about dialetheic validity is also one of them? Indeed, the view would have the great advantage that it would mean that Priest and his opponents could agree as to what is dialetheically valid and what isn't. Of course, they would still disagree about the policy of accepting all and only the inferences that are dialetheically valid; the advantage, though, is that they would understand what they are disagreeing about, they would understand what 'dialetheic validity' comes to.

The alternative understanding is that the classical model theory for dialetheic logic is not strictly correct, even extensionally, presumably because '(dialetheically) valid' is itself a dialetheic notion: some inferences *can* be both valid and not valid. This too is in principle a defensible view: the model theory could still be of use in giving the opponent of dialetheism a pretty good, if not perfect, view of what paraconsistent dialetheism is all about.

I'm not completely sure which of these best describes Priest's own attitude (though in Section 18.5 of 2006b he leans toward the latter). But to repeat: I see no problem either way.

However, the issue becomes important in connection with another issue: the relation between model theory and truth. If the model-theory is developed within set theory, two consequences follow. First, there is no model that faithfully reflects the full universe. Second, we can't be dialetheic in our assignment of values to a given sentence: we can assign it one of the values $\{1\}$, $\{0,1\}$ and $\{0\}$, but the model theory doesn't license assigning more than one such value, and we must reject any claim that the sentence has more than one such value, or that it both does and doesn't have one of the designated values. (Again, I'm putting aside the possibility of dialetheism within set theory itself.) And in that case, we can't possibly accept an identification of truth with anything model-theoretic, say with having designated value in some preferred model: for the theory has it that sentences like Q are both true and not true.

One possibility at this point would be to maintain that there is a model theory not statable in standard set theory, with a notion of designated value in which a sentence can both have a designated value and not have a designated value. But I think it is fair to say that the model theory Priest offers in standard set theory gives us little grasp of what this imagined model theory would be like.[1]

---

[1] Priest seems to agree:

Is there a metatheory for paraconsistent logics that is acceptable in paraconsistent terms? The answer to this question is not at all obvious. (Priest 2006b, p. 258)

The better thing to say is what I said on behalf of both continuum-valued semantics (in Section 5.6) and of my own theory: truth is one thing, designated value another. On this view, we shouldn't expect truth to be defined model-theoretically, or in any other way. Rather, the understanding of truth comes from the laws that it obeys. These laws may include Intersubstitutivity, as they do on some versions of dialetheism; or they may include only Intersubstitutivity outside the scope of a negation, as in Priest's preferred theories. But however one goes on this, it is by virtue of the laws of truth that we understand truth, not by a connection to the model theory. What the set-theoretic model theory primarily does is to establish that these laws of truth don't get us into trouble. (At least, that's what a Brady-like model theory would do for dialetheic theories with contraposable conditionals, and what we may hope for in the case of Priest's theories.)[2] This position, it seems to me, is perfectly satisfactory, and would protect Priest against the sort of charges considered against continuum-valued logic in Section 5.6. But of course no one who takes this line can object to the paracomplete theorist adopting the analogous line.

27.2. SOLE TRUTH AND SOLE FALSEHOOD

A common worry about paraconsistent dialetheism (T. Parsons 1990; Littman and Simmons 2004; S. Shapiro 2004) can be roughly put as follows: the dialetheist can't express the idea that something is *not* a dialetheia, or that it is solely true (true and not a dialetheia), or that it is solely false (false and not a dialetheia).

Of course, this objection can't really be correct *as just stated* (as the authors themselves are all aware): the notion of a dialetheia is certainly defined within Priest's language (as something that is both true and false), and so 'not a dialetheia', 'true and not a dialetheia', and 'false and not a dialetheia' are defined in it as well. The problem that these authors are raising is that on these definitions, the notions don't behave in accordance with how they seemed intended to behave when the theory was being explained.

There is, I think, considerable justice in the complaint, though whether it goes just against the standard explanations of dialetheism or the doctrine itself is harder to evaluate. The standard explanations strongly suggest that 'glutty', 'gappy', 'solely true', and 'solely false' are mutually exclusive, a view that we've seen that no paraconsistent dialetheist can hold. (Basically, the standard

---

[2] As I've said, we needn't rule out getting a model theory that uses dialetheic resources (perhaps a dialetheic property theory?) in which we can take a dialetheic attitude toward claims about the values of sentences. But even if we did, it would not be through such a model theory that we understand 'true': we understand it via the laws that govern it.

explanations treat paraconsistent dialetheism as if it were a classical glut theory, in much the way that some explanations of paracomplete theories treat them as if they were classical gap theories.) In my own explanation of paraconsistent dialetheism I have tried to avoid this defect in the standard explanations.

But is there still a disconnect between what dialetheists need to say in motivating their theory and what their theory allows them to say? Whichever way the dialetheist goes on the question of the validity of the inference from $\neg A$ to $\neg \text{True}(\langle A \rangle)$, we've seen that he must declare the Liar sentence Q to be both a dialetheia and not a dialetheia: in particular, it must be declared to be both a dialetheia and also solely false. So *calling a sentence solely false is not by itself sufficient to commit one to rejecting its also being true*. It might be thought that this raises a problem.

Call two claims *strongly incompatible* if the acceptance of both would commit one to everything, so that acceptance of the first rules out acceptance of the second on pain of triviality. Non-dialetheists take the ordinary negation of A, or the claim that A is false, to be strongly incompatible with A, but of course the dialetheist rejects this on the ground that a sentence can be both true and false. This seems at first like a relatively small loss: it's just that if we want to rule out the acceptance of A, we now need to say that A is *solely* false. But the problem, or apparent problem, raised by the previous paragraph is that according to paraconsistent dialetheism, the claim that A is solely false (false and not a dialetheia) *also* fails to be strongly incompatible with A, so asserting it can't be used to rule out acceptance of A. The example of Q shows this, as would various other examples. (In versions of dialetheism that assume full Intersubstitutivity, *any* dialetheia would show it.)

How terrible is this? I think it is not *as* terrible as is sometimes made out, because a number of moves are available to the dialetheist to partially capture the intended force of declaring a sentence solely false.

One move that won't in the end take us very far is the one briefly contemplated in a paracomplete context in Section 3.8: the move of using rejection and conditional rejection. Instead of merely calling a sentence solely false, which is compatible with its being a dialetheia, we *reject* the sentence; instead of saying that if conditions C obtain it is solely false, we *conditionally reject* it (reject it conditionally on the assumption C). But in analogy to the discussion in 3.8, this method of capturing the intended force of "sole falsity" claims is very limited, because it isn't extendable to richer embedded contexts. For instance, we'd like to say things like

(1) If the premise of a conditional is solely true and the consequent is solely false, then the whole conditional is solely false;

but for this to "mean what we'd like it to mean", then 'solely true' and 'solely false' in it had better "mean what we'd like them to mean", and it's hard to see how to capture the intent of (1) in terms of rejection or conditional rejection.

Fortunately, the dialetheist has more powerful moves at his disposal. For instance, just as the paracomplete theorist will typically accept all instances of excluded middle in certain "non-problematic sub-languages" (e.g. those without 'true', 'instantiates' or related terms), the dialetheist can do something similar: accept all instances of the explosion rule (or disjunctive syllogism) in such a non-problematic sub-language (and regard this as part of his theory). Given that he has done so, accepting the negation of a sentence *in that sub-language* commits him to rejecting the sentence. (Strictly, it commits him only to *either* rejecting the sentence *or accepting everything*, but I think we can take it for granted that no one will accept everything, and ignore the second disjunct.)[3] Given this, then at least as applied to "non-problematic" sublanguages, (1) will "say what it ought to say".

But how about sentences in the more "paradox-prone" parts of language, say involving 'True'? Consider for instance a contingent Curry sentence, such as

K: If what the nasty man on the screen is saying is true then I'm the Pope,

said by a nasty man who isn't the Pope and who unbeknownst to himself is the person on the screen. The dialetheist who accepts excluded middle will want to say that if the facts are as I've described, the sentence is solely false—where this is intended to rule out its being true. But just saying that it's solely false doesn't seem to convey what we mean, because on dialetheic doctrine some sentences, such as the Liar, are both solely false and also both true and false. *Prima facie*, this is a problem.

There are still moves available that don't depend on the (ultimately insufficient) idea of rejection as autonomous from acceptance. Here's one that Priest himself mentions (Priest 2006b, p. 291). (I won't take the time to explore the extent to which it could handle embedded constructions like (1); but even if not, it is of interest.) Suppose one wants to find a sentence strongly incompatible with K. As we've seen, the claim that A is solely false won't do it, since on paraconsistent dialetheist standards, that is compatible with it being true. But what if instead we had said

$$\langle A \rangle \text{ is true} \rightarrow \bot,$$

or more simply,

NA: $A \rightarrow \bot$,

where $\bot$ implies everything. This does suffice: by modus ponens, A and NA together commit one to triviality. Given that we reject $\bot$ (and that it is presumably "mandatory" to do so), accepting NA does commit us to the rejection of A.

---

[3] The use I've just made of disjunctive syllogism is legitimate, given that 'believe' is in the restricted language! (As it presumably is: I don't think any dialetheist would suggest that we might simultaneously believe and not believe the same thing.)

True($\langle NA \rangle$) thus seems rather more satisfactory as a reading of the intuitive idea of "sole falsehood" than the more obvious explication "false and not true".

This idea can be used in a great many cases of sentences in the language with 'True' that a dialetheist would intuitively want to call "solely false". But it won't work in general: for though N*A* is strong enough to be strongly incompatible with *A*, it is a bit too strong. This can be seen in the case of the Curry sentence *K* above: we can't assert N*K* (or True($\langle NK \rangle$)), for that would be effectively equivalent to the Curry sentence (relative to facts statable in the 'True'-free sublanguage).

But we can extend the idea so as to handle *K*. After all, N*A* isn't the weakest schema that is strongly incompatible with *A*; a weaker one is

$$N_2 A : \qquad [A \to \bot] \vee [A \to (A \to \bot)].$$

Accepting this commits one to rejecting *A*; and one *can* accept this when *A* is *K*. Success!

But this still doesn't handle all possible examples. Suppose that the nasty man in our story is a logician, who for some reason knowable only to logicians had instead said

K_2 It is either the case that if what the nasty man on the screen is saying is true then I'm the Pope, or else it is the case that if what the nasty man on the screen is saying is true, then if what the nasty man on the screen is saying is true then I'm the Pope.

Dialetheism seems committed to regarding this as "solely false in the intuitive sense", since its truth (together with the fact that he is the nasty man on the screen) would imply that the speaker was the Pope. But for the same reason that it is illegitimate for the dialetheist to assert N*K*, it is illegitimate for the dialetheist to assert $N_2 K_2$. We need to go to an N_3.

Where I'm heading, obviously, is that in a paraconsistent dialetheist logic there is a sequence of weaker and weaker approximations to the intuitive idea of "sole falsity". It can in fact be extended into the transfinite: not only can we define $N_{\alpha+1} A$ as

$$N_\alpha A \vee [A \to N_\alpha A],$$

but we can also define $N_\lambda A$ for limit λ, as roughly "For some $\alpha < \lambda$, $\langle N_\alpha A \rangle$ is true". (Of course we will need to invoke the subtleties analogous to those in Chapter 22 to make sense of this. For the reasons discussed there, things start to go haywire when one reaches ordinals that are undefinable or for which it is problematic whether they are definable: at that point, even clear falsehoods won't be N_α-true.) The N_α operators get *strictly* weaker as α increases, until the definitions become ill-behaved: the hierarchy of sentences K_α defined in obvious extension of the examples above can be used to show this.

(The sequence of N_α is in fact just one of many such sequences that are definable in the dialetheic languages, though which ones have this feature of "getting strictly weaker forever" depends on the details of how the dialetheist treats the conditional. One obvious alternative sequence to consider is the sequence of operators $\neg D^\alpha$, defining D^α as in the paracomplete case. As duality considerations suggest, the sequence of $\neg D^\alpha$ in the paraconsistent logics considered in Section 25.2 has essentially the same features as I've just noted for the sequence of N_α.)

It would be nice if the sequence of N_α's, or some similar sequence, "converged on the intuitive notion of sole falsehood" before the definition broke down. It's hard to make this issue very precise, since it involves an intuitive notion that resists formalization, but I think we can say the following: the extent to which the N_α's get closer to that intuitive notion depends very much on the theory of conditionals in question, and in particular on whether the conditional reduces to the material conditional in "the non-dialetheic fragment of the language". If it doesn't so reduce, we shouldn't expect anything like "convergence to sole falsehood": for instance, if the conditional reduces instead to a *modal* conditional in the 'true'-free fragment, then none of the $N_\alpha A$ will be true when A is a *contingently* false sentence of the ground language, so intuitively the N_α's will approach something more like sole necessary falsehood than sole falsehood. This is another reason why I think a dialetheist is better off with a conditional that reduces to the material conditional in the ground language: the problem of "sole falsehood" raised by Parsons, Shapiro, and Littman and Simmons is considerably less if there is such a conditional in the language.

But even in the best case, where for large α, calling $N_\alpha A$ true is very close to the intuitive idea of calling A solely false, we simply have to accept that there is no way within the language to define a notion of sole falsity that works quite as we might have expected. The dialetheist must bite the bullet, and say that the various notions that are definable are the best we can have: there just is no intelligible notion of sole falsity that works in accordance with naive intuitions.

Of course, it would be difficult for a dialetheist who takes this line to complain bitterly about the paracomplete theorist's treatment of hyperdeterminateness.

27.3. EXTENDED PARADOX?

It is well-known that there are natural ways to try to "read operators off the dialetheist model theory" in a way that would produce paradox if such operators were in the language. An obvious example is Boolean negation: for instance, in the modal model theories, there is an operation that when applied in any world to the value {0} yields {1} and when applied to either {1} or {0,1} yields {0}. If there were in the language an operator ⊬ which corresponds to this model-theoretic operation, the logic would be trivial: there would be a Liar-like sentence Y equivalent to "⊬ Y", and there would be no way to coherently evaluate it (in *any* possible world). There are many other such examples. For instance, in

Priest's logics the process of "taking the limit" of the operations that correspond to the N_α in the model theory does not produce Boolean negation, but it does produce an operation that would give rise to a Curry-like paradox if there were an operator in the language that corresponded to it. The dialetheist should claim such operations to be monsters: mere artefacts of the model theory.

If that were Priest's conclusion, though, he could not in good faith argue against the paracomplete theorists on the basis of the "monsters" that are definable in their model theories. And yet he does: for instance, in Priest 2005, p. 45.

Perhaps for this reason, Priest seems to suggest an alternative way of getting around the extended paradoxes: declare that the meta-theory contains dialetheias. (Priest 2006a, p. 98.) However, as I've argued before, there is an ambiguity in 'metatheory'. If Priest means that the dialetheist's truth theory for a dialetheic language must be dialetheic—and a look at the context of the quote from 2006a suggests that he might have meant this—then of course he is right: it is after all part of the truth theory that the Liar sentence is both true and not true, and anyone who insisted on a classical theory of truth would be missing the whole point of dialetheism. But if that's what he meant, it is irrelevant to the current question, which concerns model theory. And model theory of the familiar sort, and the sort that Priest discusses mostly when he discusses model theory, is done within standard set theory, which is presumably in an "effectively classical" sub-part of the dialetheist's language.

There is, to be sure, a program—perhaps one that would not be hard to carry out—of developing a novel model theory in the part of the language that is not effectively classical. This would best be done by using a property theory, keeping set theory classical. If that can be done, then such a model theory might be much closer to truth theory, and in terms of such a model theory we wouldn't expect there to be an analog of Boolean negation. Such a program seems a possibility for both the dialetheist and the paracomplete theorist; neither party has carried it out, but I see no clear reason to think it would be more difficult for one sort of theorist than for the other. But of course the objection above wasn't raised for such an imagined model theory, but for the ordinary model theories, done within standard set theory, which Priest actually provides.

And for ordinary model theories done in standard set theory, it seems that the only answer a dialetheist could give is the one I've given several times on behalf of the paracomplete theorist: model theory is one thing and truth theory is something else. Indeed, any set-theoretic model theory for a dialetheic truth predicate inevitably misrepresents that predicate, both because the model theory is classical and because it only involves restricted domains; but this doesn't undermine its main purpose, which is to provide a theory of validity. Given this, there's no reason to think that every operation definable in the model theory corresponds to an intelligible connective: standard set theoretic model theory contains "monsters". This, I say, is the only answer the dialetheist can conceivably give; but giving it would undermine a main part of Priest's critique of paracomplete theories.

Saying that this is the only answer the dialetheist can conceivably give is actually a slight overstatement. There is one more alternative, which I dismissed from consideration early in the chapter but which Priest seriously entertains: one could take a dialetheic attitude toward sentences in standard Zermelo–Fraenkel set theory. I leave it to the reader who is willing to take this position seriously to see whether doing so would lead to different conclusions.

References

Adams, Ernest 1975, *The Logic of Conditionals* (Reidel).
Beall, JC 2005, "Transparent Disquotationalism," in Beall and Armour-Garb 2005, pp. 7–22.
____ (ed.) 2003, *Liars and Heaps* (Oxford).
____ (ed.) 2007, *Revenge of the Liar* (Oxford).
____ and Brad Armour-Garb (eds.), 2005, *Deflationism and Paradox* (Oxford).
Belnap, Nuel 1962, "Tonk, Plonk and Plink," *Analysis* 22: 130–4.
____ 1982, "Gupta's Rule of Revision Theory of Truth," *Journal of Philosophical Logic* 11: 103–16.
Boghossian, Paul 2000, "Knowledge of Logic," in P. Boghossian and C. Peacocke (eds.), *New Essays on the A Priori* (Oxford), pp. 29–54.
Boolos, George 1985, "Nominalist Platonism," *Philosophical Review* 94: 327–44.
Brady, Ross 1989, "The Non-Triviality of Dialectical Set Theory," in Priest, Routley and Norman, *Paraconsistent Logic: Essays on the Inconsistent* (Philosophia Verlag), pp. 437–70.
Burge, Tyler 1979, "Semantical Paradox," *Journal of Philosophy* 76: 169–98. Reprinted in Martin 1984, pp. 83–117.
____ 1982, "The Liar Paradox: Tangles and Chains," *Philosophical Studies* 41: 353–66.
Cantini, Andrea 1990, "A Theory of Formal Truth Arithmetically equivalent to ID_1," *Journal of Symbolic Logic* 55: 244–59.
Cartwright, Richard 1994, "Speaking of Everything," *Nous* 28: 1–20.
Chang, C. C. 1963, "The Axiom of Comprehension in Infinite Valued Logic," *Math. Scand.* 13: 9–30.
Craig, William, and Robert Vaught 1958, "Finite Axiomatizability Using Additional Predicates," *Journal of Symbolic Logic* 23: 289–308.
Curry, Haskell 1942, "The Inconsistency of Certain Formal Logics," *Journal of Symbolic Logic* 7: 115–17.
Dummett, Michael 1973, *Frege: Philosophy of Language* (Harper and Row).
____ 1978, "The Justification of Deduction," in his *Truth and Other Enigmas* (Harvard), pp. 290–318.
Edgington, Dorothy 1995, "On Conditionals," *Mind* 104: 235–329.
Feferman, Solomon 1962, "Transfinite Recursive Progressions of Axiomatic Theories," *Journal of Symbolic Logic* 27: 259–316.
____ 1984, "Toward Useful Type-Free Theories—I," *Journal of Symbolic Logic* 49: 75–111. Reprinted in Martin 1984: 237–87.
____ 1991, "Reflecting on Incompleteness," *Journal of Symbolic Logic* 56: 1–49.
Field, Hartry 2000, "Indeterminacy, Degree of Belief and Excluded Middle," *Nous* 34: 1–30. Reprinted with new Postscript in Field, *Truth and the Absence of Fact* (Oxford 2001), pp. 278–311.
____ 2002, "Saving the Truth Schema from Paradox," *Journal of Philosophical Logic* 31: 1–27.

Field, Hartry 2003a, "A Revenge-Immune Solution to the Semantic Paradoxes," *Journal of Philosophical Logic* 32: 139–77.
____ 2003b, "The Semantic Paradoxes and the Paradoxes of Vagueness," in Beall 2003, pp. 262–311.
____ 2004, "The Consistency of the Naive Theory of Properties," in *Philosophical Quarterly*. Reprinted in G. Link, ed., *100 Years of Russell's Paradox* (de Gruyter 2004), pp. 285–310.
____ 2005a, "Is the Liar Sentence Both True and False?," in Beall and Armour-Garb 2005, pp. 23–40.
____ 2005b, "Variations on a Theme by Yablo," in Beall and Armour-Garb 2005, pp 53–74.
____ 2006b, "Truth and the Unprovability of Consistency," *Mind* 115: 567–605.
____ 2007, "Solving the Paradoxes, Escaping Revenge," in Beall 2007, pp. 78–144.
Fine, Kit 1975, "Vagueness, Truth and Logic," *Synthese* 30: 265–300.
Frege, Gottlob 1892, "On Sense and Reference." In P. Geach and M. Black, eds., *Translations from the Philosophical Writings of Gottlob Frege* (Blackwell, 1952), pp. 56–78.
Friedman, Harvey, and Michael Sheard, 1987, "An Axiomatic Approach to Self-Referential Truth," *Annals of Pure and Applied Logic* 33: 1–21.
Glanzberg, Michael 2004, "A Contextual-Hierarchical Approach to Truth and the Liar Paradox," *Journal of Philosophical Logic* 33: 27–88.
Gödel, Kurt 1931, "On Formally Undecidable Propositions of *Principia Mathematica* and Related Systems, I." Translated in Jean van Heijenoort, *From Frege to Gödel* (Harvard, 1967), pp. 596–616.
Grover, Dorothy, and Joe Camp and Nuel Belnap 1975, "A Prosentential Theory of Truth," *Philosophical Studies* 27: 73–125.
Gupta, Anil 1982, "Truth and Paradox," *Journal of Philosophical Logic* 11: 1–60. Reprinted in Martin 1984, pp. 175–235; page numbering is from reprinted version.
Hahn, Hans 1933, "Logic, Mathematics and Knowledge of Nature." In A. J. Ayer, ed., *Logical Positivism* (The Free Press, 1959), pp. 147–61.
Hajek, Petr, and Jeff Paris and John Sheperdson 2000, "The Liar Paradox and Fuzzy Logic," *Journal of Symbolic Logic* 65: 339–46.
Halbach, Volker 1997, "Tarskian and Kripkean Truth", *Journal of Philosophical Logic* 26: 69–80.
Halbach, Volker, and Leon Horsten 2005, "The Deflationist's Axioms for Truth", in Beall and Armour-Garb 2005, pp. 203–17.
____ 2006, "Axiomatizing Kripke's Theory of Truth," *Journal of Symbolic Logic* 71: 677–712.
Hamkins, Joel 2003, "A Simple Maximality Principle," *Journal of Symbolic Logic*, 68: 527–50.
Herzberger, Hans 1982, "Naive Semantics and the Liar Paradox," *Journal of Philosophy* 79: 479–97.
Horwich, Paul 2005, "The Sharpness of Vague Terms." In his *Reflections on Meaning* (Oxford), pp. 85–103.
Hunter, Geoffrey 1971, *Metalogic* (University of California).
Jackson, Frank 1979, "On Assertion and Indicative Conditionals," *Philosophical Review* 88: 565–89.

Kaye, Richard 1991, *Models of Peano Arithmetic* (Oxford).
Kleene, Stephen 1952, "Finite Axiomatizability of Theories in the Predicate Calculus Using Additional Predicate Symbols," *Memoirs of the American Mathematical Society* 10: 27–68.
Kreisel, Georg 1967, "Informal Rigour and Completeness Proofs." In I. Lakatos, ed., *Problems in the Philosophy of Mathematics* (North-Holland), pp. 138–71.
Kremer, Michael 1988, "Kripke and the Logic of Truth," *Journal of Philosophical Logic* 17: 225–78.
Kripke, Saul 1975, "Outline of a Theory of Truth," *Journal of Philosophy* 72: 690–716; reprinted in Martin 1984, pp. 53–81. Page references are to reprinted version.
____ 1976 "Is There a Problem about Substitutional Quantification?," in G. Evans and J. McDowell, eds., *Truth and Meaning* (Oxford), pp. 325–419.
Lavine, Shaughan 1994, *Understanding the Infinite* (Harvard University).
Leeds, Stephen 1978, "Theories of Reference and Truth," *Erkenntnis* 13: 111–29.
Leitgeb, Hannes 2007, "On the Metatheory of Field's 'Solving the Paradoxes, Escaping Revenge'." In Beall 2007, pp. 159–83.
Lewis, David 1973, *Counterfactuals* (Harvard University).
____ 1986 "Postscript to 'Probabilities of Conditionals and Conditional Probabilities'," in Lewis, *Philosophical Papers, vol. II*, pp. 152–6.
Littman, Greg, and Keith Simmons 2004, "A Critique of Dialetheism," in Priest, Beall and Armour-Garb 2004, pp. 314–35.
Lukasiewicz, Jan, and Alfred Tarski 1930, "Investigations into the Sentential Calculus." In Tarski 1956, pp. 38–59.
Maddy, Penelope 1983, "Proper Classes," *Journal of Symbolic Logic* 48: 113–39.
Martin, Robert (ed.) 1984, *Recent Essays on Truth and the Liar Paradox* (Oxford).
Maudlin, Tim 2004, *Truth and Paradox* (Oxford).
McGee, Vann 1989, "Applying Kripke's Theory of Truth," *Journal of Philosophy* 86: 530–9.
____ 1991, *Truth, Vagueness, and Paradox* (Hackett).
Montague, Richard, 1963, "Syntactic Treatments of Modality, with Corollaries on Reflexion Principles and Finite Axiomatizability," *Acta Philosophica Fennica* 16: 153–67.
Myhill, John 1984, "Paradoxes," *Synthese* 60: 129–43.
Parsons, Charles 1974a, "The Liar Paradox." *Journal of Philosophical Logic* 3: 381–412. Reprinted with new Postscript in Parsons 1983, pp. 221–67, and in Martin 1984, pp. 9–45. Page references to latter.
____ 1974b, "Sets and Classes." *Nous* 8: 1–12. Reprinted in Parsons 1983, pp. 209–220.
____ 1983, *Mathematics in Philosophy* (Cornell).
Parsons, Terrence 1990, "True Contradictions," *Canadian Journal of Philosophy* 20: 335–54.
Popper, Karl 1959, *The Logic of Scientific Discovery* (Basic Books).
Priest, Graham 1987, *In Contradiction* (Martinus Nijhoff). [Reprinted with new commentary as Priest 2006b; page numbers are to latter.]
____ 1998, "What is So Bad About Contradictions?," *Journal of Philosophy* 95: 410–26.
____ 2002, "Paraconsistent Logic," in D. Gabbay and F. Guenther (eds.), *Handbook of Philosophical Logic* (2nd edn) v. 6 (Kluwer), pp. 287–393.

Priest, Graham 2005, "Spiking the Field Artillery," in Beall and Armour-Garb, eds., *Deflationism and Paradox* (Oxford), pp. 41–52.
____ 2006a, *Doubt Truth to Be a Liar* (Oxford).
____ 2006b, *In Contradiction*, 2nd edn (Oxford). [Reprinting of Priest 1987 with new commentary.]
Priest, Graham, and JC Beall and B. Armour-Garb (eds.), 2004, *The Law of Non-Contradiction* (Oxford).
Prior, A. N. 1960, "The Runabout Inference Ticket," *Analysis* 21: 38–9.
Putnam, Hilary 1968, "Is Logic Empirical?," in Cohen and Wartofsky, eds., *Boston Studies in Philosophy of Science*, v. 5. Reprinted as "The Logic of Quantum Mechanics," in his *Philosophical Papers vol. 1* (Cambridge): pp. 174–97.
Quine, W. V. 1940, *Mathematical Logic* (Harvard).
____ 1960, *Word and Object* (MIT).
____ 1970, *Philosophy of Logic* (Prentice-Hall).
Ramsey, Frank 1927, "Facts and Propositions," *Proceedings of the Aristotelian Society* 7 (Suppl): 153–70.
Rayo, Agustin and Gabriel Uzquiano (eds.) 2006, *Absolute Generality* (Oxford).
Rayo, Agustin and Philip Welch 2007, "Field on Revenge," in Beall 2007, pp. 234–49.
Reinhardt, William 1986, "Some Remarks on Extending and Interpreting Theories with a Partial Predicate for Truth," *Journal of Philosophical Logic* 15: 219–51.
Restall, Greg 1992, "Arithmetic and Truth in Lukasiewicz's Infinitely Valued Logic," *Logique et Analyse* 139–40: 303–12.
____ 2007 "Curry's Revenge: the Costs of Non-Classical Solutions to the Paradoxes of Self-Reference," in Beall 2007, pp. 262–71.
Rogers, Hartley 1967, *Theory of Recursive Functions and Effective Computability* (McGraw-Hill).
Russell, Bertrand 1945, *A History of Western Philosophy* (Allen and Unwin).
Scott, Dana 1967, "Existence and Description in Formal Logic," in Ralph Schoenman, ed., *Bertrand Russell: Philosopher of the Century* (Allen and Unwin), pp. 181–200.
Shafer, Glenn 1976, *A Mathematical Theory of Evidence* (Princeton).
Shapiro, Lionel 2006, "The Rationale Behind Revision-Rule Semantics," *Philosophical Studies* 129: 477–515.
Shapiro, Stewart 2002 "Incompleteness and Inconsistency," *Mind* 111: 817–32.
____ 2004, "Simple Truth, Contradiction and Consistency," in Priest, Beall and Armour-Garb 2004, pp. 336–54.
Shoenfield, J. R. 1967, *Mathematical Logic* (Addison-Wesley).
Simmons, Keith 1993, *Universality and the Liar* (Cambridge).
____ 2003, "Reference and Paradox," in Beall 2003, pp. 230–52.
Skolem, Thoralf 1957, "Bemerkungen zum Komprehensionsaxiom," *Zeitschrift für Mathematical Logik* 3: 1–17.
Skyrms, Brian 1970, "Notes on Quantification and Self-reference." in Robert Martin, ed., *The Paradox of the Liar* (Yale), pp. 67–74.
Soames, Scott 1999, *Understanding Truth* (Princeton).
Stalnaker, Robert 1968, "A Theory of Conditionals." in N. Rescher, ed., *Studies in Logical Theory* (Oxford), pp. 98–112.
____ 1974, "Pragmatic Presuppositions," in M. Munitz and P. Unger, eds., *Semantics and Philosophy* (NYU Press), pp. 197–213.

Strawson, Peter 1950, "Truth," *Proceedings of the Aristotelian Society* 24 (Suppl): 129–56.

Tappenden, Jamie 1993, "The Liar and Sorites Paradoxes: Toward a Unified Treatment" *Journal of Philosophy* 90: 551–77.

Tarski, Alfred 1931, "The Concept of Truth in Formalized Languages" (original Polish version, without Postscript). English translation in Tarski 1956, pp. 152–267.

―――― 1936a, "The Concept of Truth in Formalized Languages" (German translation of Tarski 1931 with additional footnote and Postscript). English translation in Tarski 1956, pp. 152–278.

―――― 1936b, "On the Concept of Logical Consequence" in Tarski 1956, pp. 409–20.

―――― 1956, *Logic, Semantics, Metamathematics* (Oxford).

Van Mill, Jan 1989, *Infinite-Dimensional Topology* (North-Holland).

Visser, Albert 1984, "Four-Valued Semantics and the Liar," *Journal of Philosophical Logic* 13: 181–212.

Weir, Alan 2005, "Naive Truth and Sophisticated Logic," in Beall and Armour-Garb 2005, pp. 218–49.

Welch, Philip forthcoming, "Ultimate Truth *vis-a-vis* Stable Truth," *Journal of Philosophical Logic*.

Williamson, Timothy 1994, *Vagueness* (Routledge).

Yablo, Stephen 2003, "New Grounds for Naive Truth Theory," in Beall 2003, pp. 312–30.

Index

acceptable ordinal 252, 255n., 257, 259–60, 262, 264–5, 273, 274n.
Adams, Ernest 374n.
agnosticism: *see* ignorance

BDM ("basic deMorgan logic") 79–81
Beall, JC ix, 11n., 363, 378
Belnap, Nuel 138, 186–7, 190, 311
Berra, Yogi 10, 172, 175
Berry paradox 106–8, 270, 291
biconditionals 27, 72–3, 118n., 119, 180, 187, 276, 362, 369
 see also: conditionals
bivalence 104, 111–13, 241, 298, 303, 305, 308, 328–30, 339, 341–3
 see also: excluded middle
Boghossian, Paul 49n.
Boolean-valued semantics 156; Section 10.5; 169–71, 173, 175, 189–90, 232, 262
Boolos, George 34n., 340
boundaries of vague terms 100–1, 104, 106, 151, 240, 343n.
Brady, Ross 371n., 386
Brouwer, L. E. J. 8, 25n., 88, 97–9
Burge, Tyler 57, 58n., 190, 211n., 213, 219–20

Camp, Joe 138
Cantini, Andrea 121, 128, 144
Cantor, Georg 3, 309
Cartwright, Richard 34
categorical truth 190
Central Argument from Equivalence to Contradiction 7–8, 10
Chang, C.C. 88n.
change of logic 14–17, 67, 110–12
Church, Alonzo ix, 214n., 326n., 327n.
"circle" of ordinals 259–60, 261n., 274n.
circular predicates 7–8, 11n., 15, 19, 244
classical fragment 309, 321–31, 334–5
 see also: effectively classical
closing off a fixed point 125n., 223–4
completeness theorems 47–8, 304–5
compositional truth rules 28–9, 53, 62, 112, 126–7, 129–30, 140n., 145–6, 176–7, 183–4, 188–9, 202, 206, 243–4, 248–9, 310–11, 354

comprehension schema: *see* naive property theory
concatenation theory: *see* protosyntax
conditional assertion, v. assertion of conditional 163–4, 170, 172–5, 194, 267, 282–4, 288–90, 303–4
conditional proof (*aka* $\rightarrow$-Introd) 161–2, 172–3, 269; Section 19.1; 284–5, 286n., 288, 313
 restricted version 269, 282
conditionals
 embedded in other conditionals 84–5, 242–3, 246–9, 253, 267–70, 351, 373–4, 379
 in paracomplete logics 66n., 72–3, 81, 83–9, 94, 102, 105, 107, 112, 231, 233, 236, 240, 242–53, 256n., 261, 264–74, 276–7, 296
 in paraconsistent dialetheic logics 81, 362–3, 366, 368–75, 377, 379–83, 386–7, 390
 indicative conditionals in ordinary English 373–5
 Stalnaker and Lewis 264, 374, 381–2
 variably strict 264–6, 270
conservativeness
 over ω-models 66–8, 78, 87–9, 91–4, 97–9, 112, 127–8, 160, 231, 234–5, 237, 262–3, 294–5, 313, 322–3, 325, 342, 343n., 346
 Belnap's argument 311
consistency, belief in 203
 See also: incompleteness theorems; inconsistency; restricted truth-preservation.
contextual theories of truth 57, 58n., 190, 211–14, 216, 218–21, 225
continuum-valued semantics 86–99, 102, 104–5, 108–9, 112–13, 151, 167–8, 171, 225, 231–6, 238, 241, 256n., 270, 275–6, 369–70, 386
contraction rule (nonstructural) 84n., 268, 269n., 283n.
 structural contraction 283n., 284
contraposition of conditionals 89, 123, 193, 195, 266, 268, 270, 288–9, 362, 371–2, 374, 382–3, 386
 contraposition rule 264, 270
Convention T 28n.
Craig, William 52, 202

Curry and iterated Curry paradoxes 15, 84–7, 109, 247–8, 255, 256n., 268–72, 281–4, 289, 313–14, 370–1, 376–8, 380–1, 388–9, 391
Cut Rule 283n.
  see also: structural rules

Davidson, Donald 33n.
decency, standards of 300–2
defectiveness ix, 76–8, 95–6, 212, 225–8, 240n., 276, 351–2, 357
  autobiographical or normative remarks as surrogate for? 77–8, 96
  quasi-defectiveness 240, 357
  unified notion of? ix, 96, 228, 349–52, 357
  of concepts 310n., 344
definability (explicit)
  v. inductive characterizability 38–9
  of iterations of operators 93, Section 22.3, 389–90
  of validity 298, 300, 302, 307
  excluded middle for 106, 328–30
  paradoxes of 15, 106–8, 291–3
  see also: Tarski undefinability theorem
definite descriptions 27, 86, 97, 291–3
degree of belief
  in consistency claims 203n.
  non-classical 74–5, 139, 208–9, 364
degree-theoretic approaches to vagueness 88–9, 169, Section 15.1
deMorgan laws 8n., 9, 65n., 232–3
deMorgan logics 9–10, 65n., 79–81, 365
deMorgan-valued algebras (or lattices) and semantics 166–9, 171n., 232, 260, 276, 292, 317n.
denotation 15, 206, 291–4
designated value 65–6, 73, 83n., 85, 110, 112–13, 167–72, 232–3, 262, 267, 306–7, 343n., 368–9, 371–3, 382, 384–6
determinately operator 73, 76, 78, 88–90, 235–6, 276
  classical 151–5, 164–5
  in the context of vagueness 100, 102–4, 113
  iterations of (including transfinite iterations) 91–4, 104–5, 237–41, 270–1, 325–31, 347–9
  see also: indeterminacy; hyper-determinately; super-determinate truth
diagonalization 25–8, 31–2, 41, 84, 129n., 130n., 299, 301, 318
dialetheism: *see* paraconsistent dialetheism; truth-value gluts (classical)
direct application of rule: *see* restricted truth-preservation

disjunction elimination: *see* reasoning by cases
disjunctive syllogism 17, 65n., 80, 244n., 361, 369, 388
distributive laws, infinitary 233, 261, 317, 319
duality 11n., 74–5, 80, 127, 129, 142–6, 147n., 166, 176, 181, 183–4, 189, 191n., 197n., 216, 233, 285, 286n., 364, 368–70, 390
Dummett, Michael 8, 49n. 310n.

Edgington, Dorothy 374n.
∃-Elimination 82, 252, 261n., 267, 299, 314, 371
effectively classical 108, 110–11, 385, 391
  see also: classical fragments
epistemic interpretations of supervaluationism 151–3, 155, 175
epistemic and normative paradoxes 77–8, 95n.
  see also: validity, paradoxes of
excluded middle 8–11, 13–17, 48–51, 65, 69, 72–5, 77–8, 84–5, 95, 114, 119, 125, 127–8, 152, 162, 165, 169, 191, 209, 269, 271, 275–6, 283, 289–90, 292, 294–6, 309–12, 319–23, 328–33, 335–7, 341–2, 356, 362n., 366, 369–70, 373–4, 388
  arguments for 48–9, 310–12
  and least number principle 100–1, 107–8
  for definability 106, 328–30
  for vague predicates 101–5, 155
  for validity 109, 112, 300; Section 20.5; 321, 323, 356
  for iterations of 'determinately' 103–5, 238, 325, 328, 331–2
  in dialetheic theories 363n., 364, 378, 381, 383
  rejecting instances of 74–5, 95, 152, 165, 209, 325
  see also: bivalence
exclusion negation: *see* negation, exclusion *v.* choice
existentially committing 206–8, 291–3
explosion rule 11n., 80, 269, 287–90, 361, 362n., 369, 382, 388
expressing (as opposed to stating) agreement and disagreement 138–41, 148–9, 205–10, 212, 220–1, 351
expressive incompleteness 23, 33, 58, 73, 89, 92, 118, 309–24, 326, 338–9, 342, 353, 384
exportation rule 268–9
extensionality 3n., 11n., 296–8, 341
external theory of a fixed point 68, 125–6, 128–30, 156, 178, 187n., 222–3, 285, 368

false 23n., 66n., 70–2, 88, 123, 126–7, 140, 176, 191n., 206, 208, 216, 310, 334, 361, 365–7, 376
　see also: truth-value gaps; truth-value gluts; solely false.
FDE: see BDML
Feferman, Solomon 69, 121, 124–7, 129–30, 144–7, 156, 203n.
Fine, Kit 128n.
finite axiomatizability via truth or satisfaction predicate 52–4, 138–9, 171, 202, 205, 287
fixed points 25n.
　Brouwer 88, 97–9
　Gödel-Tarski: see diagonalization
　Kripke 58, 61–3, 65–6, 68–70, 121, 125–30, 137, 144–5, 156–60, 169, 177–82, 184–7, 189, 196–7, 217n., 222–4, 242–52, 258, 265–6, 272–4, 277, 285, 368, 371
　Yablo 244–9, 253, 272
FM ("external logic of Kleene-based fixed points") 68–72, 121–2, 125, 127, 130n., 156, 191, 215
Frege, Gottlob 3n., 11n., 37, 206–8
Friedman, Harvey ix, 119n., 121, 128, 144, 147, 161
Fundamental Theorem 251–2, 257–8, 260–1, 265, 271

Gardner, Martin 108
Glanzberg, Michael 211n., 213, 222
Gödel, Kurt vii, 3–4, 93, 118, 159, 200–1, 297, 299, 300–2, 306, 318
　See also: incompleteness theorems; self-reference
Gödel sentence 302, 306, 376, 380n.
Gödel-Bernays set theory 297
Grelling's paradox: see heterologicality
ground language 58–9, 234, 242
grounded sentences 137
Grover, Dorothy 138
Gupta, Anil 57–8, 186, 187n., 190, 213

Hahn, Hans 310
Hajek, Petr 94
Halbach, Volker 69, 185, 214n., 215
Hamkins, Joel 64n.
Henkin's paradox: see Curry paradox
hereditarily definable ordinals 29n., 255n., 328, 330, 334, 338
Herzberger, Hans 186–7
heterologicality 1, 4, 11–14, 23, 31, 118, 134–5
Heyting, Arend 8

hierarchical theories: see stratified theories of truth
hierarchy of operators ix, 91–2, 326–31, 334
　path-dependent v. path-independent 327–8
　compared to stratification 347–9
　see also: Hierarchy Theorem
Hierarchy Theorem 237–40
horseshoe rules (positive and negative) 266–7, 269, 288, 381
Horsten, Leon 69, 185
Horwich, Paul 150
Hunter, Geoffrey 191
hyper-determinately 325–6, 331, 335–6, 338–40, 343–4, 352, 389–90
hyper-dialetheism 143, 144n., 147, 160n., 179, 191–2, 199–201, 285–6, 376

identity, determinacy of 295, 297, 356
ignorance 70–2, 102, 119–22, 150–3, 172, 174, 183, 198–9, 290
importation rule 84–5, 268
impredicativity 34, 317–22, 341–3
　see also: quasi-impredicative higher order logic
inaccessible cardinals 63–4, 165, 300, 302, 312
Incoherence Principles 119–20, 123–4, 129–30, 143, 150, 155, 159, 172, 175–6, 181, 200
incompleteness theorems vii, 19, 52–3, 201–3, 226n., 286, 290, 353, 355, 376–7
inconsistency, alternative definitions of 298–9
indefinite extensibility 18, 34–6, 213
indeterminacy 19, 78, 94–6, 100–4, 120; Chapter 9; 151–5, 164–6, 171, 173–4, 199, 203, 290, 293n., 307, 321
　of identity 297
　see also: determinately operator
indexical, truth as: see contextual theories
induction
　rule v. conditional 263–4, 270, 287
　expansion as language expands 53–4, 191, 263–4, 304, 354–5
　see also: least number principle; least ordinal principle
inductive definition 33, 35–8, 44, 53, 63
　making explicit 38–9, 45, 60, 63
inductive proof 19, 50, 191, 201, 203, 286–7, 369, 377, 379
infinite conjunctions and disjunctions 92–3, 171, 210, 237–9, 316–23, 331–3, 340, 348

intelligibility 5, 12, 207, 220, 313, 315, 320–1, 323, 326, 340, 352–3, 356, 390–1
internal theory of a fixed point 68, 125, 128, 156–7, 159, 178–9, 181, 183–5, 187n., 208, 222–3, 225–8, 243, 249, 275, 368
interpretation (v. model) 45–6, 112, 305, 353n.
Intersubstitutivity Condition 232, 237, 242, 251, 256
Intersubstitutivity Principle 9, 12, 16, 65–6, 70, 72–3, 83–4, 87, 92, 95n., 104n., 112–13, 138, 151n. 210, 227, 231, 260, 263, 268–70, 275–6, 281, 283n., 288–9, 309, 311n., 313, 317, 319, 322–3, 325, 331, 345–6, 348, 351, 354, 362–74, 383, 386–7
for truth-of 12, 112, 210n., 231
Conditional 379, 383, 386
intersubstitutivity of equivalents 25n., 27, 84, 246–7, 253, 267–8, 362
intuitionist logic 8–9, 15, 65n., 109–10, 117, 161, 285, 312–13, 315–17, 319–20, 324

Jackson, Frank 374
join-irreducibility and
C-join-irreducibility 232, 260, 261n.

K_3 ("Kleene logic") 65, 79–81, 170, 368–9
Kaye, Richard 53n.
KF ("Kripke-Feferman theory"): see FM
KFS ("internal logic of Kleene-based fixed points") 65–78, 83, 88–9, 95–6, 102, 107, 111–12, 118n., 124–8, 156, 159, 209, 212, 214, 223, 225–6, 228, 231, 234, 275–6, 364, 368
Kleene, Stephen
3-valued semantics and logic 58, 65–6, 69, 79–80, 84–8, 121–2, 124–5, 127–8, 130–1, 137, 144, 157–9, 167–8, 170–1, 223–6, 228, 231–3, 242, 249–52, 258, 267, 275, 285, 304, 368
on finite axiomatization 52
ordinal notations ix, 214n., 326n., 327n.
see also: K_3.
Kleene-style gap theories 124–8, 131
see also: FM
König's paradox 106–8, 291, 293, 329–31, 335
Kreisel, Georg 46–8, 50, 67, 109, 170n., 300, 303–5, 355
Kremer, Michael 65n., 66n.

Kripke, Saul ix, 57–8, 105, 127, 144, 177, 180, 231, 242–4, 249, 265, 272–3, 275–7, 368–9, 371
on defining truth 33n., 58–9, 62, 64–5, 68–9, 164
critique of Tarski 56–7, 215
conservativeness theorem 65–7
closing off a fixed point 125n., 223–4
ghost of Tarski hierarchy 222–8
see also: fixed-points (Kripke); KFS; supervaluationist approach to paradoxes (internal); Kleene-style gap theories; supervaluation-style gap theories

Lavine, Shaughan 3n.
least number principle (classical and generalized) 100–1, 107, 111, 270,
least ordinal principle (classical and generalized) 106–8, 330, 331n., 335
Leeds, Stephen 138
Leitgeb, Hannes 356n.
Lewis, David 264, 374, 381–2
Liar sentences 23–7
contingent 24
Liar hierarchy 91–2, 237–41, 325–6, 357
hyper-Liar, super-Liar, etc. 331–49
"ordinary" v. "strengthened" 23n., 123n.
see also: strengthened Liar discourses; negation, exclusion v. choice
Littman, Greg 386, 390
Löb's paradox: see Curry paradox
logical consequence: see validity
logical necessity 42–5, 75, 111–12, 284–6, 373, 390
bivalence of? 306–7
logicism 15
LP (Priest's "logic of paradox") 66n., 80–1, 368–73, 375, 377
Lukasiewicz, Jan 84–5, 87–9, 95, 102, 104–5, 111, 122, 162, 168, 225, 231, 369

Maddy, Penelope 297–8
Maudlin, Tim 69, 121, 124–30, 132, 140–1, 144–7, 156, 212, 286
McGee, Vann 19, 69, 185, 189n.
McGee sentence 185, 189, 348n.
meaning, change of 16–17, 85, 276, 310n., 344
"meaning-constitutive" assumptions 17, 310n.
meaningfulness 12–14, 135, 206–7
see also: intelligibility
Medium-Standards Theory 370–1, 375, 380, 382–3

meta-language, relation to object language: *see* self-sufficient language
meta-theory 108–14, 354, 384–6, 391
modal semantics 246–8, 264–6, 274, 372–3, 382, 384, 390
model 40, 44–5, 49–50, 65
   v. interpretation 45–6
   class model 46
   multi-valued 66, 87–8, 97, 99, 234–5, 262–3, 275, 294, 368–70, 373, 391–2
   defined in non-classical language? 109, 112–3, 306, 312, 356–7, 385–6
model theory, significance of 63–4, 67–8, 108–14, 311–2, 343n., 353–7, 384–6, 390–1
modus ponens 66n., 80, 83n., 144, 147, 246, 266–70, 283–6, 289, 313, 363, 369–71, 373, 377–80
   and truth-preservation ix, 51, 131, 147–8, 159–60, 176, 182–3, 188, 189n., 191–3, 199, 285–6, 288n., 290, 377–80
modus tollens 362, 366, 371–2
monotonicity condition 61n., 83, 158n., 223–4, 247, 285–6,
monster operators 356, 391
Montague, Richard 131, 146, 191, 220
Montague sentence 131, 146
Myhill, John 3n.

Naive property theory 7–10, 11n., 134, 232, 294–7, 312
Naive theory of denotation 293
Naive theory of truth and truth of 12, 272
necessitation rule 162–3
necessity: *see* logical necessity
negation
   Boolean 309–12, 390–1
   exclusion *v.* choice 310–2
   weakened 73, 76, 78, 89, 95–6
   hierarchies of negation-like operators 94, 388–90
Nixon-Dean problems: *see* subscript contests
non-adjunctive logics 11n.
non-denoting singular terms 206, 291–3
normative notions 77–8, 96, 352
   see also: epistemic and normative paradoxes

ω-inconsistency 93–4, 148, 189n., 231
ω-models and ω-logic 66–7, 87, 93, 97, 125, 127, 156, 160, 170n., 184–6, 234–5, 242, 263, 294–5, 300, 368
Official Theory 271–4
operator *v.* predicate 151n., 343n.

ordinal notations viii, ix, 5, 29n., 113, 214n., 216n., 220, 227–8, 237, 275, 326–7
   see also: paths
overspill 6, 11–13, 18, 106

paracomplete 8–15, 67, 69, 72, 143, 151–2, 156, 165–6, 171, 173, 209, 213, 228, 231–357, 362, 364–5, 368–70, 375–6, 378, 381–2, 384, 386–8, 390–2
paraconsistent 10, 11n., 361
paraconsistent dialetheism vii, 10, 12, 132n., 142, 145–6, 285, 290, 353, 361–92
   without excluded middle 363n., 378, 383
paradox of acceptance and rejection 95n.
parameterized formula 38n., 85n., 233, 257–8, 260–1, 273, 341
partially parameterized formula 295
Paris, Jeff 94
Parsons, Charles 133n., 211n., 213, 222, 297–8, 341
Parsons, Terrence 386, 390
path 327–30, 333–5, 337n., 338
permissibility 128, 140–1
permutation rule 268
plural quantifiers 34n., 340–3
Popper, Karl 164n.
predicativity: *see* impredicativity; quasi-impredicative higher order logic
Priest, Graham ix, 73, 80, 290, 291, 353–7, 361–6, 368, 371–5, 376–83, 384–6, 388, 391–2
Prior, A. N. 310n.
proof, naive 376–7
proper classes 34, 46, 53, 64, 295, 297–8
properties 1–4, 18, 31, 109; sections 20.2 and 20.3; 312, 341–2, 378, 386n., 391
   conceptual *v.* natural 3, 11
   restricting comprehension for conceptual? 4–7, 10
   predicates not expressing 13–14; Section 7.5
   see also naive theory of properties
propositions 132–3, 135–7, 144, 213, 296, 313–4, 316–9
protosyntax 24–5, 27, 58, 66, 86–7
Putnam, Hilary 16

quasi-impredicative higher order logic 341–2, 356n.
Quine, W. V. 4, 11n., 25, 138, 201n.

Ramsey, Frank 138, 374
Rayo, Agustin 34, 340–3, 356n.

reasoning by cases (*aka* ∨-Elimination) 7, 10, 12, 14*n*., 79–81, 160–2, 167, 172–5, 193–4, 199, 227, 232, 244*n*., 251, 261, 267, 282, 285, 311, 319, 371, 375, 378, 382–3
recursive progressions of theories 203*n*.
reduct 234–5, 242, 263, 294
reductio ad absurdum 8–9, 122, 143, 161–2, 172, 197–8, 313–16, 320, 334, 378
Reinhardt, William 65*n*., 69, 121*n*., 122*n*.
rejection 8, 9*n*., 73–7, 94, 95*n*. 101*n*., 109, 145, 148, 152, 165, 175, 208–9, 226, 290, 325, 352, 362*n*., 364–6, 369, 371*n*., 378, 380, 382, 385, 387–9
  conditional 75–7, 96, 387
  "operator" 76–7, 94
relation 3, 295–6
Restall, Greg 93, 316–23
Restall sentence 93
restricted *v*. unrestricted languages 29*n*., 38–40, 44–5, 48, 59, 62–6, 68, 72, 88, 110, 112, 153–7, 160, 164–5, 190, 257*n*., 262, 305, 311, 340, 342, 343*n*., 355, 391
restricted truth-preservation: *see* truth-preservation (restricted *v*. unrestricted)
revenge paradoxes Section 23.3; Chapter 27
  see also: model theory, significance of; hyper-determinately; super-determinate truth
revision-rule theories of conditionals 249–53, 257, 259, 266, 271–2
revision-rule theories of truth 121, 128, 156, 163–4, 176, 186–97, 199–200, 202–6, 208, 210, 226–7, 287–90, 380
  strong, medium, dual medium and weak 188–9, 191; Sections 12.1 through 12.3; 200, 203–4, 287–9, 290*n*., 348, 380
Richard paradox 291
Roach Motel property 61, 83, 158, 196*n*., 250
Robinson arithmetic 26*n*., 53*n*., 131*n*.
Rogers, Hartley 214*n*., 326*n*.
rule-circularity 49–50, 111–12, 190–1
Russell, Bertrand 3, 106*n*.
  Russell's paradox (for properties and for sets) 1–11, 13–14, 31, 134–5, 294–6, 341*n*., 361

S_3 ("symmetric Kleene logic") 65*n*., 66*n*., 81, 170
satisfaction 38–40, 50–3, 59, 184, 201n, 213, 215, 233, 298, 309, 321, 328–9, 334, 339, 341, 347, 349
  see also: true of
Scharp, Kevin ix
Schechter, Joshua ix
schemas
  in stratified and contextual theories 220, 227–8
  use of 'true' in instances of 54, 129*n*., 203*n*., 262–3, 355
  see also: Naive Property Theory; Naive Theory of Truth
Scott, Dana 291*n*., 293*n*.
second order logic 34*n*., 46, 305, 340–3
self-reference 23–7, 58, 87, 93, 97, 130*n*., 180, 187, 231
  banning 118
self-sufficient language 18, 222–3
self-sustaining sets of sentences 97–9
"self-undermining" Sections 7.3, 8.3 and 8.4; 146, 192, 195, 196, 198; Section 12.3; 203–4, 227, 349
semantic values 59, 61, 105
  fine-grained 168–70, 189–90, 232, 248; Section 17.1; 290, 292–3, 383
  "real-world" 340–2, 343*n*., 355–6
  relation to truth 62–5, 67–8; Sections 3.4, 3.5 and 4.3; 110
  see also: ultimate value
semi-classical: *see* weakly classical
sequent calculus 82, 166*n*., 304*n*.
Shafer, Glenn 209*n*.
Shapiro, Lionel 190
Shapiro, Stewart 380*n*., 386, 390
Sheard, Michael ix, 119*n*., 121, 128, 144, 147, 161
Sheperdson, John 94
Shoenfield, J. R. 45*n*.
Simmons, Keith 211*n*., 213, 293*n*., 386, 390
Skolem, Thoralf 88*n*.
Skyrms, Brian 212*n*.
Soames, Scott 69, 71
"solely true" and "solely false" 119, 146, 362*n*., 366, 373, 378, 381–3, 386–90
soundness proofs 48–55, 190–1, 201, 203, 286, 290, 304, 353*n*., 355, 376–82, 384
stably included 187–8
Stalnaker, Robert 206, 374, 381–2
stratified theories of truth and instantiation 3–4, 5–7, 12*n*., 56–8, 110, 190–1; Chapter 14; 275, 323, 326, 341, 347–52
stratified gap theories Section 14.2, 349*n*., 350–2
stratified internal fixed point theories Section 14.3, 349*n*.

coarse *v.* fine 215–18, 349–52
Strawson, Peter 138
strengthened liar discourses 211–13, 221, 225
structural rules 10–11, 79, 269*n.*, 282–4
subscript and superscript contests 56–7, 141, 217–9, 350–1
subvaluation-style glut theories 144
super-cool entities 29–30, 34
super-determinate truth 338, 343–7, 353, 356–7
super-truth: as account of truth *v.* as account of determinate truth 120, 128, 153–4
supervaluationist approach to vagueness 101, 102*n.*, 120; Section 9.2
supervaluationist approach to paradoxes (internal) Chapters 10 through 12; 205–6, 208, 209*n.*, 210, 223–4, 226–8, 262, 287–90, 348, 380
 strong, medium, dual-medium and weak 182–5, 191; Sections 12.1 through 12.3; 200, 203–4, 287–9, 290*n.*, 348, 380
supervaluation-style gap theories 121–2, 124, 126*n.*, 128–31, 144–7, 153, 191, 215, 285
System H ("external logic of supervaluational fixed points"): *see* supervaluation-style gap theories

Tappenden, Jamie 19
Tarski, Alfred ix, 24, 84
 explicit definition of truth or axiomatic theory? 33–41, 53, 58
 hierarchies of truth and satisfaction predicates 28–30, 33–6, 42–3, 50–1, 54–5, 125*n.*, 141, 214–15, 217, 241, 271, 275, 329–30, 331*n.*
 on logical consequence 42–4
 schema, or biconditionals: *see* truth schema
 undefinability theorem 23, 27–33, 58, 64, 110, 155, 160, 165, 262, 311, 354
 see also: self-reference; stratified theories of truth and instantiation
(T-COMPL) and (T-CONSIS) 183–5, 189, 194, 197–8, 226–7
(T-Elim) 161–3, 170, 174, 180, 183, 188, 189*n.*, 192, 194–8, 202, 205, 208, 210, 224, 227, 281–2, 284–5, 287, 311*n.*, 313–15, 317, 319–20, 363–6
(T-Introd) 161–3, 170, 174, 179, 185–6, 188, 189*n.*, 192–5, 197–200, 202, 205, 207, 224, 227, 281–2, 284–5, 287–8, 311*n.*, 313, 315, 317, 319–20, 363–4, 378
(¬T-Elim) 161–2, 170, 174, 180, 183, 188–9, 190*n.*, 192, 194–8, 205–8, 224, 227, 363
(¬T-Introd) 161–2, 170, 174, 179, 188, 192, 194–5, 197–8, 205, 224, 227, 363–6
(T-IN) 121–2, 124, 126, 129, 132–6, 142–4, 146–8, 161, 214*n.*, 216
(T-OUT) 121–4, 126, 128–44, 146, 147*n.*, 156, 161, 215, 227
transparent valuation and transparent fixed point 243–7, 249, 251, 273–4
true of 1, 11–15, 23, 59, 61*n.*, 93–4, 106–8, 112, 118, 134–5, 210, 231, 233–5, 242, 263, 275, 291–4, 327, 341
 see also: satisfaction
truth
 "deflationary" or "minimal" theory 18
 role in expressing agreement and disagreement Section 7.7; 148–9; Chapter 13; 212, 220–1, 351
 generalizing role of 18, 92–4, 171, 176; Section 13.3; 220, 228, 237, 326–8, 348–9, 363, 367
 in instances of schemas 54, 129*n.*, 203*n.*, 262–3, 355
 no role in theory of understanding 354–5
 as primitive: *see* Tarski undefinability theorem
truth in a model 40; Section 2.2; 49–50
truth-preservation 19; Section 2.1; 50, 75–6, 111–12, 131, 147–8, 176, 182–3, 188, 189*n.*, 191; Chapter 12; 205*n.*, 208; Sections 19.2 and 19.3; Chapter 26
 restricted *v.* unrestricted 148, 160, 200, 203, 287–90, 376, 380–3
 super-restricted 382–3
truth schema (= Tarski schema) 30, 276, 366
 negations of instances of 369, 370, 372–3
 see also: Naive Theory of Truth
Truth-teller sentence 124*n.*, 164, 180, 271–3, 277*n.*, 342
truth-value gaps Section 3.5; 120; Chapter 7; 153, 156, 159, 174–5, 183, 187*n.*, 192, 200, 202, 205–6, 208, 210, 212–13; Section 14.2; 222–4, 282, 285–6, 345, 350–2, 386–7
 not posited in paracomplete theories 11*n.*; Section 3.5
 relation to gluts in paracomplete theories and paraconsistent dialetheic theories Section 3.5; 143; Section 8.4; 310–1; Section 24.3; 368, 371–2
 Kleene-style *v.* supervaluation-style 121–2; Section 7.2; 131, 191
 and classical logic 127–8
 harmless and relatively harmless Section 13.1

truth-value gluts
  classical 71–2, 121n., 125, 131, 142–9, 159–60, 172, 174–5, 183, 191–2, 199–200, 202–3, 205, 208, 210, 216, 282, 285–9, 361, 363–4, 368, 380–2
  in paraconsistent dialetheic theories 365–8, 371–2, 386–7
type theory 3, 12n., 29n., 35, 36n.
  quasi-impredicative 341, 356n.
  ramified 341

ultimate value 251–2, 257–8, 259, 271, 273
underspill 6, 7n., 11–14, 18, 106
universal language: *see* self-sufficient language; expressive incompleteness
Uzquiano, Gabriel 34

vagueness vii, 8n., 19, 66n., 96, 100–14, 120, 128, 150–5, 169, 209, 240–1, 264–6, 270, 276, 357
  higher order 101, 103–5, 113, 153, 240–1, 270
validity (=logical consequence) ix, 19; Sections 2.1 through 2.3; 75–6, 106n. 128, 262, 276–7; Sections 19.1 and 19.2
  weak *v.* strong Sections 10.2, 10.3 and 10.6; 267–9, 299
  of conditional assertion 164, 169–70, 173–4, 283–4
  v. necessary preservation of truth Section 2.1; 76, 111–12; Section 19.2

model-theoretic characterizations of Sections 2.2 and 2.3; 50–1, 66–8; Sections 5.6 and 10.6; 355–6
paradoxes of 109; Sections 20.4 and 20.5; 314, 355–6, 384–5
see also: excluded middle for validity; decency, standards of
Validity Argument 42–3, 47, 76, 284–6
valuation
  for conditionals 242–58, 273, 274n.
  starting 243, 249, 256, 277
van Mill, Jan 99
Vaught, Robert 52, 202
VF *see* supervaluation-style gap theories
Visser, Albert 124n.

Weak-Standards Theory 370
weakly classical (= semi-classical) viii, 10, 12, 13n., 14n., 77, 80, 149, 156, 172, 186, 196n., 203n., 208–9, 212–13, 223, 225, 241, 269, 281–2, 284–9, 320, 347–8, 362–4, 371, 381–2
Weir, Alan 283n.
Welch, Philip 270, 305, 340–3, 356n.
Williamson, Timothy 150, 270
Wright, Crispin 314–7

Yablo, Stephen 25n., 244–9, 253, 267, 270, 272–3, 277

ZF(C) = Zermelo-Fraenkel set theory (plus axiom of choice) 3, 12n., 36n., 38, 46, 52–3, 63–4, 203n., 297, 300–2, 353–6, 392.

CPSIA information can be obtained
at www.ICGtesting.com
Printed in the USA
BVHW042145111218
535410BV00007B/167/P